# RACE TRAFFIC

# RACE
# TRAFFIC

*Antislavery and the
Origins of White Victimhood,
1619–1819*

GUNTHER PECK

*Published by*
THE OMOHUNDRO INSTITUTE OF
EARLY AMERICAN HISTORY AND CULTURE,
WILLIAMSBURG, VIRGINIA,
*and the*
UNIVERSITY OF NORTH CAROLINA PRESS,
CHAPEL HILL

The Omohundro Institute of
Early American History & Culture (OI)
is an independent research organization sponsored by
William & Mary and the Colonial Williamsburg Foundation.
On November 15, 1996, the OI adopted the present name
in honor of a bequest from Malvern H. Omohundro, Jr.,
and Elizabeth Omohundro.

© 2024 The Omohundro Institute of Early American History & Culture
All rights reserved

Manufactured in the United States of America

Cover art © Adobe Stock / artistmef

Complete Library of Congress Cataloging-in-Publication Data
is available at https://lccn.loc.gov/2024023905.

ISBN 978-1-4696-7514-5 (cloth: alk. paper)
ISBN 978-1-4696-7515-2 (epub)
ISBN 978-1-4696-8054-5 (pdf)

*For my parents,*
*Russell Albert Peck and Ruth Demaree Peck*

# ACKNOWLEDGMENTS

WHEN I FIRST began researching the origins of so-called white slavery while on a fellowship at the National Humanities Center in 2001, I thought that 1865 would be the start date for my next book, a moment in time I ultimately never returned to as I investigated the complex and intertwined histories of whiteness and antislavery. My efforts to locate the historical origins of white victimhood have taken me well beyond the conceptual and geographic boundaries of the history of the U.S. West, my primary field of study as a graduate student. The inquiry propelled me first into the U.S. South and North during the antebellum era, then to the far-flung boundaries of an emerging British Empire across the Atlantic and the Mediterranean during the long eighteenth century, and, finally, back to the seventeenth century and the history of the nascent English Empire, when skin colors first emerged as methods for seeing and moving people across England's first colonies.

This empirical inquiry has sparked numerous conversations with colleagues and students and with friends and family along the way. Indeed, at each stage of my research, I have been blessed to engage the work and ideas of new cohorts of scholars and students. Although I have no doubt omitted some of the good practitioners who helped me discern this history, I am grateful, now, to be able to offer my thanks to many of them.

First and foremost, I want to thank my students at Duke University, who have not only taught me a great deal about the past but also how to talk and think about the long shadow of mercantilism and the markets in people that it organized four centuries ago. Students in three undergraduate classes—"Historicizing Whiteness," "Immigrant Dreams," and "Human Trafficking, Past to Present"—have been especially generative thinkers and have helped me hone many of the insights in this book. The following undergraduate researchers were also enormously helpful. I thank, in chronological order of their research, Julia Spinnenweber, Neha Sabharwal, Rachel Merker, Briana Nofil, Davia Young, Elijah Fox-Peck, Nicole Rapfogel, Sara Evall, Emily Nagler, Lizzy Kramer, Grace Kurtz-Nelson, and Patrick Duan for their assistance in tracking down unusual iterations of white grammar and for helping create the databases that undergird many of the findings in this book. And thanks to Josie Haile for help building the index for the book.

I have benefited from conversations with several graduate students throughout the research and writing of *Race Traffic*. For their curiosity and insights, I thank Felicia Arriaga, Eladio Bobadillo, Jessica Borsellino, Aaron Colston, Jenny Wood Crowley, Risha Druckman, Jonathan Free, Natalie Gasparowicz, Reena Goldthree, Alisha Hines, Max Krochmal, Ayanna Legros, Gordon Mantler, Brianna Nofil, Yuridia Ramirez, Lesa Redmond, Jacob Remes, Joshua Strayhorn, Vivien Tejada, Georgia Welch, Casey Williams, and Brad Wood. I offer special thanks to Nofil and Tejada, whose research into the geographies of incarceration and coercion across North America during the nineteenth and twentieth centuries have sharpened my understanding of the role of states in fomenting human trafficking.

My faculty colleagues have been generous and supportive of this research, even when they disagreed with this author about details within the narrative. For engagement with an early chapter that would in time become *Race Traffic*, I offer thanks to my colleagues at the University of Texas: Daina Ramey Berry, Judith Coffin, Julie Hardwick, Martha Newman, Robert Olwell, James Sidbury, Michael Stoff, and Allan Tully.

At Duke, I have enjoyed the generosity and wisdom of an extraordinary community of scholars. For transformative conversations about the book and specific feedback on chapters of *Race Traffic*, I thank Sarah Balakrishnan, Edward Balleisen, Nick Carnes, Bill Chafe, Sarah Deutsch, Laura Edwards, Elizabeth Fenn, Barry Gaspar, Ray Gavins, Thavolia Glymph, Michael Hardt, Wesley Hogan, Reeve Huston, Bruce Jentleson, Judith Kelley, Bob Korstad, Adriane Lentz-Smith, Justin Leroy, Cecilia Marquez, John Martin, Fritz Mayer, Sucheta Mazumdar, Andrew Nurkin, Jocelyn Olcott, Simon Partner, Jay Pearson, Dirk Philipsen, Sumathi Ramaswamy, Deondra Rose, Pete Sigal, Orin Starn, Philip Stern, Don Taylor, Susan Thorne, Timothy Tyson, Robyn Weigman, Peter Wood, and Alexandra Zagbayou. I also benefited from a manuscript workshop at the John Hope Franklin Humanities Institute at Duke in 2018. I thank FHI Director Ranjana Khanna and FHI Associate Director Christina Chia for supporting the workshop and Reena Goldthree, David Roediger, Manisha Sinha, and David Waldstreicher for coming to Duke and making the FHI conversation so generative and productive.

I have been fortunate to enjoy several fellowships over the course of investigating and writing *Race Traffic*, all of them made possible by the financial support of Duke University. I took full advantage of the research opportunities provided by the staff and librarians at the National Humanities Center in 2001–2002 to move fully into the early nineteenth century, and I thank all the fellows from the 2001 cohort, especially Winifred Breines, Deborah Cohen,

Gerald Early, Winston James, Frank Mort, John Plotz, and Jon Sensbach. In 2006–2007, I received a fellowship from the American Council of Learned Societies that enabled me to begin investigating British imperial history during the very long eighteenth century. At the Charles Warren Center for Studies in American History at Harvard University in 2009–2010, I enjoyed working back into the seventeenth century with the intellectual company and support of Kristen Block, Vincent Brown, Lizabeth Cohen, Nancy Cott, Marisa Fuentes, Joshua Guild, Walter Johnson, Paul Kramer, Jill Lepore, Edward Rugemer, Patrick Wolfe, and Cynthia Young. At the Gilder Lehrman Center for the Study of Slavery, Resistance, and Abolition at Yale University in 2017–2018, I learned a great deal from the expertise and intellectual acumen of Ned Blackhawk, David Blight, Matthew Jacobson, Jennifer Klein, Jacob Remes, Edward Rugemer, and Sasha Turner. Between 2016 and 2018, I was also a member of the Gilder Lehrman Center's inaugural working group on modern slavery. To Kevin Bales, Janie Chuang, Andrew Crane, Grace Peña Delgado, Anna Mae Duane, Genevieve LeBaron, Jessica Pliley, Joel Quirk, Jennifer Rosenbaum, Elena Shih, and Zoe Trodd, I offer heartfelt thanks for feedback on chapters of *Race Traffic* and for modeling ways to link critique with advocacy on behalf of the millions being trafficked today.

I have been invited to present portions of *Race Traffic* to several groups and benefited from the engaged responses by commentators, panelists, and audience members. I thank the following individuals and institutions for inviting me to present my work: Edward Rugemer, organizer of the Race and Atlantic Slavery in the Atlantic World to 1900 reading Group at Yale University; Sandy Darity of the Samuel DuBois Cooke Center on Social Equity at Duke University; Jefferson Cowie, convenor of a race workshop series at Vanderbilt University; Amy Dru Stanley of the Pozen Family Center for Human Rights at the University of Chicago; Laurent Dubois of the Forum for Scholars and Publics at Duke University; David Waldstreicher of the Center for Early American History at Temple University; the Department of History at Bowdoin College, for a keynote talk at the Kemp Symposium; Suzanne Katzenstein, for a symposium on human trafficking with Anne Gallagher at the Kenan Institute for Ethics at Duke University; and Julie Hardwick of the Institute for Historical Studies at the University of Texas at Austin.

Although digitized collections of seventeenth- and eighteenth-century public records have made much of the research for *Race Traffic* possible, the book could not have been written without the knowledge, expertise, and professionalism of archivists across the United States and Great Britain. I want to thank the many library workers and archivists who patiently helped me find literally hundreds of documents over the course of my research at the following libraries: the British Library; the Senate House Library at the University of London; the British National Archives at Kew; the Guildhall Library—the Library of London History; the Bodleian Old Library at Oxford University; the Sterling Memorial Library and the Beinecke Rare Book and Manuscript Library at Yale University; the Widener Library at Harvard University; the Library of Congress in Washington, D.C.; the Newberry Library in Chicago; the New York Public Library; the Huntington Library in Los Angeles; the William Andrews Clark Memorial Library at the University of California, Los Angeles; and the Perkins Library and the David M. Rubenstein Rare Book and Manuscript Library at Duke University. I offer special thanks to three librarians, all at Duke: Margaret Brille, Patrick Stawski, and Carson Holloway. Brill not only generously explained British imperial records but found ways to secure access to the newly digitized British collections while I was researching *Race Traffic*. Stawksi and Holloway have both worked closely with my students and research assistants over the past decade, while Carson helped me track down the archival homes for every illustration in the book.

Working with the University of North Carolina Press has been a delightful process. I owe thanks to Chuck Grench, who first read and engaged with *Race Traffic* as a manuscript and then generously supported having it reviewed by the Omohundro Institute of Early American History and Culture. I am deeply grateful for the support, acumen, and superb vision of Catherine Kelly, who recognized the scholarly and political promise of my manuscript long before it was ready to reach its audience. Emily Suth and Nicholas Popper have been key members of an outstanding team in support of *Race Traffic*, helping craft a haunting book cover and remaining steadfast in their enthusiasm for the book. Kaylan Stevenson is quite simply the best manuscript editor I have ever encountered. She has made *Race Traffic* a more readable and timely book, and I thank her for her rigor and candor.

At key moments of the research and writing of *Race Traffic*, I have been grateful for the timely intellectual engagement of a few key scholarly friends. At an early stage of the research for the book, Leon Fink helped me think more clearly about maritime workers and their complex relationships to the nations that ostensibly govern them, while Cindy Hahamovitch inspired me to think more critically about antislavery on a global scale. I thank Andy Neather for a long friendship stretching back, first, to the Green Room in Durham, N.C., where we first discussed politics, race, and labor, and, then, to London, where we shared questions and spirits during my research trips to British archives. My dear friend David Waldstreicher has not only read every chapter of *Race Traffic* but kindled excitement in the research and writing with each new foray into an earlier period.

Working with my hands and with fellow gardeners and maple-syrup enthusiasts, Steve Curtis, Andy Quintman, and John Zuccardy of Hamden, Connecticut, has enriched the solitary nature of writing, revising, and finishing this book. I thank them for believing in the power of ideas and of sap. Making music has also enlivened this process. My friend David Swanson interrupted me in 2019 with the comment, "You'll never finish the book if you stare at that upright bass!" He was right, and I have been playing the bass ever since. And now the book is done.

I could not have conceived of or completed this book without the support of dear friends. Brad Parham kept me laughing through long periods of writing that seemed never-ending. Michael Gallagher helped me stay grounded while building democratic engagement across North Carolina. To my oldest and best friend John Sarbanes, who gently suggested I needed to keep working on the book after hearing me summarize the work while making maple syrup in Renfrew County, Ontario, back in 2012, I offer abiding thanks. John's commitment to democratic action and the strength of transformative ideas has inspired me to finish this book, reminding me of the power of good trouble and the unfinished emancipation project that has animated multitudes across time and space.

Last, but not least, I want to thank my family for their witness and support: John and Susan Mullin; Carter and Carol Fox; Lucy Fox; Paul Fallon; Carol Jean Fallon Fox; Baylor, Jordan, Max, and Miles Fox-Kemper; my sister Demaree Peck; James, David, and Sarah Peck; my dear brother Nathan Peck; Rebecca Peck; Lindsey Peck; Cody Peck; Chris Peck and Jackie Sherman; James Peck; Caleb Lambert; Catherine Lambert; Nathaniel Lambert; and Savannah Lambert. To my nieces and nephews, I offer thanks for keeping it real through games of pinochle.

My son Gabe once observed years ago that if I would only stop checking the weather forecast for gardening or maple syrup news, I might finish this book. My son Elijah tried a different approach and became a research assistant for a summer while a student at Oberlin. My daughter, Miranda, opted to sing songs with me while I accompanied her on the bass. All three have helped me immensely, reminding me that all harvests have a season and are worth the wait.

To my beautiful thought partner in life, Faulkner Fox, words are just one way of expressing appreciation for the love that has sustained me over a two-decade book project. I have learned more from her than from any other person, living or dead. A ferocious activist, inspiring teacher, and powerful writer, she has helped me see, day in and day out, how the living ghosts of white supremacy gain strength from evasion. Her words as a playwright inspire me to see how history and imagination, properly linked without lies or malice, can change the world for the better. I look forward to the next chapter of our life together, whether or not it exists on a printed page.

My mother, Ruth Demaree Peck, and my late father, Russell Albert Peck, read every chapter of *Race Traffic* that I sent to them. Theater enthusiasts, they offered critical feedback and rumination on the ethical challenges at the heart of *Race Traffic*, wondering how and why idealism and cruelty, antislavery and injustice could become so co-mingled in the past and the present. My father, a scholar of Medieval literature, and my mother, a concert pianist, taught me how to see complexity and how to fight for social change simultaneously, a vantage that quite literally made *Race Traffic* possible. I dedicate the book to them.

CONTENTS

Acknowledgments vii

List of Illustrations xv

**INTRODUCTION**
Race Traffic, Past and Present
1

**CHAPTER ONE**
The Origins of Race Traffic
25

**CHAPTER TWO**
Ransom Traffic and Antislavery
in the Mediterranean
85

**CHAPTER THREE**
Novel Ways of Seeing Race
133

**CHAPTER FOUR**
Atlantic Slave-Servant Conspiracies
171

**CHAPTER FIVE**
Nationalizing Emancipation
in the Mediterranean
213

**CHAPTER SIX**
War, Traffic, and Race
across the British Empire
251

CHAPTER SEVEN
Trafficking, Freedom, and Race
in the Age of Revolution
295

CHAPTER EIGHT
Antislavery Nationalism and Race
349

CONCLUSION
The Radical Challenge to Race Traffic
399

APPENDIX A
The Colonial State Papers
423

APPENDIX B
Early English Books Online
433

APPENDIX C
Eighteenth Century Collections Online
439

APPENDIX D
Daniel Horsemanden's *Journal of the Proceedings
in the Detection of the Conspiracy* (1744)
449

Index 467

## ILLUSTRATIONS

### FIGURES

FIGURE 1. Richard Ligon, *A Topographicall Description and Admeasurement of the Yland of Barbados*, 1657  52

FIGURE 2. Title Page from Thomas Lurting's *The Fighting Sailor Turn'd Peaceable Christian*, 1770  87

FIGURE 3. *Turks Taking the English / Selling Slaves in Algiers . . .* , 1675  97

FIGURE 4. Robert White, after John Riley, *Aphra Behn*, 1718  137

FIGURE 5. *Imoinda and Oroonoko*, 1736  144

FIGURE 6. *Representation du feù terrible a Nouvelle Yorck . . . / Schreckenvolle feuersbrunst welchs zu Neu Yorck*, 1776  184

FIGURE 7. Title Page from [Daniel Horsmanden], *A Journal of the Proceedings in the Detection of the Conspiracy . . . for Burning the City of New-York*, 1744  185

FIGURE 8. *A Representation of a Massacre . . . Done in the Presence of the English Slaves*, 1751  215

FIGURE 9. John Faber, Jr., after Richard Phelps, *Bampfylde Moore Carew*, 1750  263

FIGURE 10. Unknown artist, *Peter Williamson*, 1759  285

FIGURE 11. *Phillis Wheatley*, 1773  301

FIGURE 12. *A Striking Likeness of Mrs. Newsham the White Negress*, 1791  313

FIGURE 13. *The Sufferer in His Prime*, 1762  319

FIGURE 14. Daniel Orme, after W. Denton, *Olaudah Equiano ('Gustavus Vassa')*, 1789  330

FIGURE 15. John Eckstein, *Sir Sidney Smith*, 1801–1802  371

FIGURE 16. *The Ship Boston Taken by the Savages at Nootka Sound, March 22, 1803* 375

FIGURE 17. *Robert Wedderburn*, 1824 400

FIGURE 18. Eugène Delacroix, *Greece on the Ruins of Missolonghi*, 1826 417

## TABLES

TABLE 1. Mentions of White Grammar by Keyword in the Colonial State Papers, 1661–1720 425

TABLE 2. Mentions of White Servants by Category in the Colonial State Papers, 1661–1720 426

TABLE 3. Mentions of Christian Servants by Category in the Colonial State Papers, 1661–1720 427

TABLE 4. Mentions of Blacks by Category in the Colonial State Papers, 1661–1720 428

TABLE 5. Mentions of Whites by Category in the Colonial State Papers, 1661–1720 429

TABLE 6. Mentions of Unruly Christian Servants versus White Servants in the Colonial State Papers, 1661–1720 430

TABLE 7. Revisions to White Grammar in the *Calendar of State Papers* by Keyword, 1870s 430

TABLE 8. Mentions of White People by Category in the Colonial State Papers, 1661–1720 431

TABLE 9. Changing Religious Affiliations and Geographic Origins of Whites Mentioned in Early English Books Online, 1651–1700 435

TABLE 10. Religious Affiliations and Geographic Origins of White People Mentioned in Early English Books Online, 1601–1700 436

TABLE 11. Religious Affiliations and Geographic Origins of White Men Mentioned in Early English Books Online, 1601–1700 437

TABLE 12. Aggregate Religious and Geographic Identities of White Subjects by Keyword Mentioned in Early English Books Online, 1601–1700  438

TABLE 13. Religious Affiliations and Geographic Origins of Whites Mentioned in Eighteenth Century Collections Online, 1701–1800  441

TABLE 14. Religious Affiliations and Geographic Origins of White Women Mentioned in Eighteenth Century Collections Online, 1701–1800  442

TABLE 15. Religious Affiliations and Geographic Origins of White Slaves Mentioned in Eighteenth Century Collections Online, 1701–1800  443

TABLE 16. Geographic Origins of Individuals of White Race Mentioned in Eighteenth Century Collections Online, 1701–1800  444

TABLE 17. Nonfictional versus Fictional White Women Mentioned in Eighteenth Century Collections Online, 1701–1800  445

TABLE 18. Nonfictional versus Fictional White Slaves Mentioned in Eighteenth Century Collections Online, 1701–1800  446

TABLE 19. Nonfictional versus Fictional Christian Slaves Mentioned in Eighteenth Century Collections Online, 1701–1800  447

TABLE 20. Grammars of Bondage in the Mediterranean by Keyword in Eighteenth Century Collections Online, 1701–1800  448

TABLE 21. Confessions and Final Statements of New York's Conspirators, 1741, in Horsmanden's *Proceedings*  450–461

TABLE 22. Thematic References within Confessions and Final Statements by Sentencing, 1741, in Horsmanden's *Proceedings*  462

TABLE 23. Thematic Differences within Confessions and Final Statements by Court Interrogators, 1741, in Horsmanden's *Proceedings*  463

TABLE 24. Thematic Differences in Confessions and Final Statements Recorded by Nichols and Lodge by Date, 1741, in Horsmanden's *Proceedings*  464

TABLE 25. Correlations between Themes in Confessions and Final Statements, 1741, in Horsmanden's *Proceedings*  465

TABLE 26. Sentencing Differences between Free and Enslaved Conspirators, 1741, in Horsmanden's *Proceedings*  466

# RACE TRAFFIC

INTRODUCTION

# Race Traffic, Past and Present

HISTORIES OF slave trafficking haunt contemporary conversations about racial injustice and what to do about it. For modern-day abolitionists, the outlawing of the African slave trade serves as the historical model that informs a broad-based coalition seeking to eliminate human trafficking. Human trafficking in the present day was defined in 2000 by the U.S. Congress's Trafficking Violence Protection Act (TVPA) and the United Nations' Palermo Protocol as modern slavery. Abolitionist author Kevin Bales estimated in 1999 that more than twenty-seven million people around the planet were suffering from modern slavery, a number that has since grown to more than forty million. For contemporary abolitionists, a diverse coalition of labor and human rights activists, conservative evangelical Christians, U.S. State Department employees, and legislators in more than one hundred countries, history is an essential tool in fighting human trafficking. Abolitionist David Batstone has used the history of the slave trade to underscore the contemporary challenge, writing that the number of modern slaves "is greater than the total of all African slaves trafficked to the Americas over four centuries." Not to be outdone in adapting the past to the present, the U.S. Congress renamed the TVPA the William Wilberforce Act in 2008, commemorating the bicentennial of the African slave trade's abolition and the British Parliament's role in that effort. Progressive history can, it seems, repeat itself.[1]

---

1. Victims of Trafficking and Violence Protection Act, Pub. L. no. 106-386, 114 Stat. 1464 (2000) (hereafter TPVA), https://nche.ed.gov/legislation/trafficking-violence-protection/; UN General Assembly, Resolution 55/25, Protocol to Prevent, Suppress, and Punish Trafficking in Persons Especially Women and Children . . . , A/RES/55/25 (Nov. 15, 2000), Protocol to Prevent, Suppress, and Punish Trafficking in Persons Especially Women and Children, Supplementing the United Nations Convention against Transnational Organized Crime | OHCHR (hereafter Protocol), https://www.ohchr.org/en/instruments-mechanisms/instruments/protocol-prevent-suppress-and-punish-trafficking-persons; David Batstone, *Not for Sale: The Return of the Global Slave Trade—and How We Can Fight It* (New York, 2007), 5, 6.

Yet historical analogies about slave trafficking also inform right-wing activists building a global white supremacist movement. The African slave trade is their point of departure for publicizing in their view a far greater crime: the history of so-called white slavery. Members of the far-right British National Party use stories about white slaves of varied origins to insist that white British subjects have no responsibility for Great Britain's crimes in its former colonies. American white nationalists similarly use images of white slavery, primarily those of indentured servants sold in colonial North America and contemporary Christian women sold to Jewish men in Israel or Muslim sheiks in North Africa, to fuse hatred of Blacks, Jews, and Muslims. For these transatlantic racists, white victimhood is a global travesty, emerging in both Atlantic and Mediterranean geographies, a crime that silences all claims to Black reparations. White slavery is an ongoing crime at home, too, they contend, fashioned by a conspiracy of liberal journalists and politically correct radicals in academia who have allegedly repressed the true history of white victimhood. Like contemporary abolitionists, modern-day white supremacists have

---

The scholarly literature on modern slavery is vast, growing, and interdisciplinary. The leading abolitionist scholar is Kevin Bales, whose work has helped generate a consensus among policymakers that modern slavery is real and requires legislative action. See Bales, *Disposable People: New Slavery in the Global Economy*, rev. ed. (Berkeley, Calif., 2012), 25. See also Siddharth Kara, *Sex Trafficking: Inside the Business of Modern Slavery* (New York, 2009). On scholars who valorize the work of the new abolitionism, see Judith G. Kelley, *Scorecard Diplomacy: Grading States to Influence Their Reputation and Behavior* (Cambridge, 2017). For more sober assessments of antitrafficking legislation, see Anne T. Gallagher, *The International Law of Human Trafficking* (Cambridge, 2010); Anthony M. DeStefano, *The War on Human Trafficking: U.S. Policy Assessed* (New Brunswick, N.J., 2007); and Janie A. Chuang, "Rescuing Trafficking from Ideological Capture: Prostitution Reform and Anti-Trafficking Law and Policy," *University of Pennsylvania Law Review*, CLVIII (2010), 1655–1728. Modern abolitionists have come under sustained critique by a variety of feminist and antiracist scholars. See Kamala Kempadoo and Elena Shih, eds., *White Supremacy, Racism, and the Coloniality of Anti-Trafficking* (New York, 2023), 64–87; Jo Doezema, *Sex Slaves and Discourse Masters: The Construction of Trafficking* (London, 2010); and Gretchen Soderlund, "Running from the Rescuers: New U.S. Crusades against Sex Trafficking and the Rhetoric of Abolition," *NWSA Journal*, XVII, no. 3 (Fall 2005), 64–87. On efforts to bring critics and practitioners into productive dialogue, see Genevieve LeBaron and Jessica R. Pliley, "Introduction: Fighting Modern Slavery from Past to Present," in LeBaron, Pliley, and David W. Blight, eds., *Fighting Modern Slavery and Human Trafficking: History and Contemporary Policy* (Cambridge, 2021), 1–33. The reauthorization of the TVPA in 2008 focused mostly on strengthening the capacity of law enforcement to prosecute human traffickers. See [Charles Doyle], "The William Wilberforce Trafficking Victims Protection Reauthorization Act of 2008 (P.L. 110–457): Criminal Law Provisions" ([Washington, D.C.], 2009).

been remarkably successful in harnessing historical analogies to their cause. Indeed, their understanding of racial victimhood has broad and growing appeal. Since 2015, white people in the United States consistently report feeling more likely than African Americans to have been victimized on account of their skin color.[2]

Although contemporary abolitionists and white nationalists use the history of the slave trade to very different political ends, both groups resist a more complex history of human trafficking. Activists and authorities working to stop human trafficking have been reluctant to consider the mischievous historical uses of antislavery. Rarely do modern abolitionists mention the white slavery campaigns of the Progressive Era in which fears of organized sex trafficking sanctioned the Mann Act of 1910 and expanded the power of federal authorities to violate the rights of its citizens. The U.S. State Department has made no

---

2. On the history of white supremacy within modern Britain, see James Rhodes and Natalie-Anne Hall, "Racism, Nationalism, and the Politics of Resentment in Contemporary England," in John Solomos, ed., *The Routledge International Handbook of Contemporary Racisms* (New York, 2020), 284–299. On the ideology, imagery, and uses of whiteness in the far-right British National Party, see James Rhodes, "Multiculturalism and the Subcultural Politics of the British National Party," in Nigel Copsey and Graham Macklin, eds., *The British National Party: Contemporary Perspectives* (New York, 2011), 64–72. On September 15, 2001, a white nationalist group in the United States called the Omdurman published a sequence of six images on the internet showing deformed Saudi men seeking to enslave white American women. The images have since been removed from the internet but are discussed in Gunther Peck, "The Shadow of White Slavery: Race, Innocence, and History in Contemporary Anti-Human Trafficking Campaigns," in Hal Brands and Jeremi Suri, eds., *The Power of the Past: History and Statecraft* (Washington, D.C., 2016), 210–216. They can also be viewed at Peck, "Welcome and Keynote Address: 'Historicizing the Origins of White Racial Victimhood,'" The Samuel DuBois Cook Center on Social Equity at Duke University, video, Apr. 12, 2017, https://www.youtube.com/watch?v=MB6bYKtbObI&t=1809s (located between the 30 and 35 minute markers). On indentured servants in America as white slaves, see David Duke, *My Awakening: A Path to Racial Understanding* (Covington, La., 1998); and Michael A. Hoffman, II, *They Were White and They Were Slaves: The Untold History of the Enslavement of Whites in Early America* (Coeur d'Alene, Id., 1991). On white people's perceptions of their own racial victimhood, see Samuel L. Perry et al., "Divided by Faith (in Christian America): Christian Nationalism, Race, and Divergent Perceptions of Racial Injustice," *Social Forces*, CI (2022), 913–942; and James Kolber, "Having It Both Ways: White Denial of Racial Salience while Claiming Oppression," *Sociology Compass*, XI, no. 2 (February 2017), 1–9. For an effort to define victimhood as the key attribute of a hegemonic whiteness, see Matthew W. Hughey, "The (Dis) Similarity of White Racial Identities: The Conceptual Framework of 'Hegemonic Whiteness,'" *Ethnic and Racial Studies*, XXXIII (2010), 1289–1309.

mention of white slavery in any of its annual Trafficking in Persons Reports since 2001 and seeks distance between its work and the demonstrably racist legacy of white slavery abolitionism during the Progressive Era. Yet by defining all contemporary victims of trafficking as slaves, policymakers valorize their own work while using images of white victimhood to justify efforts to suppress human trafficking, neglecting the fact that most contemporary victims of human trafficking are not white and many also resist the rescue offered by NGOs and governments. As in the Progressive Era, victims of trafficking are objects rather than subjects of public conversation and debates, appropriated by NGOs, government officials, and Hollywood screenwriters alike.[3]

3. The historical literature on the African slave trade is vast and has never been richer or more accessible. On the centrality of African women's kinship ties and reproduction to the history of the African slave trade, see Jennifer L. Morgan, *Reckoning with Slavery: Gender, Kinship, and Capitalism in the Early Black Atlantic* (Durham, N.C., 2021); Sasha Turner, *Contested Bodies: Pregnancy, Childrearing, and Slavery in Jamaica* (Philadelphia, 2017); and Saidya Hartman, *Lose Your Mother: A Journey along the Atlantic Slave Route* (New York, 2007). For overviews of the African slave trade, see David Eltis, *The Rise of African Slavery in the Americas* (Cambridge, 2000); and Robin Blackburn, *The American Crucible: Slavery, Emancipation, and Human Rights* (London, 2011). On African responses to the transatlantic slave trade, see John Thornton, *Africa and Africans in the Making of the Atlantic World, 1400–1800* (Cambridge, 1992); Paul E. Lovejoy, *Transformations in Slavery: A History of Slavery in Africa* (Cambridge, 2012); Sean Stilwell, *Slavery and Slaving in African History* (New York, 2014); and Toby Green, *The Rise of the Trans-Atlantic Slave Trade in Western Africa, 1300–1589* (Cambridge, 2012). The history of white slavery during the Progressive Era has received considerable scholarly attention, much of it focusing on the mischievous work of white, middle-class purity reform. See Pamela Haag, *Consent: Sexual Rights and the Transformation of American Liberalism* (Ithaca, N.Y., 1999); Brian Donovan, *White Slavery Crusades: Race, Gender, and Anti-Vice Activism, 1887–1917* (Urbana, Ill., 2006); and Jessica R. Pliley, *Policing Sexuality: The Mann Act and the Making of the FBI* (Cambridge, Mass., 2014). On immigrant efforts to adapt fears of white slavery to their advantage, see Edward J. Bristow, *Prostitution and Prejudice: The Jewish Fight against White Slavery, 1870–1939* (New York, 1982); and Gunther Peck, "Feminizing White Slavery in the United States: Marcus Braun and the Transnational Traffic in White Bodies, 1890–1910," in Leon Fink, ed., *Workers across the Americas: The Transnational Turn in Labor History* (New York, 2011), 221–244. On the work of international feminists during the white slavery scare, see Stephanie A. Limoncelli, *The Politics of Trafficking: The First International Movement to Combat the Sexual Exploitation of Women* (Palo Alto, Calif., 2010). On the undemocratic uses of antislavery ideology in both passing and implementing the Mann Act of 1910, see Pliley, *Policing Sexuality*, 70–83. For an especially clear example of self-heroizing among contemporary abolitionists, see Aaron Cohen with Christine Buckley, *Slave Hunter: Freeing Victims of Human Trafficking* (New York, 2009). The movie *Taken* (2008), starring Liam Neeson, exemplifies continuities between Progressive-Era white victimhood and

White nationalists have been ironic beneficiaries of these unfortunate facts. Speaking on behalf of so-called white slaves past and present, contemporary racists pedal stories about white victimhood while ignoring most evidence about the history of human trafficking, slavery, and the racial wealth gap that it helped engender. By almost any measure of aggregate wealth, economic opportunity, or political representation, people with fair skin color have never been more powerful, gaining rather than losing economic power over the past three decades in both the United States and Great Britain. Yet images and narratives of white slavery remain the emotive heart of contemporary white racial ideology. The idea of white slavery commands attention, an oxymoron with salacious power. The history of that oxymoron is indeed real, though not as it narrates itself, as a timeless wound that generations of white people have allegedly endured. The history of white slavery, and the idea of white racial suffering that informs it, has a particular historical origin and purpose: a revisionist effort to silence radical challenges to the political economy of enslavement and human trafficking that emerged sporadically but consistently among trafficked slaves, servants, and sailors across the seventeenth- and eighteenth-century Atlantic and Mediterranean. Whiteness became globally hegemonic, I argue, not as a direct claim of white racial superiority, but as a grievance about trafficking, one that ironically trafficked the value of white skin. Just so have white slavery abolitionists, now and in the past, expressed and contained antislavery critiques against a global capitalism that, in fact, thrives on human trafficking.[4]

---

contemporary abolitionism and white supremacy. The movie's protagonist is an innocent white virgin whose sale to a Saudi sheik in the final scene justifies a torrent of righteous violence against her Albanian sex traffickers and their accomplices. For a discussion of the movie and the racist continuities in representing victims of trafficking in the annual human trafficking reports of the U.S. State Department since 2001, see Peck, "The Shadow of White Slavery," in Brands and Suri, eds., *Power of the Past*, 214–219. On *Taken*'s broader significance, see Casey Ryan Kelly, "Feminine Purity and Masculine Revenge-Seeking in *Taken* (2008)," *Feminist Media Studies*, XIV (2014), 403–418; and Klaus Dodds and Philip Kirby, "Resurrecting the Vigilante: Paternal Sovereignty, Exceptionality, and Familial Security in *Taken* (2008) and *Taken 2* (2013)," *Critical Studies on Security*, II (2014), 245–261.

4. Among many studies of the racial wealth gap in the United States, the work of William Darity, Jr., stands out for linking both educational and financial capital. See Darity, Jr., et. al, "Beyond Broke: Why Closing the Racial Wealth Gap Is a Priority for National Economic Security," Center for Global Policy Solutions, Duke University, Durham, N.C., 2014. For a complementary analysis of the ways white supremacy was "woven into the warp and weft of earlier anti-trafficking efforts" during the Progressive Era in the 1920s, see Jessica R. Pliley, "Ambivalent Abolitionist Legacies: The League of Nations' Investigations into Sex Trafficking, 1927–1934," in LeBaron, Pliley, and Blight, eds., *Fighting Modern Slavery*, 118.

The prominence of history in contemporary debates about modern slavery necessitates a sustained historical inquiry into the first contexts when human trafficking, whiteness, and racism became interwoven. First, when and where did people with light skin color come to see themselves as white? And second, when, where, and why did ideas of victimhood become intrinsic to the meaning of white identity? Answers to these questions have been far-flung and unexpected, not sequestrable within a single nation, empire, or ocean. The Atlantic, long known as the incubator for racial slavery, was indeed vital to the articulation of white identity and the ideas of victimhood that birthed the notion of a white race. But the Mediterranean also occupied a central place in the twined histories of human trafficking, skin color, race, and imperial expansion during the seventeenth and eighteenth centuries. The emergence of so-called white people was a transoceanic phenomenon, the timing and political work of which was quite distinct in each oceanic context and also different from contemporary understandings of white racial identity. The first whites in the English language were, not exemplars of racial privilege, but political outsiders, men and women marked by human trafficking. Two groups made up the most conspicuous individuals referred to as whites during the 1670s and 1680s: English convicts who had been transported out of the nation's jails to work as indentured servants in booming Atlantic slave colonies and Muslim men and women sold as slaves in Mediterranean slave markets. Both cohorts were explicitly distinguished from Christian servants in the Atlantic and Christian slaves in the Mediterranean. These whites were not viewed as individuals or as a singular race but as discrete pieces of property, to be counted and taxed by imperial authorities.[5]

In the Atlantic, the first whites were unreliable and politically dangerous, capable of uniting with enslaved Blacks in opposition to colonial rule. In time, the language of whiteness and blackness would make it easier for English authorities in Barbados and elsewhere to make distinctions between the political status of enslaved Africans and that of indentured servants from England,

---

5. Digitization has been indispensable to this research, enabling me to trace and map the changing meaning of white grammar using a rich mixture of primary sources found in the Colonial State Papers and the databases Early English Books Online and Eighteenth Century Collections Online. For a discussion of how I have used these databases, as well as some of the interpretive challenges and risks, see Appendices A through C. On the relationship between numeracy, the slave trade, and imperial expansion, see Morgan, *Reckoning with Slavery*, 29–54; and Gunther Peck, "Counting Modern Slaves: Historicizing the Emancipatory Work of Numbers," in LeBaron, Pliley, and Blight, eds., *Fighting Modern Slavery*, 39–46.

Scotland, and Ireland, the primary group called whites across the seventeenth century. Those distinctions, however, had not yet been naturalized in the minds of colonial and metropolitan elites, nor among trafficked actors themselves, who resisted being commodified and compelled to work. Fears of cooperation between trafficked servants and slaves rippled across many English colonies. Antitrafficking emerged initially as a collaboration across lines of status and skin color, with both the enslaved and the transported, Blacks as well as whites, challenging the imperial architects of plantation slavery and mercantilist exchange. When London authorities raised an important tax on colonial sugar plantations in 1685, for example, the acting deputy governor of Barbados, Edwyn Stede, lamented that many planters had "dismissed from their service the hyred that were amongst them," increasing their reliance on trafficked servants and enslaved Africans, a dangerous combination. Previously, the "hyred" had been "a defense against our Servants, as both united, were a Curb on our Negroes." Freely hired servants steered the transported indentured servants away from finding common cause with the enslaved. Stede had a low opinion of transported white servants, however, describing them as "being but the Cleanings of your Majesty's Gaols." The distinction Stede drew between hired servants and transported convicts highlights just how closely tethered trafficked individuals and rebellion were in the minds of the architects of England's emerging empire. The greatest threat to imperial power in Barbados in 1685 was an uprising of the trafficked. "Considering the bloody temper of our Slaves," Stede concluded, "we cannot but have dreadful apprehensions of the Club and the Knife when infected by those People."[6]

The political distinctions between hired and trafficked servants and the work of skin color would change in time, as the eighteenth century witnessed the imagination of whiteness as a set of heritable rights and privileges for

---

6. Deputy Governor, Council, and Assembly of Barbados to Lords of Trade and Plantations, Sept. 14, 1685, CO 1/58, 56, enclosure I, PRO, The National Archives, Kew, U.K. (hereafter TNA). The text was summarized in the *Calendar of State Papers* nearly two centuries later as Stede saying that "we have been obliged to discharge our hired servants, who were a great safety to the Island, since they formed most part of the Militia and curbed our negroes and white servants, . . . being the sweepings of the jails." See "The Deputy-Governor, Council, and Assembly of Barbados to Lords of Trade and Plantations," Sept. 14, 1685, in J. W. Fortescue, ed., *Calendar of State Papers, Colonial Series, America and the West Indies, 1685–1688* . . . , [XII] (London, 1899), 94. The *Calendar* summary left out key details about trafficked servants briefly being "united" with hired servants while also adding white grammar to Stede's description of transported convicts. I discuss these nineteenth-century alterations to seventeenth-century documents in Chapter One, below.

all Christians of European heritage. That process, however, was resisted not only by many elites, who loathed connections with the commoners they had long exploited, but also by trafficked servants, who continued to form strategic alliances with enslaved Africans, running away from shared masters and, on occasion, plotting rebellions against common enemies. Even when whiteness became better established as an ideology of race with a set of prescriptive rights, its relationship to trafficking remained conspicuous. Indeed, when freedom became racialized as an inherent expression of a now timeless white identity, defenders of white rights made victimhood and trafficking their emotive cornerstones. In that highly elastic accounting of historical suffering, trafficking played a vital if imprecise role, a way of insisting that white suffering or white slavery was a crime whose costs far exceeded any crimes associated with the enslavement of African peoples across the Americas. That transnational and transactional calculus linked a partial critique of mercantilist political economy to white racism, a hallmark of the ideology of white supremacy that came into full flower, not with the expansion of the African slave trade in the 1680s, but in opposition to the power and potential of anti-trafficking and antislavery during an age of revolution and emancipation in the 1780s. Contemporary white nationalists similarly appropriate narratives about racial injustice and human trafficking to silence radical alternatives. In short, exaggerated claims about white victimhood are central to the political work of white racial identity in the past and the present, in each case a response to radical challenges to dominant norms of political culture and economy. White identity has never been created by skin color, even if notions of white victimhood naturalize that premise. Rather whiteness as a concept originated through political discourse about human trafficking, enslavement, and sharp conflicts over what to do about both.[7]

---

7. One of the most dramatic examples of collaboration between indentured whites and enslaved Blacks is the servant-slave conspiracy of 1741 in New York City in which four Irish immigrants, three of them servants, and twenty-six African slaves were executed as part of an alleged plot to burn colonial New York to the ground and overthrow common masters. See Chapter 4, below; and Jill Lepore, *New York Burning: Liberty, Slavery, and Conspiracy in Eighteenth-Century Manhattan* (New York, 2005). It has not helped that some historians have anachronistically described indentured servants in Virginia during the early seventeenth century as white slaves, despite that most indentured servants were known as Christian servants and only transported convicts were known as whites. Historians have similarly described European captives sold into slavery in North Africa during the seventeenth and eighteenth centuries as white slaves, even though no European captives were described as such until the early nineteenth century. On the history of so-called

Introduction

This is not the narrative we have come to expect about the history of whiteness or white supremacy. In *Race Traffic*, I explore the historical relationship between human trafficking—the buying and selling of people—and race—the idea that a person's skin color defines their intrinsic identity and value as a person. Before 1661, few people believed that skin color alone authored one's value or one's identity.[8] Other forms of difference, such as religion, nativity, national identity, and familial background, organized and justified human

---

white slaves in British history, see Don Jordan and Michael Walsh, *White Cargo: The Forgotten History of Britain's White Slaves in America* (New York, 2007). White supremacist Michael A. Hoffman goes further than Jordan and Walsh insisting all white people in colonial America were enslaved because they were white, a patently false claim. See Hoffman, *They Were White and They Were Slaves*. For anachronistic references to white slaves in seventeenth- and eighteenth-century North Africa, see Linda Colley, *Captives* (New York, 2002), 56, 59, 61; Paul Baepler, ed., *White Slaves, African Masters: An Anthology of American Barbary Captivity Narratives* (Chicago, 1999); Robert C. Davis, *Christian Slaves, Muslim Masters: White Slavery in the Mediterranean, the Barbary Coast, and Italy, 1500–1800* (New York, 2003); Giles Milton, *White Gold: The Extraordinary Story of Thomas Pellow and Islam's One Million White Slaves* (New York, 2004); and Simon Webb, *The Forgotten Slave Trade: The White European Slaves of Islam* (Philadelphia, 2020).

8. Scholarly investigations into the origins of white supremacy have given rise to a wide range of decisive historical turning points. Peter Linebaugh and Marcus Rediker highlight the Putney debates in 1659, when English parliamentarians protested the enslavement of Englishmen while assenting to the enslavement of Africans. Jennifer L. Morgan has brilliantly analyzed how notions of "heredity, motherhood, commodity, and race" became linked in the transatlantic slave trade beginning in the middle of the seventeenth century, while Kathleen M. Brown has underscored the vital importance of the passage of the Virginia servant-slave codes of 1661, which made enslavement heritable through the mother's status. Edmund S. Morgan and Theodore W. Allen have suggested Bacon's Rebellion in Virginia in 1676 was the key uprising that propelled England to leadership in the African slave trade. Peter H. Wood has elaborated how the Stono Rebellion in 1739 and its aftermath institutionalized the power of white supremacy in South Carolina, while Jill Lepore argues that the reaction to the alleged servant-slave rebellion in New York City in 1741 solidified white supremacy in New York. Peter Silver has suggested that only with wars between white people and indigenous peoples in the mid-Atlantic colonies in the 1750s did white supremacy fully emerge there. Nikole Hannah-Jones, in turn, has suggested that white supremacy was baked into the history of North American colonization from its inception, citing 1619, when the first Africans were sold to English colonists. See Linebaugh and Rediker, *The Many-Headed Hydra: Sailors, Slaves, Commoners, and the Hidden History of the Revolutionary Atlantic* (Boston, 2000), 138; Morgan, *Reckoning with Slavery*, 3; Brown, *Good Wives, Nasty Wenches, and Anxious Patriarchs: Gender, Race, and Power in Colonial Virginia* (Williamsburg, Va., and Chapel Hill, N.C., 1996), 116–136; Edmund S. Morgan, *American Slavery, American Freedom: The Ordeal of Colonial Virginia* (New York,

trafficking, enslavement, and conquest. The global expansion of human trafficking by skin color during the latter half of the seventeenth century, however, set in motion political work as profound and far-reaching as the older processes of colonization and enslavement that it amplified and recast. And yet, the historical alchemy between human trafficking, skin color, and ideas of inheritance that became known as race were neither inevitable nor natural. Rather, those linkages were peculiar as well as temporally and spatially uneven. I examine contingencies within the history of mercantile political economy and culture by considering how and why white identity would become powerful as a timeless construct, as an idea of white suffering. That formation, crafted by elite progenitors of white identity, sought to co-opt or silence alliances of trafficked and enslaved actors who were challenging racial capitalism. In so doing, I illuminate the centrality of revisionism to ideologies of whiteness as well as those ideologies' characteristic conceit: that whites were the real victims of racism in history, despite no so-called white slaves ever being trafficked or enslaved because they were white.[9]

---

1975), 316–337; Allen, *The Invention of the White Race*, I, *Racial Oppression and Social Control* (London, 1994), 44; Wood, *Black Majority: Negroes in Colonial South Carolina from 1670 through the Stono Rebellion* (New York, 1974), 308–326; Lepore, *New York Burning*; Silver, *Our Savage Neighbors: How Indian War Transformed Early America* (New York, 2008), 114; and Hannah-Jones, "1619 Project," *The New York Times Book Magazine*, Aug. 18, 2019. Jones writes that the sale of thirty Africans in 1619 proves that "anti-black racism runs in the very DNA of this country" (Hannah-Jones, "The Idea of America," ibid., 21).

9. Skin color has become an increasingly important topic of historical investigation, though most studies focus on contemporary communities of color in the United States. See Evelyn Nakano Glenn, ed., *Shades of Difference: Why Skin Color Matters* (Stanford, Calif., 2009); Mara C. Ostfeld and Nicole D. Yadon, *Skin Color, Power, and Politics in America* (New York, 2022); and Nina G. Jablonski, *Living Color: The Biology and Social Meaning of Skin Color* (Berkeley, Calif., 2012). For a comparative approach, see Edward E. Telles, *Race in Another America: The Significance of Skin Color in Brazil* (Princeton, N.J., 2004). On historical investigations of when and where skin color became incorporated into evolving notions of race, see Sujata Iyengar, *Shades of Difference: Mythologies of Skin Color in Early Modern England* (Philadelphia, 2005); Nancy Shoemaker, *A Strange Likeness: Becoming Red and White in Eighteenth-Century North America* (New York, 2004), 125–140; Roxann Wheeler, *The Complexion of Race: Categories of Difference in Eighteenth-Century British Culture* (Philadelphia, 2000); and Winthrop D. Jordan, *White over Black: American Attitudes towards the Negro, 1550–1812* (Williamsburg, Va., and Chapel Hill, N.C., 1968), 512–541. On the varied definitions of race across the eighteenth century, see Wheeler, *Complexion of Race*, 1–48; and Laura Doyle, *Freedom's Empire: Race and the Rise of the Novel in Atlantic Modernity, 1640–1940* (Durham, N.C., 2008), 12–21. On the role of religious affiliations as

To understand this historical work in the context in which it occurred, I define trafficking and enslavement as the seventeenth-century architects of mercantilism did, as distinct practices within a single political economy that stretched from the Mediterranean to the Atlantic. Rather than conflating trafficking and slavery as the TPVA and Palermo Protocol do, I sharply delineate between them. Trafficking describes the historical processes by which migrant men and women became fungible property, bought and sold by owners, who, in turn, extracted value from the bodies they purchased. Trafficking frequently involved the deployment of "force, fraud, or coercion" in organizing migrants' passages and could result in enslavement, as in the case of the African slave trade. But trafficking also facilitated forms of unfree labor that did not become slavery, as in the case of convict transportation or indentured servitude. Trafficking also thrived within nominally free labor arrangements in which migrant wage earners were commodified across borders, along with their access to particular employments in new destinations. Trafficking has existed with and without the force of law and occurs when migrants, by virtue of debts, geographic circumstance, family obligations, or illegal status, become commodities. Human trafficking, in short, has assumed varied forms in history but has been indispensable to global capitalism from the seventeenth century to the present.[10]

---

well as renegades in shaping the traffic in both Christian and Muslim captives across the Mediterranean, see Minna Rozen, *The Mediterranean in the Seventeenth Century: Captives, Pirates, and Ransomers* (Palermo, Italy, [2016]), 65–84; Nabil Matar, *Britain and Barbary, 1589–1689* (Gainesville, Fla., 2005); and Daniel Hershenzon, *The Captive Sea: Slavery, Communication, and Commerce in Early Modern Spain and the Mediterranean* (Philadelphia, 2018).

10. See TPVA; and Protocol. My definition of trafficking is narrower than the Palermo Protocol's broad language "for the purposes of exploitation" but retains the TPVA's focus on "force, fraud, and coercion" while concentrating on the coercive practices that generate commodification. Like the TVPA and the Palermo Protocol, I exclude individuals who have been smuggled and who are not sold on arrival. On distinctions between smuggling and trafficking, see Peter Andreas, *Smuggler Nation: How Illicit Trade Made America* (New York, 2013). Both corporations and states have played central roles in fomenting trafficking within nominally free wage-labor contexts. On connections between corporations' reliance on subcontracting and human trafficking, see Genevieve LeBaron, "Subcontracting Is Not Illegal, but Is It Unethical? Business Ethics, Forced Labor, and Economic Success," *Brown Journal of World Affairs*, XX, no. 2 (Spring/Summer 2014), 237–249. On the history of padrones in creating corporate systems of labor subcontracting and coercive trafficking, see Gunther Peck, *Reinventing Free Labor: Padrones and Immigrant Workers in the North American West, 1880–1930* (Cambridge, 2000).

Slavery, on the other hand, describes a condition of continuous theft in which one's body, labor, identity, skills, and progeny are stolen, whether one is formally sold at auction. Being trafficked was not a universal experience for enslaved individuals born into slave societies across the Americas, even if the fear of being sold shaped how master-slave relations functioned. For the men, women, and children kidnapped in Africa and sold into the transatlantic slave trade, bondage made up both traffic and theft, commodification and slavery. The horrific work of the slave ship, as Marcus Rediker demonstrates, was to teach Africans, first, the meaning of enslavement—that their bodies were not their own—and, second, the meaning of trafficking—that they would soon become cash. Slavery in the Americas could not function separately from the traffic in slaves, as making enslaved people fungible and movable powered economic growth and the expansion of capitalism across Anglo-American frontiers. Both made the development of racial capitalism possible across the seventeenth and eighteenth centuries. But for no servants did the experience of being trafficked, however traumatic or frequent, turn them or their descendants into slaves. The contemporary conflation of servitude and slavery would have made little sense to trafficked people or their masters.[11]

Solidarity among those who were trafficked or enslaved in the seventeenth and eighteenth centuries did not occur by virtue of their varied and shared experiences as commodities. Solidarities among trafficked people were achieved through shared sacrifice, common proximities to one another and to shared

---

11. My definition of slavery is compatible with contemporary activists' definitions of modern slavery, which exist without the formal sanction of the law. But I narrow the definition of slavery in the Palermo Protocol from that of a generalized exploitation to one of a condition of having one's labor, personhood, services, and wages continuously or perpetually stolen. I also differ from sociologist Orlando Patterson, who argues that racial slavery in the Americas was defined by natal alienation, the total rupture between slaves and their communities of origin. By that standard, there were no true slaves in the Mediterranean, as captive sailors continued to possess identities that were central to how they were trafficked as slaves and, if they were fortunate, emancipated through ransoms. On debates over the definition of human trafficking in the Protocol, see Chuang, "Rescuing Trafficking from Ideological Capture," *University of Pennsylvania Law Review*, CLVIII (2010), 1655–1728. On definitions of slavery as an irrevocable sundering of one's natal identity, see Patterson, *Slavery and Social Death: A Comparative Study* (Cambridge, Mass., 1982); and Chapter Two, below. On preparing enslaved passengers for sale, see Marcus Rediker, *The Slave Ship: A Human History* (New York, 2007), 238–239; and Emma Christopher, *Slave Ship Sailors and Their Captive Cargoes, 1730–1807* (New York, 2006), 195–225. On the misuses of history in the contemporary abolitionist movement, see Peck, "Counting Modern Slaves," in LeBaron, Pliley, and Blight, eds., *Fighting Modern Slavery*, 34–55.

masters, and local ingenuity. They are significant precisely because the legal, political, and material differences between transported servants, captive sailors, and enslaved Africans were substantial and growing over the course of the two centuries after 1619. After 1661, being purchased at auction in Virginia as an enslaved African meant something radically different than being sold as an indentured servant in the same place and time. Henceforth, the traffic in African women involved the financial value of their reproduction, with all their progeny owned by their masters. No indentured servant or transported convict, however mistreated, experienced trafficking in such fashion. Fungibility had a time limit. For sailors enslaved in North Africa, in turn, trafficking meant, not despair, but the hope that friends, relatives, and allies might be able to finance their ransom and redeem them. No such transatlantic aspiration existed for those sold at auction in the Americas, whether they were enslaved or indentured.[12]

These profound differences in the ways people were historically bought and sold not only created dilemmas among the trafficked but also sparked enduring questions about how trafficking should be remembered and historicized, how or even whether particular kinds of trafficking should be compared to one another. Some historians have been reluctant to compare racial slavery to other forms of unfree labor, for example, fearful that comparisons might imply moral equivalence. On the other hand, comparisons between servitude, transportation, captivity, and enslavement are as old as mercantilist expansion itself and have shaped how European colonization was made and contested. Rather than leave such comparisons to contemporary race traffickers, whose capacity to exaggerate an ahistorical white victimhood is limitless, I instead historicize the political work such comparisons have fostered, focusing on the geographic contexts in which human trafficking and race came to condition one another's meanings.[13]

---

12. On servants' capacity for collaboration with the enslaved in rebelling against common masters, see Susan Dwyer Amussen, *Caribbean Exchanges: Slavery and the Transformation of English Society, 1640–1700* (Chapel Hill, N.C., 2007), 158–159; Simon P. Newman, *A New World of Labor: The Development of Plantation Slavery in the British Atlantic* (Philadelphia, 2013), 96; Linebaugh and Rediker, *Many-Headed Hydra*, 124; Michael Guasco, *Slaves and Englishmen: Human Bondage in the Early Modern Atlantic World* (Philadelphia, 2014), 167; and Morgan, *American Slavery, American Freedom*, 298–299.

13. Linda Colley, for example, writes that "it is wrong to draw comparisons between the North African system of seizing and exploiting human beings and the triangular trade in black slaves," though she also insists that "it is no less appropriate to marginalise Barbary depradations [sic]." See Colley, *Captives*, 62–63. Assessing the historical relationships

To understand what trafficking meant to those who experienced it, I have turned to the narratives that trafficked people wrote or told to others about their experiences of being bought and sold, whether as indentured servants, transported convicts, captive sailors, or enslaved people torn from their communities and families of origin. Because of the spread of literacy and the printing press during the late seventeenth and eighteenth centuries, published narratives are scattered across national and regional libraries in Europe and the Americas. These sources exist within multiple manuscript collections, national archives, personal papers, imperial correspondence, and trial records. All present interpretive challenges, filled as many are with literary devices, fabricated encounters with local peoples, and memories that, at minimum, were constructed and narrated for specific purposes after the fact. Reading them as unmediated reflections on the experience of being sold, or as an archive of oral histories of the trafficked, simplifies their historical significance. Some survivors of trafficking published narratives that directly engaged the meanings of trafficking, empire, freedom, and race more broadly. Others, such as the alleged conspirators behind New York City's enslaved rebellion in 1741, became known for the words they refused to say, such as a confession to participating in a racial conspiracy to kill white people demanded of them by prosecutors as the price for their survival. In each case, I have examined the narratives of the trafficked in the political and semantic contexts that made their stories powerful and historically significant. Most trafficked and enslaved people left no individual stories or records at all. For the few whose stories have survived, I link individual narratives to the political and discursive context that produced them, discerning the choices, however limited, narrators possessed.[14]

---

between servitude and enslavement has been vexing for historians of indentured servitude as well, with some downplaying coercion among servants and others highlighting it. For those emphasizing commonalities between servitude and enslavement, trafficking features prominently. See Abbott Emerson Smith, *Colonists in Bondage: White Servitude and Convict Labor in America, 1607–1776* (Williamsburg, Va., and Chapel Hill, N.C., 1947), 67–74; Newman, *New World of Labor*, 92–100; Guasco, *Slaves and Englishmen*, 166–167; and Robert J. Steinfeld, *The Invention of Free Labor: The Employment Relation in English and American Law and Culture, 1350–1870* (Chapel Hill, N.C., 1991), 44–54. For those insisting on consent, trafficking recedes in importance. See Christopher Tomlins, *Freedom Bound: Law, Labor, and Civic Identity in Colonizing English America, 1580–1865* (New York, 2010), 80–81; and Kenneth Morgan, *Slavery and Servitude in Colonial North America: A Short History* (New York, 2001), 19–22.

14. I am indebted to Linda Colley's "captivity archive" for locating many of the trafficking narratives I discuss. See Colley, *Captives*, 15, 380–383.

Interpreting the rhetoric of enslavement among diverse trafficked actors represents a methodological challenge as vexing and important as the ethical challenge of distinguishing trafficking from slavery. Were the indentured servants who called themselves slaves exaggerating their coercion? Were the sailors captured at sea and sold to Muslim masters who insisted their slavery was worse than Egyptian bondage commenting on the African slave trade? No single political answer across time and space is possible for these comparative assessments. The reason for that is simple: the geographic and political context for trafficking mattered as much as the formal legal definitions of migrants' status in constituting the coercion they experienced. Equally important, the antislavery frameworks that trafficked and enslaved actors used to demand justice were themselves comparative in form, imaginatively crossing Atlantic and Mediterranean geographies. Consider, for example, the case of indentured servant William Okeley who set sail aboard the *Mary* of London in 1639, destined for the island of Providence in the West Indies. Just days after departing, his ship was overtaken by three Turkish ships, and Okeley, along with hundreds of other indentured servants sailing alongside him, was captured and sold as a slave in Algiers, an ordeal that Okeley would survive and eventually recount in a rare published life story, *Eben-ezer; or, A Small Monument of Great Mercy*. Okeley's account demands considerable caution as a historical source. Written from the vantage of English freedom and filled with literary inventions, his narrative nonetheless constitutes an invaluable perspective on the experience of being trafficked across two oceanic geographies.[15]

Okeley's vivid critique of trafficking was comparative in form and had a polemical aim: to encourage Christians sold to fellow Christians in the Atlantic to be loyal and obedient to their masters. His message was a direct response to the political unrest of young servants in London, who were just then protesting coercion in the servant trade, an effort that had pushed Parliament to pass legislation against the practice of spiriting in 1670. Okeley's description of trafficking was, not an unmediated reflection on his experience, but a sermon, a story meant to dissuade young Atlantic servants from protesting their experiences of being trafficked to Christian masters in the Americas. Comparison and revision shaped the creation of Okeley's narrative and changed its

---

15. William Okeley, *Eben-ezer; or, A Small Monument of Great Mercy* . . . (London, 1675), 4, 8–9, 11. On Okeley's journey and its historical significance, see Colley, *Captives*, 90–92; and Joe Snader, *Caught between Worlds: British Captivity Narratives in Fact and Fiction* (Lexington, Ky., 2000).

meaning over time. In the hands of British and American nationalists during the early nineteenth century, Okeley's story, along with most narratives of Christian slavery written in the seventeenth and eighteenth centuries, was recast as a narrative of white slavery. In 1814, Sir Sydney Smith, a retired British admiral, led a campaign among ministers and diplomatic leaders at the Congress of Vienna to create a united European assault against white slavery that would destroy the capacity of Algiers to capture and traffic European captives in North Africa. Okeley's opposition to the *"Imperious Turk"* was replotted as a racial struggle between white Europeans and racialized Muslims, despite the untidy fact that a third of the British and American navies at that moment were Black. At the beginning of the nineteenth century, abolitionism and white victimhood had become tightly twined in the Mediterranean.[16]

Tracking the changing meaning of Okeley's narrative is important, not just for the sake of historical accuracy, but for understanding when, how, and why an ideology of white victimhood became powerful. Okeley's narrative exemplifies key themes in *Race Traffic*—how trafficking insights became meaningful through comparison and how revision has become essential to the proliferation of ideas of white victimhood. At no moment did Okeley refer to skin color, his own or that of his master, nor did he describe himself as a white person, or mention white slavery. His account was published in 1675, when white grammar was quite new, reserved for transported convicts and trafficked Muslim slaves. Discerning that political context makes Okeley's narrative all the richer, precisely because he geographically traversed the Atlantic and Mediterranean theaters so important in the evolution of race traffic. Okeley's narrative exemplifies how languages of antislavery and race have frequently been imposed on trafficked subjects by political actors long after the fact, complicating the task of discerning how trafficked actors themselves perceived trafficking, skin color, and enslavement. Throughout *Race Traffic*, I keep my attention focused on questions of historical agency and cultural context, considering who articulated the language of antislavery and

---

16. Okeley, *Eben-ezer*, [A7r–v]; "An Act to Prevent Stealing and Transporting Other Children," Mar. 18, 1670, CO 389/2, 1–13, CSP, TNA. For a description of the Spiriting law as passed in Barbados in 1670, see "Six Acts of Barbados Passed in 1670," Aug. 11, 1670, CO 30/1, 75–83, CSP, PRO, TNA. On the elevation of white slavery over Christian slavery, see [Sidney Smith], *Translation of the Documents Annexed to the Report of the President of the Reunion of the Knights, Liberators of the White Slaves of Africa, Assembled at Vienna, on the 29th of December, 1814* (Paris, 1816).

skin color and to what ends. For the trafficked and the enslaved, antislavery ideology was a method for mapping and comparing their stories to other sites of coercion and bondage. Such maps were not necessarily drawn on the pages of a book, though they sometimes were, but were more often etched in trafficked subjects' imaginings about the location of freedom and its relationship to nations and empires.

By making distinctions between skin color and race as well as between trafficking and slavery, I build on the pathbreaking work of several generations of scholars to offer interventions at the intersections of multiple historical fields.[17] Three contributions anchor the book's narrative and analysis. First, I shed light on contingencies within the history of racial capitalism, finding moments when the meanings of skin color, race, sovereignty, and antislavery

---

17. The scholarship that historicizes race and its relationship to skin color and enslavement is voluminous. I am particularly indebted to Karen E. Fields and Barbara J. Fields for their conceptualization of race as an ideology that is not authored by skin color and that obscures class inequality. See Fields and Fields, *Racecraft: The Soul of Inequality in American Life* (New York, 2012), 12–15; and Allen, *Invention of the White Race*, I, 3–24. I am likewise indebted to Nell Irvin Painter, the only scholar of whiteness who has incorporated the Mediterranean into her analysis. See Painter, *The History of White People* (New York, 2010), 43–58. I am in dialogue with David R. Roediger's foundational work on whiteness and racial capitalism throughout *Race Traffic*. See Roediger, *The Wages of Whiteness: Race and the Making of the American Working Class* (London, 1991); Roediger, *Towards the Abolition of Whiteness: Essays on Race, Politics, and Working-Class History* (London, 1994); and Roediger, *Class, Race, and Marxism* (London, 2017). My debts to scholars of antislavery and abolition are also interwoven throughout the book, especially Christopher Leslie Brown's understanding of abolitionism as a transformation of political antislavery and Manisha Sinha's comprehensive history of abolition that puts Black people and interracialism at the center of her story. See Brown, *Moral Capital: Foundations of British Abolitionism* (Williamsburg, Va., and Chapel Hill, N.C., 2006); and Sinha, *The Slave's Cause: A History of Abolition* (New Haven, Conn., 2016). My distinction between human trafficking and enslavement in history has been fostered by engagement with scholars studying "modern slavery," especially Elena Shih, Janie A. Chuang, Joel Quirk, and Genevieve LeBaron, each of whom critiques the conflation of human trafficking with modern slavery. See Shih, *Manufacturing Freedom: Sex Work, Anti-Trafficking Rehab, and the Racial Wages of Rescue* (Oakland, Calif., 2023); Chuang, "The Challenges and Perils of Reframing Trafficking as 'Modern-Day Slavery,'" *Anti-Trafficking Review*, no. 5 (September 2015), 146–149, www.antitrafficking review.org; Quirk, "Evaluating the Political Effects of Anti-Slavery and Anti-Trafficking Activism," in LeBaron, ed., *Researching Forced Labour in the Global Economy: Methodological Challenges and Advances* (Oxford, 2018), 60–78; and LeBaron, *Combatting Modern Slavery: Why Labour Governance Is Failing and What We Can Do about It* (Cambridge, 2020).

were not settled by the alleged logic of the markets in people that defined the meaning of freedom to mercantile elites.[18] When indentured servants and their advocates demanded an end to kidnapping and the spiriting of servants in the 1660s, for example, English lawmakers in Parliament confronted a challenge that threatened how and whether England would become a global leader in the African slave trade. When shipping merchant Thomas Betton decided to create the Ironmongers' Slave Fund, dedicated to emancipating all "English slaves" in the Mediterranean, on his death in 1733, he could not have anticipated its impact on how Great Britain would eventually globalize emancipation for non-English enslaved people across the Atlantic. And when the formerly enslaved sailor Olaudah Equiano recast English captivity narratives as critiques of trafficking, slavery, and Christianity, he upended how unfree labor markets worked in both the Atlantic and Mediterranean theaters. Abolitionist achievements in the Atlantic also paradoxically invited the globalization of white victimhood in the early nineteenth century, when the first campaign for abolishing white slavery in the Mediterranean became powerful with military interventions against North Africa in 1815 and 1816. To see the contingencies in these historical episodes is to understand that hostility to trafficking, antislavery ideology, and race were each moving targets. *Race Traffic* examines how ideas, policies, and people moved in tandem and how people transformed antislavery, race, and the purposes of sovereignty in the process.[19]

---

18. On the expansive scope of the history of racial capitalism, see Cedric J. Robinson, *Black Marxism: The Making of the Black Radical Tradition* (1983; rpt. Chapel Hill, N.C., 2000); and Justin Leroy and Destin Jenkins, "Introduction: The Old History of Racial Capitalism," in Leroy and Jenkins, eds., *Histories of Racial Capitalism* (New York, 2021), 1–26. Much of the scholarship on racial capitalism is concentrated on the late eighteenth- and nineteenth-century Atlantic world. See overviews by Walter Johnson, "Racial Capitalism and Human Rights," in Johnson with Robin D. G. Kelley, eds., *Race Capitalism Justice*, Forum 1, *Boston Review* (2017), 105–113; Sven Beckert, "History of American Capitalism," in Eric Foner and Lisa McGirr, eds., *American History Now* (Philadelphia, 2011), 314–315; Seth Rockman, "What Makes the History of Capitalism Newsworthy?" *Journal of the Early Republic*, XXXIV (2014), 439–466; and Edward E. Baptist, *The Half Has Never Been Told: Slavery and the Making of American Capitalism* (New York, 2014). On the centrality of gender and women to the history of racial capitalism, see Gargi Bhattacharyya, *Rethinking Racial Capitalism: Questions of Reproduction and Survival* (London, 2018); Hartman, *Lose Your Mother*; and Morgan, *Reckoning with Slavery*, 15–17, 25–26.

19. "Last Will and Testament of Thomas Betton," Feb. 15, 1723, MS 17034/4, 4, Thomas Betton Charity Papers, Guildhall Library, London; and Chapter Five, below. The history of the Worshipful Company of Ironmongers of London awaits its historian. See the

Second, by demonstrating that whiteness originated in the seventeenth century within a global and imperial context, I provide an alternative to the geographically confined nature of much of the scholarship on whiteness, which has often found definitive starting points for white supremacy but missed the essential work of racial revisionism that animates the enduring power of white racial ideology. In so doing, I also offer a corrective to the scholarly focus on working-class communities during the nineteenth and twentieth centuries. Whiteness has, from its inception, been global, I demonstrate, an imperial grammar that became most powerful as an ideology by co-opting the emancipatory energy created by trafficked and enslaved actors cooperating across lines of skin color. That historical process involved narratives of victimhood that transcended one social class or one region in time. Approaches to the history of whiteness that limit it to the United States or to a particular region such as the U.S. South obscure its global origin and function, the centrality of human trafficking to its evolution, and a full historical understanding for how and why it became powerful and enduring. If only white racism were solely a southern U.S. problem, or if white nationalism could be confined to an exceptional region or nation! Viewing white racism as a geographic problem, one that can be confined to a particular geography or class, itself represents a kind of revisionism that exemplifies how whiteness has worked in tandem with national imaginaries since the late eighteenth century.[20]

---

dissertation of Catherine M. Steyer, "Barbary Pirates, British Slaves, and the Early Modern Atlantic World, 1570–1800" (Ph.D. diss., University of Pennsylvania, 2011). For a brief mention of the Ironmonger Company, responsible for administering a trust established by Thomas Betton, which became the Ironmongers' Slave Fund, see Colley, *Captives*, 120. For Equiano, see Olaudah Equiano, *The Interesting Narrative of the Life of Olaudah Equiano; or, Gustavus Vassa, the African; Written by Himself*, 2d. ed. (London, [1789]). On the emergence of white slavery abolitionism in 1814, see [Smith], *Translation of the Documents Annexed to the Report of the President*; Chapter Eight, below; John R. Jewitt, *A Journal, Kept at Nootka Sound, by John R. Jewitt; One of the Surviving Crew of the Ship Boston, of Boston, John Salter, Commander, Who Was Massacred on 22D of March, 1803* . . . (Boston, 1807); and Jewitt, *A Narrative of the Adventures and Sufferings, of John R. Jewitt; Only Survivor of the Crew of the Ship Boston, during a Captivity of Nearly Three Years among the Savages of Nootka Sound: With an Account of the Manners, Mode of Living, and Religious Opinions of the Natives* (Middletown, Conn., 1815).

20. Scholarly investigations of whiteness emerged within U.S. labor and immigration history as a debate over problems peculiar to the American nation and its working class. See Roediger, *Wages of Whiteness*; Roediger, *Towards the Abolition of Whiteness*; and Roediger, *Working toward Whiteness: How America's Immigrants Became White: The Strange Journey from Ellis Island to the Suburbs* (New York, 2005); Noel Ignatiev, *How the Irish Became White*

*Race Traffic*, finally, suggests that historians of antislavery have suffered from a teleological focus on abolitionism, misreading expressions of antislavery sentiment as rehearsals for a true abolition. Protests against human trafficking did not begin with the better-known abolitionist movement of the late eighteenth century but emerged across England's expanding mercantile domains during the seventeenth century. The prominence of antislavery arguments among the trafficked during the seventeenth century did not so much rehearse abolitionism as create a reservoir of political possibilities for those protesting trafficking and the metropolitan and colonial authorities who sought to silence or to co-opt them. A multifaceted tradition of antislavery protests across Britain's empire became a resource for the better-known abolitionists when they finally emerged, not the other way around. The power of antitrafficking and the malleability of antislavery are precisely what made the abolitionist movement a stunning and unanticipated development when it did arrive, as Black and white abolitionists successfully adapted hostility to human commerce to make antislavery a radical, emancipatory political project, though only temporarily so. Antislavery could be a vehicle for critiquing systemic injustices within racial capitalism or just as easily an insidious ideology supporting the status quo. For the trafficked and the enslaved, antislavery

---

(London, 1995); Neil Foley, "Becoming Hispanic: Mexican Americans and the Faustian Pact with Whiteness," in Foley, ed., *Reflexiones 1997: New Directions in Mexican American Studies* (Austin, Tex., 1998), 53–70; Karen Brodkin, *How Jews Became White Folks and What That Says about Race in America* (New Brunswick, N.J., 1998); Matthew Frye Jacobson, *Whiteness of a Different Color: European Immigrants and the Alchemy of Race* (Cambridge, Mass., 1998); and Ian Haney-López, *White by Law: The Legal Construction of Race* (New York, 1996). For a critique of that literature's definitional deficits, see Eric Arnesen, "Whiteness and the Historians' Imagination," *International Labor and Working-Class History*, no. 60 (Fall 2001), 3–32. For a critique of the nation-bound weaknesses of the whiteness debate, see Gunther Peck, "White Slavery and Whiteness: A Transnational View of the Sources of Working-Class Radicalism and Racism," *Labor: Studies in Working-Class History*, I, no. 2 (Summer 2004), 41–63. For scholars who have extended the timeframe and periodization for the history of whiteness, with more attention on origins as well as evolutions beyond the United States, see Nancy Isenberg, *White Trash: The 400-Year Untold History of Class in America* (New York, 2016); Painter, *History of White People*; and Isabel Wilkerson, *Caste: The Origins of Our Discontents* (New York, 2020). On the relationship between nations and races, see Jacobson, *Whiteness of a Different Color*, 39–90. On the ways white racism has gained strength as a local geography that is also broadly national and imperial, see Walter Johnson, *The Broken Heart of America: St. Louis and the Violent History of the United States* (New York, 2020); and Johnson, *River of Dark Dreams: Slavery and Empire in the Cotton Kingdom* (Cambridge, Mass., 2013).

was a strategy for daily survival, a lifeline that emboldened them to endure and to demand freedom and political rights. For the powerful, by contrast, antislavery buttressed support for royal prerogatives over human trafficking. As a currency of sovereignty as well as an indictment of its inadequacies, antislavery did not constitute a straightforward emancipatory politics but a ferociously contested tradition, the very fabric from which peoples resisted, challenged, and affirmed powers of the state. Understanding that contest sheds light on how and why white supremacy and a global abolitionist movement both gain energy from hostility to human trafficking.[21]

Throughout *Race Traffic*, I consider, like Okeley, the significance of the Mediterranean to the larger history of human trafficking and racial ideology that transformed both the Atlantic and Mediterranean regions by the beginning of the nineteenth century. At the start of the seventeenth century, the Atlantic had not yet become the dynamic engine of political, economic, and cultural change it would become. Nor were all slaveries there or elsewhere racial in form. The Mediterranean functioned as a crucial theater for building relationships between human trafficking and empire, whether for European, English, or North African actors. The comparative absence of either skin color or race in shaping the booming traffic in sailors, servants, and enslaved peoples across the Mediterranean during the seventeenth and eighteenth centuries provides a rich opportunity to see racial revisionism at work, as whiteness dramatically arrived in the wake of the slave trade's abolition. The linking of Islamophobia to fears of Black-white collaboration by 1815 emerged as a comparatively late innovation in race thinking, even while dressed in the garb of ancient tradition. The Mediterranean, though late to embrace race traffic, was not peripheral but central to the globalization of white victimhood that emerged in tandem with the abolition of the African slave trade. Challenging the pervasive existence of geographic chauvinism within both abolitionism and critiques of white supremacy—the tendency to isolate the origins of racism to a specific region and class or to nationalize the

---

21. See Brown, *Moral Capital*, 33–101; and David Waldstreicher, *Runaway America: Benjamin Franklin, Slavery, and the American Revolution* (New York, 2004), 175–209. The mischievous uses of antislavery are better known during the late eighteenth century but less so in the seventeenth century. On the varieties of political antislavery rhetoric in the American Revolution, see Waldstreicher, *Runaway America,* 176; and Eliga H. Gould, *Among the Powers of the Earth: The American Revolution and the Making of a New World Empire* (Cambridge, Mass., 2012). On the complex politics of antislavery and competition over enslaved sailors and Black freedmen during the War of 1812, see Alan Taylor, *The Internal Enemy: Slavery and War in Virginia, 1772–1832* (New York, 2013), 136–142.

achievements of antislavery—requires tracking how both whiteness and antislavery have moved, becoming conflated with places and polities over time.[22]

*Race Traffic* proceeds in both comparative and chronological fashion with chapters that alternate between the Atlantic and the Mediterranean. I begin with the emergence of skin color to describe trafficking in the Atlantic and the primacy of religious identities in shaping human trafficking in the Mediterranean, exploring the varied contexts for trafficked labor in both locales during the seventeenth century. Using the writings of sailors and transported servants, I investigate the earliest efforts by trafficked people to corral antislavery to emancipatory purposes as well as the hostile response by English political authorities to the rebellions that trafficked actors posed across the empire during the seventeenth century. Next, I investigate how critiques of trafficking fomented increasingly radical denunciations of Britain's trafficking policies and the British actors who benefited from them in the middle of the eighteenth century. The protests of enslaved and trafficked peoples in the Mediterranean pushed British authorities to articulate what they deemed national relations of rescue, while servant-slave collaborations in the Atlantic represented an extraordinary challenge to imperial authority. I then examine the remarkable culmination of antitrafficking radicalism during the late eighteenth and early nineteenth centuries. I link the emergence of that challenge to the globalization of a white-slavery discourse in the aftermath of the abolition of the African slave trade, a development that weakened the capacity of trafficked people to protest coercions associated with markets in people. Radical protests against racial capitalism would survive the emergence of a fully global ideology of white racial victimhood in both regions during the 1810s, but white slavery abolitionism expressed and contained dissent, using the bodies of trafficked whites to defend both white supremacy and the enslavement of Africans and their descendants across the Americas.

---

22. I am indebted to Ferdinand Braudel's conceptualization of the Mediterranean as a region. His analysis of the development of capitalism by states and monopolists illuminates the highly variable prices that captives and enslaved peoples commanded over time. See Braudel, *Civilization and Capitalism, 15th to 18th Century,* trans. Siân Reynolds, I–III (New York, 1982–1984); and Braudel, *The Mediterranean and the Mediterranean World in the Age of Philip II,* trans. Reynolds, 2 vols. (London, 1972–1973). On Braudel's enduring historiographical impact, see Gabriel Piterberg, Teofilo F. Ruiz, and Geoffrey Symcox, eds., *Braudel Revisited: The Mediterranean World, 1600–1800* (Toronto, 2010). On efforts to see the importance of the Mediterranean to British history, see Colley, *Captives,* 23–41; and Alison Games, *The Web of Empire: English Cosmopolitans in an Age of Expansion, 1560–1660* (New York, 2008), 47–79.

This book is not a comprehensive history of human trafficking, of racial slavery, or of whiteness between 1619 and 1819. Rather, it is best read as a series of empirically researched inquiries into how the history of human trafficking has been remembered and put to work. How can an understanding of that complex history better prepare activists to make contemporary antislavery a genuinely emancipatory project? How might recognition of the long, protracted fight by trafficked actors against commodification, enslavement, and racism reshape contemporary conversations about white supremacy? Can a better understanding of the mercurial work of white victimhood prompt a more robust movement to unmake the enduring privileges at the heart of racial capitalism? How might a better understanding of the historical role of states in fomenting human trafficking, before and after slavery's abolition, create new approaches for combatting it? If we are to learn from the past, we need to do more than make analogies with it; rather, we need to read the past on its own terms. Only then can we learn from the hard-won wisdom of the trafficked, whether enslaved, transported, or imprisoned, on how to build a political economy without human trafficking and racism at its core.

CHAPTER ONE

## The Origins of Race Traffic

WHEN A FLEMISH PIRATE named Captain John Colyn Jope arrived on board the English ship the *White Lion* in Jamestown, Virginia, in 1619, his cargo, as Englishman John Rolfe casually described it, included "not any thing but 20. and odd Negroes, wch the Governor and Cape Marchant bought for victualle." That Rolfe, a member of the governor's council and secretary and recorder general for the Virginia Company, could nonchalantly characterize the African people on board Captain Jope's ship as cargo is perhaps not surprising. Already an important figure in the young Virginia colony, he had been the first to cultivate and export tobacco to England in 1611. Yet he was also husband to the better-known Powhatan princess Pocahontas, who died several years before the *White Lion* came to Jamestown. That Rolfe, the enlightened Englishman who married across lines of color and religion, could view these Africans as worth little more than victual is jarring. These were the first Africans to arrive in North America as trafficked cargo, after all, the first of millions who would be transported across the Atlantic Ocean over the ensuing two and a half centuries. Rolfe's reaction seems especially obtuse and racist in hindsight, given the extraordinary ethical and financial impact the African slave trade would come to have on the subsequent history of both Africa and British North America. Racial slavery, and the horrific racism and violence that it would engender, appears to have commenced from the very moment Africans set foot in England's New World colonies.[1]

1. John Rolfe to Sir Edwyn Sandys, January 1619/20, in Susan Myra Kingsbury, ed., *The Records of the Virginia Company of London*, 4 vols. (Washington, D.C., 1906–1935), III, 243, also cited in Michael Guasco, *Slaves and Englishmen: Human Bondage in the Early Modern Atlantic World* (Philadelphia, 2014), 1. On the meanings of freedom and slavery in 1619 and their particular historical context, see Paul Musselwhite, Peter C. Mancall, and James Horn, eds., *Virginia 1619: Slavery and Freedom in the Making of English America*

At the time of Captain Jope's transaction, however, there was not yet any clear legal foundation for slavery in either England or its fledgling colonies. Nor did Africans immediately become the main source of unfree labor within Virginia or any of England's colonies after 1619. In Virginia and in Barbados, that work over the next half century fell primarily to indentured servants, many of them prisoners of war or transported felons, trafficked men and women whose unfree labor established both sugar and tobacco as export commodities for English planters. Although the transatlantic slave trade out of Africa was well established under Dutch and Portuguese leadership by 1619, the organized importation of enslaved Africans to England's Caribbean and North American colonies would not commence until much later in the seventeenth century. Barbados was the first English colony to turn to the African slave trade, doing so in the late 1630s, with Virginia following suit only in the 1680s, nearly seventy years after Jope struck a deal with Virginia's governor and the Cape merchant.[2]

The most salient aspect of the arrival of the "20. and odd Negroes" in Virginia in 1619, then, was the way in which the event reflected the ubiquity of human trafficking across cultural, political, and linguistic boundaries. The buying, selling, and trading of human subjects was indispensable to all imperial planning and ambition at the beginning of the seventeenth century, the reality of which Captain Jope, Rolfe, and the other Virginia officials were

---

(Williamsburg, Va., and Chapel Hill, N.C., 2019). The mythology of John Rolfe's racial liberality has a long and fascinating history that becomes visible in narratives of his alleged true love for Pocahontas. See Catherine Randolph Sheets, *Love Will Find the Way: The Marriage of John Rolfe and Pocahontas; His Letter Containing the Reasons Moving Him Thereunto* (Washington, D.C., 1907). For a good introduction to the important cultural work that the mythology of Pocahontas has performed throughout U.S. history, see Robert S. Tilton, *Pocahontas: The Evolution of an American Narrative* (Cambridge, 1994).

2. As historian Michael Guasco writes, "It still is not clear if the two dozen or so Africans" who arrived on the *White Lion* "were actually held as slaves" after Jope left. See Guasco, *Slaves and Englishmen*, 3. The landing of "20. and odd Negroes" in Virginia in 1619 was unusual not only because very few Africans came to Virginia before 1650 but also because pirates were forbidden from selling or trafficking their wares with colonial merchants throughout most of the seventeenth century. For an analysis of the slow development of African slave trafficking to Virginia before the 1670s, see Robin Law, "The Slave Trade in Seventeenth Century Allada: A Revision," *African Economic History*, XXII (1994), 59–92. On the role of Barbados in shaping Virginia colonial history, see April Lee Hatfield, *Atlantic Virginia: Intercolonial Relations in the Seventeenth Century* (Philadelphia, 2004).

well aware. Nor were they unique in that awareness.³ Rationales for trafficking people, whether transporting and selling convicts or defeated soldiers and sailors, abounded within England and northern Europe in 1600. Human trafficking likewise permeated diplomatic and commercial transactions across the Mediterranean region and beyond. Indigenous peoples trafficked humans across the Americas in 1619, as trade networks—and horses—were expanding throughout North and South America. Trafficking people provided diplomatic currency between political entities and commercial benefits to those who could traffic their defeated rivals. The form, meaning, and significance

3. The transition from indentured servitude to slavery in England's Caribbean and North American colonies has been part of a larger debate about the historical origins of racism and white supremacy in America. For Peter Linebaugh and Marcus Rediker, that moment came in 1659, when members of Parliament deliberated over a petition by English subjects who claimed to have been enslaved in Barbados. The discussion represented a turning point in "the development of the English doctrine of white supremacy," they argue, as English freedoms trumped concerns for the fate of African slaves. See Linebaugh and Rediker, *The Many-Headed Hydra: Sailors, Slaves, Commoners, and the Hidden History of the Revolutionary Atlantic* (Boston, 2000), 134, 138. Hilary McD. Beckles has averred that the passage of the Barbados slave and servant code in 1661, which established separate distinct penalties for runaway servants and slaves, was the watershed moment in making white supremacy. See Beckles, *White Servitude and Black Slavery in Barbados, 1626–1715* (Knoxville, Tenn., 1989). Edmund S. Morgan pinpointed the origins of white supremacy, not with the importation of the first Black slaves to North America, but with the decisive shift to African slavery in Virginia in the 1680s. See Morgan, *American Slavery, American Freedom: The Ordeal of Colonial Virginia* (New York, 1975), 316–337. For the colony of New York, Jill Lepore has reasoned that a political order firmly organized around white rights only emerged in the aftermath of the city's slave-servant conspiracy. See Lepore, *New York Burning: Liberty, Slavery, and Conspiracy in Eighteenth-Century Manhattan* (New York, 2005). Peter Silver, in turn, has contended that a language of white peoplehood did not come to dominate political life in the mid-Atlantic colonies of Pennsylvania and Maryland until the Seven Years' War during the late 1750s. See Silver, *Our Savage Neighbors: How Indian War Transformed Early America* (New York, 2008), 114. See also Theodore W. Allen, *The Invention of the White Race*, 2 vols. (London, 1994–1997), I, 44. Nikole Hannah-Jones has argued that the 1619 sale underscores the abiding racism that predated and helped author the U.S. nation's identity, writing that "anti-black racism runs in the very DNA of this country." See Hannah-Jones, "Our Democracy's Founding Ideals Were False When They Were Written: *Black Americans* Have Fought to Make Them True," *New York Times Magazine*, Aug. 14, 2019. For critique and discussion of that argument, see Sean Wilentz, "American Slavery and 'the Relentless Unforeseen,'" *New York Review*, Nov. 19, 2019. For a critique of Wilentz, see David Waldstreicher, "The Hidden Stakes of the 1619 Controversy," *Boston Review*, Jan. 24, 2020.

of human trafficking varied widely across the global and local borders that gave it shape and power. In none of these contexts, however, was the color of a trafficked person's skin the sole or even most noteworthy feature shaping his or her value. Conceptions of racial difference rooted in skin color, so central to the subsequent history of plantation slavery across British North America, had not yet come into being, even if human trafficking was already foundational to England's mercantile political economy.[4]

Yet seeing human trafficking as the key method for realizing imperial ambitions in 1619 does not naturalize the subsequent history of race traffic, the buying and selling of human beings based on skin color and later racial identities. On the contrary, it necessitates investigating when, how, and why skin color became prominent among the colonial and metropolitan elites who

---

4. The literature on human trafficking is not confined to one nation or to a single kind of coercive labor. On the use of transportation and enslavement as tools for reforming English and Irish felons, see Simon P. Newman, *A New World of Labor: The Development of Plantation Slavery in the British Atlantic* (Philadelphia, 2013), 31–33, 72–79. On the decline of slavery across Europe and England during the fifteenth century and its replacement with indentured labor, see Robin Blackburn, *The Making of New World Slavery: From the Baroque to the Modern, 1492–1800* (London, 1997), 54–59. On trafficking and enslavement in the Mediterranean across the early modern era, see Bernard Lewis, *Race and Slavery in the Middle East: An Historical Enquiry* (New York, 1990); Linda Colley, *Captives* (New York, 2002), 43–72; and Ferdinand Braudel, *The Mediterranean and the Mediterranean World in the Age of Philip II*, I (London, 1972). The study of slavery among Native Americans across North America has received long-overdue attention since 2000, with several award-winning books published in the field. See James F. Brooks, *Captives and Cousins: Slavery, Kinship, and Community in the Southwest Borderlands* (Williamsburg, Va., and Chapel Hill, N.C., 2002); Julianna Barr, *Peace Came in the Form of a Woman: Indians and Spaniards in the Texas Borderlands* (Chapel Hill, N.C., 2007); Ned Blackhawk, *Violence over the Land: Indians and Empires in the Early American West* (Cambridge, Mass., 2006); and Alan Gallay, *The Indian Slave Trade: The Rise of the English Empire in the American South, 1677–1717* (New Haven, Conn., 2002). See also Guasco, *Slaves and Englishmen*, 186–187. On the history of trafficking and enslavement in Africa prior to the commencement of a global slave trade and without blackness as its metric, see Blackburn, *Making of New World Slavery*, 1; and David Brion Davis, *Inhuman Bondage: The Rise and Fall of Slavery in the New World* (New York, 2006), 11–12. On African participation in the Atlantic slave trade, see John Thornton, *Africa and Africans in the Making of the Atlantic World, 1400–1800* (Cambridge, 1992); Hugh Thomas, *The Slave Trade: The Story of the Atlantic Slave Trade: 1440–1870* (New York, 1997); David Eltis, *The Rise of African Slavery in the Americas* (Cambridge, 2000), 132–136; Robin Blackburn, *The American Crucible: Slavery, Emancipation, and Human Rights* (London, 2011), 82–87; Paul E. Lovejoy, *Transformations in Slavery: A History of Slavery in Africa* (Cambridge, 2012); and Sean Stilwell, *Slavery and Slaving in African History* (New York, 2014).

first emphasized it. Whiteness and blackness emerged at different moments in colonial and metropolitan correspondence during the seventeenth century but for a related purpose: as tools for counting and seeing the value of human bodies as disposable labor. The traffic in servants and the enslaved highlighted both commonalities and stark differences between white and Black bodies. Shared between them was the reality of their trafficking, a process intrinsic to slavery but not commensurate with it. When whiteness appeared, it did so as a transactional frame, as a method for calculating the comparative financial value of transported bodies. A language of trafficking and commodification rather than a racial identity, white grammar initially conferred few if any of the rights or political, cultural, and legal privileges later associated with white supremacy. Rather, grammars of skin color enabled merchants, masters, ship captains, and metropolitan administrators to determine the value of particular groups of bodies in motion, whether for a term of years or in perpetuity.[5]

Market fungibility framed distinctions between whites and Blacks as a simple financial metric, but such reasoning also obscured the profound differences that existed in the ways most whites and Blacks were brought to market across the seventeenth century. The first Africans who came to Virginia likely never experienced even the fiction of consent, unlike indentured servants from England, many of whom were nonetheless kidnapped and trafficked to the New World. As white grammar became visible in the correspondence of colonial and metropolitan elites during the late seventeenth century, its provenance and function were uncertain, a precarious mechanism of mercantile social control. Whiteness was eschewed by the first Irish and English subjects

---

5. On efforts to create a longer periodization for the history of white racial ideology during the nineteenth and twentieth centuries, see Matthew Frye Jacobson, *Whiteness of a Different Color: European Immigrants and the Alchemy of Race* (Cambridge, Mass., 1998); and Eduardo Bonilla-Silva, *Racism without Racists: Color-Blind Racism and the Persistence of Racial Inequality in America,* 5th ed. (New York, 2018). For the seventeenth and eighteenth centuries, there has been less work. Nancy Isenberg is careful not to describe indentured servants or destitute English migrants as white until these historical actors themselves began doing so in the 1730s. However, she deploys *white trash,* a term that gained wide currency in the 1850s, to frame her longer history of class oppression. See Isenberg, *White Trash: The 400-Year Untold History of Class in America* (New York, 2016), 58–60. Don Jordan and Michael Walsh are less careful, calling all indentured servants white slaves in the seventeenth and eighteenth centuries and ignoring who used the term, when, or how rarely trafficked actors themselves embraced white modifiers. See Jordan and Walsh, *White Cargo: The Forgotten History of Britain's White Slaves in America* (New York, 2007). The best analysis of the historical emergence of white racial ideology remains Allen, *Invention of the White Race,* I, 25–45.

described as such—transported convicts and indentured servants—as well as by English elites, who recoiled from a taxonomy of skin color that connected them to the commoners they trafficked. How whiteness would work, whether those categorized as white would ratify or subvert English political authority, remained an unresolved question at the end of the seventeenth century. For English elites, the moment of genesis surrounding the development of race as a powerful and eventually hegemonic concept was not 1619 but near the end of the seventeenth century, after England began to organize and dominate the African slave trade.[6]

## The Emergence of White Grammar

Which groups of colonial subjects became linked to white grammar when it first became conspicuous in imperial correspondence during the 1670s? And what kind of political work did white grammar achieve for those deploying it? Two English-language primary-source databases—Early English Books Online, comprising thousands of published English language books, and the Colonial State Papers (CSP), a compendium of correspondence between colonial and metropolitan administrators across England's emerging empire between 1660 and 1730—provide opportunities for answering these questions during the first century of England's overseas expansion. Two larger patterns are immediately observable during the seventeenth century. First, English writers, administrators, and imperial actors made dark skin the most salient signifier when identifying peoples from Africa, referring to them either as "negroes" or as "blacks" throughout the seventeenth century. Second, English writers and imperial administrators only began deploying grammars of white skin color during the final quarter of the seventeenth century, and then in highly selective ways. Many light-skinned English people were not yet described as white by 1700, in contrast to the men and women with African origins known

---

6. On the appearance of white grammar during the 1680s, see Allen, *Invention of the White Race*, I, 29, 44; and Morgan, *American Slavery, American Freedom*, 250–270. Nell Irvin Painter does not pinpoint a particular moment or place from which white grammar appeared but highlights instead the key role of scientific racism during the eighteenth century in transforming popular understandings of the relationship between skin color and race. See Painter, *The History of White People* (New York, 2010), 59–90. Nancy Isenberg examines the varied and particular contexts from which whiteness developed in colonial America, demonstrating the extent to which class and gender relations were entwined. See Isenberg, *White Trash*, 37–42.

as Blacks and "negroes." That empirical and political disparity is vital to understanding the histories of both skin color and race.

The first and most conspicuous white subjects to appear in the English language were not aristocrats or direct beneficiaries of plantation slavery but rather cohorts of unfree and trafficked actors who were imported to perform two kinds of labor in the Americas: indentured servitude on sugar plantations and militia work in slave colonies. These white subjects had distinct roles from the people designated as Blacks, but both groups were deemed commodities by imperial and colonial administrators, assets to be moved and deployed in building English colonial power. By far, the largest category of people described using white grammar during the late seventeenth century were *white servants*, with references to them vastly outnumbering those to more general categories, such as *whites, white people, white men,* or *white women,* before 1700. Indeed, when white grammar first emerged in the 1670s, it was almost entirely connected to indentured servitude. Between 1661 and 1700, those classified as white servants made up more than half of all people associated with white grammar (see Appendix A, Table 1).

If trafficked whites were the most common and conspicuous kind of white subjects mentioned in the CSP before 1700, their political loyalties and behaviors were also the most suspect to the political authorities who highlighted their skin color. The semantic link between white servants and so-called malefactors highlights the role of imperial anxiety in shaping the emergence of white grammar. In retrospect, malefactors seem like an unlikely cohort to become connected to whiteness. Before 1680, malefactors made up a diverse group of men and women associated with political disorder and governance challenges across England and its expanding empire. Some malefactors were pirates or armed enemies on the periphery of England's colonies; others were Native peoples resisting England's colonial expansion. On the island of Antigua in 1675, for example, local "Caribbee" Indians were described as "treacherous and bloody malefactors" for having rebelled against English colonizers. The warriors were accused of having "murdered the King's subjects of both sexes, ravished women, carried away men, women, and children, kept them slaves, burned houses, and committed other enormities." Malefactors potentially threatened every English colony in 1663. Maryland authorities, for example, felt compelled to pass a local ordinance *"providing irons in each county for burning malefactors."* Over the next two decades, however, malefactors became closely associated with a particular group: convicts transported to English colonies and known almost exclusively as "white servants." Indeed, for a brief period during the 1680s, the terms *malefactors* and *white servants* were used interchangeably by metropolitan and colonial authorities. By contrast, not a single malefactor was described as a Christian servant in the CSP between 1670 and 1700. Rather, white servants were distinct from the hired servants known as Christian servants. At its inception, white grammar indicated the subject had been trafficked and was likely a transported felon.[7]

White grammar's origins in human trafficking and imperial anxiety come into sharper focus by investigating the history of the term that white servants displaced: *Christian servants*. Before the appearance of white grammar, Christian servants were discussed in a variety of ways by metropolitan and colonial authorities during the 1660s and 1670s (see Appendix A, Table 3). First, their importation had to be encouraged through the passage of legislation. Once in the colonies, they had to be counted, they had to be "provided with Armes, . . . Mustered and Trayned," and they had to be disciplined when they ran away. Occasionally, metropolitan authorities expressed concern about the health and welfare of Christian servants, as when a grand jury was convened in Barbados in 1673 to investigate "the cruel severity of some Masters and

---

7. "Col. Stapleton, Governor of the Leeward Islands, to the Committee of Council for Plantations," Dec. 20, 1675, in W. Noel Sainsbury, ed., *The Calendar of State Papers, Colonial Series, America and West Indies, 1675–1676* . . . , [IX] (London, 1893), 319–320; "The Titles of Twenty-Nine Acts Made at the General Assembly Begun at St. Mary's," Sept. 15, 1663, in Sainsbury, ed., *The Calendar of State Papers, Colonial Series, America and West Indies, 1661–1668* . . . , [V] (London, 1880), 163. Compilers of the *Calendar of State Papers* created a special subject heading for original documents authored between 1681 and 1684 entitled "Transportation of Malefactors and White Servants to the Colonies." See, for example, "Form of a Condition of Transportation," June 1681, in J. W. Fortescue, ed., *The Calendar of State Papers, Colonial Series, America and West Indies, 1681–1685* . . . , [XI] (London, 1898), 80. There are a total of eighteen documents with such a subject heading in the *Calendar* between 1681 and 1684. The best history of transported malefactors to British North America during the seventeenth century remains Abbott Emerson Smith, *Colonists in Bondage: White Servitude and Convict Labor in America, 1607–1776* (Williamsburg, Va., and Chapel Hill, N.C., 1947), 89–109. See also Cheesman A. Herrick, *White Servitude in Pennsylvania: Indentured and Redemption Labor in Colony and Commonwealth* (Philadelphia, 1926), 113–141; and Richard B. Morris, *Government and Labor in Early America* (New York, 1946), 310–326. The traffic in transported convicts was not especially profitable during the late seventeenth century as the securities required by local authorities to accept them were high. Only a perceived shortage in white labor in England's Caribbean colonies made malefactors attractive to local polities. In Massachusetts, convict labor was largely refused by local authorities. See Smith, *Colonists in Bondage*, 99–104; and Lawrence William Towner, *A Good Master Well Served: Masters and Servants in Colonial Massachusetts, 1620–1750* (New York, 1998), 9–10.

Overseers towards their Christian serv[an]ts by whose undue and inhumane Correction some have lately been destroyed." Looming over all mentions of Christian servants were anxieties about their loyalty and capacity for rebellion, with more than one-quarter of all references linked to unruly behavior during the 1670s. Beginning in the 1680s, however, the term was used in a far more specific fashion: to articulate misgivings among imperial magistrates about servants' poor treatment at the hands of cruel masters in the colonies, with laws passed "to restrain inhuman severity to Christian servants." Indeed, virtually all humanitarian concern for indentured servants in Barbados and Jamaica in the 1690s was voiced on behalf of Christian servants, with half of all references to Christian servants in the CSP expressing anxieties about their harsh treatment. As humanitarian interest in the welfare of Christian servants expanded, descriptions of Christian servants being rebellious or insolent to their masters declined. Before 1681, 24 percent of the references to Christian servants described unruly behavior, but, between 1681 and 1720, just 6 percent were unruly.[8]

By contrast, when the language of white servants became prominent, it described servants as numbered commodities. White servants were rarely mentioned by officials seeking to ameliorate the working conditions of indentured servants. Instead, authorities used white grammar to describe problems of governance and to summarize martial threats to each colony's survival, as

---

8. "Instructions for Sir Thomas Lynch," Dec. 31, 1670, CO 1/25, 107, The National Archives, Kew, U.K. (hereafter TNA), "Presentments of the Grand Jury in Barbados," July 8, 1673, CO 389/5, 163, "Instructions to Sir Nathaniel Johnson," Nov. 28, 1686, CO 153/3, 213–229. I have defined humanitarian interest in Christian servants and white servants narrowly, as language that expresses concern about inhumanity or inhumane treatment. Efforts to encourage the importation of Christian servants have not been counted as expressing humanitarian interest. See Appendix A for an explanation of the thematic categories assessed. Little humanitarian concern existed for white servants in the CSP during the seventeenth century, appearing in just 3 percent of references to them before 1700. By contrast, the percentage of references to Christian servants indicating humanitarian concern expanded from 0 percent before 1670 to 50 percent between 1691 and 1700. See Appendix A, Tables 2 and 3. Historian Katharine Grebner has located a similar transition from religious to racial signifiers in seventeenth-century English political discourse; however, Grebner argues that "whiteness" preceded the emergence of white grammar and was visible in religious iconography. See Grebner, *Christian Slavery: Conversion and Race in the Protestant Atlantic World* (Philadelphia, 2018), 51–60. On the importance of religious beliefs in shaping understandings of racial and political difference in seventeenth-century slave societies, see Jenny Shaw, *Everyday Life in the Early English Caribbean: Irish, Africans, and the Construction of Difference* (Athens, Ga., 2013).

when white servants were recruited to guard enslaved Africans or paradoxically joined ranks with enslaved Africans in rebellion against common masters. Over the last two decades of the seventeenth century, the language of white servants and Christian servants became increasingly specialized. By the first decade of the eighteenth century, white servants were more likely than Christian servants to be numbered, to be linked to militia recruitment and work, and to be unruly. Christian servants, by contrast, were far more likely than white servants to be the focus of humanitarian concern and to possess limited rights (see Appendix A, Tables 2 and 3).

Considering how the words *whites* and *Blacks* appeared as nouns in their own right sharpens the picture of how closely tethered commodification and skin color were within colonial discourse. Whites and Blacks figured as key assets in the financial preparation and imagining of new sugar plantations, enabling imperial planners to assess the comparative financial value of indentured servants and enslaved Africans and the cost of their transportation to Atlantic colonies. In 1664, for example, members of the Committee of Council for Foreign Plantations presented a report that described both indentured workers and African slaves in Barbados as "servants" but "classed" them "under two heads, blacks and whites." Known as "perpetual servants" rather than slaves, Africans were described as "blacks, bought by way of trade" who were "sold about 20*l.* a head." By contrast, "whites" who had been in "divers ways gathered up in England, few from Ireland and Scotland" were convicts "transported at the rate of 6*l.* per head" and "exchanged for commodities at different rates according to their condition or trade." In this governing body's view, no separate markets existed for servants and slaves; rather, there was a single traffic in Blacks and whites. All were fungible, the only difference between them a ratio of two-and-a-half to one, a reflection of whites' temporary status and Blacks' "perpetual" service. Skin color and trafficability similarly informed the aspirations of Sir Charles Lyttelton, a colonial sugar planter, who proposed in 1664 that "the best design for his Majesty" in Jamaica "will be a great sugar work; and for this 30 blacks and as many whites at first entering are thought sufficient."[9]

---

9. "Certaine Propositions for the Better Accommodating the Foreigne Plantations with Servants Reported from the Committee to the Council of Foreigne Plantations," 1664, Barbados, CO 324/1, 275–276, TNA, "Reasons Proposed by the King's Command for His Majesty's Settling a Plantation in Jamaica," Oct. 3, 1664, CO 1/18, 113.

A comparison of the context and meanings of the appearance of the terms *Blacks* and *whites* in the CSP illuminates the particular kinds of labor and power that imperial authorities associated with people who were known principally by skin color during the late seventeenth century. Both cohorts were closely associated with numbers. Indeed, they were the most likely groups within the CSP to be defined by numeracy between 1661 and 1720, with 64 percent of Blacks and 87 percent of whites having numbers accompany their usage (see Appendix A, Tables 4 and 5). Both terms also frequently emerged together in imperial correspondence. Blacks appear in 62 percent of all references to whites and whites appear in 48 percent of all references to Blacks. The most frequent pairings occurred when authorities discussed the planning of new plantations or military threats to English colonies. The 1690s witnessed an especially prominent deployment of Blacks in military contexts, with 61 percent of the references to Blacks associating them with military roles. Whites, in turn, were even more closely linked to military discourse, with 82 percent described as soldiers during the 1690s. Although enslaved Black men and women were officially forbidden from bearing arms in many English colonies, many were nonetheless pressed into military work by English commanders when necessitated by imperial emergencies. In 1695, for example, Jamaican authorities fended off a French attack in which they "sallied out in a body of 300 whites and 200 blacks, well armed." Skin color helped military officials navigate as well as assess imperial strengths and weaknesses, whether the trafficked soldiers they deployed were free or enslaved. It was in this context of imperial anxiety and competition that Blacks were sporadically armed by the English and that a grammar of Blacks and whites enabled commanders to narrate their military victories and losses. In the minds of imperial administrators, Blacks could be valued defenders of England's imperial investments, prized assets creating English power, and potential internal enemies all at the same time.[10]

The military challenges facing the colonial and metropolitan architects of England's colonies generated complementary ways of deploying the language of Blacks and whites. Nevertheless, while colonial authorities might call on both Blacks and whites to fight common enemies like the French, they also looked to whites to double as local members of militias and to help colonies meet population targets set in London that would harbor one white servant

---

10. Commodore Wilmot to William Blathwayt, July 26, 1695, CO 137/3, 89, TNA.

for every ten Blacks in a colony. Fears of rebellion and piracy, both of which could feature Blacks and whites arrayed against English power, tapped into anxieties about a shortage of whites able to help restore order and defend England's imperial interests. Increasingly, white grammar highlighted the value of servants as members of an armed militia. Before 1690, 43 percent of whites appearing in the CSP were associated with militia work, but after 1690, 85 percent were connected to militias (see Appendix A, Table 5). The increased emphasis on the martial capacities of whites during the 1690s encouraged many indentured servants from Barbados and Jamaica to leave the islands entirely on completing their indentures, many heading for the North American colonies of Virginia and the Carolinas, where land was more readily available. Their emigration only increased pressure on island planters and authorities to pass legislation limiting the mobility of Jamaicans and Barbadians as well as "encouraging the importation of white servants" across the Caribbean in the early 1690s. Such laws urged ship captains and planters to purchase and transport whites and white servants from England, intensifying incentives to traffic these same unfree workers. The solicitor general for the Leeward Islands observed in 1693 that "the Act for encouraging the importation of white servants" was also "encouraging the 'spiriting' away of white servants to the plantations without their consent, a practice which is very frequent and known by the name of kidnapping." One reason white grammar articulated such a strong connection to human trafficking was that white servants, whether imported as malefactors or recruited as militiamen, were understood to be commodities vital to imperial order.[11]

For colonial and metropolitan elites, then, grammars of skin color were used to articulate competing and conflicting political possibilities for imperial power. On the one hand, authorities used white grammar to underscore fears about the loyalties of white servants. In 1686, for example, Barbadian authorities called on "all masters" within the island to "keep good watches over their negroes day and night, there being signs of an insurrection of negroes and white servants." Not once during the decade did Barbadian or London authorities articulate fears of an alliance between "negroes" and

---

11. "Report of the Solicitor General on the Acts of the Leeward Islands," Oct. 12, 1693, CO 152/1, 21, TNA. On the importance of white militias in establishing slaveholder power in Jamaica and Barbados, see Edward B. Rugemer, *Slave Law and the Politics of Resistance in the Early Atlantic World* (Cambridge, Mass., 2018), 46; and Allen, *Invention of the White Race*, I, 13.

Christian servants. The language used to describe servant resistance to colonial authority—running away, teaming up with enslaved Africans, or speaking insolently to a master—shifted with the discursive emergence of white servitude. Before 1680, two-thirds of the descriptions of servant resistance to colonial masters described it as coming from Christian servants. From 1680 to 1700, by contrast, white servants made up 86 percent of the unruly servants in the CSP, as Christian servants became associated with humanitarian concern rather than rebellion (see Appendix A, Table 6). On the other hand, colonial and metropolitan authorities also passed laws encouraging the emigration of whites and white servants to the Caribbean islands as potential solutions to problems of colonial security and governance. By 1700, white grammar articulated no unitary set of politics but exemplified both elite identification with and anxiety toward trafficked whites. White servants possessed nascent rights and status as unruly commodities capable of rebellion. Christian servants, by contrast, were the colonial subjects deemed most worthy of rights and protection by the metropolitan administrators of England's expanding empire.[12]

Political uncertainty about the loyalties of these first white subjects was not limited to the imperial correspondents and elites who first deployed white grammar during the 1670s and 1680s. It also extended to the British civil servants who created an imperial archive two centuries later known as the *Calendar of State Papers*. Uncertainty over how to describe the difference between a Christian servant and a white servant is clearly apparent. The *Calendar*'s compilers frequently changed the terms they used in creating summaries of original documents authored in the 1680s and 1690s. A detailed comparison of all references to white servants in the *Calendar* with the documents in the CSP from the 1670s, 1680s, and 1690s reveals that civil servants frequently substituted the phrase *white servant* for *Christian servant* in many of their summaries of original handwritten sources. Most of these changes were focused on a key period, 1681–1698, the same timespan when white grammar

---

12. "Minutes of Council of Barbados," Feb. 16, 1686, CO 31/1, 675–676, TNA. On differences between white servants and Christian servants, see Appendix A, Tables 2, 3, and 6. Before 1700, white servants were more likely to be referred to as unruly than to be mentioned in connection with rights and privileges, a pattern that flipped after 1700. Even with that important change over time, Christian servants were substantially more likely to be associated with rights, with more than four times as many Christian servants as white servants, forty-two to nine, linked to rights between 1661 and 1700. See Appendix A, Tables 2 and 3.

was most closely connected to a discourse about servitude and servant trafficking. Some of the *Calendar* references to white servants during this decade accurately correspond to white grammar in the originals in the CSP, but many more are superimposed on references to Christian servants. Indeed, no other batch of documents in the *Calendar* displays such consistent revision among British civil servants (see Appendix A, Table 7).[13]

Why the compilers of the *Calendar* made these changes in their summaries and transcripts of original sources is a matter of speculation. Perhaps they sought to clarify the historical record by imposing what were, by the 1860s, conventional terms of an imperial whiteness onto the messy and still nascent imperial project of the 1680s. The British Empire had always been white, *Calendar* scribes might have thought, so why not make that clear in the documents at its inception? More likely, these civil servants discerned what were historical tensions over the work of white grammar itself during the 1680s, disparities that caused confusion two centuries later about how to catalogue imperial correspondence. Were all white servants malefactors? And if so, were they threats to colonial rule or redeemers of it? Since both possibilities were true, especially between 1681 and 1698, it becomes less surprising to discern how white servants vexed English colonial authorities in the 1680s and English civil servants in the 1860s. Although the precise motives of the early compilers of the *Calendar* remain unknown, the textual changes made by these civil servants provide an unusually rich example of how white grammar was revisionist, structuring the way the first English imperial archive was constructed and organized. To understand why colonial and metropolitan authorities turned to malefactors to solve problems of political economy and

---

13. The vast majority of revisions by civil servants to white grammar in the *Calendar* involve the phrase *white servant*. Together, they make up 80 percent of all the revisions to original documents (see Appendix A, Table 7). The sixty-seven references to white servants that were inaccurate in the original sources constitute just under one-quarter of all the *Calendar* references to white servants between 1670 and 1720. The revisionist character of the discourse surrounding white servants in the *Calendar* emerges more sharply when tracking the number of instances where *Calendar* compilers added white grammar to their summaries of the original documents in the CSP, with fifty-two of fifty-six such alterations linked to white servants. By contrast, no such change or confusion was apparent in the *Calendar* references to Christian servants. Indeed, every mention of Christian servants in the *Calendar* corresponds to an accurate reference in the original document. Put another way, I found no Christian servants listed in the *Calendar* corresponding to white servants in the original sources.

why white skin color was initially linked to trafficked felons, it is important to examine the larger conflicts among maritime actors over trafficking and antislavery that England's imperial expansions created.

## Trafficking, Protest, and the Politics of Antislavery, 1607–1676

In 1618, a year prior to the arrival of the "20. and odd Negroes" in Jamestown, John Rolfe reflected on the transformation that a decade of the Virginia Company's colonization had wrought on the indentured servants who had cleared the land, raised food crops, and tended the first fields of tobacco leaves grown for export. "There have beene many complaints against the Governors, Captaines, and Officers in Virginia, for buying and selling men and boies," wrote Rolfe, a practice that "was held in England a thing most intolerable." That traffic was the result of two circumstances: the selling of servants after crossing the Atlantic to pay the costs of moving them and the frequent selling of servants once they had arrived to settle the debts of their cash-strapped masters. Servant traffic in the Americas was not a single discrete event but an ongoing process linking the mobilization of English servants to planters' labor needs and financial obligations. John Smith commented on both aspects of servant traffic in 1624 in his *Generall Historie of Virginia, New-England, and the Summer Isles*. He blamed the practice of buying and selling indentures, perhaps disingenuously, on the "pride, covetousnesse, extortion and oppression" of the colony's new planters. Smith lamented not only that "men, women and children" were being sold but that profit taking inflated servants' value with no benefit to the servants: "To sell him or her for forty, fifty, or threescore pounds, whom the Company hath sent over for eight or ten pounds at the most . . . is odious." Rather than increasing the wages of indentured servants, the shortage of plantation labor intensified servant trafficking, as planters used servants as both labor and currency.[14]

---

14. "A Relation from Master John Rolfe," June 15, 1618, in John Smith, *The Generall Historie of Virginia, New-England, and the Summer Isles* . . . (London, 1624), in Philip L. Barbour, ed., *The Complete Works of Captain John Smith, 1580–1631*, II (Williamsburg, Va., and Chapel Hill, N.C., 1986), 268, Smith, *Generall Historie*, II, 329–330, both also cited in Guasco, *Slaves and Englishmen*, 167. On the importance of policing to the commodification of indentured servants, see Newman, *New World of Labor*, 92–100; Guasco, *Slaves and Englishmen*, 166–167; Christopher Tomlins, *Freedom Bound: Law, Labor, and Civic Identity in Colonizing English America, 1580–1865* (New York, 2010), 80–81; Kenneth Morgan, *Slavery*

For servants sent to the Americas, long distance mobility dramatically changed the terms of service indentured servants experienced in North America. For the English, Irish, and Scottish men and women who became the indentured servants arriving in England's North American and Caribbean colonies during the seventeenth century, being bought and sold was not unknown or unprecedented. Annual hiring fares in which adult servants and apprentices would indent themselves to a new master for a year of service were common across early modern England, and servants working on tobacco and sugar plantations technically possessed the same rights as servants in England, including the right to petition. The experience of servitude and apprenticeship in the Americas, however, was relentlessly more coercive, a trend that increased over time. First, the length of most indentures increased from one to four or five years, a response to the costs associated with transporting servants across the Atlantic Ocean. Second, few apprentices learned a skilled craft. Instead, they were tasked with clearing land and planting cash crops. In colonies devoted to growing commodities like tobacco and sugar, moreover, penalties for breach of contract and running away became much harsher than in England, as masters used severe corporal punishments to discipline runaway or rebellious servants.[15]

Colonial authorities rarely sided with servants or even heard their complaints. When authorities in Barbados did occasionally support a servant's

---

*and Servitude in Colonial North America: A Short History* (New York, 2001), 19–22; and Robert J. Steinfeld, *The Invention of Free Labor: The Employment Relation in English and American Law and Culture, 1350–1870* (Chapel Hill, N.C., 1991), 44–54.

15. Although scholars disagree on the degree of freedom that indentured servants experienced in North American colonies, they converge in recognizing that indentured servitude became more severe during the first two-thirds of the seventeenth century. Michael Guasco writes that in England's colonies, "servitude developed into something harsher after the 1620s in response to local conditions," for example, while Simon P. Newman observes that "planters found it easy to treat bound white laborers in new ways, as workers with virtually no rights, as commodities to be used with little if any restraint." See Guasco, *Slaves and Englishmen*, 164; and Newman, *New World of Labor*, 76. Christopher Tomlins similarly concludes that justices in Virginia adjudicating master-servant relations before Bacon's Rebellion "tended to be crude, cursory, and self-interested." See Tomlins, *Freedom Bound*, 267. Hilary McD. Beckles finds that Irish indentures experienced extraordinary forms of exploitation in Barbados, making comparisons of them to the island's enslaved community at least plausible if still misleading. See Beckles, "A 'Riotous and Unruly Lot': Irish Indentured Servants and Freemen in the English West Indies, 1644–1713," *William and Mary Quarterly*, 3d Ser., XLVII (1990), 514.

claims against an abusive master, penalties were not enforced. When Daniel Duncombe, an Irish servant in Barbados, tried to get his master, a ship captain named John Symonds, to pay his promised freedom dues in 1656, for example, the court agreed with him, ordering Symonds to settle with Duncombe. Yet instead of complying, Symonds gave Duncombe "a 'sound beating'" for being impertinent and extended his service. In practice, there seems to have been few limits to what masters could do to their servants in England's plantation colonies. When Barbadian planter Charles Grimlin murdered his Irish domestic servant in 1677, he was pardoned by the governor of Barbados, Sir Jonathan Atkins, who as an unpropertied official was heavily dependent on the support of Barbados's planter class. The lack of legal redress for Barbadian servants meant that severe corporal punishments were commonplace.[16]

Left with few options for challenging abusive masters in the Americas, servants turned to flight with decidedly mixed results. If apprehended, as most were, they were punished with additional years of service, a departure from English practice that only required runaways to finish the original time on their indentures. Compounding servants' woes in securing what had been customary rights in England was that many servants were young and without family advocates in English colonies. Female indentures in particular endured coercion intensified by their remoteness from their communities of origin. Trafficked for labor as well as for sex, they were exploited by male masters, who could double the length of their indentures if they became pregnant. Children born to female servants out of wedlock were almost certain to become indentured servants, saddled with apprentice contracts. Servitude never became heritable in the Americas, but, in combination with sexual violence, servant trafficking increased the leverage that masters possessed over their

---

16. Minutes of the Barbados Council, Dec. 10, 1656, Lucas MSS, microfilm, reel 1, fols. 327–338, Barbados Public Library, quoted in Beckles, "A 'Riotous and Unruly Lot,'" *WMQ*, XLVII (1990), 514–515; "Governor Sir Jonathan Atkins to Lords of Trade and Plantations," Jan. 12, 1678, in W. Noel Sainsbury and J. W. Fortescue, eds., *Calendar of State Papers, Colonial Series, America and West Indies, 1677–1680 . . . ,* [X] (London, 1896), 202, also cited in Beckles, "A 'Riotous and Unruly Lot,'" *WMQ*, XLVII (1990), 515. On the mistreatment and rebelliousness of Irish servants, see Susan Dwyer Amussen, *Caribbean Exchanges: Slavery and the Transformation of English Society, 1640–1700* (Chapel Hill, N.C., 2007), 158, 161; and Beckles, *White Servitude and Black Slavery,* 111–112. Simon P. Newman writes that "for all intents and purposes many of these bound white laborers became virtual slaves in Barbados." See Newman, *New World of Labor,* 80.

female indentures. Geographic isolation from family, new forms of severe corporal punishment, and desperate efforts to escape by running away all combined to extend servants' terms of service and to limit their ability to demand the basic necessities of life from their masters.[17]

The greater frequency of buying and selling servants in the New World intensified the capacity of masters to exploit and abuse them. The possibility of being sold weakened servants' ability to seek redress if they experienced violence at the hands of their masters. Although masters could and occasionally did sell their indentured servants in England, most servants arranged their indentures within local contexts in which masters and servants already knew one another, and auctions were rare except in cases of legal punishment. In Virginia and Barbados, by contrast, all indentures were sold at auction at least once on servants' arrival and sometimes frequently thereafter, as masters bought and sold laborers to settle debts or to dispense with rebellious individuals. If servants ran away and were apprehended, their terms were prolonged, and they were frequently sold again, as masters preferred to sell servants who had defied their power. If being sold pushed more servants to run away, so did the punishments visited on them. Servant trafficking, running away, and policing went hand in hand in England's New World colonies, explaining why legal authorities devoted so much creative energy to lengthening contracts of indenture. Servants' desperate gambits to find freedom by running away occasionally worked but more frequently fattened masters' profits with extended terms of service and additional trafficking of servants' labor and lives through sale. Servant trafficking in the Americas was profitable precisely because servant resistance to masters' abuses resulted in longer indentures and ultimately more capital for cash-poor masters.

Although the buying and selling of servants to build colonial ventures never constituted slavery, the intensification of servant trafficking invited English authorities to consider ways of using servants to create a system of domestic slavery. Even as Virginia indentures protested harsh working conditions in the early 1620s as a form of slavery, members of Parliament in London debated whether slavery itself might be formally legalized as a penal tool for reforming criminals who had committed felonies. Those "'ad[j]udged

---

17. Amussen, *Caribbean Exchanges*, 60, 61. On the importance of sexual labor in the subordination of indentured servants, see Isenberg, *White Trash*, 27–28, 67–68. On the importance of sexuality and gender in the creation of racial slavery in colonial Virginia, see Kathleen M. Brown, *Good Wives, Nasty Wenches, and Anxious Patriarchs: Gender, Race, and Power in Colonial Virginia* (Williamsburg, Va., and Chapel Hill, N.C., 1996).

to die for smale faultes' they maie be saved and Condemned as Slaves during lief and be used as in other Cuntreys unto anie Publique workes," suggested one member of Parliament in 1621, an option that already existed within England's jurisprudence. In 1547, Parliament had passed the so-called Vagrancy Statute, a law that prescribed slavery as a just punishment for poor people who refused to work and were deemed "a Vagabounde" by two justices of the peace. "Confession" of loitering, the law read "shall immediatelie cawse the saide loyterer to be marked with an whott Iron in the brest the marke of V. and adjudge the saide parsone living so Idelye to such presentor to be his Slave, To have and to holde the said Slave to him his executors or assignes for the space of twoo Yere." Unlike the policy of felony enslavement contemplated in 1621, the Vagrancy Statute was understood solely as an exemplary punishment rather than a measure to reform or improve the character of the felon. The Vagrancy Statute authorized masters to "putt a rynge of Iron abowt" the offender's "Necke Arme or his Legge for a more knowledge and suretie of the keeping of him." If the enslaved vagrant ran away and was apprehended, he or she was to be branded again, this time on the cheek or forehead and adjudged "to be the saide M[aster]s' Slave for ever." Although the 1547 statute was never enforced and the 1621 proposal in Parliament was not passed, their existence underscores the potency of slavery as a penal practice by state actors.[18]

One reason English elites did not formally enslave English or Irish vagrants is that many Englishmen, including John Smith, regarded trafficking people for profit with suspicion, associating it with despotic foreign governments. This predisposition provided indentured migrants and their advocates an opportunity to confront the intensification of servant trafficking. For many indentured servants in the Americas, the moment of sale was the most likely to spark protest, whether they had voluntarily agreed to indenture. Thomas

---

18. Wallace Notestein, Frances Helen Relf, and Hartley Simpson, eds., *Commons Debates, 1621*, VII (New Haven, Conn., 1935), 54–55, also cited in Guasco, *Slaves and Englishmen*, 161; "An Acte for the Punishment of Vagabondes and for the Relief of the Poore and Impotent Parsons," 1547, 1 Edward VI, c. 3, in *The Statutes of the Realm* . . . , IV (1819; rpt. London, 1963), 5, 8. On the 1547 Vagrancy Statute, see Guasco, *Slaves and Englishmen*, 35–36; Newman, *New World of Labor*, 31–32; David Armitage, *The Ideological Origins of the British Empire* (New York, 2000), 51; Blackburn, *Making of New World Slavery*, 57; Linebaugh and Rediker, *Many-Headed Hydra*, 18; Winthrop D. Jordan, *White over Black: American Attitudes towards the Negro, 1550–1812* (Williamsburg, Va., and Chapel Hill, N.C., 1968), 51; and Frank Aydelotte, *Elizabethan Rogues and Vagabonds* (Oxford, 1913). The Vagrancy Statute did not rely on or engender the commodification or trafficking of convicts, however, in sharp contrast with subsequent transportation policies.

Best, an indentured servant toiling in Virginia in 1623, did not object to abusive treatment by his master, Mr. Atkins, but rather being sold to settle Atkins's debts. "Atkins hath sold me," Best recalled, "like a damnd slave." It is not known whether Best willingly signed his indenture in England. His apparent surprise at becoming fungible underscores the harshness of his new geopolitical context, one that dramatically curtailed freedoms that had seemed customary in England.[19]

Best's complaint invites questions about the broader relationship between trafficking and slavery in North America at the beginning of the seventeenth century. To be trafficked "like a . . . slave" was one thing, to be a slave, quite another, a distinction Best himself acknowledged. But if Best did not believe he was literally a slave, why protest being sold like a "damnd" one? Was he exaggerating his hardship or presuming he deserved better because of his status as an Englishman? Did he believe slaves were "damnd" by nature or only by unjust men? It is impossible to know how Best might have answered these questions in 1623. The comments of his peers about slavery during the same decade, however, do provide some clues. For early Virginia colonists, slavery was a political condition only partially connected to the theft of a slave's labor. Several members of the Virginia Company deployed the language of enslavement to express their complaints about material conditions in the colony. Captain John Bargrave, an adventurer who eventually established himself as a member of England's gentry on his return, protested early efforts by the Virginia Company to regulate trade in the colony as a product of "tyrannical government in Virginia, whereby many lost their lives, and were brought into slavery." Claims of enslavement were used to protest political tyranny as well as the horrendous living conditions in Jamestown that caused the colony's early leaders to take drastic actions to survive.[20]

In the 1620s, all factions within the struggling Virginia colony used antislavery to articulate their grievances against one another. The year 1622 was an especially bad year for colonists in Virginia. That summer, Powhatan warriors killed nearly one-third of Virginia's English settlers. The Powhatan uprising not only weakened the colony's viability but also led its leadership to adopt unpopular measures policing the behavior of colonists, rationing food, and

---

19. "Notes Taken from Letters Which Came from Virginia in the 'Abigail,'" June 19, 1623, in Kingsbury, ed., *Records of the Virginia Company*, IV, 235.

20. "Petition of John Bargrave to the Privy Council," Apr. 12, 1622, in W. Noël Sainsbury, ed., *Calendar of State Papers, Colonial Series, 1574–1660* . . . , [I] (London, 1860), 28–29, also cited in Guasco, *Slaves and Englishmen*, 159.

strictly regulating trade. Indentured servant Richard Frethorne responded to the colony's privations by sending a letter to his parents in England pleading with them to free him from his indenture so he could return home. "As yor Child release me from this bondage," he wrote, a context he compared to biblical slavery, demanding that he be "freed out of this Egipt." Although Frethorne blamed the colony's misfortunes on the colonial planters who trafficked servants like him to Virginia, most planters insisted that the colony's mortality rates had little to do with their preference for planting tobacco instead of food. Starvation nevertheless made even Virginia's aristocrats slaves to hunger. Indeed, food shortages intensified the trafficking of servants. Desperate for both food and cash, masters sold servants to reduce pressure on limited household stores during long winter months.[21]

As trafficking expanded the ways masters exploited their servants, it also reshaped the meaning and consequences of Indian captivity among indentured colonists. Those connections emerge clearly in the story of the Virginia colonist Jane Dickenson, one of twenty women captured by Pamunkey warriors during the 1622 uprising. She endured a year of captivity with the Pamunkey people, a year she would later describe as slavery. Winning back her freedom amid ongoing Anglo-Powhatan warfare was exceptionally difficult. She was ransomed by Dr. John Potts, a wealthy colonist. But as Dickenson soon discovered, that emancipation did not come without transactional costs. Because she had been indentured to Dr. Potts when she was taken by

---

21. "Richard Ffrethorne; Letter to His Father and Mother," Mar. 20, Apr. 2–3, 1623, in Kingsbury, ed., *Records of the Virginia Company*, IV, 61, "Richard Ffrethorne; Letter to Mr. Bateman," Mar. 5, 1622/3, 41, both also cited in Guasco, *Slaves and Englishmen*, 159–160. For another critique of the Virginia colony's governance in 1622 using antislavery themes, see "Governor, Council, and Assembly of Virginia to the King," [February] 1623, in Sainsbury, ed., *Calendar of State Papers, Colonial Series, 1574–1660* . . . , [I], 38–39, also cited in Guasco, *Slaves and Englishmen*, 159–160. While largely rebutting Nathaniel Butler's "The Unmasking of Virginia," members of Virginia's government nonetheless acknowledged the poor treatment of servants during "Sir Thos. Smythe's government," allowing that "six, not ten, thousand persons have been transported to Virginia, who for the most part were wasted by the more than Egyptian slavery and Scythian cruelty exercised upon them by laws written in blood" ([I], 39). On the Powhatan uprising and accompanying bloodshed, see Morgan, *American Slavery, American Freedom*, 98–101; J. Frederick Fausz, "The 'Barbarous Massacre' Reconsidered: The Powhatan Uprising of 1622 and the Historians," *Explorations in Ethnic Studies*, I, no. 1 (January 1978), 16–36; and Guasco, *Slaves and Englishmen*, 183–184. On Frethorne's struggles in Virginia, see Emily Rose, "The Politics of Pathos: Richard Frethorne's Letters Home," in Robert Appelbaum and John Wood Sweet, eds., *Envisioning an English Empire: Jamestown and the Making of a North Atlantic World* (Philadelphia, 2005), 92–108.

Pamunkey warriors, Potts demanded that she pay him back in extended years of service or tender him 150 pounds of tobacco. Perhaps most disheartening for Dickenson, her husband, also an indentured servant who had died during the 1622 attack, possessed three years of unfinished service, a debt Dr. Potts now insisted fell on Jane. By extending her servitude to "the uttermost day," Dickenson complained that Dr. Potts had rendered her bondage like that of "her slavery wth the Indians." Here indeed was something new for indentured servants in the Americas. The precise value of the Dickensons' unredeemed labor—its transactional value—could no longer be suspended by death. Her story anticipates how elites would in time create a permanent class of trafficable subjects with inheritable debts. To be trafficked was not enslavement, but it facilitated a rethinking of what slavery meant and entailed in 1623.[22]

Abusive masters might be bad apples, but buying and selling people as part of a state-sponsored commerce produced grievances inherently political in nature. Given the increasingly coercive character of servitude in Barbados and Virginia by the 1620s, it is not surprising to find numerous references to servants being trafficked and claiming they had become enslaved. Like Best, servants used the language of slavery to focus their complaints on what they perceived to be the politically unjust dimensions of servitude. Servants experienced a great variety of abuses by their masters, but nearly all protested the same thing when they invoked the language of enslavement: their sale and subsequent disposability. They did so not only to highlight these perceived injustices but to gain the attention of state actors. Antislavery facilitated a political tradition for subjects unhappy with particular policies of petitioning the English crown, enlivening the claims of tyranny and slavery associated with being trafficked. As such, servant claims of enslavement ratified the right and power of political authorities to intervene and amend injustices, even while critiquing policies that were prerogatives of the crown.[23]

Servants, then, used antislavery to affirm, challenge, and even negate the prerogatives of English political authorities. Although some trafficked servants demanded justice as an inherently English right, others sought to leave

---

22. "Jane Dickinson; Petition to the Governor and Council," Mar. 30, 1624, in Kingsbury, ed., *Records of the Virginia Company*, IV, 473.

23. On servant protests across the Americas during the seventeenth century, see Steinfeld, *Invention of Free Labor*, 94–105; Richard S. Dunn, *Sugar and Slaves: The Rise of the Planter Class in the English West Indies, 1624–1713* (Williamsburg, Va., and Chapel Hill, N.C., 1972), 257; Guasco, *Slaves and Englishmen*, 257; and Linebaugh and Rediker, *Many-Headed Hydra*, 123–127.

Englishness behind altogether. The context for servant complaints about enslavement was both local and transatlantic, one in which English sovereignty was partial and in competition with numerous rivals. For Catholic indentures transported to the Caribbean by English soldiers, the most important theater of justice was, not London, but sovereign courts in Spain or even Rome. A surprising number of English troops in Jamaica, for example, defected to the Spanish during the early months of Cromwell's Western Design, his plan to subdue Spanish forces in the Caribbean in 1655. Many of these defectors were indentured servants born in Ireland but included others hailing from Holland, Germany, and Scotland, all toiling in Barbados. Whatever their national origin, these defectors claimed to have been enslaved when Spanish authorities asked them why they were changing sides. Richard Caer, a Dutch-born landowner in Barbados and a captain in the local militia, stated in Spanish to his new sovereigns that "in all the time he had been in Jamaica," which was about six months, "they hadn't given him more than one-weeks' pay and had denied him leave to go to his home in Barbados." In the face of acute hunger, "occasioned by necessity and overwork" that left several of his comrades dead, Caer deserted the English Army, even though he was a devout Protestant, stating that his commanding officers had "made them work as if they were slaves."[24]

Claims of enslavement were essential components to these labor-based imperial conflicts. Caer's protest of having been enslaved was a necessary precondition for his being accepted by Spanish authorities as a military recruit, rather than a prisoner of war. For Irish servant-soldiers, in turn, antislavery facilitated the switching of imperial masters, a problem that haunted all English imperial efforts in the Caribbean for decades. English authorities worried that indentured Irish servants would comprise a fifth column of resistance, as Irish servant soldiers frequently attacked their English masters and joined the armies of Spanish or French imperial rivals. Some of the most interesting evidence comes from Spanish language archives in San Domingo, where a number of Irish indentures sought shelter from abusive English masters

---

24. "Declaración de Ricardo Caer, de nacion olandes, natural del lugar llamado Horcon," Feb. 2, 1657, Testimonio del estado de la isla de Xamaica, noticias y auisos della deste siete de Ago de 1656, Archivo General de las Indias (AGI), Santo Domingo 178A, Seville, Spain, quoted in Kristen Block, *Ordinary Lives in the Early Caribbean: Religion, Colonial Competition, and the Politics of Profit* (Athens, Ga., 2012), 131–132, 269. On the importance of Jamaica, slavery, and the Western Design to England's imperial ambitions, see Abigail L. Swingen, *Competing Visions of Empire: Labor, Slavery, and the Origins of the British Atlantic Empire* (New Haven, Conn., 2015), 33–34, 38–42.

decades before Cromwell's conquest of Jamaica. One of those Irish Catholic refugees, John Casey, dubbed "Juan Casi" by his new Spanish masters in 1643, described the coercion that led him to flee English rule in the Caribbean. When Juan traveled to the island of Saint Kitts in 1639, he had "worked with tobacco," having been "hooked," or kidnapped, by the English from his Irish home and "held as if in captivity with various masters" for four years. When the English tried to convert him and his fellow servants to Protestantism, or "to make them heretics," he refused. At that point, John, or rather "Juan," fled "on a Spanish ship with seven other Irish servants" to San Martin and later Puerto Rico, seeking passage to Spain and eventually a way back to Ireland. Religious oppression and labor exploitation were tightly linked concerns for Casey and Irish servant runaways like him in the 1630s and 1640s. Indeed, when other Irish runaways described themselves as slaves to Spanish authorities in 1643, they, too, highlighted both political and labor abuses. Another runaway Irish servant, "Juan Garcia," stated to his Spanish interrogators that "the English treated them harshly, like slaves, and took away their rosaries." Garcia and his fellow Irishmen wanted no return to England, but, without a narrative of political enslavement, Garcias had only a tenuous claim to becoming a subject of a Catholic Spanish monarch.[25]

Location, then, was crucial to both Casey's and Garcias's accounts of enslavement and their eventual emancipation as Spanish subjects. More often, servants sought urban metropoles to make their demands for justice more visible. Distance, both temporal and geographic, from the site of one's bondage was essential to how servant antislavery worked. For their antislavery to be effective, servants needed an audience that was at least potentially sympathetic and ideally powerful, a court of law that might restrain a given master or, as in the case of Casey, an agent of a foreign power who might make all English

---

25. "Declaración de los yrlandeses que han llegada a la Isla Española y noticias del enemigos," Jan. 13, 1643, AGI, St. Domingo 87, TNI 00213453, 10, 13. Thanks to Kristen Block for sharing her case file on John Casey. On Juan Garcia, see Kristen Block and Jenny Shaw, "Subjects without an Empire: The Irish in the Early Modern Caribbean," *Past and Present*, no. 210 (February 2011), 41–42. On the treatment of prisoners of war as slaves in British imperial contexts, see Peter Way, "'Black Service . . . White Money': The Peculiar Institution of Military Labor in the British Army during the Seven Years' War," in Leon Fink, ed., *Workers across the Americas: The Transnational Turn in Labor History* (New York, 2011). Hilary McD. Beckles writes that "Irish servants . . . were seen by the English planter class as an enemy within and were treated accordingly." See Beckles, "A 'Riotous and Unruly Lot,'" *WMQ*, XLVII (1990), 511.

masters go away. Simply complaining to one's master that you felt "like a damnd slave" yielded few benefits and potential risks of reprisal from angry masters. At the same time, servants' claims of enslavement were not deployed for purely strategic purposes to effect leverage. Rather, they were advanced from a powerful and enduring moral conviction that neither servants nor any human being should ever be bought and sold. Irish servants' testimonies of kidnapping, abduction, and being "hooked" became productive for both pragmatic and idealistic reasons. Casey's story maps how servants' mobility gave rise to claims of both sovereignty and enslavement. The notion that antislavery was uniquely English during the first half of the seventeenth century reflects that nation's modest success in expanding the geography of its sovereignty and the circulation of its subjects through space. Yet that presumption was also contested at every turn by mobile actors whose protests against trafficking upended conceits at the heart of English national identity.[26]

The potential danger of servant antislavery was not resolved by English planters in Barbados turning to enslaved Africans to address their expanding labor needs on the island. To the contrary, the proximity of indentured servants toiling next to recently enslaved Africans only increased the depth of English planters' anxieties about the antislavery claims of trafficked people. The island of Barbados, the most profitable of England's colonies and the first to make the important transition to a slave society, was indeed a troubling case study for English elites. The replacement of indentured servants with enslaved labor there took time, and, for decades across the middle of the seventeenth century, servants and slaves labored together on similar tasks, serving common English masters while growing and harvesting sugarcane and exporting sugar. Their common labors invited both commentary and the first sporadic efforts to craft sharp legal distinctions between servitude and slavery. Importing enslaved Africans also invited the vexing question: Would servants collaborate with newly imported Africans and thwart common masters by resisting trafficking and enslavement at one and the same time?[27]

---

26. On the history of political antislavery as an ideological inheritance distinct from the history of abolition, see Christopher Leslie Brown, *Moral Capital: Foundations of British Abolitionism* (Williamsburg, Va., and Chapel Hill, N.C., 2006), 33–101; and David Waldstreicher, *Runaway America: Benjamin Franklin, Slavery, and the American Revolution* (New York, 2004), 198–207. On the belief that Englishness was an identity inherently antislavery in nature but still consistent with service work, see Steinfeld, *Invention of Free Labor,* 95–97.

27. On the search for workers to enslave, see Eltis, *Rise of African Slavery in the Americas,* 58–64.

For Richard Ligon, an Englishman who visited Barbados in 1647 just after planters began importing large numbers of African slaves to the island, anxieties about such collaborations between enslaved individuals and indentured servants loomed large throughout his observations about the booming English colony. Ligon's travel narrative exposed deep tensions between imperial and egalitarian impulses within English political culture during the 1640s. A bankrupted Royalist who called for the expansion of slavery in Barbados, Ligon expressed little sympathy for the ideas of radical Levellers. Yet Ligon was also appalled by the harsh living conditions that both indentured servants and African slaves endured on the island. His descriptions remain some of the most vivid in the historical record. Fed "lob-lollie," a coarse corn porridge, and an occasional potato, servants rarely received any meat, and most lived in makeshift cabins "made of sticks . . . and Plantine leaves, under some little shade that may keep the rain off." Like slaves, servants were unable to protest their treatment without experiencing corporal punishment: "If they complain, they are beaten by the Overseer; if they resist, their time is doubled. . . . Truly, I have seen such cruelty there done to servants, as I did not think one Christian could have done to another."[28]

Ligon argued that servants on Barbados were treated as if they were slaves, justifying their efforts at rebellion, especially those "whose spirits were not able to endure such slavery." They needed no English political inheritance to condone their resistance: their Christianity was all they needed, whether they were Protestant or Catholic. Ligon also condemned cruelty toward African slaves and urged planters to promote Christianity among them. He cited the case of one enslaved person, "as ingenious, as honest, and as good a natur'd poor soul, as ever wore black," who was cruelly denied the opportunity to become a Christian by planters who feared they "could no more account him a slave" if he converted. Ligon insisted that the humanity of enslaved Africans

---

28. Richard Ligon, *A True and Exact History of the Island of Barbados* (London, 1657), 31, 43–45. Ligon's firsthand observations of Barbados were both detailed and rare, particularly during the key decade of the 1640s, when enslaved Africans were being imported to replace indentured servants. Scholars have frequently cited his work. On those citing his description of a thwarted servant rebellion, see Amussen, *Caribbean Exchanges*, 158–159; Newman, *New World of Labor*, 96; Linebaugh and Rediker, *Many-Headed Hydra*, 124; Guasco, *Slaves and Englishmen*, 167; and Morgan, *American Slavery, American Freedom*, 298–299. On analyses of Ligon's racist views of African slaves, see Jordan, *White over Black*, 232; Dunn, *Sugar and Slaves*, 246–249; Beckles, *White Servitude and Black Slavery*, 125–126; Jennifer L. Morgan, *Laboring Women: Reproduction and Gender in New World Slavery* (Philadelphia, 2004), 13–15, 46–48l; and Newman, *New World of Labor*, 194–199.

was equal to that of any European subject, writing, "I beleive . . . that there are as honest, faithfull, and conscionable people amongst them, as amongst those of Europe, or any other part of this world."[29]

Ligon clearly believed abused Christian servants had a right to take up arms against unjust masters: Why not African slaves as well? Ligon sought to temper the radical implications of his moral outrage by condemning cruelty toward slaves and servants alike while insisting masters should become better Christians. He urged masters to "have a special care of" their slaves "by the labour of whose hands, our profit is brought in" by giving them more generous food rations and avoiding corporal punishment whenever possible. Christianity provided Ligon with a politically palatable vehicle for critiquing slavery while also enabling him to articulate a hierarchy directly at odds with his professed Christian universalism. Ligon advocated improved food rations, clothing, and housing for both servants and slaves, for example, while also calling for more rations for his fellow Christians. Servants, he argued, should receive a steady diet of meat, one that reversed a food hierarchy he claimed currently existed among slaves and servants. Under Ligon's plan, the "Christian servants, (which are not above thirty in number,)" on a given plantation, would receive "foure barrels of Beefe, and as much of Porke yearly, with two barrels of salt Fish, and 500 poore-Johns, which we have from New England, foure barrels of Turtle, and as many pickled Makerels, and two of Herrings for the Negres." The meat benefit Ligon proposed for Christians was temporary and transitory: "When the great Leveller of the world, Death, shall run his progresse," Ligon concluded, "all Estates will be laid even." For Ligon, Christianity both called into question and affirmed colonial rule.[30]

Ligon was both hostile to trafficking while also relying on it to map erotic and financial calculations at the very heart of the trade in servants and slaves. In so doing, Ligon exemplified values engendered by human trafficking that would in time become integral to notions of racial difference. Ligon attempted to make those values visible by creating a literal map of Barbados titled *A Topographicall Description and Admeasurement of the Ysland of Barbadoes in the West Indyaes with the M[aste]rs of the Severall Plantacons* that also featured drawings of African slaves, English soldiers, and indentured servants (Figure 1). Ligon portrayed conflicts between clothed bodies, which retained religious and national identities, and trafficked ones, which possessed values as laboring things. In the upper-right corner of the map, a fully clad and

29. Ligon, *A True and Exact History*, 45, 50, 53.
30. Ibid., 93, 113, 122.

FIGURE 1. Richard Ligon, *A Topographicall Description and Admeasurement of the Yland of Barbados in the West Indyaes*. 1657. Edward E. Ayer Digital Collection. VAULT Ayer 1000.5 .B22 L7 1657. Courtesy of The Newberry Library, Chicago

armed English soldier chases two naked Africans running toward a forest, presumably a habitat with some safety for runaway slaves. In the center of the map, virtually naked servants in rags toil with camels next to naked slaves, all of them harvesting sugarcane. Ligon's textual descriptions stress the process by which English planters mapped values onto both groups. "When they are brought to us," Ligon narrated, "the Planters buy them out of the Ship, where they find them stark naked, and therefore cannot be deceived in any outward infirmity." Trafficking, for Ligon, meant seeing slaves and servants first as exposed bodies. "They choose them as they do Horses in a Market; the strongest, youthfullest, and most beautifull yield the greatest prices. Thirty pound sterling is a price for the best man Negre; and twenty five, twenty six, or twenty seven for a Woman.... And we buy them so, as the the [sic] sexes may be equall." Making bodies fungible made them comparable, even if trafficked bodies also possessed decidedly unequal values.[31]

31. Richard Ligon, *A Topographicall Description and Admeasurement of the Yland of Barbados in the West Indyaes with the M[aste]rs. Names of the Severall Plantacions*, ibid., n.p.

Trafficking female bodies was essential to Ligon's effort to map the differential values he associated with skin color. His first description of an African slave, allegedly an African princess from the Cape Verde islands, focused on the woman's extraordinary features, characterizing her as "a Negro of the greatest beautie and majestie together that I ever saw in one woman." Ligon described her body as if at auction, observing a collection of exquisite parts while devoting particular energy to what he deemed its whitest elements, her teeth and eyes. "Her rowes of pearls, so clean, white, Orient, and well shaped, as *Neptune's* Court was never pav'd with such as these; and to shew whether was whiter, or more Orient, those or the whites of her eyes." For Ligon, the princess's whiteness, or her "Orient," made up a collection of rare and valuable things that revealed an aesthetic hierarchy between white and Black features far removed from Christian Europe. It is doubtful Ligon actually encountered an African princess on his journey. He wrote his account in 1650 while in jail for debt and under suspicion of harboring Royalist sympathies. Whiteness emerged in Ligon's narrative, not as a racial essence that English people shared, but as a trafficking fantasy associated with non-European and non-Christian women.[32]

Ligon's focus on trafficking pushed him not only to consider commonalities between servants and slaves but also to elevate the suffering of Christian servants over enslaved people from Africa. "The slaves and their posterity, being subject to Masters for ever, are kept and preserv'd with greater care than the servants," Ligon insisted, explaining that servants "are there but for five yeers, according to the law of the Iland. So that for the time, the servants have the worser lives, for they are put to very hard labour, ill lodging, and their dyet very sleight." Ligon reached this erroneous conclusion because he believed

---

[facing 1]; Ligon, *A True and Exact History*, 46–47. Literary scholars have taken the lead in analyzing how imperial encounters between European, African, and Amerindian peoples link discourses of sexuality, commerce, race, and conquest, though they focus more on the eighteenth century. See Mary Louise Pratt, *Imperial Eyes: Travel Writing and Transculturation* (London, 1992), 1–12; Srinivas Arayamudan, *Tropicopolitans: Colonialism and Agency, 1688–1804* (Durham, N.C., 1999), 190–232; and Laura Doyle, *Freedom's Empire: Race and the Rise of the Novel in Atlantic Modernity, 1640–1940* (Durham, N.C., 2008), 145–182.

32. Ligon, *A True and Exact History*, 12–13. Jennifer L. Morgan analyzes the political significance of Ligon's sexual fantasy of a Black princess with white body parts in Morgan, *Laboring Women*, 13–14. On the role of sex trafficking and reproduction to the evolution of racial slavery across the eighteenth century, see Marisa J. Fuentes, *Dispossessed Lives: Enslaved Women, Violence, and the Archive* (Philadelphia, 2016); and Sasha Turner, *Contested Bodies: Pregnancy, Childrearing, and Slavery in Jamaica* (Philadelphia, 2017).

Christian servants possessed rights that unredeemed Africans lacked. But Ligon also grounded his arguments for humane slavery within his fascination with the power of trafficking to reveal people's true value. For Ligon, trafficking people could simultaneously be wrong and uncover a hierarchy among individuals. Just as trafficking caused harm to servants and slaves, it also laid bare their shared humanity as Ligon understood it: their need to be protected by humane masters who might clothe all who were naked, even while assessing the value of their bodies. Put another way, trafficking made humanitarian calculation possible.[33]

How trafficked servants from Europe responded to newly arrived Africans is difficult to glean from the records of colonial and metropolitan elites, but the sources describing the behavior of servants and slaves, while scattered, provide clues as to how they regarded one another. When servants and slaves appear in historical records during the 1640s and 1650s, they frequently do so as co-conspirators, running away from shared masters. Whether in Barbados or in Virginia, there is also evidence of socializing and sex between servants and slaves. That sociability was a function not only of proximity—they performed similar work under common overseers and were distrusted alike by colonial and metropolitan elites—but also their shared experience of being trafficked to pay other people's debts. Being bought and sold did not make servants into slaves, but it did create a common starting point for resistance: running away and taking ownership of one's labor and mobility.[34]

The politics of trafficking and mobility explain why the earliest legal articulations of New World slavery focused on policing the collaborations between runaway servants and slaves. In 1640, Virginia's General Court sentenced three runaway "servants" who had managed to escape to the colony of Maryland, one born in Holland, another in Scotland, and the third "a negro named John Punch" of unknown origin. As punishment for running away, the Dutchman and the Scot each had an additional year of service added to their indentures as well as an additional three years of service to the colony of Virginia, likely as members of the militia. Running away also meant they would be sold at auction again, this time to pay public debts. Punch, however, was required to "serve his said master or his assigns for the time of his natural

33. Ligon, *A True and Exact History*, 43.
34. Edmund S. Morgan summarized this congruence in colonial Virginia before 1660 as follows: "It was common . . . for servants and slaves to run away together, steal hogs together, get drunk together. It was not uncommon for them to make love together." See Morgan, *American Slavery, American Freedom*, 327.

life here or else where." Punch was not described as a slave, but the differential treatment he received would soon become foundational to colonial slavery. Punch's lifetime punishment evoked the spirit of the 1547 Vagrancy Statute but with no possibility for reform or redemption. Punch's perpetual service would follow him wherever he traveled or was trafficked after 1640.[35]

In Virginia, the passage of a statute in 1661 that further legalized slavery likewise penalized servant-slave collaborations. The text of the law read "that in case any English servant shall run away in company with any negroes who are incapable of makeing satisfaction by addition of time, *Bee itt enacted* that the English so running away in company with them shall serve for the time of the said negroes absence as they are to do for their owne by a former act." By burdening the runaway servant with the transactional cost of a slave's life, the statute not only sought to make servants think twice about such collaborations but also to calculate the value of "negroes" as things, to traffic them before they even ran away together. The statute said little about how servants viewed African slaves in practice, yet its prominence indicates the depth of the problem that trafficked subjects were creating by collaborating with one another. The 1661 Virginia statute indemnified masters from any losses associated with servants claiming freedom or exercising control over their mobility. Taken together, the Punch case and the 1661 Virginia statute highlight the political rationale for creating slavery in law, stopping servant-slave collaborations and inculcating transactional values among servants who might be mulling an alliance with enslaved Africans. Transactional value, the belief that a person's worth could be measured and made visible at auction, was created, not by the invisible hand of an abstract marketplace, but by the violence associated with policing the mobility of fungible people.[36]

The transactional values associated with human trafficking remained deeply contested across the seventeenth century. During the waning days of Oliver Cromwell's Republic, an especially well-heeled group of convicted felons,

---

35. For details on the John Punch case, see "Decisions of the General Court," *Virginia Magazine of History and Biography*, V (1898), 236–237, cited in Jordan, *White over Black*, 75, n. 69. Described by Winthrop Jordan as "the first definite indication of outright enslavement" of Africans in the Americas, the context for Punch's enslavement—the effort by the Virginia court to police collaborations between trafficked African and European servants—is often overlooked. See Jordan, *White over Black*, 75.

36. "English Running Away with Negroes," March 1660, in William Waller Hening, *The Statutes at Large; Being a Collection of All the Laws of Virginia, from the First Session of the Legislature, in the Year 1619*, II (New York, 1823), 26, also cited in Morgan, *American Slavery, American Freedom*, 311; Jordan, *White over Black*, 75.

transported to Barbados in the 1650s, sought redemption from servitude by petitioning Parliament. That traditional right had become a dead letter in Barbados but still provided a sliver of hope for two felons, Marcellus Rivers and Oxenbridge Foyle, when they managed to return to London. These were not ordinary servants but "gentlemen," by their accounting, who had been condemned to die as traitors to Cromwell's Republic but were spared hanging when they were transported to Barbados in 1655. Four years later, they managed to have their petition read before the entire House of Parliament. Remarkably, Rivers and Foyle named the men responsible for their misery, "Martin Noell and Major Thomas, aldermen of London, and Captain H. Hatsell, of Plymouth," all three of whom listened as seated members of Parliament while Rivers and Foyle's petition was read by its supporters in 1659.[37]

The explosive debate that ensued juxtaposed members of Parliament who defended indentured servitude against those contemplating its similarities to slavery. The moment was already a precarious one for supporters of the Puritan Republic. For the members of the second Rump Parliament, formed after the English Army removed Richard Cromwell, Oliver's son, from power, the precise meaning of political freedom was strikingly unclear. At the heart of the debate were not only anxieties about the shape of political tyranny but conflicting assumptions about human trafficking and its exact relationship to enslavement. Martin Noell, who owned one of the largest sugar plantations on Barbados, admitted his role in transporting the petitioners, stating coolly that "I trade into those parts" and acknowledging that "I have had several persons out of Bridewell and other prisons." Noell vigorously rejected the petitioners' claim that he had enslaved the rebels, however, calling the accusations "false and scandalous. I indent with all persons that I send over," Noell continued, reflecting, "the work is hard, but none are sent without their consent. They were civilly used, and had horses to ride on." Noell sought to counter the petitioners' vivid claims of having been lowered to the level of farm animals by restoring the petitioners to the backs of horses. Captain Henry Hatsell likewise disputed the petitioners' claims. "I was present at

---

37. Petition of Marcellus Rivers and Oxenbridge Foyle, presented to Parliament, Mar. 25, 1659, cited in Leo Francis Stock, ed., *Proceedings and Debates of the British Parliament respecting North America*, I, *1542–1688* (Washington, D.C., 1924), 249. On the parliamentary debate of 1659, see Linebaugh and Rediker, *Many-Headed Hydra*, 105–109; and Guasco, *Slaves and Englishmen*, 168–171.

Plymouth when these persons were shipped. I never saw any go with more cheerfulness."[38]

For many parliamentarians, slavery was not solely about the theft of labor in the New World but the political status of English people in England. "I do not look on this . . . as a Cavalierish business," Sir Henry Vane argued, "but as a matter that concerns the liberty of the free-born people of England." "To be used in this barbarous manner," he added, "such was the case of this Thomas." Sir Arthur Haselrig concurred: "These men are now sold into slavery amongst beasts. I could hardly hold weeping when I heard the petition." For Haselrig and other supportive members in Parliament, the petition exposed a fundamental contradiction in the Puritan Republic. As Haselrig lamented, "Our ancestors left us free men. If we have fought our sons into slavery, we are of all men most miserable."[39]

The petitioners Rivers and Foyle, in turn, focused on the unlawfulness of their removal and transportation from England. Accused of bearing arms against Cromwell's armies, they insisted that many of "your distressed petitioners" never "bore arms in their lives" but were simply "picked up" by soldiers as "they travelled upon their lawful occasions." Nor were they charged with any crimes. They were "never so much as tried or examined. Yet your petitioners, and the others, were all kept prisoners by the space of one whole year, and then on a sudden . . . snatched out of their prisons." Unlawfully jailed, Rivers and Foyle were also illegally transported to Barbados after enduring a forced march through the city of Exeter. Not knowing "whither they were going," the petitioners were "all the way locked up under decks, . . . amongst horses, that their souls, through heat and steam, under the tropic, fainted in them." Perhaps the greatest injustice followed their arrival. They were sold "for one thousand five hundred and fifty pound weight of sugar a-piece, more or less . . . as the goods and chattels of Martin Noell." The petitioners concluded by protesting the unjust political authority that had produced their sale at public auction, calling on Parliament "to examine this arbitrary power, and to question by what authority so great a breach is made upon the free people of England, they having never seen the faces of these their pretended owners, merchants that deal in slaves and souls of men." The goal of their petition was

---

38. Testimonies of Martin Noell and Captain Hatsell, Mar. 25, 1659, in Stock, ed., *Proceedings and Debates of the British Parliament*, I, 250, 252.

39. Testimonies of Sir Henry Vane and Sir Arthur Hasleri[g], Mar. 25, 1659, ibid., 253, 257.

not to get Parliament to end the transportation of convicted felons but rather "to curb the unlimited power under which the petitioners and others suffer."[40]

The petitioners' demand for relief sidestepped the thorny question of what constituted slavery and its relationship to trafficking people, whether for profit or as political punishment. One of the most interesting ruptures in the 1659 parliamentary debate ensued when a parliamentarian and officer in the New Model Army Major General Richard Browne asked whether his own recent imprisonment of five years at the hands of Oliver Cromwell's government had constituted slavery. "As you are hearing the grievances of others, will you appoint a day to hear mine?" he queried. Could tyranny only be found in the grip of a despotic king or sultan, or could it also emanate from a republic? Major Robert Beake answered Browne's question expansively, "Let us compare cases. Slavery is slavery, as well in a Commonwealth as under another form." Other parliamentarians who were officers in the New Model Army agreed. Major General Thomas Kelsey rephrased the problem directly in political terms: "Tyranny is tyranny, wherever it be." Yet insights into political oppression did not produce a groundswell of support for Rivers and Foyle's petition. To the contrary, broadening the scope of slavery highlighted the dangers of hearing their petition in the first place. One army officer, a Major Knight, argued that the petition opened Pandora's box of complaints. "What will you do with the Scots taken at Dunbar, and at Durham and Worcester? Many of them were sent to Barbadoes. Will you hear all their petitions?" he asked. The prominence of transportation as a policy made this a particularly threatening conversation. Indeed, Major General Kelsey moved that the petitioners themselves be detained and their petition rejected.[41]

What began as a conversation about transportation to Barbados had become a larger reflection on the widespread practice of trafficking across En-

---

40. Petition of Rivers and Foyle, Mar. 25, 1659, ibid., 248–250. Linebaugh and Rediker have analyzed the reading of Rivers and Foyle's petition as a moment of counterrevolution when the radical promise of the English Levellers was explicitly abandoned. Rather than expressing uncertainty about the relationship between servitude and slavery, it conveyed a "convergence of ideas about slavery, race, and empire." See Linebaugh and Rediker, *Many-Headed Hydra*, 134. Rivers and Foyle did not claim rights of habeas corpus, though much of their petition can be read as a demand for such consideration from the parliamentarians hearing it. On the critical role of English sovereign authority in expanding the jurisdiction of the rights of habeas corpus in the century and a half after Cromwell's Republic, see Paul D. Halliday, *Habeas Corpus: From England to Empire* (Cambridge, Mass., 2010).

41. Testimonies of Major General Browne, Major Beake, Major General Kelsey, and Major Knight, in Stock, ed., *Proceedings and Debates of the British Parliament*, 254–256.

gland's empire, one increasingly defined by the example of racial slavery in Barbados. When Major General Kelsey responded to Rivers and Foyle by seeking to ban their right to petition, a great chorus arose in Parliament as members stood to defend that right as a cornerstone of English liberty. Sir Arthur Annesley, the first earl of Anglesey, invoked the Magna Carta directly: "I am sorry to hear Magna Charta moved against this House. If he be an Englishman, why should he not have the benefit of it?" The right to petition was as constitutive of freedom as its absence was of slavery. "If you pass this," parliamentarian Edward Boscawen warned, "our lives will be as cheap as those negroes." Boscawen's comments adroitly linked English liberties to values inscribed by human trafficking and the perceived disposability that "negroes" exemplified. Yet Boscawen was no servant or slave, even if he knew quite a lot about trafficking Africans and English convicts. He was instead a key architect of the Western Design and himself a wealthy slaveholder in Jamaica. By invoking the language of slavery to defend himself, Boscawen effectively stole the argument of the indentured petitioners Rivers and Foyle and the enslaved Africans they had found common cause with in Jamaica. "We are miserable slaves," Boscawen insisted, "if we may not have this liberty secured to us." A profound irony suffused Boscawen's speech in 1659: that it was a slaveholder who became the first member of Parliament to condemn the system of human trafficking that undergirded the development of England's empire. Boscawen's critique of human trafficking was hardly genuine. But antislavery was becoming threatening to political leaders in 1659, precisely because it could lead even slaveholders and architects of empire like Boscawen to condemn, as he put it, "the trade of buying and selling men."[42]

---

Although the backdrop of this debate was the emerging system of racial slavery in Barbados, Browne and Kelsey did not focus on race in their comments. Rather, they debated whether imprisonment for one's political views in London, by a king or by Cromwell, constituted slavery. See the testimonies of Major General Browne, Major Beake, and Major General Kelsey, ibid., 253, 254, and 255; and Linebaugh and Rediker, *Many-Headed Hydra*, 134.

42. Testimonies of Mr. Annesley and Mr. Boscawen, in Stock, ed., *Proceedings and Debates of the British Parliament*, 255, 256. On Boscawen's choice of language, see Linebaugh and Rediker, *Many-Headed Hydra*, 134; and Guasco, *Slaves and Englishmen*, 170–171. My analysis builds on the arguments of Thomas L. Haskell regarding the market-based and commercial origins of humanitarian sensibility during the eighteenth century, though I locate the timing of that emergence far earlier than did Haskell. As Haskell writes of the late eighteenth century, "What matters in the capitalist substructure is not a new class so much as the market, and what links the capitalist market to a new sensibility is not class interest

## Elite Antislavery

Servant antislavery became significant not simply because it highlighted the leverage that common actors exercised over core tenets of English political inheritance but also because it demanded a concerted response by England's political elites. That response employed antislavery rhetoric but in a form that might corral the political loyalties and behaviors of English commoners. Elite antislavery presented the monarch as a champion of antislavery who could protect the rights of his subjects as freeborn Englishmen in the midst of imperial expansion, even as a fragile English monarchy sought to expand England's role in the African slave trade and the servant trade. As such, elite antislavery posed a kind of political juggling act for those who espoused it: how to protect the consent of English and even Irish indentured servants without threatening the mercantile political economy that required their trafficking.

Complaints about the servant trade had little direct impact on colonial legislatures but did inspire sporadic efforts by metropolitan authorities to rethink England's relationship with its Atlantic colonies. On April 25, 1646, Mary Ford, a widow, submitted her "humble petition" to Parliament charging Captain Thomas Cornwallis, a former officer in Oliver Cromwell's New Model Army, with "stealing away . . . her children, and carrying them away into Maryland and seduceing them to popery and divers other fowle misdemeanours." Ford also accused Cornwallis of keeping "secret lodgeings" where he confined boys awaiting their departure. Her petition prompted the House of Commons to pass an ordinance that ostensibly reformed the servant trade by attempting to clarify the boundaries between voluntary and involuntary migration. Legislatures cautioned those responsible for the servant trade "that . . . neither force be used to take up any such servants, nor any apprentices enticed to desert their masters, nor any children under age

---

so much as the power of market discipline to inculcate altered perceptions of causation in human affairs." That sense of causation was hardly limited to capitalists but was embraced by religious radicals as well as sailors and others who resisted human trafficking at the same moment truly global markets for human cargo came into being during the late seventeenth century. Haskell focuses his argument on how the market transformed people's capacity to see, identify, and act on moral interests. The market that mattered most in the 1650s, however, was the one in trafficked servants and slaves plainly visible in Richard Ligon's observations. See Thomas L. Haskell, "Capitalism and the Origins of the Humanitarian Sensibility, Part I," in Thomas Bender, ed., *The Antislavery Debate: Capitalism and Abolitionism as a Problem in Historical Interpretation* (Berkeley, Calif., 1992), 111, 134, 136.

admitted without express consent of their parents." Even as the ordinance sought to eliminate coercion within servant traffic, however, it also blunted the radical dimensions of Ford's petition by underscoring the legality of traffic in servants. Recognizing that "there is great want of servants in the . . . plantations" of "Virginia, Bermudas, Barbados, and other places of America," lawmakers declared, "it shall be lawful for any person or persons, subjects of this kingdom, to entertain and transport from hence . . . persons . . . fit to serve or advance the trade there . . . or be employed in the said several foreign plantations." Transporting English subjects to American plantations would remain legal.[43]

Not surprisingly, servants and their advocates found coercion difficult to prove. More often than not, trafficked subjects were long gone before any charges could be filed. Securing depositions from parents of kidnapped victims was extremely challenging, as many if not most of the children stolen away to plantations possessed few opportunities to make their complaints known in a court of law. Owing to these enforcement difficulties, petitions against kidnapping and spiriting proliferated. Petitioners typically protested the injustice of particular merchants and individual kidnappers. Given how politically dangerous it was for servants to protest abusive treatment by their masters, a remarkable variety of petitions on behalf of New World servants were nonetheless presented to Parliament during the seventeenth century. Early in the summer of 1664, one Lady Yarborough protested to Parliament that a "poor boy that I had a care of about a fortnight agoe was stolen away by spirits, as they call them," the agents who used alcohol or confinement to secure a cargo of servants and then conveyed them "to ships for New England or Barbadoes." She called on port authorities to "search ships for him." After her petition was read, parliamentarian Sir Heneage Finch crafted another petition on July 12, 1664, that found "the mischiefs complained of very frequent, there being scarce any voyage to the Plantations but some are carried away against their wills." Subsequently, the mayor of London condemned "persons called 'spirits,'" who "by lewd subtilties entice away youth against the consent either of their parents, friends, or masters, whereby . . . great tumults and uproars are raised within the city to the breach of the peace and the hazard of men's lives." In London, hostility to the trafficking of servants linked the

---

43. Petition of Mary Ford, presented, Apr. 25, 1646, in Stock, ed., *Proceedings and Debates of the British Parliament*, 179, Ordinance for the Foreign Plantations, Jan. 23, 1646/7, 185–186.

protests of trafficked servants with those of masters upset that their servants had been enticed away from their households.[44]

The unusual partnership between masters and servants was successful in pushing Parliament to pass an "Act to Prevent Stealing and Transporting Other Children" on March 18, 1670. In addition to prescribing the death penalty for spirits, the act created an official register in which servants declared they were traveling of their own volition and without coercion. Enjoying the enthusiastic support of Charles II, the Spirting Act highlighted the power of antitrafficking to prompt reforms on behalf of both trafficked servants and their former masters. Taken at face value, the 1670 law made the English state a guarantor of servants' freedom. In practice, however, the creation of a servant registry only secured the formal appearance of consent. The limited effectiveness of the Spiriting Act can be discerned from the original petition that created the first servant registry in 1664 and spurred the passage of the 1670 law. Presented on behalf "of merchants, planters, and masters of ships trading to the Plantations," the petition condemned not only the "wicked custom to seduce or spirit away young people" but also the "many evil-minded persons" who "enlist themselves voluntarily to go the voyage, and having received money, clothes, diet, etc.," subsequently "pretend they were betrayed or carried away without their consents." In this telling, the central problem had become the fraud perpetrated by servants rather than the harm inflicted on them by spirits.[45]

One of the ironies of the Spiriting Act was that it rejected the testimonies of servants who claimed coercion even as it made their testimony central to

---

44. "Lady Yarborough's Petition," 1664, SP 29/109, 23, CSP, PRO, TNA, "Petition of Merchants, Planters, and Masters of Ships Trading to the Plantation to the King," July 12, 1664, CO 1/15, 31, "Memorial of the Lord Mayor and Court of Alderman to the Privy Council," 1664, SP 29/408, 117. On the history of kidnapping within a broader examination of the rights of children in Anglo-American communities during the seventeenth and eighteenth centuries, see Holly Brewer, *By Birth or Consent: Children, Law, and the Anglo-American Revolution in Authority* (Williamsburg, Va., and Chapel Hill, N.C., 2005), 273–275; and Smith, *Colonists in Bondage*, 67–86.

45. "An Act to Prevent Stealing and Transporting Other Children," Mar. 18, 1670, CO 389/2, 1–13, CSP, "Petition of Merchants, Planters, and Masters of Ships Trading to the Plantations to the King," July 12, 1664, CO 1/15, 31; "Preface" in Sainsbury, ed., *Calendar of State Papers . . . 1661–1668*, [V], xxix, "Privy Seal for Lord Chancellor Clarendon to Prepare Letters Patent . . . ," Sept. 14, 1664, 233. For a description of the Spiriting Act as implemented in Barbados in 1670 in accordance with Parliament's actions, see also "Six Acts of Barbados Passed in 1670," Aug. 11, 1670, CO 30/1, 75–83, CSP.

managing servant traffic. How exactly would English authorities know when servant migrants were telling the truth? Were claims of coercion after a vessel had departed necessarily fraudulent? These were not questions that appear to have vexed the "divers merchants, planters, and masters of ships trading to plantations," however. As long as servants signed the new registry, ship captains became indemnified against charges of kidnapping. What began as an effort by the parents and guardians of servants to protect transported and trafficked children became, in the hands of merchants and ship captains, a mechanism for policing all servants. The registry enabled ship captains to deny claims of servant abuse once in transit by pointing to a list of consenting signatures.[46]

Despite the Spiriting Act's pedagogical purpose to remind subjects that the king was against their coercion or enslavement, the servant registry obscured rather than clarified the contours of coercion in the servant trade. It shifted public scrutiny away from the profits made by planters, merchants, and ship captains to the nefarious activities of the individuals known as spirits. In the celebrated spiriting case of 1671, the first application of the 1670 law focused, not on the conduct of ship captains like Cornwallis, but instead on the deeds of five spirits, whose work implicated one another even as they protested their innocence. William Haverland, for example, swore that John Steward was guilty of "spiriting persons to Barbadoes, Virginia, Jamaica, and other places for twelve years, five hundred in a year." Top honors, however, went to William Thiene, whom Haverland claimed "in one year spirited away 840" people from London to New World plantations. Yet Haverland was himself "generally called a spirit," according to the affidavit of Mary Collins. Even as Collins's testimony implicated Haverland as a spirit, it also revealed a complex world of hardworking men and women laboring to supply impoverished men, women, and children from the neighborhoods of East London to merchants and ship captains. Some, like Thiene and Steward, were quite successful in that work, procuring thousands of people over the course of several years and amassing modest wealth in the process; others, like Robert Bayley, "an old spirit [who] lives sometimes in St. Giles and sometimes in St. Katherines and hath noe other way of livelihood but by spiriting," barely scraped by. None made as much money from the servant trade as shipping merchants or ship captains. Yet spirits received the greatest public notoriety and censure. It is not clear whether Haverland was convicted of spiriting, but, if so, he would

---

46. "Petition of Merchants, Planters, and Masters of Ships Trading to the Plantations to the King," July 12, 1664, CO 1/15, 31, CSP; Smith, *Colonists in Bondage*, 67–74.

have faced a death sentence and been transported to Virginia to be sold like other felons and so-called malefactors as an indentured servant.[47]

Perhaps the most striking feature of the legislative effort to stop spiriting was, not the creation of consensual servant migrations, then, but the sanctioning of transportation as a policy for forcibly removing England's poor and transient residents to New World plantations. Indeed, Parliament's immediate response to Lady Yarborough's petition was a proposal in 1664 "to constitute an office for transporting to the Plantations all vagrants, rogues, and idle persons that can give no account of themselves, felons who have the benefit of clergy, such as are convicted of petty larceny, vagabonds, gipsies, and loose persons, making resort to unlicensed brothels." Lest the proposal seem to contradict Yarborough's call to stop the stealing of children, it also specified that "no person under 12 years of age" should be transported "unless their friends and relations shall first personally appear at the office." The political solution to Lady Yarborough's complaint was, not the cessation of the traffic in boys to North American plantations, but the creation of an office that would guarantee those boys had consented to their travels. That consent could be given not only by the children's parents or guardians but also by children themselves once on board the ships transporting them to North America, a measure that enabled ship captains to bypass or ignore the protests of parents.[48]

The servant registry and the mechanisms for enforcing it ironically empowered ship captains and the parents and guardians of young, indentured migrants while penalizing the plebeian individuals who facilitated and even constituted the trade. Despite the registry having been enacted for their protection, perhaps the last cohort to benefit were the children shipped to plantations across the Americas. These boys and girls could now be trafficked with the official blessing of the English crown and the mercantile actors who profited from years of their unfree labor in the Americas. Indemnifying ship captains and merchants in the servant trade from the claims of young and adult indentured servants demanding redress represented a crafty solution to the vexing challenge posed by servant antislavery. At the same time, the

---

47. "Affidavit of William Haverland against John Steward for spiriting persons . . . ," February 1671, CO 389/2, 12–13, CSP, "Affidavit of Mary, Wife of Mark Collins, against William Haverland, Generally Called a Spirit," February 1671, CO 389/2, 13, "Affidavit of Tho. Stone against William Haverland for Being a Spirit," February 1671, CO 389/2, 11–12.

48. "Proposals to the King and Council," [1664?], in Sainsbury, ed., *Calendar of State Papers . . . 1661–1668*, [V], 221.

registry's existence also gave rise to new questions. Although the registry put the English state firmly on the side of ship captains worried about fraud in the servant trade, it also implicated the English crown in a child trafficking plot. If the servant registry was unmasked as a vehicle for protecting ship captains rather than children, would people see the English state as the real kidnapper?

The immediate context for Parliament's effort to regulate the trafficking of English children in 1671—English expansion into the African slave trade—suggests that elite anxieties about African slavery and English identity might have contributed to the passage of the Spiriting Act. The year 1670 was a turning point in the history of England's participation in the African slave trade. The Company of Royal Adventurers trading into Africa had only recently acquired the monopoly rights to traffic goods and enslaved Africans out of the continent in 1660, and, on January 1, 1669, the company had secured a ten-year license to purchase slaves north of the Bight of Benin, the locale from where much of the larger African slave trade originated. English participation in the slave trade grew substantially over the ensuing decades, as English planters for the first time began purchasing enslaved Africans directly from the company of Royal Adventurers, later renamed the Royal African Company in 1672, after the company had obtained the rights to build factories for housing, incarcerating, and disciplining newly purchased African men, women, and children. That infrastructure was vital to expanding England's participation in the slave trade, as illustrated by the increased number of English slave ships that arrived in Virginia during the 1670s and 1680s. Prior to 1670, just two or three slave ships had brought their human cargo directly to Virginia. During the 1670s, nine disembarked in Virginia ports, while eleven ships did so during the 1680s. That expansion brought about enormous profits for English actors as well as questions about the political character of this new power to traffic people. The Spiriting Act of 1670 did not inoculate England from concerns that its involvement in the slave trade was creating, but it did shore up the antislavery credentials of the newly restored Stuart monarchy at precisely the moment it was expanding dramatically into the most lucrative state-sponsored human trafficking endeavor in English history.[49]

49. John C. Coombs, "The Phases of Conversion: A New Chronology for the Rise of Slavery in Early Virginia," *William and Mary Quarterly*, 3d Ser., LXVIII (2011), 343. See also Alden T. Vaughan, "The Origins Debate: Slavery and Racism in Seventeenth-Century Virginia," *Virginia Magazine of History and Biography*, XCVII, no. 3 (July 1989), 311–354.

Anxieties about the troubled contradictions at the heart of England's political economy were not new to 1670 but also built on the recent history of Irish colonization and deportation. To Irish residents and migrants, the salient question was not whether the English state was a kidnapper but how many people would it kidnap to maintain its navy? English transportation was but one part of a larger process of colonization and land theft in Ireland, reflected in the plummeting rate of landownership among Irish residents, which fell from 59 percent in 1641 to just 22 percent in 1660. Estimates of how many Irish people were transported vary, but at least twenty thousand people were shipped from Ireland to New World colonies during the 1640s and 1650s. The writings of the Archbishop of Fermo, Italy, Monsignor Rinuccini, who witnessed the dramatic expropriation of Irish estates in the 1650s, afford some insight into how Catholic leaders framed these events. "While the Government were employed in clearing the ground for adventurers and soldiers," wrote Rinuccini, "they had agents actively employed through Ireland seizing women, orphans, and the destitute, to be transported to Barbadoes and the English plantations in America." Rinuccini sought to clarify the horror of Irish transportation to his elders in the Vatican by employing a comparative frame that was quite familiar to them in 1654. "Those sold to the heretics in America," he concluded, "are treated by them more cruelly than the slaves under the Turks."[50]

If the transportation of Irish vagrants, many of them children, to New World plantations highlighted the hypocrisy of parliamentary opposition to kidnapping, transportation was nonetheless perceived to be a humanitarian policy during the seventeenth century. By refusing to work, vagrants were considered by many English essayists to be criminals, frauds rather than true victims, akin to the servants who claimed to have been kidnapped at the end of their transatlantic journey. Writer Daniel Defoe justified the trafficking of vagrants in precisely such terms in 1709. The English poor, "having been long inur'd to Idleness, and the Trade of Begging, . . . will never work till the fear of Punishment obliges 'em to it," he wrote. Transportation compelled

---

50. [John P.] Prendergast, "The Official Documents Published by Mr. Prendergast," in Patrick Francis Moran, *Historical Sketch of the Persecutions Suffered by the Catholics of Ireland under the Rule of Cromwell and the Puritans* (Dublin, 1884), 327, 330. On the transportation and kidnapping of Irish peasants out of Ireland, see Beckles, *White Servitude and Black Slavery*, 49–53; Newman, *New World of Labor*, 82–83, 85–86, 96; Smith, *Colonists in Bondage*, 48–49, 163; Shaw, *Everyday Life in the Early English Caribbean*, 71–100; and Jordan and Walsh, *White Cargo*, 147–150.

vagrants to work to redeem their tarnished currency in the body politic. Defoe's arguments echoed those of political essayist and philosopher Richard Hakluyt the elder, who wrote a century earlier that transportation was a humane remedy, an opportunity for those "condempned for certen yeres in the western partes" to "be raised againe, and doe their contrie goodd service." Rather than creating a system of slavery, transportation avoided incarcerating thousands of English residents at home at hard labor, a prospect many commentators viewed as a much graver threat to English liberties. Thomas Robe reasoned in 1733 that "ill Consequences will happen, (from inflicting any kind of Slavery on free-born Subjects) which in Time may affect our Liberties." Such reasoning underscores the importance of location in obscuring the existence of a form of domestic slavery. If English subjects wore their chains in colonial outposts rather than in London, then perhaps the reality of such coercion had been mitigated. Geographic reasoning, it would seem, could solve troubling contradictions within England's political economy.[51]

But geographic reasoning did not prevent political contradictions from bubbling up to the surface anyhow, particularly those related to trafficking servants. In 1676, members of the Council of the Lords of Trade and Plantations in London praised Jamaica's new servant law as "being very necessary for the prevention of spiriting away children." The law established minimal standards of care for young, indentured servants in terms of clothing and food while also recommending that the word *servitude* not be used when discussing servants as it was "a mark of bondage." Yet in 1693, members of the council expressed anxiety that similar laws encouraging consenting servant migration to the Leeward Islands "may tend to encourage the 'spiriting' away of white servants to the plantations without their consent, a practice which is very frequent and known by the name of kidnapping." Three years later, the attorney general and solicitor general once again voiced reservations about laws designed to promote the migration of white servants to the colonies of Antigua and Montserrat that might also have the effect of incentivizing their kidnapping, which they defined as a form of slavery. These new laws "tend

---

51. Daniel Defoe, *A Brief History of the Poor Palatine Refugees, Lately Arrived in England* (London, 1709), 9–10; Richard Hakluyt, *A Discourse concerning Western Planting* . . . , ed. Charles Deane, Collections of the Maine Historical Society, 2d Ser. (Cambridge, Mass., 1877), 37, 160, cited in A. Roger Ekirch, *Bound for America: The Transportation of British Convicts to the Colonies, 1718–1775* (Oxford, 1987), 7; [Thomas Robe], "Some Considerations for Rendering the Punishment of Criminals More Effectual . . . ," Mar. 21, 1733, reprinted in [Robe], *A Collection of Political Tracts* (London, 1735), 48.

to encourage spiriting away Englishmen without their consent and selling them there for slaves, which . . . is known by the name of kidnapping." Even when passed with a humane purpose in view, servant emigration laws could incite trafficking and enslavement. Yet in the hands of English legislators and the crown, efforts to police kidnapping, even that caused by the state's own emigration laws, burnished the fiction that freedom was innately English and the king the defender of trafficking's hapless victims.[52]

Antislavery ideology, then, shaped servants' protests against coercive transportation, shipping merchants' attempts to indemnify themselves using servant testimony, and parliamentarians' actions to police kidnapping at home. The plasticity of antislavery made it useful to both subaltern and elite actors. Location and mobility were essential to how conflicts over antislavery were expressed and, at least temporarily, resolved. For servants, antislavery ideology gave them opportunities to redress grievances, even if power remained largely vested in masters' stronger access to the law. Antislavery helped focus servants' complaints on the politically unjust dimensions of transportation. At the same time, efforts to curtail the kidnapping of English servants, especially children, buttressed a political economy devoted to expanding the slave trade by securing the rights of freeborn English subjects.

Elite efforts to make antislavery work on behalf of imperial expansion could also backfire and did so in spectacular fashion in 1676, when tensions within Virginia's political economy could not be transported away. Instead, they exploded in a rebellion that for a time upended the colonial project that had pitted trafficked servants and slaves against one another. Although scholars have debated whether any consistent ideology shaped the actions of the participants of Bacon's Rebellion, the alliances between servants and slaves that it facilitated were themselves provocative to Virginia's colonial authorities.

---

52. "Journal of the Lords of Trade and Plantation," May 30, 1676, Jamaica, CO 391/1, CSP, "Report to the Solicitor General on the Acts of the Leeward Islands," Oct. 12, 1693, CO 152/1, 21, The Attorney and Solicitor General to the Council of Trade and Plantations, Nov. 11, 1696, CO 152/2, 15. On the ways in which children's political status became a vehicle for rethinking slaves' political status later in the eighteenth century, see Brewer, *By Birth or Consent*. Brewer argues that criticism of slavery in England during the late seventeenth century was muted by the sedition laws of both Charles II and James II. Debates about the potential enslavement of servants thus assumed an added interest and urgency for both Parliament and Charles II. See Brewer, "Slavery and Sedition in Britain and Its Empire," unpublished paper presented at the Triangle Global British History Seminar, Apr. 23, 2015. On the passage of the Habeas Corpus Act in 1679 and its relationship to sovereignty and royalist antislavery, see Halliday, *Habeas Corpus*, 237–246.

What began as an effort to incite hatred against Virginia's Native peoples on the colony's western frontier soon became an uprising of the trafficked against colonial masters in one of England's most lucrative colonies. The rebellion was fueled not only by class conflicts within the colony but also by the ways servants and slaves together stirred visions of a very different political economy, one in which the trafficked became, briefly, the traffickers.[53]

The rebellion began as a fight for access to land but over time morphed into a struggle over who could traffic whom, a question that cut to the heart of Virginia's political economy for all classes of Virginia's colonists as well as Native peoples like the Susquehannocks, who were waging their own campaign for power and resources across the mid-Atlantic region. The initial reaction to the news that servants, freemen, and some slaves were supporting the agitations of a young landowner named Nathaniel Bacon produced contempt rather than any concessions to their demands. The governor of Virginia, Sir William Berkeley, called them a "Rabble Crue . . . only the Rascallity and meanest of the people," with only a "very few who can either write or read." Bacon, however, offered his followers an immediate remedy to being someone else's property: the opportunity to seize, plunder, and traffic other people and other people's things. "Things have been carried by the men at the helme as if it were but to play a booty game, or divide a spoyle," Bacon wrote before the rebellion began, indicting the amoral fashion in which elite planters had amassed wealth in the colony. Now it would be the rebels' turn. Soldiers fighting for Bacon were to "have the benefitt of all plunder either Indians or otherwise," including food, livestock, guns, furs, and land itself. The power to traffic—and to enslave—was to be democratized at Native people's expense. "All Indians taken in warr" were to become the property of the taker, "held

---

53. Morgan, *American Slavery, American Freedom*, 270. There is a rich historiography on the significance of Bacon's Rebellion that has expanded, deepened, and challenged Morgan's enduring insights into the political economy of colonial Virginia. Kathleen M. Brown enriched and extended Morgan's focus on class conflicts within the colony with her pioneering investigations of gender relations and conflicts in the creation of political and racial order in the aftermath of the rebellion, while Theodore W. Allen likewise honed Morgan's insights about class antagonisms in the invention of whiteness. See Brown, *Good Wives, Nasty Wenches, and Anxious Patriarchs*; Allen, *Invention of the White Race*, I and II; and Isenberg, *White Trash*, 37–41. For critiques of Morgan's narrative and the timing of the appearance of whiteness, see Coombs, "The Phases of Conversion," *WMQ*, 3d Ser., LXVIII (2011), 332–360; and Coombs, "Beyond the 'Origins Debate': Rethinking the Rise of Virginia Slavery," in Douglas Bradburn and Coombs, eds., *Early Modern Virginia: Reconsidering the Old Dominion* (Charlottesville, Va., 2011), 239–278.

and accounted slaves dureing life." Over the course of the ensuing conflict, Bacon's soldiers did indeed plunder the unfortunate Indian communities who had forged alliances with Governor Berkeley, but planters and residents backing the governor were also fair game for plunder, a cohort that included residents of Jamestown, whose homes were burned to the ground after first being looted by Bacon's men.[54]

The violence organized by Bacon and his soldiers exposed ideological fault lines within antislavery as well as the centrality of trafficking to discussions of class interest and elite authority within colonial Virginia. Opposition to trafficking and to bonded labor was an explicit part of Bacon's appeal, even if the stated aim of the war was to steal land from Native peoples. That conflicted purpose was manifest when Bacon's soldiers set free servants and slaves of masters loyal to Governor Berkeley immediately after capturing and trafficking Powhatan Indians. It was likewise visible in the promise Bacon made to servants and slaves when they joined his army: immediate freedom to all who rejected Berkeley's political authority. As in many subsequent wars in North America, slaves willingly participated to secure their freedom. But if taking up arms fostered emancipatory aspirations, those promises proved hollow, even though Bacon and his troops were initially successful in routing Berkeley's troops and supporters. When Bacon died an untimely death just six weeks after he and his men sacked Jamestown, the contested origins of the rebellion reemerged. As Governor Berkeley sought to restore order, reinforced by soldiers from several English ships, the core of Bacon's army refused to surrender. Ultimately, they made up just one hundred men, eighty of them enslaved Africans and twenty indentured servants, all of them striving for freedom. Although some of the better-heeled rebels received amnesty from Governor Berkeley, most of these men fought to the finish only to become

---

54. The Coventry Papers of the Marquess of Bath at Longleat House, LXXVII, 95–96, 442, microfilm, Library of Congress, Washington, D.C., quoted in Morgan, *American Slavery, American Freedom*, 258, 267; "An Act for Carrying on a Warre against the Barbarous Indians," June 5, 1676, in Hening, *Statutes at Large*, II, 346, quoted in Morgan, *American Slavery, American Freedom*, 264. Scholarship on Bacon's Rebellion has resituated the conflict between classes in colonial Virginia within the larger conflicts among Native peoples in securing access to land, hunting resources, and especially control over the Indian slave trade. See Matthew Kruer, *Time of Anarchy: Indigenous Power and the Crisis of Colonialism in Early America* (Cambridge, Mass., 2021); James D. Rice, "Bacon's Rebellion in Indian Country," *Journal of American History*, CI (2014), 726–750; and Gallay, *Indian Slave Trade*.

property again, with terms of service extended, if indentured, or to be faced with severe corporal punishments, if enslaved.[55]

Bacon's Rebellion was the immediate political context in which metropolitan authorities began using white grammar to describe and count the unruly servants transported to the Americas. In the decades following the revolt, Virginia expanded its reliance on slavery, importing thousands of Africans from Barbados while devising legal mechanisms curtailing relationships between servants and slaves and between Africans and Euro-Americans more generally. In 1680, the Virginia General Assembly passed a new statute authorizing thirty lashes on the bare back "if any negroe or other slave shall presume to lift up his hand in opposition against any christian." Sexual relations between African Americans and Euro-Americans were likewise criminalized after the rebellion ended. Richard Lawrence, one of the ringleaders of Bacon's Rebellion who had freed his slaves, was publicly condemned as someone who sullied himself "in the darke imbraces of a Blackamoore, his slave: And that in so fond a Maner, . . . to the noe meane Scandle and affrunt of all the Vottrisses in or about towne." In 1691, Virginia's General Assembly passed legislation policing interracial sex involving "white women." The act called "for prevention of that abominable mixture and spurious issue which hereafter may encrease in this dominion, as well by negroes, mulattoes, and Indians intermarrying with English, or other white women, as by their unlawfull accompanying with one another."[56]

The most visible and striking legal changes in the aftermath of Bacon's Rebellion involved new laws controlling who might traffic whom in the colony. Before 1676, Native peoples in Virginia had enjoyed a measure of freedom from both trafficking and enslavement. In 1656, the Virginia General Assembly had ruled that when "Indians shall bring in any children . . . wee will not use them as slaves, but . . . bring them up in Christianity, civillity, and the knowledge of necessary trades." After Bacon's Rebellion began, Virginia lawmakers avowed "that all Indians taken in warr be held and accounted

55. Wilcomb E. Washburn, *The Governor and the Rebel: A History of Bacon's Rebellion* (Williamsburg, Va., and Chapel Hill, N.C., 1969), 85–89.

56. "An Act for Preventing Negroes Insurrections," June 1680, in Hening, *Statutes at Large*, II, 481, also cited in Morgan, *American Slavery, American Freedom*, 331; "The History of Bacon's and Ingram's Rebellion, 1676," in Charles M. Andrews, ed., *Narratives of the Insurrections, 1675–1690* (New York, 1915), 96, quoted in Jordan, *White over Black*, 79; "An Act for Suppressing Outlying Slaves," April 1691, in William Waller Hening, *The Statutes at Large; Being a Collection of All the Laws of Virginia . . .* , III (Philadelphia, 1823), 86–87.

slaves dureing life." Indians and their possessions could now be legally trafficked by colonists. In 1676/77, the Virginia General Assembly decreed that soldiers in the militia could "reteyne and keepe all such Indian slaves* or other Indian goods as they either have taken or hereafter shall take." Just as Bacon's Rebellion exemplified imperial conflicts over who could traffic whom, it also emboldened colonial legislators to weaponize trafficking, the better to police boundaries at the heart of plantation slavery. Servants who participated in the uprising not only saw their terms of service extended but were publicly sold by the parish, with proceeds supporting poor relief. Collaborations between African and Euro-Americans became more and more suspect. Rebellious behavior by servants and slaves not only warranted expanded corporal punishments but the exemplary selling of both servants and enslaved individuals as well as their personal effects for poor relief. A rebellion of the enslaved and indentured had produced, not freedom from human commerce, but tighter imperial controls over human trafficking and how those caught in its net would be managed and disciplined moving forward.[57]

## The Emergence of White Peoplehood

At first glance, the growth of white grammar in the CSP during the 1670s seems to suggest it was deliberately crafted in response to the unruly coalition of servants and enslaved actors who lead Bacon's Rebellion as well as to the dangers of servant antislavery that had pushed English policymakers to create the servant registry and outlaw spiriting. In this reading of events, white grammar appears as an effort to divide trafficked actors on the basis of skin color. Although that interpretation captures the broad outlines of mercantile political economy and culture, it ignores that white grammar did, in fact, emerge earlier, before Bacon's Rebellion, while also neglecting the close semantic connections between white grammar and human trafficking in evidence throughout the late seventeenth century. White grammar did not initially articulate racial benefits but instead status as a commodity or a transported felon, a class of trafficked actors distinct from Christian servants. Indeed, the close pairing of malefactors with white servants emerged

---

57. "An Induction to the Acts concerning Indians," Mar. 10, 1655/6, in William Waller Hening, *The Statutes at Large; Being a Collection of All the Laws of Virginia* . . . , I (New York, 1823), 396; "An Act for Carrying on a Warre against the Barbarous Indians," June 5, 1676, in Hening, *Statutes at Large*, II, 346, and "Att a Grand Assembly Begunne at Greene Spring the 20th of Ffebruary . . . ," 1676/77, 404; all cited in Guasco, *Slaves and Englishmen*, 181.

only during the 1680s, years after the uprising of the trafficked known as Bacon's Rebellion. Neither white servants nor whites were associated with rights before 1700, in contrast to Christian servants, who were linked with humanitarian concerns and rights during the 1690s. When rights do appear in association with white grammar in the CSP, they do so primarily in association with language denoting white peoplehood, accompanying individuals described as white men, white women, and white people, rather than in association with language typically denoting trafficked whites, such as white servants or, simply, whites (see Appendix A, Tables 2, 3, 5 and 8).

References to white servants and whites appear consistently after 1670, but descriptions of white people and white men were comparatively rare before the beginning of the eighteenth century. When they do show up, the identities and locations of the people so described jar present-day expectations of who white people were and where they were supposed to have existed. In 1674, British General Abraham Wood, traveling through the western regions of the colony of Virginia, for example, wrote that "eight days' journey down this river live a white people with long beards and whiskers, who wear clothing, and on some of the other rivers live a hairy people." This community of white people, likely a group of runaway servants and Europeans allied with Native people to the west of English settlement, lived with "many blacks among them" and behaved in politically unruly ways. Wood observed that they "put to death all the white and black people they take" along the western frontier. Whether white people were enemies or friends to England's colonial interests in Wood's missive is unclear: they could be both. A look at all references to white people in the CSP before 1700 amplifies the picture of semantic and political uncertainty exemplified in Wood's narrative, with half of the references to white people describing unruly behavior (see Appendix A, Table 8).[58]

After 1700, however, a sharply different taxonomy began to emerge. White people described as having rights in the CSP increased from 0 to just over 40 percent, while white people characterized by unruly behavior declined to just 5 percent, a pattern similar to changes in the semantic associations of Christian servants some two decades earlier (see Appendix A, Table 8). Additionally, the number of references to white people in the CSP expanded sharply after 1700. The emergence of white peoplehood did not accompany

---

58. Abraham Wood to John Richards, Aug. 22, 1674, 30/24/48, 94, CSP. Although the number of CSP references to white people before 1700 are small, just twelve, six of them are connected to unruly behavior. After 1700, the proportion of white people characterized as unruly drops from 50 percent to just 5 percent. See Appendix A, Table 8.

any decline in convict transportation out of London's prisons or any diminishing effort to recruit white men for militia work in England's burgeoning Caribbean colonies; trafficking remained a ubiquitous practice for all peoples identified by their skin color. Rather, references to white people after 1700 began to link white subjecthood more to rights and less to unruly behavior.

Even as a language of a white people endowed with rights displaced a language of trafficked and rebellious white servants in political conversation, however, the adoption of a taxonomy of skin color did not, in fact, solve problems of colonial governance. To the contrary, white grammar continued to convey a complex mixture of sentiments about trafficked English subjects. In 1703, English Attorney General Edward Northey sent a letter to the governor of Barbados worried lest the harshness of indenture contracts transform "white servants" into "white slaves." Northey was particularly concerned about the apparent lack of any legal process that might prevent justices of the peace in Barbados from condemning white slaves "to death" or from "dismember[ing] them arbitrarily without any form of proceeding for offences." Northey's misgivings about the harsh treatment of indentured servants were not new, as Christian servants had been the subject of numerous efforts to restrain inhumane severity by masters during the 1690s. What was new in 1703 was the term Northey used to discuss such anxiety: *white slavery*. Nevertheless, a discourse about white slaves never became prominent among colonial elites. To identify servants as white slaves magnified the political threat that they posed to colonial administrators. Although Northey's nomenclature led him, albeit briefly, to sharply question the abysmal treatment that English indentures encountered in the Caribbean, Northey was no abolitionist. Nevertheless, his probing question frankly acknowledged, or even encouraged, the possibility that enslaved Africans and servants might unite against common masters. The right not to be dismembered seems an unlikely starting point for white racial rights, but Northey's apprehension about the possibility of "arbitrary" dismemberment represents one of the first such efforts to clarify the benefit that white skin made for a trafficked servant.[59]

---

59. Sir Edward Northey to the Council of Trades and Plantations, May 15, 1703, CO 152/6, 43, CSP, Sir Jonathan Atkins to Mr. Blathway, Apr. 1, 1680, CO 1/44, 47. As references to white servants increased within the CSP during the 1690s and first decade of the eighteenth century, references to Christian servants became far more connected to a discourse of humanity and humanitarian reforms. The percentage of references to Christian servants that invoked humanitarian themes rose to 50 percent during the 1690s and to 56

Rather than responding directly to Attorney General Northey's inquiry, Colonel Joseph Jorey of Barbados crafted a letter to Northey reassuring him that the island's indentured servants had never been enslaved, causing Northey to retract his edgy comments about the political status of servants and slaves in relation to one another. It was the members of Virginia's General Assembly, however, who most effectively answered Northey's disquiet by passing a new slave and servant law in 1705, one that intensified differential punishments for any and all servants and slaves who defied colonial authority. Masters could continue to dismember enslaved people without punishment, a practice that had existed in Virginia since 1669, but corporal punishment for Christian white servants would henceforth follow a legal procedure for the first time. Masters were forbidden from whipping "a Christian white servant naked" unless they had first secured "an order from a justice of the peace." Rather than highlighting servant-slave collaborations such as running away, the statute focused on white women, one of the newest groups to emerge in CSP discourse, and their capacity to have sexual relations with men of color. The law expanded the punishments against white women that had been first articulated in the 1691 Virginia slave statute, which fined them fifteen pounds for having a child with a Black father. Now if a white woman could not pay, she would be sold at public auction herself for a five-year term of indenture, with the proceeds to go to the local parish for poor relief. White men having children with Black women, a growing if unmentioned practice across slave plantations in Virginia, were pointedly omitted from either the 1691 or 1705 statutes.[60]

The 1705 Virginia statute linked relief from capricious corporal violence against white servants to exemplary punishments against white female servants.

---

percent during the first decade of the eighteenth century. Just 3 percent of the references to white servants between 1661 and 1720 linked them to humanitarian concerns. See Appendix A, Tables 2 and 3.

60. Northey to the Council of Trades and Plantations, May 15, 1703, CO 152/6, 43, CSP; "An Act concerning Servants and Slaves," October 1705, in Hening, *Statutes at Large*, III, 448, also cited in Morgan, *American Slavery, American Freedom*, 331. On the centrality of gender and reproduction to the definition and evolution of racial slavery in Virginia, see Brown, *Good Wives, Nasty Wenches, and Anxious Patriarchs*, 116–128. Kathleen M. Brown demonstrates that the gendered foundation of racial slavery in Virginia was in place before Bacon's Rebellion. She pays less attention to the emergence of whiteness, however. On the passage and significance of the 1691 and 1705 servant and slavery statutes in Virginia, see Morgan, *American Slavery, American Freedom*, 331–338; Tomlins, *Freedom Bound*, 467–468; and Morgan, *Laboring Women*, 174.

Although the law insisted that no white woman could or should be enslaved, it simultaneously punished white women for engaging in interracial sex and put those who did in a position analogous to enslaved people. Not only was the offending white woman's servitude extended for at least seven years and her body sold at auction but her child experienced a virtual lifetime of servitude with indentures that lasted thirty years. The publicness of her trafficking paralleled another provision in the 1705 law, the public trafficking of all personal possessions that enslaved African Americans might have accumulated on plantations at auction. "All horses, cattle, and hogs, now belonging . . . to any slave," the 1705 statute read, " . . . shall be seised and sold by the church-wardens of the parish, wherein such horses, cattle, or hogs shall be, and the profit thereof applied to the use of the poor of the said parish." The power that indentured servants and enslaved soldiers in Bacon's Rebellion had briefly wielded in deciding who and what they might traffic had been decisively clarified: Blacks could not traffic whites, and Blacks and all their possessions were now all trafficable. But the lengths to which these Virginia legislators went to curtail servant-slave collaborations also suggest just how powerful antitrafficking remained in building alliances across lines of skin color and against common enemies. Indeed, the anxieties instilled by Bacon's Rebellion endured long after Bacon died and his army had been disbanded and trafficked elsewhere.[61]

How servants and slaves understood the language of white peoplehood is another story, one harder to glean from the records of the CSP. The narrative of Henry Pitman, one of a very few indentured servants to publish a captivity narrative during the late seventeenth century, offers some insights into how far and how little an elite discourse of skin color had traveled by the end of the seventeenth century. Like most indentured servants demanding redress, Pitman focused his grievances on the unjust terms of his recent sale and transportation to the Caribbean. His travails began in 1685, when he was arrested for treason for having served as a doctor with an army seeking to depose England's Catholic monarch James II. Rather than fight the charges and face the gallows, Pitman and his fellow Monmouth rebels decided to plead guilty "in hope to save our Lives." Ten years of servitude and banishment to Barbados

---

61. "An Act concerning Servants and Slaves," October 1705, in Hening, *Statutes at Large*, III, 459–460, also cited in Morgan, *American Slavery, American Freedom*, 333. On the significance of the 1705 statute beyond Virginia, see Morgan, *American Slavery, American Freedom*, 331–333; Linebaugh and Rediker, *Many-Headed Hydra*, 138; and Tomlins, *Freedom Bound*, 468–470.

was his punishment. While awaiting his deportation, Pitman recounted the same horrors of trafficking that Marcellus Rivers and Oxenbridge Foyle had experienced three decades earlier. Pitman was first "sold to George Penne," who wanted "Money to pay for our Transportation" and craftily offered "to purchase mine and my brothers freedom" in Barbados for a hefty fee. On disembarking, however, Pitman was disappointed to learn that he would be sold at auction to the highest bidder. Pitman's fleecing led him to a sweeping denunciation of servant trafficking and any form of human trafficking. "And thus we may see the buying and selling of Free-men into slavery," he reflected. Being trafficked by Protestant masters was especially galling to Pitman, even as he sought to link the "Heathenish custom" of trafficking to James II's Catholicism.[62]

Yet sectarian religious beliefs provided little enduring comfort to Pitman. Desperate to escape what seemed an impossible servitude, Pitman soon ran away from his Protestant master with the help of both servants and slaves on the island. On being recaptured, Pitman experienced, like all trafficked runaways on the island, extreme forms of corporal punishment of the kind that would later worry Attorney General Northey. Pitman was ordered to endure "39 Lashes on his bare Body on some publick day in the next Market-Town to his Master's place of abode, and on another Market day in the same Town," he was to "be set in the Pillory in the space of one Hour, and be burnt in the fore-head with the Letters F. T., signifiying Fugitive Traytor." As a felon transported to Barbados, Pitman exemplified the conflicting political possibilities associated with white servants. He and his fellow rebels were valuable commodities not only because they were compelled to serve ten years as indentures but also because they helped fill an emerging shortage of militia on the island. Pitman and his fellow rebels were also exceptionally unruly subjects whose status as both commodities and traitors had to be marked with brands on their foreheads. The initials spelled out, in permanent fashion, the political risks associated with unruly whites like Pitman, a graphic solution to the problem of visibility that the new taxonomy of skin color created and necessitated.[63]

---

62. Henry Pitman, *A Relation of the Great Sufferings and Strange Adventures of Henry Pitman, Churgion to the Late Duke of Monmouth, Containing an Account* (London, 1689), 5. On the Monmouth rebels and their complaints against servitude in Barbados, see Amussen, *Caribbean Exchanges*, 128.

63. Pitman, *Relation of the Great Sufferings and Strange Adventures*, 7, 8.

Perhaps because of that highly visible scar, Pitman did not draw attention to any advantages or potential benefits that his skin color might have provided in his narrative. Not once did he describe himself as white, nor did he claim to be worse off than his enslaved coworkers from Africa with whom he ran away. White grammar remained for the time being an elite discourse, deployed by masters to express their own mixed messages about the value of servants and their capacity for unruliness. In Pitman's case, claiming status as a white servant possessed no visible advantages in 1689, for, as yet, very few advantages for whites existed in Barbados. With "F.T." branded on his forehead, Pitman's skin quite literally marked the absence of political status, the very condition he sought to escape. Rather than referencing his skin or its color, Pitman framed his antislavery claims around two vital facts: his Christianity and his Englishness. Both were far older than Parliament's newly passed Bill of Rights (solidifying parliamentary powers such as free elections and freedom of speech for parliamentarians as well as the right of subjects to petition Parliament) or his scars, and both fostered Pitman's desire for justice and redemption. As Pitman and other servants discovered, religious and national affiliation empowered their demands for redress, even if their Englishness also made them disquieting to political authorities.[64]

Pitman might have been inspired to protest transportation by Samuel Sewall, an English compatriot in North America who authored what has been hailed as the first antislavery tract published in North America in 1700. In *The Selling of Joseph*, Sewall penned a biblical critique condemning slavery in the Americas. Quoting the book of Exodus, he referenced the unjust capture and sale of Joseph. Reprising servants' protests against trafficking across the seventeenth century, Sewall wrote, "*Joseph* was rightfully no more a Slave to his Brethren, then they were to him: and they had no more Authority to *Sell* him." "Man Stealing" was "the most atrocious of Capital Crimes," Sewall continued, a practice he deemed anathema to Christianity as well as to the English political tradition.[65]

---

64. The Buill of Rights: An Act Declaring the Rights and Liberties of the Subject, and Settling the Succession of the Crown, December 1689, HL/PO/PU 1/1688/1W & Ms2n2, Parliamentary Archives, London.

65. [Samuel Sewall], *The Selling of Joseph: A Memorial* (Boston, 1700), [1]–2. Sewall's pamphlet generated a rebuttal by a Bostonian slaveholder. See John Saffin, "A Brief and Candid Answer to a Late Printed Sheet Entitled *The Selling of Joseph*" (1701), in George H. Moore, *Notes on the History of Slavery in Massachusetts* (New York, 1866), 251. For a discussion of Sewall's essay and its immediate impact, see Bjorn F. Stillion Southard, "The Plain

Unlike Pitman and other servants who condemned the buying and selling of people, however, Sewall's religious critique of human trafficking sharply differed in his attention to skin color. Even as Sewall argued that Africans must not be trafficked or enslaved, he also believed that they could not exist as free people in North America either, a circumstance he attributed to their complexion. "There is such a disparity in their Conditions, Colour and Hair, that they can never embody with us, and grow up into orderly Families, to the Peopling of the Land," he reasoned. For Sewall, antislavery and race trafficking were inextricably linked topics, exemplifying the growing power of skin color to reveal both the humanity and the mercantile value of laboring people. The solution to abolishing the African slave trade, Sewall insisted, was to expand the traffic in white servants. "It would conduce more to the Welfare of the Province, to have White Servants for a Term of Years, than to have Slaves for Life." Forgotten for the moment in Sewall's solution to New England's labor shortage was his Christian opposition to trafficking people.[66]

Few imperial planners heeded Sewall's call to replace African slaves with white servants, perhaps because Sewall's anxieties about slavery and skin color were cut from the same epistemological cloth as Attorney General Northey's about "white slaves" in Barbados just three years later. To be sure, the two men disagreed sharply over whether Africans should be enslaved. Yet Sewall, like Northey, was deeply invested in the justness of a colonial judiciary that could evaluate the merits of people's character with a taxonomy of skin color. As one of the judges in the Salem Witch Trials of 1692, Sewall had a track record of discerning hard-to-see realities with evidence that was, at best, anecdotal and circumstantial. His efforts to see truth in Salem had been vexing to Sewall, leading him alone among his judicial peers to recant his rulings and to issue a public apology in 1697. Nevertheless, Sewall did not disavow the existence of witchcraft. Rather, he apologized for not having read the evidence properly in light of his abiding beliefs in witchcraft. Sewall's *The Selling of Joseph* similarly sought to make skin color a just and self-evident marker of

---

Style in Early Anti-Slavery Discourse: Reassessing the Rhetorical Beginnings of Quaker and Puritan Advocacy," *Quarterly Journal of Speech*, CII (2016), 3; and Mark A. Peterson, "*The Selling of Joseph's* Bostonian Antislavery and the Protestant International, 1689–1733," *Massachusetts Historical Review*, IV (2002), 3.

66. [Sewall], *Selling of Joseph*, 2. For an excellent discussion of the similarities between witchcraft and racism in the history of the evolution of slavery in North America, see Barbara J. Fields and Karen E. Fields, *Racecraft: The Soul of Inequality in American Life* (New York, 2012), 111–148.

political value, linking it to the character of laboring people in Massachusetts and their capacity for freedom, whether white or Black. Reading skin color could be redeemed if connected to an emancipatory project, one consistent with Christianity as well as the imperial needs of England's expanding empire. Here is how Sewall used his critique of kidnapping Africans to call for both the abolition of slavery and the concurrent expansion of servant traffic. If witchcraft could be abolished with better testimonies and evidence, so might skin color and antislavery be linked in ways that would establish abolitionism and white supremacy.[67]

Sewall disagreed with Northey's assessment of the legality of slavery, but his arguments stood in even sharper opposition to the testimony and witness of servants like Pitman, whose story and collaboration with African slaves defied Sewall's racist conclusions about freedom in North America. Unlike Sewall or Northey, Pitman refused to make skin color or race central to his emancipation claims. More importantly, he grounded his freedom claims in Christianity without regard to skin color, an act more audacious and dangerous than Sewall's guilt-ridden effort to condemn slavery. By questioning the Christianity of his Protestant masters, Pitman directly exposed the hollowness of the religious conceits that had justified the expansion of England's overseas empire, including English leadership in the African slave trade. When Pitman composed his narrative, religion rather than skin color continued to serve as the primary vehicle for rationalizing the violence that had made English mercantilism and imperial power possible. The English conquest and enslavement of peoples in both Africa and the Americas were but the latest military aggressions in which European powers had weaponized the gospel of Jesus Christ, repurposing it for imperial ambition and purposes. For Sewall, white peoplehood enabled him to make a principled critique of slavery that left emergent hierarchies of race and racism secure and unchallenged. Pitman, by contrast, critiqued trafficking and enslavement without reference to white peoplehood, a radical vantage that would continue to enliven servant antislavery as well as visions of sailor freedom across the Atlantic and beyond well into the eighteenth century.[68]

---

67. Sewall's apology for his errors in the Salem Witch trials in 1697 has received more scholarly discussion and attention than his essay *The Selling of Joseph*. See Eve LaPlante, *Salem Witch Judge: The Life and Repentance of Samuel Sewall* (New York, 2007); and Richard Francis, *Judge Sewall's Apology: The Salem Witch Trials and the Forming of an American Conscience* (New York, 2006).

68. [Sewall], *The Selling of Joseph*, 2.

## Conclusion

Henry Pitman protested his un-Christian mistreatment by imperial elites during a crucial moment in England's expansion of mercantile capitalism in the Atlantic. His antislavery efforts and those of trafficked servants before him should not be judged by the actions that elites took in response to them. Servant antislavery was powerful and unruly, even as officials sought to co-opt it. The Spiriting Act of 1670 passed in part with the backing of a proslavery king and a Parliament seeking to deflect anxiety and anger about England's support for the burgeoning African slave trade. The law was easily evaded by shipping merchants as the servant registry became a mechanism for their control rather than a tool of redress or justice for mistreated servants. The passing of the Spiriting Act not only diverted attention from the larger trade in servants but burnished the antislavery credentials of England's monarchs, whether Protestant or Catholic, during decades of political upheaval and geopolitical growth. If the extension of the African slave trade under the Royal African Company became a benchmark of Charles II's power as a sovereign during the 1670s and early 1680s, so, too, did antislavery become a tool of English sovereignty and its elite defenders. From one vantage, antispiriting laws helped make the African slave trade palatable, channeling discomfort about a political economy built on trafficking to a safer fiction of consenting servants.[69]

Yet Christianity and antislavery beliefs, ideas, and behavior remained unruly elements of English political culture across the seventeenth century, especially when embraced by trafficked actors on the bottom rungs of society. Although most servants and slaves did not run away together, collaborations between them proliferated throughout England's colonies. Indeed, whether punishing John Punch with perpetual service for running away with a Dutchman in 1640 or making "English servant[s]" liable for the cost of slaves who ran away with them, the earliest justifications for slavery in English colonial jurisprudence were devised as punishments for servant-slave collaborations. Even the Virginia statute that made slavery heritable through the mother's status in 1669 was passed as a solution to the crime of "any christian" committing "ffornication [sic] with a negro man or woman." Nevertheless, not all sex between servants and slaves in England's colonies was necessarily in opposition to slavery during the first half of the seventeenth century, nor were

---

69. On poor people's use of law and legal customs to their advantage, see James Scott, *Weapons of the Weak: Everyday Forms of Peasant Resistance* (New Haven, Conn., 1987).

servant protests against being bought and sold necessarily critiques of slavery or acts in solidarity with enslaved Africans. Even as most efforts by servants to escape with enslaved Africans were pragmatic in nature, the trafficking of servants and slaves and the fears inspired by collaborations between them were the central problems that drove the definition of slavery by law in England's colonies.[70]

Servant antislavery could be co-opted, but it also represented an enduring challenge to elite understandings of trafficking and empire. Servant antislavery would remain a stumbling block for colonial and metropolitan leaders, not because it was an accurate assessment of their status—servants were not, in fact, enslaved—but because it effectively galvanized protest against the trafficking of English people, the principal mechanism by which England initially developed its colonies. Servant antislavery had to be countered with carrots and sticks at every turn, by creating fictions of consent with the servant registry, by paying overdue freedom dues when absolutely necessary, and, in desperate circumstances, by even promising freedom to servants and slaves during Bacon's Rebellion. When concessions failed, punishments were called for—extended years of service, trafficking in the public square, whipping, and even dismemberment by lawful proceedings—though such violence frequently backfired.

Whiteness emerged initially, not as an answer to the reality of servant-slave collaboration, then, but as a mechanism for facilitating the movement of trafficked bodies and calculating their financial worth to geographically distant investors and rulers. Designation by skin color was less a privilege than a sign of being bought and sold, a condition that actors sought to avoid. The African slaves and trafficked sailors and servants who were caught up in the construction of a coercive empire in 1703 largely eschewed identification by skin color, along with any embrace of the financial value that the trafficking of people facilitated. For indentured servants, Christianity remained the dominant marker of English political identity at the beginning of the long eighteenth century. As such, it became a powerful tool for trafficked actors as well as a growing number of religious radicals with which to oppose English

---

70. "Negro Womens Children to Serve According to the Condition of the Mother," December 1662, in Hening, *Statutes at Large*, II, 170, also cited in Brown, *Good Wives, Nasty Wenches, and Anxious Patriarchs*, 132. On the 1661 Virginia statute, see Brown, *Good Wives, Nasty Wenches, and Anxious Patriarchs*, 132; and Morgan, *American Slavery, American Freedom*, 311.

sovereignty. White grammar mattered by 1700 certainly, but, for the colonial and metropolitan elites who invented and deployed it, white grammar conveyed contradictory and ambivalent views of the trafficked. How those at the lower echelons of England's empire used Christianity and antitrafficking to challenge English authorities is another story, one that was most prominent during the seventeenth century in the region where human trafficking had long been organized along lines of religion and nation: the Mediterranean.

CHAPTER TWO

# Ransom Traffic and Antislavery in the Mediterranean

IN 1680, a remarkable challenge to English monarch Charles II developed in the Mediterranean Sea. Unlike Bacon's Rebellion, it did not involve armed men, although Moroccan forces were preparing to conquer the crown jewel of England's imperial ambition in the region, the ill-fated colony of Tangier. Nor was it financial in nature, even if raising ransom money for hundreds of English sailors held in slavery in North Africa was draining royal coffers. Rather, the challenge came from an unlikely source: a common English sailor named Thomas Lurting. Captured by Muslim pirates, a crew of sailors from Algiers, who, like many crews in the Mediterranean, sought riches seizing and trafficking sailors and their cargoes, Lurting freed himself while his new master slept, finding a way to take his guard's cutlass. He then retook the ship in the middle of the night. When the Muslim ship captain awoke and realized he was now himself captive along with his crew, he "fell all to crying" and "desired they might not be sold." What Lurting did next would lay the groundwork for conflict with his king. Instead of selling his former captors into slavery as was the common practice, he acceded to their demands, promising them that they should not be sold. By thus "pacif[ying] them," as Lurting put it, he helped his liberated English compatriots maintain control of the vessel.[1]

Lurting's promise to the pirates would soon be put to the test, generating opposition from all quarters outside his ship and compelling Lurting and his fellow sailors to flee, not one, but two ships seeking to traffic them. Lurting's crew first encountered an English ship near the Spanish island of Mallorca,

1. Thomas Lurting, "Of George Pattisons Taking the Turks about the 8 Month 1663," May 30, 1680, in George Fox, *To the Great Turk, and His King at Argiers; Together with a Postscript of George Pattison's Taking the Turks, and Setting Them on Their Own Shoar* (London, 1680), 17–18.

whose captain not only "looked upon us as fools because we would not sell" the Muslim sailors, Lurting recounted, but told a nearby Spanish ship, "who threatened to take'em [the Muslim sailors] from us." Desperate to escape both the English ship captain as well as the Spanish, Lurting turned to his prisoners, imploring them that "they must help us, . . . which pleased the Turks very well." Lurting's refusal to sell his former captors now meant he and his fellow Englishman had to "put our selves to the hazard of the Turks" once more "to save them." Lurting succeeded in this unlikely quest, evading both the English ship captain and the Spanish privateers, retaining control of the vessel, sailing to the coast of Algiers, and returning the Muslim sailors to freedom before parting with them, as he described it, "in great Love."[2]

When Lurting returned to London, however, he was sharply rebuked by Charles II. On hearing the tale, the king insisted Lurting should not have freed his captors, for they had become the property of the English crown. Lurting had a right, even an obligation to fight for his freedom, but he also had an obligation to traffic the Muslim sailors and share that prize with his king. And here is where Lurting's actions became powerful and dangerous. After being publicly chastised, Lurting managed to get a short version of his story published as an addendum to a speech by Quaker leader George Fox. Over the next three decades, Lurting would become a leader in sailor antislavery, redoubling his efforts to turn English sailors into pacifists and to resist both English wars of conquest and the subsequent support these conflicts engendered for human trafficking.[3]

---

2. Thomas Lurting, *The Fighting Sailor Turn'd Peaceable Christian* . . . (London, 1710), 38, 39, 45.

3. The pervasive trafficking of people across the Mediterranean has begun to receive attention by scholars, who have noted its role in shaping imperial competition as well as slavery across the region. Robert C. Davis estimates that nearly one million European subjects were enslaved in North Africa between 1500 and 1800, a traffic in slaves that peaked in conjunction with Ottoman power during the seventeenth century. See Davis, *Christian Slaves, Muslim Masters: White Slavery in the Mediterranean, the Barbary Coast, and Italy, 1500–1800* (New York, 2003), 3–26. Nabil Matar, on the other hand, disputes that number, suggesting that the actual number was much lower and that England's focus on English slaves reflected cultural and political imperatives associated with England's growing empire. See Matar, *British Captives from the Mediterranean to the Atlantic, 1563–1760* (Leiden, Netherlands, 2014). Sustained comparisons of Mediterranean and Atlantic slavery, however, are comparatively rare. Although David Brion Davis observed the importance of the Mediterranean and especially of the Iberian slave trading in shaping English attitudes about race in the seventeenth century, other scholars have been reluctant to make comparisons between the regions to avoid suggesting any moral equivalencies. Linda Colley,

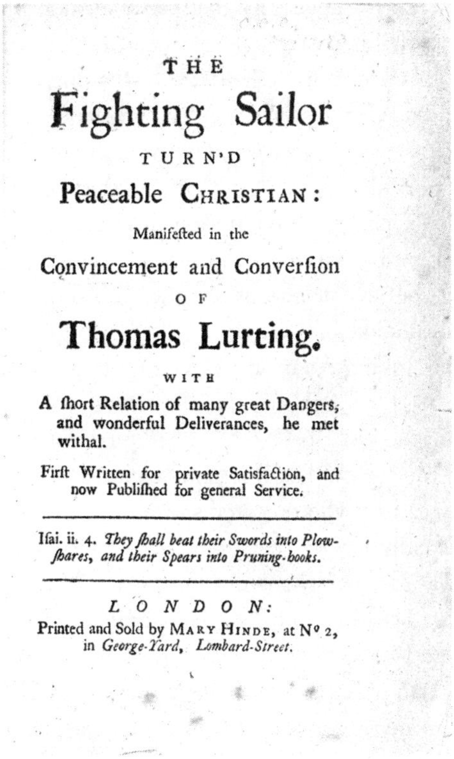

> THE
> # Fighting Sailor
> TURN'D
> Peaceable CHRISTIAN:
> Manifested in the
> Convincement and Conversion
> OF
> ## Thomas Lurting.
> WITH
> A short Relation of many great Dangers, and wonderful Deliverances, he met withal.
>
> First Written for private Satisfaction, and now Published for general Service.
>
> ---
> Isai. ii. 4. *They shall beat their Swords into Plowshares, and their Spears into Pruning-hooks.*
>
> ---
> LONDON:
> Printed and Sold by MARY HINDE, at Nº 2, in *George-Yard*, *Lombard-Street*.

FIGURE 2. Title page from Thomas Lurting, *The Fighting Sailor Turn'd Peaceable Christian* . . . (London, 1770). Courtesy of David M. Rubenstein Rare Book and Manuscript Library, Duke University, Durham, N.C.

Lurting published a more expansive biography in 1710, *The Fighting Sailor Turn'd Peaceable Christian*, in which he paired his tale of escape and redemption with a longer account of his conversion to pacifism and his struggle against impressment (Figure 2). In his extended narrative, Lurting laid out in detail how he learned to resist compulsory labor at sea and bested every English ship captain who sought to compel him to fight. A kind of primer on

---

for example, writes that "I am not suggesting that Barbary captivities and slaveries were comparable to black slavery in the Caribbean and North America. Clearly they were not." See Colley, *Captives* (New York, 2002), 63–64; and Davis, *Inhuman Bondage: The Rise and Fall of Slavery in the New World* (New York, 2006), 60–64.

how to use nonviolence to subvert English naval authority, Lurting's narrative also elaborates a strikingly radical critique of buying and selling people, whether Africans or Europeans, Christians, Muslims, or Jews. Rooted in his sincere love of Jesus Christ, Lurting's courageous freeing of his Algerine captors is the culminating act in his narrative. In retelling his experiences, Lurting indicted England's investment in human trafficking across the planet while also tarnishing Charles II's reputation as an antislavery monarch.[4]

Lurting's story is hardly typical of the captivity narratives written by English sailors during the seventeenth and eighteenth centuries. His story underscores the political stakes in struggling against both trafficking and enslavement while also linking Atlantic and Mediterranean worlds in ways that scholars have only begun to fathom and investigate. The political geography of human trafficking he described in the Mediterranean grew out of imperial rivalries across the region. English captives were but one part of a larger cohort of European sailors who reported stories of captivity and redemption that defied the allegedly transparent boundaries between empires, nations, and faiths. Race was largely absent not only from Lurting's story but also from the majority of chronicles of life in the Mediterranean written by sailors in the seventeenth and eighteenth centuries. Rather, captive sailors described themselves as Christian slaves as opposed to white or Black slaves. Sailors like Lurting struggled to make trafficking a liberatory practice, one that would benefit them individually and collectively if possible. For most sailors, the mindset traffic or be trafficked served as the informal survival guide for voyaging in the Mediterranean. Indeed, trafficking itself could be a path to freedom, a fact that made Lurting's radical critique of the practice all the more remarkable.[5]

Understanding Lurting's motivations is challenging because his actions defied not only the expectations of his contemporaries but also those of subsequent historians of human trafficking and enslavement. The pervasive forms

---

4. Lurting's struggles against impressment constitute two-thirds of his full-length book. Lurting's patron, George Fox, was more than a leading Quaker, he was one of the religious group's founders and the object of political persecution after being accused of inciting a slave insurrection in the Caribbean when he first visited there in 1671. On Fox's career, see H. Larry Ingle, *First among Friends: George Fox and the Creation of Quakerism* (New York, 1994).

5. Lurting, *Fighting Sailor*, 5–31. Lurting's expanded narrative was published repeatedly over the ensuing century and a half and was popular among subsequent abolitionists, sailors' advocates, and critics of Britain's impressment policy on both sides of the Atlantic between 1709 and the 1840s. See subsequent editions of *The Fighting Sailor Turn'd Peaceable*

of human trafficking in the Mediterranean that Lurting and his Muslim captors navigated in the seventeenth century have received only passing and partial attention by historians of slavery. One way historians of slavery have sought to make comparisons between the Mediterranean and the Atlantic has been to deploy a grammar of race, referring to the Atlantic world as a region of Black slavery and the Mediterranean as a zone of white slavery. But there are several problems with that approach. First, scholars of Mediterranean slavery have erred in anachronistically applying racial designations to human trafficking across the Mediterranean, obscuring when, where, and why certain trafficked Europeans became known as white slaves rather than Christian slaves. Second, considering each slave system as fully formed in racial terms has lent itself to assessments of which system was more severe, rather than analyses of how each shaped the other's historical evolution. Comparisons between white and Black slavery have tempted historians to participate in a kind of race trafficking after the fact, simplifying differences between the regions or dismissing slavery in the Mediterranean as an exaggeration. One of the most important distinctions between Atlantic and Mediterranean slavery, however, has been neglected: namely, the role that specific kinds of trafficking played in shaping and delimiting enslavement in both locales. There was no ransom traffic across the Atlantic, after all, certainly not for Africans sold into bondage nor for transported indentures struggling to recover lives and relations lost to them back in England. Moreover, the Atlantic traffic in both indentured servants and African slaves was state sanctioned. The ransom traffic

---

*Christian* published in 1766, 1770, 1813, 1816, and 1842. Despite the widespread appeal of Lurting's narrative, his account has only received passing mention in the historiography of Mediterranean captivity and abolition. See Colley, *Captives*, 89. Of the nearly one dozen narratives published by English sailors held captive in North Africa during the seventeenth century, only Lurting's explicitly condemned the trafficking of all sailors across the Mediterranean. Most sought ransom traffic as a path to freedom. See, for example, Thomas Sweet, *Deare Friends* [London, 1647], 669.f.11 (3), British Library, London; Francis Brooks, *Barbarian Cruelty...* (London, 1693); and Thomas Phelps, *A True Account of the Captivity of Thomas Phelps, at Machaness in Barbary...* (London, 1685). The narrative of Atlantic-bound servant William Okeley, who was captured and sold into North African slavery, is one of the more vivid links between Atlantic and Mediterranean histories. See Okeley, *Eben-ezer: or, A Small Monument of Great Mercy...* (London, 1675), 2–11. On Okeley's significance, see Joe Snader, *Caught between Worlds: British Captivity Narratives in Fact and Fiction* (Lexington, Ky., 2000); and Colley, *Captives*, 90–92. On connections between Mediterranean and Atlantic history, see Alison Games, *The Web of Empire: English Cosmopolitans in an Age of Expansion, 1560–1660* (New York, 2008), 47–80; and Matar, *British Captives*.

that ensnared Lurting in the Mediterranean, by contrast, offset the failures of state power and was predicated on moving national or religious subjects back to their points of origin.[6]

For a great many historical actors, the political and economic boundaries between the Atlantic and the Mediterranean were not black and white but permeable. Distinctions based on skin color were well established within certain portions of slave traffic in the Mediterranean long before the invention of racial slavery in the Atlantic. Skin color mattered across the seventeenth-century Mediterranean, but not as a signifier of racial identity. Skin color was a trafficable fact, a thing that concerned some buyers of captive people, and anti-Black sentiment was certainly visible across the region in the 1600s. But slavery and human trafficking were not yet organized along lines of racial difference. Instead, as Lurting understood all too well, a captive's religion, national affiliation, and family lineage structured how captivity, enslavement, and trafficking worked in the Mediterranean. For a clearer picture of the work that skin color did and did not organize in the contexts that Lurting traversed, it is helpful to examine the prevalence of non-Christian and non-European whites beyond the Atlantic during the seventeenth century.[7]

---

6. Both Robert Davis and Linda Colley have described the Europeans captured by North African pirates and enslaved there during the seventeenth and eighteenth centuries as white slaves, despite that all the English captives who wrote and published their stories during the seventeenth and eighteenth centuries described themselves as Christian slaves or Christian captives. See Davis, *Christian Slaves, Muslim Masters*; and Colley, *Captives*, 59–64. By contrast, Nell Irvin Painter adeptly locates the origins of white grammar outside of North America. See Painter, *The History of White People* (New York, 2010), 34–58. On the primacy of religious motivations and organizations in shaping ransom traffic across the Mediterranean during the early modern era, see Minna Rozen, *The Mediterranean in the Seventeenth Century: Captives, Pirates, and Ransomers* (Palermo, Italy, [2016]), 65–91; and Ariel Salzmann, "Migrants in Chains: On the Enslavement of Muslims in Renaissance and Enlightenment Europe," *Religions*, IV (2013), 391–411. On the importance of Mediterranean slave traffic to the history of European nations within the maritime region, see Nabil Matar, *Britain and Barbary, 1589–1689* (Gainesville, Fla., 2005); Daniel Hershenzon, *The Captive Sea: Slavery, Communication, and Commerce in Early Modern Spain and the Mediterranean* (Philadelphia, 2018); and Gillian Weiss, *Captives and Corsairs: France and Slavery in the Early Modern Mediterranean* (Stanford, Calif., 2011).

7. On the modernity of race, see George M. Frederickson, *Racism: A Short History* (Princeton, N.J., 2002). On the primacy of Atlantic slavery in creating race and racism simultaneously, see Peter H. Wood, *Black Majority: Negroes in Colonial South Carolina from 1670 through the Stono Rebellion* (New York, 1974). On race within the Mediterranean

## Alien Whiteness

An examination of grammars of skin color in the database Early English Books Online (EEBO), a compendium of nearly sixty thousand texts published in the English language between 1475 and 1700, highlights the importance of phenotype during the late seventeenth century as a tool for English travel writers to identify and discern trading partners. Mapping white grammar—where it appeared and to whom it was affixed—confirms many of the patterns observed in the Colonial State Papers (CSP), particularly the relationship between human trafficking and white subjecthood (see Appendix B). More surprising, however, is that white grammar delineated distinctions among peoples far beyond the borders of Europe, revealing perceived cultural differences across the expanding reaches of England's commercial interactions. Many of the whites that travel writers discussed, for example, were not English or European but members of Indigenous communities in far-flung contexts (see Appendix B, Table 9). In these texts, whiteness signified the relative color of a person's skin rather than any universalized white essence or race. This is not the cultural or political work typically associated with whiteness.[8]

Indeed, one of the most striking features of a broad survey of white grammar during the seventeenth century was how consistently it modified non-Christians and non-Europeans. In 1693, English missionary Samuel Wesley believed he had discovered something truly remarkable, "encompassed with several High Mountains in *America*, a *White People*, with long *Beards*," descendants, he imagined, of one of the lost *"Ten Tribes"* of Israel. Other

---

region, see Bernard Lewis, *Race and Slavery in the Middle East: An Historical Enquiry* (New York, 1990), 40; and Davis, *Inhuman Bondage*, 70–73. On the varied notions of race as a concept in the late seventeenth century, see Susan Dwyer Amussen, *Caribbean Exchanges: Slavery and the Transformation of English Society, 1640–1700* (Chapel Hill, N.C., 2007), 11–12. On the distinction between skin color and familial inheritance, see Karen E. Fields and Barbara J. Fields, *Racecraft: The Soul of Inequality in American Life* (New York, 2012), 50–52.

8. Histories of whiteness before the advent of the seventeenth-century slave trade highlight its power as an aesthetic criteria denoting beauty typically connected to religious and political elites in Europe or England. Rarely has it been examined as a category moving beyond Eurocentric political and religious boundaries. For a brief history of whiteness as an aesthetic frame beyond Europe, see Painter, *History of White People*, 43–58. On the "Elizabethan cult of whiteness," see Michael Guasco, *Slaves and Englishmen: Human Bondage in the Early Modern Atlantic World* (Philadelphia, 2014), 105–108.

travel writers and missionaries proclaimed similar findings. Portuguese writer Manuel de Faria e Sousa described natives in what is now Southeast Asia as a "White People, like the *Chineses,* but differing in Language." French travel writer Jean-Baptiste Tavernier confirmed the existence of Indigenous white peoples across Asia in 1680, locating "another land . . . inhabited by White people, with long Hair, habited after the *Japon* fashion." Over the course of the seventeenth century, travel writers from Europe claimed to have seen indigenous white people in every continent, with important portions of Africa inhabited by whites (see Appendix B, Table 10). Skin color was an indispensable tool in travel writers' capacity to find and comprehend cultural and political differences in virtually every corner of the planet. White grammar did not denote a singular race or even a class of trafficked workers but rather signposted cultural and political virtues among local peoples outside Europe and its Atlantic colonies.⁹

Describing aliens as possessing white skin made them legible to European explorers, a fantasy of their knowability as well as their potential trafficability. Travel writers' widespread application of white skin color to non-Europeans, however, also led to semantic confusion. Travel writer John Ogilby, publishing a historical atlas of the entire African continent in 1670, purported to have found Indigenous white people in the heart of Africa: "To the East beyond the River *Congo,* according to the relation of the *Condians,* are found white People, with long Hair." Yet he added that these white people were "not altogether white as the *Europeans.*" Similar disclaimers pervaded the text, as when describing a group of nomadic Muslims as "white People that Ride on Mules and Asses, and use Lances for Arms; but they are not altogether white, as the *Europeans.*" Ogilby articulated what were competing uses for European writers deploying white grammar in the seventeenth century. White grammar functioned as a tool that summarized common but still nascent attributes of Europeans traveling beyond Europe's borders as well as perceived cultural differences among the non-Europeans that European travelers happened on outside of Christendom. Whiteness could be both things only if it remained

---

9. Samuel Wesley, *The Life of Our Blessed Lord and Saviour Jesus Christ: An Heroic Poem Dedicated to Her Most Sacred Majesty* (London, 1693), 316; Manuel de Faria e Sousa, *The Portugues Asia; or, The History of the Discovery and Conquest of India by the Portugues,* Tome the First (London, 1695), 48; Jean-Baptist Tavernier, *A Collection of Several Relations and Treatises Singular and Curious of John Baptista Tavernier* (London, 1680), 19. The hope that explorers might find the lost tribe of Israel was a persistent myth shaping travel writing not only in Asia but also across the Americas. See Tudor Parfitt, *The Tribes of Israel: The History of a Myth* (London, 2002).

a grammar for distinguishing diverse cultural differences rather than an ideology of a pure white race.[10]

Rather than interpret the striking mixture of non-European and European actors described as white to be some kind of semantic confusion, it is far better to view white grammar as most seventeenth-century travel writers did, as a tool for describing cohorts of people with commonalities specific to occupation, local cultures, and local geography. A comparison of the whites who were European in origin with those who were non-European also reveals important continuities over the course of the seventeenth century. For most of the seventeenth century, there were substantial numbers of non-Christian white subjects in English language publications with an uneven increase in the proportion of European-born white subjects over time. Only in the final two decades of the seventeenth century did a majority of whites become Christian and European in EEBO texts (see Appendix B, Table 9). The prominence of white people and white men who were not Christian across the century is also striking. Similarly, only in the final two decades of the century did a clear majority of white people and white men emerge as Christian and European in EEBO texts (see Appendix B, Tables 10–11). By comparison, the white slaves and white women who appear in EEBO texts were dominated by non-Christians throughout the century, many of them with origins outside of Europe (see Appendix B, Table 12).

The significance of non-Christian and non-European white subjects within EEBO is twofold. First, the origins of white grammar cannot be solely explained as a response to New World racial slavery in the Americas. A grammar of whiteness was apparent in English language sources long before the English became key organizers of the African slave trade in the mid-seventeenth century. Likewise, whites were conspicuous among non-Europeans far removed from the African slave trade. The earliest references to white people in EEBO are from the 1580s and 1590s, nearly all of which are to indigenous non-Christians living in what is now Asia. When Spanish explorer Juan Gonzalez de Mendoza traveled to the Far East in the middle of the sixteenth century, for example, he discovered "white people . . . as bigge as gyants" who were "appareled like unto those of China." Second, the prominence of non-Christian whites underscores the significance of Nell Irvin Painter's claims about the eastern origins of whiteness. Painter has argued that images of white slaves from the region of Georgia were especially

---

10. John Ogilby, *Africa: Being an Accurate Description of the Regions of Aegypt, Barbary, Lybia, and Billedulgerid* (London, 1670), 418, 524.

influential in the development of racialized and racist aesthetics about the beauty of white skin. Although there are only a few scattered references to white slaves in EEBO during the seventeenth century, the seven references support Painter's eighteenth-century depiction of white slavery. Before 1700, all seven of the white slaves in EEBO were non-Christian, female, and non-European, with descriptions of them emphasizing their exotic beauty. In the fictional portrait of a white slave by the French poet and novelist Marin Le Roy Sieur de Gomberville, for example, the hero, an aristocratic "Moor" named Zabaim, had "falne [sic] in love with a white Slave; and so fondly amorous, that to behold the alterations she wrought on him, 'twas necessarily believed she had bewitched him." Other French writers like Jean-Baptiste Chardin used white slaves to portray exotic landscapes of Eastern wealth and power in the 1680s, where European observers struggled to know "how many white Slaves" the local Sultan "had in his Seraglio." French travel writer Jean de Thevenot likewise described white slaves in 1687 in ways that highlighted the transactional purpose of white grammar. "White Slaves are sold there," he began, and "every body may look upon them, touch and feel them, like Horses, to see if they have any faults."[11]

The spectacle of white slavery, combining transactional and erotic imaginings, appeared sporadically in seventeenth-century English books and publications. Images of white bodies for sale provoked considerable fascination among writers of English fiction and drama. The interest in white slaves closely parallels the ways white women appear more generally in EEBO texts across the seventeenth century. Most references to white women in the seventeenth century were to non-Christians, with a substantial portion originating from outside Europe. By contrast, roughly three-quarters of white men and nearly two-thirds of whites were Christians hailing from Europe. White people, in turn, made up a more genuinely hybrid cohort, a mixture whose diversity also turned out to have a significant temporal dimension (see Appendix B, Table 12). When the data is broken down in twenty-year periods, white people before 1681 closely resembled white slaves and white women, with a clear majority appearing as non-Christians. After 1681, white people

---

11. Juan Gonzalez de Mendoza, *The Historie of a Great and Mightie Kingdome of China*, trans. R. Parke (London, 1588), 341, 387; Painter, *History of White People*, 47; [M. Le Roy Sieur de Gomberville], *The History of Polexander: In Five Books* (London, 1647), 46; Jean-Baptiste Chardin, *The Travels of Sir John Chardin into Persia and the East Indies*, I (London, 1686), 264; Jean de Thevenot, *The Travels of Monsieur de Thevenot into the Levant in Three Parts* (London, 1687), 143.

decisively shift their appearance in EEBO, looking more like white men, with majorities originating from Europe and possessing Christian backgrounds (see Appendix B, Table 10).

Discerning why these temporal, geographic, and semantic shifts occurred is a challenging task. The changing location, frequency, and religious identity of whites, white people, and white men suggest that the 1680s and 1690s were indeed watershed decades in the evolution of white grammar. The geographic origins of the white slaves in EEBO were vastly different from the whites that colonial administrators in North America and the Caribbean discussed. All seven white slaves located in EEBO were female and Muslim, originating outside of the geographic boundaries of Europe. But both groups also shared common features too: all the white slaves in EEBO were also fungible, like transported felons and indentured servants. Although the geographic origins of female and non-Christian white slaves seem vastly different from the whites that colonial administrators in North America and the Caribbean trafficked, both groups, in fact, shared common features. They were fungible goods, living and working outside the centers of European political power and authority, and they were imperfectly connected to the Christian white people who also called themselves Englishmen. Rather than signifying a unified or purely racial essence, white grammar helped English writers and imperial administrators discern and map varied political and cultural differences on the expanding periphery of England's empire. The stark gender-based patterns within white grammar of the seventeenth century also help explain how and why a sailor like Thomas Lurting did not describe himself as a white slave during his captivity and why not a single English sailor enslaved in North Africa resorted to white grammar in their captivity accounts either. To writers and readers of English travel literature, white slaves were exotic subjects dependent on Muslim masters for survival, the very things that sailors like Lurting refused to accept when made captive. Like the white slaves that Thevenot described, English sailors protested being sold at auction in North African slave markets. Alleging themselves to be white slaves would have vitiated their claims to being redeemable.

## Ransom Traffic

In the summer of 1639, an English ship, the *Mary* of London, set sail for the island of Providence, an impoverished English colony in the Caribbean struggling with piracy and pervasive labor problems. Among the passengers on the *Mary* was a young man named William Okeley, an indentured servant who would eventually publish his story in London more than four decades later. Okeley's account of the ill-fated voyage underscores the threat that imperial competition over human trafficking imposed on everyone, sailors and passengers, venturing across the Atlantic Ocean in 1639. Just six days after setting sail from the Isle of Wight, the crew spotted three *"Turks Men of War"* in the distance. Not certain what to do—flee or fight—the *Mary*'s crew lost valuable time deciding before finally settling on escape. They were soon overtaken. After a brief skirmish in which six English sailors were killed, the *Mary* was captured by Algerine sailors, who made Okeley and his fellow servants "Prisoners at Sea." Moved from his ship to the hold of a larger Algerine vessel, Okeley encountered "many *Englishmen* in their Ships, Slaves, like our selves." After a long and dispiriting voyage to North Africa, he and his fellow captives began their life in bondage in Algiers as Christian slaves. Okeley recounted not only the miseries of his confinement but the humiliation of being sold, a process strikingly similar to accounts by indentured servants protesting their sale on the other side of the Atlantic. "We were *driven like Beasts* thither, and exposed *to Sale*," Okeley recalled, with buyers turning his body into parts, inspecting his teeth, and then using their hands to examine, touch, and assess his *"Limbs"* (Figure 3).[12]

Unlike prospective buyers at servant auctions in Providence, buyers in Algiers looked for evidence of each captive's pedigree in his or her hands. "If they be *callous and brawny*," Okeley explained, "they will shrewdly guess they have been *inured to Labour;* if *delicate and tender*, they will suspect some *Gentleman* . . . and then the hopes of *a good Price of Redemption* makes him Saleable." In the Algerine slave market, two distinct kinds of value determined the price of each captive. Buyers examined bodies for their capacity to labor but also for their ability to command a ransom. Such payments could be extracted from captives' families, churches, or governments. The uncertainty surrounding the price each captive could possibly command at ransom engendered a speculative dimension to many auctions. Expectations of rapidly paid ransoms typically proved disappointing, as transactions usually occurred only after precarious negotiations between a new master and the captive's family, friends, and government representatives. Both sellers and new owners

---

12. Okeley, *Eben-ezer*, 4, 5, 8–10. On the brief history of Providence as an English colony during the 1630s, see Karen Ordahl Kupperman, *Providence Island, 1630–1641: The Other Puritan Colony* (Cambridge, 1995); and Games, *Web of Empire*, 176. On the history of the island of Providence after Spanish control resumed, see J. H. Elliott, *Empires of the Atlantic World: Britain and Spain in America, 1492–1830* (New Haven, Conn., 2007), 180.

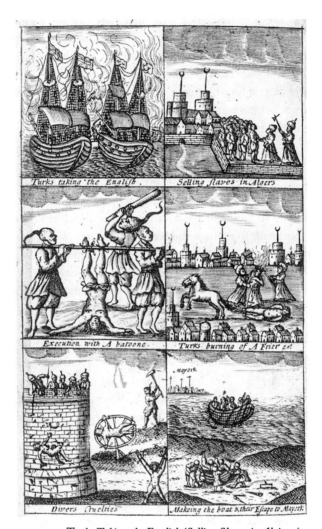

FIGURE 3. *Turks Taking the English / Selling Slaves in Algiers / Execution with a Batoone / Turks Burning of a Frierer / Divers Cruelties / Making Their Boat and Their Escape to Mayork*. From William Okeley, *Eben-ezer; or, A Small Monument of Great Mercy* . . . (London, 1675). Courtesy Beinecke Rare Book and Manuscript Library, Yale University, New Haven, Conn.

often inflated the potential value that their new charges might command through ransom traffic. For buyers, scrutinizing captives' hands was a little like digging for gold, hoping to read future profits in the texture of skin. In that endeavor, callouses mattered more than skin color.[13]

An investigation of how ransom traffic worked and evolved over time helps to discern how human trafficking fostered slavery without skin color. Here the stories left by English captives are especially revealing. In his life story published in 1704, English sailor Joseph Pitts described the process by which the "Cryer" at his first slave auction attempted to excite buyers' expectations: *"See, what a pretty Boy this is! No doubt his Parents are very Rich, and able to redeem him with a great Ransom!"* For buyers, such speculations were quite risky, as it was difficult to ascertain a sailor's familial pedigree after months at sea and likewise difficult to arrange and receive a ransom. Not only did the price of a ransom have to be negotiated with a captive's representatives after purchase but the means of making payments also had to be secured. For captives, such negotiations were inherently unfair. Enslaved individuals possessed few options if a master refused the proffered ransom or if family and friends were unable to raise the sums of money demanded. Thomas Phelps, who published his story in 1685, learned that predicament firsthand after his "Friends in *England* had taken some care for my Ransome, and had given orders to Mr. *Luddington,* an English Merchant in Barbary, to endeavor my relief if One hundred and fifty Pounds would effect it." When Phelps "profered the said Sum" to his master, however, "it would not be accepted." No ransom would ever materialize for Phelps, and he soon lost "any hopes of Redemption."

---

13. Okeley, *Eben-ezer,* 11. On the importance of ransom traffic to the experience of slavery across the Mediterranean, see Rozen, *Mediterranean in the Seventeenth Century,* 65–84; and Jennifer Lofkrantz and Olatunji Ojo, eds., *Ransoming, Captivity, and Piracy in Africa and the Mediterranean* (Trenton, N.J., 2016). Historicizing what role enslaved people have been able to deploy in shaping their commodification has been an ethical and empirical challenge for obvious reasons, not least the implication that enslaved people somehow consented to their oppression. The topic has thus received less sustained attention in histories of slavery, despite its centrality to the history of Mediterranean slavery and trafficking. On the role of captives in shaping their potential ransoms through letter writing, see Robert Davis, *Christian Slaves, Muslim Masters,* 142–148. On efforts to historicize particular forms of power and violence in Atlantic slave markets, see Walter Johnson, *Soul by Soul: Life Inside the Antebellum Slave Market* (Cambridge, Mass., 1999), 140–143; Daina Ramey Berry, *The Price for Their Pound of Flesh: The Value of the Enslaved, from Womb to Grave, in the Building of a Nation* (Boston, 2017); and Marisa J. Fuentes, *Dispossessed Lives: Enslaved Women, Violence, and the Archive* (Philadelphia, 2016). On challenges to making ransoms fungible, see Davis, *Christian Slaves, Muslim Masters,* 146–148, 164–166.

Refusing a proffered ransom payment was a gamble for masters in North Africa, who might wind up with no payment.[14]

A remarkably astute portrait of the political complexities that trafficking generated emerges from Flemish captive Emanuel d'Aranda's narrative *The History of Algiers*. D'Aranda recounted not only his captivity in Algiers between 1640 and 1642 but also that of dozens of Europeans like himself. A collective biography of the lives and experiences of his fellow captives, d'Aranda's account lays bare the web of transactional relations that shaped how captives experienced enslavement and, for the lucky few, redemption. For d'Aranda, the assessment of a captive's pedigree was the single most important factor setting their price at auction. Determining what that price might be was nonetheless a struggle. Captives with noble pedigrees typically sought to minimize knowledge of such connections, as that information only increased the size of expected ransoms. Merchants in Algiers and Morocco, by contrast, used all means available to discern such details before presenting their captives for sale in local slave markets.[15]

---

14. Joseph Pitts, *A True and Faithful Account of the Religion and Manners of the Mahammetans* (Exeter, England, 1704), 7; Phelps, *A True Account of the Captivity of Thomas Phelps*, 11. Pitts's narrative was noteworthy not only because he learned Arabic while captive but also because he claimed not to have become Muslim, even though his master tried to compel him to do so. For an excellent annotated edition of Pitts's story, see Paul Auchterlonie, *Encounters in Islam: Joseph Pitts: An English Slave in 17th-Century Algiers and Mecca; A Critical Edition* . . . (London, 2012). On the refusal in many Mediterranean captivity narratives to articulate a clear binary between Christian and Muslim, European and North African boundaries, see Stefanie Fricke, "Renegades between Christian 'Self' and Muslim 'Other': The Captivity Narratives of Joseph Pitts and Thomas *Pellow*," *Litteraria Pragensia: Studies in Literature and Culture*, XXVI, no. 51 (July 2016), 36–51.

15. Emanuel d'Aranda's narrative was originally published as D'Aranda, *Relation de la captivité et liberté du Sieur Emmanuel d'Aranda, jadis esclave à Alger, où se trouvent plusieurs particularités de l'Affrique, dignes de remarque*, 3d ed. (Brussels, 1662), before being translated into English as d'Aranda, *The History of Algiers and Its Slavery; With Many Particularities of Africk* . . . , trans. John Davies (London, 1666). Despite its rich insights and relevance to European and Mediterranean social, religious, and political history, d'Aranda's work has received little sustained scholarly attention. Dutch historian Lisa Kattenberg explores the transformation of his text from its original publication to the more widely circulated and ecumenical version that was translated into English in 1666, writing that the "tone and content . . . were radically altered" by the author and his publishers "to accommodate a concept of universal morality" and "to reach a broad and international audience." See Kattenberg, "Moslims, 'morale deuchden' en commercieel succes: Het slavernijverslag van Emanuel d'Aranda, 1640–1682," *Zeventiendea eeuw*, XXVIII (2012), 21–39. The most extensive treatment of d'Aranda's stories and their significance is in Davis, *Christian Slaves, Muslim Masters*, 85–87, 97–100, 112–116, 123–127.

Much of the work of assessing captives' potential market value was done by middlemen who visited newly arrived captives in prison while they awaited sale. According to d'Aranda, one of these middlemen was a Jewish merchant named Ciscas. Ciscas approached European captives like himself in Algiers with alcohol and kindness: *"Whence come you my Friends and Companions; assure your selves I am extreamly troubled at your misfortune. However, pray be of good courage, and do me the kindness to accept of a glass of wine which I will bestow on you."* Working with the permission of local authorities, Ciscas took European captives out of their chains to a local tavern where "the poor besotted fools, having their hearts full of grief, their bellies of Wine, and their heads warm, believ'd all the trapanning raskal said to them." Like an English spirit, Ciscas then asked whether they were *"able to give four or five hundred Patacoons for your liberty?* Some answer'd they were, nay, haply if need were, they could advance a thousand, for they had such and such friends, who would not suffer them to continue long in that miserable condition." Others without income volunteered that they had "yet a House or Tenement of Land, which should be sold rather than they would stay long in Slavery." Armed with such vital intelligence, Ciscas then shared it with prospective buyers "when they came to be sold in the Market." Ransom traffic began with a traffic in information about captives' identities.[16]

Commodification was both a cause of slavery in the Mediterranean and a pathway to redemption for many of the enslaved. D'Aranda's depiction of middlemen draws attention to their crucial role in both facilitating enslavement and redemption through exchange. The bargains that European captives struck were by no means fair or freely negotiated; they could stretch over months and even years of hard labor and privation. The problem was, not so much being trafficked, but the geography of the unfree labor market. There were few buyers in North Africa who might purchase a sailor and then return him to England. The biggest challenge from the vantage of English authorities was making transactions happen at all. Without an agreed-on price and an acceptable currency, there could be no emancipatory transaction, no way to render market values humanitarian or capable of redemption.[17]

---

16. D'Aranda, *History of Algiers,* trans. Davies, 136, 137.

17. Determining a generalized price for Christian or Muslim captives was tricky work given the varied factors that both facilitated and blocked the fulfilment of ransom payments. Ransoms were first and foremost determined by what loved ones and families could pay, not a universalized price, as for a galley slave. Robert Davis has constructed a list of

The market for captives was thus something of an illusion, a product not of the supply and demand of slaves but of highly unequal negotiations, with deception being one of a captive's only tools. Such efforts could be quite risky. D'Aranda recounted the story of a Spanish knight trying to minimize his ransom value by pretending to be "a poor Youth, born at *Ostend,* the son of a mean *Irish*-Officer." The knight chose Ireland as his place of origin, d'Aranda informed his readers, because "the said Nation is little known and not much esteem'd at *Algiers,* those of it yielding but ordinary ransomes." The knight played the part as well as he might, refusing to talk with the "Officer-slaves" to "take off the suspicion of his being a person of high quality." Yet the dangers of the knight's gamble became apparent when he was sold to Alli Pegelin, the "General of the Gallies," the ultimate destination for many indigent captives from Ireland. When Pegelin asked the knight what he might put up for his release, the captive suggested "five hundred Patacoons," a standard ransom for a common soldier, but his answer only sent the general into a fury. Suspecting that the captive was an English officer, Pegelin "order'd the Knight to have a chain of sixty pound weight fasten'd to his legge, to induce him to come somewhat neer the sum of thirty thousand Patacoons, at which he had set the Knight's ransom." For six weeks, the knight received daily beatings, including a form of torture called the bastinado, during which he sustained one hundred blows to his feet, leaving him unable to "so much as to touch the ground with his feet." In the face of such torments, he relented and agreed to offer fifteen hundred patacoons for his liberty and to be kept in a Jewish-run prison at Leghorn, Italy, "till the ransom were paid." The knight's efforts to pass as an Irish sailor failed, but he did reduce his redemption price to one-twentieth of the general's original demand. More importantly, the knight received an unexpected compensation when the Leghorn-bound ship ran aground on the coast of Spain, whereupon "all the slaves had their liberty

---

"exemplary prices" for Christian slaves across the seventeenth century, but he does not make clear whether they reflected market values separate from diplomatic considerations or those same diplomatic capacities. See Davis, *Christian Slaves, Muslim Masters,* xi–xiii. Historical documents concerning the role of Jewish middlemen in facilitating ransom traffic reflect pervasive forms of antisemitism across both Christian and Muslim sources in the Mediterranean. See Gilles Veinstein, "The Ottoman Jews: Between Distorted Realities and Legal Fictions," *Mediterranean Historical Review,* XXIV (2010), 53–65. For an overview of antisemitism in Europe, see Léon Poliakov, *The History of Anti-Semitism,* III, *From Voltaire to Wagner* (Philadelphia, 2003).

without paying anything, by means of that happy tempest escaping imprisonment at *Legorn*."[18]

The traffic in captive sailors was reinforced by a parallel traffic in convict labor, the so-called malefactors of European states, who in the Atlantic would become known in the 1680s as white servants. Ransom traffic not only relied on middlemen to finance transoceanic exchanges but also a network of prisons that supplied galley slaves to national navies across the Mediterranean. English captives represented a comparatively small portion of the larger pool of coerced laborers, as English felons transported to North America only sporadically fell into the orbit of Turkish slavery. Convicts in the Mediterranean did not acquire any racial status but, like their Atlantic counterparts, toiled in the galleys of Venetian, Spanish, French, or Algerine vessels. Once in the hold, no clear distinction separated European felons from captives taken in combat with North Africans. Christian captives, like their Muslim counterparts, endured the harsh working conditions of galleys as best they could. The daily demands of rowing made virtually all desperate for redemption, even as they were likely to remain there until perishing from overwork.[19]

For Christians laboring in the gallies, there were multiple paths in and very few out. They might have been sentenced to the galleys by Christian authorities in Venice, who were seeking to purge so-called malefactors from society's ranks. Or they might have been indentured servants like Okeley bound for Providence but captured at sea by Algerine pirates. The journal of Aurelio Scetti, an artisan from Venice who killed his wife and was sentenced to serve out the rest of his days as a galley slave during the late sixteenth century, provides glimpses of how difficult life could be for a convicted Christian felon. Scetti's only hope for redemption was escape in a storm or capture by pirates, whether Christian or Muslim. The only substantial difference between Christian and Muslim galley slaves was that Muslim ship captains were prohibited from enslaving fellow Muslims, a custom that led many Christians working in the galleys to renounce their faith.[20]

18. D'Aranda, *History of Algiers,* trans. Davies, 214, 215, 216, 217, 220, 221.

19. On the use of galley slavery among European powers across the Mediterranean, see Paul W. Bamford, *Fighting Ships and Prisons: The Mediterranean Galleys of France in the Age of Louis XIV* (Minneapolis, Minn., 1973); Lufkrantz and Ojo, eds., *Ransoming, Captivity, and Piracy;* and Gillian Weiss, "Ransoming 'Turks' from France's Royal Galleys," *African Economic History,* XLII (2014), 37–57.

20. Aurelio Scetti, *The Journal of Aurelio Scetti: A Florentine Galley Slave at Lepanto (1565–1577),* trans. and ed. Luigi Monga (Tempe, Ariz., 2004). Venice served as an important hub for the traffic in both Christian and Muslim slaves throughout the early modern era.

Religious conversion offered a risky avenue of potential escape for Christian captives. Renegades, or Christian captives who chose to convert, were worth less than Christian slaves for at least two reasons: not only could Christians be sold into the galleys of both Christian or Muslim ship captains but renegades possessed virtually no ransom value in European countries, as religious conversion effectively divorced them from the authorities that might raise ransoms for their rescue. Consequently, faith was tightly policed by masters of individual captives. D'Aranda related an account of "a French-slave belonging to *Alli Pegelin*" who "had row'd several Voyages in the Gallies" but who was "not able to brook that kind of life." Seeking relief, the French slave "desir'd *Pegelin*'s permission to renounce the Christian Religion and to embrace the Turkish." General Pegelin, however, refused to allow the enslaved Frenchman to convert "because the Renegadoes are worth much less than the Christians; for being once turn'd Turks, they are not oblig'd to row as the Christians are." Nevertheless, lack of permission did not stop the French slave from trying to convert. He assumed a Turkish habit and "gave himself the name of *Mustapha*," only to be met with a violent response from General Pegelin, who "seeing him in that equipage, call'd four slaves, who . . . cudgell'd him so long till at last he cry'd out; *My name is John, and not Mustapha; I am a Christian, and not a Turk, I will put on my Christian habit*." More than a matter of conscience, religious conversion was closely connected to the traffic in both Christian and Muslim sailors, as both European and North African masters policed how and when individual slaves converted. The enslavement of varied actors across the Mediterranean—sailors, passengers, servants, convicts, and

---

See Benjamin Arbel, *Trading Nations: Jews and Venetians in the Early Modern Eastern Mediterranean* (New York, 1995); John Martin and Dennis Romano, eds., *Venice Reconsidered: The History and Civilization of an Italian City-State, 1297–1797* (Baltimore, Md., 2002); Magnus Ressel, "Venice and the Redemption of Northern European Slaves (Seventeenth and Eighteenth Century)," *Cahiers de la méditerranée*, LXXXV (2013), 131–145; Cecil Roth, *History of Jews in Venice* (New York, 1975); and Alberto Tenenti, *Piracy and the Decline of Venice, 1580–1615*, trans. Janet and Brian Pullan (Berkeley, Calif., 1967). On the role of religious organizations and affiliations in shaping human trafficking across the Mediterranean during the medieval and early modern periods, see James William Brodman, "Community, Identity, and the Redemption of Captives: Comparative Perspectives across the Mediterranean," *Anuario de estudios medievales*, XXXVI (2006), 243–245; Molly Greene, *A Shared World: Christians and Muslims in the Early Modern Mediterranean* (Princeton, N.J., 2000); Mikhail Kizilov, "Slave Trade in the Early Modern Crimea from the Perspective of Christian, Muslim, and Jewish Sources," *Journal of Early Modern History*, XI (2007), 1–31; and Salzmann, "Migrants in Chains," *Religions*, IV (2013), 391–411.

soldiers—reflected the power of state actors to determine when, whether, and how captive subjects might be trafficked.[21]

Just how hard it could be to escape the galleys is best illustrated by d'Aranda's own personal story. His new master, "the Bassa," paid two hundred patacoons for him, "telling us he had been credibly inform'd, that we were rich and persons of quality." When the bassa learned that they "were not persons of quality, nor rich as it had been reported," he loaned them to General Pegelin, who promptly put them to work rowing as galley slaves. Here d'Aranda's fortunes reached a low ebb. Fortunately for him, the bassa still held out hope that d'Aranda possessed some ransom value, and he removed d'Aranda from the galleys and put him to work in Algiers, where he learned the "Trade" of "pounding Wheat in a Stone-mortar." He received no food from his master. Instead, he and his fellow captives were granted three hours of freedom "every day" in order "to shift for our Livelihood." D'Aranda and his peers were compelled to steal objects in town and then sell them for food to subsist. This new predicament was a reprieve from life in the galleys, though, and d'Aranda exploited every wisp of opportunity that urban slavery offered. During his daily three hours as a thief, he managed to borrow money from an Italian merchant to send letters to religious and political authorities in his home of Flanders, alerting them to his situation. In the process, he learned that seven Turkish slaves were incarcerated in Flanders and two Flemish slaves held in Algiers. With the help of his Flemish emissaries, he organized a proposed contract for the exchange of three Flemish Christian slaves for seven Turkish Muslim slaves.[22]

Making that transaction occur presented numerous roadblocks for d'Aranda that exemplifies the narrow path to freedom that ransom traffic made possible. How and where would Turkish and Flemish captives be exchanged and made free? What would prevent the emancipated from being retaken and trafficked again? Would local masters even accept a traffic in bodies divorced from money? D'Aranda recognized that the exchange might spark resistance, so he waited to negotiate his ransom until after he had "received answers from *Flanders*." With contractual assurances in hand, d'Aranda and his two Flemish compatriots approached the bassa by kissing his robe "on the Sleeve of his inner Garment (a Turkish Reverence)" and asking him respectfully "how much he would have from us." The bassa demanded "two thousand *Patacoons* at Legorn or fifteen hundred here," acknowledging the steep costs of making

21. D'Aranda, *History of Algiers*, trans. Davies, 173, 174.
22. Ibid., 11, 13, 15.

money mobile in the Mediterranean. As d'Aranda's plan for a prisoner swap in lieu of ransom money became apparent, however, the bassa strenuously resisted efforts to exchange slaves without financial compensation. After *"two Turks come from* Dunkirk" arrived in Algiers and explained the terms of the proposed slave exchange, the bassa's steward said, *"You Dogs, which of you writ into his Country to be exchanged for Turks?"* D'Aranda tried to cool tempers by lying that "nobody had written to the Country" but to no avail. The same steward threatened to "cut off" their "Noses and Ears," insisting that *"the* Bassa *will not have* Turks *for your ransome, but money."* Here indeed was the nub of the problem. On one hand, d'Aranda and his two fellow Flemish captives possessed a kind of diplomatic value, expressed in the ratio of prisoner slaves to be exchanged; on the other hand, the Turkish prisoners held no financial value to the bassa, as they could not be used as galley slaves.[23]

The solution for d'Aranda and his two enslaved compatriots was to find a way to come up with a fungible ransom for their Algerine masters. The origin of d'Aranda's ultimate ransom of five hundred patacoons came from an unlikely source: the grandmother of one of the Turkish slaves stuck in a Flanders prison, who, unlike the bassa of Algiers, had a keen interest in seeing the proposed slave exchange move forward. Remarkably, she agreed to pay a ransom for the Christian slaves to guarantee the planned exchange. The grandmother, however, bitterly resented using her money to pay for the liberty of Christians and tried to get d'Aranda and one of his compatriots, M. Caloen, to raise money to offset her investment, putting both men in chains and threatening them daily with beatings. The exchange of slaves had been arranged to take place in the Moroccan port of Tetuan, six weeks after the two Turkish slave emissaries first arrived, a period that gave the grandmother several weeks to extract money from d'Aranda and Caloen. On the night before the ship for Tetuan was to sail, the grandmother tried one final time. *"Tomorrow the Ship goes away for* Tituan," she said, *"therefore if you love your liberty, give the seven hundred Patacoons, otherwise you shall dye here like Dogs."* Having been

---

23. Ibid., 24, 25, 27, 28, 29. The diplomatic relationship between Algiers and Turkey also did not favor the Bassa receiving any compensation for having freed three Turkish slaves. Indeed, Alli Pegelin, general of the gallies in Algiers, refused an exchange requested by Turkish emissaries in 1642, pointing out the limits of Algerine sovereignty: *"You are to know, that the* Turks *take the Citizens of* Algiers *for Subjects, having subdu'd them by force of Arms, because they would have revolted."* See ibid., 29, 31. On prisoner exchanges across the Mediterranean, see Daniel Hershenzon, "'Para Que Me Saque Cabesea Por Cabesa...': Exchanging Muslim and Christian Slaves across the Mediterranean," in Lofkrantz and Ojo, eds., *Ransoming, Captivity, and Piracy*, 25–50.

counseled by a fellow "Christian Slave, named *Gregorio*" not to give in to her demands, d'Aranda and Caloen reminded her that her grandson *"is in the hands of my Companion."* Calling the grandmother's bluff worked, for the next morning they were on board a vessel bound for Tetuan, where they would be exchanged with five remaining Turkish slaves and formally freed.[24]

Yet d'Aranda's transaction remained incomplete and his freedom and that of his countrymen insecure until all parties safely reached Tetuan, a journey that accentuated the enduring political and geographic obstacles to making ransoms fungible. First, d'Aranda and his fellow Christian slaves had to pay the "Turk who was to go along with us to *Tituan*" fifty patacoons "for his pains." Then they had to pay a duty to the port authorities in Algiers before leaving. "Yet before a Christian can be dismiss'd, he is to pay a certain proportion according to his ransom" to the "Farmers of the Customs," d'Aranda explained, "to see whether the Christians who were redeemed had paid the duty." These taxes were instituted, d'Aranda wrote, with no apparent trace of irony, "to prevent the Stealing of Slaves." Once on their way, new impediments emerged daily. They soon "discover'd at Sea two other Ships, which continually followed ours." Fearing they were slaving ships, they changed course only to discover they were being pursued by "two Pirates of *Algiers*," one of them under the command of a renegade named Amet Arrais, born at Dunkirk, d'Aranda's hometown. Here, indeed, was a topsy-turvy world, one where political and religious boundaries between sovereign authority and piracy remained grey and trafficking was conducted opportunistically, with unpredictable outcomes. As if to illustrate that uncertainty, a storm drove d'Aranda's ship with its cargo of soon-to-be-emancipated Christian slaves, Turkish sailors, and Jewish merchants into rocks off the Moroccan coast. As the ship began to break apart, all hierarchies of power dissolved as slaves were released from the hold and joined a multireligious throng on deck. Turkish sailors implored "the assistance of their Prophet *Mahomet;*" Jewish merchants "address'd their prayers to *Abraham*, [*Isaac*], and *Moses;* and we *Christians* ... directed ours to our Blessed Savior *Jesus Christ*, and his glorious Mother." Fortunately, all passengers survived, swimming safely to shore as the boat sank.[25]

On finally reaching Tetuan by foot two days later, freedom for d'Aranda and his companions remained elusive. They were thrown into the city's dungeon to await the arrival of the five Turkish slaves from Flanders. Efforts to extract a higher ransom resumed, this time from local merchants who

24. D'Aranda, *History of Algiers*, trans. Davies, 43, 44.
25. Ibid., 46, 54.

directed their jailors to perform daily beatings and invoke "a thousand lyes" about promises made in Algiers, all in an effort to *"Trapan us out of our money by their malicious inventions."* The emancipatory transaction was finally concluded only after the five Turkish slaves were beaten by their steward from Flanders and two Muslim merchants intervened by putting up money as "security" to guarantee the three Christians' release from prison in Tetuan. On being set at liberty, the eight slaves met in the port city of Ceuta near the Strait of Gibraltar where they celebrated their respective freedom in a striking moment of cross-religious harmony, exchanging stories and sharing beverages and food with one another. These were "the greatest satisfactions and enjoyments, that ever we had," d'Aranda wrote, "or ever shall have, in our lives." The comity between emancipated Muslim and Christian slaves evoked the moment in Lurting's adventure when he celebrated with his former captors before setting them free on Algerine shores. Whereas Lurting rejected all forms of human trafficking, however, d'Aranda embraced ransom traffic as a means to freedom. For d'Aranda, the redemption of five Muslim and three Christian slaves vindicated the emancipatory promise of trafficking.[26]

Redemptions such as d'Aranda's were made possible not only because sailors maintained their religious, class, and national status on being captured but because they managed to make these markers fungible. Natal commodification rather than natal alienation meant that freedom could be recovered through trafficking. When one of the five Turkish slaves in Ceuta, Alli, proclaimed the morning after their celebrations that he was no longer Muslim but Christian, having *"embrac'd the Christian Religion"* in Flanders," the transaction once again ground to an abrupt halt. Alli was informed that he would not be able to return to Algiers if he remained a Christian and would instead have to go back to Europe as a slave. Alli quietly "made answer that he would return into his Country," and all talk of conversion ceased. Freedom trumped faith, unless, of course, one's faith offered a path to freedom.[27]

D'Aranda's success in working with numerous state authorities exemplifies both change and continuity in how captives in the Mediterranean secured freedom through ransom. Prisoner exchanges had become common across the region during the fourteenth century, a reflection of the power of religious intermediaries in structuring interactions between Christian and Muslim parties. The notion that a captive's national or religious identity mattered

26. Ibid., 63, 69.
27. Ibid., 70; Orlando Patterson, *Slavery and Social Death: A Comparative Study* (Cambridge, Mass., 1982), 7–8.

in securing their ransom was hardly original to the seventeenth century. The expectation that ransoms would be arranged primarily by money, however, was another matter, an outgrowth of the increasing prominence of merchants in facilitating sovereignty across the second half of the seventeenth century. Prisoner exchanges could not occur until they became financial transactions, a traffic arranged by both familial and diplomatic actors. Thus, freedom was increasingly understood to be both national and transactional simultaneously, a linkage foundational to how European sovereignties expanded their purview after 1600.[28]

## Trafficking Sovereignty

Between 1670 and 1734, the English state paid ransoms for roughly twenty-two hundred of its captive subjects in North Africa. The English crown demonstrated deep ambivalence, however, about how to conduct ransom payments and curtail prize taking. English efforts to raise ransom money ironically fueled the very same traffic the state officially outlawed. Many of these diplomatic efforts also took years, exasperating the patience of enslaved subjects and endangering the lives of the English consuls who negotiated their release. Consular officers consequently attempted to make treaties that would prohibit North African authorities from enslaving English subjects. In 1602, English and Algerine authorities signed an agreement that stipulated that "henceforth no subject of his Majesty of Great Britain . . . shall be bought or sold or made slaves in any part of the Kingdom of Algier, upon any pretense whatsoever." At the same time, consular officials endeavored to negotiate a fixed price for purchasing enslaved Englishmen in North Africa. If the traffic in English bodies could not be stopped, diplomatic actors could at least bring that traffic into line consistent with market values. Doing so would make transactional emancipations more fair, they hoped, while also strengthening the belief that markets could be a redemptive force.[29]

For captives seeking ransoms, then, the ability to become fungible was intimately connected to the capacity of states to traffic people across oceans. The well-heeled Thomas Sweet, for example, secured a ransom contract, not

---

28. On the centrality of early modern corporations to governance across England's colonies, see Philip J. Stern, *The Company-State: Corporate Sovereignty and the Early Modern Foundations of the British Empire in India* (New York, 2011).

29. "British Slaves: Extracts from Treaties," MS 17034/3, Thomas Betton Charity Papers, Guildhall Library, London.

simply because he possessed wealthy relatives, but because he petitioned Parliament for his freedom while still a captive in North Africa. Sweet had to make short letters to Parliament accomplish important political work. The first surviving letter was clearly not his first missive to Parliament. "I have written oft to *London* to Master *Southwood* of the upper ground," he began his letter, and "to *Richard Barnard* of Dukes place, *Richard Coole* of the Bankside, to Master *Linger* an Haberdasher in crooked Lane, and in that to Master *Southwood* I sent an inclosed to my Father, if living, and other Letters to my Brother and friends, if not dead." These letters produced no immediate action on Sweet's behalf, whose time as a *"Barbary* captive" had already extended to five years. "I could never heare whether any of you were alive or dead, which makes me thinke the Letters are either miscarried, or all of you deceased, or gone to other places." Why this letter, dated September 29, 1646, and sent "from Barbary," succeeded where others had failed is unclear. Certainly, Sweet's quotation of scripture and evocation of the English as God's chosen people helped his case, as did his astute appeal to religious captivity. "We did never so well understand the meaning of that Psalme, penned by those captive Jewes held in Babilonish captivity as now," wrote Sweet, continuing, *"By the waters of Babilon we sate down and wept, when we remembered thee, O Sion, when we remember thee, O England."*[30]

Sweet's letter spurred action not simply because of its religiosity and eloquence but also because he laid out a specific transactional path to redemption. "We are told there is a Merchant in London, one Mr. *Stanner* of St. Mary-Axe, that hath a Factor in *Legorne*, and one Mr. *Hodges*, and Mr. *Mico, Londoners*, that are dealers there, who are able to direct you in the readiest way for our redemption." Here were the specific "dealers" in London whose financial connections to the Jewish-run prison in Leghorn, Italy, might enable a successful ransom for Sweet in Algiers. Sweet also identified an informational pathway that might help him and his friends negotiate his ransom: "There is a Post in *London* that conveys Letters into all parts, and you may have an opportunity of letting us heare from you, if you please within a month or six weeks." Sweet knew these transactional pathways well. His master, a French renegade, had grown rich linking European captives to sovereigns across the region, pathways that Sweet had come to facilitate. "I doe keepe his bookes of Accompts and Merchandize," Sweet wrote, and "that keeps

---

30. Sweet, *Deare Friends*. The broadside, printed on the authority of the House of Commons, includes two letters, the first, dated September 29, 1646, narrates Sweet's captivity in Algiers.

me here in misery." Sweet had become indispensable to his master's business dealings as a trafficker, a predicament that made the Frenchman even less willing to negotiate Sweet's ransom. Sweet's knowledge nonetheless guided him to send his missives to Parliament, and one was finally read on April 16, 1647, more than a year after it was written in September 1646. His subsequent redemption highlights the power of both commercial networks and the English state in ransoming its subjects.[31]

Sweet's second letter reveals the efforts of his advocates in London to reconcile the tension between market values and antislavery. In it, Sweet indicated that "Master *Cason* the Parliament's Agent" had concluded a new peace with the basha of Algiers that aimed to simplify how emancipatory transactions occurred. Henceforth, "all *English* Captives (not turn'd Renegadoes) shall be redeemed at the price they were first sold in the Market for." Masters would not be able to demand more in a ransom for an English slave than they originally paid. Or that, at least, was the aspiration of "Master *Cason* the Parliament's Agent." He might also have imagined that Sweet's original sale price was substantially less than 250 pounds. Unfortunately, Sweet's master anticipated such an agreement and produced a bill of sale for 250 pounds, his demanded ransom price. Sweet's case illustrates the toothless nature of Cason's agreement, which enabled adept patrons in Algiers to appear reasonable without changing their ransom demands. England's diplomatic agreement provided little direct relief to Sweet, suggesting just how limited the English state was during the middle of the seventeenth century in managing the terms of traffic that would, in time, make it a truly formidable imperial power.[32]

Sweet's dilemma raised a broader question that vexed English authorities across the seventeenth century: What precisely was the relationship between English sovereignty and the traffic in Christian slaves in North Africa? Did that traffic highlight the shortcomings of national sovereignty, or did it expand the capacity of states to police trafficking across the Mediterranean? Could both propositions be true if the traffic in Christian slaves existed, like piracy, both as a short-term threat to European sovereignty and as an instrument of its long-term extension? When focusing on ransom traffic, sovereignty in the Mediterranean emerges less as a discrete military possession or territory than as a capacity to shape how the traffick in human beings

31. Ibid.
32. Ibid.

occurred across the inland sea and to influence the numerous political and cultural actors vying to control it.³³

If the power to traffic people and goods across water constituted a key element of English sovereignty, that imperative also sanctioned symbolic contests between sovereigns who used the bodies of emancipated national subjects to establish their claims to power. When the Moroccan prince, Mohammed esh-Sheikh es-Seghir, the "Emperor of Morocco," forged a new treaty with England in 1637, he traveled to London to celebrate its ratification. Robert Blake, an English merchant who helped arrange the emperor's visit and who went on to become a member of Parliament and the leader of Oliver Cromwell's navy, published an account of the diplomatic moment titled *The Arrival and Intertainements of the Embassador*. Blake described both the treaty and the "Redemption of three hundred and two of his Majesties poore subjects, who had beene long in miserable slavery at Salley in Barbary." Saving English captives from that spiritual purgatory, Blake claimed, had been Charles I, who "both with his Word and Purse, when they were in miserable thraldome and Slavery . . . never ceased to doe his best to comfort them."³⁴

Or so Blake insisted. The English crown was, in fact, quite stingy in comparison to continental authorities in spending ransom money for its captive subjects. Indeed, Charles I contributed no money for the ransoming of the 302 Christian slaves held up as symbols of his emancipatory reign. Rather, the new emperor of Morocco had paid their ransoms *"out of his Royall Coffers,"*

---

33. On oceanic legal regimes, see Philip E. Steinberg, *The Social Construction of the Ocean* (Cambridge, 2001); Mary Sarah Bilder, *The Transatlantic Constitution: Colonial Legal Culture and the Empire* (Cambridge, Mass., 2004); and Elizabeth Mancke, "Early Modern Expansion and the Politicization of Oceanic Space," *Geographical Review*, LXXXIX (1999), 225–236.

34. Robert Blake, *The Arrivall and Intertainements of the Embassador, Alkaid Juarar Ben Abdella, with His Associate, Mr. Robert Blake* (London, 1637), title page, 5, 16, British Library, London. For a filiopietistic but informative account of Blake's life, see [William] Hepworth Dixon, *Robert Blake, Admiral and General at Sea: Based on Family and State Papers* (London, 1852). See also Michael Baumber, "Cromwell's Soldier-Admirals," *History Today*, XXXIX, no. 10 (October 1989), 42–47. On the broader context of trafficking and piracy in shaping imperial conflicts and imperial expansion among European states during the early modern era, see Lauren Benton, *A Search for Sovereignty: Law and Geography in European Empires, 1400–1900* (Cambridge, 2009). On Ottoman statecraft and state formation, see Karen Barkey, *Bandits and Bureaucrats: The Ottoman Route to State Centralization* (Ithaca, N.Y., 1997); and Barkey, *Empire of Difference: The Ottomans in Comparative Perspective* (Cambridge, 2008).

a disbursement of *"at least* 10000. *pounds sterling."* The sultan's largesse, Blake informed his readers, emanated from his gratitude for English military aid in his recent war with the political and military leaders of New Salley, the so-called pirate's republic wreaking havoc on commerce within the Mediterranean. That help came in two forms: eighteen English slaves who had proved to be *"good* Gunners" for the young emperor and several English ships, including the "Leopard, commanded by Captaine *William Rainsborough,* who was the *Generall of the Salli Fleete."* The result of that collaboration was English military success over New Salley in 1637.[35]

A narrative of that redemptive battle was literally put on display in the streets of London in 1637, with a parade featuring emancipated slaves, the Moroccan ambassador, soldiers, ministers, merchants, and the king of England himself. The arrival of the Moroccan ambassador, with the 302 emancipated English slaves carried by boat up the Thames River, summoned a dramatic gathering of "ten Thousands of Spectators" in London, along with *"Barbary-Merchants* bravely mounted on Horsebacke, all richly apparelled, every man having a Chaine of Gold about him; with the *Sherriffes* and *Aldermen* of *London* in their *Scarlet Gownes,* with such abundance of Torches and Links, that though it were Night, yet the Streetes were almost as light as Day." The moral of the procession, if there was just one, was that only truly noble sovereigns could successfully sunder slavery and guarantee free commerce and trade. That moral was supplied directly in the preamble to *The Arrivall and Intertainements.* "Amongst the multiplicity and varieties of blessings which God . . . hath bestowed upon men," Blake wrote, *"Commerce* and *Trafficke* is to be esteemed and ranked as the chiefe happinesse." Those blessings were protected by sovereign authority at home and helped strengthen sovereign authority abroad. *"Commerce* and *Trafficke"* facilitated the spread of "civility amongst the most barbarous and rudest people" and made "peace, love, and amity with Princes and Potentates, though they are far remote from each other." But if traffic brought about the Enlightenment, why did it also lead to slavery and the proliferation of cities like New Salley, where all manner of trafficking flourished, causing great "confusion to Shipping-merchants and Merchandize?"[36]

35. Blake, *Arrivall,* 6–7, 23, 25, 31. On the role of captive taking and redemption in state formation during the seventeenth century, see Colley, *Captives,* 53; Janice E. Thomson, *Mercenaries, Pirates, and Sovereigns: State-Building and Extraterritorial Violence in Early Modern Europe* (Princeton, N.J., 1994); and Marcus Rediker, *Outlaws of the Atlantic: Sailors, Pirates, and Motley Crews in the Age of Sail* (Boston, 2014).

36. Blake, *Arrivall,* 1, 2, 9, 24.

Although the polemical purpose of the Moroccan ambassador's arrival was to ratify the triumph of sovereignty over enslavement, the principal actors in the parade complicated or contradicted those efforts. The 302 freed slaves were not all *"English, Scottish,* and *Irish,"* as Blake initially described them. They also included *"*27. *French men,"* "8. *Dutch men[,]* and 11. *Spaniards."* Their emancipation created problems for those seeking to burnish Charles I's antislavery credentials. Why emancipate the French enemy? For their part, the French slaves seem to have understood their brief symbolic value and "wisely ran away from their keepers." The Spanish and Dutch freedmen lingered, though one doubts they agreed "to love, honour, and obey *Our most Gracious King."* More provocatively, even Blake would soon abandon his support for Charles I and fight against him in the upcoming civil war. The republican aspirations creating New Salley were not so easily sundered.[37]

The difficulties the English government experienced in fashioning national solutions to the world of Christian slave traffic endured throughout the seventeenth century and the ferocious conflicts that gripped Puritans, Catholics, and monarchists across England and its kingdoms. In 1675, Charles II, Charles I's son, restored to the throne, issued yet another proclamation announcing a new agreement with the "Government of Algiers." Like the Treaty of 1602, the proclamation forbid all English subjects from sailing on vessels whose states were at war with Algiers. Those who did forfeited their rights to rescue by the English state. The new treaty represented a concession to Algerine complaints that individual English subjects, many of them gunners on foreign ships, had violated the treaty by engaging in battle with Algerine ships. Yet it also reflected an effort by the English state to control the mobility of its own subjects, whose voyages under varied national flags challenged its capacity to govern. By so doing, the English government sought to gain leverage not only with authorities in Algiers but also with its own wayward national subjects, many of whom served as mercenaries in European navies.[38]

England's control over both groups proved fleeting, however, particularly when Mediterranean and Atlantic actors collided. In 1677, two English ships bound for Virginia with 971 passengers, most of them indentured servants,

---

37. Ibid., 26. On the political tensions and contradictions posed by England's simultaneous support for expansion of the slave trade and commercial freedoms during the late seventeenth century, see Abigail L. Swingen, *Competing Visions of Empire: Labor, Slavery, and the Origins of the British Atlantic Empire* (New Haven, Conn., 2015), 83–85.

38. "British Slaves: Extracts from Treaties," Dec. 20, 1675, MS 17034/3, Thomas Betton Charity Papers.

were captured by ships from Algiers, whereupon all on board were "exposed to Sale in publick Markets for Slaves." According to a petition brought to Parliament by the "disconsolate Fathers and Wives, on behalf of their distressed Children and Husbands" in 1678, passengers and crew had been confident about a safe journey to North America when they left, all of them possessing "his majesties pass for their safe conduct" and accompanied by "a convoy attending some of them" from the English Navy. But to no avail. Perhaps because passengers and crew had presumed their passports protected them, family members addressed their concerns directly to Parliament. Petitioners protested their loved ones "being exposed to Sale" as well as the specific corporal punishments that they endured. "The said patrons do frequently Bugger the said Captives . . . and beat upon the Souls of their Feet with a Bulls Pissle, some three, four, five hundred blows, run irons into their fundaments, rip open their bellies with knives, cut their Britches a-cross, and washing them with vinegar and salt, and hot Oyl, draw them in Carts like horses . . . till they become Broken-bellied." The graphic description of dismemberment served as an extreme version of trafficking itself, a process that turned people into body parts to be assessed, poked, and commodified. Fears of dismemberment as well as sodomy were hardly new within English captivity narratives, but the explicit language of this petition and its context—being read to "the Right Honourable the Commons of England in Parliament Assembled"—made it an extraordinary and sensational account, one designed to maximize national shame and provoke parliamentary action.[39]

Human trafficking was an especially volatile topic when connected with Virginia-bound indentured servants, as critiques of the crown's capacity to enslave its own still reverberated among the king's advisers, who read the petition from the families of the captive servants in the wake of Bacon's Rebel-

---

39. Petitions of "Disconsolate Fathers and Wives, on Behalf of Their Distressed Children and Husbands," 1678, Broadside 12:12, Thomas Betton Charity Papers. On the significance of sodomy within English captivity narratives, see Colley, *Captives*, 128–132; and Hans Turley, *Rum, Sodomy, and the Lash: Piracy, Sexuality, and Masculine Identity* (New York, 1999). As a metaphor for political corruption in early modern England, see Danielle Clarke, "'The Sovereign's Vice Begets the Subject's Error': The Duke of Buckingham, 'Sodomy,' and Narratives of Edward II, 1622–28," in Tom Betteridge, ed., *Sodomy in Early Modern Europe* (Manchester, U.K., 2002), 46–64; and Joseph Allen Boone, *The Homoerotics of Orientalism* (New York, 2014). On efforts to see discussions of sodomy during the seventeenth and eighteenth centuries as case studies of homoerotic sex, see Randolph Trumbach, "The Transformation of Sodomy from the Renaissance to the Modern World and Its General Sexual Consequences," *Signs*, XXXVII (2012), 832–848.

lion. Rather than call for war against Algiers or the enforcement of English sovereignty, the petitioners instead demanded help in raising ransoms. Engaging in a ransom traffic in Christian slaves, petitioners believed, was their best hope for securing the redemption of their loved ones. Perhaps a market in manly souls could redeem their captive sons and husbands, whom royal warships and edicts failed to protect. Notions of manhood and free markets were double-edged swords for defenders of the English crown, as likely to subvert as support claims of state power and political privilege.

Religious radicals in England also seized on the opening provided by the petition made on behalf of the Virginia-bound Englishmen and the spectacle of their being tortured in North Africa. One of the most outspoken was Quaker activist George Fox, who, in 1680, published a fiery sermon entitled *To the Great Turk, and His King, at Argiers*. Though a pacifist, Fox's indignant denunciation of Muslim authorities summoned arguments for moral and religious war. "Did ever *Mahomet* give you Authority to rob, spoil, and take the Goods of them that do you no harm, and keep Captives the bodies of them, and sell them, or to beat upon the feet, belly, or back . . . because they refuse to lye with your men, as a man lyeth with a Woman?" Fox not only condemned English sailors' captivity and their sale at auction but continually linked that traffic to the practice of sodomy, effectively equating them as complementary dehumanizing practices. References to "these Abominable Impieties" and to making slaves "lye with your men as with Women" occurred with remarkable repetition in Fox's sermon, appearing twenty-two times in the first eleven pages of his text, an almost chantlike rebuke of the trafficking of Christian slaves. Unlike the parliamentary petitioners that inspired him, however, Fox did not end his sermon with a call to raise ransom money. Rather, he eschewed any participation in ransom traffic. He supported that argument by printing a brief version of former captive Thomas Lurting's story at the end of his sermon. It was here, in the context of a diatribe against sex trafficking and the emasculation of Christianity and English sovereignty, that Lurting's powerful challenge to the king's prerogatives was first made public.[40]

Although Fox's diatribe and the antitrafficking petition made on behalf of the Virginia-bound servants posed a problem for Charles II's reputation as an antislavery king, they also created an opportunity for Royalists. Supporters of the king did not condemn Fox or ignore the fate of the Virginia-bound servants. Instead, they organized a broad coalition of actors within English society to raise ransoms for the English slaves in Algiers. In 1680, the king's

---

40. Fox, *To the Great Turk, and His King at Argiers*, title page, 2, 4, 5.

ministers circulated a "Brief for Collections to Free the English Captives in Algiers" and directed it toward "Mayors, Sherrifs, Bayliffs, Constables, Churchwardens, Chappelwardens, Headboroughs, Collectors of the Poor, and their Overseers; And also to all Officers of Cities, Boroughs, and Towns Corporate, and to all other our Officers, Ministers, and Subjects." The brief recapitulated the petitioners' narrative on the circumstances of the Virginia-bound servants, focusing on the horrors of commodification and torture. "They now lead a life much worse than death, bought and sold like beasts in the market . . . and beaten daily with a certain number of stripes upon the Soals of their feet." It also accepted the petitioners' central argument about ransom traffic, that "the money needful for accomplishing their Redemption, amounts to so vast and great a sum, that our distressed subjects are utterly unable by themselves or their friends to procure the same." Churchwardens throughout England were directed to go "house to house" and "to ask and receive from all the Parishioners, as well as Masters and Mistresses, and servants as others in their families," taking a census of "all those who shall contribute thereto."[41]

The Royal Slave Fund that was established for freeing English slaves as a result of this national canvas was impressive. The sum raised, twenty thousand pounds sterling, was the largest financial commitment yet mustered by the English state on behalf of its captive subjects in North Africa. Within one year, 390 English captives had been ransomed from Algiers at the going rate of forty pounds sterling per head. Politically, the fund provided Charles II an answer to a crisis that required a decisive and highly public action on behalf of two of England's most important labor resources: North American servants and English sailors in its imperial navy. The nascent connections between the grievances of English sailors in North Africa and those of indentured servants in Virginia presented a political storm for Charles II, as threatening as Bacon's Rebellion and far worse than the individual protests that trafficked servants had posed a decade earlier. Like the servant registry, the Royal Slave Fund created an opportunity for the king and his defenders to perform their

---

41. Charles II, *A Brief for Collections to Free the English Captives in Algiers* (London, 1680), Thomas Betton Charity Papers. On the vexed relationship between the Stuarts and English captivity in the Mediterranean, see G. E. Aylmer, "Slavery under Charles II: The Mediterranean and Tangier," *English Historical Review*, CXIV (1999), 378–388. On Charles II and the African slave trade, see William A. Pettigrew, *Freedom's Debt: The Royal African Company and the Politics of the Atlantic Slave Trade, 1672–1752* (Williamsburg, Va., and Chapel Hill, N.C., 2013), 22–25.

commitment to antislavery even while expanding trafficking and enslavement across the decade.⁴²

Yet underlying problems within England's mercantile economy remained unresolved and quite visible to critics and defenders of the king. The Royal Slave Fund was only partially successful in emancipating Englishmen from bondage in North Africa. A royal proclamation entitled "The Redemption of Captives," published in 1691, celebrated the emancipatory results of the 1680 brief: *"The number of captives redeemed by help of the former Brief were about four hundred and fifty six . . . And the number of Captives still in Slavery about five hundred."* Even so, the total of redeemed captives in 1691 revealed that only sixty-six additional slaves had been ransomed through the Royal Slave Fund after its initial success in 1681, despite hundreds remaining enslaved in North Africa. As a onetime alms-giving effort, the Royal Slave Fund did not permanently change how the English crown funded its ransoming efforts. Equally important, anxieties about servants and sailors' loyalties remained pervasive, especially as servant and sailor narratives linking antislavery, Englishness, and manhood proliferatred.⁴³

## Sailor Antislavery

For thousands of English captives in North Africa, antislavery had little to do with matters of national sovereignty or endorsements by the king but a daily struggle against owners who sought to extract as much value as possible from their bodies, whether in ransom money or labor. Sailors' difficulties led them into contradictory positions regarding human trafficking, alternately critiquing the traffic that gave rise to their bondage in the first place and affirming the values of a ransom traffic that held out the promise of freedom. Sailors' ambivalence toward the traffic that both enslaved them and brought redemption only deepened over time, as the state became more involved in ransom traffic. Increasingly, toward the end of the seventeenth century, captive sailors began to frame their protests as political demands inherent to national rights, whether or not they supported the crown. Co-opting the story of national redemption championed by those who would craft Charles II in the image of an antislavery king, sailors expanded their antislavery narratives

---

42. Albert Carlos Bates, "Introduction," in *Narrative of Joshua Gee of Boston, Mass. while He Was Captive in Algeria of the Barbary Pirates, 1680–1687* (Hartford, Conn., 1943), 7.

43. William and Mary, *The Redemption of Captives*, Mar. 12, 1691, Thomas Betton Charity Papers.

to critique not only the trafficking of English subjects abroad but abuses closer to home, such as impressment.[44]

One of the most vexing conundrums posed by captive sailors related to their capacity for religious conversion, a topic that remained inherently political across the seventeenth century. Although religious authorities deemed conversion to Islam a spiritual and religious malady, the process assumed a political lexicon as well, one that conflated becoming a renegade with "turning Turk." For sailors held in captivity, the question of turning Turk was also one of labor. Because the Koran explicitly forbids Muslims from enslaving other Muslims, conversion to Islam meant, in theory, a reprieve from bondage for English sailors who chose to renounce their Christian faith. Although English authorities were loath to admit it, conversion to Islam functioned as a form of antislavery. For captured sailors, becoming a renegade offered a way of escape from the perpetual toil that Christian slaves endured as captives. Indeed, stories of Christian slaves becoming renegades emphasized these pragmatic reasons for conversion.[45]

Virtually all the sailor conversions described by Emanuel d'Aranda involved sailors seeking to escape dungeons. Conversion meant freedom from prison. Many of the conversions d'Aranda depicted went awry when looked-for freedoms either did not materialize or led to coercions even worse than what individuals had experienced as Christian slaves. In one account, two men in a Spanish prison, "soldiers at Penon de Veles, a Fortress on the *Mediterranean*," who had been "condemn'd by their Judges" to serve the rest of their lives there as convicted felons, decided to "trust to the mercy of the Moors their enemies" and "renounce the Christian faith" rather than "suffer any longer in that Fortress." Yet after escaping the prison and submitting themselves to Moorish masters, their new owners "would not suffer them to change their

---

44. On the complex relationship between political upheaval and imagining empire, see David Armitage, *The Ideological Origins of the British Empire* (New York, 2000). On the impact of colonial experiments on English political struggles and identity at home across the seventeenth century, see Games, *Web of Empire*.

45. On the history of apostasy, see Emily M. N. Kugler, *Sway of the Ottoman Empire on English Identity in the Long Eighteenth Century* (London, 2012), 17–34. On the religious and political significance of conversion to Islam during the early modern era, see N. I. Matar, "'Turning Turk': Conversion to Islam in English Renaissance Thought," *Durham University History Journal*, LXXXVI (1994), 33–41; and Matar, *Islam in Britain, 1558–1685* (Cambridge, 1998).

Religion, because a Christian slave is worth much more than a Renegado; for the former are employ'd to Row in the Gallies, and the latter are not."⁴⁶

D'Aranda's portrayal of these complex considerations places his text in sharp contrast to most English and European captivity accounts, the majority of which emphasized the violence and depravity of Muslim masters. Particularly striking in d'Aranda's text are the comparisons he drew between different forms of unfree labor in the Mediterranean region. The narrative of Spanish felons fleeing slavery in a Mediterranean fortress only to be enslaved by new Muslim masters raised an implicit question: Which was worse, confinement in a Spanish prison run by Christian authorities or laboring as a galley slave in a Muslim vessel? The captives in d'Aranda's stories rarely posed such questions directly, but their narratives evince little sense of national or religious loyalty or pride. Christian and Muslim masters all treated their trafficked prisoners harshly in d'Aranda's narratives. According to one English renegade who had been captured by Christian pirates but was imprisoned in Dunkirk, "I went . . . to the prison, where I found about a hundred Turkish slaves, kept in a Cellar, and no better treated then the Christians in *Barbary*." D'Aranda's *History of Algiers* presents an antinational and antisectarian vision of ransom traffic. No nation or religious group was better at emancipating enslaved subjects than any other. Redemptions were generated by traffic or by flight, and all polities and pirates engaged in trafficking.⁴⁷

D'Aranda's portrait of Mediterranean traffickers diverges from religious accounts that deemed renegades to be spiritual threats to Christians near and far. Consider, for example, the story of Vincent Jukes. Jukes, like Thomas Lurting, secured his freedom by rising up against his Turkish captors and successfully disarming them. Unlike Lurting, however, when Jukes and four European compatriots took control of the ship on which they were being held,

---

46. D'Aranda, *History of Algiers*, trans. Davies, 128. For Muslim masters, maximizing the financial values of the Mediterranean traffic in human beings meant minimizing conversion to Islam. Transactional values and religious imperatives thus clashed for Muslim masters and ship captains who justified Mediterranean prize taking as an opportunity to convert Christians to Islam. On the coexistence of transactional and religious values in shaping ransom traffic among Christian and Muslim slaves in the Mediterranean, see Hershenzon, "'Para Que Me Saque Cabesea Por Cabesa . . . ,'" in Lofkrantz and Ojo, eds., *Ransoming, Captivity, and Piracy*, 33–41.

47. D'Aranda, *History of Algiers*, trans. Davies, 183; Eliga H. Gould, "Entangled Histories, Entangled Worlds: The English-Speaking Atlantic as a Spanish Periphery," *American Historical Review*, CXII (2007), 764–786.

they bound their Turkish captors "one by one" and sailed the ship to Saint Lucas in Spain, where they "sold the ten living Turks, the ship and all that was in her, for six hundred pounds, which they divided amongst themselves." Clearly, for Jukes, trafficking people posed no ethical quandary. Any second thoughts Jukes might have had about the injustice of selling people were secondary to the pressing question of finding a way home to England. With 150 pounds in his possession, he arrived a comparatively wealthy sailor and soon resumed his former employment on vessels bound to Greenland.[48]

Yet Juke's return to a sailor's life in England during the 1630s proved to be an unhappy one. While captive, Jukes had joined a group of *"Renegadoes"* after his master had "used him most cruelly" and "by daily threatenings and soare beatings forced him to renounce his Christian Religion." Once having secured his freedom and financial independence, though, Juke began to suffer anxiety about having turned apostate, so much so he confessed to his local priest. Jukes's story ultimately reached the archbishop of Canterbury William Laud, who charged Puritan minister William Gouge with preaching a sermon on the occasion of Jukes's reinstatement to the church. In a sermon on the dangers of "apostacy," Gouge described Jukes's anxieties post-emancipation as a condition of ongoing spiritual bondage for having renounced Christianity. For Gouge, Juke's emancipation from enslavement was both paradoxical and partial. "Though these were sure evidences of his freedome from *Turkish* slavery, yet not so of his freedome from a farre worse slavery under sinne and Satan . . . when he renounced his Christian faith." Renouncing his Christian faith put Jukes into a condition of spiritual slavery. True emancipation could occur only through public confession and giving oneself again to Christ. If a Christian should find himself or herself in Turkish hands, it was far better to become a martyr. "Martyrdome is the most difficult, the most acceptable and honourable worke that on earth can be done," Gouge sermonized, creating "victories, triumphs, and trophies" over slavery. Here was how Turkish slavery was best defeated. As Gouge succinctly put it, martyrdom *"lead* captivity captive." Trafficking bodies for profit was one thing, trafficking souls quite another. The purpose of Gouge's sermon ultimately was, not to comment on the immorality of trafficking, but to exhort all "Mariners, Merchants, Merchants-factors" to avoid apostacy and to choose martyrdom. Martyrdom

---

48. William Gouge, *A Recovery from Apostacy; Set Out in a Sermon Preached in Stepny Church Neere London at the Receiving of a Penitent Renegado into the Church* (London, 1639), 4.

might have been a steep price to pay, but, for the true Christian, such a transaction was indeed worth the price.[49]

Nevertheless, over the course of the seventeenth century, religious polemics against becoming renegade receded in importance as renegades began to acquire political significance as a cohort capable of challenging the expansive sovereignty claims of virtually all polities trafficking goods and people in the Mediterranean. The Turkish ship captain who captured d'Aranda serves as a case in point. He was not actually born in Turkey but was rather "an English-man . . . a Renegado," who spoke to d'Aranda in Dutch on boarding his ship. He urged d'Aranda to *"have patience Brother, this is the chance of War, to day for you, and to morrow for me."* The English renegade's comment accurately assessed the transitory nature of freedom and slavery that resulted from the trafficking of kidnapped sailors and passengers across the region. As a Turkish captain born in England and fluent in both Dutch and French, this English renegade was in many respects stateless, a man without fixed loyalties to nation or religion. For both d'Aranda and his renegade master, identity was pragmatic and circumstantial, rather than innate. So, too, for Thomas Sweet's Turkish master, whose identity was likewise forged in the human-trafficking lanes of Mediterranean commerce. Although Sweet was initially taken by "a Turkes man of Warre," his master, or "Patroon," was actually "a *French* Renegado that lives in the Country," a baron who had been unable to pay his ransom and had thus converted to Islam to avoid the galleys.[50]

For English authorities, captured Irish sailors proved to be some of the most nettlesome renegades. D'Aranda recounted the work of one such *"Ireland-Renegado"* who after being captured at sea as a Catholic had converted to Islam to become a Muslim pirate from Algiers. As for many renegades sailing in the Mediterranean, finding prizes could sometimes be very slow work. This particular Irish renegade had *"been a long time abroad . . . without taking any prize"* when he devised a scheme to secure more traffic. He proposed to his captain *"to make towards Ireland, and landing there, to take Irelanders, who suspected not that there were such barbarous people in the world."* Impressed by his Irish renegade's proposal, the captain granted him a promotion to take charge of *"the management of the enterprize."* Several weeks later, the so-called Turk and his crew arrived off the coast of Ireland and *"sent fifty souldiers ashore, who*

---

49. Ibid., 3, 15, 54, 55, 57.
50. D'Aranda, *History of Algiers*, trans. Davies, 5; Sweet, *Deare Friends*.

*brought away about eight hundred men, women, and children, and afterwards sold them... for slaves"* in Algiers. Large-scale raids on coastal communities within Ireland and England by Turkish renegades were unusual during the first half of the seventeenth century but common enough to cause general precautions against them across Ireland and England's southern coastal communities.[51]

The political status of renegades became prominent because they both contested and expanded the sovereignty claims articulated by their former nations. Indeed, renegades embodied central tensions within national policies toward prize taking. By preying on Christian slaves, renegades and pirates afforded European states the opportunity to make antislavery claims about the immorality of Christian slave traffic. At the same time, renegades vastly extended the capacity of European states to police that same traffic, justifying efforts by imperial navies to traffic one another. The relationship between renegades and state authorities could thus be both adversarial and symbiotic. Although renegades were responsible for much of the traffic in English slaves, they also offered an array of services to English consular officials, facilitating ransom traffic and the liberation of national subjects on the one hand while pioneering new ways of disposing unruly national subjects on the other.[52]

The threat of turning Turk did not contradict antislavery arguments by Christian slaves but stirred captive sailors and their advocates to demand action from the English state. Sweet, held captive in Algiers during the peak of English radicalism in 1646, made state power central to his quest for liberty. He sent letters directly to his friends who were then sitting in England's revolutionary Parliament. Their impact was manifest in renewed diplomatic efforts with Algiers as well as the writings of prominent radicals like Richard Overton, who first lauded the House of Commons' concern for Sweet during the summer of 1646: "Your zeal makes a noise as farre as *Argiere*, to deliver those captived Christians." Overton used the English state's revived interest in liberating captives, however, to critique what he saw as its unjust enslavements at home: "But those whom your owne unjust Lawes hold captive in your owne Prisons; these are too neere you to thinke of." Overton focused his anger against impressment some four decades before Lurting became a pacifist sailor. "Wee intreat you to consider what difference there is, between

---

51. D'Aranda, *History of Algiers*, trans. Davies, 247, 248. On the Irish rebellion of 1641 and the subsequent repression and dispersal of Irish rebels, see Nicholas Canny, *Making Ireland British, 1580–1650* (New York, 2001); and Ian Gentles, *The New Model Army in England, Ireland, and Scotland, 1645–1653* (Cambridge, Mass., 1994).

52. Rediker, *Outlaws of the Atlantic*, 46; Stern, *Company-State*, 134–141.

binding a man to an Oare, as a *Galley-slave in Turkie* or *Argiere*, and Pressing of men to serve in your Warre." Overton emphasized the costs to family of the press and its unjust application in which sailors were surprised in the night, forced from their trades, and separated from "dear Parents, Wife, or Children, against inclination . . . to fight for a Cause hee understands not." Moreover, he argued, the costs were as enduring as they were unjust, a form of "Tyranny or cruelty" surpassed only by that "of a *Turkish Gally-Slave.*"[53]

By linking impressment to galley slavery, Overton created a radical blueprint that would bedevil English authorities across the ensuing century, contesting states' power to traffic and to enslave people simultaneously. For Overton, impressment also illustrated the despotic power of political authority over the citizenry more generally for the way it weakened people's capacity for self-improvement and self-government. In a petition to Parliament in the spring of 1647, Overton suggested that sailors were victims of a political economy dedicated to trafficking people instead of goods. The greatest villains were "the oppressive Monopoly of Merchant-adventurers," as Overton put it. Not only were they growing rich by exploiting the trafficked but their capacities were causing a "great abridgement of the liberties of the people . . . to the great discouragement and disadvantage of all sorts of Tradesmen, Sea-faring-men, and hindrance of Shipping and Navigation."[54]

Overton's remonstrances to Parliament raised a disquieting question: Was the English state a rescuer or a trafficker? Tensions within English antislavery ideology would not be resolved by Levellers or by the Stuart Restoration and the subsequent efforts of Charles II to portray himself as an emancipatory monarch. Yet that very uncertainty stimulated increasingly political adaptations of antislavery discourse by sailors and state actors alike. The growing importance of national redemption was apparent in the spate of Christian

---

53. [Richard Overton], *A Remonstrance of Many Thousand Citizens, and Other Free-Born People of England, to Their Owne House of Commons* ([London], 1646), in Don M. Wolfe, ed., *Leveller Manifestoes of the Puritan Revolution* (New York, 1944), 125.

54. Richard Overton, "The Petition of March, 1647," in Wolfe, ed., *Leveller Manifestoes*, 137. On the expansion of impressment in England during the seventeenth century, see Denver Brunsman, *The Evil Necessity: British Naval Impressment in the Eighteenth-Century Atlantic World* (Charlottesville, Va., 2013). On the Levellers, see Geoff Kennedy, *Diggers, Levellers, and Agrarian Capitalism: Radical Political Thought in Seventeenth Century England* (Lanham, Md., 2008); and John Rees, *The Leveller Revolution: Radical Political Organisation in England, 1640–1650* (New York, 2016). On Overton's key role in articulating English radicalism, see Rachel Foxley, *The Levellers: Radical Political Thought in the English Revolution* (Manchester, U.K., 2013), 23–31, 43–45, and 68–73.

slave narratives published in the wake of the creation of the Royal Slave Fund in 1680. Thomas Phelps, for example, narrated a harrowing journey through captivity before reaching freedom in England, an emancipation he attributed to religious forces: "My design and aim in all (kind Country-man and courteous Reader) is, to excite with me thy praises to our God the only deliverer, who hath delivered me from a cruel and severe Captivity." Unlike the sermonizer Gouge, Phelps gave his story a nationalistic moral: *"In a word Slavery is so strange a condition to* England, *that to touch its soil, is ipso facto* Manumission." Phelps's vision of an antislavery England was bolstered not only by his experience of bondage in Algiers but by his strong identification with the king. As "a poor, yet honest Sea-man," Phelps explicitly linked his liberty to his having "devoted my Life to the Service of His Sacred Majesty and my Country." "I know what Liberty is," Phelps explained, "now that I enjoy the immunities and freedom of my Native Country." Phelps's embrace of royalist antislavery might also have been strategic. Critiquing English authority while seeking assistance from the Royal Slave Fund was a tricky proposition after all, permitting no ambivalence or room for misinterpretation.[55]

As national redemption gained prominence in sailors' captivity narratives, so did anxieties about their political loyalties. Although Phelps critiqued the inadequacy of the diplomatic efforts to rescue English slaves, he also attempted to minimize any damage his comments might cause by professing frequent support for Charles II, a kind of anxious loyalty oath. Other redeemed captives went to even greater lengths to limit the radical implications of their emancipations. William Okeley publicly supported Charles II yet also expressed his opposition to trafficking people. Captured in 1639, long before the creation of the Royal Slave Fund, he was repeatedly sold to different masters, leading him to lose hope of ever securing freedom through ransom traffic. Instead, Okeley fled his master, a decision that nonetheless vexed him. "It might be Questioned in the Court of Conscience," Okeley wrote, "whether it were not *down-right Theft* to with draw my self from *his Service,* who had *bought* me, *paid* for *me,* . . . and *enjoy'd* me, as his own *proper Goods.*" Okeley recognized the disruptive implications of his narrative and sought to contain them by suggesting his enslavement had been, from its inception, unlawful. "My Patron's *Title* was *rotten* at the *Foundation,*" Okeley began, continuing, "Man is too Noble a Creature to be made subject to a *deed of bargain and Sale;*

---

55. Phelps, *A True Account of the Captivity of Thomas Phelps,* Dedication, Preface, 26. On the reluctance of English admirals to expand impressment during the 1680s and 1690s, see Brunsman, *Evil Necessity,* 30.

and my *consent* was never ask'd." Because Okeley had been taken, all bargains struck over his price were both illegal and immoral.[56]

Rather than denouncing slavery, Okeley attempted to soften the implications of his self-emancipation by spelling out the moral of his story in the preface. "Let all Learn from hence, *in what State soever the Providence of God shall place them therewith to be content*." Yet Okeley's narrative hardly exemplified that dictum. He also asserted that his love for liberty was deeper than any contentedness he had acquired as a slave: *"Fetters of Gold* do not lose *their Nature,* they are *Fetters still."* So Okeley committed himself to a radical course of liberty at any cost, despite his conservative world view. He reconciled the two absolutes of his narrative—deference and resistance—by creating a hierarchy of suffering between his enslavement in North Africa and the privations that servants complained of in the Americas. "Perhaps thou art *a Servant to a Christian,"* Okeley wrote in his preface. "Dost thou murmur? It shews, thou little knowest what it is to be *a Slave to an Imperious Turk."* Okeley's message was directed toward the trafficked servants who completed their intended transatlantic journeys. "Whoever has known *Turkish Slavery,* is obliged to become *a more Loyal Subject,* a more *Dutiful Child,* a more *Faithful Servant,"* wrote Okeley. "And whoever has *not known it,* is yet obliged to become *all these,* lest God make him *know it."* Okeley's admonitions represented a kind of longing for consistency that his actual journey to Algiers had long ago shattered. Put another way, Okeley's aspirations for freedom in the Mediterranean upended the duty-bound moralism of the indentured servant he had once been in the Atlantic world.[57]

These tensions between critiquing and condoning servant trafficking are manifest in the disparate ways English writers and readers deployed the term *Turkish slavery.* A comparative signifier across the seventeenth century, the phrase was only partially connected to the experience of people enslaved by Turkish masters. More often, it helped English writers assess and evaluate spiritual, political, and economic maladies that English, Irish, and Scottish people were experiencing closer to home. "We were in a worse case than

---

56. Okeley, *Eben-ezer,* 47, 48. William Okeley's narrative has received some attention from literary scholars but less so from historians of slavery or trafficking. See John Gallagher, "Language-Learning, Orality, and Multi-lingualism in Early Modern Anglophone Narratives of Mediterranean Captivity," *Renaissance Studies,* XXXIII (2019), 639–661; Paul Baepler, "The Barbary Captivity Narrative in American Culture," *Early American Literature,* XXXIX (2004), 217–246; and Daniel J. Vitkus, ed., *Piracy, Slavery, and Redemption: Barbary Captivity Narratives from Early Modern England* (New York, 2001).

57. Okeley, *Eben-ezer,* [A7r–v], 42.

any Turkish Slave," wrote Christopher Ness in 1696, when summarizing Englishmen's capacity for sin and damnation. Turkish slavery also amplified God's capacity to redeem unworthy Englishmen. Jesus's love respected no caste or class distinction, wrote Ness, but could "redeem them that were worse Galley-Slaves than those to the Turks, tied or chained to an Oar." More common were uses of the term to describe political corruption or tyranny. The English Puritan William Prynne invoked Turkish slavery to summarize the anarchy that might result by allowing soldiers the capacity to express their conscience, with each soldier "an absolute Tyrant, equall in Monarchie to the great Turke himself." Less common but no less significant were efforts to use the term to describe forms of religious and political oppression within England, as when Baptist preacher Henry Adis condemned *"the poor Peaceable people of God, that are no Turkish slaves, but the* free born Commoners of England," being *"enslaved"* by tyrants.[58]

Like these religious radicals, the Pacifist sailor Thomas Lurting struggled to find justice as he navigated Turkish slavery across the Mediterranean. In a manner reminiscent of Richard Overton's commentary on Parliament's actions in 1646, Lurting sharpened his resistance to trafficking and slavery alike by linking critiques of Turkish slavery to his abusive treatments by several English sea captains. When he published his longer narrative in 1710, following his initial report as an addendum to George Fox's pamphlet in 1680, he replotted his opposition to buying and selling people in the context of his religious conversion. An argument as much as a narrative, Lurting's account begins at the moment he was coerced into becoming a sailor: "In the Year, 1646. I being then about Fourteen Years of Age, was impress'd (or forc'd) and carry'd into the Wars in *Ireland,* where I remained about two Years in the time of the Long Parliament." As a young man, Lurting witnessed the full contradictions of English transportation policy. Ostensibly fighting a war of religious liberation for English Protestants in Ulster, Lurting was coerced into serving in Oliver Cromwell's army and found himself deporting thousands of Irish Catholic subjects to points far and near across England's expanding empire. Yet Lurting did not become a radical overnight. He served in the navy with distinction for the next decade, working his way up from common sailor to

58. Christopher Ness, *A Compleat History and Mystery of the Old and New Testament Logically Discust and Theologically Improved* (London, 1696), 130; William Prynne, *The Soveraigne Power of Parliaments and Kingdomes Divided into Four Parts* (London, 1643), 72; Henry Adis, *A Fannaticks Alarm, Given to the Mayor in His Quarters, by One of the Sons of Zion* (London, 1661), 22.

boatswain's mate with the "Command of about 200 Men" by 1655. As a naval officer, he was given the charge of disciplining a number of sailors who had become Quakers. In the process, Lurting precipitated his own long-brewing crisis with English naval authority. It started when he experienced tremendous guilt "that I have been so long Beating and Abusing" Quaker sailors "and that without just Cause!" Next, he became a Quaker himself, a decision that led to resistance from fellow officers and his ship captain, a Baptist preacher. *"When I went to the Captain, I was scarce half a* Quaker, *but by their Lyes and false Reports against me, they have made me almost a whole* Quaker." Lurting's opposition to English naval authority soon provoked a showdown with his enraged Baptist ship captain. Lurting avoided the captain's sword, he claimed, not by yielding but by "keeping my Eye upon" the captain, offering himself as "a Sacrifice" to his unyielding commitment to pacifism. Lurting's civil disobedience unnerved the captain, whose "Countenance changed Pale," and "he turned himself about from me, and went off."[59]

Lurting's spectacular demonstration of nonviolent resistance to imperial naval authority became the focus of his remaining narrative. Over the course of 1661, Lurting was pressed four times, subverting the commands of each ship captain by refusing to do any work that furthered the sale of people or the "killing of Men." In one remarkable exchange, a newly pressed Lurting argued with his captain over what work he would perform. The captain initially invited him to serve as an officer who would "stand by me," but Lurting refused. Then the captain suggested he could serve food to his fellow sailors, a job that would not hurt anyone, but again Lurting answered, "I will not do that." When Lurting refused to eat any food for five days, the captain threatened to "send thee a-shoar to Prison." Lurting responded that he was not trying to starve himself but would instead purchase food, "for I have Money in my Pocket." The captain replied that "I cannot sell the King's Victuals." Whereupon Lurting revealed his identity as a Quaker, stating, *"I cannot do the King's Work, therefore cannot eat the King's Victuals."* The frustrated captain then discharged the troublesome sailor. Lurting had accomplished something few sailors thought possible: he had reversed the press, finding a way to be expelled, reliably, from His Majesty's Service.[60]

59. Lurting, *Fighting Sailor*, A3r, 14, 16, 24.
60. Ibid., 28, 29. The historical literature on seventeenth-century resistance to European naval impressment is limited. See Brunsman, *Evil Necessity*, 30; Christopher Hill, "Impressment and Empire," in Hill, *Liberty against the Law: Some Seventeenth-Century Controversies* (London, 1996), 162–176; and Ruth Mackay, *The Limits of Royal Authority: Resistance and Obedience in Seventeenth-Century Castile* (Cambridge, 1999).

Lurting's revisions to his original story amplified the importance of sailor antislavery while transforming its power as a tool that could also be deployed against impressment and opposition to the king and to the corrupt institutions affiliated with enslavement. Most of Lurting's literary additions assumed the form of first-person speech, as when he described his plan for retaking the ship after the Turks had captured it. "Then said I, *If the* Turks *bid you do any thing, do it without grumbling, and with as much Diligence and Quickness as you can; for that pleases them, and that will cause them to let us be together.*" Describing himself in the first person not only helped Lurting to write a more vivid drama but also personalized his conflict with English authorities. In his conclusion, Lurting directly engaged Charles II, who, Lurting recalled, "came to our Ship's side" on his and his fellow captives' return to England in 1679. "The King, and the Duke of *York*, stood with the Entering Ropes in their Hands, and ask'd me many Questions about his Men of War." When Lurting explained *"how we cleared our selves"* without royal rescuers or ransoms, the king chastised Lurting, insisting that *"I should have brought the* Turks *to him."* Lurting's captors were the king's sovereign property, Charles claimed, his to be taken and sold if he so desired. Lurting justified liberating his Turkish captors by ironically affirming the rights of their sovereign authority: *"I thought it better for them to be in their own Country."*[61]

Lurting's highly personal opposition to trafficking was powerful but also introduced tensions to his revised narrative. Did Englishness strengthen his antislavery, a sign of *"ipso facto* Manumission" as Phelps put it? Or did Lurting's Englishness compromise his ability to oppose trafficking? Lurting's narrative embellishments suggest he believed that Englishness and manhood were indeed essential to nonviolence as well as opposition to impressment. During a key moment in his quest to emancipate his former captors, for example, Lurting described the Turkish sailors rising up and grabbing an axe to commandeer the boat. Calling on his compatriots to use their bare hands to disarm the Turkish sailors, Lurting exclaimed, likely with embellishment, *"They are* Turks, *and we are* English *Men, let it not be said, We are afraid of them; I will lay hold on the Captain."* Lurting and his crew relieved the Turkish sailors of their weapons yet again, and, a day later, he safely landed them on shore, free men for the time on the coasts of North Africa. Lurting's radical

---

61. Lurting, *Fighting Sailor*, 36, 46.

commitment to every sailor's freedom exemplified the extension of his English antislavery inheritance as well as his English manhood.[62]

But if Lurting linked impressment and Christian slavery in North Africa, two forms of trafficking typically sequestered from one another, he spent little time commenting on the most important site of human trafficking across the British Empire in 1709: the booming African slave trade that was transforming England and its empire. That omission seems especially noteworthy given that some Quakers in North America were at that very moment beginning to protest the African slave trade. For both Lurting and Fox, Turkish slavery remained the primary point of reference when critiquing the horrors of slavery, not because ransom traffic in the Mediterranean was worse than the African slave trade, but because that region was key to England's national aspirations. For the time being, skin color and race did not organize the traffic in slaves and captives in the Mediterranean. Skin color occasioned commentary within Mediterranean slave auctions but not as a consistent signifier denoting the totality of a person's biological inheritance. Nor was white grammar yet associated with common sailors like Lurting, unless they were working in the slave trade in Africa. To the contrary, the most likely whites to appear in the Mediterranean were not Christians but non-European Muslim men and women sold at auction.[63]

## Conclusion

Connections between the Atlantic and the Mediterranean were not abstract but obvious to William Okeley and to the Virginia-bound servants who ended up being sold in the slave markets of North Africa during the seventeenth century. Efforts to traffic or to emancipate Christian servants and Christian slaves were dilemmas for English authorities, as both groups could disrupt royal prerogatives over the profits to be gained by trafficking people. During

---

62. Ibid., 40. On the importance of masculinity to Quaker pacifism, see Erin Bell, "The Early Quakers, the Peace Testimony, and Masculinity in England, 1660–1720," *Gender and History*, XXIII (2011), 283–300.

63. On the complex role of Quaker slaveholders in both building English colonization and leading efforts to Christianize their enslaved charges, see Katharine Gerbner, *Christian Slavery: Conversion and Race in the Protestant Atlantic World* (Philadelphia, 2018), 51–60; and Kristen Block, *Ordinary Lives in the Early Caribbean: Religion, Colonial Competition, and the Politics of Profit* (Athens, Ga., 2012), 157.

the 1680s, Christian slaves in North Africa witnessed a dramatic if brief expansion of the English state's efforts to emancipate its captive citizenry. Pragmatically, the Royal Slave Fund enabled the crown to ransom enslaved captives by raising money and standardizing the cost of emancipatory transactions in North Africa. Ransom traffic was organized, imagined, and financed without reference to skin color or race, as neither improved the process of generating ransoms for particular captives. Skin color did operate within the region's ransom markets as a way of accounting for the value of non-Christian and non-European slaves, but skin color did not reveal a particular captive's family lineage, information that was instrumental in establishing an individual's ransom value. Rather, family inheritance and lineage were things to be hidden or concealed, something men like the well-pedigreed Thomas Sweet well understood. For most captives, commodification was both the sign of their slavery and their ultimate redemption. In no way did trafficking in the Mediterranean give rise to or expand race trafficking, the commodification of enslaved people's racial identities.

Yet the intensification of sailor antislavery and the English state's commitment to financing ransoms during the 1680s did not occur in a geographic or political vacuum. The 1680s were indeed a critical watershed in the emergence of both white grammar and servant antislavery. As in the Atlantic, white grammar in the Mediterranean signified one's status as a commodity, suggesting important questions about how opposition to trafficking in the Mediterranean and in the Atlantic shaped one another. Did the appearance of white grammar in relation to English convicts and indentured servants make ransom traffic more attainable for Christian slaves in the Mediterranean? Or did the increasing involvement of the English state in ransoming Christian slaves in the Mediterranean encourage Atlantic authorities to use white grammar there? Could both developments be true at the same time, a mutually reinforcing pair of historical occurrences that expressed distinct solutions to a common problem, building an empire of liberty out of an empire of trafficking?

The effort by trafficked sailors and servants to map justice suggests that the two regions were indeed mentally linked geographies. Okeley's anxieties about the implications of his self-emancipation in the Mediterranean, after all, were expressed as a concern for the fate of servants in the Atlantic. The parents and families of the Virginia-bound indentured servants who were trafficked into slavery in North Africa, in turn, played a key role in prompting Charles II to organize the Royal Slave Fund for sailors in the Mediterranean, an emancipatory project that built connections across the expanding English Empire.

Although captive sailors' emancipatory aspirations usually remained confined within one oceanic geography, they could occasionally travel shared pathways between the Mediterranean and Atlantic worlds of trafficking, as in the case of Joshua Gee. Born in Boston, Gee was captured by Algerine corsairs in 1680 and wrote his narrative "in a small but fairly legible hand" after his return to New England via London in 1688. Although he was not "redeem[ed]" through England's Royal Slave Fund, he was nevertheless its beneficiary. Gee's parents made financial arrangements for ransoming him and his brother "out of turkeish Slavery in Algier" by using the going rate established by the fund of forty pounds per boy, a rate that Gee himself discovered from a fellow slave. How else would the Gee family have been able to secure a ransom for their sons if not for the notion of a common price for an English slave taking shape across two vast oceans? And how, in turn, could the conviction that a common price for a trafficked body exist if not for the African slave trade? Yet even a commonly understood price did not a ransom transaction make. Seven years after Gee's parents sent their money in 1681, he continued to linger in captivity until he received the assistance of a judge in Boston named Samuel Sewall, who used both money and gifts to make the emancipatory transaction possible. Sewall revealed that he had received a "pair of Jerusalem Garters which cost above two pieces 8/8 (Spanish dollars) in Algiers" for his assistance in disbursing the Gee family's money to merchants in London. The Gee family seem to have learned the necessity of having gifts ready to offer all legal authorities, whether in Algiers, London, or Boston. Redemption and justice required compensation but also a transoceanic reach that brought Atlantic and Mediterranean actors into meaningful if contested connection.[64]

The idea that transoceanic markets could define the value of things, let alone deliver them, was not the product of some invisible hand. A century before Adam Smith would write his utopian account of how markets should work, English diplomats, shipping merchants, ship captains, sailors, servants,

---

64. Charles A. Goodwin, "Preface," in *Narrative of Joshua Gee of Boston*, 3, Bates, "Introduction," ibid., 7, 9, 10; Samuel Sewall, *Diary of Samuel Sewall, 1674–1729*, I, *1674–1700* (Boston, 1878), 199; Paul Baepler, ed., *White Slaves, African Masters: An Anthology of American Barbary Captivity Narratives* (Chicago, 1999). The diary of Joshua Gee was not discovered until 1926, when a rare manuscript collector found it hidden within another book that used recycled parchment from the colonial era. So-called Barbary slavery was frequently mentioned in North American sources during the Revolutionary era and early national period but only sporadically during the seventeenth century.

and slaves in the Mediterranean all struggled to fashion a political economy in which transactional freedoms might become synonymous with political freedom. The greatest obstacle that human trafficking in the Mediterranean posed to English families and sovereigns alike was arranging ransom transactions, especially when self-serving political actors, or the wind itself, interrupted them. That ransom traffic did occur was as much a product of faith, persistence, and luck as any notion of rational self-interest. Indeed, prize taking condemned most English slaves in the Mediterranean to a lifetime of toil and premature death. Turning apostate offered some hope, but for most trafficked sailors, emancipation and being sold were distinct and distant phenomena, possibilities denied to the vast majority of Muslim and Christian slaves who formed the backbone of the Mediterranean's galley fleets.

That political and economic context made the seventeenth-century aspirations of Quaker sailors like Thomas Lurting for a world rid of human trafficking even more remarkable, as transformative as the notion that a market could guide the actions of innumerable actors toward a common good. Lurting defied the authority of the English state to profit from trafficking, thereby calling into question the fiction of its blue water empire: that transactional freedoms were equal to political freedom. It was no accident that Lurting's challenge originated in the Mediterranean rather than the Atlantic, moreover, for it was here, in the congested sea-lanes of competing European and African empires, that the endemic trafficking of people fueled both substantial profits for England's mercantile empire and enduring obstacles to it. Lurting's antitrafficking was as threatening to English power as his opposition to slavery, for Charles II had already adroitly co-opted servant antislavery in the 1670s to make an empire of global traffic more possible, despite the persistent limits presented by Muslim empires in North Africa. The loss of the colony of Tangier in 1684 to armies from Morocco represented a blow to England's imperial ambitions in the Mediterranean, but it did not threaten how that empire should be constructed. Lurting on the other hand directly defied that mercantile vision, a harbinger of later antislavery activism in the Atlantic. Lurting's struggles to reimagine how an empire of trafficking might become an empire of freedom would face stiff headwinds, not only because trafficking bodies was a path to emancipation for many slaves in the Mediterranean but also because of the powerful storytelling of a new group of antislavery writers in England: the creators of the English novel. Their geographic imaginings would transform the sea-lanes of trafficking, antislavery, and race across the long eighteenth century.

CHAPTER THREE

# Novel Ways of Seeing Race

WRITING IN LONDON in 1688, in the midst of a spectacular political crisis that would reshape the face and form of English sovereignty, Aphra Behn published *Oroonoko,* a story that sought to reframe how English-speaking people viewed skin color and its relationship to both nobility and slavery. Her narrative was not only popular but would, in time, be linked to the origins of the abolitionist movement, being published in the same year as the "first definite antislavery protest in America." The protagonist of Behn's novel, Oroonoko, was neither English nor Christian but an enslaved African who led an uprising in Surinam directly confronting the inhumanity of the slave trade. The female narrator of Behn's novel also condemns the treachery of English slave traders and of white men more generally. Speaking of Oroonoko, the narrator states, "Who-ever had heard him speak, wou'd have been convinc'd of their Errors, that all fine Wit is confin'd to the White Men, especially to those of Christendom." Behn's repudiation of slave trafficking and the moral superiority of white people helps explain why her novel would become important to a global abolitionist movement. Ironies nevertheless pervade Behn's novel critique of both human trafficking and the lies her work unmasked about white skin color. For Behn, whiteness possessed dubious political value, a taxonomy at odds with her belief in nobility and its place in justifying political hierarchy. Noble genealogies—and Britain's antislavery inheritance—could be made compatible, but only if people learned to see that nobility was not, in fact, skin deep but a heritable racial essence stronger than commercial values.[1]

---

1. A[phra] Behn, *Oroonoko; or, The Royal Slave; A True History* (London, 1688), 22; David Brion Davis, *The Problem of Slavery in Western Culture* (Ithaca, N.Y., 1966), 472. The scholarly literature on *Oroonoko* and its significance to the history of both abolition and the British Empire is vast. Davis cites *Oroonoko* as one of the first and most influential abolitionist texts ever published. On the importance of *Oroonoko* to late eighteenth-century

Behn's arguments about race and antislavery seem inconsistent, but they reflect ideological tensions prevalent at the time she was writing. Genealogical inheritance had only recently become foundational to the legalization of slavery in the Americas. In 1662, Virginia legislators made slavery heritable by decreeing that the status of the child was to be determined by the status of the mother. The Virginia statute made slavery vastly more profitable to colonial planters and also centrally about the control of enslaved women's reproductive labor. Yet skin color itself remained largely absent from the Virginia statute. The children of enslaved women and English masters were not uniformly Black or identifiable as chattel on the basis of skin color. Blackness might have been increasingly understood as a sign of enslavement because of the Virginia statute, but not all enslaved men and women in the Americas shared the same phenotype. Whiteness also possessed an uncertain and as yet poorly defined relationship to genealogical inheritance or to a concept of race, as ransom traffic in the Mediterranean and the convict trade in the Atlantic made abundantly clear.[2]

For skin color to become a reliable method for seeing and conceiving political value, it had to be naturalized in narrative form, with genealogical essences made visible in the phenotype of fictional people. In plotting that ideological work, Behn both critiqued and extended a taxonomy of skin color closely related to new methods for organizing human trafficking across the Atlantic. More importantly, she deployed a concept of race in her critique of the slave trade that was distinctly at odds with the mercantile values associated with skin color throughout her story. The main crime in *Oronooko* is the

---

abolitionism, see Moira Ferguson, "*Oroonoko:* Birth of a Paradigm," in Susan B. Iwanisziw, ed., *Troping Oroonoko from Behn to Bandele* (Aldershot, U.K., 2004), 1–2. Although literary scholars have hailed the feminist and antislavery dimensions of Behn's work, others have expressed befuddlement at what one critic has described as its "discursive incoherence," a reflection of its "ambivalent critique of colonialism and slavery." See Mary Beth Rose, "Gender and the Heroics of Endurance in *Oroonoko,*" in Behn, *Oroonoko: An Authoritative Text, Historical Backgrounds, Criticism,* ed. Joanna Lipking (New York, 1997), 258, 262. On the novel's feminist dimensions, see Stephanie Athey and Daniel Cooper Alarcón, "*Oroonoko*'s Gendered Economies of Honor/Horror: Reframing Colonial Discourse Studies in the Americas," *American Literature,* LXV (1993), 415–443.

2. "Negro Womens Children to Serve According to the Condition of the Mother," December 1662, in William Waller Hening, *The Statutes at Large; Being a Collection of All the Laws of Virginia, from the First Session of the Legislature, in the Year 1619,* II (New York, 1823), 170. On the vital importance of Black women's family lineages to the creation of Atlantic slavery, see Jennifer L. Morgan, *Reckoning with Slavery: Gender, Kinship, and Capitalism in the Early Black Atlantic* (Durham, N.C., 2021), 3–6.

enslavement of people of noble birth, a race that Behn believed transcended skin color. Here were the true victims of England's empire of trafficking, the only people whose trafficking justified the revolutionary anger embedded within antislavery. Race becomes visible and therefore believable in Behn's fiction, not as a grammar of skin color, but as a story about true nobility, antislavery, and the potential harms of the marketplace. Behn sought to articulate a conception of race that would discipline the men and women who were "by Nature *Slaves*," as her narrator puts it, as well as valorize the justness of true nobility across Britain. That she used antislavery and skin color to do so made her pioneering fiction deeply ironic as well as ideologically productive, an example that would be emulated and adapted across the eighteenth century.[3]

Behn's enduring accomplishment—protesting the trafficking of men and women—was inextricably linked to novel ways of seeing race and making it compatible with antislavery. In that endeavor, Behn had creative imitators and innovators. By the 1720s, the English novel would become a crucial vehicle for critiquing harms associated with human trafficking as well as ratifying the core policies of Great Britain's expanding empire. To understand that historical accomplishment, it is important to recognize that England's first novelists became successful, not despite their ideological tensions, but largely because of them, crafting narratives that sought to reconcile conflicting elements

---

3. Behn, *Oroonoko* (1688), 204. Margaret W. Ferguson highlights the importance of trafficking to several kinds of difference, writing that "the narrative oscillates between criticizing and profiting from a 'system' of circulation which includes not only words . . . but bodies as well." See Ferguson, "Juggling the Categories of Race, Class, and Gender: Aphra Behn's *Oroonoko*," *Women's Studies*, XIX (1991), 159–181, esp. 167. Laura Brown has effectively contended that Oroonoko was a "European aristocrat in blackface." See Brown, "The Romance of Empire: Oroonoko and the Trade in Slaves," in Felicity Nussbaum and Brown, eds., *The New Eighteenth Century: Theory, Politics, and English Literature* (New York, 1987), 48. Others have pointed out the contradictory uses of race in Behn's novel. See Rose, "Gender and the Heroics of Endurance in *Oroonoko*," in Behn, *Oroonoko*, ed. Lipking, 256–264. For critiques of Brown that focus on religious motives shaping and constituting antislavery, see Derek Hughes, "Race, Gender, and Scholarly Practice: Aphra Behn's *Oroonoko*," *Essays in Criticism*, LII (2002), 1–22. *Oroonoko* has been viewed as a rehearsal for either abolitionism or for white supremacy but rarely both at the same time. On Behn's racial politics, see S. J. Wiseman, *Aphra Behn*, 2d ed. (Tavistock, U.K., 2007), 8. Susan Z. Andrade argues that *Oroonoko*'s narrator seeks to "[safeguard] racial purity" in the novel, though she leaves unclear what constitutes Behn's conception of race. See Andrade, "White Skin, Black Masks: Colonialism and the Sexual Politics of *Oroonoko*," *Cultural Critique*, no. 27 (Spring 1994), 189–214. For a discussion of Behn's class politics, see Albert J. Rivero, "Aphra Behn's *Oroonoko* and the 'Blank Spaces' of Colonial Fictions," *Studies in English Literature, 1500–1900*, XXXIX (1999), 443–462.

within Britain's commercial empire. Along the way, they invented new ways of plotting the relationships between skin color, race, and antislavery, even while supporting policies that disciplined both Black and white bodies.[4]

## Nobility under Assault: Trafficking Royal Slaves

Aphra Behn composed *Oroonoko* in the midst of a sustained crisis in the meaning of religious, political, and civil authority across England and its growing empire (Figure 4). To Behn and other supporters of the recently deceased Charles II, the world seemed to be turning upside down. Charles II's successor and younger brother James II had survived the Monmouth Rebellion, the armed Protestant revolt that sent Henry Pitman to Barbados, in 1685 only to see his monarchy crumble when he attempted to extend religious freedoms to English Catholics in the spring of 1688. The shape of religious and sovereign authority remained sharply contested across Europe and its distant colonial outposts. Discerning truth across religious, civil, class, and geographic barriers seemed to be growing harder as political conflicts roiled Britain and sparked a pervasive epistemological crisis. Exactly what did legitimate political authority look like? Could the values exemplified by mercantile markets be made clearer and more visible? How might genealogical knowledge help the architects of England's empire transform an empire of trafficking into an empire of liberty?[5]

---

4. Literary scholars have long debated whether Behn's *Oroonoko*, published in 1688, or Daniel Defoe's *The Adventures of Robinson Crusoe*, published in 1719, was the first English novel. Both texts made trafficking and slavery central points of departure for the dramatic development of their protagonists' struggles. For a discussion of the two novelists and their role in transforming notions of race and modernity in the Atlantic, see Laura Doyle, *Freedom's Empire: Race and the Rise of the Novel in Atlantic Modernity, 1640–1940* (Durham, N.C., 2008).

5. On the political intrigue and suspicion in which Behn wrote, see Toni Bowers, "Behn's Monmouth: Sedition, Seduction, and Tory Ideology in the 1680s," *Studies in Eighteenth Century Culture*, XXXVIII (2009), 15–44. For a good overview of the political history of the 1680s, see Frank O'Gorman, *The Long Eighteenth Century: British Political and Social History, 1688–1832* (London, 1997), 35–70. For a comprehensive intellectual and political history of the Glorious Revolution, see Scott Sowerby, *Making Toleration: The Repealers and the Glorious Revolution* (Cambridge, Mass., 2013). On the role of colonial actors in transforming the shape and meaning of empire during the 1680s, see Owen Stanwood, *The Empire Reformed: English America in the Age of the Glorious Revolution* (Philadelphia, 2011). On the Glorious Revolution beyond England's borders, see Jonathan I. Israel, ed., *The Anglo-Dutch Moment: Essays on the Glorious Revolution and Its World Impact* (Cambridge, Mass., 1991).

FIGURE 4. Robert White, after John Riley, *Aphra Behn*. 1718. Line engraving. © National Portrait Gallery, London

Behn did not answer these questions directly, though she did provide starting points for seeing how true nobility might redeem the nation and its antislavery inheritance. Her story begins when the hero, Oroonoko, a royal African prince, is enslaved through the treachery of an English ship captain, who uses alcohol and gifts to distract and then subdue him. Oroonoko's subsequent voyage to the Caribbean, his sale at auction, and his reunion with his enslaved wife, Imoinda, in the English colony of Surinam all underscore the depth of the tragedy that slave trafficking had perpetrated against him. The full tragedy of his circumstances emerge only in the story's finale, however, when Oroonoko leads a valiant but doomed rebellion against the slaveholders of Surinam. Oroonoko and his noble and powerful wife are betrayed and then killed, not by their white masters, but by cruel and cunning transported English convicts and enslaved Africans who refuse to follow Oroonoko in his moment of greatest need.

Like travel writers before her, Behn claimed that her tale was derived from firsthand experience. "This is a true Story," the narrator avers in the preface, about "a Man Gallant enough to merit your Protection." Behn's narrator reiterates that truth claim throughout the book, a sleight of hand that asks readers to suspend doubts about the story's evident fictionality: "I was my self an Eye-Witness, to a great part, of what you will find here set down; and what I cou'd not be Witness of, I receiv'd from the Mouth of the chief Actor in this History, the Hero himself." Behn presented her story as both literally true and a novelty, a kind of newly arrived exotic object trafficked across the ocean as authentic as any sailor's captivity tale. Romance occupies the heart of Behn's work, but the love story between the protagonist Oroonoko and his African wife, Imoinda, highlights the impossibility of an enduring love story within the institution of slavery. Here are the elements that made the first English novel: history, romance, tragedy, and, if the narrator is to be believed, truth itself.[6]

The centerpiece of Behn's narrative is a political complaint about the unlawful and arbitrary seizing of a sovereign subject's body. For Behn, the injustice of Oroonoko's enslavement hinged on two circumstances, his royal pedigree and the treacherous manner in which he was taken. He becomes enslaved when he trusts an English ship captain, a man whose business, the narrator observes, is deception. Previously, Oroonoko had himself been an active and, according to Behn, honorable participant in the African slave trade, selling dozens of enslaved Africans who had been captured in combat, prisoners of war in his father's kingdom. When peace disrupts that flow of trafficked people, the English captain lays a trap, "entertaining the Prince every Day with Globes and Maps, and Mathematical Discourses and Instruments; eating, drinking, hunting, and living with him with so much Familiarity" that he "gain'd very greatly upon the Heart of this gallant young man." The ship captain then presses his advantage with alcohol. "The Prince having drunk hard of Punch, and several Sorts of Wine" is invited on board the ship where he is encouraged to inspect the hold, at which point, the sailors, on their captain's command, "seiz'd on all his Guests; they clapping great irons suddenly on the Prince. . . . All in one Instant . . . were lash'd fast in Irons, and betray'd to Slavery."[7]

6. Behn, *Oroonoko* (1688), A5, 2.
7. Ibid., 87, 89, 90.

This story of kidnapping was quite familiar to Behn's readers in the 1680s, modeled as it was on English exposés of spiriting servants to North America as well as the complaints of Englishmen trafficked as captives in North Africa. If the story was familiar, however, the prototype for Oroonoko's character was not. Rather than model Oroonoko after a trafficked servant or a Christian captive in North Africa, Behn looked to the beheaded Charles I. Oroonoko "had heard of the late Civil Wars," the female narrator tells readers, as well as "the deplorable death of our Great Monarch." That royalist sympathy was, for Behn, a sign of Oroonoko's own natural nobility. "He had nothing of Barbarity in his Nature, but in all Points address'd himself, as if his Education had been in some European Court." He was, the narrator concludes, "as sensible of Power as any Prince civiliz'd in the most refin'd Schools of Humanity and Learning." Both African and European in his outlook, Oroonoko embodies nobility itself; he is a man whose unjust trafficking makes visible the humiliations created by barbaric subjects and an undiscerning marketplace. "We are Bought and Sold like Apes, or Monkeys," Oroonoko laments, "to be the Sport of Women, Fools, and Cowards." For Behn, Oroonoko's trafficking linked three distinct dramas from the recent news: questions about the efficacy of English sovereignty in the Mediterranean and the Atlantic, debates over the rights of trafficked servants and captive sailors, and doubts about the morality of market transactions and the expanding African slave trade.[8]

Behn's condemnation of the traffic in enslaved Africans was highly selective and partial, based on a particular set of class-based anxieties among English nobility. Like the authors and implementers of the servant registry, Behn effectively silenced and appropriated the political complaints of captive sailors and transported English servants, advancing an antislavery decidedly hostile to those same English subjects. Behn's female narrator describes indentured servants as "*Slaves* for Four Years" who socialize with African slaves "among the Negro Houses" as "a sort of Spys" on Oroonoko when they are not drunk. These English subjects, in Behn's portrayal, deserve no privileges over the noble Oroonoko. Indeed, when Oroonoko protests being "Bought and Sold like Apes," he expresses a sense of injustice at having to be "the Support of Rogues, Runagades, that have abandon'd their own Countries, for Rapin, Murders, Thefts, and Villanies." These transported felons, known as white slaves in Behn's narrative, are undeserving of freedom, as servile as the African slaves who later abandon the noble Oroonoko. Ultimately, Behn cast the blame for Oroonoko's downfall and the failure of his armed rebellion at

8. Ibid., 19, 52, 188.

the feet of the coalition of slaves and servants he sought to organize, the same coalition that was also the great fear of colonial and metropolitan authorities throughout the seventeenth century. Before his death, Oroonoko expresses regret for "what he had done, in endeavoring to make those Free, who were by Nature *Slaves*, poor wretched Rogues, fit to be us'd as *Christians* tools; Dogs, treacherous and cowardly, fit for such Masters." Some people were by nature slaves and appropriately trafficked. Unjust slavery occurred when noble bloodlines were ignored by treacherous ship captains and the rabble known as white servants. As long as one recognizes their class-bound origins and Behn's particular political agenda supporting the Stuart succession, there is no apparent contradiction within Behn's antislavery beliefs.[9]

Behn's efforts to make white skin color both validate the nobility of European aristocrats and police wayward servants and sailors paralleled the efforts of metropolitan elites during the 1670s and 1680s. Like imperial planners, she used white grammar to articulate contempt for white servants who had been transported to the colonies. She designated European actors as "white" twelve times in *Oroonoko*, with the majority of references linking white skin color to immoral behavior. Only one "white" man is singled out by Oroonoko for a kind of praise in Behn's text, an Irishman named Bannister, who ties Oroonoko to a post, builds a fire around him, and insists he "should Dye like a Dog" after leading the failed revolt. Behn's narrator describes Bannister as "a Fellow of absolute Barbarity," but, to Oroonoko, "he was the only Man, of all the Whites, that ever he heard speak Truth." The narrator condemns white people as "rude," "wild," "inhumane," and "rabble" while offering fleeting praise for the power and civilization of *"White* Nations." Nevertheless, if nations could be white and therefore civilized in Behn's novel, white people also held the potential to constitute a particularly dangerous class of people capable of threatening the integrity of the nation's embodiment: the royal family.[10]

The central ideological and narrative tension in Behn's *Oroonoko* revolves around what kind of work race could accomplish and for whose benefit. Would imperial traffic enhance the power of aristocratic bloodlines or of skin color? Behn offered Oroonoko's natural nobility and his disgraceful capture and enslavement as one answer to that question. Imperial trafficking of people by skin color ignored Oroonoko's birthright as a member of a noble

---

9. Ibid., 184, 188, 204; Rose, "Gender and the Heroics of Endurance in Oroonoko," in Behn, *Oroonoko*, ed. Lipking, 258, 262.

10. Behn, *Oroonoko* (1688), 87, 236–237, 238.

race of African rulers while unfairly privileging white English "rogues" over him. For Behn, whites were not inherently superior to Blacks because all white people were not racially equal. Her critique of the slave trade was an effort to control what skin color meant. Although Behn called into question human trafficking, she also sought to defend discrimination on behalf of noble bloodlines rather than skin color. Whiteness needed no rescue as it was part of the problem. The innate qualities associated with the concept of race, for Behn, were genealogical and familial in form, traits applicable to noble families rather than to large cohorts of people linked by skin color. Virtues associated with skin were misleading or even false. Behn's challenge was to make true nobility visible.[11]

Trafficked bodies at auction provided the best opportunity to see the virtues of noble genealogy. Those in the novel who behold Oroonoko on display are impressed by his superior mien, a quality that, in Behn's rendering, transforms how colonial actors understand and treat him. Oroonoko's master, Mr. Trefry, almost instantly recognizes his slave's nobility and humanity and grants him freedom in every way possible except legally. Oroonoko is allowed to roam the plantation like an English nobleman, read any of the books he wishes in Trefry's library, and go on extended journeys. He even hunts with the female narrator. Oroonoko's wife, Imoinda, also possesses innate qualities of beauty and nobility that are made manifest at auction. When Trefry purchases Imoinda, he renames her Clemene, but he is unable to put her to work like "a common slave" because of the noble womanhood she demonstrates while at auction. When Oroonoko first hears that his wife has survived the Middle Passage and is on the same plantation with him, he interrogates his master. "Why, being your Slave," Oroonoko asks Trefry, did "you . . . not oblige her to yield?" Trefry replies that "she disarms me, with that Modesty and Weeping so tender and so moving, that I retire, and thank my Stars she overcame me." Imoinda's conduct at auction inspires onlookers, not to lust, but to moral rectitude and antislavery. Her trafficking is a crime, not because

---

11. Ibid., 188–203. On Behn's genealogical conceptions of value and inheritance, see Catherine Gallagher and Simon Stern, "Introduction: Cultural and Historical Background," in Gallagher and Stern, eds., *Oroonoko; or, The Royal Slave* (Boston, 2000), 16–17. Some scholars have suggested Behn herself identified with a notion of white womanhood, despite the text's ambivalence toward white protagonists and antagonists. See Ferguson, "Juggling the Categories of Race, Class, and Gender," *Women's Studies*, XIX (1991), 159–181; Andrade, "White Skin, Black Masks," *Cultural Critique*, no. 27 (Spring 1994), 191, 202; and Athey and Alarcón, "*Oroonoko*'s Gendered Economies of Honor/Horror," *American Literature*, LXV (1993), 415–443.

Black women are being unjustly enslaved, but because Imoinda's nobility has been violated by the auction block itself.[12]

Translating Behn's imperative of nobility as an aggrieved race of historical actors to the British stage proved quite a different undertaking, however. Shortly after Behn died in 1689, a playwright in London named Thomas Southerne adapted *Oroonoko* for the theater. Southerne acknowledged his debt to Behn in the preface to his 1696 publication *Oroonoko: A Tragedy* while underscoring the representational difficulty that *Oroonoko* presented. "She [Behn] thought," Southerne wrote, "that no Actor could represent him [Oroonoko]; or she could not bear him represented: And I believe the last." The conceit that justified Behn's critique of trafficking was the visibility of Oroonoko's nobility. But what if natural nobility looked artificial? Could a blacked-up English actor represent a natural lord authentically?[13]

Southerne sought to resolve the dilemma, not by having a man with Black skin play Oroonoko, but by shifting the play's focus to Imoinda and changing her skin color from Black to white. Southerne accomplished that dramatic revision by making Imoinda the daughter of a European renegade from North Africa. Imoinda's father "was a White," Oroonoko explains, "the First I ever saw of your Complexion: He chang'd his Gods for ours, and so grew great." By giving Imoinda a Mediterranean origin, Southerne achieved several things simultaneously. First, Imoinda's potentially taboo love for a non-Christian Black man becomes nothing more than her recognition of Oroonoko's natural nobility. Second, Imoinda's whiteness provided Southerne's audiences with a representational proxy for seeing their own antislavery sentiment embodied on stage. Behn's Black Imoinda is a noble fighter like Oroonoko, who carries a bow and shoots and kills white people during the disastrous slave rebellion. Southerne's Imoinda, by contrast, never bears arms except when she kills herself at the end of the play, and then to save herself from being raped by white "rogues" and from raising a child who would be a slave. The villains in

---

12. Behn, *Oroonoko* (1688), 72, 131–132.

13. Thomas Southerne, *Oroonoko: A Tragedy* . . . (London, 1696), A2, 2. The play had already been written and performed in London theaters in 1695. See Robert L. Root, Jr., *Thomas Southerne* (Boston, 1981). Debates over Southerne's politics are as divided as those over Behn's view of antislavery in her novel. On Southerne's anti-Black racism, see Anthony Gerard Barthelemy, *Black Face, Maligned Race: The Representation of Blacks in English Drama from Shakespeare to Southerne* (Baton Rouge, La., 1999). For a more progressive reading of Southerne's adaptation that places him closer to the "natural rights" philosophies of "the future," see Diana Jaher, "The Paradoxes of Slavery in Thomas Southerne's *Oroonoko*," *Comparative Drama*, XLII, no. 1 (2008), 66.

Southerne's drama remain white, even as Imoinda now embodies the purity of white womanhood.[14]

The whitening of Imoinda was part of a broader intensification of racial signs that emerged throughout Southerne's play. In sharp contrast to Behn, Southerne made use of the fiercely anti-Native politics fomented in the aftermath of King Philip's War in New England and Bacon's Rebellion in Virginia, employing an attack by Indigenous peoples on local plantations to demonstrate Oroonoko's heroism and nobility as well as the governor's wickedness. Fearing an internal rebellion, the governor secures Oroonoko with the help of six planters, all the resources his limited manpower can afford. It is in this context of a war against Native peoples, a replotting of Bacon's Rebellion, that the governor extends the term *white slaves* to English and Irish indentures to explain their apparent passivity in the face of the Native attack. "There's no danger of the White Slaves, they'll not stir. . . . Some of you stay here to look after the black Slaves." All threats to plantation society, from within or from without, are racialized in Southerne's drama: so-called red savages attacking noble protagonists, enslaved Blacks in need of noble men to look after them, and white slaves not to be trusted with arms for fear they will join the enslaved to attack their masters.[15]

Skin color provides no consistent meaning or value in Southerne's play but instead poses a question about whiteness and race more broadly. Was the whiteness of white slaves a thing to be feared or rescued? The answer for Southerne depended on the social class and gender of the white subject. Little if anything links the experiences of Imoinda with the English servants known as white slaves. Although she possesses no aristocratic bloodlines, Imoinda's selfless victimhood locate her, in class terms, as a genteel English lady, a woman whose aristocratic rights and privileges are naturalized through her marriage to the noble Oroonoko (Figure 5). Imoinda's whiteness as a white slave represents her purity as well as resistance to any and all trafficking, rejecting as she does the efforts by the lustful governor to ensnare her in a marriage bargain as well as his threats to sell her in the slave market if she refuses his advances. The rescue that Imoinda's whiteness enables comes, not

---

14. Southerne, *Oroonoko*, 24. On the significance of whitening Imoinda, see Joyce Green Macdonald, "The Disappearing African Woman: Imoinda in *Oroonoko* after Behn," *English Literary History*, LXVI (1999), 71–86; Jane Spencer, *Aphra Behn's Afterlife* (New York, 2001), 233–234; and Ferguson, "Juggling the Categories of Race," *Women's Studies*, XIX (1991), 167.

15. Southerne, *Oroonoko*, 30.

FIGURE 5. *Imoinda and Oroonoko*. Frontispiece from Tho[mas] Southern[e], *Oroonoko; A Tragedy* ... (London, 1736). Courtesy of The William Andrews Clark Memorial Library, University of California, Los Angeles

from a white man, but from a nobleman named Oroonoko, who helps her refuse the grim options presented to her.

The emergence of white slaves on stage made possible new ways of seeing both whiteness and antislavery. The English servants described by the governor as "White Slaves" are unworthy of rescue and fundamentally dangerous to the plantation economy, particularly when they began to "stir," as the governor puts it. As in Behn's novel, Southerne's antislavery ideology in the play is tightly circumscribed within class boundaries, available for natural aristocrats like Oroonoko and Imoinda but unavailable to the vast majority of English servants or Black slaves. In Southerne's dramatization, references to Mediterranean captivity recast troubling questions about the political content of white-skinned bodies. Which kind of white slave would prevail in the play, Atlantic rogues or the fair daughter of a Mediterranean renegade? For Southerne, Mediterranean slaves were far more worthy of emulation than Atlantic ones. The whitening of Imoinda reflects no generalized virtue of white skin color, for it is her genealogy as the daughter of an aristocratic English renegade who "chang'd his Gods for ours" and "still commanded all my Father's Wars" that makes her a noble match for Oroonoko.[16]

Questions about the political meaning of white skin reveal not only distinct class-based understandings of antislavery ideology but differing parameters for English sovereignty. On Southerne's theatrical stage, two geographies of human trafficking and two ways of conceptualizing race collided. For viewers of Southerne's play, the choice between trafficked malefactors from the Atlantic and a noble and beautiful renegade from the Mediterranean juxtaposed two geographies for seeing the relationship between trafficking and English sovereignty. Yet that dichotomy might have been a false one, for one could express antislavery sympathy for Imoinda while still scorning white slaves from Bridewell. On stage, the contrast between white slaves and Imoinda expressed less a contradiction than complementary aspects of a common capacity: the power of particular English aristocrats to see value in the bodies of trafficked whites, whether for beauty or for labor. Like Behn, who co-opted servant protests against spiriting and trafficking, Southerne transformed a critique of tyrannical political power into a call for aristocratic rescue.[17]

Nevertheless, England's nobility could not so easily be absolved from their responsibility in building an empire of human trafficking and enslavement. Imoinda's victimhood might have summoned a politics of female rescue, but it also initiated new ways of narrating the political value of enslaved white women, stimulating new forms of antislavery rhetoric whose purpose was not scripted by Southerne. The emergence of white slaves in fiction reflected an

---

16. Ibid., 24.

17. Some of the best scholarship on the rich gendered significance and meaning within Behn's *Oroonoko*, for example, largely ignores Mediterranean motifs or connections to Atlantic "modernity." See Athey and Alarcón, "*Oroonoko*'s Gendered Economies of Honor/Horror," *American Literature*, LXV (1993), 431.

explicitly political conflict among English subjects over the meaning of antislavery and the political character of the nation that defended it. Standing in opposition to Behn's and Southerne's aristocratic antislavery were the everyday social relations and small protests of white servants and Black slaves in the Atlantic, men and women whose rumors of collaboration in Virginia and on islands like Jamaica and Barbados continued to alarm colonial and metropolitan authorities. Most of those authorities did not share the antislavery sentiments of Behn and Southerne in 1700, yet the enthusiastic response of many English readers to both the novel and the play suggest that fears of servant-slave rebellion were key starting points for the growth of royalist antislavery.

White slavery discourse works in Southerne's *Oroonoko*, not as a straightforward claim about white racial superiority, but as a method for comparing and obscuring distinct kinds of human trafficking. Although descriptions of white slaves in Southerne's play make some forms of trafficking more visible—primarily that of English women—they also obscure others, most notably the booming traffic in African women that was essential to the creation of racial slavery in New World plantations. Indeed, the disappearance of the Black Imoinda from trafficking in stagings and revisions of *Oroonoko* made it that much easier for English audiences to imagine and plot the problems of slave trafficking without Black women's bodies or voices in mind, a racist omission that would lead to important problems for white and Black abolitionists over the ensuing centuries. Even so, images of commodified white female bodies struggling not to be trafficked still held enormous power for antislavery activists and abolitionists. The question of whether Southerne's whitening of Imoinda promoted racism or abolition has been false; it accomplished both.[18]

If Southerne's success was partially owing to the way he made whiteness within noble bodies worthy of rescue, did such humanitarian sympathy extend beyond class boundaries to other trafficked subjects? Taking an inventory of how and where iterations of white slavery subsequently emerged in political and literary discourse during the first half of the eighteenth century reveals tensions between at least two kinds of white slaves and two geographies of race and skin color: a language of commodification associated with an Atlantic traffic in English subjects on the one hand and a Mediterranean language of royal ancestry, natural rights, and aristocratic rescue on the other.

---

18. Macdonald, "Disappearing African Woman," *English Literary History*, LXVI (1999), 84–86.

That inventory also suggests that although a grammar of whiteness associated with England's Caribbean slave colonies was growing in prominence, notions of whiteness associated with non-Christian actors in the Mediterranean remained powerful in shaping how English actors conceptualized the relationships between trafficking, empire, and skin color.

## Mediterranean Whiteness: Muslim Whites in Travel Writing and Fiction

Although the successful replotting of Mediterranean captivity within Aphra Behn's and Thomas Southerne's fictions might suggest that Atlantic conceptions of race had become globally dominant by 1710, references to Muslim white slaves persisted and proliferated throughout the eighteenth century. Indeed, non-Christians stand out among all categories of white subjecthood appearing in Eighteenth Century Collections Online, a large database of English-language publications (see Appendix C). By focusing on how trafficked bodies became fungible through corporal inspection, authors describing these individuals recapitulated what had become central to most servant and sailor protests against enslavement in New World plantations or North African captivity. Few descriptions of Muslim slaves, however, animated notions of antislavery.

The centers of Muslim slave trafficking were the slave markets of Constantinople and Cairo. In 1704, Dutch travel writer Cornelius de Bruyn, for example, identified two groups of white slaves in the markets of Constantinople. The first was made up of conscripted soldiers from the Russian province of Georgia who had been transported and sold by Ottoman officials into the army and navy. The second also hailed from Georgia's Muslim villages but were women who had been sold into slavery by deeply indebted parents seeking to hold onto meager landholdings. In 1711, the *Atlas Geographus,* a world history and geography text published in London, described Cairo's slave market as a "large Square where they sell white Slaves of both sexes, plac'd in Ranks against a Wall, where the Buyer feels them like Cattle to find out their Faults." In 1767, travel writer Frederick Calvert laid out the methods used to procure these white slaves in *A Tour to the East.* Most of slaves described in Calvert's work came from the Caucasus region. The most effective actors in this traffic were known as *"Lasces,"* according to Calvert, men and women who worked in clandestine fashion, like London's spirits, bribing the mayors of small towns and villages and kidnapping "all they can lay hands on" when parents were away at work. Accounts of white slaves in Muslim slave markets increasingly highlighted how their market commodification accompanied coercive recruitment.[19]

To most writers describing the phenomenon during the eighteenth century, though, white slaves were, not subjects needing rescue or redemption, but foreign and exotic actors. Calvert described one such enslaved person as someone who expressed "the utmost disdain and hatred of the Christians," so much so that she refused to "stay an hour in a Christian's house" even though she had just been purchased at auction. These trafficked men and women stood apart from the English and European sailors captured by Muslim corsairs. The whiteness of these enslaved Muslim men and women conveyed their value as commodities. Female white slaves from Georgia were prized, not for their labor or their capacity as militia, but for their appeal as objects of beauty, aristocratic refinement, erotic interest, and occasional sympathy. Whether in reference to renegades, enslaved Muslims, or transported white servants, however, white grammar signified fungibility. To be sure, some whites had secured rights and independence by the beginning of the eighteenth century, but most of them were known as Christian servants or Christian slaves.[20]

The relationship between religious traffic and white grammar is nowhere more apparent than in Antoine Galland's French translation of the medieval Arabic text *Les mille et une nuit,* which began to appear in the English language in 1706 as *Arabian Nights Entertainments, Consisting of One Thousand and*

---

19. Cornelius [d]e Bruyn, *Travels into Muscovy, Persia, and Part of the East Indies . . .* (London, 1737) (dated 1705 in the original document); Anon., *Atlas Geographus: or, A Compleat System of Geography, (Ancient and Modern) for Africa . . .* , IV (London, 1714), 115; [Frederick Calvert], *A Tour to the East in the Years 1763 and 1764: With Remarks on the City of Constantinople and the Turks . . .* (London, 1767), 71–72, 74. On De Bruyn, see Jan de Hond, "Cornelius de Bruijn (1652–1726/7): A Dutch Painter in the East," in Geert Jan van Gelder and Ed de Moor, eds., *Eastward Bound: Dutch Ventures and Adventures in the Middle East* (Amsterdam, 1994), 51–81. Calvert, the sixth baron Baltimore, called Lord Baltimore, wrote about slave markets in the eastern Mediterranean from a vantage of admiration rather than any sense of moral repugnance. Indeed, Baltimore was known for keeping his own seraglio and was eventually tried for rape. On his life and career, see Susan Lamb, *Bringing Travel Home to England: Tourism, Gender, and Imaginative Literature in the Eighteenth Century* (Newark, Dela., 2009), 46–47. For a brief overview of sex and labor trafficking out of the Caucasus during the eighteenth and nineteenth centuries, see the first chapter of Philippa Lesley Hetherington's doctoral dissertation, "Victims of the Social Temperament: Prostitution, Migration, and the Traffic in Women from Imperial Russia and the Soviet Union, 1885–1935" (Ph.D. diss., Harvard University, 2014).

20. [Calvert], *A Tour to the East,* 56.

*One Stories.* Grammars of race crop up sporadically throughout *Arabian Nights Entertainments* in connection with trafficked slaves. The phrase *white slaves* is introduced when the sultan meets the young Aladdin and his mother, who are seeking the hand of the sultan's daughter in marriage. "I cannot marry her without some valuable Consideration," begins the sultan, "I will fulfil my Promise as soon as he [Aladdin] shall send me forty Basons of . . . gold . . . carried by the like number of Black Slaves, who shall be led by as many young and handsome white Slaves, all dress'd magnificently." The whiteness of these slaves is a sign, not so much of noble lineage, but of the power of the market to commodify people, turning them into exotic and superlative things within the sultan's kingdom. "The Dress of each Slave was so rich, both for the Stuff and Jewels, that those who were Dealers in them, valued each at no less than a Million of Money." In the text, the white slaves' finery extends beyond jewels and clothing to their very bodies. "Besides the Justness of the Dress the . . . delicate Shape of each Slave was unparallell'd." These slaves' value is expressed, not in their power to labor or in their monetary worth at ransom, but in their perceived beauty and appearance as objects of rare art reflecting the prestige, wealth, and erudition of their royal masters.[21]

The publication of the English language translation of Galland's *Arabian Nights Entertainments* complicates any straightforward genealogy of white grammar as a proxy for Christian or European identities. White skin color had already been receiving commentary before Atlantic racial slavery was organized, but not solely in association with European or Christian subjects (see Appendix B, Table 12). The prominence of white grammar as a sign of both beauty and its commodification before 1700 suggests that whiteness had long been associated with the practice of trafficking wealthy non-Christian slaves. In 1647, French writer Marin le Roy Gomberville published *Polexander,* a five-volume history of a fictional protagonist from Greece who, unlike Alexander, sets his sights on Africa, rather than Asia, as a proving ground for his imperial ambitions. A sentimental romance rather than a travel guide, *Polexander* is

---

21. [Antoine] Galland, trans., *Les mille et une nuit* . . . , 12 vols. (Paris, 1704–1717), X, 54–55, 58; *Arabian Nights Entertainments; Consisting of One Thousand and One Stories . . . Translated into French from the Arabian MSS. by M. Galland* . . . , X (London, 1721), 23–24, 26, 26–27. See also Dwight F. Reynolds, "*A Thousand and One Nights:* A History of the Text and Its Reception," in Roger Allen and D. S. Richards, eds., *Arabic Literature in the Post-Classical Period* (New York, 2006), 276–279; Rida Hawari, "Antoine Galland's Translation of 'The Arabian Nights,'" *Revue de littérature comparée,* LIV, no. 2 (April 1980), 150–164; and C. Knipp, "The *Arabian Nights* in England: Galland's Translation and Its Successors," *Journal of Arabic Literature,* V (1974), 46–48.

peopled with numerous white subjects, most of them non-Christian white slaves with exotic forms of power and beauty. The first white slave to appear in *Polexander* is named Zelopa, a slave from Guinea who is "so fondly amorous, that . . . 'twas necessarily believed she had bewitched" the protagonist Zabaim. Later, Zabaim is saved by a valiant "white slave" who shields him from an attack by the villain, Perseus. In a scene that evokes Oroonoko's final moments, Perseus subsequently "fell on that trusty and generous Slave, ran him through, and . . . hack'd him in peices." Here, in the dismemberment of a valiant slave defending the nobility of the central protagonist, it is possible to discover central elements of Behn's novel forty years before it was published.[22]

The challenge of distinguishing between transactional values involving skin color on the one hand and family pedigrees of nobility on the other were merged in fictional portrayals of Mediterranean white slaves across the seventeenth and eighteenth centuries. Increasingly, white slaves were becoming associated with royal families and lineages. Yet there was little evidence in either Gomberville's romance or Galland's translation of the *Arabian Nights* that white slaves should be emancipated or rescued from their enslavement. To the contrary, their value was resolutely transactional and expensive rather than spiritual, a sign of their masters' nobility and aristocratic pedigrees.

Trafficking people, whether in the Mediterranean or the Atlantic, helped organize imperial discourse about British mercantilism after 1690. White grammar not only made the transactional value of trafficked bodies in the Atlantic and Mediterranean—whether felons, soldiers, servants, or sex slaves—visible, but also made possible methods for comparing and mapping similarities and differences among them. In the Mediterranean, discourse about Muslim white slaves created an opportunity for English actors to make the

---

22. [M. Le Roy Sieur de Gomberville], *The History of Polexander: In Five Books* (London, 1647), Book 1, 46, Book 3, 120. On the origins of *Arabian Nights*, see Reynolds, "A Thousand and One Nights," in Allen and Richards, eds., *Arabic Literature*, 270–272; and Eva Sallis, *Sheherazade through the Looking Glass: The Metamorphosis of the Thousand and One Nights* (Richmond, Va., 1999), 18–42. On the role of Iberian and Mediterranean anti-Black racism in shaping the Atlantic slave trade, see David Brion Davis, *Inhuman Bondage: The Rise and Fall of Slavery in the New World* (New York, 2006), 75. On the historical connections between abolitionism and Islamic antislavery, see Felicity A. Nussbaum, "Slavery, Blackness, and Islam: *The Arabian Nights* in the Eighteenth Century," in Brycchan Carey and Peter J. Kitson, eds., *Slavery and the Cultures of Abolition: Essays Marking the Bicentennial of the British Abolition Act of 1807* (Cambridge, 2007), 150–172. On the centrality of gender to hierarchies of enslavement within the *1001 Nights*, see Daniel Beaumont, *Slave of Desire: Sex, Love, and Death in The 1001 Nights* (Madison, N.J., 2002), 42–66.

trafficking of non-European actors legible, conjuring romances. This traffic in white bodies predated the emergence of European or British imperialism in the Mediterranean and suggests how white grammar shaped unequal power relations between Christian and Muslim polities before the early modern era. Mediterranean white slaves signified the power and prestige of noble lineages within Eastern polities, however, not the value of a cross-cultural whiteness that Muslim sultans necessarily shared with English audiences. Only when whiteness emerged as a way of renaming the Mediterranean traffic in Christian bodies during the early nineteenth century would the mischief and violence associated with Orientalism fully take hold, a historical moment centuries after stories about white slaves began circulating between the Atlantic and the Mediterranean. The work of another early eighteenth-century English novelist, Daniel Defoe, helps to illuminate the consequences of that geographic and ideological exchange.[23]

## Trafficking Mediterranean Fictions in the Atlantic: Daniel Defoe's *Robinson Crusoe*

Like Aphra Behn, Daniel Defoe has been heralded as the inventor of the English novel and remembered for the creation of a singular, adventuring male protagonist, Robinson Crusoe. That figure has had a larger-than-life impact on British culture since he first emerged from the pages of Defoe's fiction in 1719, becoming a representative of England's commercial and imperial culture over the ensuing eighteenth and nineteenth centuries. Defoe, in turn, has been heralded as one of the architects of an Atlantic imagination, a writer whose narratives have become foundational to an understanding of the peculiar mixture of freedom and coercion in Britain's expanding Atlantic empire. Like Behn, Defoe's full historical significance is best revealed by locating his work within its immediate historical and geographic context.

Defoe published *The Adventures of Robinson Crusoe* in 1719 during a watershed moment in the history of Britain's political economy, one in which mercantile economic power—and its limits—were made visible the world over through expanding networks of trafficked goods and people. Unbridled optimism in the promise of commercial trafficking helped grow British might but also precipitated a dramatic collapse in British finance shortly after the

---

23. Edward W. Said, *Orientalism* (New York, 1978). Among many critics of Said's work, Linda Colley highlights problems of ahistoricity. See Colley, *Captives* (New York, 2002), 102, 132, 316.

publication of Defoe's first novel. In 1720, the South Sea Bubble bankrupted the British government and thousands of English investors when the royally chartered South Sea Company sought to monopolize slave trafficking in the southern hemisphere and sold stock to the British public. That effort unleashed a speculative frenzy that would briefly make thousands of British actors gleeful beneficiaries of the horrific violence known as the African slave trade. When the bubble burst and royal investigations commenced in 1721, inquisitors pursued stories of corrupt transactions to the very highest seats of power in Parliament and the court of George I. Nonetheless, few if any investigators questioned the corrupt premise of trafficking people to create English commercial wealth and freedoms. When the British government and thousands of investors who had supported the South Sea Company's investments resumed their cozy relations after 1721, slavery and trafficking across the Atlantic had become more important than ever to Britain's imperial aspirations.[24]

To understand why the financial carnage unleashed by the South Sea Company did not yield a more prolonged inquiry into the violence and coercion that underwrote that speculation, it is important to examine the relationship between slavery and geography in Defoe's popular fiction. Although Britain's imperial aspirations were indeed resolutely focused on the Atlantic slave trade by 1719, the Atlantic was nonetheless a relatively new focal point, one that had only recently displaced the Mediterranean, with its enduring commercial and political quagmires, as the geographic heart of Britain's imperial aspirations. Defoe's narrative explains at one level how that geographic rethinking came

---

24. Scholars have devoted considerable attention to Defoe's literary accomplishments. He is credited with writing not only one of the first English novels but also creating protagonists who embodied the new commercial ethos at the heart of Great Britain's expanding commercial empire. Laura Doyle has largely ignored Defoe's Mediterranean starting points, however, focusing instead on the Atlantic Ocean and the African slave trade in defining the meaning of Robinson Crusoe's adventures. "What Defoe's narrative makes quietly clear," writes Doyle, "is that the slave trade—and the African person's body—enables the merging of these stories. The African is the laborer through which the Anglo-Saxon Protestant on the Atlantic turns loss into profit and captivity into redemption." See Doyle, *Freedom's Empire*, 188. The South Sea Bubble has invited diverse investigations, some on its impact on the history of finance and others on literature. For the former, see Richard Dale, *The First Crash: Lessons from the South Sea Bubble* (Princeton, 2004); and Patrick Walsh, *The South Sea Bubble and Ireland: Money, Banking, and Investment, 1690–1721* (Suffolk, U.K., 2014). On the latter, see Silke Stratmann, *Myths of Speculation: The South Sea Bubble and 18th-Century English Literature* (Munich, Germany, 2000).

to be. Knitting both seascapes into a larger imperial whole was a narrative as well as a conceptual imperative.

In *The Adventures of Robinson Crusoe,* recounted in the first-person, Defoe transformed Mediterranean captivity by transposing it into an Atlantic context in which the shipwrecked hero, Crusoe, replots the relationship between skin color, traffic, and English freedom. Crusoe's adventures are significant not only because Defoe effectively used antitrafficking to ratify both slavery and colonialism in the Atlantic but because he also did so with Mediterranean tropes. Such geographic connections did not resolve tensions within British political economy, but they minimized the anxieties brought about by a mercantile empire built on human trafficking. Defoe's narrative imagined and helped map market values across Great Britain's empire, a process that was as tension filled as it was geographically expansive. Robinson Crusoe's adventures provided one set of answers to the riddle of how an empire of trafficking might remain true to the nation's antislavery political inheritance.[25]

Slavery is the essential point of narrative departure and transformation for Defoe's famous protagonist. Even before Crusoe sets out on his life's journey at sea, his father admonishes him to avoid being "sold to the Life of Slavery for daily Bread." Yet slavery is more than a parental admonition for Defoe, the thing to be avoided. It is also the institution that animates Crusoe's ambitions as a sailor, as he hopes to become "a *Guiney* Trader" on his maiden voyage. Crusoe's plans are not immediately realized because a *"Turkish* Rover of *Sallee"* captures him and his crew and reduces Crusoe from being "a Merchant to a miserable Slave." A would-be slave trader now facing indefinite slavery, Crusoe expresses confusion about his new circumstances: "I was perfectly over-whelmed." Enslavement and trafficking inform the subsequent narrative transitions in Defoe's novel that take Crusoe from the coast of Africa to Brazil and later to a deserted island in the Caribbean from where he is finally rescued from isolation and returned to England. Crusoe manages to escape from his slavery with an enslaved Muslim boy from Spain named Xury, who

---

25. Roxann Wheeler has argued that Defoe's *Robinson Crusoe* exemplifies the "multiplicity" of cultural and political differences within Britain's empire in 1720, underscoring the centrality of Christianity and religion as "the most significant category of difference that excuses European domination and establishes the conditions for enslavement" of non-Christians. To support her argument, Wheeler focuses on where Crusoe's story begins with his surprising capture by a Sallee Rover and his subsequent enslavement in Morocco, one of the main locales for Christian slaves in the Mediterranean region. See Wheeler, *The Complexion of Race: Categories of Difference in Eighteenth-Century British Culture* (Philadelphia, 2000), 59.

becomes a trusted collaborator as they travel down the coast of Africa. Their common emancipatory journey soon collides, however, with the transactional premise behind human trafficking and freedom. Having been rescued at sea by a Portuguese slaving ship, Crusoe decides to sell Xury to the Portuguese ship captain. Crusoe confesses to feeling remorse about that act, yet he insists it is in everyone's best interest, a humanitarian resolution to their shared predicament. Xury was already a slave, after all, and Crusoe had treated him with love and appreciation. Just so did Defoe ratify the guiding rationale for Great Britain's blue water empire that an empire based on trafficking people could expand humanitarian feeling and English liberty simultaneously.[26]

Crusoe's rescue by a Portuguese slave trader carries him further into the morally fraught geography of Atlantic slavery as he travels to Brazil and there begins to make his fortune as an owner of a slave plantation growing tobacco and sugar. That accomplishment thrives, the narrator informs readers, because of Crusoe's skills as a commercial actor, as he sells a large supply of *"English* manufactures, such as Cloath, Stuffs, Bays, and things . . . to a very great Advantage," quadrupling the value of his "first Cargo." Crusoe then uses his profits to traffic the people building Britain's plantation economy. "I bought me a *Negro* Slave, and an *European* Servant also," Crusoe narrates. He becomes a successful planter but a restless one, and he soon returns to the slave trade as the captain of a slave-trading vessel, sailing back across the Atlantic to Africa. That journey ends, like his initial quest to become a *"Guiney* Trader," disastrously, with him being shipwrecked during a hurricane, the lone survivor on a deserted island in the Caribbean. Defoe orchestrates Crusoe's eventual rescue through a Native man named Friday, an individual Defoe represents as a kind of natural slave. "At length he came close to me, and then he kneel'd down again, kiss'd the Ground, and laid his Head upon the Ground . . . ; this, it seems, was in Token of swearing to be my Slave for ever." Slavery and enslaved people not only propel Crusoe on his initial journey but redeem him from isolation, framing key turning points in Defoe's narrative.[27]

The centrality of slavery to the structure of *The Adventures of Robinson Crusoe* does not mean that Defoe was solely focused on the Atlantic slave trade. For Defoe and many of his readers, English slavery in the Mediterranean

---

26. [Daniel Defoe], *The Life and Strange Surprizing Adventures of Robinson Crusoe . . .* , 3d. ed. (London, 1719), 4, 19, 20.

27. Ibid., 19, 42, 241.

transposed and resolved tensions about the meaning of slavery within Great Britain's expanding empire. The most common references to slaves or slavery in the novel are to English slaves in the Mediterranean. When slaves are cited without modifiers in Defoe's text, they are usually Englishmen or Europeans held as slaves in North Africa. African slaves in the Americas, by contrast, are consistently modified by grammars of skin color, to distinguish them from English slaves or simply the slaves who labored in North Africa, men whose geographic origins remain unspecified. Although Atlantic bondage dramatically shapes Crusoe's narrative, it is the prominence of English slavery, and Crusoe's suffering, that Defoe used to frame the ethical significance and meaning of Atlantic slavery.[28]

It would be tempting to read Defoe's juxtaposition of enslaved Englishmen and enslaved Africans as an early form of race trafficking, a comparative assessment that would become commonplace by the middle of the nineteenth century. Indeed, Defoe's weighting of English slavery over racial slavery in the Americas, which he almost never mentions by name, exemplifies a key tenet of white supremacist ideology: the fixation on white victimhood to justify violence against any and all non-white actors, no matter how historically victimized or oppressed. Yet conflating whiteness and Englishness in 1720 obscures the specific work that skin color accomplishes in Defoe's celebrated text, anachronistically imposing habits of racial thought prominent by the early nineteenth century onto the early eighteenth century. Although Friday would eventually be portrayed as having Black skin in reprintings of Defoe's novel, Friday possesses uncertain racial features in Defoe's original text of 1719. Defoe's initial description of Friday evokes Oroonoko, who possessed both dark skin and European features. Defoe writes that Friday "seem'd to have something very Manly in his Face, and yet he had all the Sweetness and Softness of an *European* in his Countenance too, especially when he smil'd. His Hair was long and black, not curl'd like Wool.... The Colour of his Skin was not quite black, but very tawny, and yet not of an ugly yellow nauseous Tawny, as the *Brazilians*, and *Virginians*, and other Natives of *America* are, but of a bright Kind of a dun Olive Colour, that had in it something very agreeable, tho' not very easy to describe." Although Defoe leaves the precise

---

28. Scholar Laura Doyle has argued that slavery was the central political and moral problem that Defoe confronted in his famous novel, a theme that has nonetheless been "consistently overlooked" by critics focused on his life in solitude on an isolated island. See Doyle, *Freedom's Empire*, 188.

geographic origin of Friday's genealogical nobility unspecified, the closest prototype for his countenance is Mediterranean, a figure plucked from some of the sentimental romances set in Barbary during the seventeenth century.[29]

Nowhere are the uneven meanings associated with skin color more apparent than in Defoe's use of white grammar. At no point during Crusoe's recounting of slavery in North Africa does Defoe describe his protagonist as white, an absence characteristic of the broader discourse about the traffic in religious subjects in the Mediterranean before 1800. When white grammar does emerge in Defoe's novel, it occurs in the Atlantic context, where Crusoe is marooned, and in the reported speech of Friday, who describes Crusoe's heavily bearded appearance. "He told me, that up a great Way beyond the Moon . . . there dwelt white bearded Men, like me, and pointed to my great Whiskers, which I mention'd before; and that they had kill'd *much Mans*, that was his Word: By all which I understood, he mean'd the *Spaniards*." As in travel writing of the early eighteenth century, white grammar emerged, not in connection with the rights and privileges of Christian actors, but in the speech of a non-citizen subject, Friday. Defoe deployed white grammar from the outside looking in as a sign, ironically, of Crusoe's alienness. When Crusoe uses white grammar, he mimics the grammatically broken form that Friday articulates, as when learning about the existence of numerous Spaniards not far from the island: *"Friday describ'd the Boat to me well enough; but brought me better to understand him, when he added with some Warmth, we save the white Mans from drown:* Then I presently ask'd him, if there was any white Mans, as he call'd them, in the Boat: *Yes,* he said, *the Boat full of white Mans.*" By ventriloquizing Friday's white grammar in the mouth of his protagonist, Defoe valorized the colonial project and cultural hierarchies that Crusoe and Friday's relationship epitomize. At the same time, he also expressed deep ambivalence about the ostensible benefits of white skin color for English subjects. Defoe did not invest Crusoe's cultural superiority in a taxonomy of skin color because he did not have to. Defoe accomplished that work by relying on older cultural referents and binaries long associated with trafficking and commerce in both the Mediterranean and Atlantic regions: Christianity and savagery.[30]

Perhaps the most important innovation within Defoe's novel is that he placed trafficking in both the Mediterranean and Atlantic worlds within a single narrative and conceptual framework, effectively encouraging compara-

---

29. [Defoe], *Life and Strange Surprizing Adventures*, 243.
30. Ibid., 255, 264.

tive assessments of labor, human trafficking, and freedom within each locale. That comparative framework expanded the utility of skin color in making cultural and geographic comparisons but stopped short of celebrating white skin color. Like Behn, Defoe was quite skeptical of the rabble associated with whiteness, strongly supporting the policy of transportation for both convicts and indigent residents of England and Ireland to New World plantations. Defoe's commitment to England's empire and the wisdom of metropolitan rule made his *Adventures of Robinson Crusoe* an exemplary text, plotting and revising ideological tensions central to Britain's mercantile expansion. In the friendship between Crusoe and Friday, Defoe justified the commercial and political freedoms underpinning Britain's empire of trafficking.

Defoe used his next two novels, *Moll Flanders* and *The History and Remarkable Life of the Truly Honourable Col. Jacque*, to elaborate the class-based anxieties so vexing to colonial and metropolitan authorities during the early eighteenth century. Indeed, both novels comment directly on the public controversies attending the passage of the 1718 Transportation Act. That law expanded and systematized the removal of prisoners from British prisons to New World plantations, a reform that Defoe staunchly defended as a humane and just alternative to long years of incarceration in British jails. Transportation was "a fair offer of Heaven to such Creatures to begin," Defoe wrote, "not only a new Condition of Life, but even a new Life itself." The Transportation Act did not expand the state's capacity to traffic or enslave its citizenry, Defoe contended, but rather represented a solution to the delicate problem of subjecting convicted felons to a lifetime of hard labor, a penal custom that "raised fears of excessive state power," as historian A. Roger Ekirch has put it, and "smacked to many of slavery." If lifelong convicts could be redeemed through a deliberate process of labor reform, perhaps so-called domestic slavery could be avoided and transformed.[31]

Defoe defended transportation as a humane policy, even as he relied on the language of slavery to describe it in his novels. Like Behn, Defoe appropriated arguments associated with servant antislavery to forge a spirited defense of both the slave trade and servant traffic. That alchemy is most visible in the preface Defoe wrote to *Moll Flanders*, where he reveals the novel's purpose clearly:

---

31. Daniel Defoe, "On the Return to England of Transported Felons," in William Lee, [ed.], *Daniel Defoe: His Life and Recently Discovered Writings* . . . , III (Hildesheim, Germany, 1968), 96, also quoted in Gabriel Cervantes, "Convict Transportation and Penitence in *Moll Flanders*," *ELH*, LVIII, no. 2 (Summer 2011), 315; A. Roger Ekirch, *Bound for America: The Transportation of British Convicts to the Colonies, 1718–1755* (Oxford, 1987), 20.

"Transportation . . . will go a great way to deliver . . . [and] will in time raise the meanest Creature to appear again in the World, and give him a new Cast for his Life." At first glance, the story of Moll Flanders seems an especially unconvincing vehicle for Defoe's polemic. Born to parents convicted as felons and living in Newgate prison, Moll lives a life that demonstrates much of what colonial and metropolitan actors deemed unruly and dangerous about so-called malefactors and white servants in the Colonial State Papers. Although the most threatening dimension of white servants—their capacity to combine with African slaves—is conspicuously absent from Defoe's fiction, Moll embodies all that colonial and metropolitan elites feared among the "sweepings of the jails." The connections between Moll's sexual independence and her criminality epitomize Defoe's distrust of female white servants' sexuality, suspicions mirrored in colonial laws policing servants' sexuality. She lived "Twelve Year a *Whore*, five times a *Wife* (whereof once to her own Brother), Twelve Year a Thief, Eight Year a Transported *Felon* in *Virginia*," readers are told in the book's subtitle. Moll's ultimate redemption to a life of truthfulness and honesty in North America, where she "at last grew *Rich* . . . and died a *Penitent*," exemplifies Defoe's argument that transportation was morally beneficent, an alternative to the charges of domestic slavery that critics of indentured servitude, kidnapping, and transportation had long leveled against British authorities.[32]

Defoe deployed white servants much as colonial and metropolitan administrators had during the early eighteenth century, as a grammar associated with regulating and policing the behavior of unruly whites whose status as trafficked actors made them dangerous and vexing to political elites. Like Behn, Defoe also focused on white female actors to intensify the political work that white grammar accomplished on behalf of elite planners and the architects of British colonial power. The emergence of white women in the

---

32. Daniel Defoe, *The Fortunes and Misfortunes of the Famous Moll Flanders* . . . (London, 1721), title page, preface, xi; Deputy Governor, Council, and Assembly of Barbados to the Lords of Trade and Plantations, Sept. 14, 1685, CO 1/58, 56, enclosure 1, CSP, PRO, The National Archives, Kew, U.K. ("sweepings"). Jean-Christophe Agnew has discussed Defoe's fiction, particularly the portrayal of Moll Flanders, as exemplifying how an imaginary of the market became disconnected from specific places or geographies, a thing as far-flung as the character of Moll herself. See Agnew, *Worlds Apart: The Market and the Theater in Anglo-American Thought, 1550–1750* (Cambridge, 1986). Agnew, however, does not consider the significance of slavery or of unfree labor markets more generally. Trafficking people exemplified the key political instability within eighteenth-century markets, a relationship of exchange making that, like theater, necessitated displays of bodies and their true values to function.

discourse about servitude and transportation did not signal the arrival of a politics of white victimhood but an elaboration of the problem that trafficked whites were causing across Britain's empire. Moll Flanders's criminal behavior and capacity to traffic her way to wealth expressed misogynistic anxieties about the power of female servants to subvert their masters' authority as well as broader fears about how trafficked actors might subvert and unmask the fictions of a blue water empire. Servants, male and female, were viewed as both building blocks of empire and potential enemies within that project, as menacing to English sovereignty as the threats posed by captive English sailors trafficked in the Mediterranean.

Defoe extended his defense of imperial trafficking policies in his novel *The History and Remarkable Life of the Truly Honourable Col. Jacque*. The hero, Jack, is an army deserter, pickpocket, and convicted felon who finds his way to the Americas. Jack's troubles begin when he falls in with a group of young men who are offered passage to London from their native Scotland. Jack and his peers are then tricked into boarding a ship by "that Kidnapping Rogue *Gilliman*," who plies them with alcohol and false promises. Having been "Trappan'd ... by wicked Merchants," Jack protests his confinement using the language of servant antislavery, as generations of petitioners had done before him. Jack asserts that he "told the Captain" he and his fellow servants "were not People to be sold for Slaves." Despite his protest, Jack is sold to a master of a large tobacco plantation in Maryland, where he works alongside white servants and enslaved Africans, both groups governed by an overseer's horsewhip.[33]

Rather than condemning the inhumanity of the servant trade and its merging with the convict transportation system, Defoe used his protagonist's success in North America to defend both the servant trade and the African slave trade. Through a series of highly improbable interventions, Jack is befriended by his master, who makes him an overseer. Initially required to use a horsewhip to "last the Slaves and Servants" under him "when they proved Negligent, or Quarrelsome, or in short were guilty of any Offense," Jack improvises an allegedly humanitarian solution to the task of maintaining order. Instead

---

33. Daniel Defoe, *The History and Remarkable Life of the Truly Honourable Col. Jacque, Commonly Call'd Col. Jack, Who Was Born a Gentleman, Put Prentice to a Pickpocket, Was Six and Twenty Years a Thief, and Then Kidnapp'd to Virginia* ... (London, 1723), 141, 142, 145. On Defoe's view of transportation as a policy and its role in shaping how he imagined and narrated indentured servitude in the Americas, see Dennis Todd, *Defoe's America* (Cambridge, 2010). Todd has argued that "Defoe's misrepresentation of indentured servitude is symptomatic of larger tensions and contradictions in his thinking" (x).

of whipping his charges, Jack grants two African slaves a pardon after first promising to whip them twice daily for not working hard enough. This act of performative mercy not only creates a more joyful plantation of slaves and servants, readers are told, but eventually leads Jack's former master to set him up on a plantation of his own, replete with happy slaves and servants. Initially reluctant to whip his former peers, Jack soon defends its necessity. "Whipping the *Negro* Slaves," he argues, "was not so much owing to the Tyranny, and Passion, and Cruelty of the *English,* as has been reported. . . . But that it is owing to the Brutallity, and obstinate Temper of the *Negroes,* who cannot be mannag'd by Kindness." Jack concludes that "if they were used with Compassion, they would Serve with Affection, as well as other Servants." Defoe plots this humane form of managing slaves as a moral progression. Humanity, for Jack, and by extension Defoe, does not reside within the community of enslaved Africans but rather with the enlightened temperament of Jack's former master, who understands that *"Negroes* were to be reason'd into things as well as other People, and it was by thus managing their Reason, that most of the Work was done."[34]

Whether notions of racial difference and the racism they engendered could be made compatible with Great Britain's antislavery inheritance remained uncertain in the 1720s. Novels harmonizing slavery, the servant trade, and commercial freedom suggested one set of answers. How trafficked Englishmen responded to these stories and what they thought about race and skin color were quite another matter. In the wake of the success of Defoe's three novels, that question gained urgency and significance, for nothing less than the author's authenticity as a truth teller was at stake. Defoe addressed that problem through his collaboration with an illiterate sailor named Robert Drury, the first Englishman to embrace the label *white slave.*

## Trafficking Whiteness:
## Robert Drury and White Slavery

The return of the sailor Robert Drury to England in 1719, after spending fifteen years in captivity on the island of Madagascar, presented a remarkable parallel to Daniel Defoe's *The Adventures of Robinson Crusoe.* When Drury

---

34. Defoe, *History and Remarkable Life of the Truly Honourable Col. Jacque,* 162, 163, 183, 190. On tensions between "servitude and self-transformation," freedom and slavery in Defoe's *History and Remarkable Life of the Truly Honourable Col. Jacque,* see Todd, *Defoe's America,* 76–117.

published his own narrative *Madagascar; or, Robert Drury's Journal during Fifteen Years Captivity on That Island* a decade later in 1729, some readers noted its striking similarities to Defoe's now-famous fiction. Indeed, generations of literary scholars presumed Drury's fantastic narrative was crafted by Defoe himself. That argument would help account for how an illiterate and young British sailor, who had forgotten how to speak English as well as read or write, could have penned such an erudite account just ten years after his return. Anthropologists studying Madagascar have confirmed the ethnographic accuracy of Drury's narrative, however, as well as historical documents detailing the life of an English sailor named Robert Drury marooned in Madagascar. Drury's narrative is perhaps best read as a collaboration between a partially literate sailor and one of England's first novelists. As such, Drury's story is not unmediated but rather a kind of oral history, filtered through Defoe's literary imagination and shaped by both men's experience with marketplaces.[35]

Why Defoe decided to tell Drury's story or what Drury sought to achieve by collaborating with him are matters of speculation and educated guesswork. As a former English naval officer, Drury was not especially wealthy. No doubt he sought financial security, the equivalent of a pension denied him during his long years in captivity, and perhaps a measure of fame by having his narrative published. The literary skills that Defoe brought to the table certainly helped sell Drury's story, though Drury's adventures were hardly the commercial success that *The Adventures of Robinson Crusoe* had become. Defoe's motives are harder to discern. Perhaps he sensed an opportunity on hearing Drury's story. The young sailor was apparently telling pieces of it in marketplaces and pubs across London. More likely, Defoe understood how Drury's life might have been already imitating art, an example he embraced. Certainly, Defoe aspired to speak and write like a sailor convincingly, and without affect. If Defoe could tell—and sell—Drury's story, what better way to honor the truth claims of his own fiction while providing a modicum of help to a maritime storyteller in distress?

---

35. For an excellent summary of the publishing history of Robert Drury's journal and the discovery of archival evidence in the 1950s that established his historical existence, see Arthur W. Secord, *Robert Drury's Journal and Other Studies* (Urbana, Ill., 1961). For skeptics who believe Defoe rather than Drury wrote it, see David Henige, "Travelling from the Truth," *Literature and History*, 3d Ser., VI, no. 2 (Autumn 1997), 89–96. For revisionists who demonstrate that Drury's journal is historically accurate, see Anne Molet-Sauvaget, *Madagascar; ou, Le journal de Robert Drury* (Paris, 1992); and Mike Parker Pearson, "Reassessing *Robert Drury's* Journal as a Historical Source for Southern Madagascar," *History in Africa*, XXIII (1996), 233–256.

The mixture of ethnographically accurate details with literary embellishments exemplifies aspirations that Defoe possessed for his novels more generally: a mixing of realistic details and truth telling with romantic subplots and Mediterranean motifs. Those combinations make Drury's narrative an especially difficult text to interpret, filled as it is with frequent references to Drury as a white slave but almost always in the third-person. The term *white slave* appears primarily in the speech of Madagascar's chiefs and masters, as if it had clear roots in the languages of Madagascar's Native peoples. What white skin color meant to the Madagascar peoples that Drury interacted with is trickier to discern. Although the slave trade had been introduced to the island more than a half century earlier by Portuguese slave traders, there are no terms for white or Black skin color in the glossary of the "Madagascar LANGUAGE" that Drury provided. The words for *white* (*sute*) and *white man* (*verzarbar*) possess no common linguistic features. The ethnographic details in Drury's narrative might have established that Drury lived in Madagascar, but it also seems quite unlikely that the term *white slave* or its equivalent was ever used there. Rather, the phrase appears to have been adopted by Defoe after Drury's return to England.[36]

Defoe's embellishments enrich the significance of white grammar in Drury's narrative. Like Behn, Defoe used white grammar to articulate a sharp critique of the racism of white people in England. That effort was enhanced by the distance between Madagascar and England, a vantage that enabled Defoe to give voice to what had long been visible in English travel writing but rarely articulated, the perspective of non-Christian whiteness so prominent in the observations of European travel writers across the seventeenth and early eighteenth centuries. As lapsed or skeptical Christians, Drury and Defoe were both unencumbered by the constraints associated with English slaves seeking redemption by religious authorities in North Africa. The narrator did not seek any public penance for having forsaken Christianity. To the contrary, Drury's experience as a non-Christian emboldened him in decrying injustices

---

36. Robert Drury, *Madagascar: or, Robert Drury's Journal, during Fifteen Years Captivity on That Island . . .* (London, 1729), 203, 457, 464. For a discussion of the ethnographic accuracy of Drury's journal, see Pearson, "Reassessing *Robert Drury's* Journal," *History in Africa*, XXIII (1996), 233–256. See also Colley, *Captives*, 14–15. Distinctions of skin color certainly existed across the Sahel of Africa long before the establishment of the Atlantic slave trade, though there is little linguistic evidence of that pattern in Madagascar before the late eighteenth century. On the opportunities and challenges of historicizing race across North Africa and the Middle East, see Bruce S. Hall, "Reading Race in Africa and the Middle East," *Antropologia*, VII, no. 1 (2020), 33–44.

he perceived in Great Britain. After praising the sincerity of his master, Ry-Nanno, Drury remarks, "I wish, that our Christian Priests, who build so much on a more than ordinary Knowledge of God's Will, would make their Lives Examples, as his was; and teach Princes, and others too, to be in Reality so truly just, honourable, and good as this gallant black Prince was in all his Actions; and yet I question not, but he must be call'd an illiterate Heathen." Like Behn, Drury interrogates the cultural and racial superiority of English people. "We white People have a very contemptible, and mean Opinion of these Blacks; and a great One of ourselves," comments Drury, "but if an impartial Comparison was to be made of their Virtue, I think, the Negroe Heathens will excel the white Christians." Like Southerne's Imoinda or Defoe's Friday, the protagonist critiques the notion of a cross-class white identity from the outside looking in, as a renegade who rejects the idea that commoners and nobility should be lumped together.[37]

Although born a commoner, Drury aspired to become a nobleman within Madagascar, a status he sought to claim by trafficking others. When Drury helps his owner and chief, Deaan Mevarrow, defeat a rival prince in battle, he is awarded the defeated chief's daughter as a prize. Drury promptly falls in love with her and arranges to be married to her, even though both were enslaved. "SOME of my Readers will, perhaps, wonder how I could so passionately love a black Woman," Drury begins, "but let them consider, I had been several Years in the Country, and they were become natural to me." "Then," Drury continues, "she was very handsome, of a middle Stature, streight and exactly shap'd, her Features regular, and her Skin soft, fine, and delicate, as any Ladies in *Europe*." Drury's critique of white beauty relies on a detailed description of the young princess's body, one that resembles a slave auction. Drury, or perhaps Defoe, sought to efface the uncomfortable fact that Drury had kidnapped his wife by insisting, improbably and awkwardly, that his marriage was consensual. "I did not design to make a Slave of her, but a *Valle*, or Wife," Drury explains, before then arranging a marriage ceremony for himself and his wife as if they were free.[38]

Drury's narrative was hardly the first English travel narrative to harness the idea of romantic love to a larger project of imperial expansion. In so doing, his story illustrates an important but often neglected fact within narratives of trafficked actors: traffic in women organized the stakes of war and exchanges among men. Rather than acknowledge that foundational premise, Drury

---

37. Drury, *Madagascar*, 211, 229–230.
38. Ibid., 228.

uses the fiction of their consensual marriage to assert his own proprietary knowledge of his wife's culture and racial identity, effectively trafficking her blackness as his own. After deciding that he will marry the captured prince's daughter, Drury reassures his bride's mother that he "would take more Care of her than of myself, and tho' I was not a black Man, I had as tender a Heart as any black Man whatever." Drury's dubious claim to possess blackness is not contingent on skin color but on the consequences of his allegedly consensual marriage to a Black woman. His marriage is indeed a fiction, one no more nor less powerful than those invented by Behn to make apparent the visibility of noble races. Drury's assertion that he has "as tender a Heart as any black Man" bears similarities to Behn's insistence that truly noble blackness can be known by white Europeans, even as both authors put that claim to work by critiquing the prejudices of cross-class whiteness. Drury concludes, "for they [Blacks], certainly, treat one another with more Humanity than we do." Humanity emerges in opposition to trafficking, Drury insists, even if trafficking is precisely how he acquired his beloved wife.[39]

Drury's resistance to white racism, then, does not make him immune to the benefits afforded by trafficking his or other captive's identities. Drury's fantasy of possessing a Black heart and his professed ability to see the truly noble value of his wife both ironically rely on a transactional accounting of her beauty, one that evokes the very traffic that brought her to Drury in the first place. These tensions between love and value, traffic and humanity, racial beauty and racialized rights could not be contained within the improbable fiction of true love that Drury and Defoe offered their readers. When Drury acquires a chance to escape his cruel master, Deaan Mevarrow, he urges his wife to flee with him. Yet when she refuses, Drury makes clear his intention to leave his beloved behind, despite his former promises. Drury recognizes the unequal consequences of his decision: "But to part with her, and leave her in Slavery, and perhaps, to be ill-us'd on my Account, was a mortifying Stroak to me, for I lov'd her sincerely." Nevertheless, Drury concludes, leaving her behind was "a Necessity."[40]

---

39. Ibid., 225, 230. On Drury's insistence on being truly in love, see Wheeler, *Complexion of Race*, 208. On the political work of desire within colonial encounters and the travel literatures they produced, see Mary Louise Pratt, *Imperial Eyes: Travel Writing and Transculturation* (London, 1992). Pratt's brief description of Defoe's expropriation of sailors' skills in crafting global knowledge is especially useful in assessing how Defoe might have viewed his collaboration with or ventriloquism of Drury's life story. See ibid., 15, 29, 30.

40. Drury, *Madagascar*, 256. On the careers of radical abolitionists Gerritt Smith and James McCune Smith, see John Stauffer, *The Black Hearts of Men: Radical Abolitionists and the Transformation of Race* (Cambridge, Mass., 2001), 1.

Over the ensuing narrative, Drury makes clear why abandoning his wife was a "Necessity." Her continued presence with him would have precluded his return to England, the very nation he so strenuously critiqued as a white slave with a "Black" heart. The political meaning of Drury's white skin changes as he moves from the more isolated southern half of Madagascar, where he had been shipwrecked, to the north, where pirates and imperial navies dock. As the value of Drury's white skin changes, so does the meaning and prominence of slave trafficking to the varied local chiefs who own Drury. At the beginning of Drury's captivity, prize taking among Madagascar's peoples primarily reflects local geographic desires and needs. All the enslaved men and women captured by Deaan Mevarrow work for their new masters. Captives perform household chores, such as digging yams, cooking, and cleaning, while stolen cattle are butchered or added to existing herds. Few captives are sold or become fungible. Captives are trafficked for labor or for diplomatic purposes, not for ransom or market values.

By the end of Drury's account of his fifteen-year slavery in Madagascar, the purpose of war and captive taking has shifted to meet the growing demands of a transatlantic slave trade. Taking captives remains the object of war, but now captives' values are market based, part of a much larger oceanic traffic in European goods that slave traders bring to Madagascar. "This being the general Custom all over the *Island*, the King of each Place makes Terms, and settles one universal Price, to which all the People are oblig'd to conform; and this renders Trading very easy, and free from Quarrels and Disturbances." The prices established by Madagascar's local rulers were not, in fact, universal, as local polities struggled for advantage with one another by exploiting access to the slave trade and slave traders. The significance of an international slave market, however, meant that older traditions of prize taking now had to conform to newer notions of a universal price. The belief that a universal price for enslaved captives minimized war was not unique to Drury's narrative but pervaded metropolitan discourse about the slave trade. To John Locke, humanitarian and market values were not antithetical to each other but one and the same.[41]

That ideological starting point is manifest in the ways Drury's labor changes as he moves closer to outposts shaped by the African slave trade. As

---

41. Drury, *Madagascar*, 430. For John Locke's proslavery views, see Davis, *Problem of Slavery*, 118–121. For a more nuanced reading of Locke's distinctions between slavery and tyranny, see Mary Nyquist, *Arbitrary Rule: Slavery, Tyranny, and the Power of Life and Death* (Chicago, 2013), 326–328.

he nears sites of slave trafficking, his view of trafficking and the humanity of market transactions becomes more beneficent. In southern Madagascar, Drury is tasked with agricultural labor devoid of any transactional value. He spends his time "looking after Cattle, digging of wild Yams, and improving of Honey." He forages for his own survival and that of his master, who confiscates all that he gathers. His second master, Rer Vove, charges Drury with martial duties, giving him "a Blunderbuss" and making him "a Guardian over several of my late Country-folks, bidding me shoot any who should attempt to run away." Drury has become an overseer, in effect, not on a plantation but on a long journey to the sea, where several of his former cohorts will be trafficked into international slave markets. Having successfully shepherded fellow slaves to market, Drury earns a promotion when he is "made Captain of my Master's Guard," a position of social and diplomatic importance. His work now requires political acumen as he helps local actors navigate the obstacles posed by transatlantic slave trading.[42]

As Drury's labor becomes more intrinsically connected to the same imperial trade routes that brought him to Madagascar, his own transactional value as a slave steadily increases. When Drury toils as Deaan Mevarrow's slave, digging wild yams and gathering honey, King Samuel attempts to acquire him by offering Mevarrow "a handsome young Man, capable of doing him more Service, or a Buccaneer Gun." Mevarrow acknowledges that the price was fair, as "a Buccaneer Gun is the Price of a Slave," but he refuses the offer, indicating, "I will not take two for him." Drury eventually escapes Mevarrow's control, only to become a slave to a new master Rer Vove, who, he states, refuses an offer of "six Slaves for me." When another local ruler closely tied to the slave trade offers to pay *"three Slaves"* for Drury, he replies that his master *"would not take three Times three for me."* Nevertheless, Drury is eventually sold, this time to Rer Moume, who finally allows Drury to be emancipated through sale to British captain William Mackett. Mackett asks Drury, *"What he must give for my Ransom?"* Drury's reply—"only a Gun for a Present, to be kept in Remembrance of me" and "Powder, and Flints, and a Case of Spirits"—should not obscure his value, however, to his African masters. For all of them, he represented improved diplomatic ties with British merchants conducting the transatlantic slave trade.[43]

Drury's experience of emancipation through sale is at first confusing both to him as well as his African peers, for he is not initially recognized as an

---

42. Drury, *Madagascar*, 214, 372, 379.
43. Ibid., 208, 209, 214, 268, 272, 280, 284, 429.

Englishman or a white man by Captain Mackett. "I star'd at them," Drury writes, "as if I had never seen a white Man cloath'd before; and what added to the Wildness of my Appearance, I was naked except the lamber, my Skin swarthy, and full of Freckles, my Hair long, and felted together, so that I really made a frightful Appearance to them." When Captain Mackett learns that Drury had been English as a boy and named Robert, Drury explains, "they soon restor'd me to an *European* form." For Drury, purchase by Mackett means a change in physical appearance as well as political identity as he experiences emancipation from slavery and returns to England as his own master. Drury's rapid transformation from a naked white slave to a well-dressed Englishman makes him unrecognizable to his former master Rer Moume. Drury's identity only becomes clear after he "kneel'd and kiss'd his [Rer Moume's] Knee." In Drury's story, the power of slave trafficking to author a transactional identity for both African slaves and Englishmen appears supreme. The Atlantic slave traffic could transform alien whiteness and, with it, the messy world of prize taking in the Mediterranean with a single, transparent transaction. For Drury's Black friends and one former master, by contrast, being purchased by Mackett means the loss of their names, transportation in irons through the Middle Passage, and a lifetime of slavery in the Americas. In the face of these radical disparities, Drury, the onetime social critic, falls silent.[44]

Yet Drury's racial and political identity nonetheless remain uncertain after his emancipation. On his return to England, he does not recognize any of the people in the village where he grew up, and he discovers that his parents have died. Soon Drury is sailing back to Madagascar, just one year after leaving, a sailor in search of someone or something. Readers learn soon enough what Drury is looking for on his return to Madagascar, not his former wife, but a boat filled with more than two hundred Black bodies sailing to North America for sale as slaves. "In ten Weeks Time we got our whole Complement of Slaves here, and sail'd from hence January 7," Drury recounts, completing his journey into the very heart of the Atlantic slave trade that had already transformed him from an alien white slave into an English slave trader. "We touched at *St. Helena* and at *Barbadoes;* from thence to *Rappahanack* River in *Virginia,* where we sold our Slaves, took in *Tobacco,* and then sail'd for *E[ngl]and,*" arriving on September 11, 1720, he reports, a speedy circumnavigation of the trafficking triangle that, more than any other route, was growing the British Empire. If Drury harbored any anxiety about his new role as a

44. Ibid., 429, 431.

central player in the slave trade in Madagascar, he did not articulate it in his narrative.[45]

Drury's transformation into a slave trader represents a strikingly different turn than the one taken by Thomas Lurting, even if both men were responding to common dilemmas generated by English power and the growing slave trade that fueled it. How and in what context might an empire built on slave trafficking emancipate its loyal subjects? How could the British Empire link its growing military might to a corresponding moral and humanitarian authority? For Lurting and Quakers like him, the solution to these questions was to disavow slavery and all forms of human trafficking, even if that meant disobeying the king's commands. For Drury, the solution was to become a humanitarian slave trader. It is possible to see an inkling of that path when Drury is still a white slave, seeking to account for why local peoples in Madagascar generally distrust white men. The reason for that, he informs readers, is their ill-treatment by pirates and by "the *French*," who "made Slaves of them" and "inverted the whole Order of their Government." A nationalist and a humanitarian, Drury explains that most French sailors are "chiefly ignorant Seamen, who pretended thus to rule" and "regarded neither Morality, Civility, nor common Decency; making no Distinction of Persons, confounding all Order, and treating every black Man as if he was a Brute." English slave traders like Drury, by contrast, "went ashoar, and took Care of some of our Slaves, who were sick," and confronted those who abused slaves.[46]

When two of Drury's female slaves are exploited by their former Black master, Drury goes "directly to the King's Brother, telling him, *I would take Care no white Men should ever come to trade there again.*" To Drury, the former white slave, the slave trade is a blessing for Madagascar's leaders, a reward to be bestowed on those who are fair to the British and their subjects and denied to those who, like Deaan Mevarrow, remain savage in their treatment of white and Black people. Drury knows that he is a humanitarian precisely because he can critique the racism of English ladies as well as the cruelty of chiefs like Deaan Mevarrow. His critiques of inhumanity in the slave trade have become blind to skin color and therefore universal, he now believes, as holistic as the workings of the true market itself. That sense of universal value is based on the erasure of Drury's Black wife, however, as well as the denial of sexual violence and trafficking endemic to the African slave trade. Just so

---

45. Ibid., 431, 454, 455.
46. Ibid., 282, 440. For a similar discussion of tensions within Drury's claim to be humanitarian, see Wheeler, *Complexion of Difference*, 222.

did Drury and Defoe's imaginings of universal values in newly raced bodies, white as well as Black, bolster notions of humanitarian intervention and humanitarian slavery simultaneously.[47]

## Conclusion

Between 1680 and 1730, a profound transformation in how colonial and metropolitan elites saw and understood the meaning of both skin color and race began to take hold across Great Britain's expanding empire. Yet the deployment of white grammar in the late seventeenth century did not constitute or create an ideology of white racial privilege for several reasons. So-called whites remained closely connected to the trafficked servants and the non-Christian aliens that imperial authorities and travel writers continued to fear and observe from afar. The English writers Aphra Behn and Daniel Defoe played a key role in transforming the work that both race and skin color performed in ratifying the political economy of mercantile capitalism. Making race visible was not a simple process of reading skin color, though, as both Behn and Defoe expressed deep misgivings about the political virtues of whites and white people more generally. Central to their narrative work were portrayals of human trafficking in which noble pedigrees were made visible at auction and the state's trafficking policies for servants, convicts, and slaves were ratified and expanded. In the process, they dramatically heightened the visibility of white skin color, linking it paradoxically to both antislavery and to ideological defenses of Britain's empire of slave trafficking.[48]

Indeed, the meanings associated with skin color and race remained inconsistent and contradictory in Behn's, Thomas Southerne's, and Defoe's writings. Did race express a genealogy of family lineage, or an identity based on the color of people's skin? That uncertainty found geographic expression in the ways writers portrayed the meaning of white skin among non-Christians living beyond England's imperial borders. For many English writers, the Mediterranean remained a generative locale for seeing white grammar in the early eighteenth century, but only for non-Christian subjects. In the Atlantic, white grammar was associated with trafficked subjects whose value was transactional rather than religious or political. English novelists and dramatists, in turn, circulated white grammar beyond its Atlantic and Mediterranean

---

47. Drury, *Madagascar*, 442, 450, 454–455.
48. See Doyle, *Freedom's Empire*, 183–184; and Wheeler, *Complexion of Race*, 173–174.

contexts, making skin color more prominent and powerful as an imperial tool for mapping imperial freedoms and aspirations. The novel intensified connections between white grammar and antislavery ideology, a twining that also displaced Christianity as the primary marker of difference and power across Great Britain's growing empire.

Ideological tensions within the form and meaning of race and skin color, however, did not diminish the political work each accomplished in Great Britain's empire of trafficking during the early eighteenth century. White grammar both expressed and contained class conflicts over trafficking policies and antislavery politics. Although Behn's *Oroonoko* might have been linked to the origins of an abolitionist movement, its political character reflected a particular understanding of class politics and hostility to white slaves that would both nurture and bedevil the abolitionist movement over the ensuing century. Aristocratic antislavery both appropriated servants' antislavery protests and erased enslaved Black women's trafficking and subjecthood. Just so did the Black Imoinda and Drury's Black wife in southern Madagascar disappear without a backward glance by white authors seeking to contrive an emancipatory racial and national identity.

How plebeian British actors understood race, antislavery, and national identity during the early eighteenth century is a far more complex story. As the first self-described English white slave in Africa, Robert Drury provides some tantalizing starting points, even as he struggled to reconcile English commitments to antislavery and the transatlantic slave trade. At the same time, his narrative should be read with caution, not only because Defoe might have been the author but also because Drury was rare in adopting white racial modifiers during the eighteenth century. Most plebeian storytellers refused to employ the language of race entirely in their accounts. More importantly, convicts, servants, and enslaved Africans continued to find ways to collaborate across Great Britain's expanding empire. It was these collaborations that stoked the fears from which the notion of a white race would emerge later in the eighteenth century.

CHAPTER FOUR

## Atlantic Slave-Servant Conspiracies

During the hot summer of 1741 in New York City, a well-publicized trial transfixed the attention of the bustling port's diverse residents. Earlier that spring, a series of fires had scorched buildings along New York's commercial waterfront, arousing suspicions of arson. More ominously, rumors circulated of a conspiracy to overthrow British colonial authority. Over the course of the next several months, eighty-eight people would be found guilty of a plot to kill hundreds of "white People" and to invite Spanish or French troops to take over the port. Thirty people would ultimately be sentenced to death by hanging, twenty-six enslaved people of African descent and four Irish immigrants, three of them indentured servants. The two principal conspirators, an African-born slave named Ceasar and an Irish saloon owner called John Hughson, were found guilty and hung in the public square even before the trial had concluded. Their dead bodies were allowed to swing for weeks after their execution, prompting a growing crowd of New Yorkers to comment on their shape and appearance. That conversation fascinated and perplexed Daniel Horsmanden, one of the three judges presiding over the trial. He went on to publish a detailed record of the investigation. Composed in an effort to silence critics who doubted the existence of a racially motivated conspiracy, his proceedings faithfully recorded all of the trial testimony as well as details of the executions.[1]

---

1. [Daniel Horsmanden], *A Journal of the Proceedings in the Detection of the Conspiracy Formed by Some White People, in Conjunction with Negro and Other Slaves, for Burning the City of New-York in America, and Murdering the Inhabitants* . . . (New York, 1744), 88. For a modern collection of the primary documents, see Serena R. Zabin, ed., *The New York City Conspiracy Trials of 1741: Daniel Horsmanden's Journal of the Proceedings with Related Documents* (Boston, 2004). On the power of fear in New York in 1741, see Jason T. Sharples, *The World That Fear Made: Slave Revolts and Conspiracy Scares in Early America* (Philadelphia, 2020), 98–122. The definitive history of the event remains Jill Lepore, *New York Burning: Liberty, Slavery, and Conspiracy in Eighteenth-Century Manhattan* (New York, 2005). See also Zabin, *Dangerous Economies: Status and Commerce in Imperial New York* (Philadelphia, 2009); Peter Charles Hoffer, *The Great New York Conspiracy of 1741: Slavery, Crime, and*

Onlookers described the spectacle of two swinging bodies, one white the other Black, as a "Miracl[e]" with troubling implications. Hughson's "Face, Neck, Hands and Feet, were of a deep shining Black, rather blacker than the Negro placed by him," Horsmanden remarked. "The Hair of *Hughson's* Beard and Neck (his Head could not be seen, for he had a Cap on) was curling like the Wool of a Negro's Beard and Head," and "the Features of his Face were of the Symmetry of a Negro Beauty; the Nose broad and flat, the Nostrils open and extended, the Mouth wide, Lips full and thick." "As to *Ceasar*, (who . . . was also of the darkest Complexion)," Horsmanden observed, "his Face was at the same Time somewhat bleach'd or turned whitish; insomuch that it occasion'd a Remark, That *Hughson* and *he* had changed Colours." "The Beholders," he concluded, "were amazed at these Appearances." Soon, all ranks came to the see the bodies "in order to be convinced by their own Eyes, of the Reality of Things so confidently reported to be, at least, wonderous Phænomenons."[2]

Yet Horsmanden could not clarify what kind of phenomenon was occurring in New York's public square. What did Hughson's and Ceasar's respective posthumous blackening and whitening signify? The success of a new racial taxonomy of skin color that could reveal innate political vices and virtues? Or were New Yorkers imagining that freedom and character were capacities that ran deeper than skin color, commanding both the living and the dead? Could bodies, whether living or decomposing, be read for clues as to their spiritual value? Horsmanden did not answer these questions, but the evident transformation of Hughson's corpse confirmed what Horsmanden had been saying about him throughout the trial, that deep down his essential character was so evil as to make him "blacker than the Negro." The body of Ceasar, however, like many living African subjects in New York, frustrated Horsmanden. Why would one of the archvillains of a conspiracy aimed at "killing . . . white People" become white after the fact? Did Ceasar's transformation mean that Horsmanden's many convictions of African slaves had been wrong, that the Africans hung in the public square were innocent? Horsmanden, in a rare moment, did not try to fix the meaning of Ceasar's and Hughson's decomposition, commenting only that "whatever were the Causes

---

*Colonial Law* (Lawrence, Kans., 2003); Andy Doolen, "Reading and Writing Terror: The New York Conspiracy Trials of 1741," *American Literary History*, XVI (2004), 377–406; and Richard E. Bond, "Shaping a Conspiracy: Black Testimony in the 1741 New York Plot," *Early American Studies*, V (2003), 63–94.

2. [Horsmanden], *Journal of the Proceedings*, 123–124.

of these Changes, the Facts are here related, that every one may make their own Conjectures upon them." Horsmanden might have been uncertain as to the precise meaning of skin color at this critical juncture, but he remained convinced that a hierarchy of racial values existed in the bodies of New York's laboring classes. Perhaps here was the true miracle, that Horsmanden and at least some New Yorkers believed they could discover transparent racial signs in the color of putrefying bodies, if only they looked hard and long enough.[3]

Horsmanden was hardly alone among mid-eighteenth-century British colonial and metropolitan authorities in trying to make a hierarchy of political virtues visible in the skin color of trafficked bodies. As in the late seventeenth century, authorities deployed white grammar to accomplish seemingly contradictory ends across the Empire during the first half of the eighteenth century. They sought to determine transactional value in trafficked bodies on the one hand and to distinguish the legal and political rights such bodies possessed outside market calculations on the other. They did so even as the subjecthood of white grammar was becoming more diverse, with references to white men, white women, white people, and white inhabitants eclipsing the prominence of white servants in colonial and metropolitan discourse.

The semantic history of whiteness brings together topics often viewed as separate or as antagonistic: things and rights. Their linkage within discourses about skin color near the middle of the eighteenth century suggests that white rights were themselves transactional in nature and origin, not at odds with commercial calculation, but expressions of market logic. White rights, whether articulated as transactional or as humanitarian, could indeed be connected and harmonized. Put another way, whites had superior rights, not because they were necessarily above calculation, but because they possessed superior worth.

The transactional foundations to both rights and racial identity created dilemmas for trafficked actors seeking freedom and attempting to navigate emerging ideas of racial hierarchy. Did emancipation mean embracing or resisting taxonomies of skin color? In the celebrated trial of Irish indentured servant James Annesley in 1743, the unlikely heir to one of the largest landed fortunes in Great Britain at the time, skin color and familial inheritance were juxtaposed as lawyers for both the plaintiff and the defendant labored to turn first one and then the other to their advantage. Like the violence that spread across New York City's waterfront, the uncertain outcome of the trial hints at the incompleteness of a racial order at mid-century, not only in North

3. Ibid., 74, 123–124.

America but across Great Britain. Struggles for freedom among the trafficked defined the evolving meanings of antislavery ideology and skin color within both England and North America during the 1740s. In the investigations into the New York fires in 1741 and the legal battle over Annesley's inheritance in 1743, trafficked people defied elite efforts to control them and their visions of freedom. Their resistance to trafficking and to grammars of race did not emerge in isolation but in relationship to broader transoceanic stirrings against British mercantile power.[4]

## Grammars of a White Racial Order, 1700–1760

To contextualize the struggles over the meaning of skin color, race, and antislavery evident in the New York conspiracy proceedings and the Annesley trial, it is helpful to locate them within a broader eighteenth-century discourse about white peoplehood. An examination of white grammar as it appears in Eighteenth Century Collections Online (ECCO), a digitized compendium of more than two hundred thousand eighteenth-century English language texts, reveals the expanding use of white grammar across the century and underscores the rising importance of white grammar to the subjecthood of a diverse cohort of European and colonial American actors.

From the first two decades of the eighteenth century, 1701 to 1720, to the second two, 1721 to 1740, the number of whites referenced in published sources nearly doubled before rapidly accelerating in the following two decades. Between 1741 and 1760, mentions of whites rose to almost five times the number of whites as in each of the previous two decades, then roughly doubled every two decades thereafter for the remainder of the century. The nearly thirty-three-fold increase in the number of whites referenced in ECCO between the first two decades of the century and the last two far outpaced the expansion of print culture (see Appendix C, Table 13). The frequency of references to white women in ECCO provides a similar though distinct picture of semantic change. After nearly doubling between the first two decades and the second two decades of the century and holding steady in the middle two decades,

---

4. On shared efforts by sailors, servants, and slaves in the Atlantic slave economy to limit imperial power across the eighteenth century, see Peter Linebaugh and Marcus Rediker, *The Many-Headed Hydra: Sailors, Slaves, Commoners, and the Hidden History of the Revolutionary Atlantic* (Boston, 2000). On the politics of mobility that sailors and the enslaved experienced separately and together in the Atlantic, see Julius S. Scott, *The Common Wind: Afro-American Currents in the Age of the Haitian Revolution* (London, 2018), 3–7.

references to white women grew exponentially during the last four decades, more than doubling every twenty years (see Appendix C, Table 14). With regard to both whites and white women, white grammar became commonplace in the aftermath of the events explored in this chapter.

The percentage of whites referenced in published source material who were both Christian and European in origin also steadily climbed over the course of the eighteenth century, as the expanding use of white grammar accompanied a clear shift in the religious and geographic origins of individuals described as white. Whereas at the beginning of the century, almost one-quarter of the 77 whites mentioned in ECCO were non-Christian and 16 percent were non-European, by the end of the century, fully 98 percent of the 2,551 references to whites were both Christian and European in origin (see Appendix C, Table 13).

The semantic shift in the type of individuals associated with white grammar paralleled the emergence in the 1780s of a notion of a white race that was also Christian and European. The earliest references to people of a white race in ECCO either specify African and Asian origins or no geographic origin at all, with just five of eighteen such instances identifying people of European descent before 1780. Yet in the last two decades of the eighteenth century, a clear pattern emerges, where those described as being members of a white race consistently possess European origins (see Appendix C, Table 16).[5]

To appreciate what actors in the early 1740s understood about whiteness, however, it is important to review the range of anxieties and aspirations associated with white skin during the early eighteenth century. The connection between white grammar and a global traffic in convict labor evident in the seventeenth century is still plainly manifest in descriptions of penal labor in both British and European contexts during the first decades of the eighteenth century. In Spain, convicts frequently ended their lives working as galley slaves, a tradition of punishment harsher than transportation to Barbados in the estimation of many British authorities. Criminals in Spain's colonies were likewise compelled to work but were described as whites rather than as galley slaves. In 1717, French writer, explorer, and military spy Amedee Frezier

---

5. That the phrase *white race* has a history distinct from white grammar and one that emerges much later in time suggests the unevenness of racial thinking across the eighteenth century. For a different periodization of the term focusing on the beginning of the eighteenth century, see Theodore W. Allen, *The Invention of the White Race*, I (London, 1994), 89–90; and Isabel Wilkerson, *Caste: The Origins of Our Discontents* (New York, 2020), 43–45.

used white grammar as a shorthand for penal labor on a small Spanish island off the coast of what is now Chile named Valdivia. "This punishment being equivalent to that of the Galleys in *Spain*, the Name of La Galera, or the Galley, is given to the West Point of the Island. . . . Baldivia is . . . the Galley for the Whites." By using the language of the galleys to describe penal labor in the New World, Frezier linked Mediterranean and Atlantic geographies of coercion, even if race remained secondary within the Mediterranean region across most of the eighteenth century. In 1732, French physician Charles Gabriel Dellon similarly described connections between convicts and galleys within Spain's colonies: "Those among the Prisoners who were not Christians . . . and those who were Christians, as well Whites as Blacks, were led into a House which was hired on Purpose in the town, to be there instructed" for subsequent work in the "galleys." Commodified subjects identified by their skin color, whether Christian or non-Christian, needed to be policed in the Americas, even if this took the shape of penal landscapes rather than galley service.[6]

The twining of white grammar to global markets in trafficked people apparent in the frequent references to white servants in the late seventeenth century, then, carried over into the eighteenth century. English essayist David Black, for instance, connected white grammar to both trafficked people and commodities in his description of a "sort of Manufacture called Galloway-Whites" in northern England in 1706, a type of textile manufactured there. In 1734, William Loughton, the compiler of a new British dictionary entitled *A Practical Grammar of the English Tongue*, summarized the semantic link between color and commodities succinctly when assessing the importance of traffic: "We also say the Goods, the Whites, the Blacks." Perhaps anticipating the confusion generated by a commercial taxonomy that changed adjectives into nouns, the linguist continued, "but these are set for Names, or Substantively, Things and Colours being understood." The transformation of

---

6. [Amedee Francois] Frezier, *A Voyage to the South-Sea, and along the Coasts of Chile and Peru in the Years 1712, 1713, and 1714* . . . (London, 1717), 194; Charles Gabriel Dellon, *The History of the Inquisition, as It Is Exercised at Goa* (London, 1732), 53. Frezier's work was translated into English from the French in 1714. Frezier was both an explorer and an imperial spy. See Lucille Allorge, *La fabuleuse odyssée des plantes: Les botanistes voyageurs, les jardins des plantes, les herbiers* (Paris, 2003), 331–342. Dellon was sentenced to the galleys after being imprisoned in Daman and Bassien, India. On his insights into both enslavement and trafficking, see Ananya Chakravarti, "Mapping 'Gabriel': Space, Identity, and Slavery in the Late Sixteenth-Century Indian Ocean," *Past and Present*, no. 243 (May 2019), 30–32.

adjectives into objects was easier than the violent process by which human beings were transported across oceans, redesignated as slaves and servants, and then sold to masters. Here perhaps was the attraction for Loughton in crafting a taxonomy of linguistic values that, like numbers, made imperial aspirations about a global marketplace of things seem natural and inevitable rather than violent and contested.[7]

Yet if trafficked whites remained things in the minds of many by the 1720s, they were also becoming objects of humanitarian concern. After 1690, efforts to protect indentured servants from abusive treatment by masters were increasingly voiced in terms of rights for Christian servants. White servants, in turn, only slowly became associated with rights talk, an increase that became more visible as Christian servants receded from public discussion after 1700 (see Appendix A, Tables 2 and 3). The shift in terms suggests the emergence of clearer legal advantages associated with being white in a slave society. By the end of the 1720s, the wider use of white grammar had rippled outward throughout the British Caribbean and colonial South Carolina and Virginia. Humanitarian interest in white servants was expanding even as the traffic in indentured servants and transported felons boomed after the passage of the Transportation Act in 1718.

Fears of collaboration between trafficked and enslaved people nonetheless persisted through the 1720s and 1730s and continued to play an important role in shaping perceptions of white servitude. Indeed, the 1730s witnessed several major rebellions of enslaved and indentured people across Great Britain's slave colonies in the Americas. The Maroon War in Jamaica between 1730 and 1732 constituted a substantial uprising of enslaved men and women who used remote regions of the island to remain beyond the control of British authorities. In 1738, rumors of a slave insurrection involving an alliance between enslaved Africans and Irish servants terrified elites in Savannah, Georgia, and indirectly set the stage for an even larger uprising a year later in South Carolina, the Stono Rebellion. In that remarkable event, enslaved people sought not only the end of slavery but land, like indentured servants, as freedom dues, storming through the countryside of South Carolina en route to an imagined place of freedom in Spanish Florida. The militia mustered to fight

---

7. David Black, *Essay upon Industry and Trade, Shewing the Necessity of the One, the Conveniency and Usefulness of the Other, and the Advantages of Both* (London, 1706), 7; William Loughton, *A Practical Grammar of the English Tongue; or, A Rational and Early Introduction to Speaking and Writing English Correctly and Properly* (London, 1734), 70.

these rebellions pitted white servants against enslaved actors, until they briefly joined forces in Savannah in 1738 and on the waterfront of New York in 1741.[8]

Examples such as these made many authorities distrustful of the loyalties of all white subjects, even those imported to serve in militias during the 1730s. "My white men," began Thomas Peters in a letter to the governor of Jamaica in 1732 during the Maroon War, were "far from answering my expectation." Sent by gentlemen planters, they proved to be "a parcel of cowardly obstinate unable fellows who neither good words nor bad will do any good, some of whom are already run." In 1729, William Gooch, the governor of Virginia, located transported convicts near the top of an impressive list of internal threats to the colony. "We are in no small danger from our slaves," he began one letter to the Council of Trade and Plantations, recounting how one group had burned a barn to the ground after being punished for having assembled "together in a riotous manner." Worse than enslaved Africans, however, were the "pernicious crew of transported felons," Gooch contended, men and women who "are yet more intollerable." They, too, used arson to settle scores against masters they despised, burning the house of one Thomas Lee "in an instant . . . to the ground" as well as "a young white woman . . . in her bed." Gooch expressed class-based fears about the loyalties of whites in gendered terms, with a young white woman the victim to be mourned and rebellious male convicts the immoral whites to be policed.[9]

Given the mixture of imperial anxiety and aspiration shaping the use of white grammar, it is not surprising to see how it could both convey nascent

---

8. Linebaugh and Rediker, *Many-Headed Hydra*, 193. On the 1731 uprising in Jamaica, see Edward B. Rugemer, *Slave Law and the Politics of Resistance in the Early Atlantic World* (Cambridge, Mass., 2018), 133. On the Stono Rebellion, see Peter H. Wood, *Black Majority: Negroes in Colonial South Carolina from 1670 through the Stono Rebellion* (New York, 1974); and Mark M. Smith, ed., *Stono: Documenting and Interpreting a Southern Slave Revolt* (Columbia, S.C., 2005). 4. On the power of rumors of rebellion as well as actual armed uprisings, see Scott, *Common Wind*; and Vincent Brown, *Tacky's Revolt: The Story of an Atlantic Slave War* (Cambridge, Mass., 2020).

9. "Capt. Peters to Governor Hunter," Mar. 22, 1732, in Cecil Headlam and Arthur Percival Newton, eds., *The Calendar of State Papers, Colonial Series, America and West Indies, 1732* . . . , [XXXIX] (London, 1939), 94; "Lt. Gov. Gooch to the Council of Trade and Plantations," Mar. 26, 1729, in Headlam and Newton, eds., *The Calendar of State Papers, Colonial Series, America and West Indies, 1728–1729* . . . , [XXXVI] (London, 1937), 333. Gooch has received little sustained scholarly attention beyond filiopietistic accounts of the prosperity he ushered in for white residents of Virginia as governor. See Percy Scott Flippin, "William Gooch: Successful Royal Governor of Virginia," *William and Mary Quarterly*, 2d Ser., V (1925), 225–258.

racial rights on the one hand and forms of punishment against trafficked white subjects on the other. In 1703, legislators in the Leeward Islands called for the creation of public instruments that would explicitly discipline raced actors on the island: "And for the regulating many Enormities frequently committed by the Inhabitants of this Island, as well Whites as Blacks, and more especially in and about the Town of Saint *Johns*, a Cage, Pillory, Stocks, Whipping Post, and ducking Stool, are much wanting." Whites might be members of the militia protecting plantations from a slave revolt, until they were not. Precisely because whites were associated with political rights on the one hand and enduring fears of alliances among commodified subjects on the other, they were also the focus of exemplary punishment in highly public settings. White servants might have been protected from severe corporal torture such as dismemberment, but, in Saint Johns, the whipping post was explicitly designed for whites as well as Blacks.[10]

Two cohorts of rebellious whites, pirates and transported convicts, remained especially vexing to colonial authorities long after the emergence of political privileges for white subjects. European commentators consistently drew attention to the diverse skin colors of maritime workers on pirate ships as part of what made them threatening. "The said Pirates did in one Afternoon set fire to, and burn the Prosperous and Speedy Return" in the Indian Ocean, wrote Israel Phipeny and Peter Freeland in 1705, with a crew of "about 250 Men, Whites and Blacks." Off the coast of Chile four decades later, a pirate ship from Callao was similarly described as having "fifty-three sailors on board, both whites and blacks," while, near Jamaica, the crew of a Spanish privateer became "so irritated" in taking an English slaving vessel, "the Ogden, Tristram of Liverpool," in 1746, that "on Boarding her they killed all both Whites and Blacks, during which the Ship sunk." Maritime navies across the Americas possessed sailors hailing from Africa, yet writers rarely commented on the varied complexions of European navies. Rather, pirates were the sailors whose political status and mixtures of skin color stood out as noteworthy and threatening. Whites and Blacks together, allied against imperial rule—this was the transgression that made white pirates and white convicts fit for exemplary punishments.[11]

---

10. "An Act for Regulating the Towns and Harbours . . . ," May 8, 1703, in *Acts of Assembly Passed in the Charibbee Leeward Islands; From 1690, to 1730* (London, 1734), 123.

11. Israel Phipeny and Peter Freeland, *The Innocency of Captain Green, and His Crew, Vindicated from the Murther of Captain Drummond* (London, 1705); George Anson, *A Voyage Round the World, in the Years MDCCXL, I, II, III, IV* (London, 1748), 164; "Ships Taken

Throughout the early eighteenth century, then, British authorities deployed white grammar to express both aspirations for imperial control and their deepest anxieties about its efficacy. As a tool of governance, white grammar could be used to plot and discern hoped-for political order in an unruly colony like New York as well as to make sense of distinctions among alien subjects on the distant peripheries of European power. That dual usage helps explain why authorities continued to rely on white grammar to make distinctions among non-Christian and non-European subjects during the first half of the eighteenth century. The "Japonians," French travel writer Jean Crasset noted in 1705, for example, "are generally strong, robust and inured to the exercise of War." "The Chinese call them Whites," he observed, "tho' they rather incline to an Olive colour. Those of the taller Stature, and more majestick Carriage, are naturally Proud, and seem Born to Command." White grammar helped eighteenth-century European travel writers discern political differences among competing non-Christian actors just as it had in the seventeenth century, facilitating the mapping of commercial and political values among foreign actors. "Thus the greater part of those who at this Day are called the *Whites* and sometimes *Mogols*, in Indoustan," observed Italian writer Niccolao Manucci in 1709, "are rather the Descendants of Persians than Tartars." An anonymous English travel writer commented in 1742 that Persian actors had "divided themselves into two Factions, distinguished by Nature, that of the *Blacks* and that of the *Whites*." Although alien whiteness was declining in prominence by the 1740s, it still functioned as a tool for assessing imperial assets, whether in the far East or across the Ottoman Empire.[12]

Even as travel writers used white grammar to articulate commercial and political imperatives within Britain's blue water empire, however, white grammar also reflected geographic knowledge that was highly uneven and incomplete. Before 1720, the locales where white servants appear were geographically split between the jails of London and the colonial outposts where

---

by the French and Spaniards, June 1746," *British Magazine; or, The London and Edinburgh Intelligencer* (Edinburgh, Scotland), July 1747, 340. Historians studying maritime labor have noted the interracialism of maritime labor and especially of pirate crews. See Linebaugh and Rediker, *Many-Headed Hydra*; and Scott, *Common Wind*, 38–75.

12. Jean Crasset, *The History of the Church of Japan* (London, 1705), 5; [Niccolao Manucci], *The General History of the Mogol Empire, from It's Foundation by Tamerlane, to the Late Emperor Orangzeb* . . . , [ed. or comp.?] F. F. Catrou (London, 1709), 99; Anon., *The Compleat History of Thamas Kouli Khan* (London, 1742), 86. On Manucci, see Sanjay Subrahmanyam, "Further Thoughts on an Enigma: The Tortuous Life of Nicolò Manucci, 1638–c.1720," *Indian Economic and Social History Review*, XLVI (2008), 35–76.

they worked across Caribbean and North American plantations. By the 1730s, references to white servants, white people, white men, and white women emerged primarily in relation to colonial actors. This led at least one colonial correspondent to imagine by 1749 that whiteness was, itself, an American invention and vernacular. "All the colonies want more people," William Douglass began, "and whites; natives of America, do not well bear transplantation." Just so did a grammar originally associated with non-Christian actors become synonymous with Euro-American colonial subjects. From the vantage of metropolitan elites, alien whiteness could be connected to Christians, particularly if they were malefactors who resided on the outer edges of Great Britain's expanding empire across colonial America.[13]

Geographic insights about local peoples, so vital to mapping imperial power and knowledge, were also elusive. In *The History of the Revolution in the Empire of Morocco*, published in 1729 by English ship captain John Braithwaite, the author used white grammar to try to simplify complex political affiliations within Morocco. "The Whites, particularly to the People of Fez, who are all Whites," the author notes, are "chiefly of the Race of Renegado Jews." Here white grammar describes both skin color and the religious peoplehood of Morocco's Jewish residents, whom Braithwaite characterized as a race. That assessment is rooted, not so much in Braithwaite's perceptions of phenotype, as in his recognition of an older and more pervasive discourse about skin color among local Muslim and non-Muslim actors. Braithwaite's observations are filled with semantic complexities that contradict any singular or unified understanding of race based on skin color. If a renegade religion known as Judaism constituted a race, what relevance did skin color possess to that identity?[14]

---

13. William Douglass, *A Summary, Historical and Political, of the First Planting, Progressive Improvements, and Present State of the British Settlements in North America* (London, 1749), 235. A Scottish-American physician who moved from Scotland to Boston in 1716, Douglass described whiteness as a construct of North American origin. His vision linked anti-blackness to hatred of Native American communities, describing Indians in 1749 as "a gregarious sort of man-brutes." See Douglass, "A Discourse concerning the Currencies of the British Plantations in America," ed. Charles J. Bullock, *Economic Studies*, II, no. 5 (October 1897), 280. For a short biography of Douglass, see William P. Trent and Benjamin W. Wells, eds., *Colonial Prose and Poetry* (New York, 1901), 125.

14. John Braithwaite, *The History of the Revolutions in the Empire of Morocco, upon the Death of the Late Emperor Muley Ishmael* . . . (London, 1729), 8; Bruce S. Hall, *A History of Race in Muslim West Africa, 1600–1960* (New York, 2011), 2–3. Moulay Ismaïl Ben Sharif's (1672–1727) dedication to trafficking goods and people across the Mediterranean and his successful capture of Tangier as well as numerous English and European captivity narratives earned him notoriety during the late seventeenth and early eighteenth centuries. See

As white grammar became more prominent by the middle of the eighteenth century, alien whiteness continued to shape perceptions of non-Christian as well as Christian whites. For many British writers, white skin represented a political status of uncertain value precisely because it remained associated with non-European Muslim actors. For European travel writers, geographic context mattered a great deal in determining who was white as well as what work white skin color accomplished. Did whiteness mark politically dangerous status as a trafficked malefactor or the relative advantages that Arab actors wielded over sub-Saharan Africans in Morocco? Or perhaps white grammar summarized the political virtues of being British, a visible sign of what British subjects deemed their birthright as freeborn British subjects? What makes such questions confounding is that the provenance of race itself was shifting from a genealogy of family inheritance to a set of rights rooted in skin color.[15]

In 1736, a periodical entitled the *London Magazine: and Monthly Chronologer* printed an essay by an English member of Parliament under the pseudonym "Julius Florus" directly interrogating the origin and meaning of white identity

---

Linda Colley, *Captives* (New York, 2002), 36, 52, 60–62; Adam R. Beach, "African Slaves, English Slave Narratives, and Early Modern Morocco," *Eighteenth-Century Studies*, XLVI (2013), 333–348; and Nabil Mater, "Introduction: England and Mediterranean Captivity, 1577–1704," in Daniel J. Vitkus, ed., *Piracy, Slavery, and Redemption: Barbary Captivity Narratives from Early Modern England* (New York, 2001), 5–6, 12–13, Thomas Phelps, "A True Account of the Captivity of Thomas Phelps (1685)," 193–217. On Moulay Ismaïl's understanding of skin color in the context of the slave trade across the Sahara, see Isabella Alexander, "Waiting to Burn: Spanish-Maghribi Relations and the Making of a New Migrant Class," *Journal of North African Studies*, XXIV (2019), 152–174.

15. Non-Christians living on the boundaries of Britain's expanding empire also continued to be described as white during the first half of the eighteenth century. Bruce S. Hall has traced a long history of skin color distinctions in sub-Saharan Africa "well before the arrival of Europeans," concluding that "there are African histories of race that do not obey colonial logics." He found that "Sahelian writers made a fundamental distinction between 'whites' . . . who claimed Arab pedigrees, and 'blacks'" from the sub-Saharan regions of West Africa in the seventeenth century. See Hall, *History of Race*, 2. Whether skin-color discourse across the Sahel signified modern racial understandings, however, is another question. See Nicholas Hudson, "From 'Nation' to 'Race': The Origin of Racial Classification in Eighteenth-Century Thought," *Eighteenth-Century Studies*, XXIX (1996), 247–264. Moulay Ismaïl is currently popular among contemporary white supremacists focused on white slavery in North Africa. Repurposing all Christian slaves as white slaves, they ignore that Muslims were the primary whites enslaved in North Africa during the 1730s. For a sensational account that popularizes those inaccuracies, see Giles Milton, *White Gold: The Extraordinary Story of Thomas Pellow and Islam's One Million White Slaves* (New York, 2004).

for all British subjects. "But if I should say, that the Majority of our People are Whites," the author argued, "I could not prove what I asserted, and yet I should look upon him as a very whimsical, or a very disingenuous Gentleman, that would deny it, and assert that the Majority of our People were Blackamores." The more complex reality of skin color, the writer insisted, was its unknowability. He could not prove the majority of English people were "brown" any more than he could prove they were white. More provocatively, Florus questioned whether British aristocrats were even the best ones to deploy new conceptions of race, insisting that "a Country Gentleman" was a better judge of whether British people possessed a race and what color they were. By raising such lines of inquiry as to which English subjects were fit to see race, let alone embody it, Florus challenged how skin color was being deployed and by whom during the 1730s. The answers to his queries were not academic but vital to the survival of trafficked actors across the Atlantic.[16]

## New York's Conspiracy to "Kill the White People," 1741–1745

In the dry and windy spring of 1741, thirteen fires ravaged key parts of colonial New York's wooden waterfront, raising fears that arsonists were seeking to destroy the entire city (Figure 6). Those fears were fed not only by the dramatic nature of the fires themselves but also by rumors of a servant-slave conspiracy that wafted through the air like the smoke across the city's waterfront. Nearly all the evidence amassed to convict and execute the thirty African and Irish conspirators was circumstantial, with convictions relying on the testimony of a single sixteen-year-old Irish indentured servant named Mary Burton. Insights into how servants and slaves themselves viewed the conspiracy survive, but primarily in the highly mediated trial record that Daniel Horsmanden, one of the three judges in the case, assembled three years after the principal leaders of the alleged conspiracy swung for weeks in the town square. Horsmanden published his *Journal of the Proceedings* in 1744 to silence critics who claimed that there had been "no Plot at all" (Figure 7). Horsmanden's goal was to make the villainy of the conspirators visible, to give "those who had not the Opportunity of seeing and hearing" the trial a chance to see, in plain terms, just what that racial villainy looked like. To that

---

16. "Journal of the Proceedings and Debates in the Political Club . . . ," *London Magazine: and Monthly Chronologer,* January 1743, 10, 12. See also, Great Britain, Parliament, House of Commons, *The History and Proceedings of the House of Commons* . . . (London, 1743), 210.

FIGURE 6. *Representation du feù terrible a Nouvelle Yorck... / Schreckenvolle feuersbrunst welchs zu Neu Yorck...*, 1776. The Miriam and Ira D. Wallach Division of Art, Prints and Photographs: Print Collection, The New York Public Library. "Representation du Feu terrible a Nouvelle Yorck" New York Public Library Digital Collections, https://digitalcollections.nypl.org/items/510d47e3-b9b0-a3d9-e040-e00a18064a99

end, Horsmanden attempted to make skin color a form of evidence, a sign of conspiracy. The guilt of the enslaved Africans in question, Horsmanden claimed, was as natural as their skin color. "The Æthiopian might assoon [*sic*] change his Skin," argued Horsmanden, then prove his innocence. For Horsmanden, all the evidence gathered during the trial buttressed his principal contention about skin color. Namely, all masters of "Negroes" were to "keep a very watchful Eye over them, and not to indulge them with too great Liberties, which we find they make Use of to the worst Purposes, caballing and confederating together in Mischief, in great Numbers."[17]

Central to Horsmanden's work was his effort to weaponize the language of whiteness, to make it support his claim that the purpose of the conspiracy was to kill masters and white people by means of arson or direct violence. Typical of the forty-two confessions and final statements that Horsmanden coerced from the conspirators was that of an enslaved African American man named

17. [Horsmanden], *Journal of the Proceedings*, v, vi.

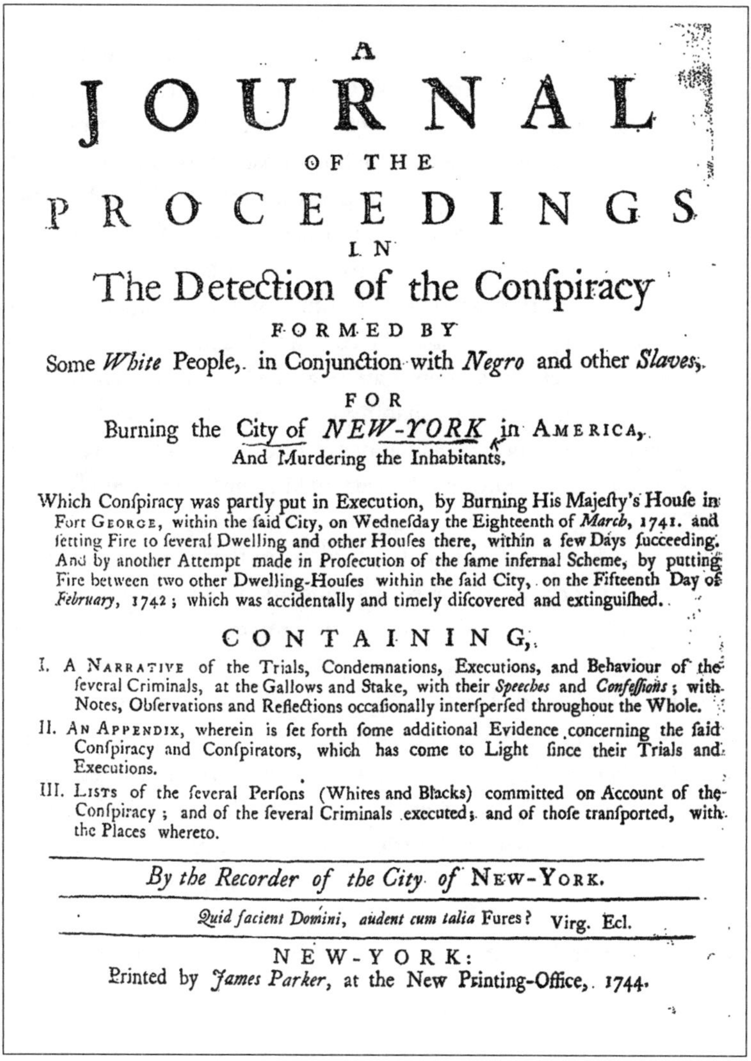

# A JOURNAL

OF THE

# PROCEEDINGS

IN

## The Detection of the Conspiracy

FORMED BY

Some *White* People, in Conjunction with *Negro* and other *Slaves*,

FOR

Burning the City of NEW-YORK in AMERICA,
And Murdering the Inhabitants.

Which Conspiracy was partly put in Execution, by Burning His Majesty's House in Fort GEORGE, within the said City, on Wednesday the Eighteenth of *March*, 1741. and setting Fire to several Dwelling and other Houses there, within a few Days succeeding. And by another Attempt made in Prosecution of the same infernal Scheme, by putting Fire between two other Dwelling-Houses within the said City, on the Fifteenth Day of *February*, 1742; which was accidentally and timely discovered and extinguished.

CONTAINING,

I. A NARRATIVE of the Trials, Condemnations, Executions, and Behaviour of the several Criminals, at the Gallows and Stake, with their *Speeches* and *Confessions*; with Notes, Observations and Reflections occasionally interspersed throughout the Whole.

II. AN APPENDIX, wherein is set forth some additional Evidence concerning the said Conspiracy and Conspirators, which has come to Light since their Trials and Executions.

III. LISTS of the several Persons (Whites and Blacks) committed on Account of the Conspiracy; and of the several Criminals executed; and of those transported, with the Places whereto.

By the Recorder of the City of NEW-YORK.

*Quid facient Domini, audent cum talia Fures?* Virg. Ecl.

NEW-YORK:
Printed by *James Parker*, at the New Printing-Office, 1744.

FIGURE 7. Title page from [Daniel Horsmanden], *A Journal of the Proceedings in the Detection of the Conspiracy Formed by Some White People, in Conjunction with Negro and Other Slaves, for Burning the City of New-York in America, and Murdering the Inhabitants* ... (New York, 1744). Newberry Library Special Collections. Courtesy of The Newberry Library, Chicago

Will, alias "Ticklepitcher," who swore an oath on June 12, 1741, that he was "to burn the Town; to burn the Fort; to burn Stone-Street . . . and to kill the white People as they came to extinguish the Flames." Will's confession represented one of several overlapping plots that emerged from the testimonies and confessions that Horsmanden and his fellow prosecutors elicited from those they interrogated. The language of whiteness was present in each version of the conspiracy but was most important to the so-called "Negro Plot," which dominated the attention of juries and prosecutors throughout the trial.[18]

A careful perusal of the confessions and final statements that conspirators offered to prosecutors suggests that the context of each confession—who recorded it, who conducted the interrogation, and where the interrogation took place—mattered a great deal in shaping its content as well as the outcome for the individual confessor. Horsmanden carefully noted the circumstances under which each conspirator confessed, making possible an analysis of the commonalities and differences among them. A total of eighty-four individuals made confessions or offered final statements in the *Proceedings*, with some conspirators having occasion to record a confession more than once, making for a total of 111 final testimonies included in Horsmanden's published report (see Appendix D, Table 21). An additional twenty-seven individuals were convicted without recorded testimonies, including conspirators who did not speak a language that court recorders understood, as in the case of some of the *"Spanish Negroes."* The contexts in which the surviving confessions were made varied dramatically. Some were taken down "at the stake," as enslaved conspirators prepared to die with little or no hope for reprieve or redemption through their words. Others were made at a stage where the accused conspirator could still hope to avoid execution by naming additional conspirators, resulting in transportation out of the colony to distant slave outposts in Spanish and French colonies.[19]

---

18. Ibid., 71. Jill Lepore has described four overlapping plots: the "Negro Plot," that encompassed the confession of slaves like Will; the Hughson plot, which constituted the campaign by Irish tavern owner John Hughson to persuade slaves to burn New York and to help install him as the new governor of the colony; the Spanish plot, which involved the assistance that Spanish and French sailors would bring to the rebellion; and the "Priest's Plot," which described the role of an Irish Catholic priest in fomenting a rebellion of African slaves and Irish Catholics against the tyranny of British masters in New York. See Lepore, *New York Burning*, 157, 160, 179–180. On the plot led by the Irish priest John Ury, see [Horsmanden], *Journal of the Proceedings*, iii, vi, 95–96, 134, 142–143, 149–153.

19. According to Daniel Horsmanden, the phrase *Spanish Negroes* was circulated among crowds of New Yorkers looking for vengeance in the wake of the fires: "There was a Cry

A comparison of the confessions of slaves who were subsequently executed with those who were transported out of the colony is striking. Just one of the twenty-two confessions of conspirators who were executed mentions a plot to "kill white People." Nearly half of the confessions generated by transported conspirators, by contrast, indicated they planned to kill white people. Sharper still were differences between the transported and the executed in whether they used the language of freedom. Just 8 percent of the transported confessed to antislavery aspirations compared to 55 percent of the executed, who indicated freedom as their primary goal (see Appendix D, Table 22).[20]

Explaining the disparities between the confessions of the transported and the executed requires looking closely at who recorded them. Although Horsmanden compiled the entire trial documentary record, he did not author all the documents published in the *Proceedings*. Just 42 of the 111 confessions and final statements were recorded by him. Thirty-six testimonies were transcribed by two constables hired by the court, Mr. Nichols and Mr. Lodge, while an additional 33 were taken down by the Grand Jury and two city aldermen, George Moore and John Schultz, who became increasingly critical of Horsmanden's methods and investigation as the trial dragged on. The vast majority of those confessing their crimes to Horsmanden framed their conspiracies in terms of whiteness and a plan to kill white people, in sharp contrast with the confessions recorded by the other court officials. Fully 67 percent of Horsmanden's transported conspirators used the language of killing white people in their confessions, while just 28 percent of those interrogated by Nichols and Lodge did (see Appendix D, Table 23).[21]

---

among the People, *The Spanish Negroes; The Spanish Negroes; Take up the Spanish Negroes.*" See [Horsmanden], *Journal of the Proceedings*, 7.

20. Ibid., 2, 47, 66. Although only 111 confessions from eighty-eight individuals are recorded in Horsmanden's *Proceedings*, a total of 121 African slaves were convicted of participating in the slave conspiracy. Whether Horsmanden intentionally excluded thirty-three slave confessions is unlikely, as some of the principal conspirators who were executed, such as John Hughson and Ceasar, for example, refused to give confessions. In general, Horsmanden was quite scrupulous in reproducing court proceedings and testimony, with only minor meddling in the way his key witness, Mary Burton, was presented. For a discussion of the accuracy of Horsmanden's court records, particularly his role in shaping the authorship of slave confessions, see Lepore, *New York Burning*, 122–126.

21. The disparity among confessions grows even larger when one considers the time frame in which they were taken down. During the first week of Nichols's and Lodge's work, just 13 percent of the confessions used the language of whiteness. By the last week of their work on the conspiracy trial, however, that had changed, as Nichols and Lodge

But why would Horsmanden require enslaved men to confess to a racial conspiracy as a precondition for saving their lives? To answer that question, it is necessary to dig deeper into the relationship between competing conspiracy narratives within the trial testimonies and the confessions. At least four conspiracy languages emerged in the 111 confessions and final statements that conspirators produced during the trial, two of them favored by prosecutors and one favored by the unrepentant conspirators who would be executed. The first and most prevalent was that of a conspiracy to kill masters. The second most frequently mentioned conspiracy, also favored by the prosecutors, referenced "killing white people," while the third most prominent involved international and imperial actors, especially Spanish and French sailors, who, it was feared, planned to join with rebelling African slaves and Irish servants to overthrow the provincial government of New York. The least common confessional language was that of freedom, words that emphasized opposition to slavery as the central motive and purpose behind burning New York's homes and main fort.

In the confessions that conspirators offered, however, striking discrepancies appear between and among the conspiracy narratives. This is particularly apparent when the confessions are sorted by the kind of language within each conspiracy. First, the language of the Spanish conspiracy and that of killing masters were quite compatible. Conspirators who confessed to being part of a broader international conspiracy against New York's provincial rulers were more likely to employ the language of killing masters than the total percentage for all confessions, and vice versa. Conspirators confessing to wanting to kill their masters were also more likely to note connections to Spanish conspirators than the total percentage for all confessions. By contrast, the languages of whiteness and antislavery were inversely correlated. Conspirators referencing freedom and antislavery were far less likely to employ the language of killing white people or killing masters than the total percentage for

---

transcribed confessions with language that was almost exactly in sync with those performed by Horsmanden. Now almost two-thirds of Nichols and Lodge's confessions used the language of whiteness, nearly half admitted desiring to kill their masters, and roughly one-third linked the conspiracy in New York City to the anticipated interventions of both French and Spanish sailors (see Appendix D, Tables 23 and 24). The only remaining disparity between the confessions obtained by Horsmanden and those by Nichols and Lodge is in the percentage that framed the confessor's actions as a demand for freedom and liberty. Overall, just two of Nichols and Lodge's thirty-six confessors, or 6 percent, claimed freedom or liberty motives, compared to nine, or 21 percent, of Horsmanden's. Clearly, a learning curve had occurred in the way Nicholas and Lodge recorded slaves' confessions.

all confessions, while conspirators confessing to a desire to kill their masters rarely used the language of freedom as a motive (see Appendix D, Table 25).

These disparities in the discourse contained within the confessions suggest that white grammar was deployed by prosecutors like Horsmanden to extract a moral lesson from the trial: namely, that the conspiracy was, not motivated by antislavery ideology or patterns of cooperation between servants and slaves, but rather by racial depravity. To Horsmanden, the languages of freedom and antislavery were dangerous precisely because of their capacity to unite conspirators across lines of skin color and status, bringing together African slaves with free Black and Irish servants against a common cohort of masters in maritime New York. Confessions that highlighted racial motives, by contrast, particularly that of killing white people, simplified the threat posed by the cooperation among trafficked people at the heart of New York's many fires. Instead of an antislavery rebellion that united slaves and servants against common masters, Horsmanden's conspiracy involved a single malevolent white saloon owner, John Hughson, a man "whose Crimes made him blacker than a Negro," and a cohort of wicked and gullible Black slaves, whose racial hatreds against white people justified tightened legal punishments against both free Blacks and African slaves. Horsmanden sought to make all villainy and conspiracy in the trial racialized, even if that meant describing a white conspirator as a race traitor, or "the Scandal of his Complexion."[22]

The challenge for Horsmanden was not only to persuade African slaves to confess to a conspiracy of killing masters and white people but also to use whiteness to vilify and exonerate distinct groups of white people. Horsmanden articulated the ways colonial elites had long deployed white grammar. On the one hand, he enumerated white people as the great repository of political virtue in New York, well-educated men and women like himself, ostensibly above partisanship, whose enlightened mien and values embodied, naturally, all the values that Horsmanden was defending in his trial investigations. The whiteness of these white people was neither transactional nor genealogical. No single English family in New York monopolized the racialized virtues that Horsmanden championed. Rather, all of New York's diverse European and American-born residents at least potentially exemplified them, all residents, that is, except tavern owner John Hughson; John Ury, the closeted Catholic Priest; and Ceasar's Irish mistress, Peggy. For them, Horsmanden employed white grammar, not to mark political virtue, but to signal its absence, a mark of infamy similar to that visited on white malefactors and convict servants

---

22. [Horsmanden], *Journal of the Proceedings*, 58.

transported to the British Caribbean and to North American plantations. Hughson's and Peggy's crimes transformed their status, making them whites who were "the Dregs and Disgrace of their Complexion," "worse than the Negroes."[23]

These diverging class-bound assessments of white people created moments of persistent tension and even suspense in trial testimonies. That confusion was particularly apparent among the English and Irish witnesses of low social status and rank, whose political virtues were most suspect by Horsmanden. Were they members of the virtuous white people whose liberties were so gravely menaced by the conspirators? Or were they whites like Hughson and Peggy, whose class-based villainy made them dangerous, a "Disgrace" to their complexion? Consider, for example, the testimony of William Kane, an Irish-Catholic soldier who was garrisoned at the main fort at New York when it burned to the ground on Saint Patrick's Day in March 1741. After Kane was implicated in the conspiracy by Horsmanden's primary witness, Mary Burton, he confessed to having participated in the plot to burn New York and "to kill the principal People." Like Hughson, Peggy, and other white conspirators, Kane initially refused to describe the plot as a racial one and made no mention of the race of any of his fellow conspirators. With his own fate hanging literally in the balance, however, Kane exhibited a learning curve in using white grammar quite similar to the court employees, Nichols and Lodge, who likewise began to record the language of killing masters and white people in the confessions they took down (see Appendix D, Table 24). Kane's redemption was secured in his fifth and final deposition, when he implicated several soldiers, all of them Irish, who worked with him at the fort in a newly racialized conspiracy. Kane testified that "David Johnson swore . . . that he would help to burn the town, and kill as many white People as he could." Here was the language of race war that Horsmanden demanded, far better than the conspiracy against the town's "principal people" that Kane initially described.[24]

But how could whiteness function simultaneously as a sign of political virtue and a method for policing whites? Despite Horsmanden's efforts to ignore or suppress evidence of a conspiracy for freedom among both African slaves and European-born servants, antislavery claims bubbled to the surface in nearly all the trial testimonies of the Black and white conspirators who were put to death. Some of the most provocative testimony was provided by Peggy,

23. Ibid. 61, 195.
24. Ibid., 127, 139.

Ceasar's Irish Catholic mistress. Like her condemned African counterparts, Peggy refused to use race as a factor in describing the motives of her fellow conspirators. "If the Fire did not succeed," she claimed in her first confession, the plan was "that they should steal all they could from their Masters," after which the ringleader, one John Romme, "would carry them to a strange Country, and give them their Liberty, and set them free." No references to killing masters or to killing white people appear in Peggy's confession. Though it would later be challenged by one of Horsmanden's cooperating witnesses, Peggy's story was not only plausible but demonstrates a keen understanding of the geography of slave and servant resistance in North America. The "strange Country" that Peggy referenced was, not France or Spain, but the swamps of interior North America still under Native American control. Her ringleader, Romme, said "he would make his Escape and go to North-Carolina, Cape Fear, or somewhere thereabouts; or into the Mohawks Country, where he had lived before." Although Mohawk Country and the Cape Fear River no longer survived as landscapes of resistance to slavery and servitude in 1741, Peggy's recollection underscores the enduring power of that idea. Such an imaginary had guided the dramatic uprising of enslaved peoples in South Carolina who tried to fight their way out of South Carolina during the Stono Rebellion to a utopian locale of freedom in Florida just two years prior. Peggy's words, work, and family ties, in turn, literally and imaginatively embodied the connections between poor whites and enslaved Africans that Horsmanden's racial conspiracy sought to obliterate. Among the many victims of Horsmanden's prosecutions was Peggy's newborn baby, son of Ceasar. By the trial's end, both his parents would be executed in New York City's public square.[25]

Horsmanden had initially sought to make Peggy, a woman with close ties to virtually all the known conspirators, his star witness. Although her association with Ceasar made Peggy abhorrent to Horsmanden, her status on the margins of New York's maritime world also made her testimony and reflections extremely valuable. Peggy, however, proved deeply loyal to her employer, Hughson, to her lover, Ceasar, and to all the key African freemen and slaves who drank and danced at Hughson's tavern, resolutely refusing to implicate

---

25. Ibid., 22–23. On understanding how an imagined geography of freedom for enslaved people might overlap with or bisect settler colonialism, see Tiya Miles "Beyond a Boundary: Black Lives and the Settler-Native Divide," *William and Mary Quarterly*, 3d Ser., LXXVI (2019), 417–426. On territorial aspirations within the Stono Rebellion, see Wood, *Black Majority*.

them in any race-based conspiracy. For that resistance, Peggy paid with her life, refusing the pardon that Horsmanden and others repeatedly offered her.

Horsmanden was far more successful in persuading another female Irish servant to cooperate with him. Mary Burton at sixteen years of age was quite similar to Peggy. Young and Irish, she was dependent on Hughson for shelter and board and possessed considerable familiarity with the enslaved Africans who came to Hughson's tavern. Like Peggy, Mary also faced an uncertain economic future with dim prospects, either as a free laborer or a wife. Marriage was unlikely for Mary, as she "had been got with Child by her former Master" and had years of unredeemed work still on her indenture to Hughson. Peggy, by contrast, experienced success trafficking "stolen Goods" that Ceasar brought her, which granted her a measure of economic independence unknown to Burton. Perhaps it was a similar desire for economic independence that motivated Mary when she decided to cooperate with Horsmanden in the weeks after the thirteen fires mysteriously broke out across New York City in late March. Rather than trafficking stolen goods, Mary instead trafficked stories of a conspiracy to kill white people. Her testimony proved decisive in condemning virtually all the principal actors in the celebrated trial. Mary's depositions secured guilty convictions against Peggy; Hughson and his wife; scores of African slaves, including many of the principal actors; a number of Irish soldiers like Kane; and an Irish-born priest, John Ury, who allegedly taught them all.[26]

Burton was not directly compensated by Horsmanden for her depositions, but the dividends her testimony created were nonetheless real and substantial. First, she obtained the peculiar satisfaction of radically turning the tables on her master and mistress, both of whom publicly humiliated her during Ceasar's trial in March 1741 by claiming she was "a vile, good-for-nothing Girl . . . that had been got with Child by her former Master." Second, Burton was, in fact, directly compensated for her testimony after the trial concluded, claiming a reward of one hundred pounds sterling that had been offered to anyone assisting in "the discovery" of evidence in May 1741. Much of Horsmanden's published trial record defends her credibility as his star witness. The young woman, he conceded, "had a remarkable Glibness of Tongue," for she "uttered more Words than People of her supposed Education usually do." Despite numerous contradictions in her testimony over the course of the trial,

---

26. [Horsmanden], *Journal of the Proceedings*, 4.

Horsmanden insisted that "she was intitled to . . . the Reward offered by the Proclamation for the Discovery" of evidence.[27]

Burton's testimony about a conspiracy of enslaved Black people to kill white people became the template for virtually every confession that Horsmanden extracted from African slaves over the course of the trial, yet she proved remarkably inconsistent in her own devotion to a narrative about racial conspiracy. Although Burton was the first to describe a plot among slaves to "kill and destroy" the "white People," she also frequently mentioned a plot to "destroy all the People." Indeed, the most consistent aspect of Burton's depositions is the regular manner in which she alternated between racial and nonracial conspiracies. Burton's uneven attention to white grammar in her depositions partially reflects the shifting targets of her testimony. When implicating African slaves, she regularly recounted a plot to kill white people, but, when condemning conspirators who were not enslaved, she abandoned the language of racial conspiracy, a sign perhaps of her own confusion about whether white skin conferred status and rights or a kind of shame on its bearers.[28]

The conflicting, class-bound meanings of whiteness were brought into the open during the final weeks of the trial when Irish soldiers, like Kane, and the Irish priest, Ury, sought to defend themselves against Horsmanden's accusations by questioning the racial integrity of his chief witness, Burton. Ury provided one of the cleverest and most spirited defenses of any of the accused. Horsmanden claimed Ury "chiefly kept Company with the Irish Servants" and had plotted the nefarious uprising of Black and white conspirators by calling for "burning the Town, and killing the White people." Instead of resisting the language of whiteness, Ury embraced it, along with arguments about the villainy of poor whites. "If I am a Priest as you take me to be," Ury

27. Ibid., 4, 201, 204.
28. Ibid., 13, 27. On April 22, Burton described a conspiracy to kill and destroy "white People." On May 13, she mentioned a plot "to destroy and murder the People." The next day, Burton returned to a narrative about "murdering the white People," but, in her next deposition on May 29, she outlined a plot to "burn the whole Town." Five days later, Burton maintained her story of a plot "to burn the whole Town," but, on June 25, she once again reverted to a plot whose central purpose was "killing the white People of this City." On June 26, Burton recounted a plot in which "the People were to be murdered," but, on July 5, she insisted that Kane and others sought to "kill all the white People." Her final deposition, on July 9, focused on the role of whites like Kane in the conspiracy but dropped the language of whiteness, returning yet again to the language of killing people more generally. See Ibid., 13, 28, 37, 56, 95, 98, 126, 131, 132.

asked the judges and jury, "I could not be so foolish as . . . to bind myself with a Cord for Negroes or what is worse, profligate Whites, the Scum of this Earth, superior in Villany to the Knights of the Post to make an Halter for me." Ury's argument took Horsmanden's claims at face value and turned them to his advantage. Ury claimed he was far better than "the Scum of this Earth," those "profligate Whites" like Burton, whose testimony might convict him. Ury's best hope for acquittal, he gambled, was to insist on his rights as a virtuous white person.[29]

Burton's testimony was ultimately successful in condemning Ury to the gallows, but her own deployment of whiteness changed in the wake of Ury's testimony as he waited in prison to be hanged. Henceforth, Burton reserved her wrath for elite whites like Horsmanden and would-be gentlemen like Ury, whose arguments about white "Scum" seem to have stung the young, indentured servant. Even as "there arose great Clamour against Mary Burton" for having falsely accused dozens of slaves and Irish soldiers, Burton insisted on naming new names. According to Horsmanden, "she had suggested to some that there were White people of more than ordinary Rank above the Vulgar, that were concerned." To the grand jury, Burton "intimated withal, that there were some People in Ruffles . . . that were concerned." The class-bound politics of whiteness were indeed coming home to roost for Horsmanden and his fellow judges, who "were very much astonished" by Burton's latest discoveries. Rather than pursuing these new leads or reexamining the many convictions that her words about killing white people had brought about, Horsmanden and his fellow judges acted promptly to silence Burton, concluding "that this Girl had at length been tampered withal." Henceforth, the charges against Irish soldiers named by Burton were dropped, all of whom walked free when their hearing before the judges occurred on August 31, 1741. If men with "Ruffles" might be white scum, and servants like Burton truly the most virtuous, then the revolution that Horsmanden feared might be arriving after all.[30]

Horsmanden's need to silence Burton produced fresh doubts about the existence of the conspiracy and spurred him to meticulously prepare the trial records for publication in 1744. As Jill Lepore has demonstrated, most of Horsmanden's work was faithful to other surviving legal records with one important exception. Horsmanden altered the texts associated with Peggy's and Burton's depositions, casting doubt on the integrity of Peggy's words and improving Burton's credibility before she turned on elite whites, the "People

29. Ibid., 159, 162.
30. Ibid., 204.

*in Ruffles.*" A careful perusal of whiteness discourse within conspirators' testimonies further demonstrates that Horsmanden's campaign to exonerate himself began long before his effort to publish the proceedings in 1744. Horsmanden's machinations to prove the existence of a race war, with a plot to kill masters and white people, shaped the trial, as he sought to convict the accused of conspiracy and to distract skeptics from seeing his own shoddy judicial work. Horsmanden's quest was, not simply to make a racial hierarchy visible, but to have the final word about what the conspiracy meant, even if Ceasar's body refused to cooperate.[31]

The unethical nature of Horsmanden's manipulation of trial evidence—taking evidence through torture, the rampant use of hearsay as hard evidence, and extraordinary forms of witness intimidation—has led Lepore to conclude there is no reliable evidence of any slave conspiracy in New York City in 1741, only a record of a witch hunt, with a host of African victims condemned by Horsmanden and his unreliable witness, Burton. Yet both possibilities could have been true, gross prosecutorial misconduct and a conspiracy that briefly united New York's African slaves and Irish servants in a plot against common English masters. Rather than dismissing Horsmanden's evidence as fabrication, it would be better to read it as part of an unequal dialogue between Horsmanden and the people he convicted and policed, one in which he deployed racial ideology to try to silence the antislavery sentiments and claims of New York's unrepentant conspirators as well as to exonerate his own questionable conduct. Here, Horsmanden's evidence underscores the political stakes in who authored narratives about race and antislavery. Yet the power of counternarratives rooted within a transatlantic community of trafficked subjects could not be diminished by guilty verdicts or hangings in the public square.

Glimpses of those counternarratives emerge not only in the prominence of antislavery language among the conspirators who were hanged or burned at the stake but also in the ways six Spanish slaves from Africa sought freedom by embracing a Spanish identity. Before being condemned, the six Spanish prisoners demanded to be remanded to Spanish authorities, claiming they had been wrongly enslaved by an English privateer named Captain Lush. "Afterwards," according to Horsmanden, the Spanish slaves pretended "to have been Free-men in their own Country" and "began to grumble at their hard Usage of being sold as Slaves." This was the primary injustice that the Spanish slaves protested in their testimonies, not the unfair accusations that

31. Ibid., 204.

led to their arrest as slave conspirators. Their freedom demands not only tapped into broader maritime complaints by sailors of various national stripes about being trafficked by privateers and sold unfairly as slaves but also constituted an excellent legal strategy. If they could establish their claims to being Spanish freemen, all evidence by enslaved persons against them and submitted by Horsmanden would have to be rejected. The Spaniards also used their ignorance of the English language to their advantage, challenging the legal validity of Burton's testimony. "The Prisoners all protested they could not speak English; and as . . . they could speak only in a Tongue which she did not understand, how could she tell what passed between them in Conversation at Hughson's?" The Spanish slaves' logic was not only astute but revealing of a broader critique of forced labor, racism, and trafficking available to transoceanic migrants.[32]

Horsmanden had a hard time dismissing these Spanish prisoners' powerful claims, many of them rooted within the larger imperial contests so visible in Mediterranean trafficking. Lots of people were listening to their testimony, moreover, in contrast to those confessions recorded only at the stake. Initially, Horsmanden tried to portray the Spanish slaves as ringleaders of a racial conspiracy, relying on the testimony of Burton, who claimed they planned to kill white people. In his own opening arguments, Horsmanden described them as subjects whose blackness explained their participation in the conspiracy. "Gentlemen, It cannot be imagined that these silly unthinking Creatures (Hughson's black Guard) could of themselves have contrived . . . so direful and destructive a scheme." By referencing the armies of enslaved Black Africans known as the Black Guard who played vital roles in supporting Muslim political authorities in North Africa, Horsmanden highlighted the enduring power of the Mediterranean traffic in slaves and imperial politics in defining how British actors perceived threats in the Atlantic. Yet such arguments did not address the Spanish slaves' demand for rights as sovereign subjects of Spain. To the contrary, Horsmanden's reference to an imperial arena known for unjust trafficking ironically fueled their justice demands.[33]

Horsmanden's effort to refute Spanish sovereignty led him into some of his most convoluted arguments as a prosecutor. He responded to the Spanish Blacks' claim of unlawful enslavement by insisting on the legality of trafficking captive people taken on the high seas. "Nothing appear'd to the Court of Admiralty," Horsmanden argued, "to shew that they were Freemen." Horsman-

32. Ibid., 7, 78.
33. Ibid., 73.

den's legalistic rebuttal sidestepped thorny questions about what precisely made trafficking a foreign national captured at sea legal. More troubling, Horsmanden's reasoning valorized complaints that a host of actors, from English sailors and African slaves to kidnapped English servants, had made against enslavement. Horsmanden's contention was only plausible if one refused the Spaniards' assertion that they were subjects of Spain, a claim that Horsmanden made by pointing to their skin color. To be Spanish was to be white, in Horsmanden's accounting, a starting point that denied the basis for these sailors' protests against enslavement. By arguing against the power of national maritime sovereignty, however, Horsmanden ironically undercut his own imperial logic about the need to support England's colonial leadership in New York.[34]

Sensing that he had opened the door to a host of antislavery challenges to the trafficking of people at sea, Horsmanden doubled down on his claim that the Spanish prisoners were racially depraved and therefore without citizenship status. "They had been severally sold and disposed of; by which means they were discharged from Confinement in Prison; and thereby have had the Opportunity of caballing with other wicked, mischievous, and evil disposed Persons, as well White-Men as Slaves." Horsmanden's closing remarks represent a remarkable shift in his legal case. First, he conceded many of their political claims. "Be they Freemen or be they Slaves," Horsmanden now contended, they still participated in the conspiracy and deserved to be hung. Instead of denying their claim to have been trafficked, Horsmanden emphasized their status as trafficked and "disposed" subjects whose experiences made them open to the evil arguments of other trafficked subjects, whether "White-Men" or African slaves. In so doing, Horsmanden extended arguments first made by colonial authorities in the Caribbean half a century earlier about the character and nature of the threats posed by trafficked people. At the same time, Horsmanden sharply resisted linking whiteness to slavery. "White-Men" and "Slaves" were mutually exclusive categories for Horsmanden in 1744. To discuss white slaves in the New York City slave revolt would have created a very dangerous category indeed, making the class commonalities between servants and slaves explicit, the very project he so adroitly and persistently resisted by coercing slaves into making confessions about killing white people.[35]

The racialized political order that Horsmanden sought to ratify in his *Proceedings*, then, remained elusive for several reasons. First, most of the

34. Ibid., 117.
35. Ibid., 83, 117.

participants within New York's servant and slave conspiracy refused to use whiteness in their testimonies or did so reluctantly to secure a sentence of transportation rather than hanging. Such reluctance did not mean that nominally white people like Peggy were somehow impervious to racism or that they lived in harmony with the numerous free and enslaved Africans who peopled maritime ports throughout British North America. Rather, their reluctance points to an important but neglected fact about trafficked people across Britain's maritime world: rather than embracing taxonomies of skin color or emerging ideas about racial difference, most commoners resisted being raced and the terms of commodification that racial language signified. For British servants like Burton who did claim some of the benefits of deploying whiteness, those gains were tempered by profound and enduring class realities. Invoking whiteness could be used to indict a host of African slaves, some of them better educated than Burton, or to get rid of a noxious white master and mistress. When Burton refashioned whiteness to try taking down whites who wore wigs, the story line grew tense indeed. Whiteness, like trafficked whites, was unruly.

To Horsmanden's chagrin, the instability of the racial order was manifest not only in the resistance of individuals like Ceasar, Hughson, and Peggy, but even in the testimony of his star witness. No wonder that many New Yorkers remained deeply skeptical of the existence of a racial conspiracy to kill white people by the end of the trial. The "Miracl[e]" that New Yorkers witnessed in the putrefying bodies of Ceasar and Hughson—that dead bodies might change their racial nature after death—further undermined the hierarchy that Horsmanden craved. Horsmanden's conspiracy trial had worked, but not as a spectacle of an emerging racial order. Despite his ability to secure a conviction in every instance he desired, Horsmanden's meticulous trial record only served to showcase the continued threat posed by Blacks and whites as well as how an international cohort of trafficked actors at sea might be summoned to support them. Word of the New York City conspiracy and its aftermath quickly spread across the British Empire, fueling fears of larger slave insurrections, especially servant-slave cooperation in Britain's booming sugar colonies. Determining how critically other colonial and metropolitan authorities viewed Horsmanden's evidence is a more challenging matter. Although Horsmanden shared many of the same interests and aspirations as the British gentry who were invested in the slave trade, most British subjects in 1744 lived at some distance from enslaved Africans and the slave trade. As such, the central anxiety Horsmanden confronted of an alliance between enslaved Africans and indentured Irish servants might have seemed less pressing to the

British readers of Horsmanden's *Proceedings*, however interesting the story he recounted. In fact, few readers purchased Horsmanden's publication outside vested parties in New York.³⁶

Yet it would be wrong to imagine that race and slavery were primarily colonial concerns and not intimately connected to the transformation of British society and culture, as several scholars have suggested. White grammar is indeed conspicuous in the correspondence between colonial and metropolitan elites in the Colonial State Papers, as British elites struggled to control, define, and restrict its meanings, even as there exists little evidence in the 1740s that commoners, whether residing in Great Britain or its growing colonies, had yet fully embraced or accepted a racial identity based on white skin color. An even better-known legal battle at the time, the celebrated struggle of James Annesley, an indentured servant unfairly sold into so-called slavery in the American colonies, helps to illuminate how men and women in the British Isles understood white grammar in the 1740s.³⁷

## The Color of Nobility and the Traffic in Rogues

In the fall of 1743, a remarkable trial fixated residents of Dublin, Ireland, and London, England. The plaintiff was a young man, James Annesley, who claimed to be a nobleman and heir to the Annesley estate in Northern Ireland. At twenty thousand acres, it was one of the largest landed estates in all of Great Britain. The defendant was Richard Annesley, James's uncle, legal heir to the vast family fortune that his brother, Arthur, the fourth baron Altham, had left to him when he died fifteen years earlier. Richard Annesley, the sixth earl of Anglesea and seventh viscount Valentia, was, in 1743, one of the most powerful men in Great Britain and perhaps the wealthiest Protestant who claimed Northern Ireland as his ancestral residence. James, by contrast, was a poor sailor and former indentured servant, transported to Pennsylvania as a boy where he labored for thirteen years "as a common Slave," having been banished there by his uncle who desired his inheritance. Predictably, Richard

---

36. Lepore, *New York Burning*, 220. For a reconstruction of the geography of New York's enslaved community, see Ibid., Appendices A and B, 233–259.

37. On the impact of slavery on English culture and political economy during the second half of the seventeenth century, see Susan Dwyer Amussen, *Caribbean Exchanges: Slavery and the Transformation of English Society, 1640–1700* (Chapel Hill, N.C., 2007); and Abigail L. Swingen, *Competing Visions of Empire: Labor, Slavery, and the Origins of the British Atlantic Empire* (New Haven, Conn., 2015).

denied James's assertions, insisting that James was his brother's bastard son, an unruly child who exemplified the "black" temperament and character of his Irish mother, a milkmaid named *"Juggy Landy."*[38]

The Annesley trial became a well-known drama throughout England and Ireland in 1743, not only because the financial stakes were so high but also because the cultural and political stakes were so substantial. Could a transported servant, born in Ireland, find justice in an English court of law? Was class status heritable? These questions resonated for a great many actors in Great Britain during the mid-eighteenth century, particularly migrant subjects like James Annesley, who were compelled under less-than-optimal circumstances to accept indentures and transportation across the Atlantic. Although James sought to secure a large political and economic inheritance, his life experiences as a transported felon were central to how people thought about him. Not only James's birthright but the merits of transportation as a policy, not to mention the testimonies of dozens of Irish Catholic women called on to defend the veracity of his claims, hung in the balance.

Concerns about the unfairness of transportation or the mistreatment of Irish subjects were hardly new to residents of Great Britain in 1743. What made the Annesley trial especially significant was, not that it provided definitive answers to either of these concerns, but the novel ways both sides in the trial framed their demands as an argument about race and its meaning. Although attorneys for both the plaintiff and the defense differed over crucial facts—the identity of James Annesley's mother, for example—both sides explained the moral legitimacy of their client's birthright in terms of racialized inheritances. At the same time, the two sides diverged over how they employed race, raising key questions about its provenance and meaning for British subjects in the 1740s. These questions, which had first emerged in the context of the traffic in transported English and Irish subjects during the late seventeenth century, were central to truth claims within the Annesley trial.

38. Anon., *A Plain Historical Account of the Tryal, between the Honourable James Annesley . . . and the Right Honourable the Earl of Anglesea, Defendant* (London, 1744), 6, 123, 135; [James Annesley], *Memoirs of an Unfortunate Young Nobleman, in Which Is Continued the History of Count Richard, Concluding with a Summary View of the Tryal; Part the Second* (London, 1743). Annesley's life and writings have been retold uncritically as an example of the oppression of Britain's poorer classes. See John Van der Zee, *Bound Over: Indentured Servitude and American Conscience* (New York, 1985), 194–208. A. Roger Ekirch has written the definitive history of the Annesley trial that locates it within the broader context of inequalities within Georgian England as well as colonial America. See Ekirch, *Birthright: The True Story That Inspired Kidnapped* (New York, 2010).

Were the Annesleys a race in their own right, a noble lineage whose virtues were apparent in Richard's and James's pedigrees and inheritance? Or were the Annesleys powerful by virtue of their superior whiteness, a family whose birthright claims rested on skin color as much as pedigree?

Questions about the race of English and Irish nobility did not emerge solely from trial testimony but also from James Annesley's efforts to publicize his side of the story. A savvy self-promoter, Annesley wrote and published his life story, *Memoirs of an Unfortunate Nobleman*, in three parts, maximizing publicity both ahead of his trial and after. In these volumes, Annesley laid out his birthright claims while also detailing his hardships and fanciful adventures in North America. His memoir fueled public interest in his legal claims, giving rise to numerous reprintings of his story and the trial's legal documents. Questions about the provenance of race were not new to British subjects in 1743, but the forums for hearing and seeing the dilemmas presented by the Annesley trial, whether James's memoir, reprinted court testimony, or essay accounts of the legal proceedings, all expanded how British readers discussed, imagined, and saw nobility and skin color. The significance of Annesley's trial was manifest not only in the size of the paper trail that it created but in the narrative strategies he deployed in protesting trafficking, demanding justice, and selling copy.[39]

Annesley's contrived memoirs, republished trial testimony, and legal arguments and depositions together constitute challenging evidence. With the prominent exception of A. Roger Ekirch, most historians have dismissed Annesley's published biographies as "sentimental fiction," unreliable melodrama far less useful than the legal records generated by the famous trial. Taken together, Annesley's legal documents and melodramatic narrative provide an exceptionally rich window into how and where racial discourse worked in Georgian England. One reason historians have dismissed *Memoirs of an Unfortunate Young Nobleman* is that much of it was probably made up, including Annesley's competing love interests, a "young *Indian* Maid" of the Iroquois nation and his master's daughter, Maria, who after being spurned by James gets pregnant "by one of her Father's white Slaves." Like Thomas Southerne in his theatrical reworking of *Oroonoko*, Annesley reserves the term *white slaves* for indentured servants at the bottom of the social order. Annesley, for his

---

39. On the conservative nature of English antislavery, especially as articulated by aristocrats like Annesley, see Nicholas Hudson, "'Britons Never Will Be Slaves': National Myth, Conservatism, and the Beginnings of British Antislavery," *Eighteenth-Century Studies*, XXXIV (2001), 559–576.

part, frequently describes himself as a "slave" but attaches aristocratic modifiers rather than those of skin color to descriptions of his plight, referring to himself as "the noble Slave." As in earlier fictional accounts about the traffic in servants and slaves, themes of interracial romance intensify the prominence of racial signifiers, even if one's noble birthright remained the most important race to be trafficked within England during the mid-eighteenth century.[40]

Throughout his memoir, James Annesley deployed competing forms of racial value, one transactional the other ancestral, to burnish ideas about his worth as a trafficked subject. Both ideas of race, the noble Annesley line and the transported white, reside in the same person. Unlike servants and sailors who protested the systemic abuses created by spirits or the press-gang, however, Annesley attributed his suffering to the innate wickedness of his uncle. Like Daniel Horsmanden, Annesley suggested that some people were evil by nature, especially his uncle, Richard Annesley. With little sense of irony, James predicted that future generations of readers would "look upon it as fictitious . . . that Nature ever cou'd produce a Monster such as Count Richard. . . . In the Character of this Count, there is not one white Line—all is black and horrid." Fictions were indeed powerful—and malleable—as Annesley understood, though they could also create dramatic inconsistencies in his narrative and trial arguments. If Count Richard's aristocratic blood lines made him "black and horrid," after all, why was James deserving of a royal inheritance? Annesley addressed that vexing question by portraying himself as a cross-class hybrid, a common nobleman who was able to inspire chants among his vassals of *"Long live the Heir* of Altamont—*our own true Lord."*

---

40. Ekirch, *Birthright*, xxii; [James Annesley], *Memoirs of an Unfortunate Young Nobleman, Return'd from a Thirteen Years Slavery in America . . .* , Part I (Belfast, Ireland, 1743), 22, 23, 24, 27. There were several editions of Annesley's memoirs published in 1743. I have cited the Belfast edition as it was the closest to the contested estate and the community of people who subsequently show up in published trial testimonies. The language of slavery varied in the editions of Annesley's memoir. Only in the Belfast edition does a mention of indentured servants as "white Slaves" appear. For another version of the romantic subplot and mention of a "young Indian maid," see [James Annesley], *Memoirs of an Unfortunate Young Nobleman, Return'd from a Thirteen Years Slavery in America . . .* (London, 1743), 91, 117. In Ekirch's retelling of Annesley's story, the trial revealed the corrupt underbelly of aristocratic rule in Georgian England, one that routinely put profit and legal title ahead of justice and morality. Largely neglected by Ekirch, however, are the complex battles over the provenance of race and whiteness that elites and commoners deployed during the trial.

Like Aphra Behn in her novel *Oroonoko,* Annesley skillfully appropriated critiques of the servant trade and adapted them to a shared project of aristocratic rescue. Annesley sutured imperial tropes of English travel literature together with populist critiques of kidnapping, linking his romance with an Indian princess to an explicit comparison with Turkish slavery. "The Hardships of an *American* Slavery," he averred were "infinitely more terrible than a *Turkish* one, frightful as it is represented." Annesley located his own noble self, rather than trafficked servants or enslaved Africans, as the key victim of the morally reprehensible system of American slavery, putting his enslavement to work on behalf of landed elites in Ireland. His use of Mediterranean slavery was especially effective in fostering the highly selective antislavery sentiment needed to win his legal battle.[41]

Yet, even as Annesley's Orientalist literary thefts might have helped him sell copy, they did not determine the outcome of his court battle. James's claims to ancestral lineage rested on the testimony of numerous Irish and English subjects, most of them women, whose memories proved to be crucially important for judges and jury members trying to answer the same question: Was James Annesley, informally known as Jemmy, a noble heir or a bastard? Lawyers on both sides of the Annesley case focused on the meanings and merits of his experience as a poor commoner, especially his time as a kidnapped servant and, before that, as a neglected child walking the streets of Dublin. For those testifying on behalf of the defendant, Uncle Richard, Jemmy's experience as a commoner was visible proof of his non-noble blood. In a subsequent edition of Annesley's memoir published in 1747, Annesley described the arguments for his Uncle Richard against him, animating their efforts to make his footloose behavior as a young boy a sign of his illegitimate origins. "He was untowardly, vicious and incorrigible.... He rambled down to *Ross,* my Lord's Estate, where he and his Mother were well known, and was treated and consider'd as my Lord's *Bastard*." Defense lawyers also cast doubt on the credibility of the testimony of numerous female witnesses, appealing to the class biases of the judge. "I say, my Lord, with great Submission," queried the attorneys, is it "impossible for a rational Man to conceive that a Transaction of this Kind should be an absolute Secret to them [this noble family], to their Friends, Neighbours, and Tenants, and indeed Secret

---

41. [Annesley], *Memoirs of an Unfortunate Young Nobleman . . . ; Part the Second* (London, 1743), 29; [Annesley], *Memoirs of an Unfortunate Nobleman,* Part 1 (Belfast, 1743), 38; [Annesley], *Memoirs of an Unfortunate Young Nobleman* (London, 1743), 63.

to all the World, except a few inferior Persons, who now appear to give point blank Proof of it"?[42]

Lawyers for James, by contrast, used accounts of his life on the streets to spotlight the cruelty of his father, Lord Altham, and James's resilience in simply surviving. When his father sent him away to an isolated house in the country and circulated rumors that he was dead, the young boy nonetheless found his way back to town. "He was a little too sprightly to be confined in that manner," the plaintiff's lawyers claimed, "and being denied Admittance into his Father's House, he roved about from Place to Place . . . for the Space of two Years." At every stage of his young life, servants and other common folk helped him survive. When his father separated him from his mother, he lived "in the Care of Servants," and, when his uncle assumed the title of fifth baron Altham after James's father died, "there were Murmurings among the Servants" implicitly challenging the chicanery of James's aristocratic elders. At stake in these diverging legal strategies was not only Annesley's birthright but the integrity and honor of the poor, largely female group of Catholic witnesses testifying on his behalf. If common servants and other "inferior persons" could be believed by well-heeled male Protestant jurors and judges, then surely justice would prevail in the Annesley trial.[43]

Or would it? The irony of James Annesley's populist rhetoric was that his effort to have common people's voices heard was simultaneously a campaign to bring an "unfortunate" nobleman to his title, redeeming Protestant rule in Northern Ireland more broadly. If James Annesley mobilized class allegiances in selling his memoir in 1743, he also vindicated an older concept of race that valorized the inherent nobility of ancient blood lines. Annesley accomplished that complex ideological work, not with arguments, but by presenting his body as a piece of evidence for his birthright claim. *"Now I remember,"* an old friend explained, that *"the young Chevalier James de Altamont had a very particular Mark about him, which I have often taken notice of when we happen'd to wash together. . . . If you have that Mark, it may serve to corroborate the rest."* When Annesley heard this, he "immediately stript and gave him the sight of this indelible Proof," leading his chastened friend to exclaim, *"There needs no more—you are the real Chevalier* James de Altamont—*the true Count* de Anglia!" That recognition of nobility functions as a transformative moment

42. [James Annesley], *Memoirs of an Unfortunate Young Nobleman, Return'd from a Thirteen Years Slavery in America . . .* , III (London, 1747), 20, 26.

43. Ibid., 5, 8, 9.

in Annesley's memoir, recalling the auction that had originally defined his slavery and victimhood.[44]

Lawyers for Uncle Richard, by contrast, sought to contradict testimony about James's body by using notions of skin color to disprove his nephew's nobility. Because defense lawyers conceded that James was the son of the deceased Lord Altham, the focus moved to recalling the physical features of his dead wife, Lady Altham, and sundering any potential links between James and her body. One Margaret Hodgers testified that Lady Altham was "a tall Woman, and of a swarthy Complexion," unlike Jemma. For Uncle Richard's lawyers, such testimony was helpful, as James apparently possessed hair that was fair or "Flaxen" colored. The remarkable inconsistencies in the testimonies of the defense witnesses, however, and their general confusion as to what skin color signified, complicated their task. Although some witnesses such as John Turner, a personal steward to the defendant, Uncle Richard, described Lady Altham as being a "big Boned large Woman" whose hair was "not Jet Black, but Brown," others, such as Christopher Brown, recalled that "her Hair was always powder'd" and "as to her Complexion, he could give no Account." Perhaps the most confused and revealing testimony came from Bartholomew Furlong, a witness for the plaintiff, who, when cross-examined by defense lawyers, described Lady Altham as "being a tall Woman, with good Complection and Features." When asked to elaborate about "what he meant by Complexion," Furlong backtracked and "said the Colour of her Face" was "not very white nor fair, but a little red." He continued nervously that "his own Wife is alive and a brown Woman" and "that her Ladyship was of a brown Complexion and somewhat towards black." Furlong's attempts to clarify what he was saying about Lady Altham's body only intensified his anxiety. He "thought her Ladyship handsome" but insisted that "his own Wife was more pleasing to him," even while observing that "her Ladyship had more white than his Wife." If Furlong associated whiteness with beauty, he nonetheless undercut that claim by stating he desired his own darker wife more. Skin color signified trafficable qualities in the bodies of Christian women, Furlong believed, just as it did among trafficked Muslim women in Mediterranean slave markets.[45]

Furlong's contradictory testimony was not simply a result of rattled nerves, then, but a telling reflection of the cultural uncertainties surrounding the

---

44. [Annesley], *Memoirs of an Unfortunate Young Nobleman* (London, 1743), 167, 168.
45. Anon., *A Plain Historical Account of the Tryal*, 10, 17, 29, 30, 39, 40, 41, 138.

relationship between skin color and race among both witnesses for the plaintiff as well as the defense. On the one hand, skin color seemed quite disconnected from any notion of Annesley's aristocratic pedigree. Lady Altham's complexion was described variously as swarthy, a little red, brown, and almost Black, suggesting no stable phenotype for the Annesley line. On the other hand, many witnesses, with the prodding of defense attorneys, mapped blackness as a sign of Annesley's bastardy and what they claimed were his poor Irish Catholic origins. Several witnesses claimed that Annesley's wet nurse as a young boy, Joan Landy, an illiterate Irish Catholic laundry maid, was also his mother. Nicknamed *"Juggy Landy,"* she was described as a "strait black Girl" who lived in extraordinary filth and poverty. According to several defense witnesses, Lord Altham knew she was James's mother but rued her tainted Irish Catholic pedigree. Martin Kneefe, a local blacksmith, recalled that "his Lordship swore, *God damn the Bastard, he has too much of his Mother Juggy Landy's Blood in him to be good!*" By deeming Irishness a racial trait, a thing in her blood, Lord Altham made his bastard son unredeemable, prompting him to say frequently "that he would rather give five hundred Pounds he had had that Child by an *Englishwoman.*" Other witnesses also described James's Irish inheritance in terms of phenotype. After Landy returned to work in Lord Altham's house, young James was put under the care of another Irish wet nurse, this one a "Dairy-Maid . . . called . . . *Black Kate.*" Perceptions of blackness in the bodies of Irish wet nurses mapped evolving ideas of race as a kind of contagion, one that could be imbibed, like breast milk, into the blood of infants like James. Thus it was that the local Protestant minister, Michael Downs, after noting that James could not speak English but only Gaelic when he arrived at his school, "believed he was a black Child."[46]

The contradictory testimonies of virtually all witnesses on the relationship between skin color and race provided a flawed foundation for mounting a legal defense of Richard Annesley's claims. Consequently, they disappeared

---

46. Ibid., 123, 135, 136, 139, 145. Revisionism is one of the consistent ironies in the history of race as a concept. The notion that Irish Catholics were a degraded race, articulated by Protestant elites during the 1730s seeking to legitimate their power in Northern Ireland, in time became foundational to arguments by Irish Catholic white nationalists who now claim that the degradation and enslavement of the Irish race trumped the historical oppression of all other groups caught in New World slavery. See Sean O'Callaghan, *To Hell or Barbados: The Ethnic Cleansing of Ireland* (Dingle, Co. Kerry, Ireland, 2001). For a stinging critique, see Jerome S. Handler and Matthew C. Reilly, "Contesting 'White Slavery' in the Caribbean: Enslaved Africans and European Indentured Servants in Seventeenth-Century Barbados," *New West Indian Guide,* XCI (2017), 30–55.

from the defense lawyers' closing arguments. Rather than using phenotype to justify Uncle Richard's noble status and rights to the estate, his lawyers intensified their attack on the inferior class of the plaintiff and his witnesses. "This is an Affair ushered in . . . by very mean People, by *Mary Doyle*, a Chamber-maid, and *Elinor Murphy*, a Landry-maid . . . from the meanness of their Offices in the Family, they could not be employed about the pretended Birth" of Lady Altham's son. The "meanness" of these "inferior Persons," defense lawyers maintained, rendered them not credible. Richard's lawyers featured the bastard's alleged illegitimate mother, Landy, in similarly demeaning terms, as "a mean, loose and unsound Woman, one greatly addicted to Lust . . . who constantly and frequently admitted to her Embraces mean Men." Why, the defense counsel asked, would Lady Altham entrust her only son, heir to a substantial fortune, "to nurse to a Whore, a mean beggarly Woman, and one who had been a Whore to her Lord"? The answer was "plain," the defense counsels concluded; "the Plaintiff was not her Son" but her husband's bastard. Putting him on a boat to North America was no crime but precisely how transportation was supposed to work. "The Plaintiff was a Vagabond, and if the Defendant had any Hand in transporting him, it was to serve his Country," Richard's lawyers argued.[47]

The defense of servant transportation as a morally justifiable and even patriotic practice articulated long-standing arguments in favor of the policy. Yet that defense also provided James's lawyers their central argument in their summary to the jury. Rather than recap the testimony of the women who witnessed Lady Altham's delivery of a birthmarked baby named James, lawyers for the plaintiff hammered Uncle Richard for having kidnapped and transported his nephew to America, making Richard's conduct proof that James was indeed the rightful heir to the Annesley fortune. Why else would Richard have sought to remove his nephew from Dublin against his will? The plaintiff's lawyers' final arguments hinged not on racializing James or his Irish witnesses but on showing that James had indeed been coerced. James was, in his lawyers' summation, an "innocent Youth" who had been "transported, and sold into Slavery." He was not a common criminal but "very young when he was transported, a meer Boy, about twelve Years of Age, and then in no Capacity to assert his Right." Rather than condemn the policy of transportation outright, Jemma's lawyers cleverly maintained that the absence of any friends and family giving their formal consent to the boy's departure in

47. Anon., *A Plain Historical Account of the Tryal*, 187, 189, 200, 201.

1727 proved that "the Plaintiff must have been put on board the Ship, in the secret, forcible kidnapping Manner."[48]

When seven hours of final arguments had been concluded and the chief justice gave his instructions to the jury, the complex questions about the provenance of race and the meaning of skin color had been reduced to a simple one: Had James Annesley been kidnapped, transported, and trafficked against his will, as his lawyers contended? "You are to consider," the chief justice began, "whether the Committing an unlawful Act of Spiriting away or transporting a Boy against his Consent carries any Weight, if it does, you are to consider within yourselves what could be the Inducement to commit that Act, and if you believe that the Act was committed, you will judge accordingly." The jury of twelve "Gentlemen," all of them wealthy Protestant landowners, returned with a unanimous verdict: "We find for the Plaintiff." James Annesley's legal victory vindicated not only his Irish Catholic witnesses but also a genealogical understanding of race. In winning his court case, James Annesley not only sundered his uncle's faulty lineage claims but also defeated his effort to use a new taxonomy of racial value that blackened people living in Ireland and whitened English aristocrats.[49]

Nevertheless, skin color also pervaded Annesley's campaign for vindication. One catches a brief glimmer of this in his lawyers' efforts to locate Annesley's slavery in the Caribbean rather than Pennsylvania. The shipping merchant who transported Annesley to Pennsylvania, one Mr. Stephenson, was described as someone who "traded to the *West-Indies* with Servants among other Goods." Annesley's lawyers then incorrectly stated that his slavery took place in the heart of England's Caribbean plantation economy, asserting that he had been put "on board a Transport Ship, which . . . carried [him] to the River *Delaware* in the West-Indies, where he was sold as a common Slave." The frequency and ubiquity of that mistake evoked an explicit comparison between Annesley, the wronged lord, and the bodies of "common Slave[s]" in the Caribbean. The crime Annesley endured was not only having been trafficked but also having had to toil among African slaves, a racist lament that would grow in power and visibility over time.[50]

James Annesley's lawyers succeeded, then, in making specific questions about his noble race speak directly to broader geopolitical concerns about the

48. Ibid., 205, 212, 220.
49. Ibid., 225, 227.
50. Ibid., 6, 67.

traffic in both servants and slaves. As in Southerne's theatrical reworking of *Oroonoko*, Annesley twined antislavery sentiment with aristocratic privilege in both his memoir and court testimony. His freedom came, not from any solidarity with fellow servants or sailors, but from recognition by a former classmate, who was now the commanding officer on board his ship, as the noble heir to Altham. Annesley's memoir celebrates a dubious connection between antislavery discourse and the rights of Great Britain's aristocracy. The question of what a noble race looked like was not simply a matter of ideological definition—what race did or did not signify—but the product of who used the concept, what they meant by it, and to what end. James Annesley's triumph in racing himself as a nobleman reflected his peculiar class circumstance, even if his inheritance remained in doubt during the trial. With some of the best lawyers in the land making his case, he possessed unusual freedoms and privileges. Saloon owner John Hughson and Ceasar's mistress Peggy, both Irish-born subjects like Jemma, possessed no such advocates. Like Irish radicals before and after them, they would swing together on the gallows for their willingness to stand together with enslaved Africans seeking freedom in another land.

## Conclusion

It is not known whether Daniel Horsmanden read about James Annesley's remarkable trial as he was compiling his *Proceedings* during the summer and winter of 1743, nor what loyalties or sympathies he might have possessed. It is possible, however, to speculate as to how Horsmanden might have reacted to Annesley's trial as well as to the testimonies of the Irish servants and women supporting James's claims in court. Unlike James, Horsmanden viewed the policy of transportation favorably, and his efforts to use it as a humane instrument expanded his capacity to inscribe white grammar into the forced confessions of transported conspirators. Likewise, Horsmanden would have found the logic of Richard Annesley's defense lawyers—that the meanness and blackness of most of James's witnesses disqualified their reliability—both persuasive and handy, as he also sought to manage the testimonies of Irish actors under oath. Yet it is doubtful Horsmanden would have been troubled by the outcome of the Annesley trial, for it ultimately vindicated the power of Protestant rulers over common Catholic subjects in Northern Ireland. That James had effectively earned his nobility by having it tested as a "common Slave" in North America echoed Horsmanden's own aspirations to be a colonial leader, a man whose power had been won, he believed, not by birth, but by hard work and dogged persistence. Therein lay much of Horsmanden's aspiration in publishing his detailed and painstaking *Proceedings* in 1744.[51]

Both Horsmanden and James likewise possessed common goals in making race a tool that would clarify their noble purposes. Although they differed sharply over what race meant—skin color or familial inheritance—they cohered in seeing it as a powerful signifier, one in which hidden cultural traits were made manifest within the physical appearance of individual bodies. For James, claims to the Annesley name and fortune hinged on specific marks on his body and the ways they had been read, seen, and remembered over the course of his lifetime. In both Annesley's memoirs and his subsequent trial, proof of his nobility began with an examination of his exposed body, a process akin to being trafficked at auction. Horsmanden similarly sought to make questions of intrinsic character visible in the appearance that bodies stripped of clothes and cultural artifacts assumed during and after trial. In that endeavor, the peculiar pattern of Hughson's decomposition exemplified for Horsmanden the promise of racing bodies, the hope that each body's true value would become manifest through public exposure. Just so did both trials recapitulate the intimate historical connection between race and the trafficking of slaves and servants, whether for sale at market or on display in the stocks as cautionary punishments. Horsmanden and James succeeded in making competing racial imaginaries visible in both trials.

Yet those who had been trafficked consistently refused to use grammars of skin color in their testimonies. Although Annesley deployed white grammar briefly in his original memoir when describing the indentured servant Maria's marriage to one of her "Father's white Slaves," not a single one of the poorer Irish witnesses in the Annesley trial, whether testifying for or against the defendant Uncle Richard, referenced whiteness when describing themselves or any of the key actors in the case. Lawyers for Uncle Richard might have attempted to use race to link Irish culture to blackness, but even defense witnesses eschewed referencing skin color in their testimony. If Irishness was a race, it had little direct connection as yet to whiteness. When trafficked witnesses, whether servants or slaves, used racial language in Horsmanden's *Proceedings*, by contrast, they did so for a particular purpose—to spare their lives. The consequences of not inhabiting a racial conspiracy in their confessions were indeed stark. They faced death by hanging or by burning. Taken together, the Annesley trial and Horsmanden's published record highlight the

---

51. Lepore, *New York Burning*, 220.

elite origins of racial grammar, whether as skin color or as familial genealogy. White grammar remained limited in its purview among English-speaking commoners on both sides of the Atlantic, language that in the minds of many trafficked actors was linked to the same policies of transportation they were resisting or seeking to escape.

The common and unresolved focal point for both trials was not only what work race might do but for whom. For that question, the political and cultural status of Irish women loomed large. Indeed, in both trials, outcomes hinged on the political status of key Irish women. Were Mary Burton's memories of a conspiracy to kill white people more believable than the loyalty of Peggy to her lover, the African conspirator Ceasar? What influence did the Irish nursemaids Juggy Landy or "Black Kate" have on James, the young nobleman? If the status of specific Irish women proved decisive in shaping the outcomes of both trials, the differences among these women are perhaps as revealing as their similarities. In Annesley's case, the believability of "Black Kate" led to his political redemption, despite that his memoirs featured aristocratic antislavery sentiments and romantic tropes at the heart of the famous play and novel *Oroonoko*. For the "Newfoundland beauty" from Ireland, Peggy, by contrast, love for a Black man sent her to the gallows without a backward glance from Horsmanden. As Peggy and the Spanish sailors and African slaves who remained committed to finding a landscape of freedom somewhere in North Carolina's Great Dismal Swamp discovered, resisting race and the political authorities determined to make it visible was deadly business indeed.

If the outcomes of the Annesley and Horsmanden trials were definitive for those accused of crimes, the questions each trial raised about the relationship between skin color and race, the purposes of antislavery rhetoric, the political status of Irish women, and the efficacy of transportation as an imperial policy were far harder for colonial or metropolitan authorities to answer in 1744. Taken together, the two trials amplified grave doubts about transportation, even as the number of convicts sent to New World destinations from the British Isles and from Europe soared during the 1730s and 1740s. Were British authorities effectively enslaving their own? Such anxieties were not new in 1744 but had been growing steadily for decades as antislavery ideology became ever more central to the political identity of British subjects, whether trafficked servants, impressed sailors, or elite planners and architects of the mercantile political economy.

Indeed, British subjects of all backgrounds were embracing as never before the notion that to be British was to be free from enslavement. In 1740, Thomas Arne put to music James Thompson's now-familiar ode, "Rule Britannia." As the chorus repeats over and over, *"Rule* Britannia, *rule the waves;* Britons *never will be slaves."* First performed on the stage in London in 1740, Arne's composition quickly became a standard drinking and fighting song among British sailors and British subjects at home and abroad. Such sentiments could elicit dangerous consequences for British authorities seeking to build an empire on the backs of transported felons, indentured servants, African slaves, and impressed sailors. To understand how British authorities responded to the newly emboldened freedom demands of their mobile subjects, it is necessary to return to the Mediterranean region, where thousands of English slaves toiled without recompense.[52]

52. *Alfred: A Masque* (London, 1740), 42; A. Roger Ekirch, *Bound for America: The Transportation of British Convicts to the Colonies, 1718–1775* (Oxford, 1987), 118; David Armitage, *The Ideological Origins of the British Empire* (New York, 2000), 173. Ekirch argues that commercial rather than penal considerations shaped the size of the flow of convicts to North America. As such, transportation functioned, not so much as a policy driven by the supply of felons, but as a demand-oriented market that benefited particular shipping merchants in both England and North America. The first performance of "Rule Britannia" on the British stage occurred in late July 1740. See "Last Night Was Perform'd," *London Daily Post, and General Advertiser,* Aug. 2, 1740, [1], and "On Friday Last Was Perform'd," Aug. 5, 1740, [2], cited in "The Celebrated Ode in Honour of Great Britain Called Rule Britannia," *Musical Times and Singing-Class Circular,* XLI, no. 686 (Apr. 1, 1900), 228–231.

CHAPTER FIVE

# Nationalizing Emancipation in the Mediterranean

English sailor Thomas Troughton's voyage to the Mediterranean Sea began like many others in the fall of 1745, with hopes of good weather, lucrative prize taking, and a return to London in the spring, with wealth and stories of adventure to share with family and friends. Sailing under the command of Captain Richard Veale on the *Inspector Privateer*, Troughton and his fellow sailors, hailing from across Europe and Africa, were forthright and unapologetic about their ambition to make their fortunes by seizing and trafficking the people and goods of non-English sailing vessels. Initially, they met with success, "taking two prizes," one a French ship, *La bella morea*, whose goods and crew were deposited at Gibraltar, the profits to be split once the captured goods had been sold. Yet Troughton's journey soon took a dramatic turn for the worse after the New Year. First, tensions between Captain Veale and his crew threatened to cut short their prize-taking venture, as several sailors, upset over the unequal distribution of prize money, fomented a mutiny against Captain Veale. Sensing that a harsh reaction might further undermine his command, Veale did not execute the accused mutineers, Daniel Gullet and George Sampson, but instead agreed to have the two "put on board the Rupert, for breeding a Mutiny." Far worse than sailor disgruntlement, however, was the force of wind and weather. "In a very brisk Gale," the *Inspector Privateer* "sprang a Leak" the day after leaving Gibraltar. For three days, Troughton and the remaining crew, made up of eighty-seven sailors, kept the sinking ship afloat "by plying our Pumps Night and Day." Realizing that "she would inevitably sink in a very short Time," Captain Veale decided to take his chances on the shores of Africa and ran the ship "a Ground in *Tangier Bay*."[1]

---

1. Thomas Troughton, *Barbarian Cruelty; or, An Accurate and Impartial Narrative of the Unparallel'd Sufferings and Almost Incredible Hardships of the British Captives, Belonging to the Inspector Privateer, Capt. Richard Veale, Commander* . . . (London, 1751), 9, 10, 16. Until

Perhaps because Tangier had once been an English colony, Troughton hoped that "we should find a favourable Reception, and immediate relief from the *Moors*." Instead, as Troughton later recounted, "the inhuman, barbarous *Moors* came down upon us, like ravenous Lions, ready to devour their Prey." Troughton soon found himself shipped to Morocco, where he worked as a slave for Sultan Mulay Abdallah, a bondage that lasted almost five years before his ransom could be negotiated and eventually paid. Troughton's published story, *Barbarian Cruelty; or, An Accurate and Impartial Narrative of the Unparallel'd Sufferings and Almost Incredible Hardships of the British Captives, Belonging to the Inspector Privateer, Capt. Richard Veale, Commander,* closely resembles the plotlines of numerous captivity tales that had been previously published in England, with descriptions of the inhumanity of the Moors and horrific working conditions building the sultan's fortress (Figure 8). What made Troughton's story distinct was his pointed critique of English diplomatic efforts to emancipate him as well as his stinging rebuke of Captain Veale's authority and leadership. According to Troughton and the sixteen sailors who signed a deposition supporting the veracity of his account, their bondage was needlessly extended by the corrupt and class-bound actions of British consular officers and Captain Veale, who secured his own freedom by selling out his crew. That crime was worsened by the British state, Troughton contended, which did not even pay their ransom but instead relied on a private English charity, the Ironmongers' Slave Fund, to fulfill its national duty.[2]

Troughton's captivity and the diplomatic controversies he detailed provide an unusually rich window into the power of sailor antislavery in the evolution of Britain's human trafficking policies across the Mediterranean in 1751. To

---

recently, Thomas Troughton had not received the scholarly attention he deserves. One excellent dissertation discusses his journey and struggle in more detail. See Catherine M. Styer, "Barbary Pirates, British Slaves, and the Early Modern Atlantic World, 1570–1800" (Ph.D. diss., University of Pennsylvania, 2011), 42–45, 77–79, 248–250, 272–273. See also Bernard Capp, *British Slaves and Barbary Corsairs, 1580–1750* (New York, 2022), 46, 50, 109, 152. Gullet and Sampson were not alone in resisting Captain Veale. Before their attempted mutiny, ten sailors were reported to have fled the ship while at dock in Lisbon and then later at Gibraltar.

2. Troughton, *Barbarian Cruelty*, 10. On the importance of Tangier to English aspirations for empire in the Mediterranean during the seventeenth century, see Alison Games, *The Web of Empire: English Cosmopolitans in an Age of Expansion, 1560–1660* (New York, 2008); Karim Bejjit, ed., *English Colonial Texts on Tangier, 1661–1684: Imperialism and the Politics of Resistance* (London, 2015); and Nabil Matar, *Britain and Barbary, 1589–1689* (Gainesville, Fla., 2005); Capp, *British Slaves and Barbary Corsairs*, 172–178. On English

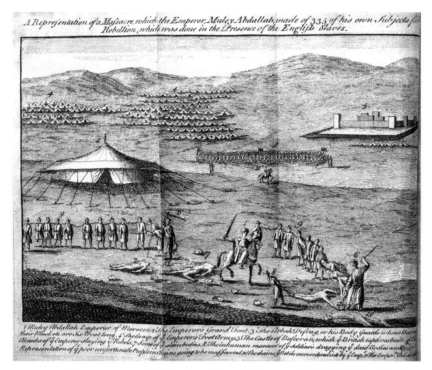

FIGURE 8. *A Representation of a Massacre, Which the Emperor Muley Abdallah Made of 335 of His Own Subjects for Rebellion, Which Was Done in the Presence of the English Slaves.* From Thomas Troughton, *Barbarian Cruelty; or, An Accurate and Impartial Narrative of the Unparallel'd Sufferings and Almost Incredible Hardships of the British Captives, Belonging to the Inspector Privateer, Capt. Richard Veale, Commander . . .* , 2d ed. (London, 1751), Plate 3. Courtesy of The Huntington Library, San Marino, Calif.

---

enslavement in Tangier and North Africa more generally, see G. E. Aylmer, "Slavery under Charles II: The Mediterranean and Tangier," *English Historical Review*, CXIV (1999), 378–388. The reign of Sultan Mulay Abdallah was marked by political instability in Morocco, as he fought his brothers to keep his position. He was unseated seven times between 1729 and 1748. For a brief discussion of his reign, see Abdallah Laroui, *The History of the Maghrib: An Interpretive Essay,* trans. Ralph Manheim (Princeton, N.J., 1977), 271–276. Little has been published on the Ironmongers' Slave Fund, but there have been a few articles and dissertations that examine its role in the Mediterranean. See Suzanne Schwartz, "Ransoming Practices and 'Barbary Coast' Slavery: Negotiations relating to the Liverpool Slave Traders in the Late Eighteenth Century," *African Economic History*, XLII (2014), 59–85; and Styer, "Barbary Pirates, British Slaves, and the Early Modern Atlantic World," 198–199, 259–260, 296–297.

understand the full significance of Troughton's story, it is necessary to first examine how and why sailors on British vessels hailing from widely varying linguistic, cultural, and political backgrounds came to demand nationalized efforts at emancipation by English authorities by the middle of the eighteenth century. Indeed, the motley crew that benefited from Troughton's critique and advocacy included Thomas Jones, an African-born man and one of the first Black sailors to be emancipated from slavery by the English crown. Yet little was made of Jones's skin color by those arranging his ransom, nor did the skin color of any of the English slaves held in bondage with Troughton become relevant to the diplomatic negotiations that led to their collective emancipation. The political economy of sailor trafficking in the Mediterranean at mid-century is revealing of how and why race trafficking was not central to the evolution of British antislavery in the region or to its national ambitions there.[3]

## English Slavery *in the Mediterranean*

The 1740s were an especially challenging decade for the diverse sailors traversing the ocean under the Union Jack. Conspiracies among enslaved and trafficked individuals, many of them seamen, circulated across Britain's Atlantic empire, while war with Spain taxed the manpower needs of Britain's imperial navy across the Mediterranean. Aware of the political and material pressures being placed on the empire's sailors in both regions, British authorities sought to create incentives that would keep and build the sailing workforce at the heart of their imperial ambitions. Toward the end of the War of Jenkins' Ear, George II issued a proclamation attempting to ensure the rights of English sailors to claim prizes at sea, part of a recruitment effort to keep the nation's best sailors in the Royal Navy without impressing them. The recent war had witnessed the dramatic expansion of impressment. In effect, Britain succeeded in its global military campaigns with forced labor. Sailors were compelled to fight, but they were also guaranteed the right to traffic and profit from any and all goods they captured at sea. In "An Act for the Better Encouragement of Seamen in His Majesty's Service, and Privateers, to Annoy the Enemy," passed in March 1744, George II declared that "Seamen, Marines, and Soldiers . . . in His Majesty's Pay, and . . . Privateers,

---

3. On the vital importance of Mediterranean traffic to the evolution of British mercantilism and its imperial capacities, see Games, *Web of Empire*, 71.

shall have the sole Interest and Property of . . . every Ship, Vessel, Goods, and Merchandizes" that they might seize. The same law also endeavored to protect the king's material interests in such prize taking, devising a series of rules for adjudicating the messy questions about property ownership that emerged from a war in which English battleships were repeatedly captured and recaptured over the course of individual naval campaigns. George II's proclamation clarified what obligations privateers owed to the British crown, yet it did little to spell out what duties the crown owed its English sailors enslaved in North Africa. Such concerns were vexing not only because hundreds of British subjects were taken captive annually by North African privateers during the 1740s but also because impressment had expanded dramatically across the Empire during its recent conflicts with Spain and France.[4]

During the 1740s, British sailors looked to the rhetoric of antislavery to both demand freedom from masters in North Africa and to challenge the new Impress Service, which many sailors deemed a form of English, or domestic, slavery. The new service relied on land-based actors across England and Ireland to function. These included local "mayors, magistrates, justices of the peace, and bailiffs," each of whom received "£3 for every able seaman" they raised for the Royal Navy. The recruitment of local officials as traffickers for the British Navy lit a match to a fuse that held the potential to spark violence for local officials, as happened in the case of the Knowles Riot in Boston in 1747. There, sailors and their supporters resisted the impressment of forty-six of their number by seizing the local officials responsible for their captivity. Condemnations of impressment as a form of English slavery in the 1740s were becoming explosive, capable of thwarting or expanding the power of George II and His Majesty's Royal Navy.[5]

A comparison of the terms used to describe human trafficking in Mediterranean slave markets between 1701 and 1800 helps to afford a crisper picture of

---

4. George II, *Anno Regni Georgii II; Regis Magnæ Britanniæ, Franciæ, and Hiberniæ, Decimo Septimo; At the Parliament Begun and Holden at Westminster, the First Day of December, . . . 1741 . . .* (London, 1744), 691; Denver Brunsman, *The Evil Necessity: British Naval Impressment in the Eighteenth-Century Atlantic World* (Charlottesville, Va., 2013), 48.

5. On the history of the Impress Service in Great Britain during the 1740s, see Brunsman, *Evil Necessity*, 76–82. On the 1747 Knowles Riot, see Peter Linebaugh and Marcus Rediker, *The Many-Headed Hydra: Sailors, Slaves, Commoners, and the Hidden History of the Revolutionary Atlantic* (Boston, 2000), 214–217; and Brunsman, *Evil Necessity*, 228–235. On enslaved people's participation in the 1747 riot, see Jared Ross Hardesty, *Unfreedom: Slavery and Dependence in Eighteenth-Century Boston* (New York, 2016), 127–129.

what the phrase *English slavery* meant to sailors like Troughton. Throughout the century, the practice was variously characterized as Christian slavery, English slavery, or white slavery. Religious modifiers were far more prominent than national or racial ones in framing how English readers interpreted sailors' captivity in the Mediterranean. Over the course of the century, there were more than five times as many references to Christian slaves in the Mediterranean as there were to all white slaves and English slaves combined. Although that ratio declined over the course of the century, falling from nearly twenty-five times as many Christian slaves as white and English slaves at the start to less than four to one by century's end, neither references to white slaves nor English slaves eclipsed those to Christian slaves (see Appendix C, Table 20).

If references to white servants had largely replaced those to Christian servants in Britain's Atlantic colonies by 1720, no such trend occurred in the discourse about captives in the Mediterranean for a couple of reasons. First, white slaves in the Mediterranean were not reliably Christian in identity. Rather, they made up an enduring mixture of non-European and non-Christian actors throughout the century. Between 1761 and 1780, for example, just 21 percent of the white slaves appearing in Eighteenth Century Collections Online were Christian, suggesting why white slavery discourse in the Mediterranean was not well suited to displace writings about Christians enslaved in North Africa (see Appendix C, Table 15). The modest increase in references to white slaves is partially attributable to the salience of fictional sources, especially the successive reprinting of *Arabian Nights Entertainments* after 1721, a narrative in which all the white slaves in the text are Muslim. Over the course of the century, 42 percent of all mentions of white slaves were fictional (see Appendix C, Table 18). Christian slaves, by contrast, were less likely to appear in fiction, with fictional mentions of Christian slaves making up just 32 percent of all mentions of Christian slaves. Descriptions of Christian slaves, both fictional and non-fictional, moreover, contained very few references to skin color, with just 66, or 6 percent, out of all mentions of Christian slaves, fictional and non-fictional, making any mention of blackness or whiteness (see Appendix C, Table 19). Christian slaves who appeared in fictional texts were more likely than Christian slaves appearing in non-fictional sources to be accompanied by modifiers of skin color, however, suggesting that the correlation between fiction and articulations of skin color was visible even in the Mediterranean, where trafficking by race was scarce compared to the Atlantic. References to *English slavery* picked up after 1780, not because of any absolute increase in the numbers of English sailors captured at sea, but because abolitionists had begun to use the term to elicit sympathy for African men and women owned by English masters. If English slaves were worthy of rescue from North Africa, why not African slaves from North America (see Appendix C, Table 20)?[6]

A comparison of the distinct semantic meanings associated with Christian slaves and English slaves sheds additional light on the political context in which sailors like Troughton demanded national forms of emancipation. Authors described the plight of English slaves most often as a political problem that required particular diplomatic solutions. To be an English slave usually meant that a foreign government, rather than a merchant or a particular private slaveholder, had taken possession of an English subject's liberty. That political fact created commonalities across national enslavements, as English essayist Joseph Browne revealed when commenting on the similarities between English slavery and that experienced by other European powers:

> But I would fain know what Difference there is between *French Slavery* and *English Slavery*, *Danish Slavery* and *Italian Slavery*, etc.
> ... The Slavery is the same, whether we form it our selves, or receive it from a *Foreign Power*.

In the Mediterranean theater, English slavery, like Italian or French slavery, was a condition characterized by confinement and ownership by North African political leaders. Most authors who used the language of English slavery also presupposed the individuals in question were Christians, differentiating

---

6. For white slaves as Muslims in *Arabian Nights*, see, for example, *Arabian Nights Entertainments; Consisting of One Thousand and One Stories . . . Translated into French from the Arabian MSS. by M. Galland . . .* , X (London, 1721), 24, 25, 28. On reprintings, see, for example, *Arabian Night Entertainments: Consisting of One Thousand and One Stories . . . Translated into French from the Arabian MSS, by M. Galland . . .* , 7th ed., 12 vols. (Dublin, 1728); *Arabian Nights Entertainments: Consisting of One Thousand and One Stories . . . Translated into French from the Arabian MSS. by M. Galland . . .* , 10th ed., 4 vols. (Dublin, 1776); *Arabian Nights Entertainments: Consisting of One Thousand and One Stories . . . Translated into French from the Arabian MSS. by M. Galland . . .* , 4 vols. (Manchester, England, 1777); *Arabian Nights Entertainments: Consisting of One Thousand and One Stories . . . Translated into French from the Arabian MSS. by M. Galland . . .* , 14th ed., 4 vols. (London, 1778); *Arabian Nights Entertainments: Consisting of One Thousand and One Stories . . . Translated into French from the Arabian MSS. by M. Galland . . .* , 13th ed., 3 vols. (Edinburgh, 1780). Of 342 Christian slaves appearing in fictional sources, 36, or 10 percent, were accompanied by racial modifiers, compared to 30, or 4 percent, out of 711 Christian slaves in non-fictional sources. See Appendix C, Table 19.

between national loyalties while minimizing religious differences among enslaved Europeans. Such national descriptions of slaveries were the inevitable consequence of the widespread practice of prize taking among European powers, a by-product of war and prisoner exchanges.[7]

Authors describing the plight of Christian slaves, by contrast, were more likely to emphasize their need for religious rescue, precisely because of the anxieties that accompanied being enslaved to Muslim masters. Rarely did discourse about Christian slaves focus on diplomatic actors as agents of rescue or redemption. More commonly, authors expressed concern that Christian slaves might be forced to convert to Islam, thereby removing them from consideration for redemption or ransom. One redeemed Christian slave from England worried in 1713 about the "deplorable ignorance of some Christian slaves who have been a considerable time in *Barbary*," believing that "the seducer *Mahomet* was sent by God; and that he did such Miracles." More common are accounts of Christians subjected to despotic masters and torture. Such themes had long characterized discourse about sailors' bondage in North Africa and remained essential within conversations about Christian slavery across the eighteenth century.[8]

These semantic trends put into relief the choices that Troughton made as a writer at mid-century. He was unusual in describing himself as both a Christian slave and an English slave, but the reasons he did so are clear. He sought to foreground political themes in his story and the centrality of consular ac-

---

7. Joseph Browne, *State Tracts: Containing Many Necessary Observations on the State of Our Affairs at Home and Abroad: With Some Secret Memoirs*, I (London, 1715), 124. On Browne's career, see Katarzyna Kozak, "Joseph Browne: Literature and Politics in Early Eighteenth Century England," *ANGLICA: An International Journal of English Studies*, XXVIII, no. 1 (2019), 39–43. On evidence of an additional author to *State Tracts*, see Robert J. Allen, "William Oldisworth: 'The Author of *The Examiner*,'" *Philological Quarterly*, XXVI (1947), 161–162, 174–175.

8. Simon Ockley, ed., *An Account of South-West Barbary: Containing What Is Most Remarkable in the Territories of the Kingdom of Fez and Morocco . . .* (London, 1713), 125. On the variety of factors shaping English conversions to Islam, see Claire Norton, "Lust, Greed, Torture, and Identity: Narrations of Conversion and the Creation of the Early Modern Renegade," *Comparative Studies of South Asia, Africa, and the Middle East*, XXIX (2009), 259–261. On Ockley, see Adam R. Beach, "African Slaves, English Slave Narratives, and Early Modern Morocco," *Eighteenth-Century Studies*, XLVI (2013), 348 n. 21. Ockley's *Account of South-West Barbary* is discussed in Nabil Matar, "Introduction: England and Mediterranean Captivity, 1577–1704," in Daniel J. Vitkus, ed., *Piracy, Slavery, and Redemption: Barbary Captivity Narratives from Early Modern England* (New York, 2001), 18; and Gerald MacLean and Matar, *Britain and the Islamic World, 1558–1713* (Oxford, 2011), 151–152.

tors in his delayed emancipation. Evoking the popular refrain of the song "Rule Britannia" that Englishmen *"never will be slaves,"* Troughton focused his story as a demand for national relations of rescue. Sailors' awareness of the possibility that they could be captured and trafficked by North African pirates or press-gangs of their own government while at sea helps to explain the significance of political themes in their understanding of liberty and slavery. The coerced labor that enslaved English sailors performed in North Africa changed little between 1650 and 1750, but the perception that they were experiencing slavery at the hands of negligent government officials, their own in particular, was growing. Although Troughton was unusual in calling himself an English slave, his protest of political injustices anticipated the expansion of antislavery sentiment into abolitionist arguments after 1780.[9]

Given the expansion of white grammar in the Atlantic world across the eighteenth century, one might also expect Troughton to have deployed white grammar to forge his political critique of Great Britain's diplomatic actors. Recognizing that white slavery in the Mediterranean remained associated with trafficked Muslims in 1750, however, explains why Troughton eschewed any explicit notion of racial suffering. References to skin color do appear occasionally in Troughton's narrative, as when he described the power of the Black Guard, young men born into bondage in French West Africa, transported to Morocco across the Sahara, and trained to be the sultan's personal bodyguards. Like travel writers before him, Troughton used skin color to assess and categorize cultural distinctions among varied African peoples in Morocco. But Troughton was unusual among authors of non-fiction writing about Christian slavery in his determination to deploy grammars of skin color. The sharpest political distinctions he drew reflected differences between captives and their new masters, men whose depravity was rooted in tyrannical authority rather than differences of skin color.[10]

9. *Alfred: A Masque* (London, 1740), 42. For expressions of political antislavery in Troughton's narrative, see Troughton, *Barbarian Cruelty*, 19, 103–104, 131. On the origins of the celebrated patriotic song "Rule Britannia," written by James Thompson and set to music by Thomas Arne, see Todd Gilman, *The Theatre Career of Thomas Arne* (Newark, Del., 2013), xiv, 2–3. The first performance of the song on the British stage occurred in early August 1740. See "Last Night Was Perform'd," *London Daily Post, and General Advertiser*, Aug. 2, 1740, [1], and "On Friday Last Was Perform'd," Aug. 5, 1740, [2], cited in "The Celebrated Ode in Honour of Great Britain Called Rule Britannia," *Musical Times and Singing-Class Circular*, XLI, no. 686 (Apr. 1, 1900), 228–231.

10. Troughton, *Barbarian Cruelty*, 90–91. The history of the Black Guard in Morocco has been linked to questions about the role of skin color and race within Islamic societies more

The question whether Europeans constituted a race did not explicitly engage Troughton, though he did articulate revealing anxieties about the relationship between skin color and enslavement. Troughton assessed his experience in terms of Atlantic slavery at the beginning of his narrative, when describing the hard labor he was called on to perform in Morocco. "We were forced to do double Duty, by which means our Skins were so blister'd, Day after Day . . . that our Hides were all perfectly tann'd," Troughton observed. He then made an explicit, and to him troubling, comparison. "Had it been possible for our most intimate Acquaintance to have seen us, they never would have known us, but took us rather for *Negroe* Slaves than *European* Captives." Atlantic slavery had begun to race these British captives, after all, transforming their physical appearance into that of "negroe slaves" caught in the Atlantic slave trade. Slavery was indeed racialized in Troughton's thinking, even if he toiled in the Mediterranean.[11]

Nevertheless, political and conceptual differences in the political economy of trafficking in the Atlantic and Mediterranean regions continued to shape distinct meanings for skin color and family pedigree in each locale across the eighteenth century. For trafficked migrants in the Atlantic, avoiding designation by skin color was impossible by the middle of the eighteenth century. To be an African slave in Barbados meant you were a Black whose every move was watched and policed. Likewise, to be a transported convict, one of the first and most conspicuous individuals to be identified as white in Britain's slave colonies, was to stir up fears of sedition and rebellion. At the same time, to be white in the Atlantic was increasingly becoming a thing shared by all European-derived colonists, even as servants and slaves resisted trafficking and notions of racial order. Being bought and sold as an English sailor in the Mediterranean, by contrast, fueled, not race traffic, but instead a market in political and religious identities. In the Mediterranean, common seamen, whatever their origins, were not yet commodified by skin color. They pushed back against enslavement, not by eschewing or embracing race, but

---

broadly during the early modern era. See Chouki El Hamel, "'Race,' Slavery, and Islam in Maghribi Mediterranean Thought: The Question of the *Haratin* in Morocco," *Journal of North African Studies*, VII (2002), 29–52; and Beach, "African Slaves, English Slave Narratives, and Early Modern Morocco," *Eighteenth-Century Studies*, XLVI (2013), 333–348.

11. Troughton, *Barbarian Cruelty*, 62–63. On the trans-Saharan slave trade in North Africa, see Ronald Segal, *Islam's Black Slaves: The Other Black Diaspora* (New York, 2001); Elizabeth Savage, ed., *The Human Commodity: Perspectives on the Trans-Saharan Slave Trade* (Portland, Ore., 1992); and Bernard Lewis, *Race and Slavery in the Middle East: An Historical Enquiry* (New York, 1990).

by demanding that religious orders and nations emancipate their subjects. Those demands would, in time, transform how prize taking was regulated by states in the Mediterranean and elsewhere, as the British state responded to its sailors' demands and the nation's manpower needs by expanding how antislavery worked and for whom.

## Organizing National Relations of Rescue, 1700–1750

At the beginning of the eighteenth century, the British government sought to minimize Christian slavery in North Africa by creating better ways for regulating ransom traffic. On June 28, 1698, the British government and the dey of Algiers concluded a new treaty of peace and commerce. Updating a half dozen consular agreements signed between 1662 and 1691, the 1698 treaty sought to avert royal-funded ransoms associated with shifting and ever-expanding costs. The 1698 treaty authorized a pass system whereby British ships carrying official authorization could not only "pass freely" if stopped by an Algerine ship but avoid being "stopped, taken, or plundered." According to the treaty, sailors and crew presenting the pass, which contained the "seal of His Majesty or Lord High Admiral," could not be "seized, nor the men made slaves" to Algerine subjects. Nor could captured English sailors carrying a pass be transferred for sale to a non-Algerine actor. The 1698 treaty stipulated that the pass "shall not permit them to be sold within the Territory of Algiers." The treaty addressed the uncertainty over whether captive English sailors trafficked for ransom were slaves by outlawing both the trafficking and the enslavement of English sailors by any Algerine actors.[12]

On the face of it, the treaty of 1698 defended the demands of both captive and nominally free British sailors by requiring Algerine authorities to refuse to traffic or sell any British people or their goods. By insisting that no subjects of "His Majesty of Great Britain shall be bought, or sold or made slaves in any part of the Kingdom of Algiers," the British state clearly and unequivocally denounced the trafficking of its subjects in Algiers. As such, the treaty resembled the form and function of the Spiriting Law of 1670, which established a clear principle for policing the booming servant trade. In the attempt to curtail the activities of spirits, national authorities were ostensibly

---

12. "Extracts of Treaties between Great Britain and Algiers," June 20, 1698, Articles 3 and 9, MS 17034/3, Thomas Betton Charity Papers, Guildhall Library, London. On events leading up to the 1698 treaty, see Nabil Matar, *British Captives from the Mediterranean to the Atlantic, 1563–1760* (Leiden, Netherlands, 2014), 184–187.

obligated to support only consensual indentures and impose the death penalty on those who seduced and trafficked English servants against their will. The pass system, like the servant registry, sought to secure what could only be deemed consensual and free labor relations for its sailors on the move. Indeed, the pass system went further than the servant registry in suggesting that the trafficking of British sailors amounted to slavery and was, according to the treaty, immoral and illegal.[13]

Many of the treaty's details, however, are revealing of the English state's anxieties over its fiduciary responsibilities in enacting relations of rescue for its captive and trafficked sailors. The pass system nominally protected sailors from being enslaved, but it also responded to a particular challenge confronting the English state posed by mobile sailors. Was the government responsible for rescuing all English sailors, even those who had become pirates or been forced to convert to Islam? A subsequent treaty amendment in 1700 was added by the dey of Algiers, which stated that "if any ship of England be seized, not having a pass, the goods in that ship shall be prize." The heart of the amended treaty, then, did not so much abolish prize taking as assert control over which English ships could lawfully board and plunder other ships and which English ships and sailors, in turn, might be legally plundered. The pass system deployed a novel strategy for English authorities short on manpower. Through its enactment, Algerine predations could be used to enforce compliance with English mercantile policy across the Mediterranean and Atlantic. By inviting Algerine ships to traffic English ships and sailors without passes, the treaty extended the reach of England's regulatory capacity, even mandating that Algerine authorities rescue English sailors who were shipwrecked on the coast of Algiers. A second imperative of the 1698 treaty was to indemnify English authorities from ransom demands precipitated by the crown's own unruly and footloose subjects. Those indemnifications extended not only to English and Irish renegades plying Mediterranean waters but also to those resourceful and loyal English sailors who succeeded in making their escape without diplomatic interventions. If Christian captives managed to board English ships of war stationed in Algerine harbors, the 1698 treaty stated that English consuls or ship commanders were "not obliged to pay anything for the said Christians."[14]

---

13. "Extracts of Treaties between Great Britain and Algiers," June 20, 1698, Article 3, MS 17034/3, Thomas Betton Charity Papers.

14. "Copy of Confirmation of the Treaty with Algier (1682), and the Additional Articles," Aug. 17, 1700, in Cecil Headlam, ed., *Calendar of State Papers, Colonial Series, America*

The 1698 treaty exemplifies the deeply ambivalent relationship that English authorities possessed toward their own highly mobile sailor subjects at the beginning of the eighteenth century. Historians have debated whether English policy regarding the crown's enslaved subjects in North Africa was mean or simply impecunious. But focusing on the motives of consular officers misses the larger context and purpose of English treaties with North African polities at the dawn of the eighteenth century. With these agreements, English authorities hoped to expand the capacity of the English state to regulate traffic across burgeoning Mediterranean trade routes. The English pass system in the Mediterranean was but one of several policies designed to regulate the flow of people and goods involving English ships and sailors. English passes also produced revenue for the English treasury. Such fees were a necessary expense for shipping merchants, a cost associated with prize taking not only in the Mediterranean but across all oceanic trading routes.[15]

For English sailors in the Mediterranean, however, the pass system did not materially enact nationalized relations of rescue for the simple reason that nations only partially organized the booming traffic in goods and people across the region. Naval authorities described captors at sea as pirates, as enemies of sovereign authority. As such, they supported official diagnoses of the root cause of the trafficking of Englishmen, describing it as a symptom of piracy rather than the result of Mediterranean-wide national policies toward prize taking. Sailors, by contrast, expressed skepticism and even hostility toward the emancipatory claims of national authority. As the radical Quaker Thomas Lurting made explicit in his published captivity account, sovereign authorities displayed, not so much indifference to the plight of enslaved sailors, but a blind eye to the true source of the problem, the chief traffickers of sailors at sea. For Lurting and sailors like him, pirates represented less of a threat to freedom than sovereign authorities, all of whom organized human trafficking and only belatedly implemented national relations of rescue and emancipation.[16]

---

*and West Indies, 1700* . . . , [XVIII] (London, 1910), 665; "Extracts of Treaties between Great Britain and Algiers," June 20, 1698, Articles 6 and 11, MS 17034/3, Thomas Betton Charity Papers, "Extracts of Treaties between Great Britain and Algiers," 1700, Article 2, MS 17034/3.

15. Linda Colley, *Captives* (New York, 2002), 53; Matar, *British Captives*, 44–45. On the variety and complexity of British policies comprehended within the term *mercantilism*, see Philip J. Stern and Carl Wennerlind, eds., *Mercantilism Reimagined: Political Economy in Early Modern Britain and Its Empire* (New York, 2014).

16. See Thomas Lurting, *The Fighting Sailor Turn'd Peaceable Christian* . . . (London, 1710); and Chapter Two, above.

If the pass system offered a crafty solution to the challenges of national governance in the Mediterranean, in practice it strengthened the hand of pirates across the region. Although the pass system enacted transparent distinctions between royally sanctioned crews and renegades from England, many English and Irish pirates somehow managed to obtain official passes, to the great consternation of English authorities. Abuses of the pass system ironically invited Algerine ships to ignore English passes altogether and to traffic all English subjects captured at sea as well as their passes. If English sailors were sailing under the flag of an enemy nation after all, "the enslavement of such men was within the terms of the treaties and was viewed as punishment." Efforts to harness the power of Algerine corsairs to buttress England's capacity to regulate its own produced contradictory results at best. That many of the crews on board His Majesty's ships were only partially English created additional confusion and invited further predations at sea.[17]

A clear sense of how confounding questions of national belonging could be emerges through an examination of diplomatic tensions between Morocco and Great Britain in the wake of the Algerine treaties. Unlike Algiers, Morocco signed no diplomatic agreements with Great Britain until 1721, when a law was passed specifying that "passengers taken by any of the Emperor of Morocco's cruizers . . . shall immediately be set at liberty." Rather than frame a hard-to-enforce commitment to antislavery, Great Britain's new treaty with Morocco focused instead on the rights of seamen and others sailing under the British flag, insisting that all persons be free from arbitrary detention. The treaty stated "that all passengers of whatever nation they may be belonging to . . . shall be entirely free without being detained, molested, robbed, or receiving any damage" from Moroccan vessels. Such language made sense given the multinational character of the sailor crews working aboard His Majesty's ships, but that diversity also created frustration for North African privateers. No less than the dey of Algiers remarked through a translator in 1699 on the phenomenon that "an English vessele thats abroad . . . should have above two thirds strangers when not one third Englishmen on board." Even Britain's adversaries expressed angst with the motley crews that were growing Britain's imperial advantages at sea.[18]

---

17. Matar, *British Captives*, 45.
18. "Treaties with Morocco," Feb. 23, 1721, Article 1, MS 17034/3, Thomas Betton Charity Papers, "Extracts of Treaties with Morocco," 1734, Article 3, MS 17034/3; The Dey of Algiers, Apr. 9, 1699, SP 71/4/5, The National Archives, Kew, U.K., quoted in Matar, *British Captives*, 45. On British-Moroccan diplomacy in 1721, see MacLean and Matar, *Britain*

To simplify the challenge that both trafficking and piracy produced for English officials, the new treaty encouraged Morocco to treat all non-English nationals on ships flying the Union Jack as British sailors. In 1734, British consular officials succeeded in forging an agreement with Morocco in which the rights of persons "navigating under the English flag," whether from Spain or Hanover, Germany, shall "be considered and esteemed as English natural subjects" by Moroccan ship captains. For sailors, the purview of British sovereignty was expanding along with British naval power during the eighteenth century. That expansion effectuated a pervasive and enduring manpower shortage within Great Britain's navy, one that encouraged a reformulation of how Mediterranean naval authorities understood British subjecthood for the Empire's multilingual and multiracial sailors.[19]

Relying on multilingual sailing crews was one aspect of the expansion of British sovereignty. Enacting relations of national rescue for Britain's diverse captive sailors was quite another. None of Britain's treaties with Morocco or Algiers created mechanisms by which British sailors already captive should be redeemed or released. Neither antislavery sentiment nor the pass system stopped prize taking by pirates or by Algerine and Moroccan vessels. The 1721 treaty between Morocco and Great Britain, like the Algerine treaty in 1698, was negotiated and signed only after protracted bargaining to redeem British slaves. Rather than abolishing prize taking, these treaties relied on the same Muslim corsairs they ostensibly condemned to enact British sovereignty claims.[20]

The multinational character of virtually all sailor crews in the Mediterranean Sea helps explain why relations of emancipation remained stubbornly organized along religious rather than national lines among many European powers during the early eighteenth century. Emancipating Spanish slaves, after all, elided differences between Muslim and Christian captives hailing from the Iberian Peninsula. Indeed, most of the ransom money for Spanish

---

*and the Islamic World,* 152; and James A. O. C. Brown, *Crossing the Strait: Morocco, Gibraltar, and Great Britain in the 18th and 19th Centuries* (Leiden, Netherlands, 2012), 37–38, 98, 125. John Windus, the British ambassador to Morocco in 1721, published an account of his diplomatic mission to Morocco the same year the treaty was ratified. See Windus, *A Journey to Mequinez; The Residence of the Present Emperor of Fez and Morocco; On the Occasion of Commodore Stewart's Embassy Thither for the Redemption of the British Captives in the Year 1721* (London, 1725).

19. "Extracts of Treaties with Morocco," 1734, Article 13, MS 17034/3, Thomas Betton Charity Papers.

20. Matar, *British Captives,* 288.

captives remained confined within religious boundaries, raised by Catholic religious orders across the Iberian region. By contrast, the Church of England deployed its resources only sporadically on behalf of English slaves, even when the political and religious loyalties of captive English sailors to the Church of England were never in doubt. In 1720, English naval chaplain Thomas Pocock published a sermon making precisely that point. "It must be observ'd," he wrote, "that the *English* are in a worse condition than those of any other *Christian Nation*. . . . In all Popish Countries there are . . . no churches without a Box . . . for the reception of money . . . for the *Redemption* or *Relief* of *Captives*." In England, he observed, "the Protestant Slaves are seldom bless'd with *publick* Contributions." Lacking relief from their own church, English captives were also frequently ignored by the crown. Captives with means were able to purchase redemption through *"private"* ties, while the rest were "condemn'd to the Obedience of inhuman *Laws*, and to the Company of Beasts, Infidels, and *Renegadoes*." Pocock drew attention to the weakness of British relations of rescue, even as he sought to realize nationalized emancipations that would bring relief and "Charity to our suffering Brethren and Countreymen."[21]

Ransom work for British captives in the Mediterranean nonetheless expanded along national lines over the course of the eighteenth century. To understand how and why, consider the importance of nationalist stirrings even within critiques of British policy. Pocock might have exposed the anemic antislavery efforts of Great Britain's religious authorities, but he also animated a vision of a morally redeemed British nation defending and rescuing its captive sailors. Pocock was no Quaker, but his sermon bears striking similarities to Lurting's story. Both narrators positioned Englishness in opposition to prize taking, slavery, and the political authorities who sanctioned such activity. The task of creating nationalized relations of rescue was first and foremost a work of imagination, and questions bedeviled these efforts. Would the crown lead or react to the demands of its sailors? Were all able seamen

---

21. Thomas Pocock, *The Relief of Captives, Especially of Our Own Countreymen; Humbly Offer'd to the Consideration of the Directors of the South-Sea Company, and to Those Who Have Been Directed by Them* (London, 1720), 9, 21–22, 26. On Pocock, see Matar, *British Captives*, 44, 144. On the power of religious intermediaries in financing emancipations for Christian slaves, see Matar, *British Captives*, 47; Colley, *Captives*, 1–20, 51–54; and Madeleine Dobie, *Trading Places: Colonization and Slavery in Eighteenth-Century French Culture* (Ithaca, N.Y., 2010).

equal in the eyes of the crown when raising money for ransoms or negotiating diplomatic rescues? Which British actors would facilitate these humanitarian transactions? The efforts of a particular shipping merchant to create national relations of rescue for all English slaves in the Mediterranean help to provide some answers.

### Financing Emancipation: Thomas Betton and the Ironmongers' Slave Fund

Toward the end of Thomas Pocock's influential sermon in 1721, he called on wealthy Englishmen to take the lead in raising ransom money for their enslaved "Brethren and Countreymen" in North Africa. "We seem to live in a time where there is no want of money," Pocock observed, urging Britons to expend their riches "in creditable and necessary acts of Charity, and for the relief of despairing *Captives*." As an exemplar of such charity, Pocock singled out the philanthropic work of one "Mr. *Adams,*" a shipping merchant who not only traded goods in the Mediterranean but also raised substantial money for ransoming dozens of British slaves. It is not known whether Thomas Betton, another English shipping merchant, listened to or read Pocock's sermon, but, when he died on February 15, 1723, just a year after Pocock published his sermon, Betton devoted his entire fortune of several hundred thousand pounds sterling to create a charity under the supervision of the "Ironmonger's Company" of London, with "one full half part of the interest and profit of my whole estate yearly and every year . . . for the redemption of British Slaves in Turkey or Barbary." Another quarter was devoted to "Charity Schools in the City and Suburbs of London where the education is according to the Church of England," while the final quarter was divided between a hospital and maintenance for mariners' widows and children "not exceeding ten pounds a year to any family." The plights of enslaved sailors abroad and their dependent families at home should not be separated from one another even if families already were, Betton believed, and his trust sought to create enduring support for both.[22]

The creation of the Ironmongers' Slave Fund, as it came to be known, transformed how British authorities responded to the ongoing threat of their

---

22. Pocock, *Relief of Captives*, 24–25, 26, 30; "Last Will and Testament of Thomas Betton," Feb. 15, 1723, MS 17034/4, 2, Thomas Betton Charity Papers.

sailors being captured at sea. Although large sums of money had previously been devoted to ransoming British captives, such outlays had been reactive and episodic, reflecting the particular needs and demands of British captives and their advocates. Captives with wealthy family members or political leverage in London fared better than average sailors, many of whom languished in captivity for years. Now, a permanent fund existed whose primary purpose was to pay ransoms for all British slaves in North Africa and the Ottoman Empire. That such a fund was created by a private fortune should not obscure its decidedly public purpose. Betton's will stipulated "that all persons acting in the capacity of British subjects . . . who should have the misfortune to fall into captivity in Turkey or Barbary are entitled to be redeemed out of the trust funds of this estate." Precisely because Betton deemed the problem to be national in nature and origin, he charged the executors of his will with fulfilling a manifestly public task without regard to rank or station.[23]

Yet how the new Ironmongers' Slave Fund would complement the work of government officials remained unclear. For trustees of the slave fund, the first challenge was to make sure that any financial transactions would indeed achieve the intended result of freeing British slaves. When a large group of captive British sailors needed public ransom money in 1733 and approached the fund, its trustees sought advice from their lawyer, councilor "D. Ryder," who urged the company to find "a person of integrity" who might be "trusted with the money." That special agent would also "keep an exact account of the Names and Familys of Slaves redeemed, the respective times when, the places where . . . and the prices for which they were redeemed." The political and geographic dilemma of making captives fungible was hardly new to the families of captive British sailors or to the British government in 1733. For

---

23. "Last Will and Testament of Thomas Betton," Feb. 15, 1723, MS 17034/4, 2, Thomas Betton Charity Papers. The Ironmongers' Company has not yet been the subject of an academic history, though it is prominently mentioned in Colley, *Captives*, 120. A company history was written at the end of the nineteenth century, as the Ironmongers' charitable work through the Thomas Betton Trust wound down. See T. C. Noble, *A Brief History of the Worshipful Company of Ironmongers, London, A.D. 1351–1889: With an Appendix Containing Some Account of the Blacksmiths' Company* (London, 1889). The best academic investigation into the work of the Ironmongers' Slave Fund is Styer, "Barbary Pirates, British Slaves, and the Early Modern Atlantic World." Styer locates the fund in a broader story of the relationship between British sovereignty and piracy in the Mediterranean across the early modern period.

trustees of the slave fund, however, finding a "person of integrity" was just the first hurdle to enacting national relations of rescue.[24]

Determining a fair price for English slaves, one that slaveowners in Algiers or Morocco would accept and abide by, was quite another conundrum. In the spring of 1733, wardens of the Ironmongers' Slave Fund, Robert Godshall, Henry Trent, and Dan Cockrell, designated two merchants living in Gibraltar, "Mr. Holraide and Mr. Pearson," to make arrangements for the sale of British slaves then being held in Algiers. To support that endeavor, the wardens persuaded the Ironmongers' Company to use two thousand pounds to pay "thirty pounds per head for the redemption of the 62 slaves." Ironmonger wardens instructed their representatives to reach out directly to George II's emissary in Morocco, Vice Consul John Leonard Sollicoffre, who also sought to secure a new treaty with Morocco. "We think ourselves obliged to let you know that we have in our hands a sum of money," began a letter to merchants Holraide and Pearson, and "we therefore desire you to act in concert with . . . John Leonard Lollicopse in order to obtain the liberty of the 62 persons . . . together with an authentic certificate of each of their names, their families, and the ships on which they were taken." Wardens for the Ironmongers' Company saw their efforts to be fully compatible with official diplomatic efforts, but they also sought distance from official channels, hoping to secure the ransom of British captives without public visibility, which, they feared, would increase the size of the ransoms. "We make no doubt but you will do your utmost to husband the money," wrote Ironmonger wardens to merchants Holraide and Pearson, "so as to get them freed on the cheapest terms possible. . . . We recommend the greatest frugality and above all things desire it may be a secret to the Moroccans that the slaves are redeemed by a public purse."[25]

National relations of rescue would have to remain private for the time being, Ironmonger wardens believed, exemplifying tensions within mercantilist political economy and culture. Blue water mercantilism was premised

---

24. "Questions and Answers," Feb. 27, 1733, MS 17034/4, 2, Thomas Betton Charity Papers.

25. Robert Godshall, Henry Trent, and Dan Cockrell to Mr. Holraide and Mr. Pearson, Mar. 4, 1733, MS 17034/3, 10–11, Thomas Betton Charity Papers. Godshall was also a local political leader, serving as the sheriff, alderman, and lord mayor of Bishopgate Ward in London, positions that gave him some insight into how local almsgiving worked. For mention of Godshall's offices, see *The Ancient Remains, Antiquities, and Recent Improvements, of the City of London . . .* , I (London, 1830), 178. On John Leonard Sollicoffre, see Matar, *British Captives*, 147–148.

on the notion that freely negotiated transactions, whether purchasing goods, spices, or people, would result in national and imperial greatness for Great Britain as well as complementary forms of moral and financial value. The notion that humanitarian charitable transactions should be cheap, that there should be no values but moral and market ones when purchasing and freeing British slaves, is revealing of tenets at the heart of both British antislavery and its ongoing commercial revolution. The Ironmonger wardens' instructions to purchase precisely sixty-two English slaves proceeded, not from any accounting of the actual number of British subjects held in bondage, but simply their calculation as to how many slaves two thousand pounds sterling ought to purchase. Their guidepost was the price of an African slave in the Atlantic, which during the latter half of the 1720s had averaged just over thirty pounds per slave but had recently slumped to roughly twenty-three pounds per head during the early 1730s. In 1733, Ironmonger wardens deemed thirty pounds to be a generous price for an adult slave, one they calculated as being slightly above fair market value. For Ironmonger trustees, market values for slaves did not preclude humanitarian motives but made them possible.[26]

The material and ideological connections between Ironmonger wardens and the Atlantic slave trade become even clearer when examining the accounts of the slave fund. The two thousand pounds dedicated to liberating British slaves in 1733 came directly from the Ironmongers' Company's "public stocks, bonds, and government securities," over half of which were invested in the South Sea Trading Company. Focused on the African trade across the southern Atlantic, the South Sea Company benefited from mercantile diplomacy, in particular the Treaty of Utrecht between Spain and Britain that expanded the South Sea Company's access to Spanish ports in the southern Atlantic. That political fix also resulted in a dramatic speculative bubble that drove the price of the South Sea Company's stock to record heights and

---

26. David Eltis, Frank D. Lewis, and David Richardson, "Slave Prices, the African Slave Trade, and Productivity in the Caribbean, 1674–1807," *Economic History Review,* XLVIII (2005), 679. For a similar analysis of how British officials used the challenges of redeeming British slaves to devise better "imperial regulations and control" over the "commercial behavior of Britons" during the eighteenth century, see Styer, "Barbary Pirates, British Slaves, and the Early Modern Atlantic World," v. Styer, however, confines her analysis to the Mediterranean. Like Colley and others, she anachronistically describes English captives as white slaves across the early modern period. See also Haskell, "Capitalism and the Origins of the Humanitarian Sensibility, Part 1," in Thomas Bender, ed., *The Antislavery Debate: Capitalism and Abolitionism as a Problem in Historical Interpretation* (Berkeley, Calif., 1992), 111.

subsequent collapse in 1720. By 1733, the South Sea Company had refocused its energies on slowly building British slave-trading posts with Iberian partners across South America, terrain that had formerly been managed by Spain and her New World colonies. The money conveyed by Ironmonger agents to emancipate English slaves in Morocco in 1733, then, came directly from profits derived from trafficking African bodies across the Americas. Ironmonger charity on behalf of British slaves in Morocco was made possible by the capital and market values of the Atlantic slave trade.[27]

Material and conceptual connections across the Atlantic, however, did not help Ironmonger trustees negotiate a consistent price for redeeming British slaves in the Mediterranean. The problem that Ironmonger agents confronted in North Africa was not so much ideological but transactional. Their chief concern was, not how to justify an antislavery mission with profits from slave trafficking, but how to persuade the owners of British slaves in Morocco to accept ransoms of just thirty pounds per head. The British merchants Holraide and Pearson had little interaction with the Moroccan authorities who controlled the fate of some 144 British slaves. They were instead dependent on the hard work of George II's exclusive agent, Sir Charles Wager, in negotiating a ransom with the sultan of Morocco's main agent, the "Bashaw of Tetuan." Wager ultimately succeeded in arranging a transaction for the liberation of 144 enslaved compatriots, but at a much higher cost than the Ironmonger wardens had expected. Merchants Holraide and Pearson tried to break the news gently, suggesting that emancipating just sixty-two slaves at thirty pounds per head was both impractical and arbitrary. "We were all desirous to facilitate as far as possible the Liberty of our unhappy Countrymen," Holraide and Pearson wrote, "so we were inclinable to believe you might

---

27. Godshall, Trent, and Cockrell to Holraide and Pearson, Mar. 4, 1733, MS 17034/3, 7, Thomas Betton Charity Papers. The South Sea Company stocks belonging to the Ironmongers' Company were divided into two groups, shares of "Original South Sea Stock," worth four thousand pounds sterling, and shares of new "South Sea Stock," valued at sixty-five hundred pounds. Collectively, they constituted more than half the total capital of the Betton Charity holdings. On the Treaty of Utrecht in 1713, see Hugh Thomas, "The Treaty of Utrecht and the Slave Trade," in Trevor J. Dadson and J. H. Elliott, eds., *Britain, Spain, and the Treaty of Utrecht, 1713–2013* (New York, 2014), 52–56. On the history of the South Sea Company, see Anne Murphy, *The Origins of English Financial Markets: Investment and Speculation before the South Sea Bubble* (New York, 2009); Helen J. Paul, *The South Sea Bubble: An Economic History of Its Origins and Consequences* (New York, 2011); Richard A. Kleer, "Riding a Wave: The Company's Role in the South Sea Bubble," *Economic History Review*, LXVIII (2014), 264–285; and Thomas, *The Slave Trade: The Story of the Atlantic Slave Trade: 1440–1870* (New York, 1997), 235–246.

acquiesce in your limit." Not having time for such permission, Holraide and Pearson lent their support to Wager to get all "one hundred and forty-four then alive" out of Morocco. As Holraide and Pearson sheepishly explained, "The King ordered that he [Wager] should go and settle the Ransom with all the particulars relating to the peace with the Bashaw at Tetuan, who there exacted from him an extravagant ransom of 87, 10 pounds per man." According to Wager, the total cost of ransoming the 144 living slaves "came to twelve thousand six hundred pounds," a sum that did not even include the expense of the diplomatic gifts necessary to make the transaction possible in the first place, an added cost to the king of "3700 pound."[28]

The final ransom bill, eight times what the Ironmonger wardens had initially authorized, challenged their basic expectations about how a humanitarian market in slaves worked. The price reflected neither the labor power of enslaved workers nor the calculations of supply and demand at the heart of the transatlantic African slave trade. Instead, the price was the result of Wager's deft political calculations that weighed the cost of ransoming the entire batch of loyal sailors versus the protracted cost of negotiating ransoms for discrete groups of sailors over time. Wager explained the importance of these factors in his correspondence with the British Admiralty Office. The ransom price was high, he acknowledged, but also the best that he or anyone could have struck, because the sultan of Morocco Mulay Abdallah had been deposed by members of his own army during the final negotiations. When the sultan's remaining chief surrogate, "the Bashaw of Tetuan," offered to finalize the negotiated transaction, Wager jumped at the offer, repeating the bashaw's argument that "he run the hazard of his head in suffering the Captives to embark . . . lest the new King should have stop'd the Captives to make a new bargain."[29]

Because Wager understood the ransom price of eighty-seven pounds was the result of political rather than market calculations, he also recognized that it would take diplomatic efforts to make the transaction palatable back home in London. To that end, Wager outlined two imperatives for his subordinates in the British Admiralty Office to tackle as they awaited the arrival of the redeemed British captives. The first was for the emancipated men to thank

28. Holraide and Pearson to [Robert] Godshall, Dan Cock[eri]ll, and Wardens of the Ironmongers' Company, Nov. 6, 1734, MS 17034/4, Thomas Betton Charity Papers, Sir Charles Wager to Admiralty Office, Sept. 27, 1734, MS 17034/4.

29. Sir Charles Wager to Admiralty Office, Oct. 29, 1734, MS 17034/4, Thomas Betton Charity Papers.

both the king and members of the Ironmongers' Company personally and collectively, a reprise of the successful theater created by emancipated slaves on behalf of Charles II in 1680. Wager gambled that thanking the Ironmongers' Company would increase pressure on them to offer additional funds to defray the greater-than-anticipated cost of ransoming all 144 British slaves. "I have talked with Mr. Scope of the Treasury about the most proper way for an application to the Ironmonger Company," Wager wrote in the same missive, inviting the "clerk of the said Company . . . to call upon him at the Treasury in the privy Garden." Wager hoped to persuade the Ironmongers' Company to devote "half the sum of their fund" toward the redemption of these British slaves, a request that would have saddled the Ironmongers with three-quarters of the total cost.[30]

Wager might have expected resistance from the Ironmongers' Company, but he was deeply dismayed by their refusal to pay any additional money for the emancipated British sailors. Wardens of the company viewed Wager's request as not only an unreasonable bailout but as an infringement on their control over Betton's charity. To meet Wager's request would have meant selling off half the fund's assets and damaging the company's capacity to administer "transactions of charity" to future British subjects enslaved in North Africa. The company responded to Wager's calculated risk with inaction and silence during the spring of 1735. Forcing Wager's hand, the wardens insisted on remaining steadfast to their original commitment of two thousand pounds.[31]

Seven months after British slaves marched in procession to the Ironmongers' Hall in London, Wager sought to turn Ironmonger resistance to his advantage by encouraging George II to demand "under his Majesty's Privy Seales" direct control over funds designated for the redemption of British slaves. On July 15, 1735, George II issued an extraordinary letter to the Ironmongers' Company laying out two arguments. The first charged Ironmonger wardens with having failed to discharge their legal obligations, asserting that "very considerable Sums of Money are remaining in your or some of your

30. Sir Charles Wager to Admiralty Office, Nov. 7, 1734, MS 17034/4, Thomas Betton Charity Papers.

31. Ultimately, the two thousand pounds were not used to pay any of the ransom money but to defray costs that diplomatic actors incurred in trying to arrange the transaction. As the two British merchants designated by the Ironmonger wardens to assist them in Tetuan, Morocco, wrote, the draft of two thousand pounds "will be sufficient for what the ambassador may want . . . very suitable credit for incidents he could not so conveniently have drawn on the treasury for." See Mess. Hatfield and Bosville to Master of Wardens of Ironmongers' Company, Mar. 13, 1735, MS 17034/3, Thomas Betton Charity Papers.

hands, custody, possession, or power which should and ought to be applied and disposed for the Redemption of . . . our Subjects . . . taken Captives and carried into Slavery." The second insisted Ironmonger wardens should no longer have sole power "to pay and defray the Charges attending the said Redemptions." The king's letter concluded with an endorsement of Wager and his authority over the negotiation and payment of emancipatory transactions. "KNOW ye therefore that we are confiding in the fidelity and care of Sir Charles Wager . . . and have nominated him to ask, demand, and receive of you . . . the sums of money . . . remaining in your hands," the king warned. Here, indeed, was a direct political challenge to the Ironmonger wardens, one that raised the question of who could enact national relations of rescue. The king's letter insisted that the king's ministers alone could authorize truly national relations of rescue.[32]

The king's letter prompted a long meeting of the entire Ironmongers' Company on August 4. Unable to formulate a strong response that would protect both the company's finances and its prerogative as stewards of the slave fund, Ironmonger members "deferred" action "to the next Court." Over the next two years, members of the Ironmongers' Company were consumed by issues sparked by the king's challenge and Wager's empowered demands for money. The central question, posed by Ironmonger members and their distinguished lawyer, Tory member of Parliament Nicholas Fazakerley, cut to the heart of the slave fund's function: "Whether the Company are obliged to pay the money as directed by Warrant of privy seal, or follow the donor's will and redeem the captives themselves?" Ironmonger members sought to reconcile two imperatives manifestly in tension, a devotion to principles governing slave markets and a commitment to enacting nationalized relations of rescue. The unspoken premise of Fazakerley's question was that the company could have redeemed these captives themselves, presumably at fair market values, had not the king's minister interfered.[33]

Fazakerley sought to preserve the company's independence while still fulfilling its emancipatory obligations. "The Company, being trustees . . . cannot

---

32. Robert Tothill [for King George] to the Masters and Wardens of the Worshipful Company of Ironmongers, July 15, 1735, MS 17034/4, Thomas Betton Charity Papers.

33. Sir Charles Wager to the Masters and Wardens of the Worshipful Company of Ironmongers, Aug. 5, 1735, MS 17034/4, Thomas Betton Charity Papers, Nicholas Fazakerley to Charles Wager, Feb. 17, 1736, MS 17034/4, 19–20. On Fazakerley's career as a Tory member of Parliament, see "Fazakerley, Nicholas" in Romney Sedgwick, ed., *The History of Parliament: The House of Commons, 1715–1754*, II (New York, 1970), 27–28.

pay the money as directed by the Warrant," Fazakerley stated, but "they must execute the trust mentioned in the Donor's will." Fazakerley recognized that "this part of the Trust may be troublesome to the Company," given the challenge of being a public fund without the necessary backing of the British state. As a solution, he suggested relying on the British courts, specifically a "Court of Equity," which might "direct the money as it grows due to be paid to a proper person appointed by the Crown from time to time for the purposes mentioned in the will." Such a mechanism would also "indemnify" the company from any future liabilities occasioned by British ministers like Wager, who might once again demand access to the entire fund if ransom money was proffered.[34]

Fazakerley's opinion became influential in shaping the Ironmongers' Company's subsequent responses to the king's demands while also emboldening Wager. In the spring of 1737, Wager filed a complaint with the attorney general alleging that "sums of money and other considerable estates had been given to the Company in Trust for the Redemption of his Majesty's subjects taken captives and carry'd into slavery which had not been applied to the Charitable intent of the donor." Worse, Wager claimed, "the Company in combination with its wardens and clerks have not only converted these Money and estates to their own uses, but refused to discover what they were and when and by whom given and how applied so that the charitable intent was frustrated." With Wager's complaint in mind, Ironmonger lawyer William Brown counseled the company to vigorously defend Betton's will. "I think it would be proper to . . . insist upon the Trust . . . and likewise to deny the charges of concealment and misapplication suggested by the information." Equally important, Brown argued the company be open to the possibility that a court of equity might "go as far as to direct an account . . . touching the application of the interest . . . towards the redemption of Slaves."[35]

Fazakerley and Brown succeeded in persuading the Ironmonger wardens to defend the "charitable trust" against the king but also convinced the king's attorney general to dissuade Wager from pursuing his complaint in court. As it turned out, both sides took some comfort from the aborted legal showdown. "As nothing further appears to have been done in the Information at the relation of Sir Charles Wager," Ironmonger lawyer Ryder wrote, "it is

---

34. Fazakerley to Wager, Feb. 17, 1736, MS 17034/4, 19–20, Thomas Betton Charity Papers.

35. Sir Charles Wager, Complaint, June 7, 1737, MS 17034/4, 21–22, Thomas Betton Charity Papers, William Brown to Ironmonger Wardens, Aug. 6, 1737, MS 17034/4, 22–23.

presumed that the proceedings were abandoned." Yet Wager's efforts yielded some fruit for the cash-poor crown. "The letters of Privy seal extend to money only," Ryder continued, "and not to real estates . . . while the will and decree direct annual profits only to be distributed." In the future, the crown could use its executive powers to make direct demands on the Ironmongers' Slave Fund, but only for the interest that had accrued on the Betton Trust's stocks and cash assets.[36]

To avoid future disputes with the crown over its financial assets, the Ironmongers' Company began investing earnings from the Betton Trust in real estate. In 1742, Ironmonger investors targeted rural locales near London, especially recently enclosed commons landscapes with reliable rent revenues. Topping the list of acquisitions were "Marsh lands," to which tenants needed access but which were also relatively modest in price and possessed strong "value" according to George Carter, a "proprietor of an estate in the locale of Eastham" who helped Ironmonger investors. Earnings from Ironmonger marsh lands, however, were not used to pay ransoms for British slaves but instead to fund the "Charity schools" run by the Betton Trust among London's poorest residents. The ironies of such investments—making money from recently dispossessed freeholders, some of them swelling the ranks of London's poorer classes, to better fund and equip the city's charity schools—paralleled similar ironies in the slave fund's reliance on Atlantic slave trafficking. If Ironmonger wardens perceived any hypocrisy in these money circuits, they did not express it, nor profess any anxiety about how their desire to indemnify the company from potential liabilities, whether British slaves awaiting ransom or starving British commoners in London, contradicted the Betton Trust's charitable intentions. Rather, members of the Ironmongers' Company deemed market value and moral value to be intertwined suppositions, things that could or should increase prosperity and freedom for British subjects.[37]

The national relations of rescue that Ironmonger wardens supported, then, were partial at best and riddled with tensions over what "transactions of charity" should cost and how they should be realized. In the wake of the legal battle with Wager over control of the slave fund, the Ironmonger wardens more willingly embraced the idea of directly honoring financial requests from the crown to emancipate British slaves as long as the capital requested did not exceed the income produced by the fund's stocks and annuities, roughly

36. D. Ryder to Ironmonger Wardens, Nov. 3, 1737, MS 17034/4, 24, Thomas Betton Charity Papers.

37. George Carter, Affidavit, July 19, 1743, MS 17019, Thomas Betton Charity Papers.

two thousand pounds every other year. That amount was insufficient to pay the ransoms of all British slaves held in North Africa. That said, the notion that relations of rescue should be nationalized by the end of the 1730s had gained prominence even among Ironmonger wardens, though sharp differences remained over how such ransoms should be transacted and to whose benefit. Market values, after all, remained abstract and meaningless without the messy and time-consuming work of diplomacy.[38]

The limitations of Ironmonger antislavery became manifest in who Ironmonger wardens counted as a British slave in the wake of their confrontation with Wager. In 1738, they received a request to pay the ransoms of "eight British slaves." Having learned that the market in British slaves had to be adjusted upward, Ironmonger wardens authorized a payment of "50 pounds a head, which was extended to 60 pounds in case it could not be done under." Two thousand pounds were procured by the company to pay the cost of redemption and any additional costs associated with making the transaction possible. All went well until the spring of 1739, when "a doubt arose whether Irishmen might be properly deemed British subjects" and therefore "proper objects of the Betton's charity." At least four of the provided eight names—"Gerrat Farril, John McGuire, and his wife and child"—were Irish, a discovery that led Ironmonger wardens to retract their ransom money. In a subsequent meeting, wardens decided only English slaves could be redeemed by the Ironmongers' Slave Fund, despite the language in Betton's charity about freeing "British slaves." Over the next decade and a half, Ironmonger wardens refused to pay the ransom for even a single captive Irish sailor.[39]

Historian Linda Colley has cited Ironmonger hostility toward emancipating Irish captives as an example of the enduring religious and cultural divisions within British national identity during the mid-eighteenth century.

---

38. The Ironmongers' Company records indicate that the slave fund brought a return of roughly 5 percent annually, which in 1740 consisted of just over £1000 pounds sterling on the £20,500 principal.

39. Sir Charles Wager to the Masters and Wardens of the Worshipful Company of Ironmongers, July 1738, MS 17034/4, 24, Masters and Wardens of the Worshipful Company of Ironmongers to Sir Charles Wager, May 2, 1739, MS 17034/4, 25, Meeting of the Worshipful Company of Ironmongers, June 5, 1739, MS 17034/4, 26. In a letter dated March 29, 1750, Ironmonger wardens objected to a request for funds from Britain's designated ambassador to Morocco, Mr. Latton, on the grounds that "in the number of the fourscore prisoners now detained there may probably be some Irishmen." See Masters and Wardens of the Worshipful Company of Ironmongers to Ambassador Latton, Mar. 29, 1750, MS 17034/4, 33, Thomas Betton Charity Papers.

Ironmonger partiality highlighted the importance of human trafficking to fault lines within British antislavery ideology as well. If Ironmonger wardens believed in a universal price for slaves, they did not believe Irish captives were redeemable. Because they possessed no fungible value to wardens, they were also unable to be emancipated. That assessment was not strictly financial in nature but rooted in exclusionary cultural and political assumptions about the British nation and who constituted it. Ironmonger warden and lawyer Fazakerley, a member of Parliament who opposed any efforts to ameliorate the suffering of Irish peasantry or to allow Jewish residents in England to become naturalized citizens, exemplified that viewpoint. For Fazakerley, antislavery and the transactions of charity that nurtured it were reserved for a particular group of subjects within Great Britain, Protestant English men, preferably naval officers, with aristocratic pedigrees.[40]

Disputes over who would receive ransom money nevertheless helped animate an important expansion in the capacity of Great Britain to emancipate its captive sailors in North Africa. Perhaps the best evidence of that expansion can be found in the documentary evidence created by one of the English sailors whom Ironmonger wardens helped emancipate in 1750, Thomas Troughton. After years of dithering over who would fund Troughton's ransom and that of his eighty-seven fellow crew members, the Ironmongers' Company agreed in 1750 to make the largest ransom payment in its history, providing the British treasury £7,647, nearly half of the treasury's total outlay, to the emperor of Morocco in the spring of 1750. Before reaching that agreement, Ironmonger wardens repeatedly sought ways to minimize their financial exposure, insisting that no Irishmen be part of the crew and that there "be proof made that they were all Britons, before they apply the money." At no point did the wardens insist that the British subjects be white. When Thomas Jones was redeemed to London with Troughton in the fall of 1749, a sailor whose freedom, like Troughton's, was procured by Ironmonger stock sales of the South Sea Company, Ironmonger wardens duly noted that he was Black but offered

---

40. Colley, *Captives*, 120. On Fazakerley's opposition to Jewish naturalization, see Bystander, *A True State of the Case concerning the Good or Evil Which the Bill for the Naturalization of the Jews May Bring upon Great-Britain; With Some Remarks on the Speeches of Sir J-B-d, and H-s Fra-y, Esq.; Upon the Said Bill* (London, 1753). On the larger backlash that the Jewish naturalization bill stirred up, much of it a transformation of antitrafficking discourse, see Dana Rabin, "The Jew Bill of 1753: Masculinity, Virility, and the Nation," *Eighteenth-Century Studies*, XXXIX (2006), 157–171.

no objection to his emancipation. The other Black sailor in Troughton's crew, "John Armatage, a Black," remained unredeemed, but only because he "turn'd Moor" along with twenty others just months before the delayed transaction occurred.[41]

Very little is known about Jones's story, how he became one of the first enslaved Black men to have his freedom purchased by the British crown, or what happened to him on his return to London. One thing is certain, though. He was not alone as a Black man sailing under the Union Jack during the eighteenth century. Indeed, one in ten sailors working on British slave ships during the eighteenth century were Black, men whose skills made them indispensable actors in shaping the transoceanic slave trade. In the Caribbean, a pervasive manpower shortage pulled even higher numbers of African and Native American sailors into the Royal Navy. During the winter of 1743, in the midst of an especially acute labor shortage brought about by the War of Jenkins' Ear, the governor of Jamaica, Edward Trelawney, found that five British vessels had more Black sailors than white. Three others possessed "an equal number of white Men and the other colours," a circumstance that Trelawney believed foretold danger for the sugar trade and the need for "some check" on impressment. For penurious Ironmonger wardens, however, the race of these redeemed English slaves was less important than their loyalty to the crown. They approved of Jones's redemption to England in 1749 because he was a devoted subject of George II, having long suffered as a British slave.[42]

## Transacting Emancipation: Thomas Troughton's Ordeal

For Thomas Troughton, the suggestion that his belated redemption exemplified the strength of national relations of rescue would have seemed ironic if not insulting. Central to his captivity narrative *Barbarian Cruelty*, after all,

---

41. "Transfer to the British Exchequer," Mar. 29, 1750, MS 17034/4, 33, Thomas Betton Charity Papers; Troughton, *Barbarian Cruelty*, 15, 16.

42. Edward Trelawney to the Admiralty, Dec. 21, 1743, Admiralty Papers, 1/3817, The National Archives, Kew, U.K., quoted in Brunsman, *Evil Necessity*, 116. On sailors of African descent in Great Britain's eighteenth-century navy, see Marcus Rediker, *The Slave Ship: A Human History* (New York, 2007), 229, 349; Paul Gilroy, *The Black Atlantic: Modernity and Double Consciousness* (Cambridge, Mass., 1993), 12–14; Peter Linebaugh, "All the Atlantic Mountains Shook," *Labour/Le travailleur*, X (Autumn 1982), 87–121; and Julius S. Scott, *The Common Wind: Afro-American Currents in the Age of the Haitian Revolution* (London, 2018), 73–76.

was a stinging indictment of the incompetence of British diplomatic efforts to emancipate him and his multiracial peers, a saga of unjust class privileges claimed by British officers against the common sailors who made up the core of the Royal Navy. Troughton began his captivity narrative conventionally enough, with praise for the British monarch who helped end his "Slavery under the arbitrary and despotic Government of *Muley Abdallah*, Emperor of *Fez* and *Morocco*." The stated purpose of his narrative was also nationalist, to emphasize the benefits of being British and to praise political leaders like George II for their steadfast commitment to their subjects' freedom and liberty. *"Happy ought every* Briton *to think himself, who enjoys his Freedom without Controul, under the mild Government of his present Majesty King* GEORGE," stated Troughton in his "Preface to the Reader." But Troughton's story departed from convention in several important respects. Rather than simply asserting his tale was *"true, and authentic,"* Troughton presented his narrative in the form of a deposition sworn under oath to the lord mayor of London, Francis Cockayne, on April 22, 1751. *Barbarian Cruelty* was more than a believable story; it was a legal argument, one Troughton's publisher, R. Walker, feared might engender claims of libel from his former captain. Troughton's legal motives were spelled out in an additional deposition, this one signed by fifteen *"Brother Slaves,"* who agreed to *"aver, that all the Surprising Incidents therein related are real Facts, without any Exaggerations to render our Cases more deplorable than they were."* The sixteen sailors made up a decidedly plebeian lot. Three of them could not sign their names, and only one, Ozborn Noble, possessed a trade worth mentioning, that of *"Carpenter."* The rest were common seamen, men whose collective legal endorsement effectively bolstered Troughton's grievances.[43]

What inspired these legal instruments within Troughton's narrative? Troughton did not specifically accuse any of his countrymen of treason, but two elements in his story—his description of Captain Richard Veale's actions and those of British consul William Pettigrew—warranted Troughton's legal strategy. Shortly after being captured, Troughton recounted that they were visited by the English consul, one "Mr. *Petticrew*," while still in port

---

43. Troughton, *Barbarian Cruelty*, title page, A2, 3, 4, 6, 7, 8. For a brief discussion of Troughton's captivity and struggle for legitimacy in the eyes of his political superiors, see Colley, *Captives*, 90–91. On the broad array of framing tropes for English captivity narratives during the eighteenth century, see Norton, "Lust, Greed, Torture, and Identity," *Comparative Studies of South Asia, Africa, and the Middle East*, XXIX (2009), 260–261; and Joe Snader, *Caught between Worlds: British Captivity Narratives in Fact and Fiction* (Lexington, Ky., 2000).

at Tangier Bay. At first, Consul Pettigrew offered all eighty-seven captive crew members hope of a quick escape, informing them that "he would send us Ropes to scale the Walls of the Town in the night, and carry us off in a Settee." After a meeting between the consul and Captain Veale, in which Pettigrew entertained him at his house "in as handsome a Manner as possibly he could," however, a second announcement brought despair to Troughton and his captive shipmates. As Troughton reported, the message stated "that there were no Hopes of our getting out of the Country, or of being released from our approaching State of Slavery, till the Government of *Great-Britain* had discharged an old Debt that was in Arrear . . . for the Ransom of a certain number of Captives . . . seventeen Years since." On learning of those outstanding diplomatic debts, "our Officers . . . formed a Project to make their Escape; and, with the Assistance, as well as the Consent of the Captain of the *Phoenix* Man of War, their Attempt was crown'd with Success." Rather than staying with his crew, Captain Veale "sent us Word to lay still, and the Consul would come the next Day, and carry us all off with flying Colours; but instead of that, they made their own Escape." Troughton's emancipation did not come "the next Day." It took more than four years to arrive.[44]

Troughton's bitterness at being abandoned by his captain infused every page of his subsequent account. As soon as Captain Veale's escape became manifest, Troughton wrote, "a whole *Legion* of *Barbarians* swarm'd about us . . . and breathed Revenge for their Disappointment." Blamed for Captain Veale's escape, Troughton and his fellow sailors were immediately placed in "the Town-Goal . . . with all the publick Marks of Infamy and Contempt by the *Moors*, and were used worse than a Pack of Dogs." Troughton framed his misery and that of his compatriots in terms that British readers, accustomed to tales of unjust imprisonment or spirited malefactors, would have clearly understood. "The Cells at *Newgate*, destin'd for the Reception of the worst of Criminals, could not stand in Competition with this loathsome Place," Troughton wrote. The prison, incidentally, had been built by English indentured servants some seventy years earlier. Troughton then reminded his readers how and why he and his fellow sailors had landed there. "As the Consul had abandoned us, we knew not where, or from whom to seek the least Manner of Redress." Troughton and his peers managed to avoid starvation but

---

44. Troughton, *Barbarian Cruelty*, 17, 18, 19. On William Pettigrew and his contributions to British policy with North African partners, see Nicholas B. Harding, "North African Piracy, the Hanoverian Carrying Trade, and the British State, 1728–1828," *Historical Journal*, XLIII (2000), 31–32, 41.

only through the intervention of a local Muslim merchant in Tangier, "who had some Share of Humanity in him" and who helped them obtain "a License . . . to beg in the Day-Time, with a Guard to follow us, about the Town." Unnamed Moors, with no interest in them but that of common humanity, performed far better than Consul Pettigrew.[45]

Consul Pettigrew's actions during Troughton's long captivity further diminished his station and standing. Four months after being transferred to the mainland and forced to work long hours for his new master Mulay Abdallah, Troughton expressed hope that an impending visit by the consul might change his and his fellow captive's miserable circumstances. Yet when Pettigrew met with the sultan, he was rebuffed, with Mulay Abdallah insisting on negotiating directly with British ambassador William Latton. Pettigrew, Troughton recalled, "took his leave of the Emperor without taking the least Notice . . . of us." "He was not above one Mile Distance from the very Castle, where we were hard at Work," Troughton continued, "yet he could not find Time to give us the least Opportunity of speaking to him." Desperate to create some plan for redemption, Troughton sent Consul Pettigrew a letter outlining one way of procuring money for ransom. "We sent, on the 1st of July, a Letter to him, in which we enclosed a Letter of Attorney, to enable him to recover for us, in our Names, the Prize-Money for a *French* Vessel, of which we had made ourselves Masters, before our unfortunate Shipwreck." Consul Pettigrew responded in a letter, reprinted in Troughton's narrative, pledging "to collect some Charity at *Gibraltar*," where their prize ship had been taken. Nevertheless, as Troughton dryly commented, "This Letter . . . and the Power of Attorney which we sent with it, did us no Manner of Service." Troughton did not elaborate but implied that Pettigrew simply pocketed their prize money.[46]

Even as Troughton expressed his unhappiness with Pettigrew, he nonetheless held out hope that more powerful British officials, perhaps Ambassador Latton, might yet redeem him and his fellow crew members. Hearing that Ambassador Latton was in Gibraltar, Troughton and *"sixteen young Captives"* managed to send a letter to him, appealing for immediate aid in the fall of 1746. Facing starvation because their masters had not provided them even with daily bread, Troughton claimed that *"if it was not for the small Subsistance we have from the Spaniards and Portuguese, we must certainly have perished."* Troughton then articulated their dilemma to Ambassador Latton in stark

---

45. Troughton, *Barbarian Cruelty*, 19, 20, 21.
46. Ibid., 48, 49, 50.

terms. They had been presented with a choice to either convert to Islam or starve outright. *"It is a most terrible thing for any* Christian *to think on,"* wrote Troughton at the end of his letter, *"that a Man must be forced to turn and renounce his God and King for the Want of Subsistance."* Troughton's request was simple enough. He desired a small amount of money, not to pay ransoms, but to sustain the sailors while ransoms might be arranged. Troughton was again sorely disappointed. Although the ambassador responded to Troughton's letter, little changed for Troughton or his compatriots. "We were prodigiously deceived," Troughton concluded, adding with a touch of sarcasm that "we had the Hard Fortune to remain in Slavery upwards of four Years after his Excellency's Arrival at *Gibraltar.*"[47]

Troughton's ensuing narrative recounts spectacles of brutal violence, horrific labor, and brief moments when hopes were raised and dashed by self-serving British diplomatic actors. He acutely understood the challenges inherent in making a ransom transaction between distrustful parties. As 1747 wore on to 1748, the main obstacle to redemption was not simply an absence of money from British consular authorities but anxiety about how a ransom transaction itself could even be arranged. On February 4, 1749, Moroccan leader Bashaw Hamet, deputized by Sultan Abdallah to facilitate a transaction, arranged a meeting with Ambassador Latton of Great Britain. The much-anticipated transaction, however, fell apart over how, when, and where the transaction should occur. Latton insisted that "he would not pay him 'till they, and their Fellow Slaves, were embark'd.'" "I fear," Ambassador Latton explained to Troughton and twenty-five others still in bondage, that "when he has got the Money, he will not send you away." Such fears were not unfounded, as negotiations over each British slave's price had resulted in the murder of the previous ambassador, John Leonard Sollicoffre.[48]

Although Troughton began his narrative by condemning the selfishness of British diplomatic actors, his critique grew more complex over the course of his story. He emphasized the political difficulties inherent in ransom transactions while also acknowledging the crafty role that Pettigrew played in

---

47. Ibid., 103, 104, 106. Troughton's criticisms notwithstanding, some British diplomatic officers labored mightily to secure his release and that of his compatriots. William Latton allowed himself to be taken into custody as a security while awaiting the long-delayed ransom funds from the Ironmongers' Slave Fund. On the challenges faced by Latton and consular officers more generally in North Africa, see Styer, "Barbary Pirates, British Slaves, and the Early Modern Atlantic World," 142–143, 259–262.

48. Troughton, *Barbarian Cruelty,* 172.

arranging ransoms for himself and his peers. Rather than waiting on stalled talks with the sultan of Morocco, Pettigrew saw an opportunity with one of the sultan's chief advisers, Bashaw Hamet, who was "impatient to have an End put to . . . our Captivity." Pettigrew knew that Hamet desired to "be in Esteem with the Governor of *Gibraltar*, and have a greater Share of the Trade from thence he had before." Pettigrew arranged for the arrival of a boat with the ransom money in late March 1749. When Hamet hesitated, Pettigrew exploited his insecurity by asking him, *"When do you imagine to get the Money into your Hands? Do you think that the Government of Gibraltar will send the Money a second Time?"* The consequences of a failed transaction, Pettigrew noted, could be deadly as well as disastrous for commerce in Hamet's locale. *"When the Merchants of Gibraltar come to understand you are not a Man of your Word, they will not think themselves safe to carry on the least Commerce with this Town."* Pettigrew's arguments persuaded Hamet, who "ordered that we should depart, which was joyfully obey'd by us." On December 9, 1749, after nearly five years of captivity, Troughton and his thirty-six remaining compatriots boarded the H.M.S. *Sea Horse*. Offering Pettigrew "three Huzza's," Troughton recounted, he and his compatriots set sail for "our Native Country." The lessons readers drew from Troughton's account were thus powerful and contradictory. His narrative condemned the cowardice and inaction of British officials while simultaneously recounting their importance to his ultimate redemption. Troughton likewise denounced the "inhuman barbarous *Moors*" in Morocco but devoted several portions of his book to sympathetic descriptions of their religiosity, food customs, and marriage practices. In short, Troughton's story exemplifies key dilemmas that confronted Great Britain's expanding imperial project: how to map intertwined geographies of freedom and slavery while reconciling humanitarian, market, and national values with one another.[49]

Troughton's engagement with that challenge becomes especially visible in his effort to include a moral toward the end of his narrative, one "with Advice to our Countrymen who intend to travel, or reside in *Barbary*." Would he reinforce his class-based critique of British officers like Captain Veale and Consul Pettigrew? Or would he simply reiterate his condemnation of Moorish inhumanity? Was there a single lesson that encompassed both narrative emphases? Troughton's conclusion is significant for what he emphasized and what he ignored. In his final pages, he condemned, above all, the custom of trafficking people for profit. "This inhuman Custom, of giving Money for the

49. Ibid., 10, 169, 181, 200.

Destruction of one another, and also buying a Man to have him intirely at his Disposal," Troughton concluded, was not only a crime against humanity but one uniquely rooted in the political life of Moroccan culture, "practised all over this Empire, both among the *Moors* and *Jews*." By describing the practice of trafficking people as an "inhuman custom," Troughton seemed to embrace the abolitionist sentiments of Thomas Lurting, but he stepped back from making an abolitionist critique of all human trafficking. Troughton did not condemn the Atlantic slave trade or even mention slavery in his final remarks. Rather, he condemned the same ransom traffic that led to his emancipation, complaining of the "barbarous Custom" in which the "bought Man is frequently tortured in the cruelest manner, to make him discover what Money he has."[50]

For Troughton, inconsistencies between his narrative and the moral truths he proffered were reconcilable within a larger vision of national relations of rescue, as long as they were justified as universal in form and purpose. His final critique of prize taking in the Mediterranean and the trafficking of ransomed subjects it generated linked national and universal interests, indicting the tyrannies of "Arbitrary Government" and defending British liberties under the nation's benevolent monarch. For Troughton and his fellow sailors on board the *Inspector Privateer*, antislavery and nationalism were twined commitments that required, at a minimum, ship captains ready to defend the liberty and freedom of their crew and royal officials who would emancipate captive subjects without prejudice to rank, station, skin color, or the cost of their ransom. Troughton's antislavery nationalism expressed, not just the interests of one political monarch or even the democratic aspirations of its sailor subjects, but the broader moral force of humanity itself. The authority Troughton imagined and helped generate was simultaneously national and versatile in form, universally opposed to trafficking and resolutely British.[51]

## Conclusion

Across Great Britain and its expanding empire by 1750, expectations that the nation should emancipate its captive subjects were becoming ever more persistent and powerful, even as national relations of rescue remained contradictory and partial in practice. Conflicts pervaded every effort to expand national emancipations. Thomas Troughton's vision was sharply distinct from that

50. Ibid., 211, 213.
51. Ibid., 212.

articulated by wardens of the Ironmongers' Company, whose slave fund made transactional values rooted in slave trafficking the foundation of humanitarian intervention. By contrast, Troughton never articulated what a fair price for his ransom should be, only that human trafficking itself was unjust and immoral. Troughton's hostility to human trafficking made his narrative both inspiring and ironic, given the initial purpose of his voyage with Captain Richard Veale. Troughton, like Thomas Jones, was indebted to unnamed and unknown Africans whose passages across the Atlantic made possible the capital for his ransom transactions. Troughton and his fellow sailors' ordeal in North Africa hardened and honed their moral sensibilities and commitments as they refused the self-serving bromides that varied British diplomats proffered them while languishing in captivity. Troughton's critique of trafficking put him at odds with both his Ironmonger emancipators as well as their principal adversary, Sir Charles Wager, who sought to garner the entire Ironmongers' Slave Fund for royal coffers. Wager's ultimate solution to the political challenges of emancipating British slaves in North Africa was to better renumerate sailors and privateers who successfully trafficked foreign vessels in the first place. As the first lord of the Admiralty in 1740, Wager authored George II's "Act for . . . the Encouragement of Seamen to Enter into His Majesty's Service," which provided greater property incentives for British sailors to join the Royal Navy during wartime. Wager's answer to British slavery was not less trafficking but more of it, with greater numbers of British sailors plying the seas as traffickers producing national wealth.[52]

Political and ideological tensions between sailors and naval authorities pervaded discussions of British slavery in North Africa as well as impressment campaigns across Britain's expanding empire. Despite his differences with the Ironmonger wardens, Wager was quite sympathetic to the antislavery claims that Troughton and his fellow sailors articulated, prompting him to try reforming how the navy impressed its sailors. Rather than create a royal press service that could use legal channels to manhandle potential recruits, Wager championed the creation of a registration system that would, he claimed, create a fair and systematic method for determining when and how often and for how long British sailors served in the Royal Navy. Wager's effort to level the playing field for sailor recruitment failed, however, because opponents

---

52. "An Act for the More Effectual Securing and Encouraging the Trade of His Majesty's British Subjects to America, and for the Encouragement of Seamen to Enter into His Majesty's Service," 1740, in Danby Pickering, *The Statutes at Large, from the Ninth to the 15th Year of King George II . . .* , XVII (London, 1765), 360–370.

charged that such a registry would be "the most flagrant barefaced attempt upon the liberties of his majesty's subjects throughout all his dominions, that ever was brought into parliament." Just so did defenders of British liberty ironically strengthen the legal capacity of press-gangs to traffic sailors on land and at sea. As in debates over the Spiriting Act of 1670, all sides claimed to be defending essential British liberties. The demand for national relations of rescue would expand the capacity and reach of the British Impress Service as well as sailors' expectations for emancipation.[53]

Wardens of the Ironmongers' Slave Fund, like Troughton, raised more questions than they answered about the relationship between nation, slavery, and liberty in Great Britain's expanding empire in 1750. Nowhere were their competing commitments to market liberties, humanity, and national redemption more sharply put to the test than in the very next emancipation case that the Ironmonger wardens considered. In 1757, wardens were asked to disburse funds on behalf of "Stephen Clement, a Slave in Barbary," as the case was named by a recordkeeper in Ironmongers' Hall, London, yet details of the case quickly complicated that description. Clement, who might indeed have once been a "slave in Barbary" emancipated by the Betton Trust as his letter claimed, was not, in fact, writing from Barbary but instead from the seaside town of Abingdon, England, on behalf of his son, a young man also named Stephen Clement, by "trade a breeches maker." Dated June 17, 1757, Clement's letter detailed a familiar tale of spiriting in which Stephen "the younger" was "decoyed by a person in London who after some talk persuaded him to go on board a ship which the poor unfortunate young man did." There he encountered "fourteen more who had been . . . kidnapped to go to Maryland, there to be sold for a Slave for the term of Five Years, and never saw his Deceiver no more." Unlike many parents whose teenaged children were kidnapped, Clement managed to find out where his son was living, having been "sold for a Slave to a Gentleman to work at Plantation Business, whose name is Nicholas Dorsey at Washington, near Ethredge Landing" in the colony of Virginia. His request was simple and straightforward; he wanted the Ironmonger wardens to use the Ironmongers' Slave Fund to purchase his son's freedom "that he may have his liberty."[54]

The request was simple, perhaps, but not straightforward. The merchants

---

53. W[illia]m Cobbett, *Cobbett's Parliamentary History of England* . . . , XI (London, 1812), 421–422, also quoted in Brunsman, *Evil Necessity*, 42.

54. "Papers Related to a Slave Stephen Clement, 1755," June 17, 1757, MS 17034/4, Thomas Betton Charity Papers.

and kidnappers in this case were not pirates from North Africa but shipping merchants whose business dealings traversed the Atlantic and the Mediterranean. With his plea for help, Clement asked a pointed question. Could the Betton Trust, which had already emancipated Clement from North Africa, also emancipate his son from bondage in North America? It is not known how the wardens of the slave fund responded, though they most certainly took his petition seriously, as Clement's letter was also signed by John Eldridge, the mayor of London and an honorary member of the Ironmongers' Guild. If they funded Clement's request, they did not do so publicly, as the file title suggests recordkeepers wanted it to be understood as "a Slave in Barbary." Wardens of the slave fund likely did not want to set a precedent that would potentially expand the number of emancipation demands by the thousands. But Clement's letter, and the possibility that Clement the younger was freed from servitude with Ironmonger funds, demonstrates just how powerful the idea of an emancipatory national slave fund had become. If British slaves in North Africa could be emancipated by a nationally designated fund, why should not deserving British slaves be emancipated in every corner of the British Empire? If liberty was indeed a birthright of every British subject, then why should not relations of emancipation be globally imagined wherever a British subject, white or Black, languished in chains? Sailors and servants had long engaged that possibility but never more so than during the ensuing decade when trafficked British subjects and literary innovators gained greater access to printing presses and to the larger literary marketplace, the subject of the next chapter.[55]

55. Ibid. On how poetry and the novel sustained and enlarged antislavery feeling during the middle of the eighteenth century, see Robin Blackburn, *The American Crucible: Slavery, Emancipation, and Human Rights* (London, 2011), 154–155. Blackburn leaves underexplored, however, how novels encoded class biases of an elite antislavery and intensified racial imaginaries.

CHAPTER SIX

## War, Traffic, and Race across the British Empire

In 1757, former indentured servant Peter Williamson published a dramatic life story entitled *French and Indian Cruelty* that chronicled the varied ways commoners across the British Isles could become captives during the middle decades of the eighteenth century. "*Stolen* from his *Parents*" by shipping merchants in Aberdeen at the tender age of eight he claimed, Williamson was then "sent to PINSYLVANIA, where he was sold as a SLAVE," an indentured servant by another name, along with fifty other young boys. Yet Williamson's years as a captive did not end with the completion of his indenture to a Quaker master. When the Seven Years' War broke out between France, England, and their respective Native American allies, Williamson, now a soldier, was taken captive by Delaware Indians and forced to march with them and other British soldiers into Canada. There he was sold to French military authorities, who sent Williamson to a prison in Montreal. Mercifully, his third captivity was brief, and Williamson was soon returned to Britain in a prisoner exchange between the warring countries. On stepping foot on his native soil, however, he became a military conscript and was "order'd to *Plymouth-Dock*, to be draughted into other Regiments." Williamson's final captivity, this time to the British Army, ended when he was discharged after demanding a pension for his years of suffering as a captive among the Indians and as a prisoner of war in Montreal. British authorities, however, were not sympathetic, especially after an officer in his old regiment claimed that he had deserted the army before being taken by the Delaware.[1]

---

1. Peter Williamson, *French and Indian Cruelty; Exemplified in the Life and Various Vicissitudes of Fortune, of Peter Williamson, a Disbanded Soldier* (York, England, 1757), title page; Williamson, *French and Indian Cruelty* . . . , 2d ed. (York, England, 1758), 103–104. On the history of the Delaware people during the eighteenth century, see Jean R. Soderlund, *Lenape Country: Delaware Valley Society before William Penn* (Philadelphia, 2015), 177–193. Unlike other Native peoples in the Southeast, they did not take captives among their

By linking captivities well known to British commoners into a single story, Williamson mapped geographies of labor and coercion that were intrinsic to British imperial expansion during the eighteenth century. Along the way, he articulated a critique of several British policies that were essential to its imperial business, condemning the traffic in children to North America, the transatlantic trade in indentured servants, the forced labor of British soldiers and sailors, and the anemic or nonexistent relations of rescue that existed for all three groups. A legal advocate for children and for trafficked servants on both sides of the Atlantic, Williamson was politically dangerous in 1757, a figure capable of exposing two of the central fictions undergirding Britain's expanding blue water Empire: that servants and children had consented to their migrations and that broader transoceanic markets for goods and people were free rather than despotic and corrupt. At the very moment Britain was expanding its imperial power through war, Williamson was stubbornly bent on debunking the ideological premise that the Empire was free, fair, and humane.[2]

Williamson was also one of the first plebeian actors in Britain to embrace notions of race in the telling and selling of his story about trafficking and

---

Native rivals in the region. On the impact of the Seven Years' War on Delaware autonomy, see ibid., 202–203. Although Williamson claimed to be eight on his departure, parish records indicate he was actually thirteen. See Timothy J. Shannon, ed., *Peter Williamson, French and Indian Cruelty: A Modern Critical Edition* (Edinburgh, 2023), x.

2. Linda Colley briefly discusses Williamson's narrative in the broader context of British imperial captivities across the British Empire. See Colley, *Captives* (New York, 2002), 191–192. Williamson has become the subject of serious scholarly inquiry. See Timothy J. Shannon, *Indian Captive, Indian King: Peter Williamson in America and Britain* (Cambridge, Mass., 2018); and Shannon, "King of the Indians: The Hard Fate and Curious Career of Peter Williamson," *William and Mary Quarterly*, 3d Ser., LXVI (2009), 3–44. Shannon demonstrates that most of what happened in Williamson's life did occur, with the important exception of his captivity among the Delaware. See Shannon, *Indian Captive, Indian King*, 56–58. Before Shannon published his work, scholars debated whether Williamson's text was accurate, rather than what his narratives meant. See, for example, Douglas Skelton, *Indian Peter: The Extraordinary Life and Adventures of Peter Williamson* (Edinburgh, Scotland, 2004). Other scholars focused on Williamson's Indian captivity in isolation from other captivities such as his kidnapping. See, for example, Tim Fulford, *Romantic Indians: Native Americans, British Literature, and Transatlantic Culture, 1756–1830* (New York, 2006), 52–53; Pauline Turner Strong, *Captive Selves, Captivating Others: The Politics and Poetics of Colonial American Captivity Narratives* (Boulder, Col., 1999), 195–200; and Troy O. Bickham, *Savages within the Empire: Representations of American Indians in Eighteenth-Century Britain* (New York, 2005), 61–64.

empire. He used descriptions of suffering white women to burnish his antislavery claims against Aberdeen's shipping merchants. More noteworthy, he deployed theatrical devices, including donning Indian headgear and warpaint, to sell and promote his inexpensive book. On a portable stage near public marketplaces across Scotland, Williamson dressed as a Delaware Indian, performing what he claimed were authentic songs and dances that he had observed among his captors. Although Williamson condemned the Delaware as "infernal" and "inhuman," he also professed to admire them and to know their culture intimately. "No People have a greater Love of Liberty," Williamson remarked, a sentiment that helped him sell revised and expanded editions of *French and Indian Cruelty* faster than Aberdeen merchants could confiscate and burn them.[3]

Williamson's racism and his radicalism were not antithetical but tightly interwoven elements in his stories about human trafficking and the manner he promoted them. Pretending to be an Indian emboldened rather than hampered Williamson in achieving his main political purpose. His aim was to sell a narrative of white suffering that denounced an entire class of shipping merchants along with the English political authorities who protected them. Indeed, Williamson used his sensational captivity narrative to assemble one of the first kidnapping archives in the English language. After Aberdeen's shipping merchants challenged his veracity and destroyed his stockpile of books, Williamson published an expanded version of *French and Indian Cruelty* in 1762 that included a forty-page appendix made up of dozens of depositions by kidnapped children and their parents. That archive documented the crimes and everyday cruelties of the trade in children in Scotland, pioneering new ways of telling and selling these important and neglected stories. By trafficking the suffering that white people allegedly endured because of their skin color, Williamson animated the essential lie that would become foundational to the ideology of white victimhood and to the notion that white people constitute a race.[4]

---

3. Williamson, *French and Indian Cruelty*, 2d ed. (1758), 13, 14, 26; Philip J. Deloria, *Playing Indian* (New Haven, Conn., 1998).

4. Peter Williamson, *French and Indian Cruelty* . . . , 5th ed. (Edinburgh, Scotland, 1762), title page. The frontispiece introduces the expanded volume as "The Fifth Edition with large Improvements." On eighteenth-century romances of Indian cultures, see Fulford, *Romantic Indians;* Karen Ordahl Kupperman, *Indians and English: Facing off in Early America* (Ithaca, N.Y., 2000), 92–100; and Deloria, *Playing Indian*, 10–37. Most analyses of plebeian appropriations of indigeneity focus on the nineteenth century. On fraternal groups such as the Improved Order of Red Men, see Deloria, *Playing Indian*, 62–68; and

Interpreting Williamson's words and actions present methodological challenges that cut to the heart of historicizing race and white supremacy. No single writer, after all, invented white victimhood or authored white supremacy. Williamson's narrative and his theatricality in selling it nevertheless establish him as a figure that in retrospect was ahead of his time. As a popularizer of both white suffering and minstrelsy, he revised imperial history to naturalize and justify his anger against political elites. A populist more than a century before the People's Party was organized, Williamson gleefully broke political rules for conveying truth, combining personal grievances with cultural fictions, mixing voices, genres, and authorship in the writing and selling of his books. With his capacity to traffic images of racialized suffering in his fiction and his outfits and performances selling it, moreover, Williamson bears a strong resemblance to subsequent race traffickers in Great Britain and the United States. Like them, Williamson became visible by ferreting out and condemning corruption, even as he burnished a reputation among friends and foes alike for being, as one critic put it, a professional liar.[5]

Yet to fully grasp Williamson's historical significance, it is necessary to see him, not as an originator of white working-class racism a half century before the Industrial Revolution, but as the product of his historical context on terms he himself would have understood. Ultimately, he was a wartime critic of imperial policies whose primary weapon was his small printing press. Although little was truly original about Williamson's words and actions, he exemplified

---

Gunther Peck, "Manly Gambles: The Politics of Risk on the Comstock Lode, 1860–1880," *Journal of Social History*, XXVI (1993), 701–723. On the importance of Indian costumes to agrarian radicals in the United States, see Reeve Huston, *Land and Freedom: Rural Society, Popular Protest, and Party Politics in Antebellum New York* (New York, 2000), 3–4, 117–119.

5. Examples of race trafficking, that is, promoting white racism by trafficking stories of white victimhood, are vast and woven throughout American and British history over the past two centuries. Among many examples in the United States, see discussions of Tom Watson in C. Vann Woodward, *Tom Watson: Agrarian Rebel* (New York, 1963); George Wallace in Dan T. Carter, *The Politics of Rage: George Wallace, the Origins of the New Conservatism, and the Transformation of American Politics* (Baton Rouge, La., 1995); and Donald Trump in Ta-Nehisi Coates, "The First White President: The Foundation of Donald Trump's Presidency Is the Negation of Barack Obama's Legacy," *Atlantic*, CCCXX, no. 3 (October 2017), 74–87. Among examples in Great Britain, see the discussion of Richard Oastler in Gunther Peck, "Labor Abolition and the Politics of White Victimhood: Rethinking the History of Working-Class Racism," *Journal of the Early Republic*, XXXIX (2019), 89–98; and Nigel Farage in Satnam Vinden and Branden McGeever, "Racism, Crisis, Brexit," *Journal of Ethnic and Racial Studies*, XLI (2018), 1802–1819.

a kind of authorship that was indeed new among plebeian actors, combining literary and legal devices to make himself and his story visible. By the middle of the eighteenth century, expanding access to printing presses and to print culture opened up opportunities for men like Williamson to traffic their narratives and to sharpen their attacks on the same elites who had initially deployed grammars of skin color nearly a century before. A growing audience for captivity literature also empowered actors from humble backgrounds to publish stories that sought not only redress but also fame and fortune. Their published narratives, however, are not unmediated windows into the lives of transient and trafficked actors but hybrid sources, combining biographical experiences with literary devices. Print culture could both amplify and co-opt plebeian voices like Williamson's, suggesting the limits of looking to the literary marketplace to challenge imperial fictions about trafficking and skin color.[6]

Williamson's significance becomes clearer through an examination of the imperial context within which he produced his narrative. He was not the first indentured servant to sell his own story about being trafficked. Several servants and sailors also published narratives around the same time that narrated and sometimes condemned the experience of transportation, impressment, war, and the suffering that British commoners endured as access to the commons was restricted across Great Britain. These publications presaged no immediate revolution in how indentured servants understood their political rights, but they did dramatize questions and dilemmas important to nearly all transient commoners, whose labor and loyalties remained vital to British identity and the expansion of British power. In a nation that celebrated the notion that "Britons *never will be slaves,*" why were so many subjects trafficked to distant corners of the empire under the British flag? How might trafficked actors fight back against the imperial policies responsible for so much

---

6. The historical literature on English print culture in the early modern era is vast. For ways to historicize books, printing presses, and their audiences, see Elizabeth L. Eisenstein, *The Printing Press as an Agent of Change: Communications and Cultural Transformation in Early-Modern Europe* (Cambridge, 1979); Adrian Johns, *The Nature of the Book: Print and Knowledge in the Making* (Chicago, 1998); and Leslie Howson, *Old Books and New Histories: An Orientation to Studies in Book and Print Culture* (Toronto, 2006). On the Seven Years' War, see Fred Anderson, *Crucible of War: The Seven Years' War and the Fate of Empire in British North America, 1754–1766* (New York, 2000); and Peter Silver, *Our Savage Neighbors: How Indian War Transformed Early America* (New York, 2008), 95–125.

coercion? Would the literary marketplace advance or thwart their aspirations? And what role if any would skin color play in shaping how plebeian authors trafficked their tales of suffering?[7]

## Trafficking Rogues:
### Servant Tales from the Bottom Up

In 1743, the same year that James Annesley defended his inheritance and Daniel Horsmanden completed his trial compendium, former indentured servant William Moraley presented his misadventures as an indentured servant to the public in a narrative entitled *The Infortunate: The Voyage and Adventures of William Moraley, an Indentured Servant*. Moraley's difficulties began when his father died and his mother disinherited him after remarrying. Like Annesley, Moraley had been born into Britain's burgeoning gentry class. After being disinherited, he sued his mother to reinstate his inheritance. When he failed, Moraley decided to "sell myself for a Term of Years into the *American* plantations," a period of servitude he described as "Voluntary Slave[ry]." Moraley's intentions in publishing his autobiography were not to win legal redress but to use his wit and irony to settle scores and eke out some earnings as a storyteller. Moraley's "Design in prefixing this *Preface*," as he put it, was "to return the Worthy Gentlemen of *Newcastle*, and Parts adjacent, my most sincere and hearty Thanks for the many Favours they have bestow'd on me, undeservedly. At present, I have no other Way to retaliate them." Whether recounting the inconsistencies of philanthropic authorities or the criminal activities of prison officials at Newcastle, Moraley laced his tale with sarcasm. He used his penal correction to burnish his credentials as a truth teller, someone who could expose imperial hypocrisies from the inside out.[8]

---

7. *Alfred: A Masque* (London, 1740), 42. On the origins of the celebrated patriotic song "Rule Britannia," written by James Thompson and set to music by Thomas Arne, see Todd Gilman, *The Theatre Career of Thomas Arne* (Newark, Del., 2013), xiv, 2–3. The first performance of the song on the British stage occurred in late August 1740. See "Last Night Was Perform'd," *London Daily Post, and General Advertiser*, Aug. 2, 1740, [1], and "On Friday Last Was Perform'd," Aug. 5, 1740, [2], cited in "The Celebrated Ode in Honour of Great Britain Called Rule Britannia," *Musical Times and Singing-Class Circular*, XLI, no. 686 (Apr. 1, 1900), 228–231.

8. William Moraley, *The Infortunate: or, The Voyage and Adventures of William Moraley* . . . (Newcastle, U.K., 1743); William Moraley, *The Infortunate: The Voyage and Adventures of William Moraley, an Indentured Servant*, ed. Susan E. Klepp and Billy G. Smith, 2d ed. (University Park, Pa., 2005), 3, 14, 28, 106. Historians Klepp and Smith have published

Precisely because Moraley was both educated and downwardly mobile, he proved to be an unusually perceptive observer of the traffic in servants. He found his labor recruiter, or spirit, during an acute moment of family stress and conflict. When his lawsuit failed, Moraley wandered to London, casting an appearance that reflected his increasingly desperate circumstances. "I was dress'd at that Time in a very odd Manner. I had on . . . an old worn out Tye Wig, which had not been comb'd out for above a Fortnight; an unshaven Beard; a torn Shirt that had not been wash'd for above a Month; bad Shoes and Stocking full of Holes." Looking like a caricature of the landed gentry but still a strong young man, Moraley was an ideal target for one of London's labor recruiters. In his recounting, his recruiter was "sincere" and earnest rather than morally wicked, a hardworking young man like him trying to make a living. "Perhaps you may imagine I have a design to inveigle you," his spirit began, "but I assure you I have none; and if you will accept a mug of beer, I will impart what I have to propose to you."[9]

Moraley's sympathetic rendering of his spirit's work contradicted stock portrayals of these key villains of the transatlantic servant trade. Moraley listened to his spirit carefully, well aware of the pragmatic ways the commerce of migration functioned. Before responding to the offer of a beer from his spirit, Moraley indicated he had already decided to travel to North America. "Not caring what became of me," after not hearing from his mother, "it enter'd into my Head to leave *England*, and sell myself for a Term of Years into the *American* plantations." To that end, Moraley sought out the main labor market for indentured labor in London, the Royal Exchange, where he hoped to "inform myself, by the printed Advertisements fix'd against the Walls, of the ships bound to *America*." Moraley happily accepted the offer to drink "two Pints of Beer" before his spirit "paid the Reckoning." Once on board, Moraley encountered a host of "Brother Adventurers" who "seem'd very dejected, from whence I guess'd they repented of their Rashness." Although Moraley noted that trickery was central to the traffic others experienced, he chose to enjoy his temporary bounty, however dearly bought in years of service. "Soon after, Dinner was brought on the Table, which consisted of stew'd Mutton Chops.

---

an annotated edition of Moraley's biography that sets the details in his narrative in their historical context. They write that "Moraley is most often a credible reporter" (111). For an additional assessment of Moraley's narrative and its authenticity, see Gwenda Morgan and Peter Rushton, *Eighteenth-Century Criminal Transportation: The Formation of the Criminal Atlantic* (New York, 2004), 100–101.

9. Moraley, *The Infortunate*, ed. Klepp and Smith, 14.

... I ate very heartily, and wash'd down the mutton with about two Quarts of Small Beer." Rather than see himself as a victim, Moraley deployed an almost clinical view of the transactions that transformed his life.[10]

Moraley's realism also led him to withhold the consent that enforcers of the servant registry demanded at the beginning of his voyage. When British authorities twice asked him whether he was acting freely or had been coerced, Moraley did not answer, revealing his skepticism about official fictions of freedom. The authorities left Moraley on the ship, concerned only that he might say no. When he accepted his allotment of clothes for the voyage, authorities took his action to be a *yes* for the servant registry. His description of the attire, however, was clinical and damning. "Every adventurer had his Apparel given him for the Voyage, which was, a Sea Jacket, two coarse chequ'd Shirts, a Woollen Waistcoat, two coarse Handkerchiefs, one Pair of Hose, a Woollen Cap, and pair of bad new Shoes." The bargain clearly had been a poor one, revealing the hollowness of British authorities' self-justifying efforts to ensure all had chosen servitude. If Moraley refused to make an explicit condemnation of transportation as a policy or the servant trade, he also avoided the convenient targets that government defenders relied on. In the process, Moraley confirmed essential facts about the transatlantic trade in servants that authorities labored to conceal. Spirits worked hard to fill merchants' ships, and debts were a crucial means for leveraging would-be servants to sign indentures. Pervasive poverty rather than moral negligence fomented coercive mobility.[11]

Moraley used antislavery language, not to exaggerate coercion, but to illustrate plainly what commodification and sale as an indentured servant looked and felt like. "Our Cargo consisted chiefly of Voluntary Slaves, who are the least to be pitied. I saw all of my Companions sold of[f] before me; my turn came last, when I was sold for eleven Pounds." Moraley made a clear distinction between his experience and that of the African slaves with whom he toiled and shared a common master. Being trafficked voluntarily enabled him to see both commonalities and differences between himself and enslaved men and women from Africa. On the one hand, he noted that "Negroes and bought Servants" were alike "clad in Osnabrigs, both coat, waistcoat, breeches, and Shirt, being of the same piece," signs that they were to be used for hard labor and to be sold. Two centuries before Edmund S. Morgan observed that planters in the Americas were "labor barons," Moraley recognized

10. Ibid., 13–14, 16, 17.
11. Ibid., 18.

that planters became "the richest farmers in the world, paying no rent, nor giving Wages either to purchased Servants or Negro Slaves; so that instead of finding the Planter rack-rented . . . you will taste of their Liberality." But Moraley also acknowledged asymmetries between servants and slaves, observing that "the Condition of the Negroes is very bad, by reason of the Severity of the Laws. . . . For the least Trespass, they undergo the severest Punishment. . . . If they die under the Discipline, their Masters suffer no Punishment, there being no Law against murdering them."[12]

Indeed, Moraley was haunted by the cruelty of the racial slavery that he witnessed as an indentured servant. The spectacle of violence against the enslaved hung about him, day and night, tempering any sense of his own victimhood. "One Night as I was in Bed with my Fellow Servant," Moraley recounted, "I perceiv'd something coming across the Floor, like a Ghost, in White, with a black Face. . . . It came to the Bedside . . . and stared me in the Face. . . . When I said, *Lord! why do you come here?* It answer'd, *Nothing with you,* as I well remember, and then went away." When Moraley mentioned the visitation to his master's family, he learned that the ghost was "a Negro killed some Years since by her Master," a reference to an actual murder in 1686, when English slaveholder James Wills killed his African bondswoman. Although the murder produced a trial in which one witness testified to having "heard still many Lashes" and her "Crying out," saying he "heard full a hundred stripes or lashes," Wills received no punishment. The memory of that injustice, as Moraley's recounting made clear, lived on among slaves, servants, and even some masters, long after the events occurred. Moraley's desire to be absolved of crimes intrinsic to racial slavery was quite unusual among English colonists, yet his connection of the meanings of servitude and slavery was not; rather, it was a coupling with a long history.[13]

Comparing the traffic in servants to that of slaves framed the larger meaning and purpose of Moraley's narrative. His comparisons, however, were not

---

12. Ibid., 28, 35, 57, 58; Edmund S. Morgan, *American Slavery, American Freedom: The Ordeal of Colonial Virginia* (New York, 1975), 120.

13. Moraley, *The Infortunate,* ed. Klepp and Smith, 47; H. Clay Reed and George J. Miller, eds., *The Burlington Court Book: A Record of Quaker Jurisprudence in West New Jersey, 1680–1709* (Washington, D.C., 1944), 57, also cited ibid., 139. James Wills's murder of his slave stirred controversy not only because he was a Quaker but also because it underscored the violence that was intrinsic to slavery. See Kristin Block, "Cultivating Inner and Outer Plantations: Property, Industry, and Slavery in Early Quaker Migration to the New World," *Early American Studies,* VIII (2010), 529–530; and Andrew T. Fede, *Homicide Justified: The Legality of Killing Slaves in the United States and the Atlantic World* (Athens, Ga., 2017), 77–78.

limited to North America. Moraley also described Turkish slavery, linking his own transportation and sale to the trauma endured by a Spanish sailor in North Africa named Alonso Tellez de Almenara. Captured by Moroccan pirates in 1710, then sold into *"Barbarian* Slavery" under the sultan of Morocco, Almenara's guards not only fastened "a Chain of twenty three Pounds Weight" about his legs but set him to work building a palace for the king. Moraley presented Almenara's story in the first person, as if Almenara himself was recounting the events. "We were forced to climb up Ladders and Scaffolds loaden with Mortar and Timber besides our Chains, that before Evening we were so wearied, as is impossible to express." Any thought of rebellion was quashed by the presence of "six hundred Blacks of his [the King's] Guard," who supervised every phase of their work with whips and shouts. The location of the reference to "Blacks of his Guard" within Moraley's narrative, coming just after his comment about "Voluntary Slaves" and just before his ghost vignette, suggests a meaning only partially located in North African piracy, though. For servants claiming enslavement in North America, Moraley had a pointed response. North Africa was where real slavery involving Europeans existed. Furthermore, masters who murdered their Black slaves with impunity should beware and consider what might befall them in North Africa, where a powerful class of Black overseers policed Europeans.[14]

Moraley's adaptation of narrative traditions common to British travel writing underscores how human trafficking in the Mediterranean and Atlantic regions conditioned one another's histories across the eighteenth century. His narrative also exemplifies how plebeian writers adapted fictional devices to their stories without sundering the authorship of the message of their tale. Moraley's inclusion of a North African captivity account was especially provocative because he refused white grammar in drawing comparisons between Atlantic and Mediterranean bondage. Rather than relying on race, Moraley used the experience of being trafficked to make disparate stories of enslavement comparable and legible, whether the subject was a freshly arrived "Voluntary Slav[e]" in Philadelphia, a "Negr[o]" sold in the Americas, or a sailor sold into *"Barbarian* Slavery" in North Africa. His skepticism about the humanitarian purpose of transportation, as well as his identification with the suffering of African slaves, marked him as a politically radical maritime worker, precisely the kind of subject that Horsmanden feared. His differences with Williamson are also telling. Both men effectively critiqued British

14. Moraley, *The Infortunate*, ed. Klepp and Smith, 37, 38, 39.

policies that encouraged human trafficking, but Moraley eschewed using race or hierarchies of suffering to do so.

Moraley relied on comparisons between slavery in North Africa and his "Voluntary" slavery to map and expand a political reality far larger than his own experience. Wardens of the Ironmongers' Slave Fund engaged in a similar kind of mental mapping when they grappled with the moral and financial significance of Stephen Clement's slavery in North America in 1757. Their respective maps, however, reveal conflicting insights about where, how, and why people should become property. Travel writing, early English novels, antislavery ideology, grammars of skin color, and transoceanic markets all performed similar work at one basic level; they made the value of far-flung trafficked actors visible and therefore meaningful through comparison. Yet these values created more questions than answers. How should one compare indentured servitude or slavery in Barbary to African slavery? Which values should British state actors defend or regulate? In seeking answers to these questions, trafficked servants learned from each other's spoken narratives as well as from published ones like Moraley's. They learned not only what to say but how to say it, a process more influenced by servants than by fiction writers.

Moraley's knowledge of Mediterranean slave narratives also raises different questions about the nature of authorship in his text. Where and how in North America did Moraley learn the story of a Spanish sailor captive in North Africa, and why did he include it in his narrative? One answer is that Almenara, or a version of him, might have briefly been Moraley's master in Philadelphia. Toward the end of his narrative, Moraley indicated he had avoided his creditors by living "as a servant with a *Spanish* Gentleman named *Don Roderigo de Almeria*." This master might have been the inspiration for the story about Almenara, or Moraley might have met someone like him whose story took him from *"Barbarian* Slavery" all the way to Philadelphia. Moraley was an expert storyteller, a trade that literally kept him alive while on the move. "I was welcome every where, though unknown," Moraley wrote, "always endeavoring to ingratiate myself into the People's favour by a modest and decent Behaviour, which, with relating Stories when desir'd . . . gain'd me the Reputation of an intelligent Man, though upon Occasion I could rake with the best of them, and change my Note as proper Time offer'd." Moraley survived as a "Tennis-ball of Fortune," as he put it, as a trafficker in stories of itinerant life, yet another reason, perhaps, Moraley presented Almenara's narrative as his own. It likely worked better in the first person and was one he had heard and then repeated in his wanderings through North America. As a teller of others' stories, Moraley revealed his intimate connection to a broader world of itinerant actors, "tennis-ball[s]" like him who survived by their wits, exposing the fallacies of Britain's empire of trafficking even as they bounced.[15]

The story of another British commoner, Bampfylde-Moore Carew, illuminates the challenges that trafficking one's own story presented for plebeian individuals. Originally published in 1745, *The Life and Adventures of Bampfylde-Moore Carew* presents Carew as a well-bred but downwardly mobile Englishman whose transience and adventuring enable him to critique British pieties about the nation's political economy (Figure 9). Carew's narrative exemplifies many of the same itinerant virtues that Moraley celebrated but with one important difference. Carew was a "Mumper," a profession in which he "concealed himself under the Disguises of Poverty, [and] Misery" and appealed to rich people for alms. Carew sometimes passed "for an unfortunate Farmer or Grazier, in a neat, rustick, plain Dress; at others, by the help of a pair of Trowsers, Jacket, etc. for a ship-wreck'd Seaman; To-day, a Foremast-man, tomorrow, (with some Alteration and Improvement of Habit) for a boatswain, mate, or master." Carew was no ordinary mendicant. Armed with details of disaster victims' lives, Carew played his parts with exuberance, extracting large sums of charity from wealthy dupes. When challenged by one gentleman about his professed story as a shipwrecked seaman, Carew undertook a voyage to Newfoundland to "enable himself to face the Shipwrecked Story with Confidence, and come off with Applause and success." Although his voyage yielded few adventures and lots of seasickness, he returned to England a much-improved impersonator of shipwrecked seamen, "keeping chiefly on the Sea-Coast in the Counties of *Devon, Somerset, Dorset, Hants, Kent* and *Sussex*, being everywhere treated with great Hospitality and Compassion," and collecting an "abundance of money." If art imitated life, Carew sought to make a perfect imitation of the commoners whose travails he literally embodied.[16]

---

15. Ibid., 40, 72, 75, 79.

16. Bampfylde-Moore Carew, *The Life and Adventures of Bampfylde-Moore Carew, the Noted Devonshire Stroller and Dog-Stealer; As Related by Himself during His Passage to the Plantations in America* . . . (Exeter, England, 1745), i, 20, 23, 31, 129. On Carew's career, see Morgan and Rushton, *Eighteenth-Century Criminal Transportation*, 78–85; Tim Hitchcock, "Tricksters, Lords, and Servants: Begging, Friendship, and Masculinity in Eighteenth-Century England," in Laura Gowing, Michael Hunter, and Miri Rubin, eds., *Love, Friendship, and Faith in Europe, 1300–1800* (New York, 2005), 177–196; and Joanna Innes, "The Role of Transportation in Seventeenth and Eighteenth-Century English Penal Practice," in Carl Bridge, ed., *New Perspectives in Australian History* (London, 1990), 1–24.

FIGURE 9. John Faber, Jr., after Richard Phelps, *Bampfylde Moore Carew*. 1750. Mezzotint. © National Portrait Gallery, London

In so doing, Carew lived the life of a vagrant, "commonly lying in Barns and Outhouses, in Blankets and Bedding which they also carried with them." At the same time, he experienced little enduring deprivation because of his transience, living "always in great Plenty," a vantage few displaced commoners would have claimed. Carew chose when, where, and how he moved and to whom he would be sold, choices not available to most transient people. Carew took a measure of pride throughout his *Life and Adventures* in successfully garbing himself as "a most deplorable Object of Charity," or in describing himself as a thing, a piece of "supercargo," as he frequently put it. Carew's evasion of the actual hardships brought about by transience and trafficking were manifest when he was readied for sale as an indentured servant after being transported to Newfoundland. He promptly jumped ship, rowing to shore in a canoe and living off the commons in Newfoundland in summertime until he found a way back to England.[17]

With lying and imitation central to Carew's craft, his narrative raises important questions about truth and artifice in his stories. If he lived like a beggar while imitating one, had he effectively become one? By sailing with endangered ship crews in order to retell their disaster stories, had Carew not become a sailor? Mumping might not have turned Carew into an actual beggar, but it did make him an astute observer of how itinerant men and women made their way by trafficking themselves to survive. Along the way, Carew portrayed trades that were under assault across Britain's countryside. His descriptions of his characters read like a who's who list of the economically precarious in Georgian England: he "returned to the Character and habit of a Jack-Tar," he "passed among the Colliers for a Tinner," "he used this Trade of making and selling Matches," he practiced the "Trade, Art, and Mystery of Rag-gathering," and he "passed for a broken Shopkeeper, obliged to abscond for Debt." Like Williamson, Carew sold "Songs and little Two-penny histories, *Tom Thumb, Jack the Giant-Killer,* and such other little Romances." As a seller of "Two-penny histories," Carew represented his actual profession, for a brief moment, without artifice: he was a trafficker of stories about Britain's footloose commoners.[18]

Rather than dismiss Carew's stories as frauds, it would be better to consider the targets of his satirical pranks, the English political authorities who were policing the mobility of poor people, whether in the countryside or in port cities. Wandering was feared by local religious and political officials across Great Britain during the middle of the eighteenth century, particularly as displaced tenant farmers grew in number with the enclosure of common lands. As enclosure intensified, local authorities passed laws to require all travelers to hold a pass, issued by a local mayor or church warden, that sanctioned one's movement. Without a pass, you officially became vagrant and could be

---

17. Carew, *Life and Adventures*, 6, 19, 127.

18. Ibid., 13, 20, 53, 92, 147–148. On the historical phenomenon of fraudulent identities as a problem related to transience and the spread of capitalism in the English countryside, see Tobias B. Hug, *Impostures in Early Modern England: Representation and Perception of Fraudulent Identities* (Manchester, U.K., 2009); and Patricia Fumerton, *Unsettled: The Culture of Mobility and the Working Poor in Early Modern England* (Chicago, 2006).

forced to work in a poor house or be transported to North America as a felon. In Dublin, where James Annesley resided as the *"Heir of Altamont,"* fully 50 percent of the felons who were transported to North America had been arrested as wanderers, vagrants who had been caught traveling without passes. In this context, Carew's capacity to dispense legal challenges at will made him something of a folk hero. In virtually every guise he donned, Carew managed to secure alms from rich residents and passes from local officials who were moved by the "deplorable Object" that Carew presented. Carew turned the pass system to his advantage by "making Use of many false and forged Passes, and frequently by applying to Church-Wardens and Officers of Parishes." Rather than curtailing transience, the pass system stimulated Carew's mobility. On returning from Sweden, Carew presented the mayor of Newcastle with forged "Letters or Certificates," "who thereupon . . . gave him a Pass for the West of *England.*"[19]

Carew took particular delight in hoodwinking "the King's Officers" who were trying to police the smuggling and trafficking of contraband goods arriving from English colonies. In one of his most satisfying tricks, Carew pretended to be a sailor, or a "Jack-Tar," who was connected to an incoming ship laden with contraband goods captured on the high seas. The "King's Officers" paid Carew handsomely for his information, offering him several pounds, free lodging and meals, and lots of alcohol. Carew slipped away before the "Sham-Informations" were discovered only to repeat the ruse on another set of king's officers he encountered in the next town, sowing "great confusion . . . in all the Sea-Ports in the West of England." Carew likewise took full advantage of a "Recruiting Serjeant" for the British Royal Navy, who saw Carew and was "tempted by the engaging Height and Size of his Body." After accepting an offer of drinks at a local alehouse, Carew gave the recruiting officer the slip during a water break, as the new recruits marched out of town. Carew then repeated the scam in the very next town. This time the navy recruiting officer

---

19. [James Annesley], *Memoirs of an Unfortunate Young Nobleman, Return'd from a Thirteen Years Slavery in America . . .* , Part I (Belfast, Ireland, 1743), 38; Carew, *Life and Adventures,* 9, 126, 127. For a broad overview of the struggles of English commoners against enclosure and the relationship of those struggles to antislavery ideology, see Peter Linebaugh, *The Magna Carta Manifesto: Liberties and Commons for All* (Berkeley, Calif., 2008), 94–95. On the transformation of the Scottish countryside near Aberdeen, see Neil Davidson, "The Scottish Path to Capitalist Agriculture, 1: From Crisis of Feudal Agriculture to the Origins of Agrarian Transformation, (1688–1746)," *Journal of Agrarian Change,* IV (2004), 227–268; and Davidson, "The Scottish Path to Capitalist Agriculture, 2: The Capitalist Offensive, (1747–1815)," *Journal of Agrarian Change,* IV (2004), 411–460.

offered Carew a speech before peppering him with more alcohol. "It was a shame," the recruiting officer began, "for a man of so . . . well-proportioned a Body, and of Youth . . . to travel the Country in Quality of a common Vagrant, and to lie liable to the Lash of the Law." Carew was then "prevailed upon to enlist," only to escape at the first march out of town. Playing the king's officers for fools, Carew critiqued their methods and claims to moral authority. The antagonists Carew exposed and individually triumphed over were, not the hardworking spirits, but the officers and magistrates who enforced impressment and criminalized vagrancy with the "Lash of the Law."[20]

The politics of Carew's *Life and Adventures*, then, were decidedly hostile to the varied policies of the British state toward its own transient subjects, especially the pass system, the servant registry, vagrancy laws, and impressment. The historical backdrop running through all of Carew's adventures were the everyday tragedies associated with an enclosure movement that deprived thousands of commoners access to livelihoods on public lands. The commons emerged in numerous anecdotes within Carew's broader narrative as a landscape that might temper the harshness of English transportation policies. When Carew escaped sale as an indentured servant in Newfoundland, he did so by heading into the forests of Newfoundland, where he "could with great Ease kill Partridges or Curlews to suffice his Appetite, and support him-self . . . for the Woods afford great Plenty of those Fowls." On his return to England, he met with a "Company of Sailors" who, like him, also took sustenance from the fragmented commons that survived in the English countryside. They were "loitering along the Road, in a weak and feeble Condition, gathering Blackberries to satisfy their Hunger." Carew understood the commons not only as a resource for hungry transients but as a set of customary rights of access to the land and to passage across it.[21]

Carew's critique of enclosure, transportation, and impressment animated

---

20. Carew, *Life and Adventures*, 67, 70, 89, 92, 97–98. The 1740s and 1750s were decades of especially acute resistance to impressment, particularly in North American colonies. One of the most dramatic uprisings against impressment occurred in Boston in 1747, the so-called Knowles Riot. On the rich currents of antislavery informing that uprising, see Denver Brunsman, *The Evil Necessity: British Naval Impressment in the Eighteenth-Century Atlantic World* (Charlottesville, Va., 2013), 226–235.

21. Carew, *Life and Adventures*, 135, 149 [157] (the pagination restarts after 152 with 145). On rethinking how to historicize migrant labor and nature as parts of a global commons, see Gunther Peck, "Migrant Labor and Global Commons: Transnational Subjects, Visions, and Methods," *International Labor and Working-Class History*, no. 85 (Spring 2014), 118–137.

a more universal critique of abusive political power beyond the boundaries of the British Isles. After escaping impressment on an Irish ship during another episode, Carew wandered across the countryside of Europe, where he "set himself to begging again, and was kindly treated by the Natives and Inhabitants," even though he remained "a stranger" to the languages of most local inhabitants. When in Italy, Carew took notice of a "most melancholy and dismal Spectacle . . . that of upwards of two hundred *Turkish* Slaves, whom the *Dutch* had sold to the *Muscovites,* who were fastened to each other by strong and heavy Chains of Iron, and worked in the Quarries near the town of *Ravel.*" His portrayal of trafficked Muslim prisoners, enslaved by Christian and European masters, was shocking because their presence reversed conventional depictions of Turkish cruelty in the Mediterranean. In Carew's assessment, the villains fomenting this traffic in slaves were, not Muslim pirates or Moroccan sultans, but other Europeans, the Dutch and the Russians. For Carew, the greatest threat to commoners' liberties were autocratic political authorities, whether Christian or Muslim. Indeed, the other "shocking Sight" Carew recounted in Italy was that of an English citizen, a "Boatswain of one of the Czarina's Men of War," being "drawn Limb from Limb" after fraternizing with a fellow English sailor aboard a different boat. Carew's experiences with European autocracy made him long "to be at his Liberty in his native Country," even as he remained steadfastly antiauthoritarian and critical of Britain's trafficking policies.[22]

Carew articulated his radicalism with few references to skin color or to the enslavement of Africans across the Americas. Slavery only briefly emerged within Carew's narrative when he described Turkish citizens sold by the Dutch to Russians building resort homes and palaces in the Italian town of Ravenna. Skin color likewise received limited attention, with no mention made of white or Black people. The single exception to that pattern was Carew's brief description of the society of "Gypsies," the cohort that Carew credited with teaching him to survive on the move as a mendicant. Carew described them as members of a "Tawny Society," which Carew joined after an initiation ritual in which he and the gypsies temporarily "coloured their Hands and Faces with a Liquor made of the green Shells of Walnuts, which they carried about with them for that Purpose in Bottles." Carew described his subsequent decision to become transient as an "Alteration of his Complexion, occasioned by the Walnut Shells," a transformation that caused his parents to "not at first know him." When Carew stained his face with green

---

22. Carew, *Life and Adventures,* 121, 122, 123, 124.

paint, he aligned himself with transient commoners who explicitly opposed the king's policies of both enclosure and transportation. The ritual recalled efforts by English commoners across the eighteenth century to protest enclosure in disguises that subverted imperial control and sovereignty. Carew's subsequent adoption of counterfeit identities was similarly intended to humiliate the English gentry and Britain's legal authorities, whose policing of transient commoners provided the fodder for the narrative energy, humor, and justice in Carew's writings.[23]

The radicalism within Carew's narrative, however, would be as short-lived as its author. Carew himself passed away in 1748, just three years after his book was published. Within months of his death, Robert Goadby, a commercial playwright, would recast Carew's character and story and republish it as *An Apology for the Life of Mr. Bampfylde-Moore Carew, Commonly Called the King of the Beggars*. Three changes distinguish Goadby's revision: the addition of racial signifiers in narrating Carew's exploits as a "Mumper"; the replotting of references to Turkish slavery, making European rather than Muslim bodies objects of sympathy; and a quieting of all critiques against Britain's expanding middle and commercial classes. These changes not only turned Carew's story into a popular and widely read text but also suggest how the literary marketplace could co-opt servants and sailors seeking to challenge political authority.[24]

Like James Annesely and Aphra Behn before him, Goadby put servant antislavery to work to defend, rather than critique, the freedoms of Britain's growing class of commercial gentry. The revised premise of Goadby's narrative was that Carew was now a natural king whose power had been ratified by the consent of his gypsy peers. The new Carew was, not simply a mendicant, but an elite populist, elected "KING of the BEGGARS" by campaigning

---

23. Ibid., 4–5, 8, 144. On the origins of blackface during early nineteenth-century minstrelsy shows, see David R. Roediger, *The Wages of Whiteness: Race and the Making of the American Working Class* (London, 1991); and Eric Lott, *Love and Theft: Blackface Minstrelsy and the American Working Class* (New York, 1993). Peter Linebaugh has described the fight to preserve access to the commons by English commoners in 1722 by blacking up as "an important moment in the development of white supremacy." If the Waltham Black Act made blacking up a crime, however, it did not simultaneously "racialize crime" for the simple fact that whites had already been connected to convicts through convict transportation. Race remained tenuously connected to skin color across Great Britain in 1722, more likely used to modify family lineages than the cross-class power arrangement known as "white supremacy." See Linebaugh, *Magna Carta Manifesto*, 96.

24. [Robert Goadby], *An Apology for the Life of Mr. Bampfylde-Moore Carew . . .* , 2d ed. (London, [1750?]).

against the notion of aristocratic inheritance and privilege. "For what is *Birthright?* what is *Inheritance,*" Carew asks an assembled throng of gypsy voters, "when put in the Scales against the choicest of Blessings, PUBLICK LIBERTY?" Goadby's question, in Carew's voice, directly addressed the central tension within the recently concluded Annesley trial, harnessing the same class politics that had garnered support for an aristocratic commoner. No longer did Carew perform pranks at the expense of wealthy commercial actors or imperial authorities. When a wealthy gentleman was hoodwinked, Goadby made sure the fun remained lighthearted and was drained of any political menace. In one vignette, Carew pretends to be a destitute miller, securing alms from a good-natured gentleman named Mr. Pleydell. On succeeding, however, the new Carew returns to Pleydell's house and reveals his true identity. "Mr. *Pleydell* said, he well *remember'd such a poor Object: Well,* replied our Hero, *that Object was no other than the expert Ratcatcher now before you;* at which all the Company laugh'd very heartily." Soon both men retire to a local alehouse where Pleydell admires Carew's ability to cross class boundaries for humor's sake, a pleasurable pastime for both men as well as an opportunity for them to reflect on their wisdom, charity, and liberality. In Goadby's hands, Carew's narrative of counterfeit identities falls victim to Carew's own methods.[25]

Goadby's recasting of Carew in Annesley's image was made explicit when he invented a meeting between the two men. Carew comes upon Annesley at a local alehouse while traveling in Northern Ireland. The two men "had been Schoolfellows . . . at Tiverton," the narrator informs readers, and they begin drinking together with "several Officers" and ship captains. Annesley and Carew are alike well-bred Englishmen with a commoner's touch, and they are also both skilled mumpers. "One of the Captains ask'd him [Annesley], *If he could get him a good Pointer? Ay, ay that he can,* replies my Lord, *for, by my Saoul Mon, he* [Carew] *and I have stole many a Dog, and lay in many a Hay-Tallet, in our youthful Days.* Then turning to Mr. *Carew,* [Annesley] told him, *His Fame was spread as much in* Ireland *as* England." Carew visits with Annesley for several days at his estate, where, readers are told, "our Hero receiv'd great Civilities from the *Irish* Gentry," culminating with a festive hunt on Annesley's newly enclosed holdings. Speeches against birthright notwithstanding, the king of the beggars appears to enjoy meeting Annesley and his guests, who find Carew "to be an excellent Sportsman." Perhaps enclosing the commons had been a good thing after all.[26]

25. Ibid., title page, 41–42, 61.
26. Ibid., 160, 161, 162.

Goadby's revision paired antislavery ideology with a celebration of enclosure and landed privilege in England. The heroes of Goadby's story are not plebeian itinerants, the shipwrecked sailors who foraged for wild blackberries in Carew's narrative, but ship captains and merchants who emancipate the king of the gypsies from his "Slavery" in North America. Indeed, Goadby's most substantial revision is the addition of a single, one-hundred-page chapter detailing Carew's transportation as a convict, an interlude that draws more tightly the connections between the new Carew and Annesley. Arrested as a vagrant and transported to Maryland, the king of the beggars initially avoids being sold by escaping the newly arrived ship. He is then discovered by some ship captains, who, instead of turning him in for a reward, offer to pay for his freedom. Goadby's Carew refuses their generous offer, however, and is soon retaken and "obliged to undergo a cruel and shameful Punishment." His master puts a "heavy Iron Collar" on him, "which in *Maryland* they call a *Pot-Hook,* and is usually put about the Necks of the runaway Slaves." Once again, ship captains intervene and show Carew a path to escape. He is eventually saved by so-called "*friendly* Indians." Returning to England, he shares a laugh and more drinks with the same captains. An imperial fantasy in which the superiority of English gentlemen and shipping merchants is amplified by adoring loyal natives, Goadby's tale is as improbable as it is conventional and devoid of political critique.[27]

Goadby was, in fact, deeply invested in defending the values of a merchant class in England, leading him to deploy a new taxonomy of racial value that could naturalize and defend them. The intensification of racial signifiers is apparent throughout his revised *Apology*. Goadby relocated the origins of the gypsies from Sherwood Forest in England to Africa, deriving "their Original from the *Egyptians,*" while reframing Carew's joining of the gypsies as a racial transformation, a mingling "*of the* Ermin *with the Spots of the* Aethiops." Throughout Goadby's subsequent recital of Carew's travels, skin color signposts political virtues and vices, many emerging from accounts of Indian-settler violence in North America. At the same time, Goadby framed his treatment of race as more authentic than the high-minded literary efforts of the novelist Henry Fielding. When describing Carew's wife, Goadby praised the naturalness of her whiteness, critiquing Fielding's description of the white heroine in *The History of Tom Jones, a Foundling*. "Here was Whiteness which no Lillies, Ivory, nor Alabaster could match." Rather

27. Ibid., 9, 91, 92.

than criticizing the Impress Service or the British Empire's policies of transportation, Goadby satirized Fielding, ironically, for his inauthentic depiction of white skin color.[28]

The most revisionist aspect of Goadby's narrative was his dramatic recasting of Turkish slavery. Rather than expressing sympathy for the plight of trafficked Turkish slaves, who were also Muslim subjects, Goadby inverted the story, making the Turkish slaves Christians who suffered at the hands of Turkish slaveholders, not Turks enslaved by Europeans, as in Carew's original story. Joined by "five or six of his Subjects . . . with Chains about their Middle," the new Carew appears in his final counterfeit as an unfortunate sailor "who had been taken and made Slaves of by the *Sallee Rovers*." As proof of Turkish cruelty, Carew points to marks on the bodies of the Turkish slaves that were made "by a hot Iron" and recalls "an Instance of their [the Turks] barbarous Cruelty, [when] they exposed the Mouth of one of the Company to all Beholders, wherein appeared no more than the Stump of a Tongue." Goadby trafficked a familiar image of Turkish cruelty to his readers in terms that were accessible to defenders of Atlantic slavery, suppressing the radical implications of Carew's critique of European slave trafficking.[29]

The transformation of Mr. Bampfylde-Moore Carew from a footloose vagrant who challenged imperial authorities to a defender of enclosure and racial hierarchy between Carew's original narrative and Goadby's recasting of his story reflects stark differences between each author. Goadby's text exemplifies how ideas of white supremacy became powerful, not as assertions of the legitimacy of elite rule, but as revisions and co-optations of plebeian voices. The intensification of racial motifs in Goadby's narrative is associated with a transformation of antislavery discourse quite familiar within literary culture, where subaltern critiques of imperial power and policy are replaced by romances of the freedoms and privileges of the gentry. Whiteness and elite antislavery expand in tandem in Goadby's publication, reprising ideas within Defoe's and Behn's fictions. Goadby's revisions, then, were not especially original in 1749 but exemplify how some fiction writers succeeded by effectively blaming transportations' victims and defending trafficking as a policy.

One of the most popular defenses of transportation to be published in the wake of Goadby's co-optation of Carew's narrative was entitled *The Fortunate*

---

28. Ibid., i, 1, 31; Henry Fielding, *The History of Tom Jones, a Foundling*, 6 vols. (London, 1749), II, 11.

29. [Goadby], *An Apology for the Life of Mr. Bampfylde-Moore Carew*, 226.

*Transport; or, The Secret History of the Life and Adventures of the Celebrated Polly Haycock*, published by an anonymous author in 1750. The heroine, Polly, closely resembles the lead character in Defoe's *Moll Flanders*. Like Defoe, the writer uses the narrative of the unruly behavior of a female servant to ratify transportation as a humane policy, effacing the particular violence female servants endured as trafficked subjects. Born into a life of crime, Polly is "brought up among Pickpockets, transported for Felony," and becomes successful across the Atlantic, where she "rolls in Ease, Splendor, and Luxury." Like Moll, Polly owes her success to her ability to traffic older wealthy men. She marries three aging planters en route to becoming a plantation owner herself. Eventually, she comes to possess hundreds of servants and slaves. Unlike Defoe's plucky heroine, Polly experiences no moral transformation over time. She is a protagonist who only "laughs at dull Moralists, who would persuade Mankind that the Way to be happy is to be good . . . wise and prudent." Polly never treats her slaves or servants humanely, a defect she carries with her when she returns to London with her newly found fortune. "Unhappily for her, she has brought Home with her too much of the Spirit of the Planter," the narrator observes, "a Disposition to use her Servants with great Severity, and scarce any Share of Humanity."[30]

Humanity is geographically circumscribed in *The Fortunate Transport*, stunted by colonials like Polly, who find reward for their peculiar "Creolian" mixture of cruelty and cunning. Polly's immoral gains suggest the corruption of transportation by colonial slave societies rather than by metropolitan administrators in London, as criminals in the Americas reap benefits for all the wrong things. The moral of the narrative, if there is just one, expresses itself as an anxiety about the degrading influence of plantation slavery on Great Britain. "I have heard all Creolians complain of their *English* Servants with great Warmth, as if there were no such Thing as good or honest Servants in the Island of *Britain*," the narrator opines in the final pages, "but the Truth of the Matter is, they treat free-born *Englishmen* as they do Negroes and Felons in the Plantations, and expect the same Submission from the one as the other." The cruelty of slavery is an American virus, the author contends, even as he mimics the racialized grievances that Creoles exemplify. Only British masters, the narrator concludes, "behave with Candour and Humanity

---

30. Anon., *The Fortunate Transport; or, The Secret History of the Life and Adventures of the Celebrated Polly Haycock, Alias Mrs. B----, the Lady of the Gold Watch* (London, [1750?]), 4, 42–43. The phrase "Price One Shilling" appears on the cover page.

towards our Servants, which we are bound to do as Men and Christians." Here, Christian servants are not racists but humanitarians in contrast to the corrupted creoles known as whites.[31]

The lesson of Polly Haycock's narrative was not only geographic but also misogynistic, blaming white servant women in the colonies for the perversion and cruelties of an otherwise humanitarian empire. Indeed, the author of *The Fortunate Transport* articulates a distrust of trafficked women, whiteness, and any humanitarian sympathies associated with them. The key turning point in the narrative occurs when a local magistrate witnesses the spectacle of Polly being whipped after she prepared a poor meal for her master. "The Sight of a fine Woman in that dismal Figure, with an old Negro labering her with an unmerciful Cat-and-nine-Tails, rais'd in the Justice all the Sentiments of Humanity, that good Nature could suggest." Polly's suffering at the hands of a man of color evokes the same mixture of racism, pornography, and "Sentiments of Humanity" that Williamson would invoke a decade later. Yet the satiric purpose of the passage distinguishes it from Williamson's narrative, as the narrator soon reveals that the magistrate was so moved by the sight of "using a white Servant in that cruel Manner" that he fell in love with Polly and emancipated her. She promptly robs him of "about a hundred and fifty Guineas" and flees the island. Sympathy for a trafficked white woman betrays the jurist. If cruelty toward slaves and servants was a colonial disease, according to the author, so was whiteness a gendered delusion, enabling rogues like Haycock to appear as people they are not, in Haycock's case, as a member of the virtuous English aristocracy, the only truly noble race within the British Empire.[32]

Here are familiar conflicts over the provenance of race and racial value, only now expressed with a gendered and geographic twist. Cruelty is white, female, and spatially rooted in colonial contexts where slaveholding rogues like Polly become powerful. The danger for the author is that Polly's so-called virtues might spread, like a contagion, to England. The revisionist conceit that Polly Haycock naturalized for metropolitan British writers and readers was that whiteness was itself a colonial invention, despite that metropolitan governors were the first to deploy such language when exporting felons from

---

31. Anon., *Fortunate Transport*, 43–44.

32. Ibid., 34, 38, 44. On broader connections between violence and humanitarian sympathy, see Karen Halttunen's fine essay, Halttunen, "Humanitarianism and the Pornography of Pain in Anglo-American Culture," *American Historical Review*, C (1995), 303–334.

London's jails to the Americas in the 1680s. Metropolitan writers blamed the cruelty of slavery on white servants, while simultaneously reaping the material benefits of the traffic in both servants and slaves. Just so did this British writer of fiction use geography and gender to divert attention from more troubling questions posed by the trafficking of unfree people across Britain's empire.

It is uncertain whether Peter Williamson read or heard of Polly Haycock's narrative, but he similarly displayed the body of a suffering white woman in the third edition of *French and Indian Cruelty* published in 1758. After freeing himself from Delaware Indians following his capture during the Seven Years' War, Williamson and his fellow soldiers interrupt a party of Delawares who had been attacking Anglo-American settlers. In his depiction of the dramatic spectacle, he portrays a stunning scene of white female victimhood that distilled the moral and emotional focus of his revised narrative. "Behold one nurtured in the most tender manner . . . quite naked, and in the open woods, encircling with her alabaster arms and hands a cold rough tree, whereto she was bound, with cords so straitly pull'd, that the blood trickled from her finger's ends!" Williamson used this image of an anonymous white woman's naked body to justify subsequent violence against the Delaware and to highlight the rewards that masculine rescue proffered. The captain who found her "for a long time could do nothing but gaze upon and clasp her to his bosom," readers are told, "raving, and tearing his hair like one bereft of his senses." When the captain belatedly clothed the naked girl, she "recovered her dissipated spirits, the repossession of which she manifested by eagerly fixing her eyes on her dear deliverer." Rescue had been achieved, and now revenge could be wrought by Williamson and his company. He recounted how they scalped the white woman's fleeing Indian captors without remorse, a "bloody, though agreeable piece of work." The pornography of witnessing a white woman's naked body and the subsequent violence he and his fellow soldiers perpetrated against Delaware Indians were merged events within Williamson's narrative.[33]

The prominence of white female victimhood and racialized violence in Williamson's revised narrative raise questions about the veracity of his text. Scholars investigating Williamson's biography have concluded that he was

---

33. Peter Williamson, *French and Indian Cruelty* . . . , 3d ed. (Glasgow, 1758), 36, 37. The history of Native American conquest has long been plotted as a story of Anglo-American victimhood, a key part of the mythology of the North American frontier. See the work of Richard Slotkin, especially Slotkin, *Regeneration through Violence: The Mythology of the American Frontier, 1600–1860* (Norman, Okla., 1973); and Slotkin, *The Fatal Environment: The Myth of the Frontier in the Age of Industrialization, 1800–1890* (New York, 1985).

not, in fact, captured by Delaware Indians, making his scene of white female suffering an imagined interlude. Yet from where did Williamson's story and imagery originate, if fabricated? And what if anything was novel about his portrayal of white female suffering? A careful examination of the changing meanings of white women in Eighteenth Century Collections Online suggests some starting points for understanding the historical significance of Williamson's inclusion of this episode. First, Williamson's narrative was published on the cusp of a dramatic expansion in published references to white women and to white grammar more generally during the eighteenth century. Between 1700 and 1760, references to white women increased consistently but slowly. Between 1761 and 1800, however, the number of white women in print dramatically expanded, doubling or tripling every two decades, resulting in a more than sixfold increase from the middle two decades of the century to its final two decades (see Appendix C, Table 14).

Williamson's text was also published in the wake of a striking semantic transformation in the meanings of white womanhood. That change comes into sharper focus if references to "white women" in fiction and literature are viewed separately from those found in political and legal documents. First, fictional references to white women highlight the enduring prominence of alien whiteness before 1760. Before 1780, 76 percent of the white women appearing in fiction were not Christian, a figure that fell dramatically in the final two decades of the century to just 12 percent (see Appendix C, Table 17). Like the renegade-born Imoinda in Thomas Southerne's *Oroonoko*, these white women possessed noble lineages and were also noteworthy for their beauty, as in Galland's popular translations of *One Thousand and One Arabian Nights*. Appearances by white women in fiction, whether noble actors awaiting rescue or objects of sexual fantasy and desire, comprised the majority of such references during the first six decades of the eighteenth century. Although the political meanings of these fictional white women varied, none were deemed politically dangerous or associated with punitive discipline.

---

Historians of British imperial history have been crucial in getting British historians generally to make race and conquest more central to narrating nineteenth-century cultural and social history within the nation, though less successfully for the eighteenth century. See Catherine Hall, *Civilising Subjects: Colony and Metropole in the English Imagination, 1830–1867* (Chicago, 2002); and Hall and Keith McClelland, eds., *Race, Nation, and Empire Making Histories, 1750 to the Present* (Manchester, U.K., 2010). On the ongoing power of pornographic violence in constituting racial ideology, see Bell Hooks, *Writing beyond Race: Living Theory and Practice* (New York, 2013), 123–130.

References to white women in non-fictional publications, by contrast, emerged in far greater numbers during the middle decades of the eighteenth century and were far more likely to be Christian than in fictional accounts (see Appendix C, Table 17). Paradoxically, however, these white women were also controversial actors, with politically dangerous allegiances according to the documents published between 1720 and 1760. More than one-third of all non-fictional references to white women described them as actors warranting punishment rather than rescue. Consider, for example, the servant laws that Maryland's colonial assembly published in 1727 that became models across several North American and Caribbean colonies. Maryland's colonial legislators declared "that any White Woman, whether Free or Servant, that shall suffer herself to be got with Child by a Negroe or other Slave, or free Negroe, such Woman . . . if free, shall become a Servant for and during the Term of Seven Years; if a Servant, shall finish her Time . . . [and] shall again become a Servant, for and during the Term of Seven Years." Anxieties about sexual relations between servants and slaves were especially acute in the mid-Atlantic colonies, with Virginia, Pennsylvania, Delaware, and New Jersey each passing similar laws to Maryland's. Indeed, laws seeking to police the behavior of white women in North American colonies grew more punitive over the ensuing decades. In 1723, authorities in Bermuda proscribed equal punishments to white women and Black men whether slave or free who bore children together. "The said Justices of the Peace shall, and may order" both the offending "White Woman" and "such Negroe, or other Slave, to be publickly whipt, at their Discretion, under the Gallows by the common Hangman," legislators decreed. In Delaware, a law published in 1752 aimed at curtailing sex between white female servants and Black slaves proscribed that the offending white woman "be publickly whipt with Thirty-nine Stripes on her bare Back, and well laid on, at the common Whipping-Post." Offspring of such unions, despite having a nominally free mother, were also effectively unfree. Whether born in Maryland, Pennsylvania, Delaware, or Bermuda, the children of white female servants and Black slaves were deemed indentured servants until the age of thirty-one, the fungible property of their mother's master.[34]

---

34. "An Act relating to Servants and Slaves," in Maryland, *A Compleat Collection of the Laws of Maryland* . . . (Annapolis, Md., 1727), 112; "An Act against Bastardy," 1723, in Bermuda, *Acts of Assembly, Made and Enacted in the Bermuda or Summer-Islands, Continued to 1736* (Bermuda, 1737), 90; "An Act against Adultery and Fornication," in Delaware, *Laws of the Government of New-Castle, Kent, and Sussex, upon Delaware* (Philadelphia, 1752), 77;

The discourse surrounding white servant women's labor and sexuality across the middle decades of the eighteenth century, then, revealed, not so much white privilege, as the gendered foundations of the class-bound anxieties that colonial legislators and leaders had long expressed about alliances between their servants and slaves. When white servants coupled with free Black servants or Black slaves, they transgressed the racial order that elites like Daniel Horsmanden and others desired and policed but which, for all their repressive work, remained maddeningly elusive. White grammar, moreover, continued to express contrasting dimensions of white experience. Whites at once possessed racialized rights, articulated as limits on the liberties that masters could take with their servants on the one hand, but were liable to punishments that sought to discipline their behavior and freedoms on the other. Laws policing female servants' behavior highlighted just how tethered the bodies of servants and slaves remained in the minds of many colonial elites, especially in Maryland and Pennsylvania, where servants still worked in proximity to enslaved Africans. Deemed things as well as subjects, white women still held out the capacity to combine with slaves as sexual partners or as workers, which marked them as threats to colonial political order, threats that would in time transform how authorities saw and legislated the sexuality of white male servants as well. Within two decades of the passage of laws policing white servant women's sexual relations with Black men, similar laws were passed policing white male servants' relationships with Black women, making the sexuality of both male and female servants a key site of labor control.[35]

Semantic and narrative differences between white women in fiction and in legal discourse represented, not so much ideological confusion, as a reflection

---

"An Act concerning Servants and Slaves," in Virginia, *An Abridgement of the Publick Laws of Virginia, in Force and Use, June 10, 1720* . . . (London, 1728), 84; "An Act for the Better Regulating of Negroes in This Province," in Pennsylvania, *A Collection of All the Laws of the Province of Pennsylvania* . . . (Philadelphia, 1742), 338–339.

35. "Act relating to Servants and Slaves," Apr. 26, 1715, in Maryland, *Abridgement and Collection of the Acts of Assembly of the Province of Maryland, at Present in Force* . . . (Philadelphia, 1759), 76. The best analysis of the gendered foundations to the economic power of southern slaveholders over both slaves and indentured servants remains Kathleen M. Brown's *Good Wives, Nasty Wenches, and Anxious Patriarchs: Gender, Race, and Power in Colonial Virginia* (Williamsburg, Va., and Chapel Hill, N.C., 1996), 194–201. Brown demonstrates that the policing of interracial bastardy among white servant women emerged in the last three decades of the seventeenth century in Virginia, well before similar laws were passed in the mid-Atlantic states.

of the conflicting purposes to which metropolitan and colonial authorities imagined white womanhood. The actions of female indentured servants in resisting the unwanted sexual advances of their masters as well as their capacity to bear children with free or enslaved Blacks directly challenged prerogatives at the heart of colonial political economy, but fictional portrayals of white female victimhood also represented one elite answer to the problem of white women's unruliness. Better to see white women as perfect victims who could be spoken on behalf of or rescued than to have to listen to or engage with unruly white women and their disobedient behavior. Tensions over the behavior of white servants, male and female, had long been visible in fictions about Britain's American colonies, expressed in the gendered differences between white male slaves in Southerne's *Oroonoko* and the beautiful Imoinda, the innocent but non-Christian white slave. The white female heroine in *French and Indian Cruelty* was similar to the fictional representations of white women that had appeared in print over the previous half century in most respects, save one. Beautiful, innocent, and awaiting rescue, Williamson's protagonist was also Christian and poor, a subject closer in background and historical context to the white female indentured servants whose sexuality colonial elites so conspicuously policed during the 1730s and 1740s. Her nakedness marked her as a sexual object in the hands of non-white male actors, a theme that runs across a majority of references to white women during the eighteenth century. Unlike white female servants, however, the whiteness of Williamson's fictional hero made her worthy of rescue, an object whose skin color sanctioned paternal authority rather than subverting it or requiring punishment. Put another way, Williamson managed to put white womanhood to work on behalf of a political project that linked racialism and radicalism, a war simultaneously against savagery and Aberdeen's trafficking merchant class.

The political and literary contexts for Williamson's portrayal of servant trafficking, Indian captivity, and white suffering in *French and Indian Cruelty*, then, were each well established by 1757. White grammar was primarily deployed by elite writers and colonial and metropolitan administrators to organize imperial investments or to ratify prescriptions for preserving them in slaveholding societies. Whites were trafficked things who could be moved, whether initially to build colonies as tobacco or sugar workers or later to protect the investments of slaveholders and shipping merchants as convicts or overseers who might serve as militiamen. Discourse about white women, in turn, expressed elite ambivalence about whites as a trafficked class. On the one hand, white women were associated with unruly servant women, whose bodies and sexuality, authorities believed, needed to be policed. On the other hand, white women were also being reimagined as emblems of a united race of whites, metonyms for a race whose visible suffering might unite disparate classes into a common political project. Both formulations were articulated primarily by British elites rather than plebeian actors, whether they resided in London or the colonial contexts where alliances of enslaved and trafficked people were most visible and dangerous. In each instance, whiteness was a thing attributed to people lower than one's rank or in other parts of the British Empire, a language of attribution rather than self-identification. Whiteness, in short, was considered an ambivalent sign, an indication of one's status as a trafficked subject, eschewed by those with noble pedigrees and common origins alike.

## British Wars and Race

Peter Williamson's narrative was not simply a product of the literary context he navigated in Aberdeen, however, but also a response to the Seven Years' War, a military conflict that changed how British actors at home and abroad perceived the power and provenance of skin color and the British Empire. Unlike previous wars dominated by national and religious imperatives, the Seven Years' War witnessed the emergence of race as a key tool for justifying and explaining Britain's imperial engagements. The meanings of race varied dramatically by context. Wartime violence between British settlers and France's Algonquin allies across Pennsylvania stirred up colonists to invoke race as a means to rationalize their military campaigns against Native peoples. Africans in Jamaica known as the Coromantee, in turn, used the language of race to rouse enslaved people against their island masters. The dramatic uprising made racial conflicts within the larger imperial war visible and unavoidable, even as leaders of the rebellion killed enslaved Black people acting in support of the British during the conflict. This was the larger imperial context in which Williamson wrote, performed, and trafficked his story of captivity, kidnapping, and white victimhood.[36]

The idea of a war on behalf of race nevertheless remained a double-edged and imperfect rationale for articulating or expanding British power in 1760.

---

36. Peter Silver has argued that Europeans and their descendants in North America did not embrace a white racial identity until the middle decades of the eighteenth century, largely in response to the violence engendered by pervasive wars between English settlers and Native peoples. See Silver, *Our Savage Neighbors*, 114, 116, 122.

Defining British military expansion as a war for white people left out key actors within the British Navy, the Black sailors who kept the Union Jack afloat during times of war and made the African slave trade feasible in times of peace. Imperial arguments on behalf of the whiteness of British power in 1760 likewise undermined the alliances Britain sustained with Native peoples across the Americas, self-serving though they might have been. The concept of race war permitted little room for British officials and Native allies to maneuver, a framing that ignored the very real middle ground that characterized imperial engagements and negotiations across North America during most of the eighteenth century. In Jamaica in 1760, in the midst of a major slave rebellion, the logic of a war between whites and Blacks was especially dangerous to Britain's imperial interests, as that framing minimized the vital role that enslaved men and women played in resisting the Coromantee. The pragmatic realities of British colonial rule in Jamaica and across the Caribbean did not mean racism was becoming less central to British imperial power or to slavery in 1760, only that the language of whiteness poorly expressed the logic for British hegemony, ignoring internal divisions within categories of skin color in Britain and its Atlantic colonies.[37]

When Williamson first published *French and Indian Cruelty* in 1757, war rather than race was central to his narrative, the reason why he believed his story mattered. Little on the title page of his first edition is indicative of the importance either race or radical antislavery would come to have on the book's eventual success. The title established it as a wartime polemic, with only an indirect reference to the crimes of Aberdeen's shipping merchants in the subtitle: "*stolen* from his *Parents* and sent to PINSYLVANIA, where he was sold as a SLAVE." Williamson described himself more prominently as "A Disbanded Soldier" whose experiences in battle provided the best reason to purchase and read his account, including "an accurate and succinct Detail, of the Operations of the FRENCH and ENGLISH Forces, at the Siege of OSWEGO." Nor did race

---

37. On the idea of a larger race war between enslaved Africans and white slaveholders that preceded and superseded the Seven Years' War, see Vincent Brown, *Tacky's Revolt: The Story of an Atlantic Slave War* (Cambridge, Mass., 2020). On the power of racial imaginaries among the enslaved, see Trevor Burnard, *Jamaica in the Age of Revolution* (Philadelphia, 2020); and Marjoleine Kars, *Blood on the River: A Chronicle of Mutiny and Freedom on the Wild Coast* (New York, 2020). On the fears such conspiracies generated among British settlers and planters and their role in crafting white racial identity, see Jason T. Sharples, *The World That Fear Made: Slave Revolts and Conspiracy Scares in Early America* (Philadelphia, 2020); and Silver, *Our Savage Neighbors*, xviii–xxv.

appear in the description of his narrative. Cruelty was a disease shared equally by Great Britain's imperial enemies, whether they were French or Indian. The outcome of the Seven Years' War, moreover, remained uncertain. The British defeat at Oswego in 1756 was one of a string of victories by an alliance of seasoned French troops and their Native American allies who together possessed the upper hand across the interior of North America. Great Britain's advantages at sea, with a larger navy and more efficient system of impressing and retaining its sailors, had yet to play a decisive role in the war's outcome.[38]

Over the course of the Seven Years' War, however, the conflict's purpose and rationale changed for those fighting it. Race became more prominent in the war's prosecution and retelling, even as military victories complicated the work race might do for British power. Why the Seven Years' War, as opposed to previous military conflicts such as the War of Jenkins' Ear, initiated that change is a challenging question to answer. British participation in the slave trade, after all, had long been established, but the prominence of race—and whiteness—in descriptions of the Seven Years' War and its significance grew steadily over the conflict's duration. Local factors certainly played an important role in that transformation, as battles between Native Americans and colonists in Pennsylvania and New Jersey began to be understood in racial rather than religious terms. In Jamaica, the Coromantee deliberately used race and emancipation as key parts of their military strategy and organizing, a rehearsal for subsequent uprisings of the enslaved in Haiti and elsewhere across the Caribbean. These battlefields made the work of race not only visible but unavoidable in defining the purposes of both the war and the nation.

These shifting ideological stakes reflected a larger transformation in Britain's imperial capacities just before the start of the Seven Years' War, one driven in part by conflicts within Britain's military. In the face of sailors' mounting critiques of the Impress Service and demands for national relations of rescue, British military authorities revised the Articles of War. The new articles published in 1749 tightened military discipline and sought to curtail desertion; they were the political counterpoint to Thomas Troughton's and Will Jones's concurrent pleas for emancipation from slavery in Morocco. In attempting to reduce the number of British sailors who would ever become captives, Article IX mandated that British sailors "fight courageously" and prescribed death if any person "in the Fleet, shall treacherously or cowardly yield, or cry for Quarter." For sailors, war had literally become a fight to the

---

38. Williamson, *French and Indian Cruelty* (1757), title page.

death, an ideological condition in which surrender or even questioning the premise of war were punishable by death. Older justifications for military engagements between ships such as trafficking prizes had shifted. Previously, sailors knew that military skirmishes at sea could mean that they and their cargoes might become trafficked. That transactional premise structured for how long and how fiercely opponents might fight one another. Today's victors might be tomorrow's captives. In the new Articles of War, British authorities removed sailors and ship officers from any ownership of those calculations, insisting they fight to the death and claiming control of all prize taking. Henceforth, "No Person . . . shall take out of any Prize or Ship, or Goods seized for Prize, any Money, Plate, or Goods." The admiralty alone would adjudicate who and what was sharable among fighting crews. Trafficking people and goods across oceanic spaces, long a feature of Britain's mercantilism, had become resolutely national in the new articles, with the power to traffic people and expressions of sovereignty tightly linked. Any sailor or ship captain who shared prizes without the king's explicit permission now became a renegade. The new Articles of War were conspicuously silent on why British soldiers should fight so courageously, stressing only that sailors and soldiers should do so. For sailors like Williamson demanding pensions, British authorities were becoming more rather than less skeptical, as the new articles suggested that the truly courageous should have died in battle. For soldiers and sailors returning from war, trafficking their narratives of suffering was the one arena left open to them to make their demands known.[39]

Two other narratives, one by a fellow British soldier and another by a fellow indentured servant published around the same time as Williamson's, illustrate some of the increasingly racialized signposts that plebeian actors possessed when narrating captivity and the experience of being trafficked during war. British soldier Henry Grace published his story of sacrifice at the conclusion of the Seven Years' War, a narrative that closely resembles Williamson's in detail and in purpose, Grace's effort to secure a pension. A disbanded soldier like Williamson who had also been conscripted, Grace was likewise captured by local Indians and spent months in captivity. He, too, described and performed Indian dancing, though, in his case, he performed on pain of death. While traveling with a "Part of the *Five Nation* Indians" near Niagara Falls,

---

39. Articles VII and IX, in Great Britain, Parliament, *A Bill for Amending, Explaining, and Reducing into One Act of Parliament, the Laws Relating to the Government of His Majesty's Ships, Vessels, and Forces by Sea* [London, 1749], 5.

Grace complained that they "used me very barbarously, making me dance for their Diversion, as long as I was able to stand or go, and do any Thing else as they pleased." Grace "bore all with Patience," until his Indian owners "agreed to sell" him "for four hundred Livres and a Cask of Rum that held sixteen Gallons and a half" to a Frenchman near Montreal, beginning a four-and-a-half-year indenture in which he "was forced to work at all Kinds of Husbandry." On finally returning to Great Britain, Grace was reunited with his military company but was promptly discharged on "the 10th of *February*, 1763, with the Loss of ten Year's Pay and Cloathing." Like Troughton and Williamson before him, Grace mourned the failure of national authorities to count his time as a captive as a form of national service. Grace did not secure his pension, despite his poignant plea on the final page of his narrative: "I submit my Case . . . to the Consideration of the Humane and Benevolent, hoping for some Relief." Nor did Grace sell many copies of his book.[40]

German indentured servant Gottlieb Mittelberger published his memoir just one year before Williamson did and similarly detailed a traumatic narrative of "man stealing." Sold as an indentured servant in Pennsylvania, he published his story to warn his compatriots about "the wretched and grievous condition of those who travel from Germany to this new land." Like Williamson, Mittelberger described the process of being sold in Philadelphia as "slavery" and commented on the culture of local Indian peoples and the power of white people pretending to be Indian in their revelries. Yet the differences between Williamson and Mittelberger's tales are equally telling. Mittelberger was interested in witnessing the cultural performances of local Indian peoples, especially the ways religious enthusiasm brought different peoples together, as when "our evangelical ministers have baptized and confirmed many adult persons, both white and black." Able to play the harpsichord, Mittelberger used music to create connections between diverse Christian performers. He also possessed a dim view of those who pretended to be Indian while living in Philadelphia: "On the first and second days of the month of May," Mittelberger observed, "there is general merry-making in Pennsylvania, in which the unmarried of both sexes chiefly take part. All amuse themselves with playing, dancing, shooting, hunting, and the like. Such unmarried persons as are born in the country adorn their heads with a piece of fur of some wild animal. With these the young men walk about the

---

40. Henry Grace, *The History of the Life and Sufferings of Henry Grace* . . . (Reading, England, 1764), 35, 51, 52, 55, 56.

city, crying 'Hurrah! Hurrah!' . . . These are called Indians." Mittelberger noted the revelry but did not imitate or admire it.[41]

Unlike Mittelberger, Williamson was persuaded by the energy and enthusiasm of the street revelers known as "Indians" in Philadelphia, yet he only partially appreciated the power of playing Indian when he first returned to Aberdeen and published *French and Indian Cruelty* in 1757. Little about the Delaware Indians appears within the lengthy title to his first edition. By 1758, he had added his description of the rescue of a naked white girl with "alabaster" arms. By 1759, he had revised the fourth edition to include a frontispiece featuring him dressed in Delaware Indian garb with subtitles highlighting colonists' suffering, including "a particular Account of the *Manners, Customs,* and *Dress,* of the SAVAGES; of their *scalping, burning* and other *Barbarities,* committed on the ENGLISH in NORTH-AMERICA" (Figure 10). Williamson had learned that playing Indian was an effective tactic both for selling copy and enraging Aberdeen's merchants. Williamson's narrative had become more radical and more racial over time.[42]

The changes to Williamson's way of representing his narrative, however, depended less on his desire to appropriate literary culture than on the necessities of fighting a protracted legal battle with Aberdeen's shipping merchants. In 1758, just after Williamson published his second edition of *French and Indian Cruelty,* sales were abruptly interrupted by shipping merchant Alexander Cushnie, whose legal complaint described the book as a "scurrilous and infamous libel" that "highly hurt and prejudged" the shipping merchants of Aberdeen. Cushnie and his fellow shipping merchants demanded that Williamson "be exemplarily punished in his person and goods" and that "the said pamphlet, and whole copies thereof ought to be seized, and publicly burnt, in terror of others to commit the like." To that end, authorities confiscated Williamson's entire stock of unsold books, excised the offending portions

---

41. Gottlieb Mittelberger, *Gottlieb Mittelberger's Journey to Pennsylvania in the Year 1750 and Return to Germany in the Year 1754* . . . , trans. Carl Theo. Eben (Philadelphia, 1898), 16, 59, 112; Deloria, *Playing Indian.* For a review of the literature on immigrant middlemen in fomenting migrations as well as the moralistic literature that presumes all such labor contractors are "unscrupulous," see Adam McKeown, "How the Box Became Black: Brokers and the Creation of the Free Migrant," *Pacific Affairs,* special issue, "Opening the Black Box of Migration," LXXXV (2012), 21–45.

42. Williamson, *French and Indian Cruelty* (1757), title page; Williamson, *French and Indian Cruelty* . . . , 2d ed. (1758), title page; Peter Williamson, *French and Indian Cruelty* . . . , 4th ed. (London, 1759), frontispiece and title page.

FIGURE 10. Unknown artist, *Peter Williamson*. 1759. Etching. © National Portrait Gallery, London

describing Aberdeen's shipping merchants as man stealers, and even compelled Williamson to recant the publication of his book. Such lawsuits across the first half of the eighteenth century were not uncommon in Georgian England; many were brought by the British state itself, which sought to curtail criticism of the slave trade and slavery. Rather, they constituted one response to the growing capacity of footloose actors like Williamson to make their mark with publications that cost a shilling.[43]

Yet Aberdeen's shipping merchants misjudged Williamson's tenacity. Instead of backing down, he published all the legal documents produced by his trial. In an exposé titled *State of the Process*, he acknowledged signing a recantation of his book but insisted he had been "incarcerated in the tolbooth of Aberdeen until he granted the foresaid writing and declaration" and was "threatened . . . with corporal punishment." Nor did Williamson stop there. He sought damages against Aberdeen's merchants, including "restitution of the value of the books seized, amounting to 650 in number, at one shilling each" while demanding "further damages" as he had been "branded with the name of an imposter, and suffered the infamy of banishment." Williamson also refuted the merchants' claim that he had consented to his migration. "At the time he was carried off, he was at most but nine years of age, and consequently incapable of consent." Williamson was "secreted and kept under close confinement during the whole time the ship remained in the harbor, while his brother and relations were enquiring after him through the whole country."[44]

Believing that publicizing the legal record would only validate his claims, Williamson recounted the legal arguments deployed against him by the Aberdeen merchants. In the lawsuit, Cushnie argued that Williamson had not been tricked or decoyed but had "voluntarily engaged himself, along with other boys, to a ship-master . . . who was then going to America." Cushnie also objected to the particular manner in which Williamson constructed his larger narrative. "If he had only told a wonderful story of his adventures on the other side of the globe, however destitute the story might have been of truth," Cushnie stated, it would have been "no crime." The real crime, according to Cushnie and his fellow Aberdeen merchants, was that Williamson blamed them for his kidnapping. "He might have said, that this was done, without fixing the guilt of it upon the merchants of Aberdeen; or if he wanted

---

43. [Peter Williamson and Alexander Cushnie], *State of the Process, Poor Peter Williamson, against Alexander Cushnie, and Others* [Edinburgh, 1761], 4, 5.

44. Ibid., 5, 6, 7.

to be more particular, he might have said, that it was the ship-master who did it." Williamson understood that Cushnie's arguments, denying coercion in the servant trade on the one hand while insisting others should be blamed for it on the other were inconsistent, and he explained his desire to use the merchants' words against them.[45]

To that end, the most powerful portion of Williamson's legal tract was the inclusion of forty depositions by local individuals who corroborated the details of his story and provided chilling accounts of the coerced transportation of minors to Pennsylvania. A kind of preview to abolitionist Thomas Clarkson's antislavery investigation, the depositions Williamson collected were unadorned with the embellishments and rhetorical flourishes that characterized his own narrative. Instead, deponents detailed the daily struggles that afflicted impoverished parents when "provisions were dear and scarce." Margaret Ross provided an especially vivid account of the kidnapping of her twelve-year-old son, James, whom she sent to Aberdeen on "an errand" one day. James did not return. Having been offered a "stripped vest-coat" in exchange for signing up to go to America by a merchant named "Mr. Copland," he was kept in a barn outside of town for eight days along with a group of other boys while Copland and other agents sought to fill a vessel bound for the plantations. During the day, James "had liberty to go through the town with other boys, and they used to go in companies beating the drum," helping Copland to decoy more boys with sociability, fancy clothes, and music. Margaret looked for her son in vain but had the good fortune to see him in church eight days after she sent him to Aberdeen. "She came to the chapel in Gallowgate to hear worship, and she saw her son there, and got hold of him, and carried him home with her to Loan-head." When four men, representing the merchant Alexander Grey, subsequently showed up at Margaret's home, her husband got up and went with them. They told him he could "get back his son" if he were able to "pay seven pounds Scots, for the expence of maintaining" him, a sum Margaret and her husband could not afford to pay. They traveled to Aberdeen to speak with the mayor, known as the "provost of the town." The merchant argued that James had agreed to be transported and that "the boy complained that his mother was not good to him." James, it seems, had been a willing recruit, perhaps liking his new friends and fancy jacket. Margaret, in turn, insisted that Grey had taken their son without their consent. The provost reconciled these competing claims by sending James

45. Ibid., 8, 10.

home with his parents but requiring that Grey's debt be paid with a promissory note. When James's father "grew rich, he would cut stones for him, he being a stonecutter."[46]

Margaret Ross's deposition in particular reveals the desperate circumstances that led many women and minors to be transported abroad. James clearly did not like living at home, as Margaret by her own admission had to "g[e]t hold of him" and "carr[y] him home." But James's emancipation also cost the family dear, with James's father incurring a significant debt in the process. James's days with his parents were, in fact, numbered. Margaret "kept her son at home a considerable time with herself," but, on a return trip to Aberdeen, disaster struck again when James "was taken up (as she was informed) by one Lunen in Aberdeen, who went over with boys, and her son, a trader to the Plantations." Margaret tried to free him again, but, before he was sent away, "he was put into the tolbooth," a kind of prison for debtors. Times were especially hard, Margaret deposed, as "provisions were very dear and scarce, and many were difficulted to get their bread," and Margaret was unable to persuade local authorities to release James or to pay the debts he had incurred to the trader, Lunen. Facing grinding poverty and deepening debt, Margaret "gave him her blessing before he went away," stating "she never saw him since." The family was unable to rescue their son a second time. At the end of her deposition, Margaret insisted that she and her husband "were in condition to have maintained her son, and never consented to his being carried off." Her deposition underscored the grim choices that she and many servant families faced and that traders exploited.[47]

Not every deposition so richly charted the ways rural poverty fostered servant traffic, but those Williamson assembled cohered in exemplifying the varied ways traders fleeced and silenced their impoverished charges. Robert Reid recalled that he "heard musick and a great noise in said barn" when he went "to see the country boys, who were going over to Philadelpia." Isobel Wilson similarly remembered visiting a "malt-barn to see one Peter Ley, who had engaged to go to America" and was surprised to see "the barn full of boys and men, to the number of 50 and upwards as she believes, and that they had a piper amongst them." Coercion was intrinsic to the traffic in both minors and adult servants. Phrases such as "he was taken up at Aberdeen, and carried to the plantations" appear in many depositions. The active collaboration of local magistrates with Aberdeen's merchants is also a common theme. When

---

46. Deposition of Christian Finlater, ibid., 24, Deposition of Margaret Ross, 18, 19, 20.
47. Deposition of Margaret Ross, ibid., 19, 20.

Margaret Ross visited her son James in a barn outside town, she noticed that the single entrance and exit to the barn was guarded by "an *officer*," who remained impervious to the calls of boys demanding "shoes, and other necessaries that they wanted." When the shoemaker William Jamison discovered that his ten-year-old son had gone "amissing" in 1741, he went to town and found "a great number of boys . . . diverting themselves." He, too, followed them to a barn on the outside of town. When he was prevented from reaching the barn by an "overseer," hired by the merchant John Burnett to watch over the boys, Jamison decided to inform the local magistrates. Warned by local people "that it would be in vain for him to apply to the magistrates to get his son liberate; because . . . the magistrates had a hand in those doings," he instead "went home," where he called on his master and landlord, William Gordon, the second earl of Aberdeen, for intervention. The earl agreed to force the merchant Burnett to return Jamison's son from Maryland "under the penalty of 50 *l.* Sterling." Unfortunately for Jamison, the earl died before his son was returned, and Jamison never learned "whether his son" was "dead or alive."[48]

Jamison's story draws attention to the inherently political context of mobility in the countryside, much of it coercive, that shaped the fate of tenant farmers and children alike. When Lord Aberdeen died, Jamison became a soldier and "was sent over to Flanders, where he served some years." On his return, he discovered that the merchant Burnett had himself "become bankrupt" but had also "left the country," leaving Jamison no path to pursue in finding his only son. Jamison's efforts echoed those of Peter Williamson's parents, who also actively resisted their son's transportation. When Peter's father, James, discovered that Peter was missing, he "made search for him . . . in the country, but could not find him." Francis Fraser, an acquaintance of both Peter and his parents, stated that "James Williamson and his wife . . . made a clamour for the loss of their son" but to no avail. James was not destitute, Fraser indicated, and could have supported "his children and his family," having "a plough going on Upper Balnacraig . . . and likewise . . . a plough going in Hirnley." James and his wife nevertheless had no legal recourse to recover Peter when they discovered he had been taken. Peter's father "shed many salt tears on that account," a bitterness he took to his grave. Neither he nor his wife were alive when Peter returned to his native Britain.[49]

---

48. Deposition of Robert Reid, ibid., 14, Deposition of Isobel Wilson, 14, Deposition of John Wilson, 13, Deposition of Margaret Ross, 20, Deposition of William Jamison, 21, 22, 23.

49. Deposition of William Jamison, ibid., 23, Deposition of John Wilson, 12, 13, Deposition of Francis Fraser, 13.

Williamson's kidnapping archive presented an unflinching and radical account of the coercive practices used by shipping merchants as well as the daily tragedies that befell rural commoners as they struggled to survive enclosure during a season of endless foreign wars. Unlike older parliamentary condemnations of kidnapping, the deponents focused, not on wicked spirits, but on an entire class of actors and their political supporters. The depositions shifted the center of attention away from individual parents to the dilemmas that all impoverished parents faced as they sought to reclaim their children from merchants and traffickers. For Williamson's deponents, parents and their kidnapped children were never to blame. All had been victimized by Aberdeen's shipping merchants, who transported sons and daughters against their parents' will with the blessing of local jurists and magistrates.

Williamson's deponents nevertheless differed from him in one crucial respect. Not one of them made any reference to white people, or to white suffering, and they only rarely mentioned skin color in their narratives. This was true of deponents who were kidnapped to North America and those who managed to avoid being kidnapped. In a tale evocative of the story of James Annesley, George Johnston, a printer in Edinburgh who was transported against his will at the age of six and "sent over to Virginia by an uncle" in the year 1740, for instance, did not denigrate the enslaved Africans he toiled alongside. He commented instead on the oppressive daily conditions that all trafficked people faced. All were "harshly used by their masters," according to Johnston, "and kept upon a very course diet, so that they are often forced to desperate measures, and to make away with themselves." Such efforts, Johnston reported, were highly unlikely to succeed. Runaways, when apprehended, were "whipped for so doing, and adjudged to serve a year longer than otherwise . . . obliged to do." Such coercion did not originate in North America, Johnston insisted, but began with the brutal treatment indentured servants experienced at the hands of Aberdeen's shipping merchants. The absence of any sense of white racial privilege in kidnapped servants' depositions does not indicate the absence of anti-Black racism, however, only the limited extent to which trafficked actors had embraced a white identity by 1760.[50]

The one principal exception to the absence of references to racial language in the testimonies collected by Williamson is the account of Charles Ewan, a chair maker in Edinburgh, who at twelve years old resisted the efforts of an agent of the shipping merchants to decoy him onto a boat set to sail for North America. Ewan initially agreed to the spirit's enticements, accepting "a dram

50. Deposition of George Johnston, ibid., 16, 17.

and a piece of biscuit, and . . . a new coat." When he told some friends of his good fortune, however, "they told him that he was a fool, for he would be sold to the blacks and they would eat him." Ewan's testimony reveals racialized fears in Scotland regarding the political economy in North America, where Blacks allegedly ruled over whites, in this case, eating them like uncivilized savages. From Charles's vantage, racial slavery and Indian conquest were both threats to whites in North America, a world turned upside. That fear, however racist in Charles's articulation, reflected the systemic and far-reaching ways that human trafficking and capitalism in the British countryside were transforming the world commoners had once known. Those fears appeared as a kind of folkloric knowledge to Ewan, magical thinking that helped him escape from his would-be kidnappers.[51]

Initially published as a separate pamphlet entitled *The State of the Process* in 1761, Williamson's kidnapping archive did not sell well as a stand-alone document, so he appended it to his new and expanded fifth edition of *French and Indian Cruelty* in 1762, merging at once his newfound raced theatricality in selling his narrative with his legal campaign on behalf of trafficked children. The combination was especially galling to Aberdeen's merchants. Robert Thomson, the town clerk of Aberdeen, recalled that Williamson set up his book stand in "the ordinary place where gentlemen meet to do business, commonly called the Plain-stones, and that he never saw any creamers or chapmen expose books at that place before or since." The problem was not only that Williamson sold his books without legal permission but that he brought his theatricality to the public marketplace and to private homes. Shipping merchant Alexander Carnegie grew enraged when he "saw the said Peter Williamson hawking and selling copies . . . in George Mackie's house . . . where he was exhibiting himself to company in the Indian dress." Other merchants condemned Williamson being "carried out in a street-chair in the Indian dress," while Francis Nicoll, the town sergeant in Aberdeen, was horrified that Williamson used his performances to hoodwink local aristocrats, "acting to Sir Alexander Gordon and some Ladies in the Indian dress." For shipping merchants in Aberdeen, Williamson's Indian feathers, his kidnapping archive, and his books filled with white women needing rescue had made local marketplaces themselves unruly and dangerous places for the original architects of child trafficking out of Aberdeen.[52]

---

51. Deposition of Charles Ewan, ibid., 15–16.
52. Deposition of Robert Thomson, 49, Deposition of Alexander Carnegie, 29, Deposition of Robert Brand, 30, Deposition of Francis Nicoll, 32.

## Conclusion

In 1760, as commoners across Great Britain struggled against enclosure and enslaved Jamaicans were rising in rebellion against white people, an anonymous abolitionist writing under the pseudonym J. Philmore published a pamphlet condemning the African slave trade. In a short work entitled *Two Dialogues on the Man-Trade*, Philmore declared that "the man-trade is a wicked trade," citing the systemic existence of "men-merchants" who steal "their own countrymen" before selling them to European shipping merchants. Philmore's rhetoric closely paralleled that of trafficked servants in Peter Williamson's kidnapping archive, underscoring the emotional toil of "man-stealing" on both parents and children who were forever lost to one another. Yet Williamson's and Philmore's narratives of human trafficking differed in one crucial respect. Williamson believed skin color authored race and one's capacity for suffering. Philmore insisted that the "black-skin'd and the white-skin'd" were not separate races but all members of "the same species, all of the human race." Human suffering from trafficking was universal, Philmore insisted, with "humanity" itself necessarily bigger and deeper than skin colors or nations. "A patriot, or a lover of his country, is a brave character," Philmore wrote, but the foundation of humanity lay with individuals who saw themselves as "a citizen in the world" rather than "as a citizen of England."[53]

Philmore was not the first abolitionist to condemn "man-stealing," but the parallels between his essay and the servant narratives that condemned kidnapping even as Tacky's Revolt shook Jamaica suggest an interplay between abolitionist thought, plebeian protest, and slave resistance during a key moment of wartime mobilization during the eighteenth century. Whether Williamson read Philmore's essay or either author had fully absorbed accounts of the ongoing slave revolt in Jamaica, the spectacular expansion of Williamson's fifth edition of *French and Indian Cruelty* in 1762, with the inclusion of the kidnapping archive, extended key arguments against slavery and the inhumanity of trafficking. Additionally, although Philmore and Williamson differed in how they deployed skin color, both framed their critiques of British policy and imperial power with conceptions of race as their starting points. By contrast, most plebeian actors protesting enslavement and trafficking in the middle decades of the eighteenth century did not mention skin color. Henry

---

53. Anon., *Two Dialogues on the Man-Trade* (London, 1760), 3, 7, 9, 13, 14, 20.

Grace remained silent on the question altogether in his narrative, while William Moraley, Bampfylde-Moore Carew, and Gottlieb Mittelberger harnessed anger against "man-stealing" by blaming imperial actors and policies rather than prioritizing skin color or any notion of whiteness.

Philmore's and Williamson's writings, taken together in their immediate historical context, highlight an important dilemma that actors seeking to challenge, change, or transform injustices within Great Britain's empire of trafficking faced after 1760. Exactly how might race be repurposed to fight imperial power, mercantilism, and even racism? Could Christianity and the nation state similarly become vehicles for reimagining the meaning and purpose of British power? If the literary marketplace intensified racist formulations of elite antislavery, could it nevertheless empower the varied demands of plebeian individuals and former slaves for justice? As the penny press was amplifying the voices of radical actors during an age of revolution, these questions would become ever more pressing after 1760, not only for the trafficked and enslaved men and women who continued to challenge British power. Henceforth, protests and rebellions would focus less on refusing race than on using it to fight slavery and trafficking. The differences between Philmore and Williamson forecast a coming fight over how to deploy race, as well as what work trafficking and race would do in tandem, a combustible mixture that was as powerful as it was unpredictable.

Williamson's significance cannot ultimately be measured by the immediate consequences of his book or lawsuits, then, but by the ways he linked radicalism to definitions of race and to dilemmas created by literary culture. The theater and the penny press generated highly unequal opportunities for plebeian men like Williamson. Moraley and Carew both found possibilities and perils in trafficking their narratives. Although it expanded the capacity of some to critique British policies, the penny press also enabled theatrical professionals like Robert Goadby to appropriate and distort the stories of transient people circulating across the British Empire. Williamson achieved publishing success by actively experimenting with literary devices and racial grammar associated with fiction. Even as it would be tempting to locate him in a genealogical narrative as the author of racial minstrelsy, for example, doing so would misconstrue where his innovations came from and what he was attempting to do with them. Donning the headdress of a Delaware Indian did not indicate nostalgia for a preindustrial world for the simple reason that most of England's artisans and tenant farmers still eschewed white identity even as they fought enclosure, impressment, spiriting, and kidnapping, much as they had done for the previous century. Williamson's performances exemplified dilemmas about skin color and race for opponents of imperial trafficking that were still becoming visible over time. How could or should plebeian suffering and enslaved people's resistance be linked or intertwined? No single answer or method was apparent to abolitionists or the trafficked and the enslaved on either side of the Atlantic at mid-century. The strength of their varied answers was nonetheless powerful, manifest in the depth of reaction they inspired among the wily modernizers of Britain's empire of trafficking over the ensuing half century.[54]

---

54. Jean-Christophe Agnew, *Worlds Apart: The Market and the Theater in Anglo-American Thought, 1550–1750* (Cambridge, 1986), 149–194. For a sweeping and inspiring narrative of that resistance project, see Peter Linebaugh and Marcus Rediker, *The Many-Headed Hydra: Sailors, Slaves, Commoners, and the Hidden History of the Revolutionary Atlantic* (Boston, 2000). On the "psychological wage" connected to white workers' fully articulated racial consciousness during the Reconstruction era, see W[illiam] E[dward] Burghardt Du Bois, *Black Reconstruction: An Essay toward a History of the Part Which Black Folk Played in the Attempt to Reconstruct Democracy in America, 1860–1880* (New York, 1935), 687; and Roediger, *Wages of Whiteness*, 97.

CHAPTER SEVEN

# Trafficking, Freedom, and Race in the Age of Revolution

IN THE PORT CITY of Boston in 1773, as a national independence movement gained strength across North America, a young enslaved African woman named Phillis Wheatley published a book of poems that established her as a rising star among a transatlantic community of readers. In a poem dedicated to "William, Earl of Dartmouth, His Majesty's Secretary of State for North America," Wheatley praised Dartmouth's appointment as a victory for American freedom: "No more, *America*, . . . shall thou dread the iron chain, / Which wanton *Tyranny* with lawless hand / Had made, and with it meant t'enslave the land." A patriot, Wheatley championed the idea of America as an antislavery nation. She also anchored her condemnation of political tyranny in her experience of the African slave trade that had violently wrested her from her family as a child in Africa in 1761. "Snatch'd from *Afric's* fancy'd happy seat" as an eight-year-old girl, Wheatley recalled the bitter pangs of family separation: "What Sorrows labour'd in the Parent's breast!" Wheatley's poem pointedly contradicted imperial efforts to justify the African slave trade as a lawful traffic in African felons and prisoners of war. More provocatively, Wheatley linked the purpose of the emerging American nation to the cause of abolition.[1]

Wheatley did not cede faith or flags to her opponents. She instead fashioned a radical rethinking of what Christianity and nations meant as well as what antislavery should look like. A devout Christian who believed sincerely in the emancipatory power of the gospel, Wheatley also found strength in the intellectual inheritance of the Enlightenment, a body of knowledge she mapped onto the ancient Mediterranean. Wheatley located inspiration in ancient poets like Virgil and Terence, connecting them to timely and pressing questions about antislavery and the nation. Could Christianity become a

---

1. Phillis Wheatley, *Poems on Various Subjects, Religious and Moral* (London, 1773), 73–74.

resource for justice instead of dominance? Could race be repurposed to fight racial slavery and redeem the nation? These questions helped propel Wheatley to fame as a poet, even if many American patriots confounded or misread her vision.[2]

A revolution in rights for the enslaved and the trafficked was not a foregone or even foreseeable outcome in 1773, even if the political outlines of a national independence movement against tyranny and slavery had clearly emerged across North America. Wheatley and abolitionists like her did not transform the newly organized United States into an antislavery nation. Far from it, proslavery forces would succeed in containing the political possibilities being produced by radical advocates of antislavery. The U.S. Constitution sanctioned slavery with the counting of all enslaved people as three-fifths of a person, an adaptation of the skin-color discourse first adopted by the seventeenth-century mercantile elite to the need to preserve and expand the political power of slaveholders in the new Republic. Racialized numeracy, fueled by human trafficking, continued to dominate how national planners discussed the political significance of the enslaved and how they weaponized skin color. Disciplining internal enemies remained one of the central tasks for state authorities across North America, even as a new nation took shape led by American patriots who claimed they had been enslaved by British tyrants. Trafficked servants and the migrant poor, those subjects most likely to be deemed "paupers, vagabonds, and fugitives from Justice" in the Articles of Confederation in 1781, were explicitly exempted from the benefits of citizenship. State legislatures similarly remained skeptical of such individuals' fitness for civic membership. In 1788, New York legislators passed an "Act for the Better Settlement and Relief of the Poor" that empowered local authorities to deport any "stranger likely to become a charge," while any sailor who could not "give a good account of himself" was to be sent "back again to the place from whence he . . . came." Even as the servant-slave rebellion of 1741 faded as a public memory, New York's political authorities took care

---

2. Wheatley's life story has remained something of a mystery to historians, as she left very few documents outside of the poems that she published. For a masterful telling of her life, see David Waldstreicher, *The Odyssey of Phillis Wheatley: A Poet's Journeys through American Slavery and Independence* (New York, 2023); Vincent Carretta, *Phillis Wheatley: Biography of a Genius in Bondage* (Athens, Ga., 2011); Henry Louis Gates, Jr., *The Trials of Phillis Wheatley: America's First Black Poet and Her Encounters with the Founding Fathers* (New York, 2003); and B. B. Thatcher, *Memoir of Phillis Wheatley: A Native African and a Slave*, 2d ed. (Boston, 1834).

to prevent the formation of future alliances between servants, former sailors, and the enslaved.[3]

Yet precisely because a transatlantic movement for the abolition of the slave trade emerged in tandem with the new nation, antislavery remained a sharply contested discourse across Britain and the United States during the 1770s. Moreover, trafficked, enslaved, and recently emancipated actors were key participants in the war for American independence, fighting on both sides to realize the meaning of antislavery nationalism. Here, indeed, was something new and paradoxical. The sacrifices, aspirations, and visions of enslaved and trafficked actors helped create a new nation even as these individuals were excluded from citizenship. The Age of Revolution brought about genuine but unequal opportunities for subaltern patriots, as Black soldiers became indispensable to the success of General Washington's army and a young Black poet challenged the white men known as founding fathers over how sovereignty and emancipation might be woven together. Wheatley's poems were idealistic and strategic at the same time, bending the arc of political antislavery to the cause of abolition.[4]

Even as Wheatley's unfinished fight to realize an emancipatory political project within the emerging nation provides a point of departure, she was not alone in her opposition to human trafficking. The protracted and occasionally heroic efforts of other trafficked subjects—slaves, sailors, and servants—to fight the various forms of human trafficking intrinsic to Great Britain's and the United States' political economies before the abolition of the African slave trade in 1807 raise questions about how plebeian actors could disrupt entrenched policies at the heart of British and North American political economy. For many slaves, sailors, and servants, resistance to being trafficked made abolitionism a logical extension of their individual struggles. Yet hostility to trafficking did not necessarily sanction antislavery protests or hostility to racism. If radicals like Wheatley linked antitrafficking and antislavery, others used the concept of race to sequester the significance and possibilities

---

3. Articles of Confederation, 1781, art. IV; "An Act for the Better Settlement and Relief of the Poor," Mar. 7, 1788, in *Laws of the State of New-York, Passed by the Legislature of Said State, at Their Eleventh Session* (Albany, N.Y., 1788), 123, 129. On the Three-Fifths Compromise, see U.S. Constitution, 1787, art. I, Section 2, Clause 3.

4. For a brief but effective overview of Wheatley's interactions with Thomas Jefferson and George Washington, see Gates, *Trials of Phillis Wheatley*, 37–38, 44–48; and Waldstreicher, *Odyssey of Phillis Wheatley*, 288–304.

of both antitrafficking and antislavery sentiment. An examination of how the concepts of race and antislavery were changing during the late eighteenth century helps to illuminate that complex work.[5]

## The Geography of Antislavery

The war for American independence engendered a stew of polemical diatribes on both sides of the Atlantic questioning the purpose, legitimacy, and nature of just political authority. Both sides adapted notions of antislavery to bolster their cause, with each condemning the other as enslavers or hypocrites, exaggerating claims of enslavement in the process. The meanings of antislavery multiplied in the years leading up to the war for American independence. The Stamp Act, which directly levied taxes on printed materials across Britain's North American colonies in 1765, sparked an explosion of antislavery sentiment. Stephen Hopkins of Rhode Island, for example, insisted in 1765 that "those who are governed at the will of another, . . . and whose property may be taken from them by taxes, or otherwise, without their own consent, and against their will, are in the miserable condition of slaves." A decade later, as violence between colonists and British troops escalated over the issue of taxation, defenders of British prerogatives excoriated colonial arguments about being enslaved. In a pamphlet entitled *Taxation No Tyranny*, British essayist Samuel Johnson asked the biting question, "How is that we hear the loudest yelps for liberty among the drivers of negroes?" If all colonists were enslaved by parliamentary taxation, then all were also hypocrites, Johnson concluded. Slavery was entrenched in every British colony in 1775, including Massachusetts. Antislavery nationalism became significant in the leadup to the war for American independence, not because of a groundswell of abolitionist sentiment, but because it was geographically myopic and therefore politically effective in equating moral virtues and vices with national identities. For Hopkins, America was the seat of liberty and freedom and London a sinkhole of corruption and tyranny. For Johnson, America was the cauldron of hypocrisy and slavery. Only London could genuinely defend freedom.[6]

---

5. Especially compelling are the claims of Karen E. Fields and Barbara J. Fields, who argue that there can be no separating race from racism. Good science cannot, in turn, flow out of junk science. See Fields and Fields, *Racecraft: The Soul of Inequality in American Life* (New York, 2012).

6. [Stephen Hopkins], *The Rights of Colonies Examined* (Providence, R.I., 1765), 4; Samuel Johnson, *Taxation No Tyranny; An Answer to the Resolutions and Address of the American*

As tensions between London and its North American colonies intensified after the passage of the Stamp Act in 1765, racial language and imagery became more prominent in protests against British policy. In Boston, blackness became a vehicle for patriots to excoriate protesters deemed less than fully militant. In one anonymous letter to the editor of the *Boston Evening-Post*, a writer called for crowd action against those who sought to redress the Stamp Act through petitions, describing them as *"slavish."* They should be humiliated instead, the writer insisted, offering to "furnish a sufficient quantity of black paint, to cover them with their proper colour," averring that he would "strictly enjoin the operator to give them a double blackness, to distinguish them from their *superior slaves*, whose sable appearance is natural. . . . These *slaves* do not groan, they are content, only desiring an 'ALLEVIATION.'" For this patriot, blackness, however militant, was a sign of servility and shame. The writer stood in opposition not only to those who would petition the king but also to the scores of Africans and African Americans who had been participating in protests against the Stamp Act in the streets of Boston. Indeed, when street protests resumed a few weeks later, Boston's Black residents were ordered to stay home and not participate, an effort to make clear, as historian David Waldstreicher has so aptly put it, that "there would be no confusion about whose liberty was at stake." Antislavery could be antislave or simply anti-Black, a racial division that Boston's crowds nevertheless routinely ignored over the coming decade. As the African American Crispus Attucks, the first American to die during the Boston Massacre of 1770, amply demonstrates, antislavery nationalism was not owned by white patriots.[7]

---

*Congress*, 3d ed. (London, 1775), 89. On the importance of antislavery and enslaved people in shaping the American Revolution and its outcome, see David Brion Davis, *The Problem of Slavery in the Age of Revolution, 1770–1823* (Ithaca, N.Y., 1975), 272–285, 299–306, 311–326; Christopher Leslie Brown, *Moral Capital: Foundations of British Abolitionism* (Williamsburg, Va., and Chapel Hill, N.C., 2006), 209–258; Seymour Drescher, *Abolition: A History of Slavery and Antislavery* (New York, 2009), 105–145; Simon Schama, *Rough Crossings: Britain, the Slaves, and the American Revolution* (New York, 2006); and Manisha Sinha, *The Slave's Cause: A History of Abolition* (New Haven, Conn., 2016), 34–64. On Wheatley's response to the Stamp Act, see Gates, *Trials of Phillis Wheatley*, 86; and Waldstreicher, *Odyssey of Phillis Wheatley*, 57–71. For a discussion of the antislavery debate that Johnson's broadside intensified, see Staughton Lynd and David Waldstreicher, "Free Trade, Sovereignty, and Slavery: Toward an Economic Interpretation of American Independence," *William and Mary Quarterly*, 3d Ser., LXVIII (2011), 597–630.

7. "Cambridge, October 15, 1765," *Boston Evening-Post*, Oct. 28, 1765, Supplement, [1]; "To the Publishers," *Boston Evening-Post*, Sept. 23, 1765, [1]; Waldstreicher, *Odyssey of Phillis*

For the young and still enslaved Wheatley, articulating antislavery was both life affirming and dangerous, as likely to yield humiliation and violence as any personal gain or freedom. Tackling racism against Africans represented an especially risky challenge. Wheatley cultivated curiosity about her literary skills by tapping into the growing rivalries between antislavery supporters on either side of the Atlantic. The notion of genius was central to her initial success as a poet. In a proposal to publish a book of her poems circulated by newspaper editors in 1772, Wheatley trafficked the idea of her remarkable intellect to generate interest, writing that "PHILLIS, a Negro Girl," would compose the book "from the strength of her own Genius, it being but a few Years since she came to this Town an uncultivated Barbarian from *Africa*" (Figure 11). Although Wheatley trafficked the idea of her genius, she did not invent or own that discourse. Perceptions of Wheatley's brilliance could challenge racism as well as affirm it, as she became the exception that exemplified racist exclusions. Wheatley's concession to having arrived in Boston as "an uncultivated Barbarian," a nod to imperial hubris and racism, might have been necessary for her to be seen and heard in a literary marketplace that commodified the origins of all mercantile goods, whether Virginia tobacco or a trafficked and enslaved girl from Africa. Origins mattered, but who she was and what she would become in America mattered more. That narrative was central to Wheatley's poems and how she presented them. "It is hoped Encouragement will be given to this Publication," she concluded, "as a reward to a very uncommon Genius, at present a Slave." A slave, though not for long, Wheatley would write her way to emancipation.[8]

Wheatley's poems became well-known, fueling a transatlantic competition among her readers to claim her genius as their own. Wheatley's readers used geography to explain why her poems mattered and who they were as readers. British reviewer John Langhorne was condescending toward Wheatley in 1773 but sang her praises when condemning the hypocrisy of her American

---

Wheatley, 67. On Attucks's significance to the coming Revolution, see Mitch Kachun, *First Martyr of Liberty: Crispus Attucks in American Memory* (New York, 2017); and Brian Deming, *Boston and the Dawn of American Independence* (Yardley, Pa., 2013), 152–162.

8. "Proposals for Printing by Subscription, a Collection of Poems," *Censor* [Boston], Feb. 29, 1772, [2]; "Proposals for Printing by Subscription, a Collection of Poems," ibid., Mar. 14, postscript, [2]; "Proposals for Printing by Subscription, a Collection of Poems," ibid., Apr. 11, supplement, [4]; Phillis Wheatley, *Complete Writings,* ed. Vincent Carretta (New York, 2001), 165–167; Kirstin Wilcox, "The Body into Print: Marketing Phillis Wheatley," *American Literature,* LXXI (1999), 14. On Wheatley's efforts to secure subscriptions, see Waldstreicher, *Odyssey of Phillis Wheatley,* 139–143; and Gates, *Trials of Phillis Wheatley,* 22.

FIGURE 11. *Phillis Wheatley, Negro Servant to Mr. John Wheatley of Boston.* Frontispiece from Phillis Wheatley, *Poems on Various Subjects, Religious and Moral* (London, 1773). Courtesy of David M. Rubenstein Rare Book and Manuscript Library, Duke University, Durham, N.C.

owners. "We are much concerned to find that this ingenious young woman is yet a slave. The people of Boston boast themselves chiefly on their principles of liberty. One such act as the purchase of her freedom, would, in our opinion, have done them more honour than hanging a thousand trees with ribbons and emblems." American readers, in turn, celebrated Wheatley's genius and love of freedom as singularly American virtues. In a footnote to his pamphlet *An Address to the Inhabitants of the British Settlements in America, upon*

*Slave-Keeping* of 1773, patriot Benjamin Rush called attention to Wheatley's extraordinary accomplishments, quoting an anonymous author: "There is now in the town of Boston a Free Negro Girl, about 18 years of age, who has been but 9 years in the country, whose singular genius and accomplishments are such as not only do honor to her sex, but to human nature." Human nature was on the side of the emerging American nation, apparently, and Wheatley's voice amplified its virtues, even if Rush failed to realize Phillis was still enslaved by the Wheatley family. Narratives of Wheatley's genius, then, bolstered antislavery nationalism on both sides of the Atlantic.[9]

Whether an American patriot or a British genius, Wheatley unmasked conceits at the very heart of Anglo-America's larger empire of trafficking, from London to Boston to New York to Charleston. She did so craftily, even while praising metropolitan or colonial officials. Wheatley's poem lauding the selection of William, earl of Dartmouth, as the new secretary of state for North America, for example, directly linked the patriot's fight to the rights of enslaved people across the Americas. For Wheatley, slavery was not a metaphor. Sundering it meant more than ending taxation without representation; it meant overthrowing the traffic in enslaved families that had brought her to America. The Dartmouth poem was even more remarkable for the context in which she composed it: as an answer to the skepticism of Thomas Wooldridge, a British bureaucrat who had publicly cast doubt on whether she had actually written her poems. In 1772, he demanded that she write one in his presence to prove her authorship. The resulting fifty lines underscore Wheatley's capacity to turn the spectacle of her racialized genius to her advantage. Reversing the premise that Black or enslaved Americans could not be patriots, Wheatley instead claimed "The Patrio't's [sic] breast" as her own, describing its powerful effects. "Then Shall the Race of injur'd Freedom bless / The Sire, the Friend, and messenger of Peace." The race that Wheatley defended was, not created by skin color, but by patriots whose freedoms had been injured. She later revised the manuscript version of the poem for inclusion in her published volume of poetry.[10]

---

9. "Art. VII; *Poems on Various Subjects, Religious and Moral* . . . ," *Monthly Review; or, Literary Journal*, XLIX (December 1773), 457–459, reprinted in Mukhtar Ali Isani, "The British Reception of Wheatley's *Poems on Various Subjects*," *Journal of Negro History*, LXVI (1981), 147–148; [Benjamin Rush], *An Address to the Inhabitants of the British Settlements in America, upon Slave-Keeping* (Philadelphia, 1773), 2–3; Waldstreicher, *Odyssey of Phillis Wheatley*, 189.

10. Wheatley, *Complete Writings*, ed. Carretta, 128–129. For a transcription of the exchange, see Thomas Wooldridge to the Earl of Dartmouth, Nov. 24, 1772, in William H.

For Wheatley, racism against Africans posed an existential threat to the nation she imagined. Her commitment to an American national identity rooted in antislavery empowered her to engage with the most powerful figures in the emerging nation, even before the American colonies officially declared independence. In a letter addressed to George Washington in 1775, Wheatley both praised the Continental army and put General Washington on notice. She suggested that other nations were watching to see how he treated his Black troops, valiantly fighting for the cause of American liberty: "And so may you, whoever dares disgrace / The land of freedom's heaven-defended race! / Fix'd are the eyes of nations on the scales, / For in their hopes Columbia's arm prevails." There was just one race in Wheatley's poem, that of the freedom-loving American. Columbia's arms would rise or fall according to how well American patriots respected the scales of justice and protected all Americans born in this "land of freedom," regardless of skin color.[11]

Washington received Wheatley's poem in December 1775, during tense negotiations with his Black troops. At the time, they were demanding to be incorporated into the Continental Army. The question had grown more urgent after the last royal governor of Virginia John Murray, fourth earl of Dunmore, promised to emancipate "indented Servants, Negroes, or others (appertaining to Rebels)" if they would serve in the British Army, the same motley crew that British officials had recently blamed for the Boston Massacre. Rather than respond to Wheatley's poem, Washington initially ignored it. When he finally replied, he had brokered a political compromise with his Black troops. Although they would continue to serve in the army, any future recruitment of free Black patriots was to be curtailed. General Washington praised Wheatley's poem in a private letter to her at the same time that he pointedly avoided engaging with its radical premise.[12]

Wheatley has not, until very recently, been remembered as a radical Christian, an effective opponent of racism, or even an ardent abolitionist, in part

---

Robinson, *Phillis Wheatley and Her Writings* (New York, 1984), 454. The importance of this dialogue was first pointed out by James A. Rawley, "The World of Phillis Wheatley," *New England Quarterly*, L (1977), 666–670. See Waldstreicher's discussion of the Dartmouth poem in Waldstreicher, *Odyssey of Phillis Wheatley*, 169–174.

11. Wheatley, *Complete Works*, ed. Carretta, 88–90.

12. "Proclamation by His Excellency the Governor of Virginia," Nov. 7, 1775, in William J. Van Schreeven, Robert L. Scribner, and Brent Tarter, eds., *Revolutionary Virginia: The Road to Independence*, IV ([Charlottesville, Va.], 1978), 334–335; Thomas J. Steele, "The Figure of Columbia: Phillis Wheatley Plus George Washington," *New England Quarterly*, LIV (1981), 264–266.

because some of her poems lauded political leaders who were slaveholders or denigrated Africa as a continent. In one of her most anthologized poems, "On Being Brought from Africa to America," published in 1768, for example, she wrote: "'TWAS mercy brought me from my *Pagan* land, / Taught my benighted soul to understand / That there's a God, that there's a *Saviour* too: / Once I redemption neither sought nor knew." At first glance, Wheatley seems to be offering a concession to racism. By expressing gratitude to her white masters for the gift of Christianity, Wheatley appears to ratify the moral efficacy of the slave trade and her enslavement to ostensibly good Christian masters like Susannah Wheatley. Yet posthumous critics of Wheatley have neglected the context in which she wrote and published her poem. At the time, she was just fourteen and dependent on Susannah Wheatley for survival. They have also failed to acknowledge the indictment she levied against racist Christians in the final stanza of the same poem. "Remember, *Christians, Negroes,* black as *Cain,* / May be refin'd, and join th' angelic train." By critiquing the slaveholders' gospel, which used biblical references to Cain and the alleged marks among his descendants to justify slavery, Wheatley challenged the racism that relied on Christianity to rationalize slavery and the slave trade.[13]

Wheatley's opposition to racism became more visible as her celebrity grew. Her vision of a single American race living in an emancipated nation was especially threatening to Thomas Jefferson. Living in France during the Revolution, Jefferson was well aware of Wheatley's reputation, one that had become especially prominent after the philosopher Voltaire commented in 1774 that Wheatley proved that "genius, which is rare everywhere, can be found in all parts of the earth." Jefferson, by contrast, denied Wheatley was even a poet, writing in his *Notes on the State of Virginia* that "religion, indeed, has produced a Phyllis Whately; but it could not produce a poet. The compositions published under her name are below the dignity of criticism." If Wheatley was not a genius, Jefferson defensively argued, then her powerful claims about an antislavery nation could be ignored. Although Jefferson condemned slavery, he also insisted on the superiority of the white race, his attempt to control the work that antislavery was accomplishing within the new nation.[14]

---

13. Wheatley, *Complete Works,* ed. Carretta, 13. "Whatever references [Wheatley] made to her African heritage were derogatory, reflecting her status as a favored house slave and a curiosity," wrote Black literary critic Dudley Randall in the early 1960s. See Randall, "Black Poetry," in Addison Gayle, Jr., *Black Expression: Essays by and about Black Americans in the Creative Arts* (New York, 1969), 109–114, also cited in Gates, *Trials of Phillis Wheatley,* 77.

14. Voltaire to M. Le Baron Constant de Rebecque, Apr. 11, 1774, in [Louis Moland, ed.], *Oeuvres complètes de Voltaire . . . ,* new ed., XLVIII (Paris, 1882), 594–595 (le génie,

Eight years before Jefferson published his famous *Notes on the State of Virginia*, however, Wheatley had written a poem in 1777 that would live on, silently exposing Jefferson's hypocrisy in condemning slavery while espousing and naturalizing racism.

> Say, why this insult and disgrace—
> So freely thrown on Afric's race;
> Or shall we, wondrous author! own,
> That insult can from *thee* be thrown?
> Our different hue tho' nature gave,
> Does colour constitute the *slave*?

For Wheatley, skin color was a natural fact. But slavery remained profoundly unnatural, an affront to "Afric's race" as well as the new nation. By fashioning a poetry of dissent that was as patriotic as it was enduring, Wheatley transformed her approach to both race and racism during her short career, shifting from her earlier efforts to valorize an American race committed to freedom to a defense of "Afric's race." That shift was as pragmatic as it was ideological, a recognition that the war over American independence had bolstered both antislavery and racism, a paradox only if one conflates political antislavery with support for abolition. By 1777, Wheatley, sadly, knew better.[15]

## From Skin Color to Race

Thomas Jefferson's insistence that even illiterate whites were racially superior to a Phillis Wheatley represented a relatively new development in the way political elites linked white skin color to the concept of race. Just two decades before Jefferson denied Wheatley's brilliance, the provenance of whiteness for British subjects had remained uncertain. Elites had eschewed connections with the commoners known as whites, while plebeian actors refused

---

qui est rare partout, se trouve aussi en tout climat), quoted in Voltaire, "A Negro Woman Who Writes Very Good English Verse . . . ," in William H. Robinson, ed., *Critical Essays on Phillis Wheatley* (Boston, 1982), 33; Thomas Jefferson, *Notes on the State of Virginia by Thomas Jefferson with Related Documents*, ed. David Waldstreicher (Boston, 2002), 175–181. On Wheatley's skill in navigating the racism of her detractors, see Henry Louis Gates, Jr., *Figures in Black: Words, Signs, and the "Racial" Self* (New York, 1987), 17–18; and Waldstreicher, *Odyssey of Phillis Wheatley*, 307–310.

15. "Messieurs Powars and Willis, Please to Insert the Following Reply . . . ," *Independent Chronicle and the Universal Advertiser* (Boston), Feb. 12, 1778, [2].

trafficking and racial designations simultaneously. By the end of the century, however, whiteness had become more fully recognizable as a thing that all people with lightly complected skin necessarily possessed, whether they were or had been trafficked. That transformation was especially clear in the changing meaning and visibility of the term *white race*, which proliferated in published English language texts across the second half of the eighteenth century.

Before 1750, the phrase *white race* had appeared sporadically and most frequently in connection with non-Christian and non-European actors. In 1710, for example, Jesuit travel writer Balthazar Tellez described a group of people in Ethiopia who "for want of Improvement and through too much mixing with Barbarians . . . became . . . very brutal," as being members of a "white Race." Travel writers deployed the phrase to lump together a great variety of non-English actors, the boundaries around which were inclusive rather than exclusive. A compendium of British and European travel writing published in 1734 as *The Present State of the Republick of Letters* demonstrates just how far-flung and transcontinental the meaning of the phrase could be when used by European travel writers: "It is well known that the Children of *Noah* were white: that the Descendents of *Japhet* inhabited the Islands in the Mediterranean, the Northern Part of *Asia*, and all Europe: that the Posterity of *Sem* possess'd great Part of *Asia*, as far as the River *Cophen* in *India;* and that the Race of Cham settled in Palestine, Egypt, and the Coast of *Africa*, now call'd *Barbary*, and formerly *Lybia*, *Numidia*, and *Mauritania;* all which People are of the white Race." This white race incorporated peoples from diverse locales and skin colors, stretching across several continents. The description did not signify an immutable identity that was superior to others but a local character that a people could gain or lose over time. "Tho' at first these People were of a white Race," wrote Tellez of the Ethiopians, "they lost their Colour and turn'd Black." Some travel writers believed such transformations could be achieved during a single lifetime.[16]

16. Balthazar Tellez, *The Travels of the Jesuits in Ethiopia* . . . (London, 1710), 65; Auguste Malsert, "Memore sur l'origine des négres et des americains," *Present State of the Republick of Letters* (London), July 1734, 65. On the peculiar publication history of the *Present State of the Republick of Letters*, see Norman S. Fiering, "The Transatlantic Republic of Letters: A Note on the Circulation of Learned Periodicals to Early Eighteenth-Century America," *William and Mary Quarterly*, 3d Ser., XXXIII (1976), 642–660. Roxann Wheeler has written that "the assurance that skin color was the primary signifier of human difference was not a dominant conception until the last quarter of the eighteenth century, and even then individuals responded variously to nonwhite skin color." See Wheeler, *The Complexion of Race: Categories of Difference in Eighteenth-Century British Culture* (Philadelphia, 2000), 7.

In the wake of the Seven Years' War, however, a sharply divergent understanding of what constituted a white race emerged in the correspondence and publications of British colonial officials. One of the most influential writers was Thomas Pownall, former governor of Massachusetts, who asserted in 1765 that there were three irreducible races among humankind, each a different species with "essential properties, distinct and different each from the other." "These three different species of race," he explained, "are—The white race—the red—the black. It is not barely the colour of these two first, which distinguishes them; the form of their skull, and their hair, where there has been no mixture, is specifically different from each other. . . . The black race has wool instead of hair, as also a form of skull different from each." Pownall's taxonomy linked external phenotypes to internal structure and character, positing permanent and essential differences between whites and two internal enemies, one red and one Black. That rendering was both politically productive and successful over time, providing a new and effective way for rationalizing the conquest of Native peoples and the expansion of the slave trade. It came into full flower, not at the point of contact between African, European, and Native American peoples in the seventeenth century, but in the wake of a protracted war that remade the shape and geography of political sovereignty across the interior of North America.[17]

Pownall was not the sole originator of the idea of a single racial hierarchy of white, red, and Black peoples in North America. A young writer named Benjamin Franklin published his "Observations concerning the Increase of Mankind" in 1755, describing what would soon become a familiar taxonomy. Franklin lamented that the "Number of purely white People in the World" was "proportionably very small." "Why increase the Sons of Africa, by Planting them in America," Franklin opined, "where we have so fair an Opportunity, by excluding all Blacks and Tawneys, of increasing the lovely White and Red?" Franklin's racism, like much Enlightenment thinking, was expressed as a universalized claim rather than a parochial reaction to the

---

17. Thomas Pownall, *The Administration of the Colonies*, 2d ed. (London, 1765), 155. Pownall published six editions beginning in 1764 over six consecutive years. See G. H. Guttridge, "Thomas Pownall's *The Administration of the Colonies*: The Six Editions," *William and Mary Quarterly*, 3d Ser., XXVI (1969), 31–46. On Pownall's tenure as governor, see John A. Schutz, *Thomas Pownall, British Defender of American Liberty: A Study of Anglo-American Relations in the Eighteenth Century* (Glendale, Calif., 1951), 182, 197; and S. Max Edelson, *The New Map of Empire: How Britain Imagined America before Independence* (Cambridge, Mass., 2017), 114–115.

violence associated with "clearing America of Woods." Yet Franklin voiced uncertainty about the exact work that white complexion accomplished, apparent in his anxieties about whether the "Palatine Boors" could ever "acquire our Complexion." The number of pure white people was indeed very small, he fretted, in part because he excluded all of Pennsylvania's German people from the "Complexion of my Country." One might think of Franklin's arguments about a white race as an experiment, an effort to tie a particular cohort of Englishmen in Pennsylvania to the benefits of an allegedly superior racial identity. The problem was that people with lightly complected skin were so varied, so demonstrably unfit for the political benefit of the doubt that Franklin imagined white skin to create. From its inception, the idea of a white race was imagined as a kind of political aspiration out of sync with its local context. Franklin was less an originator than an imitator of colonial and metropolitan elites, who were anxious about undeserving whites and their impact on the political "Complexion" of the country.[18]

The emergence of species-based formulations of a white race, then, recast older imperial concerns about internal enemies, some of them European in origin. Revisionist in form and internally contradictory, descriptions of a unitary white race in the late 1750s and 1760s hardly constituted a cohesive theory of racial difference. Inconsistencies abounded in the meaning of the term, even as its use exploded twenty-fold across English language texts between 1760 and 1790. If the white race was an immutable thing, why was it still shaped by climate? Inequality, hierarchy, and political difference persisted within efforts to define a geographically expansive white race. Conceptions of alien whiteness among non-Christians and non-Europeans continued to

---

18. Benjamin Franklin, "Observations concerning the Increase of Mankind" (1755), in Leonard W. Labaree, ed., *The Papers of Benjamin Franklin*, IV (New Haven, Conn., 1961), 233–234. On the role of the Enlightenment in cementing racist conceptions of skin color difference, see Robin Blackburn, *The American Crucible: Slavery, Emancipation, and Human Rights* (London, 2011), 145. On the Britishness of Franklin's observations, see John M. Murrin, "The Jeffersonian Triumph and American Exceptionalism," *Journal of the Early Republic*, XX (2000), 1–25. On the role of Franklin's thinking in the evolution of a white nation, see Steve Martinot, *The Machinery of Whiteness: Studies in the Structure of Racialization* (Philadelphia, 2010), 95; and Richard H. Immerman, *Empire for Liberty: A History of American Imperialism from Benjamin Franklin to Paul Wolfowitz* (Princeton, N.J., 2010). On Franklin's connections to trafficking and capitalism, see David Waldstreicher, "The Vexed Story of Human Commodification Told by Benjamin Franklin and Venture Smith," *Journal of the Early Republic*, XXIV (2004), 268–278; and Waldstreicher, *Runaway America: Benjamin Franklin, Slavery, and the American Revolution* (New York, 2004), 138.

circulate, even as notions of white racial superiority gained greater traction. In his *Natural History*, written and published in French during the 1750s and 1760s, French scientist and naturalist George-Louis Leclerc, comte de Buffon, reiterated the popular belief that "in the same race of men, the greater or less degree of black depends on the heat of the climate. Many ages might ... elapse before a white race would become altogether black." Even as white races were reimagined as singular essences, older notions of racial malleability persisted. Race might be innate, yet it could also be lost. Speaking of native South Africans, Buffon insisted that "the Hottentots are not real negroes, but a people of the black race, approaching to the whites, as the Moors of the white race do to the black." Lest there be any confusion produced by that semantic geography, Buffon insisted that "these Hottentots ... form a species of very extraordinary savages." Buffon believed that race, for the Hottentots, was more powerful than skin color, a thing transcending the transactional values that had made skin color a marker of difference in the first place.[19]

If the growth of scientific conceptions of whiteness seemed to eclipse older mercantile discourse, in practice no clear binary separated the two. Scientific racism was an important variation on how grammars of skin color had long functioned as a means of facilitating the trafficking of people and bolstering efforts to legitimate hierarchies of value among those trafficked. What was new in the late eighteenth century was how the concept of a white race transformed the work that skin color had previously done within commercial and colonial contexts. Scientific whiteness posited a timeless and natural boundary between whites and all other colors while simultaneously entrenching transactional conceptions of the value of whiteness. That complex work made racial mixing especially noteworthy to travel writers, philosophers, and naturalists, opportunities to see what the unstable fiction of race truly meant.

One of the most popular of these racial-mixing tropes was the so-called *white negro*. The term first became widely known in London after Voltaire's works were translated into English in 1762. His observations about an albino

---

19. [George-Louis Leclerc, comte de Buffon], *Barr's Buffon; Buffon's Natural History; Containing a Theory of the Earth, a General History of Man, of the Brute Creation, and of Vegetables, Minerals, etc.*, IV (London, 1792), 296, 306. On Buffon's significance to the history of racial taxonomies and nation, see Nicholas Hudson, "From 'Nation' to 'Race': The Origin of Racial Classification in Eighteenth-Century Thought," *Eighteenth-Century Studies*, XXIX (1996), 252–255; and David Bindman, *Ape to Apollo: Aesthetics and the Idea of Race in the 18th Century* (London, 2002), 61–68. For Buffon's broader life story, see Jacques Roger, *Buffon: A Life in Natural History*, ed. L. Pearce Williams, trans. Sarah Lucille Bonnefoi (Ithaca, N.Y., 1997).

man born in Africa whom he met on the streets of Paris in 1744 presented Voltaire with an opportunity to clarify what he understood the relationship between skin color and race to be. Voltaire argued the "White Negro" was scientifically distinct from the white race, a being "which resembles ours no more than a pointer does a greyhound." Voltaire's understanding of race highlighted differences in phenotype but rooted them in observations about the intrinsic value of African bodies. The "white negro" was, not a racial hybrid, then, but simply a "negro," a member of an inferior species distinct from the white race. Race was an essence deeper than skin color, Voltaire insisted, even as he maintained that skin color remained essential to seeing species of peoples.[20]

Voltaire's circular reasoning, a form of magical thinking, connected race as a scientific discourse to imperial exchanges and mercantile political culture. His description of "white negroes" captivated the attention of writers across Europe, including scientists within London's Royal Society, fusing racial spectacle with scientific authority. In 1765, the Royal Society exhibited a "white Negro" to its members, a boy whose "father and mother . . . are perfectly black." The young fair-complexioned boy was put on display to invite discussion about the alleged facts of racial difference, connecting older notions of race as a genealogy of family inheritance to one defined by skin color. The article describing the exhibition was reprinted in 1774 in a publication called the *Weekly Museum; or, Instructive Entertainer*, edited by the popularizer Robert Goadby of Bampfylde-Moore Carew fame, along with descriptions of several other "white negroes." Goadby's reprinting of the Royal Society's article on the exhibition, like Voltaire's portrait of a "white negro," linked metropolitan readers to the ratification of race as a trafficking spectacle. Here

---

20. "Relation concerning a White Negro . . . ," in "Miscellaneous Pieces of M. de Voltaire," in Voltaire, *The Works of M. de Voltaire; Translated from the French* . . . , trans. T. Smollett et al., XXII (London, 1762), 6, 9, 10 [188, 191, 192] (note: the pagination restarts with the "Miscellaneous Pieces" after page 180); Andrew Curran, "Rethinking Race History: The Role of the Albino in the French Enlightenment Life Sciences," *History and Theory*, XLVIII, no. 3 (October 2009), 166–171; Temi Odumosu, "Burthened Bodies: The Image and Cultural Work of 'White Negroes' in the Eighteenth Century Atlantic World," *American Studies in Scandinavia*, XLVI, no. 1 (January 2014), 31–50. On Voltaire's racism, see Blackburn, *American Crucible*, 146; William B. Cohen, *The French Encounter with Africans: White Response to Blacks, 1530–1880* (Bloomington, Ind., 2009), 83–85; and Christopher L. Miller, *The French Atlantic Triangle: Literature and Culture of the Slave Trade* (Durham, N.C., 2008), 7–8, 27, 73.

curious readers learned the meaning of skin color and race imaginatively, as if they were scientists inspecting bodies, seeing them as scientific and transactional facts simultaneously.[21]

Descriptions of "white negroes" were but one part of a broader genre of popular science writing that was in the process of recasting travel literature as scientific discovery. Such literature frequently focused on finds within the newly mapped interiors of the continents of Africa and North and South America. Science writing thus enabled European travelers to discern cultural and political differences among colonized peoples, framing them as objective truths. Exhibitions of "white negroes" in European markets evoked public slave auctions in Britain's colonial port cities, the commerce at the heart of racial slavery. Voltaire ignored the violence undergirding these public displays even while universalizing the marketplace's benefits. Many of the seemingly contradictory features of the Enlightenment that scholars have struggled to make sense of, such as its simultaneous naturalization of racism and universal human rights, for example, possessed common ties to oceanic markets and the forms of traffic they sanctioned. Human trafficking and scientific discourse were never truly separate.[22]

Observations about human sexuality played a key role in transforming ideas of racial difference into science, making a traffic in female bodies central to both scientific and racial knowledge. Typical were the discoveries of nature writer N. Burt, who published his *Delineation of Curious Foreign Beasts and Birds, in Their Natural Colours* in 1791, a companion to his weekly exhibit

---

21. "An Account of the White Negro Shewn by the Royal Society: In a Letter to the Right Honourable the Earl of Morton, President of the Royal Society, from James Parsons, M.D.F.R.S.," *Philosophical Transactions* . . . (London), 1765, 45–53; "An Account of the White Negro . . . ," in *The Weekly Museum; or, Instructive Entertainer* (London), 1774, no. 4, 83–85.

22. On the importance of popular science discourse to a decisive shift in British thinking about race, see Wheeler, *Complexion of Race*, 29. See also Anthony J. Barker, *The African Link: British Attitudes to the Negro in the Era of the Atlantic Slave Trade, 1550–1807* (London, 1978). For an intellectual history of the Enlightenment that highlights the role of particular radical thinkers, see Jonathan I. Israel, *The Radical Enlightenment: Philosophy and the Making of Modernity, 1650–1750* (New York, 2001); and Israel, *Enlightenment Contested: Philosophy, Modernity, and the Emancipation of Man, 1670–1752* (New York, 2006). Israel, however, devotes just one chapter to the topic of race in Enlightenment thought. For a perceptive critique of such ahistoricity, see Samuel Moyn, "Mind the Enlightenment: Jonathan Israel's Epic Defense of the 'Radical Enlightenment' Has the Dogmatic Ring of a Profession of Faith," *The Nation*, May 12, 2010.

outside the theater district of London. Burt addressed his book "to the curious" and contained chapters entitled "The Black and White Negro" and "The White Negro Woman," the latter being a light-skinned African American woman named Amelia Newsham who had been "exhibited in England near forty years." Born in Jamaica to "remarkably black" parents, Amelia came to England at the age of nine, sent "as a present" to her mother's masters' son. Newsham was then sold to new masters "who exhibited her in Castle Street, near Hemming's Row, King's Mews, and then in various parts of England." Newsham invited onlookers to inspect her body for signs of its true racial character, making the question of her racial identity vivid and profitable. After being baptized at Exeter, she determined herself to be free, whereupon she continued exhibiting herself as a means of making money, only quitting the public stage after "she married an Englishman" and started a family.[23]

Discerning Newsham's perspective on being placed before the public eye is challenging. Whether her earnings in the marketplace remained hers is unclear. What is apparent is that she used the stage to engage her audiences' understanding of the morality of race. She was not, in fact, silent as a trafficked subject. "From black parents, how could I exist?" she reportedly asked, continuing, "My nose, my lips, my features all explore, the just resemblance of a Blackamoor." Yet in virtually the same breath, Newsham challenged her viewers' assumptions about the political status of enslaved women. "In me you see the Almighty's wondrous Power," she told her curious onlookers, "His potent arm can all things overthrow, and crush the world to nothing at one blow." Just so did Newsham use Christ to defy earthly authority and hierarchies of race.[24]

Or so readers are told, for Burt's publication was meant to persuade Londoners to come and see his exhibits. An amateur artist, his publication also included an engraving of Newsham, sandwiched between images of "curious foreign beasts" in nature, including a "Segatair" and a "Royal or Crown Bird." Captioned "a striking likeness of Mrs. Newsham the White Negress. 1791,"

---

23. N. Burt, *Delineation of Curious Foreign Beasts and Birds in Their Natural Colours; Which Are to Be Seen Alive at the Great Room over Exeter Change, and at the Lyceum, in the Strand* (London, 1791), 3, 25, 33, 34. Amelia Newsham's life is analyzed in Temi Odumosu, "Burthened Bodies," *American Studies in Scandinavia*, XLVI, no. 1 (January 2014), 45–50.

24. Burt, *Delineation of Curious Foreign Beasts and Birds*, 33, 34. Burt is not widely known but is described as "an amateur artist" in Odumosu, "Burthened Bodies," *American Studies in Scandinavia*, XLVI, no. 1 (January 2014), 47.

FIGURE 12. *A Striking Likeness of Mrs. Newsham the White Negress.* From N. Burt, *Delineation of Curious Foreign Beasts and Birds, in Their Natural Colours* . . . (London, 1791), [Unnumbered page between 32 and 33]. The British Library, London

Burt's image of Newsham portrayed her clad in a fine dress, looking away from the reader's gaze (Figure 12). Were Newsham's words the script of her crowd-seeking employer? Although details remain opaque, what is clear from the varied descriptions of Newsham is that she possessed exemplary power in the minds of her onlookers, a subject whose skin color invited reflection on the changing meanings of racial origins and character. In that regard, her similarities to Wheatley—her Christianity, exceptional characteristics, and her antislavery message—suggest the highly mediated nature of agency for all enslaved women.[25]

Newsham's significance comes into sharper focus in the writings of physician and botanist Robert John Thornton, best known for his richly illustrated studies of the sexual capacities of Carl Linnaeus's botanical discoveries. He commented directly on Newsham's physical attributes in his book *Medical Extracts*. "In the *white Negro*, born of black parents, exhibited in LONDON," he observed, "the nose . . . was flat, exactly resembling that of a black, and the lips were thick, and the skull prominent from behind. No doubt, therefore, remained of this woman having been born of negro parents." To Thornton, Newsham exemplified the utility of race in classifying the "variety of the human species." She had been "universally described by all travellers as a race of *low* STATURE, of a *feeble* make, and *incapable* of *enduring* the *slightest* FATIGUE," he explained. Newsham's invocation of a powerful God notwithstanding, Thornton focused on Newsham's physical attributes to make her race visible and natural to onlookers. She might have appeared white, but she was, in fact, Black, he insisted. Racial hierarchies were deeper than skin color, even if they relied on skin to be knowable.[26]

Thornton nevertheless seems to have absorbed the emancipatory energy Newsham's speeches induced. After describing her ancestry, he asked in a footnote, "Would the TRADERS IN HUMAN FLESH feel some confidence in selling this *white* negro woman?" Now Newsham's white skin stimulated an argument against trafficking. Thornton sought to clarify the confusion in a footnote that accompanied his concluding sentence about Newsham's racial inheritance. "It is melancholy to observe the pains white men have been at," he began, "to represent the *black race* as a lower species of animal, to confound them with the monkey; or if men, to degrade them into beings destined by . . . PROVIDENCE to become the *slaves* of such as boast the names of *Christian* and *European!*" His effort to reconcile racial classification with human rights and the gospel led him to question the very merits of the Enlightenment project he was so invested in as a botanist. "If it shall be said that the 18th

---

25. Burt, *Delineation of Curious Foreign Beasts and Birds*, title page, 31, 32–33, and 35 [the caption for the Newman image appears on an unnumbered page between 32 and 33]. Whether Phillis met Amelia during her trip to London is unknown, but their stories temporally collided and amplified one another in London's literary marketplace during the 1780s.

26. [Robert John Thornton], *Medical Extracts: On the Nature of Health, with Practical Observations: And the Laws of the Nervous and Fibrous System* . . . , new ed., III (London, 1796), 437, 438.

century was an enlightened period," he concluded, "your deeds will be adduced to disprove the assertion." For Thornton, slaveholders rather than botanists were responsible for the ethical travesty at the heart of Britain's empire, a conviction that ignored the messy connections between those cohorts across Britain's colonies.[27]

The discourse surrounding "white negroes" illustrates the emerging power of scientific racism to classify trafficked peoples, not only Africans but also English felons. In 1791, philosopher Jeremy Bentham condemned transportation as the "White-negro trade," a form of state-sponsored trafficking in which "prisoners" were "abandoned to the uncontrouled and uncontroulable discretion of a single despot." Like Peter Williamson, Bentham excoriated an entire class of mercantile actors, not just individual traffickers. "Unhappily where conduct is buried in darkness," Bentham wrote, "it is by the class only that the individual can be judged." Unlike seventeenth-century originators of white grammar, however, Bentham did not condemn these convicts as malefactors but instead championed their suffering by highlighting their whiteness. These whites were not supposed to be treated like enslaved Africans, no matter how egregious their crimes. Trafficking and victimhood went hand in hand. Here was a key piece of white racial ideology that would gain visibility over the ensuing half century, precisely as abolitionist arguments gained power. Indeed, Bentham himself called for the abolition of slavery in the Americas.[28]

## Maritime Antitrafficking, 1765–1792

The narratives created by a motley crew of sailors, transported convicts, enslaved Africans, and emancipated slaves across the British Atlantic during the late eighteenth century continued to refuse the language of racial victimhood articulated by both Thomas Jefferson and Jeremy Bentham, even as trafficking remained central to the stories they told. Although most of the narratives

---

27. Ibid., 437–438.
28. Jeremy Bentham, *Panopticon: or, The Inspection-House* . . . (Dublin, 1791), 396. On the *Panopticon*, see Janet Semple, *Bentham's Prison: A Study of the Panopticon Penitentiary* (New York, 1993). On Bentham's views on slavery, see Davis, *Problem of Slavery*, 355–358. On Bentham's view of convict labor, see R. V. Jackson, "Jeremy Bentham and the New South Wales Convicts," *International Journal of Social Economics*, XXV (1998), 370–379. For a reassessment of Bentham's view of the slave trade, see Frederick Rosen, "Jeremy Bentham on Slavery and the Slave Trade," in Bart Schultz and Georgios Varouxakis, eds., *Utilitarianism and Empire* (Lanham, Md., 2005), 33–56.

generated by trafficked actors remain obscure in print culture, collectively, they reflect the growing capacity plebeian actors enjoyed to challenge and reshape the relationship between states, trafficking, and enslavement. Some identified themselves as abolitionists, while others protested or resisted trafficking and slavery as individuals. Whether they advanced ideas central to abolition or antislavery nationalism, their narratives reframed how subjects and citizens discerned the relationship between human trafficking, enslavement, and national freedom during the late eighteenth century.

The sailor Robert Barker published his life story in 1758, like Henry Grace, in hopes of securing a pension from British authorities in recompense for the trials and tribulations he endured aboard the *Thetis Snow*. He published a slightly expanded version of his story with illustrations in 1762 as well as sought legal redress against the *Thetis Snow*'s abusive captain, who had left him blind in one eye and unable to support himself. That injustice and his compelling indictment of cruelty within the slave trade anticipated key arguments among British abolitionists and would, by the 1790s, make Barker well-known among them. His nemesis as a sailor was a man named Washbutt, the first mate who replaced his captain after the latter abruptly died on their journey to Africa. Insecure and inexperienced, Washbutt soon turned on Barker, whom he suspected of plotting a mutiny against him on behalf of poorly fed and malnourished sailors. That suspicion was unfounded, Barker insisted, as he refused, when asked by a mutineer, to "hoist Jolly Roger." But Washbutt soon "clapt a pistol" to Barker's head and "ordered" him "to be put in irons and chained to a post." Barker spent the remainder of the voyage from Africa to the Americas in chains.[29]

Barker survived the horrific journey because of the skills of enslaved Africans sailing the vessel as well as discrete acts of courage made by enslaved Africans below deck. "We . . . set sail with the assistance of our own slaves,"

---

29. [Robert Barker], *The Unfortunate Shipwright: or, Cruel Captain; Being a Faithful Narrative of the Unparallel'd Sufferings of Robert Barker, Late Carpenter on Board the Thetis Snow of Bristol, in a Voyage to the Coast of Guinea and Antigua* (London, 1758), 15, 18; [Barker], *The Unfortunate Shipwright: or, Cruel Captain; Being a Faithful Narrative of the Unparallel'd Sufferings of Robert Barker . . .* (London, 1762). The biography was frequently republished over the course of the eighteenth and early nineteenth centuries. It was enlarged and revised in 1795 and again in the immediate aftermath of the abolition of the slave trade in 1809. For the revised and expanded edition, see Barker, *The Genuine Life of Robert Barker . . .* (London, 1809). On Barker, see Marcus Rediker, *The Slave Ship: A Human History* (New York, 2007), 391 n. 39, 394 n. 7, 401 n. 14; and Philip Edwards, *The Story of the Voyage: Sea-Narratives in Eighteenth-Century England* (Cambridge, 1994), 152.

Barker related, because the "bad conduct, ill usage, and wicked contrivances" of Washbutt and the ship's doctor had reduced the crew of twenty to just three men, a result of sailors' "death, sickness and desertion." After Barker was initially imprisoned, his only advocates were the ship's "head negroes, who spoke very good English," and who at "diverse times requested to know what offence I had committed to be thus barbarously treated." Washbutt's answer, that "he had reason enough, and that was sufficient," provided little help to Barker, although it did reveal a grudging acceptance of the necessity of these men's labor as "head negroes." The crew's enslaved Black sailors repeatedly saved Barker's life. When Washbutt tried to starve Barker to death, excluding him from even sharing in the slaves' rations, Barker reported that the enslaved sailors pitied "my lamentable circumstances" and "took all opportunities to assist me privately with part of their provisions." Such acts of humanity, as Barker defined them, were indeed dangerous. When the doctor discovered the enslaved sailors passing Barker food, Washbutt "whipped them himself severely." Nevertheless, the discrete gifts of sustenance to Barker continued, and he survived the traumatic voyage.[30]

The power of these acts of charity was visible in the extraordinary efforts Washbutt and the doctor took to suppress them. "The negro women and girls," Barker recounted, were ordered by the doctor "to haul me backwards and forwards by the privities" on deck, an ordeal that humiliated both Barker and the female slaves. Still, it did not stop the passage of food to Barker. What Barker described as the humanity of the ship's enslaved people was also well organized, the result of communication between enslaved people who might have believed he could help them as a mariner were a rebellion to occur. Keeping Barker alive might have also expressed genuine sympathy for him, as no larger rebellion ultimately developed. When the *Thetis Snow* reached Jamaica, the circumstances of Barker and his enslaved African helpers diverged. They were sold at auction while he was abandoned at the wharf, a disabled refuse sailor with no wages.[31]

Barker vowed never to forget these acts of moral courage made by the unnamed African sailors and captives onboard his ship, and he gave them a prominent place throughout his narrative. Barker believed that Washbutt had murdered Captain Pope, the original captain to secure the profits of the voyage and then tried to blame Pope's death on him and the ship's enslaved cargo. "It is the opinion of the learned," Barker wrote, "that the captain's

30. [Barker], *The Unfortunate Shipwright* (1758), 20–22, 26.
31. Ibid., 28.

death did not proceed from the effects of negroes poison, but European." Barker also claimed that Washbutt had defrauded the owner of the *Thetis Snow* of any profits from the slaving voyage by illegally smuggling in "seven hundred weight of ivory." Barker's campaign aimed to expose more than two bad apples in the slave trade. He also sought to upend the unjust circumstance that a ship captain's word was law, a custom that effectively silenced any claim to injustice that a common sailor might have. Barker's story enabled him to press charges successfully against Washbutt, securing a measure of justice for one abused sailor though not for the African men and women who had risked their lives to save his. Barker was awarded a pension of three shillings and sixpence per week for the remainder of his life, "payable by the merchants' hospital." The abiding sense of injustice against slave ship captains and the larger slave trade made Barker's narrative popular as abolitionists gained followers across the 1780s and 1790s. Central to the book's appeal were the solidarities Barker documented between himself, enslaved African sailors, and the English mariners who supported him in London when battling Captain Washbutt in court. "I applied to the shipwrights, both in his Majesty's and the merchant's yards, for relief," Barker wrote, continuing that they "assisted me very much . . . well knowing money to be the sinews of law."[32]

For Barker, the ship was both prison and opportunity, a container of surprising solidarities and unimaginable cruelty. That complexity nurtured Barker's sense of justice across lines of color and nation. He expressed his humanity and capacity for suffering visually in the 1762 edition of his memoir on the title page, a block cut in which he appears waving from shore to a ship with the caption, "The Sufferer in His Prime" (Figure 13). The image presented Barker as a skilled carpenter with a hoped-for stake in a mercantile world that would soon betray his expectations. Barker's portrait bore similarities and sharp differences with another plebeian writer publishing in 1762, Peter Williamson. Both men fully occupy the frontispieces of their books, but Barker is unadorned in his block cut, a plain ship's carpenter without feathers, headdress, or props. He had more in common with the deponents in Williamson's kidnapping archive, who, like him, eschewed literary tropes, white grammar, or any sense of racial victimhood. Suffering was not racialized for Barker; rather, it was universal in form and power. If true humanity was raced in his narrative, it was Black, the only community that consistently exemplified true

---

32. [Barker], *The Unfortunate Shipwright* (1762), 39–40; [Barker], *The Unfortunate Shipwright* (1758), 32, 34, 38.

FIGURE 13. *The Sufferer in His Prime*. Frontispiece from [Robert Barker], *The Unfortunate Shipwright: or, Cruel Captain; Being, a Faithful Narrative of the Unparallel'd Sufferings of Robert Barker, Late Carpenter on Board the Thetis Snow of Bristol, in a Voyage to the Coast of Guinea and Antigua* (London, 1762). Courtesy of The Library of Congress, Washington, D.C.

generosity. Unlike Williamson, Barker used visions of humanity across lines of skin color and status to fight slavery, racism, and his own personal injuries simultaneously.[33]

Barker was successful in his campaign for legal redress and for public recognition, a remarkable achievement given how many British mariners suffered with personal injuries and unanswered demands for redress from the British state in the wake of the Seven Years' War. One measure of Barker's success was not only the indictment of his nemesis Captain Washbutt in court but also the publication of a follow-up volume in 1766 entitled, *The Second Part of the Unfortunate Shipwright; or, The Blind Man's Travels through Many Parts of England, in Pursuit of His Right*, "published according to Act of Parliament," as stated on the volume's title page. In it, Barker chronicled his struggles as an itinerant almsgiver, a narrative ostensibly similar to that of Bampfylde-Moore Carew, except that Barker insisted his suffering was genuine and politically transformative. Barker's demands for justice resonated across a growing portion of Britain's reading public, an accomplishment that built on the successes, though not the excesses, of authors like Peter Williamson. Like him, Barker used the universalized power of antislavery to advance direct claims on the British state in the 1770s. As it turned out, Barker was not the only former mariner who would describe the deleterious impact of the slave trade on the British Navy.[34]

When the transported felon William Green published his narrative in 1775, he similarly highlighted the power of universalized humanitarian values. Green outlined a familiar tale that began with youthful indiscretions. Apprenticed to a master artisan, the young Green ignored his parents' and his master's wishes and ran away to join a gang of unemployed youth living in Sherwood Forest. Unlike Carew, Green and his entire cohort were soon arrested and punished with transportation to Maryland to serve a seven-year term of indenture. Their misery began as soon as they set sail for the Americas. "We soon lost sight of land," Green recalled, "and the next morning we were put under deck for fear of rebelling." Confined for the rest of the voyage, Green was let on deck only briefly with the other convicts, just "six at a time." He and his fellows received rations that barely sustained them, for they sailed with "a most wicked crew as ever went over." Green did not blame the sailors of the convict

33. [Barker], *The Unfortunate Shipwright* (1762), frontispiece.
34. Robert Barker, *The Second Part of the Unfortunate Shipwright; or, The Blind Man's Travels through Many Parts of England, in Pursuit of His Right* (London, 1766), title page.

ship for his misery, however, but lumped himself and his fellow felons along with the wicked crew, for "most . . . did smoak" on board the ship and "all did swear." Conditions and rations improved briefly on their arrival in Maryland. By the command of the captain, Green reported, "We were all ordered to wash ourselves and comb our hair, and shave off our beards." Yet his recital of their ensuing sale at auction encapsulated key grievances against trafficking: humiliating bodily inspections, stripping of clothes, treatment like beasts, and the weakening of their identities as British subjects. "The next day we were put all on shore in couples, chained together and drove in lots like oxen or sheep," Green recounted, before arriving at the auction block. "They search us there as the dealers in horses do those animals in this country, by looking at our teeth, viewing our limbs, to see if they are sound and fit for their labour." Green had been "very well dressed" despite the long voyage, but, he complained, "they stripped me of all my cloathes and gave me lousy rags to put on my back."[35]

Like other trafficked felons, Green looked to the sea for a measure of freedom once his servitude began. His master rented him out to whaling vessels, where he earned wages that he split with his master. "I was put a whaling, and I liked it very well," Green recalled. He survived his servitude with the help of fellow sailors. His greatest comfort came from a friendship he forged with another transported felon turned sailor, Anthony Atkinson, who wept "bitterly" when they were separated on completion of Green's term of service. That friendship was born in common suffering. "What shall I do when you are gone," Atkinson asked, continuing, "I have nobody here to speak to as I have to you." So important was this maritime bond that Green made his eventual reunion with Atkinson two years later the key moment in his emancipation story. "As soon as the news reached my ears," Green wrote of Atkinson's return, "I was in a transport of joy." The cruelties of being trafficked as a transported felon were finally overcome, not by law, but through maritime friendship, one laced with homoerotic overtones. "I ran immediately on board to see him," Green wrote, and Atkinson "fell upon me for joy and wept. Oh! . . . The love that was kindled in each heartin [sic] unspeakable."[36]

35. William Green, *The Sufferings of William Green, Being a Sorrowful Account, of His Seven Years Transportation* . . . (London, 1775), 5–6. There exists little scholarship on Green's life or his biography. For a brief mention of Green, see Nicole K. Dressler, "The 'Vile Commodity': Convict Servitude, Authority, and the Rise of Humanitarianism in the Anglo-American World, 1718–1809" (Ph.D. diss., Northern Illinois University, 2018), 114–116.

36. Green, *Sufferings of William Green*, 9, 10, 11.

Green's narrative, however, was not intended to challenge transportation as a policy. Although he made frequent references to humanity throughout, he framed his story as an admonition to the lawless. "Ye that are just beginning to break the laws, I give you warning now before it is too late, flee everything that hath a tendency to bring on punishment." To readers who ignored this warning, Green offered his only invocation of slavery. "For be assured that like horses you must slave, and like galley-slaves will you be used." Green never mentioned Africans or African Americans, a striking omission given his proximity to enslaved people in Maryland and at sea. Whether his mention of Mediterranean galleys was racist by omission remains a matter of speculation. On the one hand, much of Green's narrative evoked the horrors of the Middle Passage and the suffering inflicted on enslaved Africans, a kind of narrative theft. On the other hand, Green did not create a hierarchy of suffering in his text, nor did he suggest that trafficking people was moral. It could only be justified on pedagogical grounds, Green insisted, as a legal punishment for illegal acts. From that vantage, the trafficking and enslavement of Africans was both illegal and immoral, even if defenders of the trade insisted otherwise. Like Phillis Wheatley, Green animated religious imperatives and interventions: "Make the Scriptures your daily study, read, mark and inwardly digest them, then you need not fear let what will approach you." Just so would evangelicals like Wheatley and Green Christianize the social and political order, whether in Britain or America.[37]

The meaning and significance of Green's narrative emerges with greater clarity when read in connection to a popular ballad that closely mirrored its substance and detail. James Revel's *The Poor Unhappy Transported Felon's Sorrowful Account of His Fourteen Years Transportation at Virginia in America* relayed his experience as a transported convict in rhyming verse. "Some view'd our limbs turning us around, / Examining like horses if we were sound. . . . Some view'd our teeth to see if they were good, / And fit to chew our hard and homely food." Whether Revel adapted Green's prose or the other way around, the lack of a publication date makes it impossible to determine a definitive sequence. It is clear that Revel's verse was circulating by 1780, suggesting that Green's story had become linked to a folkloric retelling of the transported

---

37. Ibid., 15, 16. Some of Green's arguments are also set forth in Granville Sharp, *A Representation of the Injustice and Dangerous Tendency of Tolerating Slavery* . . . (London, 1769). It is not known whether Green and Sharp met, but Sharp would likely have been supportive of Green's rights as a servant. On Sharp's legal cases defending the rights of African slaves within England, see Andrew Lyall, *Granville Sharp's Cases on Slavery* (Oxford, 2017).

felon's suffering. The form of Revel's story, a poetic ballad, also indicates the story had wide appeal among the felons building Great Britain's empire, even after the war for American independence had shut down the convict trade.[38]

Revel's ballad differed in two key respects from Green's narrative with the description of Revel's labor in Virginia and his inclusion of African slaves as principal actors. Rather than working as a maritime whaler, Revel toiled in tobacco fields on a slave plantation. "My fellow slaves were five transports more, / With eighteen negroes which is twenty four, / Besides four transport women in the house, / To wait upon his daughter and his spouse." Revel emphasized commonalities with the people of African origin he labored alongside. "We and the negroes both alike did fare, / Of work and food we had an equal share." Humanity was on their side, Revel insisted, in direct opposition to their abusive English master. "Much hardship then I did endure, / No dog was ever nursed so before," Revel complained, continuing, "More pity then the negroe slaves bestow'd, / Than my inhuman brutal master show'd." Such sympathies across lines of skin color and trafficking had long terrified colonial authorities, but the unusual prominence of this master's inhumanity as the source of servant-slave solidarity marks Revel's ballad as a late eighteenth-century invention.[39]

That more radical purpose was manifest in the explicit linkages Revel forged between enslaved Africans and transported English convicts as well as his critique of transportation as a policy. "My countrymen take warning e'er too late, / Lest you should share my unhappy fate, / Altho' but little crimes you

---

38. James Revel, *The Poor Unhappy Transported Felon's Sorrowful Account* (London, n.d.), 4, 5. Although the British Library lists the probable publication date of Revel's ballad as 1780, some details suggest an older origin, among them Revel's claim in one edition that he was sold in "Raphannock county," which stopped being a county in 1691, near the town of Wicomico, Virginia (ibid., 5). See Revel, "The Unhappy Transported Felon's Sorrowful Account of His Fourteen Years Transportation at Virginia in America," ed. John Melville Jennings, *Virginia Magazine of History and Biography*, LVI (1948), 180–194. Revel's ballad has attracted scholarly interest. See Gwenda Morgan and Peter Rushton, *Eighteenth-Century Criminal Transportation: The Formation of the Criminal Atlantic* (New York, 2004), 89–92; Revel, "The Poor, Unhappy Transported Felon," in Paul Lauter, ed., *The Heath Anthology of American Literature*, 4th ed., I (Boston, 2002), 267–275; and Revel, "The Poor Unhappy Transported Felon's Sorrowful Account of His Fourteen Years of Transportation at Virginia in America," in Susan Castillo and Ivy Schweitzer, eds., *The Literatures of Colonial America: An Anthology* (Malden, Mass., 2001), 230–235. On the role of the Mediterranean convict trade in an Atlantic context, see Alison Games, *The Web of Empire: English Cosmopolitans in an Age of Expansion, 1560–1660* (New York, 2008), 145–146.

39. Revel, *Poor Unhappy Transported Felon's Sorrowful Account*, 5, 6.

here have done, / Think of seven or fourteen years to come." Unlike Green, Revel did not counsel obeying the law because it was just. Rather, he did so because transportation so unfairly punished poor people. Revel's ballad linked felons to enslaved people, condemning transportation as a policy precisely because it was inseparable from the slave trade, whose sailors were frequently convicts sent abroad. "Forc'd from your friends and country to go, / Among the negroes to work at the hoe, / In different countries void of all relief, / Sold for a slave because you prov'd a thief." Revel's ballad, like many narratives written by trafficked individuals in the late eighteenth century, was remarkably free from hierarchies of suffering, especially when compared to the exaggerated claims of antislavery advanced by British and American elites. To be sure, not all trafficked servants, felons, and sailors viewed themselves as abolitionists, but nearly all who published accounts in the 1770s and 1780s condemned the trafficking of people, adding heft, energy, and momentum to abolitionist demands for an emancipatory nationalism on both sides of the Atlantic.[40]

## Toward Abolishing Race Traffic in the Atlantic

When the young Cambridge graduate Thomas Clarkson plotted his unlikely campaign to abolish the African slave trade using firsthand testimonies from its participants, he could not have foreseen how timely or how narrow the window for his intervention would be. The moment for political rupture and transformation was quite short, the immediate aftermath of a war fought over the meaning of national freedom and slavery and the months before the French Revolution gave rise to fears of political subversion that would postpone consideration of the abolition of the slave trade. Clarkson compiled *The Substance of the Evidence* in the fall of 1788, using the insights of mariners and enslaved Africans as his authorities. Clarkson's depositions exposed crimes of trafficking that were systemic in nature, immoral results of an entire class of historical actors. Clarkson sought to remove any hint of fiction in his work, seeking to be "disinterested and unbiassed" and insisting that he would "propose the same queries to all." *The Substance of the Evidence* worked, like good horror writing, by combining several villains into one familiar body: that of the treacherous English slave ship captain. Clarkson used the English slave ship captain to dramatically upend readers' expectations about Englishness,

40. Ibid., 8.

white people, and Christianity. Each deposition began with revelations of coercion in the recruitment of sailors, followed by manifestations of treachery in the slave trade, and concluded with examples of inhumanity on slave ships.[41]

Clarkson's first exhibit mirrored claims made by Phillis Wheatley, debunking the notion that British slave traders were merely purchasing prisoners of war who had already been enslaved. Clarkson presented the testimonies of three African brothers, Little Ephraim Robin John, Amboe Robin John, and Ancona Robin Robin John. In 1767, the three men were invited onto an English slaving ship, the *Indian Queen*, to discuss terms of trade. Ephraim, Amboe, and Ancona soon learned that "we were deceived." The captain, a man named Bevan, "who gave us liquor to drink," briefly left the cabin on board the ship, only to return "attended by his mate and people, armed with pistols and cutlasses, threatening us with death if we made any resistance." The Robin John brothers fought back nevertheless. As Amboe was "struck and cut by the said Captain Bevan and his officers," he asked Beven a question that overturned any notion of English cultural superiority: "'O Captain Bevan, what fashion this for white men to kill black man so?'" Outside the ship, a slaughter ensued in which Bevan's crew "seize[d] all the people of the old Town," killing all who resisted. Those captured were subsequently carried to the West Indies and sold into slavery.[42]

Ephraim's deposition recast virtually every signpost of political or religious virtue within English captivity narratives. The treacherous pirates were, not Algerines, but English ship captains. The key protagonists, in turn, were African and Irish maritime workers. Ephraim only survived because an Irishman, one "Captain O'Neil," took pity on Ephraim on hearing his story and pledged to "carry me to my country," Ephraim relayed, after helping him escape from his English master in the West Indies. Ephraim and his brothers remain religiously devout actors throughout, invoking a providential God at the beginning of their deposition. "God is a rewarder of those who do well, and an avenger of those who do ill," the three brothers declared. Religious radicals like Wheatley and Thomas Lurting could not have said it better.[43]

Clarkson's first deposition established themes that would recur in many subsequent testimonies, including the treachery of English slave ship captains

---

41. Thomas Clarkson, *The Substance of the Evidence of Sundry Persons on the Slave Trade* ... (London, 1789), iv, v.
42. Ibid., 5, 6, 7.
43. Ibid., 6, 8, 9, 10. Captain O'Neil is also mentioned as "Captain O'Neill" (9).

and the coercive treatment of English sailors working in the slave trade. In the second deposition, an English "third mate" concluded that the slave trade was "the grave of our marine," with just eight of twenty-five seamen returning at the end of a voyage in 1768. "The treatment, which the seamen experience in the slave vessels, in point of corporal punishment, is not easy either to be credited or described. They are kicked and beaten about," the third mate revealed, for trifling reasons. He recalled an especially violent episode involving a Black seaman who "had shipped himself at Bristol as cook. . . . They beat and bruised him with hand-spikes: they struck him also repeatedly with the rice-stir . . . [and] compelled him to work at the copper in chains." The cook eventually died, an ostensibly free Black sailor indistinguishable from the enslaved Africans struggling in irons below deck.[44]

The depositions Clarkson assembled made clear that the cruelties of slave ship captains were not confined to Black bodies. All sailors, Black and white, experienced a "want of shelter" on slave ships. One Irish sailor named Lawrence Smithie became sick with the "flux" and was beaten after being unable to "get into the head rails to ease himself." When a few days later he became "so emaciated and weak as to be forced to crawl upon his hands and knees," he asked the captain for "a little nourishment to sapport him." Instead of offering food, the captain "beat him cruelly with a stick, and drove him forward on the main deck, where he was found dead the next morning." This same captain also tyrannized his English-born sailors, including a mariner named Edward Hilton from Liverpool. Like Smithie, Hilton had the temerity to ask for food and was beaten by the doctor who struck him in the eye with his cane, occasioning "the loss of it." Shortly after, the captain ordered Hilton to get in a boat "in a rough and brutal manner" and commanded another sailor to "take that 'white negro Hilton with [him], and to put him on shore any where.'" Hilton expired twelve hours later on the coast of Africa.[45]

The captain's reference to "that 'white negro'" conveyed the abiding contempt that had long shaped British elites' treatment of transported felons. He deployed the term derisively, to mock the agency that sailors allegedly possessed. From this captain's perspective, his crew were all "negroes," bodies to be worked, sold, and discarded like the cargo they were delivering. When Hilton's value as a laboring body was destroyed by the doctor, his only remaining utility was as a living warning to fellow sailors who dared to ask for

44. Ibid., 12, 16, 17.
45. Ibid., 56–58.

more food. Keeping him alive was expensive, however, so he was discarded. Better to maximize the disciplinary value of his punishment by leaving him to die.[46]

Depictions of such cruelty were not new to English readers, as accounts of torture defined most Barbary Coast narratives. What was new across all of Clarkson's depositions was the identity of the perpetrator, the English slave ship captain, whose cruelties ravaged slaves and sailors alike. Clarkson surveyed the coercive nature of sailor recruitment in ways that echoed and amplified the treachery so many Africans experienced in the slave trade. "Seamen have a great aversion to the Slave trade," wrote one mariner. "They are in general procured by crimps.... These get them into debt, and then put them into gaol, from which there is no escape but in the hold of a Guinea-man." Virtually all the sailors interviewed by Clarkson entered maritime service from prison, felons like James Revel. If a sailor aboard a slave ship survived the voyage to the West Indies, he was by no means safe on arriving there. The fate of the blinded Hilton awaited even the luckiest of slave ship sailors. "On their arrival, however, in the West Indies, the Captain and Officers seem to relax a little from their barbarity, and to become kind," recalled one sailor. "They give the seamen leave to go on shore," he explained, "but if they stay longer than forty-eight hours (which it is presumed they will do after so fatiguing a voyage) they are then termed deserters, and are not permitted to come on board. This method they take ... to cheat them of their wages." None of these sailors claimed to be slaves, but their testimonies consistently bespoke commonalities across lines of skin color. "Turned adrift, without money and friends, and with ulcers and Guinea worms in their feet, they are ... found begging about the wharfs, in the extremity of distress, forming that body of people ... known by the name of wharfingers." Some refuse sailors simply died "in empty sugar casks," whites with no value as commodities. Others were "taken in by the negroe women, out of compassion," and "healed in time." Such depositions made clear that the sufferings of these sailors possessed common origins to that of the slaves they transported. All were part of an empire that transformed men and women, white and Black, into disposable things.[47]

46. Ibid., 58. Emma Christopher also cites Edward Hilton's narrative and testimony in her book Christopher, *Slave Ship Sailors and Their Captive Cargoes, 1730–1807* (New York, 2006), 113.

47. Clarkson, *Substance of the Evidence*, 17, 21, 24, 60. Marcus Rediker also noted the sympathy offered to excluded sailors in the British Caribbean who were kept alive by the

Clarkson's *Substance of the Evidence* produced a political uproar because it effectively crushed most signposts of English moral authority. By denouncing England's murderous slave trade and the racism that sanctioned it, mariners' depositions revealed a community of interest between trafficked sailors and African slaves, actors that metropolitan and colonial authorities had long sought to keep separate. Cruelty in their recruitment forged potential alliances between the enslaved and the convicted. Sailors condemned the coercion that brought them to slave ships, whether by the manipulations of spirits or the policy of transportation that moved them from prison directly to the slave ship. These arguments echoed older alliances between maritime actors, whether white servants and African slaves in Barbados in the 1680s or Irish-African cohorts plotting conspiracies on the waterfront of New York City in 1741.[48]

Unlike the maritime radicals Ceasar and Peggy, however, Clarkson was no enemy of the British Empire but a firm believer in its morally beneficent purposes. For Clarkson, as for many abolitionists, trafficking was the key factor shaping both their critique of British power and their confidence in its redemptive capacity. Slave trafficking could never be made reconcilable with humanitarian premises. It was the source of the worst cruelties within the Empire. Yet British culture and Christianity could also save African peoples from themselves, Clarkson contended, particularly if Africans embraced the gospel of free labor, the belief that trafficking one's labor was both efficient and moral. "The slave trade too has been hitherto an insuperable impediment to the civilization of the Africans," wrote Clarkson. "But the new commerce would have a contrary effect. . . . It would gradually alter their opinions and habits. It would soften and polish their manners, and would bring them to a state of refinement." Free labor would, like Christianity, function as a civilizing project, expanding the moral authority of Englishmen and Africans alike. "This civilization would be productive of the most beneficial effects to ourselves: for in proportion as we civilize a people, we *increase their wants*, and we should create therefore . . . another source of *additional consumption of our manufacturers*." Clarkson's candor about the self-serving benefits of free labor

---

generosity of enslaved Jamaican women. See Rediker, *Slave Ship*, 351–352. Friedrich Engels described English factory wages as leading to starvation, a form of slavery akin to chattel slavery in 1845. See Engels, *The Condition of the Working Class in England* (1845), ed. Victor Kiernan (London, 1987), 114.

48. On the radicalism within the depositions of sailors and ex-slaves in Clarkson's *Substance of the Evidence*, see Sinha, *Slave's Cause*, 101.

makes it hard not to see the imperial interests within his abolitionist vision. Trafficking one's labor for wages was not intrinsically evil, Clarkson insisted, only trafficking slaves.[49]

British abolitionists sharply disagreed with their critics over how to make British imperial power moral and enduring. All sides of the slavery debate nevertheless affirmed common assumptions about the stakes of the slave trade. As in the United States, those stakes were moral, religious, and, above all, national in scope, with abolitionists conflating the health of the nation with that of its maritime work force. Traffic was essential to evolving understandings of slavery, skin color, and race on both sides of the Atlantic Ocean. The political success of abolitionism would rest on how well its advocates could redefine national identity and the relationships it sanctioned between trafficking and sovereignty.

## Olaudah Equiano, Maritime Radical

The only evidence more compelling in condemning the slave trade than the depositions of enslaved actors and slave ship sailors in 1788 was the life story of Olaudah Equiano, an emancipated African mariner turned Christian. *The Interesting Narrative of the Life of Olaudah Equiano*, first published in the spring of 1789, made its author a transatlantic celebrity, going through nine reprintings in just six years and being translated into French, Dutch, and Spanish. Equiano's personal narrative was not the first to condemn the institution of slavery in the Americas (Figure 14). It was, however, the sharpest and certainly the most effective critique of slavery yet published in the English language in 1789, transforming the power, reach, and capacity of abolitionism on both sides of the Atlantic. Equiano's success was also attributable to his identification with Great Britain and what he deemed the Empire's fundamentally moral and Christian purpose. Equiano was a radical Christian and a patriot, making him a formidable opponent of the African slave trade.[50]

Like British sailors held in bondage in North Africa, Equiano protested being trafficked as much as being enslaved. Although he reported being well

---

49. T[homas] Clarkson, *An Essay on the Impolicy of the African Slave Trade* (London, 1788), 115. On Clarkson's vision of free labor, see Davis, *Problem of Slavery*, 382.

50. Olaudah Equiano, *The Interesting Narrative of the Life of Olaudah Equiano; or, Gustavus Vassa, the African; Written by Himself*, 2d. ed. (London, [1789]); Equiano, *The Interesting Narrative of the Life of Olaudah Equiano, or Gustavus Vassa, the African*, ed. Shelly Eversley (New York, 2004). On the publishing history of Equiano's narrative, see the

FIGURE 14. Daniel Orme, after W. Denton, *Olaudah Equiano ('Gustavus Vassa')*. 1789. Stipple engraving. © National Portrait Gallery, London

treated by his masters, he complained bitterly about his kidnapping in Africa, when he was "first torn away from all the tender connexions that were naturally dear to my heart." Being trafficked was inextricably linked to his separation from his sister, a loss that pushed him to the brink of suicide on his subsequent passage across the Atlantic. Refusing to eat and having to be force-fed during the journey, Equiano arrived in the West Indies sick, emaciated, and unsalable. With no one willing to purchase him, Equiano became known as a refuse slave. He was shipped to Virginia, where ship captains hoped he would make enough of a recovery that his body might become fungible. This time they were modestly successful, and the young Equiano was sold for a mere thirty pounds.[51]

Over time, Equiano learned skills as an enslaved mariner that would enable him, against considerable odds, to eventually earn enough money to purchase his freedom, buying and selling things in local markets. Trafficking goods and people were essential to his survival and his experience of both coercion and freedom at sea. For Equiano, the adult sailor, crimes connected to slave trafficking, kidnapping, and resale remained the most visible threats to

---

introduction by Robert Reid-Pharr, "Introduction," in Equiano, *Interesting Narrative*, ed. Eversley, xv–xviii. On Equiano's autobiography's impact on subsequent slave narratives, see Frances Smith Foster, *Witnessing Slavery: The Development of Ante-bellum Slave Narratives* (Westport, Conn., 1979), 47–52; Henry Louis Gates, Jr., ed., *The Classic Slave Narratives* (New York, 1987); Dwight A. McBride, *Impossible Witnesses: Truth, Abolitionism, and Slave Testimony* (New York, 2001), 120; and James H. Sweet, "Mistaken Identities? Olaudah Equiano, Domingos Álvares, and the Methodological Challenges of Studying the African Diaspora," *American Historical Review*, CXIV (2009), 279–306. On abolitionists' efforts to cast their arguments as quintessentially British and Christian during the 1780s and 1790s, see Brown, *Moral Capital*, 295–297; and James Walvin, *An African's Life: The Life and Times of Olaudah Equiano, 1745–1797* (New York, 1998), 151. Equiano's dual identity as both African and English has fostered a rich debate among scholars over whether he was born in Africa or the Americas. See Vincent Carretta, *Equiano the African: Biography of a Self-Made Man* (Athens, Ga., 2005); and Paul E. Lovejoy, "Autobiography and Memory: Gustavus Vassa, Alias Olaudah Equiano, the African," *Slavery and Abolition*, XXVII, no. 3 (2006), 317–347. On the conceptual limits of the Equiano origins debate, see James Sidbury, *Becoming African in America: Race and Nation in the Early Black Atlantic, 1760–1830* (New York, 2007); Sidbury, "From Igbo Israeli to African Christian: The Emergence of Racial Identity in Olaudah Equiano's Interesting Narrative," in Stephan Palmié, ed., *Africas of the Americas: Beyond the Search for Origins in the Study of Afro-Atlantic Religions* (Leiden, Netherlands, 2008), 79–106; and Sweet, "Mistaken Identities," *American Historical Review*, CXIV (2009), 303–304.

51. Equiano, *Interesting Narrative*, ed. Eversley, xxx.

his personhood, long after his Middle Passage experience. Equiano paid his owner nearly seventy pounds to become his own master, yet he faced constant anxiety about being reenslaved. After saving the crew of his ship during a storm off the coast of Georgia, Equiano soon found himself in peril when "I was beset by two white men, who meant to play their usual tricks with me in the way of kidnapping." Equiano survived, but John Annis, a free Black cook also on board his ship, was not so lucky. He was kidnapped by slave dealers. As Equiano recounted Annis's tragic fate, the captain, perhaps receiving a bribe, gave his consent to the kidnapping, despite the protest of crew members. Equiano did everything in his power to help Annis, a British subject with no Ironmongers' Slave Fund to support him, calling on the abolitionist Granville Sharp to intervene while petitioning lawyers in London to secure a writ of habeas corpus that might free him from Saint Kitts. When these legal efforts failed, Equiano risked his life and returned to Saint Kitts, where he "whitened" his "face that they might not know" him in order to investigate. Equiano's efforts did not stop Annis's former owners from torturing the cook, however, and he died just two months after returning to enslavement.[52]

Equiano's decision to embrace British political culture and Christianity created enduring tensions within his narrative. Although he condemned the slave trade for its "tendency . . . to debauch men's minds, and harden them to every feeling of humanity," he also briefly participated in the same traffic. Like Clarkson, Equiano defended the possibility of creating a humanitarian British Empire in Africa, one organized around free trade and free labor rather than slave traffic. To that end, toward the end of his narrative, Equiano joined his English patron, one Dr. Irving, in fitting out "a plantation at Jamaica and the Musquito shore." That project meant sailing to Africa "on board a Guinea-man, to purchase some slaves to carry with us, and cultivate a plantation; and I chose them all of my own countrymen, some of whom came from Lybia." Equiano struggled to explain the moral purpose of these human purchases. "I accepted of the offer, knowing that the harvest was fully ripe in those parts . . . of bringing some poor sinner to my well-beloved master,

---

52. Ibid., 161, 185–186. Equiano's story illuminates how freedom could be achieved through arduous "physical and spiritual exertions," as scholar Robert Reid-Pharr put it, "the result more of a complicated set of emotional and financial machinations." See Reid-Pharr, "Introduction," in Equiano, *Interesting Narrative*, ed. Eversley, ix–x. On the activism and radicalism of sailors in colonial and Revolutionary New York, see Jesse Lemisch, *Jack Tar vs. John Bull: The Role of New York's Seamen in Precipitating the Revolution* (New York, 1997).

Jesus Christ." Trafficking bodies to harvest souls was an unhappy bargain for Equiano. Perhaps that is why he was so keen to secure people from his own region, the better to bridge the gap he knew so well between being an object and a Christian subject.[53]

Yet these tensions were neither new nor unique to Equiano. Like Phillis Wheatley, Equiano wrestled with how to make patriotism an emancipatory force. Equiano's keen appreciation of the crimes connected to trafficking people led him to see both commonalities and sharp differences with his fellow British sailors. Their most powerful shared fear, beyond sailing into a hurricane, was waking to the sound of the press-gang boarding their ship at dawn. "Immediately the press-gang came on board," Equiano recalled of one encounter, "with their swords drawn, and searched all about, pulled the people out by force, and put them into the boat," a scene that evoked his original kidnapping in Africa. "The man that found me held me up by the heels while they all made their sport of me," Equiano wrote, recalling that he was "roaring and crying out all the time most lustily." By linking impressment to his kidnapping in the slave trade, Equiano made clear there could be no African slave trade, no empire built on traffic, without impressed sailors and kidnapped Africans, both subject to oceanic trafficking.[54]

Equiano was also unsparing in his criticism of the racism of white people. He understood that racism was not intrinsic to white skin but to a person's geographic proximity to slave trafficking and their class position. The West Indies was an especially vexing locale, one which enabled white men to purchase and kill any African slave with impunity. Such cruelty was the product of particular local laws, Equiano insisted, such as one in Barbados that required white men to *"pay into the public treasury fifteen pounds sterling"* for

---

53. Equiano, *Interesting Narrative*, ed. Eversley, xxxiv, 103, 213, 216.

54. Ibid., 52. On Equiano's views of impressment, see Daniel James Ennis, *Enter the Press-Gang: Naval Impressment in Eighteenth-Century British Literature* (Newark, Del., 2002), 127–132. Colonial governors feared that impressment would increase the necessity of using Black sailors and Native peoples to field national navies, heightening racist fears of rebellion in sugar colonies especially. After years of intensive impressment during the War of Jenkins' Ear, for example, Governor Edward Trelawny of Jamaica performed a survey in 1743 of the British naval ships at Port Royal and discovered more than half the sailors were Black or Native American. Sailors of all colors resisted the press, as Equiano's narrative suggests, whether they were enslaved Africans. If enslaved sailors experienced sailing as a "pathway to freedom" as Denver Brunsman indicates, it was nonetheless in a context of maritime discipline, trafficking, and limited freedom. See Brunsman, *The Evil Necessity: British Naval Impressment in the Eighteenth-Century Atlantic World* (Charlottesville, Va., 2013), 116, 122.

killing another man's slave. Equiano described the law as "at once unmerciful, unjust, and unwise; which for cruelty would disgrace an assembly of those who are called barbarians." The practice of selling newly captured African people and their children at auction, reducing the humanity of African and African-descended subjects to so much tonnage, however, overshadowed all other cruelty, even that of the law. No indentured servant or impressed sailor, no matter how mistreated, experienced commodification in such fashion. The sight of those auctions haunted Equiano long after his own sale. "I have often seen slaves, particularly those who were meagre, in different islands," Equiano recalled, "put into scales and weighed, and then sold from three-pence to six-pence, or nine-pence a pound." These so-called refuse slaves were valued like slaughtered food or livestock. For Equiano, it was market thinking that turned African people into so many body parts. Worse, the cruelty of the slave market was not even visible to buyers and sellers; rather, it had become a habit of thought. Equiano's insight into the dehumanizing nature of the slave trade is perhaps no more vividly recalled then in his description of his master's horrified reaction to the traffic in refuse slaves. The very man "whose humanity was shocked at this mode" of selling people, Equiano wryly observed, himself "used to sell such by the lump." Equiano's observation of his master's belated shock was doubly troubling, exposing his master's deformed sense of humanity as well as the moral form it assumed. Here, indeed, was a mischievous and powerful critique of market morality.[55]

---

55. Equiano, *Interesting Narrative*, ed. Eversley, 101, 102, 103. On the moral superiority of Black humanity over white in Equiano's narrative, see McBride, *Impossible Witnesses*, 120. See also Jesús Benito and Ana Manzanas, "The (De-)Construction of the 'Other' in *The Interesting Narrative of the Life of Olaudah Equiano*," in Maria Diedrich, Henry Louis Gates, Jr., and Carl Pedersen, eds., *Black Imagination and the Middle Passage* (New York, 1999), 47–56. On the centrality of reproduction to the financial assessment of enslaved people's bodies, see Daina Ramey Berry, *The Price for Their Pound of Flesh: The Value of the Enslaved, from Womb to Grave, in the Building of a Nation* (Boston, 2017), 12–17. According to Berry, the "last four decades of the 18th century were crucial" in the creation of market prices for enslaved women that explicitly commodified the value of future progeny, a very different metric than the weight of an enslaved person for sale (12). On the category of "refuse slaves" and its relationship to the silences that market "values" enacted on Africans in the slave trade, see Marisa J. Fuentes, "'Refuse' Bodies, Disposable Lives: The Ethical Practice of History" (lecture, The Race and Slavery Working Group, Gilder Lehrman Center for the Study of Slavery, Resistance, and Abolition at the Whitney and Betty MacMillan Center for International and Area Studies, Yale University, October 2017). On the limits of transactional frames for recovering the history of enslaved women, see Fuentes, *Dispossessed Lives: Enslaved Women, Violence, and the Archive* (Philadelphia, 2016).

Humanity, of course, had only recently begun to be understood as a community that possessed inalienable rights and values. That historical development reflected not simply the emergence of markets, with their ostensibly universalized values, but also the work of humanitarians, most of them Black and enslaved, who insisted on defending their humanity and that of others even while chained in the holds of ships, as William Green well understood. Equiano's invocation of the rights of "humanity" was both radical and ironic, as double-edged as his adoption of antislavery values and Christianity in the name of defending the British Empire. Himself a trafficked subject, Equiano defended the universalizing values associated with global markets. At the same time, no formerly enslaved writer better captured the barbarity associated with market logic in the slave trade.[56]

If the West Indies was an especially corrupt place, however, Equiano experienced the Mediterranean, by contrast, as a region relatively free of racism, though still marked by prize taking and captivity. In 1768, his work as a free sailor took him on a voyage to Villa Franca, Nice, Leghorn, the Archipelago Islands, and Turkey, among other destinations. His interactions with Greek people were especially beneficent. They "treated me always with great civility. In general I believe they are fond of black people." Yet even as he noted the comparative lack of racism in the Mediterranean, Equiano remained aware of the varieties of human trafficking and slavery that distorted freedom there, haunted by the spectacle of "the galley-slaves, whose condition . . . is truly piteous and wretched." He expressed particular dismay on witnessing "how the Greeks are, in some measure, kept under by the Turks, as the negroes are in the West Indies by the white people." Equiano created no hierarchy of suffering in his comparisons of galley slaves, subjugated Greeks, and African slaves. Instead, comparisons and similes enabled him to discern and map the signature harms of trafficking and enslavement wherever he traveled. Indeed, throughout Equiano's narrative, geography and mobility form essential parts of his political vision and moral imagination, enabling him to show and explain how human trafficking and racism created bottlenecks of violence across Britain's expanding Empire.[57]

---

56. For an analysis of the relationship between trafficking and antislavery in the Atlantic context, see Philip Gould, *Barbaric Traffic: Commerce and Antislavery in the Eighteenth-Century Atlantic World* (Cambridge, Mass., 2003).

57. Equiano, *Interesting Narrative*, ed. Eversley, 171, 172. Robert Reid-Pharr highlights the importance of Equiano's skills as a sailor to his larger historical significance, especially his quest to find freedom in a world equal parts commercial and coercive. See Reid-Pharr,

## Expanding National Emancipations in the Mediterranean, 1776–1807

In 1789, the political economy of human trafficking and enslavement in the Mediterranean remained distinct from the Atlantic, even if comparisons between the two regions had grown more frequent and commonplace. For Africans enslaved in the Atlantic, the Mediterranean appeared beneficent, a region of respite from the unrelenting racism of Atlantic enslavements. Yet the Mediterranean also challenged truisms connected to Atlantic abolitionism. Trafficking could precipitate slavery or be instrumental to emancipation for captives seeking ransoms. In contrast to the Atlantic, race was not a defining feature of human trafficking in the Mediterranean, nor was hostility to being bought and sold a precondition for antislavery or emancipation. The relationship between slavery and trafficking in the region was especially problematic, given the reliance of European powers on penal transportation to provide a labor force for national navies. U.S. independence would further complicate trafficking and relations of ransom and rescue in the region, as the fledgling republic's naval recruitment strategies and its comparatively generous naturalization laws drew sailors from many nations to the American flag. Mediterranean mariners would come to play a vital if largely unheralded role in expanding antislavery even while demanding the extension of Anglo-American sovereignties, an important rehearsal for larger Atlantic transformations. At the same time, U.S. naturalization law introduced race as a category into the process by which sailors switched nationalities to become American sailors, whether in the Atlantic or the Mediterranean.

Mariners' demands for stronger relations of national emancipation in the Mediterranean were hardly new when war broke out between Britain and its colonies in the mid-1770s. That conflict, however, reshaped how sailors and diplomatic officers understood emancipation, freedom, and national identity. For sailors flying under the new American flag, the immediate consequence of national independence was the loss of even modest protections that had been secured by Britain's treaties with Morocco and Algiers. American sailors were now fair game for trafficking by both renegades and Algerine and Moroccan navies, and many were soon captured and set to work as slaves. The

---

"Introduction," ibid., xvii. On the ways Equiano imagined nations beyond European frameworks and on behalf of African peoples, see Alexander X. Byrd, "Eboe, Country, Nation, and Gustavus Vassa's *Interesting Narrative*," *William and Mary Quarterly*, 3d Ser., LXIII (2006), 123–148.

resulting diplomatic crises for the United States, not to mention the staggering debt incurred to North African polities across the 1790s in paying sailors' ransoms, produced logistical challenges for the U.S. government, not only for the American treasury but also for the American Navy, which could not emancipate its captive sailors effectively and struggled to fill its ranks. Putting additional pressure on the U.S. government to protect American sailors' maritime freedoms were Great Britain's diplomatic ties to North African polities and the British government's history of organizing relations of rescue for its sailors.

For British sailors, the United States' successful bid for independence opened up an avenue of escape from Britain's increasingly oppressive Impress Service. As British naval impressment expanded across the 1790s to meet the demands of the Royal Navy's global campaign against French power in the wake of the French Revolution, some British sailors claimed to be American to avoid British press-gangs on shore. Others jumped ship to avoid Britain's compulsory military service. It did not help British press-gangs that the American Navy forbid impressment and recruited its work force with better pay and greater rewards for service. Sailors' defections encouraged British press parties to board and search U.S. vessels looking for English sailors, even if such forays risked escalating the labor conflict into war with the United States.

U.S. naturalization laws also attracted British sailors to American ships. The 1790 Naturalization Act declared that all "free white person[s]" could become citizens after establishing residence in the United States for just two years. Excluded from naturalization were a diverse group of people referred to collectively as non-whites, including persons from Africa, Asia, the Americas, and parts of Europe, and European-born whites who had emigrated to the nation as indentured servants or transported felons. Such actors might become American citizens in time, but only after they were no longer indentured or in debt, requirements that excluded a great many immigrant subjects. For sailors with lightly complected skin color, however, the 1790 Naturalization Act was remarkably open, with no formal requirements for proving two years of residence. Indeed, it was the very expansiveness of the 1790 law that led Great Britain to begin boarding American ships in search of escaped sailors.[58]

---

58. "An Act to Establish an Uniform Rule of Naturalization," Session II, Statute II, chap. III, Mar. 26, 1790, in Richard Peters, ed., *The Public Statutes at Large of the United States of America, from the Organization of the Government in 1789, to March 3, 1845 . . .* , I (Boston, 1845), 103–104. The white racial status at the heart of the 1790 Naturalization Act

In the young United States, birthright citizenship and race were linked from the nation's very inception. That fact reflected not only the centrality of slavery and enslaved people to the form and structure of the U.S. Constitution but also the importance of whiteness to the passage of the 1790 Naturalization Act. The phrase "free white person[s]" invites consideration of the political status of unfree whites, those trafficked men and women whose political loyalties had long been vexing to colonial and metropolitan authorities. By excluding free Blacks and unfree whites from naturalization, American framers cemented a foundational but often hidden boundary between free white citizens and whites who had been trafficked and were deemed unfree. Although framers of the law might have wanted whiteness and freedom to be synonymous, they were manifestly not so, either in law or in elite discourse about the people. That is perhaps why President George Washington made no mention of free white persons when discussing the need for a uniform naturalization law in 1790. The phrase appeared in American newspapers only after the naturalization bill had become law in March 1790. That absence suggests caution in presuming that whiteness had already become a de facto political currency that bound southern and northern legislators to one another in 1790. The political need for such a currency was certainly real enough, particularly as debates over slavery, the slave trade, and the Three-Fifths Compromise created strikingly divergent footings for political union between slave and non-slave states. But there were far too many unfree whites in the land, too many rebellious and landless actors of uncertain political loyalty, to make whiteness alone the sole requirement for naturalized citizenship. Although the 1790 Naturalization Act highlighted enduring class inequalities among the people called whites in the United States, the law also set in motion a long and complex historical process by which new immigrants to the United States sought citizenship rights, whenever possible, by claiming to be free and white, despite being treated as outcasts and aliens.[59]

British naturalization law, by contrast, had evolved in relation to the specific needs of foreign-born merchants from Europe, not the needs of its

---

has been hailed as an important starting point for subsequent North American immigration history, but few have investigated the circumstances of its framing and passage. On the importance of the 1790 Naturalization Act to immigrant whiteness over succeeding generations of arrivals, see Matthew Frye Jacobson, *Whiteness of a Different Color: European Immigrants and the Alchemy of Race* (Cambridge, Mass., 1998), 18–19.

59. "The President's Speech to Both Houses of Congress," *New-York Packet,* Jan. 9, 1790, [3].

increasingly heterogenous navies. In 1674, British naturalization law reserved the privilege of naturalization for merchants who were living and working in London or other British centers of oceanic trade. Subjects had to be *"of the Age of Eighteen years or above"* and had to *"have received the Sacrament of the Lord's Supper, within one month"* before any bill would be brought before Parliament. Such naturalized subjects also had to profess political fealty, to *"take the Oath of Supremacy, and the Oath of Allegiance, in the Parliament-House."* The process of naturalizing *"Alien Merchants"* precipitated resistance to their rights as English subjects. In a *History of Naturalization*, likely authored by then attorney general Samuel Pepys in the late 1670s, fear and mistrust surrounded the status of naturalized subjects. "The greatest part of them are not intended to inhabit with us," the *History* lays out, "but, like Summer-Birds, when they have filled their Pockets, or if trouble or War arise, they will not forget their Fathers Land . . . [and] may be instruments of great inconvenience to His Majesty and His *Natural-born Subjects*." Naturalization in Great Britain granted transactional privileges for participating commercially within the nation but did not establish British citizenship. Fears of British sailors becoming Muslim remained powerful. Even so, few diplomatic or consular actors believed naturalization instilled enduring political loyalties. Such arrangements were deemed to be expedient rather than ideological, as were the ransom monies raised by British authorities.[60]

Even as the 1790 Naturalization Act enticed white-skinned British sailors, it nevertheless stood as a barrier to Black sailors. Black British sailors seeking work on U.S. ships faced particular dilemmas. Should they work for an American navy even if they were not granted citizenship? Would Black sailors be ransomed by American authorities if they could not claim birthright citizenship? As in Great Britain, an acute need for skilled maritime labor drove considerations by individual ship captains. The U.S. Navy had little incentive to turn its back on Black sailors, who might have considered themselves Americans despite being exempted from any benefits from the 1790 Naturalization Act. These dilemmas made skin color increasingly relevant to

---

60. *The History of Naturalization, with Some Remarques upon the Effects Thereof, in Respect to the Established Religion, Trade, and Safety of His Majesties Dominions* (n.p., [1680?]), [1], 3. Pepys's name appears on the undated original in the Bodleian Library, MS Rawlinson, c. 342, Oxford, though it is not certain whether he is the author of the document. It was likely published in 1674, the same year as a related document: *A Proclamation by the King Prohibiting His Majesties Subjects to Go out of This Kingdom into the Service of Any Foreign Prince or State without License* (London, 1674), MS Rawlinson, c. 342, no. 346, Bodleian Library.

conversations about national emancipation in the Mediterranean, setting the stage for dramatic conflicts between each nation over the loyalties of their sailors, Black and white.

Although the British Navy experienced manpower losses to American ships after the fighting in the American Revolution ended in 1783, Britain nonetheless possessed superior financial, military, and political capacities for emancipating its subjects in North Africa. The Ironmongers' Slave Fund's investments in the transatlantic slave trade over the previous half century had been quite profitable, generating spectacular growth. The fund had increased from thirteen thousand pounds in 1725 to "nine hundred and seventeen thousand, two hundred and fifty-eight pounds" by 1811. Political factors in the Mediterranean also presented expanding opportunities for British authorities. In 1765, British consuls had successfully strengthened diplomatic agreements with the deys of Algiers and Morocco regarding the emancipation of all captive British subjects laboring in their territories. In theory, the cost of ransoming captive British sailors was to be calculated by the sole cost of their food and board during their captivity in Morocco.[61]

Moreover, for both British authorities and Ironmonger wardens, the notion that transactions of charity should represent fair market values discouraged any explicit consideration of skin color or race in organizing ransom traffic in the Mediterranean. Skin color provided little guidance, after all, in distinguishing the ransom values that particular sailors might command. Rethinking British national identity as a racialized birthright might have possessed some appeal for nationalists working within British consular services or the Ironmongers' Company, but that vision directly conflicted with the labor imperatives of an imperial navy that relied on sailors hailing from many nations and locales.

No surge in Ironmonger-funded emancipations, however, occurred across the final decades of the eighteenth century for both logistical and political reasons. First, the price of emancipating British slaves in North Africa had grown substantially during the American Revolution, rising steadily from two hundred pounds per captive in 1776 to roughly three hundred pounds per captive in 1784 to four hundred pounds in 1792, and, finally, to five hundred pounds by 1799. Although the 1765 treaty protected English mariners from being trafficked by Moroccan authorities, it did not restrain local banditti

---

61. "Financial Papers," 1725–1811, MS 17019, Thomas Betton Charity Papers, Guildhall Library, London, "Articles of Peace and Commerce between Great Britain and Algiers," Aug. 3, 1765, MS 17034/3.

from demanding high prices for the British sailors who fell into their hands. A similar escalation governed the ransoming of American captives after 1789. Such escalation in prices, fueled by the scarcity of maritime labor and continuing political instability in North Africa, caused Ironmonger wardens to balk at the requests that British consuls in North Africa made for their funds.[62]

Second, as British consul Charles Logic put it, Ironmonger wardens yearned for "a fixed price for the redemption of Christian Slaves according to their quality, so much for a Captain, so much for a mate, and so on." That no such apolitical market for Christian slaves ever existed in North Africa did not deter them. The Ironmonger wardens' desire for an invisible hand that would guide market transactions might have been brought about by the growing popularity of Adam Smith's *Inquiry into the Nature and Causes of the Wealth of Nations* (1776), which imagined markets as objective, rational, and enlightened forces. The prices commanded for sailors held captive in the region, however, did not reflect the power of invisible hands. Rather, they were governed by the same tense negotiations between diplomats, sailors, and political authorities in North Africa that Thomas Troughton had protested. The preferences of Ironmonger wardens during the 1780s and 1790s for financing emancipations for British slaves at fixed prices remained out of step with both the labor demands of Britain's imperial navies as well as the Empire's political requirements for expanding beyond national boundaries.[63]

How then did British authorities broaden their commitments to defending the liberties of their captive sailors while also effectively competing with their new American rival? That task was complicated not only by Britain's impressment policies but also the empire's continuing support for transportation and a booming convict trade. For British diplomat Logic, disposing of

62. "Financial Papers," 1725–1811, MS 17019, Thomas Betton Charity Papers.
63. "Substance of the Conversation with Consul Logic and the Worshipful Company of Ironmonger Wardens," Nov. 16, 1784, MS 17034/3, articles no. 4–5, Thomas Betton Charity Papers, "Samuel Bosanquet, Esquire, Deputy Governor of the Turkey Company to M. Tho Silk, Master of the Ironmongers Company, about Redemption of Slaves," Dec. 20, 1792, MS 17034/4, 22, John Falcon to the Masters and Wardens of the Worshipful Company of Ironmongers, June 18, 1799, MS 17034/4, 23; Adam Smith, *An Inquiry into the Nature and Causes of the Wealth of Nations* . . . , 2 vols. (London, 1776). For Smith and slavery, see Brown, *Moral Capital*, 157–160; Davis, *Problem of Slavery*, 351–356; and Spencer J. Pack, "Slavery, Adam Smith's Economic Vision, and the Invisible Hand," with an appendix by Robert W. Dimand, "Adam Smith and the Late Resolution of the Quakers of Pennsylvania: A Response to a False Report," *History of Economic Ideas*, IV, nos. 1/2 (1996), 253–269.

rebellious British subjects through transportation and finding sailors among transported convicts made the task of organizing transactional emancipations for English captives challenging and even self-defeating. For more than a century, galley slavery had functioned as an international penal institution for European powers, the final destination for felons and political prisoners across Europe and North Africa. Even though galley ships were declining in importance by the end of the eighteenth century, European nations continued to transport felons and political prisoners to Mediterranean locales. Spain's efforts to build a prison for transported felons in Oran, Africa, during the 1780s, for example, was simply an attempt at a new solution to an old problem. Such efforts resulted in more questions than answers for nations seeking to emancipate national subjects. How should European authorities view imprisoned malefactors? Were felons subjects to be shunned or prisoners to be freed? Should Britain discipline or emancipate former felons, especially when trafficking them abroad had long been a successful containment policy?

The changing geography of Britain's transportation policy suggests anxiety about how to answer these questions. For decades, British officials had used transportation to solve two problems simultaneously: exporting rebellious English, Scottish, and Irish subjects from the nation and redressing a labor shortage in its American colonies. In the Mediterranean region, neither of those goals seemed realizable. Creating a British traffic in felons to the Mediterranean would have compounded challenges to British governance there, aggravating piracy and weakening the British state's capacity to emancipate British slaves. Given these predicaments, British officials bypassed Gibraltar and the Mediterranean altogether in 1788, turning to Australia for its new convict trade. Trafficking felons continued to be profitable for British authorities, even though the costs associated with the African slave trade were growing. The political and economic benefits of trafficking imprisoned people, whether British or African, remained substantial.[64]

Competition for sailors' loyalties, then, did not change how Britain responded to or emancipated its captive sailors in North Africa. The actions

---

64. On the role of transportation and the convict trade in the founding of the British colony of Australia, see Stephen Nicholas and Peter R. Shergold, "Transportation as Global Migration," in Nicholas, ed., *Convict Workers: Reinterpreting Australia's Past* (Cambridge, 1988), 28–42; and Alan Atkinson, *The Europeans in Australia: A History*, I, *The Beginning* (Melbourne, 1997), 3–118. For a broader history of penal transportation and European imperial expansion, see Clare Anderson, "Transnational Histories of Penal Transportation: Punishment, Labour, and Governance in the British Imperial World, 1788–1939," *Australian Historical Studies*, XLVII (2016), 381–397.

of sailors operating under the Union Jack during the late eighteenth century, however, did transform the shape and look of Britain's relations of rescue. The case files of the Ironmongers' Slave Fund furnish a rich record of negotiation about what British relations of rescue and emancipation should look like and who might benefit from them. In late 1772, wardens of the Ironmongers' Company received an emancipation request from the crew of a British slave ship, the *Lark*, "belonging to the port of Liverpool," that had been shipwrecked and "cast away on the Coast of Barbary." The letter, written by one of the *Lark*'s crew, John Downward, emphasized privations that would have been familiar to Ironmonger wardens. Downward and "his fellow sufferers [were] treated with scanty food . . . full, hard labor, and every bitter circumstance of a severe and abject slavery." Downward also made new claims in his request, namely that their miseries had been "aggravated in the utmost extent by the consideration of their being Englishmen, and as such distinguished not as freemen only, but above all other freemen upon Earth." Downward demanded not just to be ransomed, he also wanted the protection of his political birthright. He and his crewmates soon received an eight-hundred-pound grant for their "emancipation." Although fund managers still insisted on a full accounting of the emancipation expenses incurred in Morocco— charity had to remain transactional in form—the process took less than a year, a dramatic improvement compared to the delays experienced by Troughton. Sailors' arguments for national relations of rescue were becoming impossible to ignore.[65]

The successful expansion of sailors' demands for national relations of rescue was made vividly apparent by none other than Thomas Troughton a full quarter century after his first emancipation from Algiers. On December 20, 1776, as many of his maritime compatriots were being impressed to fight upstart Americans in North America, Troughton began a new captivity when Moroccan captors boarded his storm-battered ship. His latest ordeal as a Christian slave would last 457 days, a long time but much shorter than his previous captivity. His circumstances were far different from his first captivity, as fragmentary correspondence between British consuls and wardens of the Ironmongers' Company reveal. In contrast to previous disbursements, the bulk of the eight hundred pounds devoted to freeing Troughton and his crew was applied to settling "Accounts of Subsistence, Cloathing, and Expenses" as well as costs associated with moving them from Morocco to Tangier and eventually to Gibraltar. In contrast to his prior captivity, Troughton was well taken care of

---

65. "To the Worshipful Master, Warden, and Livery of the Company of Ironmongers of the City of London," June 16, 1772, MS 17034/14, 32, Thomas Betton Charity Papers.

by the British consul, Logic, who not only paid the crew's lodging and board but even maintained their employment hierarchies within the naval service. According to Logic's accounting, the captain of the *Sally*, George Duncan, received eleven shillings per day while in captivity, the first mate Henry Delano nine shillings, and each of the "seamen" six shillings throughout their captivity. Troughton's older exposé of official corruption might have persuaded Logic to spare no expense in compensating the crew of the *Sally*. Leaving little to chance, Logic secured a signed affidavit from all thirteen crew members before they left Gibraltar in 1779 stating that "we were subsisted, cloathed, and maintained by order of Charles Logic . . . Consul General in the Empire of Morocco." The value of Englishness had been made accountable, preempting the need for Troughton to traffic another narrative damning authorities.[66]

During the last decade of the eighteenth century, sailors on board ships flying the Union Jack continued to challenge British consuls to find new ways to fund their emancipations, expanding who was viewed as a British slave. In 1792, Logic again presented a new list of eight "British and Irish Subjects" to Ironmonger wardens for their consideration. But these sailors possessed transnational labor histories and political identities that vexed Logic and Ironmonger wardens alike. Five of the sailors, hailing from England, Scotland, and Ireland, it was discovered, had first been "detected smuggling in Spain" and "transported to Oran for 10 years" as Spanish felons. Many of these captives were also "Deserters from the Army," though they still claimed to be British patriots. After refusing to serve in the Spanish fleet and deserting from Gibraltar, they sought "escape to Barbary rather than serving an enemy to Great Britain." Such narratives constituted a dilemma for Ironmonger wardens. Should the slave fund emancipate English and Irish sailors who had become Spanish malefactors? How would they know whether their professed loyalty to Great Britain was now sincere? What if Ironmonger wardens paid the ransom of an English felon who had fallen into Barbary captivity? Logic used transactional thinking to suggest an answer: "I should presume the Seamen would be the first redeemed as the most useful and valuable." But valuable to whom or to what? Seeking to express "Charity and Humanity" toward his countrymen, Logic simultaneously recommended an imperial assessment of their value as sailors. Ironmonger wardens were sympathetic to

---

66. "Accounts of Subsistence, Cloathing, and Expenses," Dec. 20, 1776, MS 17034/3, Thomas Betton Charity Papers, "Account of Money Received of the Ironmonger Company by J. Snyder, Esquire, for the Redemption of Christian Slaves and the Expenditures Thereof," January 1779, MS 17034/3.

English antislavery but also skeptical of sailors' stories, fearing their funds might undermine transportation as a policy.[67]

For many English-born captive sailors, sailing under a foreign flag or being transported to Oran as Spanish felons did not prevent them from trying to secure British relations of rescue. Their continued suffering in North African prisons only expanded support for a broader emancipation policy in the Mediterranean. "Some of these poor wretches must then continue in slavery," concluded Sam Boranguet in 1792, a lawyer working for the Turkey Company, a private group seeking to identify potentially redeemable and therefore trafficable Christian slaves in North Africa. At the same time, British impressment policies complicated the meaning of these captivities and sailor emancipations, especially those experiencing mandatory naval service under British colors on returning home. In 1799, the recently emancipated crew of the British ship, the *S.S. Alexander*, for example, never made it to London. Instead, they began service on board a new British ship, the *Hydra*, at Gibraltar. Four of these sailors were Spanish nationals, having been previously captured as a prize by the British ship, the *Speculator*, before becoming enslaved to Moroccan masters when the *Speculator* wrecked. When the newest British captain offered them work at Gibraltar, one wonders how free they felt to say no. For these Spanish sailors, being trafficked remained a precondition for survival. For Anthony Peunio, even that precondition remained elusive. "Discharged as unfit for service" after two years of grueling slavery in Africa, Peunio was compelled to leave the *Hydra*, a refuse sailor "whom they did not hear of afterwards." Emancipated by the Ironmongers' Slave Fund, this masterless sailor was now free to starve.[68]

## Conclusion

Like the sailor Olaudah Equiano, Phillis Wheatley viewed the Mediterranean as a region that created freedom opportunities for those held within the grip of the Atlantic slave trade. Both writers conceptualized freedom

---

67. Charles Logic to Ironmongers, July 1, 1792, MS 17034/4, Thomas Betton Charity Papers. Logic was also mentioned by captive American sailors who had been born in England. See James Leander Cathcart, *The Captives* . . . , compiled by J. B. Newkirk (La Porte, Ind., [1899]), 3–6, 34–35. For a discussion of *The Captives*, see Martha Elena Rojas, "'Insults Unpunished': Barbary Captives, American Slaves, and the Negotiation of Liberty," *Early American Studies*, I (2003), 159–186.

68. Sam Boranguet to Ironmonger Company, Dec. 28, 1792, MS 17034/4, 22, Thomas Betton Charity Papers, "W. Johnston, Esquire, Ironmongers, London," Nov. 23, 1807,

and slavery as geographies, particular places defined by the forms of trafficking that carried them from Africa to New World slaveries and to London. Although Wheatley never traveled to Greece or experienced the kind of hospitality there that led Equiano to imagine a political economy without racism, her knowledge of the Mediterranean ancients emboldened her, even as an enslaved teenager, to see the Atlantic world from the outside in, as a region that could be navigated and piloted toward freedom. What Equiano and Wheatley would have made of the dilemmas that Mediterranean sailor Anthony Peunio encountered are matters of educated guesswork. Certainly, Equiano would have recognized the dangers that a refuse sailor like Peunio experienced, as he commented on such cruelties in his writings. Wheatley never directly described her Middle Passage to America nor the experience of nearly becoming a refuse slave in Boston as a sick and emaciated arrival there in 1761. Yet she, too, was no stranger to the displacements and privations that enslavement and trafficking induced.

Wheatley also surely understood the doubled-edged nature of having to traffic one's labor and one's words to survive. Her emancipation from slavery was a remarkable achievement, a reflection of her skills as a poet as well as her capacity to sell the story of her enslaved genius. Freedom nevertheless brought its share of heartache and formidable challenges to Wheatley. In 1778, as the young nation she defended fought to realize its independence, Wheatley struggled to be seen, heard, or published. She placed no less than six advertisements in local Boston newspapers that year seeking advance subscriptions for the publication of a second volume of poetry. That book would have provided her income as well as the opportunity to engage some of the unfinished challenges that antislavery nationalism posed for patriots of all stripes. Lacking the British support that had formerly enabled her to publish her first volume, however, Wheatley was unable to secure enough financial

---

MS 17034/4. The Turkey Company was a joint-stock company also known as the Levant Company, in existence since 1581 and involved with all forms of trade between the Ottoman Empire and Christian merchants across Europe. On the Levant Company, see Despina Vlami, *Trading with the Ottomans: The Levant Company in the Middle East* (London, 2015), 1–2. British defenders of empire cast the company as an emancipatory force within the Ottoman Empire. See J. Theodore Bent, "The English in the Levant," *English Historical Review*, V (1890), 654–664. On the adverse impact of the traffic in Christian captives on the cloth and cotton trades across the eighteenth century, see Michael Wagner, "The Levant Company under Attack in Parliament, 1720–53," *Parliamentary History*, XXXIV (2015), 293–313.

subscriptions to publish her second volume. In the same year, 1778, Phillis married a free Black man named John Peters, who, like her, also strove to market his labor. In 1784, after years of hardship trying to make a living as a skilled free Black artisan, Peters ended up in debtor's prison. Phillis, in turn, was forced to work in a boarding house, and her health soon gave out. She died in December 1784, penniless and alone, after her third child had perished.[69]

For servants as well as the enslaved, the geography of freedom remained elusive. No nation, however emancipatory its creed or its founding mythologies, was a guarantor of liberty. Antislavery nationalism was not so much a lie as a contested discourse that fueled the aspirations of trafficked and enslaved people as well as efforts by elites to burnish the moral authority of the nations they were creating. Each cohort sought to define what nations meant and what they owed their migrant subjects. As the political currency of Britishness became more closely affiliated with notions of antislavery during and after the American Revolution, the capacity to be emancipated as a British slave expanded dramatically. That transformation helps explain how a disabled Spanish sailor might be emancipated by Ironmonger wardens and then discarded at Gibraltar while dozens of enslaved English nationals, having shipped out under different foreign flags, died in North Africa during the 1790s. British slaves now made up a remarkably diverse cohort, men whose loyalties to any given nation consisted first and foremost to the flag flapping above their ship on any particular voyage. Filling the labor needs of both British and America navies necessitated hiring foreign-born sailors of varied backgrounds. Like Equiano, these sailors expanded the meanings of both antislavery and sovereignty simultaneously, even as their individual stories confounded the nationalistic narratives trafficked by consular officials.

Trafficked American and British subjects played key roles in expanding the purview of antislavery policies across the Mediterranean during the 1790s. The disavowal of both impressment and transportation as policies by the American nation were, not empty gestures, but reforms that benefited all American sailors, including many naturalized British sailors who switched flags. Black sailors in both nation's navies continued to make up key portions of each polity's labor force, even if they struggled to secure rights. Although British and American authorities alike defended and expanded the African slave trade, they also affirmed the belief that market transactions could give

---

69. "Wheatley's freedom," writes Henry Louis Gates, Jr., "enslaved her to a life of hardship." See Gates, *Trials of Phillis Wheatley*, 68.

rise to enduring freedoms. Commercial and political liberties were thus intrinsically linked, making efforts to finance the emancipations of captive sailors at market rates a new and dramatic expansion of the rights of the trafficked as well as of Anglo-American sovereignty. That commitment in the Mediterranean, emerging a decade and a half before the abolition of the African slave trade, was fueled by both pragmatic and ideological factors, the insatiable labor needs of each nation's navy, and the power of sailors' antitrafficking and antislavery arguments and demands.

Narratives of resistance to both trafficking and enslavement highlighted the diverse challenges that maritime laborers confronted as they hunted for niches of freedom. Across both the Atlantic and the Mediterranean, maritime actors managed the best of unequal bargains, resisting enslavement by protesting trafficking until being trafficked presented a window of opportunity. That maritime storytelling tradition also transformed the larger transatlantic abolitionist movement during the late eighteenth century. Resistance to trafficking and to enslavement were neither consistent nor necessarily radical, as some antislavery narratives exemplified core tenets of liberal political economy. Indeed, Wheatley, Thomas Clarkson, and Equiano each supported the creation of free wage labor relations in Africa. Yet buying one's freedom could also generate narratives that transformed dominant paradigms to radical political ends. Dilemmas over how to make the suffering of the trafficked visible and to what ends their suffering should be put became ever more pressing in the wake of Wheatley's and Equiano's literary successes. The suffering of the enslaved could both inspire and antagonize patriots of all stripes at the dawn of the nineteenth century, furthering movements for emancipatory change as well as war between antislavery nations.[70]

---

70. On Equiano as a devotee of liberal political economy, see Laura Doyle, *Freedom's Empire: Race and the Rise of the Novel in Atlantic Modernity, 1640–1940* (Durham, N.C., 2008), 10, 183–184. Doyle presumed that Equiano and Daniel Defoe's purposes were the same because they advocated transactional emancipations. Defoe defended and naturalized the humanity of slavery and market economies, however, while Equiano used his humanity to indict them both.

CHAPTER EIGHT

# Antislavery Nationalism and Race

IN THE IMMEDIATE aftermath of Britain's successful naval bombardment of Algiers and the liberation of several thousand enslaved Christians there during the fall of 1816, a remarkable standoff occurred between British and American sailors in the port of Naples, Italy. Nathaniel Toms, mate of the British schooner *Ann*, apprehended a "Blackman" who had allegedly stolen a piece of leather from his ship that was docked in the city's port next to several of His Majesty's ships recently returned from Algiers. When Toms tried to prevent the sailor from leaving his vessel, a "scuffle ensued in which the said Blackman struck me a violent blow in the face and attempted to get away but was prevented by the crew of the schooner." What happened next became a matter of heated dispute, but certain facts emerged across all accounts. Toms tied the accused thief to the mast of the British ship's quarterdeck and began to whip him as punishment for theft and for hitting a British ship's officer. The flogging of the Black man incited a dramatic reaction by American sailors watching from shore, who recognized their comrade and immediately boarded the docked British ship. "Soon after an officer in United States Uniform came on board who called himself a Yankee," John Bell, the *Ann*'s master, recalled. The officer said, "'You have been flogging an American seaman' and added much aggravating language." Although the unnamed Black American was freed, he was soon pushed into the water by "a man who knocked him off the plank."[1]

Over the next week, American sailors and officers repeatedly attacked and confronted the *Ann*'s officers while on shore in Naples, "quarrels" according to the local Italian police that materially ruined "the tranquility of the city." The escalation of violence was so severe that even the nearby British proconsul at Messina, seeking to minimize the diplomatic damage, admitted that the fighting "appears to have been much more serious than we even first imagined." At

---

1. Deposition of Nathaniel Toms, Mate of the Schooner *Ann*, Sept. 16, 1816, PRO 30/7/2, 506, The National Archives, Kew, U.K (hereafter TNA).

the heart of the American sailors' anger was the spectacle of one of their own being flogged by an English ship's officer, violence that demanded retribution. "You are a damned consummate rascal," an American naval officer named Armstrong yelled at the British captain John Bell two nights later at a sailors' pub, continuing, "Who gave you authority to flog our man?" When Captain Bell insisted that he had not himself touched the American, a fight ensued in which Bell was nearly strangled to death and stabbed when a host of American sailors, officers, and common seamen overpowered the British ship's officers and punished the offending captain. That a Black American sailor could ignite the solidarity of these American seamen was not directly commented on by the British mariners, but the importance of race loomed large in their defensive telling of events. "I did not know what country the Blackman belonged to," Toms insisted, and "only chastised the Blackman as a thief and should have done the same to any man whatever dedicated in thieving." Captain Bell similarly insisted the flogging of the American sailor was not intended to be a national or racial insult, stating, "I did not know what country the Blackman belonged to, so help me God." The American sailors were the problem, according to Toms, because they had been insolent and violent in their response to Captain Bell. "They used the most abusive language to Captain Bell," protested Toms, calling him frequently a "Buggar," "coward," "scoundrel," and, perhaps most provocatively, a "Coward Blackguard."[2]

Blackness and national honor were thoroughly intertwined in both American and British accounts of the conflict. Unresolved in the surviving sources were the exact motives of the American sailors. Were they protesting the racism of a British ship's officer? What exactly did the American sailors mean by calling Bell a "Coward Blackguard?" What Black and white American sailors variously thought is important but elusive. Uncontradicted by any of the surviving sources, however, was that the flogging of a Black sailor ignited an extraordinary show of solidarity among Black and white American mariners, a show of force also closely connected to their professions of patriotism. That fact made sense of the recent past, as Black sailors had played a vital material and symbolic role within the navies of both Great Britain and the United States during the recently concluded War of 1812. In that conflict, ironies had permeated each nation's effort to use antislavery ideology against the other.

2. Andrew Douglas to British Admiralty, Sept. 20, 1816, PRO 30/7/1, 117, 134, 141, TNA, Deposition of John Bell, Master of the Schooner *Ann*, Sept. 16, 1816, PRO 30/7/2, 506–507, Sept. 18, 1816, 507–509, Deposition of Nathaniel Toms, Mate of the Schooner *Ann*, Sept. 16, 1816, PRO 30/7/2, 506.

Although British polemicists defended a humanitarian empire, taking credit for abolishing the African slave trade, slavery still flourished in all of Britain's colonies. American nationalists, in turn, defined the war as an antislavery campaign against British impressment and unlawful trafficking, even while an internal slave trade blossomed across the Deep South. For American sailors doing battle with British mariners in Naples, yet another set of wartime lessons had been learned: that the rights of American sailors, Black and white, were worth defending, and no British ship's captain had the right to flog an American sailor. The American sailors' militancy confounds any straightforward assessment of the relationship between antislavery, nationalism, and race.

This Mediterranean battle has largely escaped the attention of Atlantic historians of slavery, race, and abolition. Occurring near an obscure outpost of British power, it was geographically removed from the main foci of abolitionist struggle in North America and Great Britain. Yet these mariners' efforts to fight for an interracial nation that would defend their rights had immediate and long-lasting significance, raising questions about maritime solidarities and their relationship to antislavery and nationalism at the start of the nineteenth century. How did the abolition of the African slave trade, deemed a victory over the most nefarious traffic in human history, affect the rights of trafficked people after 1807? And what impact did the abolition of the slave trade have on the meaning and geography of white racial ideology? Examining the surrounding geographies of water, nation, and race helps to illuminate what Black and white American sailors were up against in Naples in 1816. Their battle in the Mediterranean was not, in fact, separate from those of their peers in the Atlantic or in the port cities where plebeian communities were devising new strategies for resisting tyranny. For maritime actors who were trafficked, impressed, enslaved, or formerly enslaved, the abolition of the slave trade dramatically reconfigured the relationships between nations and race. Although the abolition of the slave trade ended the legal trafficking of Africans across the Atlantic, it did not end race trafficking. By 1816, the Mediterranean region, a kind of holdout to trafficking whiteness in 1800, had become one of the primary sites for its global articulation and hegemony. Understanding the transformation of how, when, and why white slavery replaced Christian slavery as the inhuman traffic to be abolished in the Mediterranean after 1814 begins with an exploration of the neglected importance of the Mediterranean to the British-led abolition of the African slave trade in 1807.[3]

3. On Black sailors' struggles for U.S. citizenship rights during the first half of the nineteenth century, see Martha S. Jones, "Marin et citoyen: Être noir et libre à bord des navires

## Abolishing the African Slave Trade, 1805–1807

For both British and American abolitionists, geographic knowledge and imagination were essential to the campaign to abolish the African slave trade. Supporters of Britain's 1807 Abolition Act, which outlawed the African slave trade, called it a victory, not just for enslaved people, but for the continent of Africa itself. "Hail, woe-worn Africa! let grief no more," began one poem published under the alias "R" entitled "Verses on the Bill for the Abolition of the Slave-Trade." Shame and grief were geographic in form and content, with Great Britain housing both: "Detested traffic!," began another verse, "which, to Britain's shame, / So long has tarnish'd her commercial name." American abolitionists similarly nationalized the evils of the African slave trade, even while ignoring its monstrous American counterpart, the internal slave trade across North America:

> Who manufactures thumb-screws? Who the scourge?
> Whose navies shield the pirates o'er the surge?
> . . . .
> It is England,—merciful and mild!
> . . . .
> Who trade in tortures, profit draw from pain,
> and even whose mercy is but love of gain!

These abolitionists, whether English or American, turned ideas about the geography of British freedom upside down, highlighting the slave trade's British accents and origins. The ethical truths of the African slave trade were coming home to haunt the British nation, a geographic linkage that abolitionists pressed in their campaign to provoke Parliament to action.[4]

Questions over how to enforce an ambitious international ban on the African slave trade similarly assumed a geographic form. Earlier efforts to abolish the slave trade in 1805 suggest genuine uncertainty among British

---

états-uniens avant la guerre civile," *Le mouvement social,* no. 252 (Juillet–Septembre 2015), 93–112; Kate Masur, *Until Justice Be Done: America's First Civil Rights Movement: From the Revolution to Reconstruction* (New York, 2021), 119–151; Paul A. Gilje, *Free Trade and Sailors' Rights in the War of 1812* (Cambridge, 2013), 186, 331–333; and Leon Fink, *Sweatshops at Sea: Merchant Seamen in the World's First Globalized Industry, from 1812 to the Present* (Chapel Hill, N.C., 2011), 50–54.

4. "R," "Verses on the Bill for the Abolition of the Slave-Trade," *Monthly Magazine; or, British Register* (London), May 1, 1807, 359–360; "To England, on the Slave-Trade," *Port Folio,* New Ser. (Philadelphia), Dec. 27, 1806, 400.

abolitionists about how as well as where to focus Britain's policing energies. One proposed 1805 bill concentrated on policing trafficking in slave societies in the Americas, specifically "prohibiting the Importation of Slaves (except in certain Cases) into any of the Settlements, Islands, Colonies, or Plantations on the Continent of *America,* or in the *West Indies*." Another proposed bill in 1805 called for abolishing the trafficking of people with dark skin, making it unlawful "to export, transport, send, carry, or convey . . . any Negro or Mulatto Slave or Slaves." Race trafficking, not just the African slave trade, needed to be abolished if justice was to prevail across the oceans that sustained the dynamic and still growing British Empire. Yet both bills failed because of a lack of political support as well as the logistical challenges they presented. Policing all the Americas was a daunting task, especially in the wake of Britain's recent loss to the new American nation. An Order in Council made that same year restricting slave importation highlighted the enormity of the task at hand: namely, preventing "any Slave or Slaves to be landed upon any of the Coasts, or imported or brought into any of the Ports, Harbours, Creeks, or Roads, or within the Limits, Jurisdictions, and Territories of any of the Settlements, Islands, Colonies, or Plantations on the Continent of *America* or in the *West Indies*." Forbidding the trafficking of all slaves, in turn, opened up separate problems for enforcement. Were all enslaved Black sailors at sea to be counted as contraband and forfeit to British authorities? The first 1805 bill attempted to clarify that question by specifying an important exception: "that nothing herein contained shall prevent or be construed to prevent any Slave from being employed either in Navigation, Fishing, or any other his ordinary Business or Occupation upon the Seas, provided a Licence be had for that Purpose." Although licensing all maritime actors, regardless of skin color or nationality, had long been an elusive imperial ambition for British authorities, abolishing enslaved Black maritime labor was quite another story. A better instrument or target for the abolitionists was needed.[5]

5. "A Bill to Prevent the Importation of Slaves, by Any of His Majesty's Subjects . . . ," Aug. 15, 1805, Bills and Acts, no. 91, Nineteenth-Century House of Commons Sessional Papers 1806, I, 275, 284; "A Bill for the Abolition of the Slave Trade, at a Time to Be Limited," Feb. 19, 1805, Bills and Acts, no. 31, Nineteenth-Century House of Commons Sessional Papers 1805, I, 33; "Copy of an Order of His Majesty in Council . . . Made for Prohibiting the Importation of Slaves into Any of the Settlements, Islands, Colonies, or Plantations, on the Continent of America, or in the West Indies . . . ," Aug. 15, 1805, House of Commons Papers, no. 84, Nineteenth-Century House of Commons Sessional Papers, 1806, XII, 303. Surprisingly little has been written on these failed bills to abolish the slave trade. On the passage of the 1807 Abolition Act, see David Brion Davis, *The Problem of*

The Mediterranean, a region with a rich history of building imperial power through prize taking and trafficking, would provide abolitionists with an important precedent for how the work of abolishing the slave trade might be accomplished. During England's brief foray into building an imperial outpost at Tangier during the 1670s, much of the colony's business was made up of processing ships and cargoes taken by English ship captains. At Tangier, English authorities first condemned incoming prizes as forfeited rather than stolen loot, then ship captains redistributed the goods among their crews, sharing and consigning what had not been already forfeited directly to the crown. Such practices had long fueled English dreams of expanding control over commerce and piracy in the Mediterranean. Although the loss of Tangier proved a setback to Britain's imperial ambitions in the region, it did not impede the mechanism for expanding British sovereignty through forfeiture and traffic. In the campaign to abolish the African slave trade, prize taking by privateers would not be outlawed but redirected toward abolitionist ends.[6]

Several clauses in the 1807 Abolition Act highlight its connections to the informal and formal practices of prize taking that had long been prevalent in the Mediterranean. Clause B "for seizing and Forfeiture of Slaves unlawfully carried" relied on the practice of Mediterranean prize taking in which the goods and people of any given ship captured at sea were first condemned as trafficable cargo and then "forfeited to His Majesty." Clause C, "providing for Slaves captured or seized," expressly linked the practices of war and prize taking to the abolition of the slave trade. Acknowledging that the seizure or detaining of "Ships" or "Vessels" in "present or future Wars" was inevitable,

---

*Slavery in the Age of Revolution, 1770–1823* (Ithaca, N.Y., 1999), 32, 412; Christopher Leslie Brown, *Moral Capital: Foundations of British Abolitionism* (Williamsburg, Va., and Chapel Hill, N.C., 2006), 432, 441; and W. E. B. Du Bois, *The Suppression of the African Slave-Trade to the United States of America, 1638–1870* (New York, 2007).

6. On the 1807 Abolition Act's reliance on forfeiture and prize taking, see Richard Anderson and Henry B. Lovejoy, "Introduction: 'Liberated Africans' and Early International Courts of Humanitarian Effort," in Anderson and Lovejoy, eds., *Liberated Africans and the Abolition of the Slave Trade, 1807–1896* (Rochester, N.Y., 2020), 4–7; Benjamin N. Lawrance and Richard L. Roberts, eds., *Trafficking in Slavery's Wake: Law and the Experience of Women and Children* (Athens, Ohio, 2012); Padraic Xavier Scanlan, "The Rewards of Their Exertions: Prize Money and British Abolitionism in Sierra Leone, 1808–1823," *Past and Present*, no. 225 (November 2014), 115–116; Scanlan, *Freedom's Debtors: British Antislavery in Sierra Leone in the Age of Revolution* (New Haven, Conn., 2017), 70–71; Christopher Lloyd, *The Navy and the Slave Trade: The Suppression of the African Slave Trade in the Nineteenth Century* (New York, 2007); and W. E. F. Ward, *The Royal Navy and the Slavers: The Suppression of the Atlantic Slave Trade* (New York, 1969).

the 1807 law put the practice of prize taking to work. "It is necessary and expedient," legislators declared, "to encourage . . . Captors, Seizors, and Prosecutors." With the signing of the 1807 Abolition Act, British slave ship captains, the villains of the abolitionist Thomas Clarkson's exposés, were transformed into enforcers of a powerful moral crusade that would now eliminate slave trafficking out of Africa as well as any slave traffic between Britain's colonies in the Caribbean and the Americas. The law further empowered British ship captains in the Royal Navy to seize the cargo and belongings of any ship involved in the slave trade while placing a series of financial penalties on ship captains caught exporting enslaved people from Africa. Those found guilty of breaking the law would be fined fifty pounds sterling for every trafficked African apprehended and one hundred pounds for every British subject engaged in such traffic. Just so did human trafficking in the Mediterranean transform how policymakers imagined and then enforced the abolition of the transatlantic slave trade across the planet.[7]

By making the slave trade illegal through humanitarian prize taking, the 1807 Abolition Act sought to make state-organized trafficking consistent with an antislavery project. Even as the act insisted that enslaved people could no longer be trafficked or "sold, disposed of . . . or dealt with as Slaves," it nonetheless treated enslaved people as "Property in the same manner as Negro Slaves." Enslaved individuals in the hold of a slave ship who found themselves rescued by a privateer or Royal Navy vessel would not be immediately emancipated. Rather, they would first be declared cargo that had been forfeited. "All Slaves, and all Natives of *Africa*," legislators declared, "for the purposes only of Seizure, Prosecution, and Condemnation as Prize or as Forfeitures" shall "be considered, treated, taken, and adjudged as Slaves and Property in the same manner as Negro Slaves have been heretofore considered." Framers of the new law ostensibly offered captive cargoes a choice. Ship captains were authorized "either to enter and enlist" the "Natives of *Africa*" into "His Majesty's Land or Sea Service, as Soldiers, Seamen, or Marines, or to bind

---

7. "A Bill, (as Amended by the Committee), Intituled, An Act for the Abolition of the Slave Trade," [1807], Bills and Acts, no. 92, Nineteenth-Century House of Commons Sessional Papers, 1806–1807, I, 47, 48, 49, 53; [William Wilberforce], "Proceedings of the British Parliament Respecting the Slave Trade," *Literary Magazine, and American Register* (Philadelphia), January 1807, 25–28. On the use of forfeiture to avoid property claims by slave traders, see Maeve Ryan, "'A Most Promising Field for Future Usefulness': The Church Missionary Society and the Liberated Africans of Sierra Leone," in William Mulligan and Maurice Bric, eds., *A Global History of Anti-Slavery Politics in the Nineteenth Century* (London, 2013), 37–58.

the same ... whether of full Age or not, as Apprentices, for any Term not exceeding Fourteen Years." Emancipation from the slave trade and expansion of the British press were thus fused into one policy, a linkage anticipated by the compulsory service of emancipated British slaves in the Mediterranean during the 1790s. Whether becoming a British sailor made the "Natives of *Africa*" genuinely free was a more challenging question. Certainly, indentures and apprenticeships were better options for captive Africans than working as lifelong slaves on sugar plantations, with all their progeny enslaved, but authors of the 1807 act also openly acknowledged that coercion was built into the prize taking that ostensibly ended the African slave trade. "Any Indenture of Apprenticeship duly made and executed," the law stated, "shall be considered, treated, and dealt with in all respects as if he had voluntarily so enlisted or entered himself." The sleight of hand is startling: "as if he had voluntarily so enlisted." The text of the new law did not reconcile the troubling ironies that forced enlistment created. Although Africans captured as forfeited cargo rejoiced to escape the fate of their enslaved brethren in Caribbean sugar fields, they were not free to resist their supposed emancipators in the form of British ship captains.[8]

By replacing slavery with involuntary contracts of indenture and apprenticeship, the 1807 law forecast a larger transition from enslavement to indentured servitude across Britain's empire over the nineteenth century. Defenders of slavery had argued that white indentured labor could not possibly perform the work of African slave labor. Yet they overlooked that indentured servitude had long shaped the fortunes of Europe's imperial projects. When the

---

8. "A Bill, (as Amended by the Committee), Intituled, An Act for the Abolition of the Slave Trade," [1807], Bills and Acts, no. 92, Nineteenth-Century House of Commons Sessional Papers, 1806–1807, I, 49. On the relationship between humanitarian and imperial interests, see Lauren Benton, "Abolition and Imperial Law, 1790–1820," *Journal of Imperial and Commonwealth History*, XXXIX, no. 3 (2011), 355–374; Benton and Lisa Ford, *Rage for Order: The British Empire and the Origins of International Law, 1800–1850* (Cambridge, Mass., 2016); Bronwen Everill and Josiah Kaplan, eds., *The History and Practice of Humanitarian Intervention and Aid in Africa* (London, 2013); Everill, *Abolition and Empire in Sierra Leone and Liberia* (London, 2013); Clare Anderson, "After Emancipation: Empires and Imperial Formations," in Catherine Hall, Nicholas Draper, and Keith McClelland, eds., *Emancipation and the Remaking of the British Imperial World* (Manchester, U.K., 2014), 113–127; and Robin Law, "Abolitionism and Imperialism: International Law and the British Suppression of the Atlantic Slave Trade," in Derek R. Peterson, ed., *Abolitionism and Imperialism in Britain, Africa, and the Atlantic* (Athens, Ohio, 2010), 150–174. On the dilemmas emancipated Africans faced as newly indentured labor, see Anita Rupprecht, "'When He

African slave trade was abolished in 1807, a boom in the trafficking of convict and indentured labor ensued across British territories, returning Britain's imperial planning to its original formulations before 1650 while still benefitting from slave labor. That the Mediterranean, a region that had long resisted the racing of maritime labor, became a proving ground for the abolition of the slave trade represented no irony but the central importance of trafficking, war, and empire to humanitarian imagination.[9]

By using prize taking to abolish the African slave trade, British ship captains now possessed the moral pretext to board virtually any ship in the world, even those not at war with Great Britain. At the same moment, wartime measures against France also enhanced Great Britain's capacity to enforce its new humanitarian project of abolishing the slave trade. Just a few months before the passage of the 1807 Abolition Act, the crown passed an Order in Council that prohibited "Trade to be carried on between Port and Port of Countries under the Dominion or usurped Controul of France and her Allies." If a neutral ship did not first pay a duty to the British government and obtain a license before docking in a French port, it would become a "lawful Prize." This order in council extended the moral authority generated by antislavery to expansive forms of prize taking in which British naval officers

---

Gets among His Countrymen, They Tell Him That He Is Free': Slave Trade Abolition, Indentured Africans, and a Royal Commission," *Slavery and Abolition: A Journal of Slave and Post-Slave Studies*, XXXIII (2012), 435–455; Patrick Harries, "Slavery, Indenture, and Migrant Labour: Maritime Immigration from Mozambique to the Cape, c. 1780–1880," *African Studies*, LXXIII (2014), 323–340; and Tara Helfman, "The Court of Vice Admiralty at Sierra Leone and the Abolition of the West African Slave Trade," *Yale Law Journal*, CXV (2006), 1122–1156. On the coercive dimensions of slave trade liberation, see Emma Christopher, "'Tis Enough That We Give Them Liberty'? Liberated Africans at Sierra Leone in the Early Era of Slave-Trade Suppression," in Robert Burroughs and Richard Huzzey, eds., *The Suppression of the Atlantic Slave Trade: British Policies, Practices, and Representations of Naval Coercion* (Manchester, U.K., 2015), 55–72.

9. On the expansion of the trafficking of indentured servants out of Africa after the abolition of slavery across Great Britain's empire in 1833, see David Northrup, *Indentured Labor in the Age of Imperialism, 1834–1922* (Cambridge, 1995). On the role of indentured labor across Britain's empire before and after the abolition of the slave trade, see P. C. Emmer, ed., *Colonialism and Migration; Indentured Labour before and after Slavery* (Dordrecht, The Netherlands, 1986); and Paul E. Lovejoy and Nicholas Rogers, eds., *Unfree Labour in the Development of the Atlantic World* (London, 1994). On the importance of war making and military actors in demanding constitutional forms of governance in the early nineteenth century, see Linda Colley, *The Gun, the Ship, and the Pen: Warfare, Constitutions, and the Making of the Modern World* (New York, 2022).

could search, and seize, any ship in the Atlantic or Mediterranean, whether or not a state of war existed with another nation's navy. British seizures were not all successful, nor were they just in the eyes of the French or other neutral countries. Nevertheless, the relationship between Britain's moral capital and its war-making power were self-evident to critics and supporters of Britain's empire alike in 1807.[10]

Whether emancipating enslaved Africans in a French ship or liberating captive British sailors sailing under foreign flags, antislavery ideology lay at the heart of Britian's new open-ended sovereignty claims, both complicating and broadening the reach of relations of rescue for those caught in Mediterranean slavery. Ironmonger wardens and British consuls alike labored to resolve tensions between these commitments across the Mediterranean. Should they pay the ransom of all sailors working under British colors or just British-born sailors sailing under foreign flags? After the passage of the 1807 Abolition Act, British authorities began taking into custody any and all British slaves they could find in North Africa, lumping sailors of any nationality sailing under the Union Jack with British-born sailors working in foreign navies. Yet evidence of that expanded commitment appears even before the 1807 Abolition Act became law in May. In January 1807, British consul James Green persuaded Ironmonger wardens to support emancipating two "Englishmen" among the crew of an American ship that had recently shipwrecked in southern Morocco. "There are two Englishmen among the crew, who I cannot claim officially, they being wrecked under American colors," Green explained. However, "though they are at present Americans, having sailed under that flag," he argued, they were still "a very desirable object for the Ironmonger Company." Because the American consul had "declined interfering," Green anticipated, "these two unfortunate men will I foresee experience a long continuance in Slavery unless ransomed privately by your bounty."

---

10. "Order in Council, Prohibiting Trade to Be Carried on between Port and Port of Countries under the Dominion or Usurped Controul of France and Her Allies," Jan. 7, 1807, House of Commons Papers, no. 5, Nineteenth-Century House of Commons Sessional Papers, 1808, X, 51. On the history of Orders in Council, see Reginald Horsman, *The Causes of the War of 1812* (New York, 1962), 39–42, 97–156, 196–202, 244–261, 267. On the role of national interests and imperial competition in creating opportunities for abolitionists, see Brown, *Moral Capital*, 459–461. For a triumphalist account of the British Navy's role in the abolition of the slave trade, see Peter Grindal, *Opposing the Slavers: The Royal Navy's Campaign against the Atlantic Slave Trade* (London, 2016). For a nuanced view of reciprocities between antislavery work and British sovereignty, see Jean Allain, "The Nineteenth Century Law of the Sea and the British Abolition of the Slave Trade," *British Yearbook of International Law*, LXXVIII (2007), 342–388.

With his request, Green linked humanitarian and nationalistic goals. By paying the American sailors' ransoms, Ironmonger wardens not only liberated the two men but made them English again, expanding the reach and power of a redeemed British sovereignty.[11]

### Sailors' Rights and Antislavery Nationalism, 1803–1816

Nevertheless, Britain's expanding sovereignty claims following the abolition of the slave trade did not take place in a vacuum. Rather, they took place amid not only war with France but also ongoing competition with the United States over the loyalties of maritime workers. That competition was fueled by the labor needs of each polity's navy as well as the mobility of those same maritime actors, whose capacity to desert frustrated maritime officials. The purpose of Britain's new impressment policies, enacted in 1803, was to redress the British Navy's pervasive labor shortage and to defeat France at sea by imposing an effective blockade across the European mainland. The geography of the new policy was strikingly different from previous impressment efforts by His Majesty's Impress Service, with press-gangs now boarding other nations' ships at sea. The new impressment policy relied on tactics developed in the Mediterranean for prize taking that would become central to efforts to abolish the slave trade just four years later. Yet the new British press was directed mostly against American ships, with nearly ten thousand American sailors pressed into the British Navy between 1803 and the outbreak of the War of 1812. These same British press-gangs also accelerated desertions of British sailors to American vessels. By 1812, when war resumed between the two nations, nearly half of the most skilled sailors in the American navy were British sailors who had deserted, some nine thousand sailors in total. In the years leading up to the War of 1812, the abolition of the British slave trade and impressment together brought about remarkable expansions in Britain's presumptive capacity to violate the sovereignty of other nations by searching for particular human cargoes, whether British deserters or enslaved Africans.[12]

British impressment also incited political controversy, fueling an expansion of antislavery claims by defenders of sailors' rights within the United States. Just three months after Britain enacted the abolition of the African slave trade, a British warship, the HMS *Leopard*, demanded to board a poorly

---

11. James Green to James Pellatt, Jan. 28, 1807, MS 17034/4, Thomas Betton Charity Papers, Guildhall Library, London.
12. Gilje, *Free Trade and Sailors' Rights*, 174, 178.

defended American ship, the USS *Chesapeake*, in search of British deserters. Before the American flag could be lowered, the better-armed British warship attacked the USS *Chesapeake*, killing three American sailors and wounding eighteen others. The crew of the HMS *Leopard* then boarded the frigate and removed four British deserters before sailing away from the badly damaged ship. The violence, known as the Chesapeake Affair, prompted immediate demands for war against Great Britain, with crowd actions in American ports featuring ferocious condemnations of both Britain and impressment, a kind of rehearsal for the War of 1812. Some of the most intense calls for war came from the maritime community of Norfolk, Virginia, which refused to resupply British ships needing water and food before traversing the Atlantic. Antislavery language shaped condemnations of impressment as well as what to do about it. Typical was the editor of the *American Citizen* who described impressment in the British Navy as "a service as severe as the slavery of Algiers."[13]

Comparisons to slavery had long shaped perceptions of trafficked labor, but the meanings of such comparisons were not timeless or absolute. They were closely tied to the particular historical contexts in which they were invoked. The Chesapeake Affair occurred just three months after the 1807 Abolition Act became law, with British maritime crews now emboldened by their nation's antislavery mandate. Yet critics of British impressment also turned antislavery ideology into a potent weapon against British action. By comparing impressment to slavery in Algiers, the editor of the *American Citizen* maximized his condemnation of Britain's alleged hypocrisy while avoiding the elephant in the room that would have complicated the picture of American antislavery: the fact that racial slavery was flourishing across both the United States' and Britain's sugar colonies. That evasion was apparent in the newspaper coverage of the Chesapeake Affair in which two of the four "British" deserters were men of color born in North America, one a "colored man" from Massachusetts and the other an "Indian looking man" from Maryland. Few newspapers paid attention to their nativity or skin color, perhaps because doing so would have raised important questions about how they had become British in the first place. Perhaps they were formerly enslaved Americans who had joined the British in exchange for freedom in the recent war for

---

13. "Republican Meeting," *American Citizen* (New York), Feb. 27, 1809, [2], also cited in Gilje, *Free Trade and Sailors' Rights*, 181; Gilje, *Free Trade and Sailors' Rights*, 73, 156–159, 175–187; Alan Taylor, *The Internal Enemy: Slavery and War in Virginia, 1772–1832* (New York, 2013), 122–138, 176–213.

American independence? If so, then these British deserters had a very different story to tell about American antislavery and where it came from. The lack of commentary about these sailors' racial status does not indicate any transcendence of racism; rather, it points to just the opposite. In this instance, comparisons between impressment and slavery in Algiers evaded the facts of Native American conquest and racial slavery booming across the nation.[14]

The political work associated with antislavery nationalism became more belabored when conflicts erupted between the United States and Britain over the loyalties of Black sailors. In 1811, a Black British sailor deserted to the USS *Essex* while docked in a British port. When members of a British press-gang demanded the return of the sailor, the American ship captain John Smith "politely gave him up." When the same sailor chopped off his hand rather than return to British naval service, a Virginia newspaper editor concluded, in racist fashion, that the sailor possessed "a complexion incompatible with freedom." Yet the same editor also praised the British sailor's drastic action to rebuke the cowardice of Americans for not standing up to British impressment, calling the violence a "manly act." "A nation of six millions of souls submits to British impressment," the editor lamented, "while a 'black seaman,' *maims himself* to break his yoke." Such contradictory claims exposed deeper cracks within antislavery nationalism in the United States that no explication about manhood could rectify. How, after all, could this British Black sailor be an embodiment of American liberty and someone possessed of a complexion "incompatible with freedom"?[15]

The presence of free Black sailors in both the U.S. and British Navies in the lead-up to the War of 1812 dramatized the complex political stakes of Black sailors' rights on both sides of the Atlantic. That political potential pushed many American newspaper editors to focus on the experiences of white sailors when writing about British impressment. One especially popular poem, entitled "The Poor Woman's Dwelling, *or Thomas and Mary,*" retells the story of a young white couple's struggles with the violence of the British press-gang. The poem features a melodramatic reunion between Mary, who had been "broken-hearted, / since hearing the British had dragg'd you away," and her

---

14. "This Answer Was Written Jan. 7, 1807," *National Intelligencer, and Washington Advertiser* (Washington, D.C.), July 29, 1807, [3], quoted in Robert E. Cray, Jr., "Remembering the USS *Chesapeake:* The Politics of Maritime Death and Impressment," *Journal of the Early Republic,* XXV (2005), 463–467, quoted in Gilje, *Free Trade and Sailors' Rights,* 181.

15. "Heroism," *Farmer's Repository* (Charles Town, [W. Va.]), May 10, 1811, [3], quoted in Gilje, *Free Trade and Sailors' Rights,* 186.

husband, Thomas, who opined "sad, my dear Mary, was my situation, / When sunk to a slave!—torn from children and thee! / I wish'd but for power to 'whelm the whole nation, / And sink them in flames to the depth of the sea." The poet intensified Thomas's antislavery fury with descriptions of his suffering at the hands of unjust British ship captains. As Thomas laments, they:

> Drag me up to the gang-way, and strip my back bare
> . . . .
> Yes, Mary, they flogg'd my bare back till I fainted,
> And when I recover'd they flogg'd me again.

By concentrating on the flogging of a patriotic white man, the poem marshalled antislavery iconography for the American cause while simultaneously displacing the most common victims of corporal punishment in the United States: enslaved African Americans for whom flogging was a daily menace and threat to survival. In the eyes of British defenders of a humanitarian empire, such efforts to fashion the United States, a slaveholding republic, as a defender of the globe's trafficked classes exemplified American hypocrisy.[16]

On both sides of the Atlantic in 1812, then, antislavery sentiments were expressed as intrinsic expressions of national loyalty as well as justifications for acts of aggression and war against hypocritical nations. The War of 1812 began, like the American Revolution, as a polemical conflict over the meaning of slavery and each nation's authority to traffic people. The U.S. Navy's inability to stop or break a suffocating British blockade of North America was balanced by the fact that throughout the war British sailors deserted their navy for the United States. Although the war was initially a military debacle for the United States, the young republic's eventual victory did lead to the suspension of Britain's impressment of U.S. sailors, with just five cases of impressment reported in the decade after the war's conclusion. British desertions, on the other hand, revealed unsettling questions about the legitimacy of antislavery nationalism in Britain at the conclusion of its wars with the United States and with France in early 1815.[17]

---

16. "The Poor Woman's Dwelling, *or Thomas and Mary*," *Cabinet* (Schenectady, N.Y.), Jan. 20, 1813, [1]; Gilje, *Free Trade and Sailors' Rights*, 185–186; Masur, *Until Justice Be Done*, 170, 181, 182; Fink, *Sweatshops at Sea*, 10–25.

17. The abolition of the African slave trade under British leadership was also partial, precisely because of national interests and enduring demands for enslaved labor across North America. On challenges to enforcement of the Abolition Act of 1807, see Michael Cotey Morgan, "The Ambiguities of Humanitarian Intervention," in Hal Brands and Jeremi Suri, eds., *The Power of the Past: History and Statecraft* (Washington, D.C., 2016), 181–207.

It was in this context that both American and British navies resumed their focus on the trafficking of sailors in the Mediterranean in the summer of 1815. The U.S. Navy was the first to engage its Mediterranean adversaries, going to war with Algiers on June 17, even as Napoleon was preparing to fight and lose his final battle at Waterloo. The cause of the second war between the United States and Algiers was similar to the first in 1803, the capture and enslavement of American sailors. During the War of 1812, Britain had urged Algiers to resume its prize taking of American goods and sailors. With the war's end, the United States turned from resisting impressment and fighting British warships to liberating its sailors from captivity in North Africa once more. Though the fighting was short and decisive, the diplomatic resolution to the United States' second war with Algiers remained uncertain, as European powers at the Congress of Vienna had yet to determine the shape of the post-war peace across the Mediterranean and beyond.

A joint British-Dutch bombardment of Algiers on August 27, 1816, a year later, under the military leadership of the commander-in-chief of Britain's Mediterranean fleet, Sir Edward Pellew, brought clarity to the expanding geography of British antislavery. Precipitated by the killing of some two hundred fishermen from Corsica and Sardinia by the dey of Algiers who were under British protection, the conflict resulted in the eventual emancipation of some three thousand plus sailors. The diplomatic response to the British-led bombardment was decisive: a new treaty that outlawed the enslavement of any Christian in Algiers and the fulfillment of an elusive dream for Ironmonger wardens, the articulation of a fair and consistent price for all remaining enslaved British sailors in Algiers. Transactional antislavery and imperial power had finally become twined, even if at the end of a gun barrel.[18]

---

On analyses of the African slave trade that take into account slave trafficking before and after the abolition of the slave trade, see Leonardo Marques, *The United States and the Transatlantic Slave Trade to the Americas, 1776–1867* (New Haven, Conn., 2016). On the role of impressment in the War of 1812, see Horsman, *Causes of the War of 1812*, 21, 27–30, 84–95, 101–112, 122, 139–145, 219–221, 260–267; Gilje, *Free Trade and Sailors' Rights*, 99–110; and Fink, *Sweatshops at Sea*, 10–22. On the war more broadly, see Alan Taylor, *The Civil War of 1812: American Citizens, British Subjects, Irish Rebels, and Indian Allies* (New York, 2010). Taylor writes that in 1807 "antislavery served imperial power as well as moral principle, ennobling Britain's dual struggle to expand her global empire of commerce and defeat Napoléon" (116–117).

18. Frank Lambert, *The Barbary Wars: American Independence in the Atlantic World* (New York, 2005), 123–156, 179–202; Lawrence A. Peskin, *Captives and Countrymen: Barbary Slavery and the American Public, 1785–1816* (Baltimore, Md., 2009), 71–89, 187–210. On the

The full significance of the international nature of this British-led emancipation effort only became apparent, however, when the identity of the emancipated sailors become known. Roughly two-thirds of the 1,642 sailors initially emancipated at Algiers, some 1,110 individuals, were "Neapolitans and Sicilians," with an additional two hundred captives hailing from Spain. A smattering of Dutch, Greek, German, and even French slaves were also liberated by Pellew, though just thirteen Englishmen were emancipated by their compatriot. Nevertheless, the international scope of the British-led emancipation effort did not silence European or American critics of British power in the Mediterranean or the Atlantic, even though none of the emancipated Christian slaves or their consular charges refuted the claim that imperial antislavery in Great Britain had wrought a decisive change in Mediterranean slave trafficking.

The full significance of the event is revealed in an obscure pamphlet produced by the Ironmonger wardens that foreshadowed a significant reframing of Mediterranean slavery from a problem of Christian slavery to one of white slavery. Seeking to capitalize on their modest role in this emancipation effort, Ironmonger wardens published an account of the company's part in the successful ransoming of the crew of the brig *Surprise*. The short book *A Narrative of the Shipwreck of the British Brig, "Surprise," of Glasgow* exemplified the Ironmonger wardens' abiding support for transactional forms of emancipation. More significantly, a second title page celebrated Pellew's naval victory as one that effected "the Grand and Signal Achievement of the Utter Abolition of Christian Slavery." British sovereignty, it seems, had liberated the entire continent of Europe. But was the bombardment of Algiers an abolitionist victory over Christian slavery or an imperial triumph over white slavery? The diplomatic conversations that immediately preceded the bombardment and shaped its meaning serve to illuminate Britain's wartime accomplishment.[19]

---

British-Dutch bombardment of Algiers, see Seymour Drescher, *Abolition: A History of Slavery and Antislavery* (New York, 2009), 235–237; and Stephen Taylor, *Commander: The Life and Exploits of Britain's Greatest Frigate Captain* (New York, 2012), 270–295. For a discussion of the massacre of Sicilian fishermen, see ibid., 260–265.

19. *A Narrative of the Shipwreck of the British Brig, "Surprise,"* . . . *on the Coast of Barbary,* . . . *and Subsequent Captivity of the Passengers and Crew,* . . . *until Ransomed by the Worshipful Company of Ironmongers* (London, 1817), title page, 11–12. For a celebratory history of Britain's military victory in 1816, see Tom Pocock, *Breaking the Chains: The Royal Navy's War against White Slavery* (Annapolis, Md., 2006), 67; and Grindal, *Opposing the Slavers*. On the nationalistic aims of the U.S. war with Algiers in 1815, see Oded Löwenheim, "'Do Ourselves Credit and Render a Lasting Service to Mankind': British Moral Prestige,

## Toward White Slavery Abolitionism

At the Congress of Vienna in 1815, retired British Navy admiral Sir William Sidney Smith called for the creation of an international "amphibious force" that, "without committing any flag, . . . shall . . . have the important duty of watching, stopping, and pursuing all the pirates" along the coasts of North Africa. The purpose of this international armada was humanitarian rather than imperial or national, Smith insisted, an opportunity to fulfill timeless and twined imperatives: abolishing slavery, conquering Islam, and making "commerce perfectly secure" in the Mediterranean. "The White Slaves in Africa," Smith contended, were "hapless captives who toil in chains, under a scorching sun and under the blows of their fanatical and inexorable taskmasters." According to Smith, some fifty thousand sailors, working under varied European flags, were currently toiling as white slaves in North Africa, awaiting rescue from antislavery government authorities. Himself a knight, Smith called on "Christian Knights" across Europe to join him in his self-styled crusade at the Congress of Vienna. Smith impressed not only a defeated adversary, the French ambassador to the Ottoman Empire, Charles Francois de Riffardeau, marquis de Riviere, who complimented his plan for its "incalculable" moral value, but also traditional allies like the governor of Genoa, the chevalier de Revel, who called on British leaders to "take upon herself the noble functions of the Order of Malta." To many European government ministers, Smith made sense of the centuries-old traffic in human labor across the Mediterranean, one in which Christians and Muslim sailors raided each other's ships, seized cargo, and sold all captured subjects into slavery.[20]

---

Humanitarian Intervention, and the Barbary Pirates," *International Studies Quarterly,* XLVII, no. 1 (March 2003), 23–48; and Frederick C. Leiner, *The End of Barbary Terror: America's 1815 War against the Pirates of North Africa* (New York, 2006), 152–171.

20. W[illiam] Sidney Smith, "Memorial on the Expediency and the Means of Putting an End to the Piracies of the Barbary States, presented by Sir W. Sidney Smith, to the King of Sardinia [ . . . ]," in [Smith], *Translation of the Documents Annexed to the Report of the President of the Reunion of the Knights, Liberators of the White Slaves of Africa, Assembled at Vienna, on the 29th December, 1814* (Paris, 1816), 3–13, "Copy of a Letter from the President of the Reunion of the Knights, Liberators of the White Slaves in Africa, to the First Minister of His Majesty the King of Sardinia," 25–26, "Extract from a Letter of His Excellence the Chevalier M. the Marquis De Riviere," ibid., 17, 21. On Smith's campaign at Vienna, see Löwenheim, "'Do Ourselves Credit and Render a Lasting Service to Mankind,'" *International Studies Quarterly,* XLVII (2003), 39–43; Gillian Weiss, *Captives and Corsairs: France and Slavery in the Early Modern Mediterranean* (Stanford, Calif., 2011), 147–153; Tom Pocock, *A Thirst for Glory: The Life of Admiral Sir Sidney Smith* (London, 1998); Jerome Reich,

Yet Smith's embrace of an allegedly timeless Christian chivalry should not obscure what was indeed new about his campaign. Smith was the first British military authority to describe the traffic in religious and national subjects across the Mediterranean as white slavery. Nevertheless, Smith's racial revisionism flew in the face of several facts. Many Christian sailors operating under European flags and held captive in North Africa were Black; few if any Muslim masters in North Africa possessed Black skin; and there were no laws in the region fixing servitude or enslavement in terms of race. Although Smith failed to head the international armada he envisioned, his abolitionist campaign against white slavery was dramatically successful and enduring, emboldening American, British, and Dutch naval authorities to take military action against Morocco and Algiers in 1815 and 1816. His efforts initiated more than a century of intensified European imperial action in North Africa that, like his call to arms, rationalized political and military aggression as humanitarian intervention. Equally consequential but less commented on, Smith's racial revisionism transformed how abolitionists, government actors, and trafficked subjects discussed the traffic in humanity across the Mediterranean region. The million or more sailors trafficked in North African slave markets between 1500 and 1800 would henceforth be remembered as white slaves.[21]

The key to the success of Smith's racial revisionism, however, lies beyond the Mediterranean region. The campaign to abolish Christian slavery in 1816 had, in fact, become a far more complex political challenge than Ironmonger wardens realized when they celebrated Admiral Pellew's decisive naval victory. Consider first that millions of African and African American slaves in the Americas had recently become Christians. That transformation had begun more than a century earlier but accelerated and gained prominence with the abolition of the slave trade in 1807. Henceforth, slave societies in North and South America and the Caribbean would have to become more humane, a project that supporters of the abolition of the slave trade conflated with bringing Christianity to enslaved communities. The total abolition of

---

"The Slave Trade at the Congress of Vienna—A Study in English Public Opinion—," *Journal of Negro History*, LIII (1968), 129–143; Brian E. Vick, *The Congress of Vienna: Power and Politics after Napoleon* (Cambridge, Mass., 2014), 195–226; and Ian Clark, *International Legitimacy and World Society* (New York, 2007), 38–60.

21. On anachronistic descriptions of North Africa's Christian slaves as white slaves, see Paul Baepler, ed., *White Slaves, African Masters: An Anthology of American Barbary Captivity Narratives* (Chicago, 1999).

Christian slavery in 1816 consequently had become a far more radical and expansive demand. Smith's version of the story, the one that would prove enduring, provided one solution to the increasingly radical implications of that older religious campaign. By focusing on the alleged whiteness of Christian captives, Smith limited the liabilities of abolishing Christian slavery by minimizing obligations to emancipate enslaved Black subjects who had become Christian.[22]

White slavery abolitionism also adroitly built on an older competition between Great Britain and the United States to reframe the relationship between antislavery ideology and national identity to each side's geopolitical advantage. Smith's deployment of white grammar represented an important departure in British officials' efforts to answer the vexing political and ideological challenge of American nationalism. Formerly, the prominence of whiteness in articulations of American peoplehood had provided fodder for British polemicists, who used such rhetoric to dismiss the legitimacy of American antislavery claims. Americans were the primary inventors of racism and political hypocrisy, the cruel Creoles who had made slavery so visibly immoral and had sullied their antislavery inheritance. Now Smith directly co-opted the ideas and arguments of prominent Americans about the Mediterranean. Although Smith made no mention of Benjamin Franklin, his intervention was indebted to Franklin's discussion of slavery in the Mediterranean. In 1790, Franklin had published a scathing indictment of British hypocrisy by using satire to offer an endorsement of British impressment entitled "On the Slave Trade." Writing in the guise of Sidi Mahomet Ibrahim, an Algerine nobleman, Franklin argued that emancipating "Christian slaves" in North Africa would wreak havoc on North Africa's community and economy, ventriloquizing Southern and Caribbean slaveholders who likewise insisted that the abolition of the slave trade would destroy slavery itself. European powers had no moral authority to condemn Christian slavery, Sidi, Franklin's alter ego, continued: "Even England treats her sailors as slaves, for they are, whenever the government pleases, seized and confined in ships of war, condemned not only to work, but to fight for small wages, or a mere subsistence."

---

22. On the central role of African American churches in the life and survival of Southern Black communities, see Albert J. Raboteau, *Slave Religion: The 'Invisible Institution' in the Antebellum South* (New York, 2004). For an historiographical overview of scholarship on Black churches, see Sylvia R. Frey, "The Visible Church: Historiography of African American Religion since Raboteau," *Slavery and Abolition*, XXIX (2008), 83–110.

Franklin's adroit satire killed two birds with one satiric stone, linking North African and British oppressions while inviting a process by which both antislavery sentiment and racial ideology could move as political currencies. That alchemy became a useful precedent for Smith, another ambitious diplomatic actor like Franklin, who used Mediterranean slave trafficking to seek power and recognition.[23]

Smith was hardly the first British nationalist to deploy whiteness in his effort to revise the nation's history of human trafficking. English radical William Cobbett also called up the specter of white slavery in his polemical critique of William Wilberforce. As the campaign to abolish the African slave trade heated up in 1805, Cobbett mocked the inability of Quakers and leading abolitionists to condemn or even mention the "system of government, by which the parish paupers in England have been swelled in number to more than a million." Cobbett decried these and other coerced European actors as white slaves in his writings, exposing what he saw as the selectivity and geographic omissions within abolitionists' commitment to antislavery. He intensified his use of the term in the fall of 1814, using it to describe groups of poor European men and women who had been trafficked by their own political leaders or governments. "If these strenuous advocates for the abolition of the African Slave Trade were *genuine* patriots," Cobbett began in 1814, "they would be as eager to contribute for the diffusion of knowledge among the illiterate and uncultivated Irish, as they are to promote expensive missions to the coast of Africa." Contemporary white slave traffic involved the deliberate political and economic oppression of "the natives of Ireland" by leaders keen on "procuring lucrative posts in the State for themselves and a few select friends." Like Smith, Cobbett deployed whiteness to describe the trafficking of British subjects, leading him to elevate the moral significance of the suffering of white slaves above that of African slaves. The liberation

---

23. Benjamin Franklin, "On the Slave Trade," Mar. 23, 1790, in Franklin, *Works of the Late Doctor Benjamin Franklin, Consisting of His Life Written by Himself; Together with Essays Humorous, Moral, and Literary* . . . , II (London, 1799), 101, 103. "The American, transformed into the defender of all liberties," wrote historian David Waldstreicher, redefined slavery as "all unfree, bought labor," accusing Great Britain of "founding their great empire on the slavery of soldiers and sailors who are also forced to cause the violent deaths of others." See Waldstreicher, *Runaway America: Benjamin Franklin, Slavery, and the American Revolution* (New York, 2004), 197. For an excellent analysis of the role of antislavery, race, and national competition in fomenting the War of 1812, see Alan Taylor's brilliant *Internal Enemy*, 115–121. See also Eliga H. Gould, *Among the Powers of the Earth: The American Revolution and the Making of a New World Empire* (Cambridge, Mass., 2012), 145–177.

of so-called white slaves in Ireland, Cobbett concluded, possessed "infinitely more importance than liberating all the negroes in the world."[24]

If arguments such as Cobbet's conditioned diplomats and citizens to be receptive to retired admiral Sir William Sydney Smith's campaign in 1815, it was the immediate military conflict between the United States and Great Britain that gave the greatest impetus to Smith's racial revisionism. When Smith surveyed the ongoing challenges to British sovereignty and moral authority in the Mediterranean region in 1814, he assessed the enduring limits to British power that North African corsairs presented as well as the moral quandary that American polemicists had forged in the recent war over impressment. Rather than rebut their claim, Smith co-opted it. Linking sailor's rights to free trade, Smith embraced America's cause in the War of 1812, demanding that *"the outrages of African corsairs"* against European sailors must henceforth stop as a precondition for safe commerce between "all civilized nations." Smith believed the only humane and enduring basis for international "peace and amity" was to support the abolition of all slaveries in the region. Like Cobbett, Smith insisted that a greater crime was being inflicted on Europe's own imperial navies, a desecration of the "nation's property."[25]

---

24. "Slave Trade," *Cobbett's Weekly Political Register* (London), Mar. 9, 1805, 372; "The Inquisition," *Cobbett's Weekly Political Register*, Sept. 3, 1814, 293–293, 300. On Wilberforce's key role in the passage of the Abolition Act of 1807, see Davis, *Problem of Slavery*, 421–445; Brown, *Moral Capital*, 438–449; and Manisha Sinha, *The Slave's Cause: A History of Abolition* (New Haven, Conn., 2016). On Wilberforce's life, see William Hague, *William Wilberforce: The Life of the Great Anti-Slave Trade Campaigner* (Orlando, Fla., 2007); Adam Hochschild, *Bury the Chains: Prophets and Rebels in the Fight to Free an Empire's Slaves* (Boston, 2005); and John Pollock, *Wilberforce* (New York, 1978). For an account that heroizes Wilberforce by ignoring the abolitionist movement, see Eric Metaxas, *Amazing Grace: William Wilberforce and the Heroic Campaign to End Slavery* (New York, 2007). On Cobbett's polemic against Wilberforce in 1804, see Marcus Wood, "William Cobbett, John Thelwall, Radicalism, Racism, and Slavery: A Study in Burkean Parodics," *Romanticism on the Net*, XV (August 1999), https://www.erudit.org/en/journals/ron/1999-n15-ron427/. On Cobbett's racism, see Arthur Scherr, "'Sambos' and 'Black Cut-Throats': Peter Porcupine on Slavery and Race in the 1790's," *American Periodicals: A Journal of History, Criticism, and Biography*, XIII (2003), 3–30. On Cobbett's life, see G. D. H. Cole, *The Life of William Cobbett*, G. D. H. Cole: Selected Works, V (1924; rpt. London, 2011); Daniel Green, *Great Cobbett: The Noblest Agitator* (Oxford, 1985); and Leonora Nattrass, *William Cobbett: The Politics of Style* (Cambridge, 1995). On Cobbet's reaction to American narratives of the War of 1812's outcome, see Gilje, *Free Trade and Sailors' Right*, 281.

25. Smith, "Memorial on the Expediency and the Means of Putting an End to the Piracies of the Barbary States," in [Smith], *Translation of the Documents*, 9–11. On the impact of "free trade and sailors' rights" in the Mediterranean, see Gilje, *Free Trade and Sailors'*

Smith's campaign on behalf of Europe's white slaves was well timed to maximize its political impact on European conversations about slave trafficking and sovereignty. As the former admiral of the British Navy who had defeated Napoleon's navy at the Battle of Acre in 1799, Smith's diplomatic status in Vienna was nonetheless quite tenuous (Figure 15). He possessed no official sanction from the British government, having been recently dismissed by the navy while stationed in Sardinia. Smith had invited the king of Sardinia to board his vessel and negotiated directly with the sovereign over a disputed ship that had sailed into Sardinian waters. Smith might have earned praise for his diplomatic gamble had he not also attempted to bill Britain's foreign office for "table-money." Smith defended his violation of diplomatic protocol by arguing that he had "succeeded in re-establishing harmony" with the king, insisting that "on such an occasion, a man of my rank in the world, independent of the flag, could not set a 'leg of mutton and turnips' before such guests." This was not Smith's first such breach of the navy's chain of command. In 1792, he had quit the Royal Navy and served for two years as a mercenary for the king of Sweden, commanding the Swedish navy and earning himself a Swedish knighthood in the process. This time, Smith's British superiors were less forgiving. In May 1814, the hero of Acre was dismissed from the Royal Navy.[26]

Smith's dubious diplomatic status led him to take risks at the Congress of Vienna, which began in November 1814. By agitating on behalf of Europe's white slaves and writing letters to dozens of fellow knights and military officers, he used whiteness and antislavery to try to regain the political footing he had recently lost in Sardinia. His correspondence, published with help from French friends after Britain's military intervention against Algiers in 1816, revealed his unrelenting efforts to link white victimhood to the ongoing diplomatic effort to abolish the African slave trade. "At a time when the means of effecting the abolition of the Slave Trade on the western coast of Africa are under discussion," Smith began his letter to all diplomats and military officials, "it is [a] matter of astonishment that no attention is paid to the northern coast" of Africa, where "no mariner can navigate . . . the Mediterranean,

---

*Rights*, 172–175, 339. For the language of "Free Trade and Sailors' Rights," see "Copy of a Challenge," *Providence Patriot* (R.I.), Aug. 20, 1814, [1]. On sailors as "the nation's property," see Fink, *Sweatshops at Sea*, 9–34.

26. Sir W. Sidney Smith to Wm. Hamilton, July 16, 1814, in John Barrow, ed., *The Life and Correspondence of Admiral Sir William Sidney Smith, G.C.B*, II (London, 1848), 361, 362, 364.

FIGURE 15. John Eckstein, *Sir Sidney Smith; Possibly Ahmad Pasha al-Jazzar ('Jazzar or Djezzar Pasha') and Two Unknown Men*. 1801–1802. Oil on canvas. © National Portrait Gallery, London

or even the Atlantic in a merchant vessel, without . . . being taken by the pirates, and carried as a slave into Africa." Smith had become a defender of the Mediterranean and of whiteness simultaneously. The governor of Genoa was persuaded by Smith's pivot, answering that "compassion for the blacks is worthy of praise, but there are other men my dear Admiral, who require it from us, as the Africans under whom they suffer are still more barbarous than the Europeans who carried on the negro slave trade."[27]

Smith's pairing of whiteness and antislavery transformed how participants discussed the abolition of the slave trade at the Congress of Vienna. The Count de Vallaise, a minister for the king of Sardinia, expressed hope that Smith's campaign might precipitate unified action by European powers, "whether for the abolition of the Slave Trade or for the suppression of the piracies of the Barbary States." The practical impact of Smith's call to arms, however, was to make it easier for European leaders to avoid taking effective international action against the African slave trade. Although the Congress of Vienna officially condemned the African slave trade, its action was a hollow victory for abolitionists. France continued to outfit and run slaving vessels from West Africa to the New World for another two decades, despite its military defeat under Napoleon. Although Britain remained the leader in abolishing the African slave trade as well as so-called white slavery in North Africa, Smith's racist campaign weakened a coordinated international effort to police the slave trade out of Africa, encouraging individual ship captains to continue trafficking enslaved Africans to the Americas.[28]

For Smith, the campaign to emancipate "the white slaves in Africa" failed to achieve its objectives, even if European powers and the United States scored military victories over Algiers. A diplomatic renegade, he remained an embarrassment to a British admiralty that had already fired him. Unlike Cobbett, Smith was not seeking to critique the powerful but to curry favor with them, to insinuate himself into the august company of Europe's reactionary sovereigns. Linking white grammar to abolition was a political experiment, a form of hucksterism similar to Peter Williamson's Indian feathers. Unlike

27. Smith, "Memorial on the Expediency and the Means of Putting an End to the Piracies of the Barbary States," in [Smith], *Translation of the Documents*, 3–4; M. the Chevalier Count de Revel, "Extract of a Letter from M. the Chevalier Count de Revel, Governor of Genoa, to Sir Sidney Smith, Dated from Turin, the 9th Nov. 1814," in [Smith], *Translation of the Documents*, 19.

28. "Letter from Mons. the Cound De Vallaise, Minister of His Majesty the King of Sardinia, to Sir Sidney Smith:--," in [Smith], *Translations of the Documents*, 15.

Williamson, however, Smith's embrace of whiteness sundered the historic ties he had established with Muslim actors. Smith's military victory at Acre, after all, had occurred when he commanded a fleet of Turkish ships. Similarly, as the commander of Sweden's national navy, Smith had worked to free Turkish prisoners laboring in galley slavery. As Great Britain took the lead in the effort to abolish the African slave trade in 1806, however, Smith had adopted racist filters to describe Turkish and Muslim actors in the Mediterranean. "A few shells from the Pompée," he boasted in one letter, "dispersed the Asiatics." Here, then, was Smith's most enduring accomplishment, the adroit blending of white victimhood, antislavery, and a military power that would soon *"rule the waves,"* even as America and Britain battled for supremacy over white slavery abolitionism.[29]

## John Jewitt, White Slave for an American Empire

What common sailors in the Atlantic and the Mediterranean thought of antislavery nationalism and whiteness in 1807 and again in 1815 are different stories. Both Black and white sailors defected to the national flag that best preserved their rights and liberties as maritime actors, whether they were deemed citizens by law or by custom. Conflicts between British and U.S. authorities over the loyalties of Black sailors represented a potent flash point for national rivalry and conflict, one that reflected clashing national policies over abolition and war. Competition over the loyalties of Black sailors was also fueled by sailors' mobility and how they took advantage of the opportunities each nation provided. Racism flourished within both national navies, even as Black sailors exercised power as mariners, making their presence central to how antislavery and sovereignty were seen, imagined, and enacted.[30]

---

29. "Copy of a Letter from the President of the Reunion of the Knights, Liberators of the White Slaves in Africa, to the First Minister of His Majesty the King of Sardinia," Jan. 10, 1814, in [Smith], *Translation of the Documents*, 25; Rear-Admiral Sir Sidney Smith to Vice-Admiral Sir John Thomas Duckworth, [Feb. 19, 1807], in Barrow, ed., *Life and Correspondence of Admiral Sir William Sidney Smith*, II, 223; *Alfred: A Masque* (London, 1740), 42. The first performance of "Rule Britannia" on the British stage occurred in early August 1740. See "Last Night Was Perform'd," *London Daily Post, and General Advertiser*, Aug. 2, 1740, [1], and "On Friday Last Was Perform'd," Aug. 5, 1740, [2], cited in "The Celebrated Ode in Honour of Great Britain Called Rule Britannia," *Musical Times and Singing-Class Circular*, XLI, no. 686 (Apr. 1, 1900), 228–231.

30. "Mr. Taggarts' Address to His Constituents, on the Subject of Impressments," *New-York Spectator*, Feb. 27, 1813, [2].

The broader impact of white slavery abolitionism after 1815 can be assessed by examining the life, career, and published narratives of a common seaman, John Jewitt. Jewitt became the first American sailor in the wake of Sir William Sydney Smith's campaign to describe himself as a white slave. At first glance, Jewitt was an unlikely candidate for such a dubious distinction. Born in England, he was sailing under American colors off the coast of Vancouver in 1803 when disaster struck. His ship was captured by local Nootka Indians, part of the Makah people in the Pacific Northwest (Figure 16). He was then sold and enslaved by a Nootka chief named Maquinna for two years. Throughout his captivity, Jewitt kept a journal, which he published on his escape, a remarkably unadorned record of his daily struggle to survive. In that sixty-page daily captivity log, published during the run-up to the abolition of the African slave trade in 1807, Jewitt never once described himself as a white slave, experiencing few of the adventures that would soon grace the pages of *A Narrative of the Adventures and Sufferings of John R. Jewitt; Only Survivor of the Crew of the Ship Boston.* That volume, published in 1815 with the assistance of Richard Alsop, a troubled Yale graduate with literary aspirations, would become popular as a sensational narrative of white victimhood.[31]

Few clues in Jewitt's published *Journal* of 1807 predicted it had much potential to become a commercial success. "Printed for the author," Jewitt's volume possessed no preface nor editorial comment, and the text seems to have been the actual diary he managed to maintain while a captive. Absent in it were any of the religious or national signposts that accompanied most Indian captivity narratives of the eighteenth century. John Williams's iconic captivity narrative

---

31. John R. Jewitt, *A Journal, Kept at Nootka Sound, by John R. Jewitt; One of the Surviving Crew of the Ship Boston, of Boston, John Salter, Commander, Who Was Massacred on 22D of March, 1803* . . . (Boston, 1807); Jewitt, *A Narrative of the Adventures and Sufferings, of John R. Jewitt; Only Survivor of the Crew of the Ship Boston, during a Captivity of Nearly Three Years among the Savages of Nootka Sound: With an Account of the Manners, Mode of Living, and Religious Opinions of the Natives* (Middletown, Conn., 1815). On Jewitt's captivity within the larger history of the Makah people, see Joshua L. Reid, *The Sea Is My Country: The Maritime World of the Makahs, an Indigenous Borderlands People* (New Haven, Conn., 2015), 47–50. For a discussion of Maquinna and the *Boston*'s crew, see also Lissa K. Wadewitz, *The Nature of Borders: Salmon, Boundaries, and Bandits on the Salish Sea* (Seattle, Wash., 2012), 31. Richard Alsop did not live to see the success of his work, dying in 1815. On Alsop's life, see "Richard Alsop (1761–1815)," in Samuel Kettell, ed., *Specimens of American Poetry* (Boston, 1829). See also "By Critical and Biographical Notice Richard Alsop (1761–1815)," Bartleby, https://www.bartleby.com/96/155.html. Jewitt's account has recently been reprinted. See John R. Jewitt, *White Slaves of Maquinna: John R. Jewitt's Narrative of Capture and Confinement at Nootka* (Surrey, B.C., 2000).

FIGURE 16. *The Ship Boston Taken by the Savages at Nootka Sound, March 22, 1803.* From John Jewitt, *A Narrative of the Adventures and Sufferings of John R. Jewitt; Only Survivor of the Crew of the Boston, during a Captivity of Nearly Three Years among the Savages of Nootka Sound* . . . (New York, [1815?]). Courtesy of David M. Rubenstein Rare Book and Manuscript Library, Duke University, Durham, N.C.

from 1707, for instance, was typical of many such texts, highlighting the religious purpose of his narrative: "The wonders of divine mercy, which we have seen in the land of our captivity, and deliverance therefrom, cannot be forgotten." Jewitt, by contrast, offered no moral homilies or even an implicit purpose to his journal. Most of it constituted a log of daily chores and burdens. Typical was the entry for August 20, 1804, which read: "Fine and clear weather. Natives fishing." More tantalizing were entries that hinted at his dependence on the ruined ship for his survival within a food-challenged community in which starvation seemed to be always near. August 9, 1804, read: "Employed making copper rings from bolts which I got out of the ship. I made out very well with them, for one ring I could get three salmon, which enabled me to live well while the copper rings lasted." A chronology as much as a narrative, Jewitt's *Journal* did not sell well, in large measure because it did not offer his readers much in the way of religious, racial, or national pedagogy.[32]

As an accurate historical rendering of one man's experience of captivity, however, Jewitt's *Journal* is invaluable. That Jewitt's journal survived at all is a remarkable fact, given the suspicion and hostility his writing incited in his master, Chief Maquinna, who "told me, that if he ever caught me writing my journal any more he would burn it, for he said I was writing bad about him." Maquinna was indeed perceptive, though Jewitt spared him most of the moral condemnation that Christian captives traditionally bestowed on their captors. Although Maquinna killed his ship captain and most of his crew, Jewitt understood that he had survived because of Maquinna's intercession. Jewitt gained the chief's favor by making knives and harpoons for him to aid his efforts to capture whales. "Last night our chief informed me he was concerned for his life, because there were no fish to be caught." When Jewitt created a new harpoon out of steel and Maquinna caught a whale the

---

32. Jewitt, *A Journal Kept at Nootka Sound*, title page, 28–29; John Williams, *The Redeemed Captive Returning to Zion* . . . (Greenfield, Mass., 1793), ii. On Williams's life, see John Demos, *The Unredeemed Captive: A Familiar Story from Early America* (New York, 1994). The historical literature on Native American captivity narratives and their meaning is vast. On their importance to the evolution of both national and racial identities, see June Namias, *White Captives: Gender and Ethnicity on the American Frontier* (Chapel Hill, N.C., 1993). Namias, however, anachronistically describes a white racial identity in the captivity texts published before 1700. On the history of trafficking and enslavement among Native peoples, see Juliana Barr, *Peace Came in the Form of a Woman: Indians and Spaniards in the Texas Borderlands* (Chapel Hill, N.C., 2007); and James F. Brooks, *Captives and Cousins: Slavery, Kinship, and Community in the Southwest Borderlands* (Williamsburg, Va., and Chapel Hill, N.C., 2002).

next day, "the chief was very much delighted with the harpoon I had made for him." That goodwill saved Jewitt's life when lean times returned. "The common natives were always for killing us," Jewitt wrote of himself and his other surviving shipmate, John Thompson, a sailmaker, "but the chiefs would not consent to it." Like captives before him, Jewitt condemned the savagery of his captors but focused that enmity on the daily habits of the Nootka people. "Our sufferings amongst these savages are incredible, for they are the most filthy people in the world."[33]

Unlike authors of older captivity accounts, Jewitt possessed little hesitation in describing himself as a slave. "When the Chief called me on deck and told me that I must be his slave and work for him and he would spare my life . . . I of course assented." In his subsequent entries, Jewitt sometimes used slavery to describe his state of captivity, as when he described "the slavery of savages who had stript us of our clothes and our provisions." More frequently, he deployed the word to describe the arduous work he performed. One typical entry read: "Employed as slaves cutting fire wood." This frame would later become tightened over time to read simply, "Employed as slaves," shorthand for being "hewers of wood and drawers of water." In contrast to narratives of sailor captivity in North Africa or servants' descriptions of their sale at auction, Jewitt's use of slavery language was neither comparative nor focused on his sale. At no moment did Jewitt invoke privileges associated with his skin color or indicate that he suffered more because he was white or Christian. Other slaves of Native origin in Jewitt's *Journal* also suffered from arduous work, and Jewitt lamented their poor treatment as much as his own. "We two poor Christians are in a distressful situation," Jewitt wrote on March 17, 1805, continuing, "This day one of the slaves died, and he was thrown out of the house as soon as the breath was out of his mouth, which is a custom amongst the natives." Jewitt's identification with this unnamed slave's dispensability suggests a deeper set of antislavery convictions. Nevertheless, his *Journal* is remarkably free of editorializing, even when it seems hard-earned by virtue of his misery and unceasing work.[34]

---

33. Jewitt, *A Journal Kept at Nootka Sound*, 9, 19–22. On Jewitt's relationship with Maquinna and his role among the Nootka, see Reid, *Sea Is My Country*, 27–50.

34. Jewitt, *A Journal Kept at Nootka Sound*, 4, 6, 37, 40. During the month of February 1805, Jewitt described his labor as slavery on six different occasions, a cold month in which the seasonal demand of finding, chopping, and splitting burnable wood was most burdensome. Yet not all labor was so designated even in this bleak month, as when Jewitt also recorded that he was "employed mending the long boat." See Ibid., 38–39.

Jewitt's disregard for literary flourishes or artifice are manifest not only in the absence of white grammar but also in his decidedly unromantic description of his marriage to a young Indian woman in 1804. From the outset, Jewitt described the event as a symptom of his enslavement. "This day our chief bought a wife for me, and told me that I must not refuse her, if I did he would have both Thompson and myself killed." Jewitt protested that it was "very much against my inclination to take one of these heathens for a partner" but conceded that it would likely "be for my advantage . . . for she has a father who always goes fishing." Food, rather than love, sex, or companionship, seemed to have been foremost in Jewitt's thinking. When marriage did not bring him his hoped-for sustenance and he was compelled to work without American clothes, Jewitt continually protested to Maquinna, who finally relented six months later. "Being very sick and down hearted, our chief gave me liberty to dispense with the girl that he had forced me to take for a partner, which I did with great satisfaction." Just what Jewitt meant by "dispense with" was not explained; it was the last time, however, she was mentioned in his journal. Jewitt's marriage stood in sharp contrast to the narrative presented by the so-called white slave Robert Drury. Jewitt professed no love but instead acute embarrassment by the lack of consent in the union.[35]

Other clues indicate that Jewitt was, like many British and American sailors at the time, critical of both trafficking and of slavery. His disavowal of his marriage might have reflected his discomfort with the explicit sexual traffic that had created it. His wife had been purchased by the chief, one of several transactions involving Indian women that Jewitt noted in his journal. Jewitt's contempt for being trafficked seems to have been bound to gender norms rather than any sense of racial privilege. When an American ship finally arrived and he found his way on board, Jewitt continued to condemn trafficking, prevailing on the American ship captain not to sell or to punish Maquinna, lest it instigate more war and bloodshed. Although Maquinna was briefly detained, leading many of his people to fear that "their chief was

---

35. Ibid., 30, 40. On marriage practices among the Nootka people, see Wadewitz, *Nature of Borders*, 47–51. There is a substantial literature on intermarriage among Native peoples of Canada. See Susan Sleeper-Smith, *Indian Women and French Men: Rethinking Cultural Encounter in the Western Great Lakes* (Amherst, Mass., 2001); Sylvia Van Kirk, *Many Tender Ties: Women in Fur-Trade Society, 1670–1870* (Norman, Okla., 1983); and Jennifer S. H. Brown *Strangers in Blood: Fur Trade Company Families in Indian Country* (Norman, Okla., 1996).

a slave," Jewitt succeeded in having his new ship captain return Maquinna to his people unharmed. Jewitt was no abolitionist. Yet his distaste for slavery and for trafficking structured his reactions to bondage and to his eventual emancipation on an American ship.[36]

In *A Narrative of the Adventures and Sufferings of John R. Jewitt*, published eight years later with the help of Richard Alsop, Jewitt's retold story became strikingly different in content, tone, and substance. Perhaps the most significant transformation involved Alsop's depiction of Jewitt's enslavement. Jewitt was no longer a slave because of the arduous work he was forced to undertake. Instead, Alsop highlighted the significance of Jewitt's skin color to his captivity and suffering. The term *white slave* first appears after an incident between the sailmaker Thompson and Maquinna's eldest son, an eighteen-year-old chief in the making, who was struck by Thompson after the son "provoked him by calling him a *white slave*." White slavery was a provocation quite separate from the actual work Jewitt and Thompson performed, a racial insult that worsened Jewitt's enslavement. Jewitt was so offended that he protested directly to Maquinna. Although the chief "was thus favourably disposed towards us, I took an opportunity to inform him of the ill-treatment that we frequently received from his people, and of the insults that were offered us by some of the stranger tribes in calling us white slaves and loading us with other opprobrious terms." In Alsop's new rendering, Maquinna was sympathetic to Jewitt and to Thompson's racialized pain. "He was much displeased and said that his subjects should not be allowed to treat us ill, and that if any of the strangers did it, he wished us to punish the offenders with death."[37]

Alsop also introduced racial signifiers throughout the text, describing Nootka Indian women as white women who were sexually desirable. Jewitt continued to protest his marriage to a Nootka woman in Alsop's new narrative, but now he had a choice in the matter, one that led him to choose a seventeen-year-old daughter of a chief from a neighboring tribe. "Her complexion was, without exception, fairer than any of the women," Jewitt related, "with considerable colour in her cheeks; her hair long, black, and much softer than is usual with them; and her teeth small, even, and of a dazzling whiteness, while the expression of her countenance indicated sweetness of temper and modesty." Although Jewitt had ignored the color of Nootka Indians' skin in his *Journal*, Alsop made it central to the *Narrative*'s descriptive power. Like

36. Jewitt, *A Journal Kept at Nootka Sound*, 47.
37. Jewitt, *White Slaves of Maquinna*, 60, 134.

Daniel Defoe, Alsop crafted his white slave protagonist as a willing participant in marriage traffic, ratifying the broader imperial transactions wrought by conquest.[38]

Jewitt's wife was not the only Nootka woman whose beauty Alsop expressed in terms of skin color. "As to the women, they are much whiter" than the men, Alsop wrote, continuing, "many of them not being darker than those in some of the southern parts of Europe. They are in general very well looking and some quite handsome." The aesthetic criteria with which Alsop described Nootka women rested directly on the tradition of alien whiteness from the Mediterranean, now transposed to the Pacific Northwest. Alsop's whitening of Nootka women was one part of a larger Orientalist revision of Jewitt's story, a transformation visible in descriptive details about Chief Maquinna and his wife. She was characterized as being "uncommonly well formed, tall, and of a majestic appearance: her skin remarkably fair for one of these people, with considerable colour, her features handsome and her eyes black, soft, and languishing." Maquinna, in turn, was described like Muslim nobility from North Africa or the Ottoman Empire. "It was curious to see," Alsop wrote, "how these people seat themselves with their feet under them crossed like Turks." Images of Maquinna in Alsop's narrative highlight these Orientalist motifs, transforming the traditional Nootka basket cap into a turban.[39]

Alsop's literary embellishments brought Jewitt's story into dialogue, not with the antitrafficking narratives of actual mariners, but with older fictional depictions of white slaves in British literary culture. Alsop's portrayal of Thompson was similar to the unruly indentured servants in Aphra Behn's play who betrayed and killed the noble Oroonoko. Thompson's contempt for the Nootka people not only threatened Jewitt but also the racial nobility of the fair wives and daughters of Nootka chiefs. In Behn's and Alsop's narratives, tensions among white slaves complicated their pedagogical purpose. Behn's white slaves raised the question whether whiteness was to be feared or emulated. Alsop's white slaves performed similar work. Who was more worthy

38. Ibid., 146; Mary Louise Pratt, *Imperial Eyes: Travel Writing and Transculturation* (London, 1992), 8–9.

39. Jewitt, *White Slaves of Maquinna*, 35, 74, 147; Edward W. Said, *Culture and Imperialism* (New York, 1993), 132–160; "Preface," in Hilary Stewart, ed., *The Adventures and Sufferings of John R. Jewitt, Captive of Maquinna* (Seattle, Wash., 1987), 7. For the traditional Nootka basket cap transformed into a turban, see the painting by C. W. Jefferys, *John Jewitt, Captive of Chief Maquina at Nootka*, 1803, 1953, reproduced in Jefferys, *The Picture Gallery of Canadian History*, II, *1763 to 1830* (Toronto, 1945), 99.

of Jewitt's trust? The Indian chief Maquinna, with whom Jewitt shared a noble refinement? Or Thompson, his fellow white slave, whose intolerance threatened their mutual survival? Although Jewitt's white slavery ostensibly cast him in opposition to all Nootka people, his sympathies for Maquinna and the whitened Nootka royalty he admired suggest greater sympathy for Native nobility. In both texts, whiteness pacifies antislavery sentiment that might have challenged national or imperial order. Alsop's literary embellishments co-opted two ideological hurdles for the young American Republic: the threat of Native American power, on the one hand, which Alsop domesticated by transposing Mediterranean whiteness onto Maquinna, and plebeian democracy on the other, embodied by the mariner Thompson, whose hot temper contested the enlightened rule that Maquinna and Jewitt briefly crafted together.[40]

Alsop's version sold quite well by publishing standards of the day, going through three printings in 1815 alone and selling more than nine thousand copies by 1817. The book was well reviewed and praised in 1815, ironically, for its "higher claim to authenticity," with one reviewer singling out Alsop for special praise, "a literary gentleman of Connecticut, who has scrupulously abstained from all digression or embellishment of style." Those 140 additional pages of embellishments in the new volume paled in comparison to the adornments that Jewitt himself brought to the text in the months after its publication, however. Not only did the former captive travel across six states by horse and wagon with a supply of his leather-bound books, he also, like Peter Williamson, performed at local book fairs, reenacting parts of the book and providing curious onlookers with performances of Nootka dance and song. Jewitt's efforts to market his book led him to collaborate with a playwright named James Nelson Barker to create a dramatic version of his "adventures and suffering." In the spring of 1817, Jewitt starred in his own theatrical production entitled *The Armourer's Escape; or, Three Years at Nootka Sound*. The play was composed of seven scenes, including a depiction of his ship, the *Boston*, the murder of the crew, a war dance, a procession and "dance of young Nootkian girls," and several Nootka ceremonies. According to the Philadelphia Theater playbill in 1817, the play concluded with Jewitt singing

---

40. For a similar analysis of the political work of frontier fiction, see Richard Slotkin, *The Fatal Environment: The Myth of the Frontier in the Age of Industrialization, 1800–1890* (New York, 1985).

"The Nootkian War Song" and "The Song of the Armourer Boy," melodies that paired Jewitt's roles as an authentic Indian and an honest blacksmith.[41]

Jewitt's and Barker's collaboration in creating a protagonist who quite literally staged his own rescue did not occur in a literary vacuum. Jewitt's theatricality constituted a kind of greatest hits of race traffic within English language literary culture. The figure of Thompson resembled the dangerous and morally repugnant white slaves of Thomas Southerne's and Behn's fiction; the female bodies of Nootkan royalty recalled the exotic white slaves of Aladdin and European travel writers; and the humanitarian white slave John Jewitt evoked Robert Drury, whose shared critique of white racism became a defense of white racial superiority. And, of course, Jewitt himself resembled Peter Williamson, who also sold copy by appropriating Native peoplehood. These antecedents underscore the remarkably consistent theatrical roles that white slaves played for book-minded English-speaking audiences across the long eighteenth century. Each of these fiction writers used white slaves to generate popular forms of antislavery sentiment while ratifying racial differences that also made for good theater and spectacle.

Yet it was Jewitt's and Barker's immediate political and cultural context that made them politically transformative. An examination of the terms *white slave* and *white slavery* in British and American newspapers and periodicals between 1730 and 1820 illuminates the political work that both terms played in engendering new perceptions of race and trafficking. So-called white slaves appeared sporadically in Anglo-American periodicals and newspapers across the eighteenth and early nineteenth centuries, linked primarily to servants, felons, conscripted soldiers, or, increasingly, to partisans protesting political tyranny. One of the oldest descriptions of white slavery came from Moses Bon Sàam, a West Indian freedman whose 1735 speech about the rights of British slaves was frequently reprinted with the rise of the abolitionist movement in the late eighteenth century. Asked whether British slaves in the West Indies should wait until English residents and masters saw them as equals,

---

41. Stewart, ed., *Adventures*, 7; "Reviews: *A Narrative of the Adventures and Sufferings of John R. Jewitt* . . . ," *Analectic Magazine* (Philadelphia), June 1815, 495; Playbill for the Philadelphia Theater, Mar. 21, 1817, Historical Society of Pennsylvania, featured in Stewart, ed., *Adventures*, 183. James Nelson Barker was best known for his play about Pocahontas. See J[ames] N[elson] Barker, *The Indian Princess; or, La Belle Sauvage* . . . (Philadelphia, 1808). See Eliana Crestani, "James Nelson Barker's Pocahontas: The Theatre and the Indian Question," *Nineteenth Century Theatre*, XXIII (1995), 5–32. On Barker's sexualizing of Native women, see Jeffrey H. Richards's introductory essay to Barker's *Indian Princess* (1808) in Richards, ed., *Early American Drama* (New York, 1997), 109–112.

he responded with the question, "What were *These* [European citizens] a Hundred Years past, but *white Slaves,* to a Monarch?" Unlike the taunts that Nootka Indians allegedly made toward Thompson and Jewitt, Sàam's question animated a broader abolitionist project, one that linked the struggle for freedom among West Indian slaves to the political struggles of numerous exploited groups within Europe. Other descriptions of white slavery during the late eighteenth century also exemplified the growing power of abolitionist arguments, but through opposition to them. The London paper, the *British Evening Post,* for example, deployed the term *white slavery* in 1788 to critique abolitionist claims. "The Day-Labourers of England, Ireland, and Scotland, are . . . much greater Slaves than any of the African Blacks, with this Difference only, that the former are Slaves to a Variety of Masters, the latter, perhaps, only to three or four." American papers, in turn, used white slavery to describe the plight of transported felons and redemptioners. The *New York Packet* summarized emigrants from Ireland as being "most of them redemptioners or white slaves." Most American newspaper references to white slaves were published in New England, with the state of Connecticut one of the most prominent locations for white slavery discourse before 1815, a fact that might have influenced Alsop when revising Jewitt's *Journal.*[42]

During the second decade of the nineteenth century, a remarkable transformation in the volume, geographic range, and meanings of the terms *white slave* and *white slavery* occurred within both American and British newspapers. In the months immediately following the March 1815 publication of Alsop's revised narrative of Jewitt's captivity and the conclusion of the Congress of Vienna, references to white slavery dramatically increased across all American and British newspapers. Some of that discourse reflected Sir

---

42. See Moses Bon S[à]am, "The Speech of Moses Bon Saam . . . ," *Gentleman's Magazine* (London), January 1735, 23, reprinted in *Freeman's Journal; or, The North-American Intelligencer* (Philadelphia), Aug. 27, 1788, [1–2], and *New-York Packet* (New York), Oct. 28, 1788, [2]; "To the Printer of the St. J. Chronicle," Dec. 26, 1787, *St. James's Chronicle; or, British Evening-Post* (London) Feb. 9–12, 1788, [2]; "Edinburgh, July 13," *New-York Packet and the American Advertiser,* Sept. 16, 1784, [3]. Some have suggested that Sàam's speech was a fabrication, written by a white abolitionist. See León-François Hoffmann, "An Eighteenth Century Exponent of Black Power: Moses Bon Sàam," *Caribbean Studies,* XV, no. 3 (October 1975), 149–161; and Thomas W. Krise, ed., *Caribbeana: An Anthology of English Literature of the West Indies, 1657–1777* (Chicago, 1999), 101–102. On the prominence of Connecticut in white slavery discourse of the early nineteenth century, see descriptions of *"white slaves* of Connecticut," in "The Democrat," *Democrat* (Boston), June 20, 1804, [2]; and "Connecticut Politics," *Witness* (Litchfield, Conn.), Nov. 6, 1805, [2].

Sydney Smith's campaign on behalf of Europe's white slaves in North Africa, but Alsop's narrative also prompted its own burst of white slavery discourse, as many newspapers reviewed Jewitt's book. Perhaps more significant were changes in the geography and forms of white slavery discourse with no connection to Jewitt or Smith. White slavery stories were especially conspicuous in describing narratives of North American captivities to Native peoples. One of the most discussed and reprinted newspaper stories of 1815 featured a settler named Henry Bird who was captured and ill-treated by Indians as a white slave but finally escaped to tell and sell his tale. His account closely paralleled Alsop's revision of Jewitt's narrative but made no attribution to either party. Bird had, it seemed, become one of the first plebeian authors to describe himself as a white slave without help from a fiction writer, a celebrated novelist, or an axe to grind against a smug class of shipping merchants. White slavery was becoming a timeless and geographically expansive thing, a trope without a history or accountability.[43]

The extraordinary proliferation of white slavery discourse in 1816 initiated new discursive possibilities and meanings for both whiteness and antislavery, with captive sailors in the Mediterranean and the Atlantic, European captives across North America, and English and Irish transportees shipped to Australia all now appearing as white slaves. In the wake of the abolition of the slave trade and ensuing wars between Anglo-American rivals, white slavery had become truly global, a kind of universalized currency of white victimhood. In the year 1816 alone, more stories featuring white slaves were published in English-language newspapers in North America than in the entire previous century. The majority of these accounts featured condemnations of the white slave trade in the Mediterranean, the last region on the globe to be understood in terms of race traffic. Captives who had hitherto been known and seen solely in religious or national terms now had to negotiate their bondage through the lens of white suffering. The semantic shift was as abrupt as it was large. Before 1815, not a single American or British newspaper story described Anglo-American men or women enslaved in North Africa as white slaves. The only white slaves in the Mediterranean to appear between 1725 and 1814 in British or North American newspapers were Muslim men and women sold in eastern slave markets. In 1816, white slaves comprised Christian sailors, national treasures of increasingly virile American, British, and European

---

43. See "The Adventures of Henry Bird," *Columbian Register* (New Haven, Conn.), Nov. 11, 1815, [4]; and reprints in *Farmer's Repository* (Charlestown, [West Va.]), Nov. 16, 1815, [1]; and *Providence Patriot and Columbian Phenix* (R.I.), Nov. 18, 1815, [1].

nation states. Christian slavery had indeed been abolished, but not in the ways Ironmonger wardens had anticipated.[44]

For the thousands of Black and white sailors working within the national navies of Great Britain and the United States in the Atlantic in 1816, such Mediterranean developments might have seemed irrelevant to more immediate challenges such as securing their liberty as sailors and citizens or simply avoiding impressment. Yet for Black and white American sailors across both locales, the possibility of linking opposition to an abusive English mate on the *Ann* in Naples or to a broader antislavery project suffered an enduring setback. With the rise of white slavery as the dominant frame for organizing stories about human trafficking across the globe, the burden would increasingly fall on Black sailors in both nations to justify and explain their opposition to trafficking and to slavery. The stories about slavery and nation that two Black mariners sought to traffic in the wake of Napoleon's defeat demonstrate how Black sailors responded to the planet's first white slavery pandemic.[45]

## Black Sailors and Humanitarian Empire, 1816

Like Olaudah Equiano, British Black sailor William Nelson believed passionately that slave emancipation and British naval power were linked forces during the early nineteenth century. As the personal servant to British vice admiral Horatio Nelson, the commander of the British fleet that decisively destroyed Napoleon's combined French-Spanish fleet at the Battle of Trafalgar in 1805, William occupied a powerful but precarious position within the British Royal Navy. The naval victory at Trafalgar not only conclusively established British hegemony at sea over the next century but laid the military

---

44. I have relied on the database America's Historical Newspapers to track the emergence and expansion of white slavery discourse within American newspapers of the eighteenth and early nineteenth centuries. Between 1730 and 1815, there were 126 references to the keywords *white slaves* or *white slave* in the digitized American newspapers within the database. In 1816, there appeared 140 references to white slaves during the calendar year alone. Typical was the mention of Sir Sidney Smith's campaign and his call to create "the Knights, Liberators of the White Slaves in Africa." See "Barbary Powers," *Albany Advertiser* (New York), Oct. 2, 1816, [2].

45. On the risks of reenslavement for Britain's Black sailors after 1807, see Charles R. Foy, "'Unkle Sommerset's' Freedom': Liberty in England for Black Sailors," *Journal for Maritime Research*, XIII (2011), 21–36. On similar challenges for Black American sailors, see Masur, *Until Justice Be Done*, 137–139.

foundation for Great Britain's capacity to abolish the African slave trade just two years later. William Nelson's life seemed to exemplify the emancipatory possibilities of a Black man's identification with British maritime power. Born enslaved in the West Indies, he was "taken from slavery" there by British flag officer Horatio Nelson "when he was seven years old" and then trained to be a sailor and companion to Nelson throughout his ensuing naval career. Vice Admiral Nelson suffered a mortal wound during the Battle of Trafalgar, however, one that left William Nelson without a secure position in the Royal Navy. He continued to work as a common sailor, but, in 1812, his ship, the HMS *Belona*, was captured by Algerine pirates on an expedition to Alexandria, Egypt, in search of cotton. For the next three and a half years, as Britain battled both French and American navies, William Nelson struggled to survive as a slave in North Africa. He was emancipated only in 1816, when the British commander-in-chief of the Mediterranean, Sir Edward Pellew, bombarded Algiers and secured the freedom of some three thousand Christian slaves, the same men celebrated as white slaves in both British and American newspapers that fall.[46]

The exact publication date of William Nelson's narrative, *Particulars of the Hardships and Sufferings of William Nelson,* is not known. Most likely, he sent it to print after his return to London and after Pellew became Lord Exmouth in recognition of his naval success at Algiers. William's narrative never became a commercial success like Jewitt's. Indeed, just one copy survives in the British Library, where it was for some years incorrectly filed and presumed lost. Although the publication of his story did not reshape public discourse

---

46. William Nelson, *Particulars of the Hardships and Sufferings of William Nelson, Servant to the Late Lord Nelson, and Served under Him at the Battle of Trafalgar, Who Was Afterwards Taken Prisoner by an Algerine Galley in 1812, While on a Voyage to Alexandria for Cotton, When after Enduring Slavery for Three Years and Nine Months Was Rescued by Lord Exmouth, in 1816, Who Was Eye-Witness to the Following Cruel and Barbarous Treatment* (London, [1820?]), Biography 74/d.1, British Library, London. Because of the rarity of Nelson's published narrative, little has been written about him by scholars, though a good deal more is known about his British master, Horatio Nelson. On Horatio Nelson's life, see Roger Knight, *The Pursuit of Victory: The Life and Achievement of Horatio Nelson* (London, 2005). On Nelson's role in the abolition of the slave trade, see Christer Petley, "The Royal Navy, the British Atlantic, Empire, and the Abolition of the Slave Trade," in John McAleer and Petley, eds., *The Royal Navy and the British Atlantic World, c. 1750–1820* (London, 2016), 97–116. On Nelson's racism toward Black sailors, see Afua Hirsch, "Toppling Statues? Here's Why Nelson's Column Should Be Next," *Guardian*, Aug. 22, 2017.

about slavery, race, and trafficking, it offers a rare window into the thinking of a Black British sailor at precisely the moment white slavery discourse was transforming the public conversation about British sovereignty, antislavery, and race across the British Empire.

As it had been for legions of English sailors before him, Nelson's enslavement in North Africa was traumatic, not only for the violence and coercion he endured but also for the ways it challenged assumptions about his religious and national affiliations. In contrast to previous English slaves who published their narratives, Nelson expressed no interest in providing a travel account of the local customs and culture of his Algerine captors. Nor did Nelson articulate any sense of reciprocity or cultural affinity with his African masters. Instead, his account represents one of the most exacting and totalizing condemnations of Christian slavery ever penned in the English language. A chronicle of extraordinary cruelty, Nelson's narrative features a diverse host of Christian victims, all butchered or dismembered by their Muslim captors. English, American, French, and Swedish sailors, gentlemen, ladies, and their children alike suffer horrific acts of violence in Nelson's story, a collective portrait that both sanctioned Great Britain's recent war against Algiers as well as highlighted commonalities among diverse Christian slaves. Nelson's response to white slavery framing was clear and unambiguous: he rejected it, insisting he was a Christian as well as a British slave. Race played little part in his recounting of his or others' suffering.

Nelson presented Christian suffering, his own and others', in an ecumenical manner, moving from English victims to recently vanquished French rivals in the Napoleonic wars. After detailing how an "English sailor" was tortured and killed for having complained about the food—his captor "taking a penknife" and thrusting it "under his thumb nails loosening them, and then taking a pair of pincers, and tearing them off, one by one," all the while the man was "bound . . . with iron bars head to foot"—Nelson then described the horrific stripping, killing, and dismemberment of an English family, whose female members refused to "marry any gentleman of the Algerine nation." Each description of torture followed a similar pattern: a graphic spectacle of violence, followed by the protest of a loved one, and then repetition of the same cruelty. "The gentleman after the death of his wife could not refrain from speaking, when they immediately bound him down and scalped him." Meanwhile, "the servant seeing his master in that miserable state, asked for a little plaster." The dey instead "ordered his tongue to be cut out," and "they both bled to death and were taken for prey to the fowls of the air." Next came a French family, followed by a French sailor, a group of Americans, a Dutch family, and, finally, a Swedish sailor.[47]

Nelson focused on the nakedness of these Christian prisoners, elevating not only Christian nations but female victimhood in the process. His use of the language of savagery, as well as his frequent descriptions of scalping, suggest that he was adapting North American tropes to his account, the geographic inverse of Alsop's revision of Jewitt's story. Unlike Williamson or Alsop, however, Nelson explicitly avoided describing either his own skin color or that of his fellow Christian captives. He sought instead to emphasize the singular depravity of his Muslim captors, striving to create sympathy for his former antagonists in Europe. Christians of all nationalities were equally vulnerable to the cruelty of the dey, a point he underscored in his description of the suffering of a companion to a Swedish slave recently murdered. "His comrade was tied up by the heels and flogged on the soles of his feet with oak staves, till the blood streamed from his ears, nose, and mouth," a reprise of that notorious instrument of torture, the bastinado. "They beat him till we could not see whether he was black or white, owing to the blood flowing over his body." Humanity was Christian and necessarily multiracial and multinational in Nelson's story, made visible, not by skin color, but by Muslim cruelty.[48]

For Nelson, the experience of imperial war and captivity created profound dilemmas about how to narrate and manifest his own freedom credentials. Like Equiano, he embraced Christianity and Englishness to attack slavery of every kind. Unlike Equiano, Nelson also strongly disassociated himself from Africa, adopting hierarchies of suffering that demonized the Muslim peoples who held him in captivity there. "My Christian reader, I often hear of the cruelties of this country," Nelson wrote, evoking the recent controversy over the African slave trade as well as convict transportation, "but I assure you," he continued, "the greatest punishment here is not to be compared to the smallest of the Algerine Nation." Nelson portrayed the violence of his Muslim captors defensively, to silence anxieties about Britain's slave-trading past and its role in the convict trade. Nelson eschewed a language of white victimhood when condemning his Muslim tormenters for obvious reasons. Yet his narrative illustrates how hierarchies of racialized suffering could confine the ways a Black mariner defended his humanity as a Black man without ties to the continent of Africa.[49]

47. Nelson, *Particulars of the Hardships and Sufferings of William Nelson*, Biography 74/d.1.
48. Ibid.
49. Ibid.

The British Parliament's abolition of the African slave trade in 1807 generated new predicaments for Black and white maritime workers opposed to slavery. Even as war making in the name of fighting slavery expanded after the abolition of the African slave trade, it also placed Black sailors like Nelson in positions that required them to make unhappy choices. For Black mariners, fighting to defend a Christian nation that was increasingly racialized as white gave rise to enduring predicaments, whether or not they were captured by Algerine pirates. How should a Black mariner articulate his national status or defend his rights as a British national? Could literary conventions, long associated with white skin color and aristocratic antislavery, be repurposed to emancipatory ends? For Black mariners like Nelson, Faustian bargains with empire shaped where freedom might be imagined as well as how a mariner might promote that vision. The story of Nelson's story is telling. There is little evidence that he was able to sell his narrative to a broader audience. He did not own his own printing press like Peter Williamson, and his patron, Lord Nelson, was dead, depriving him of any benefits from or access to a literary culture that might have transformed his visibility.[50]

For the American-born Black sailor Robert Adams, securing freedom was similarly connected to the question of where to present his narrative to a broader reading public. Adams, in fact, presented two versions of his story, one to a British reading public and another to an American audience. As an illiterate sailor destitute on a wharf in London in 1816, Adams's immediate dilemma was, not abstract or philosophical, but transactional. What could he secure from an English employee of the Royal African Company, Samuel Cock, who seemed very interested in the fact that he had traveled to Timbuktu during his enslavement? Previous efforts to traffic his tale as so many Christian slaves had done before him had yielded little personal benefit. After being emancipated by an American and a British consul in Mogadore, he managed to reach Cadiz, Spain, where he told his story to an American from Boston, but that version of his journey had not yet been made public and would only be published as a response to the sensational account that the British writer Cock first printed in the summer of 1816. Jared Sparks, American editor for the *North American Review*, would dispute Adams's claim to having made it to the "Interiour of Africa" at Timbuktu and publish his version of Adams's life in the summer of 1817. Taken together, the two accounts of Adams's plight raise doubts about whether Adams even traveled to Timbuktu

50. Taylor, *Internal Enemy*, 137–166.

or the "Interiour of Africa." Their disparities also signal the surprising power and importance of one Black sailor's testimony in assessing how a destitute Black sailor might traffic his way to some kind of emancipation and freedom in the wake of the slave trade's abolition. Rather than reading them as white fictions or as unmediated expressions of Black identity, it would be better to read them as windows into the possibilities and limits that race traffic and antislavery nationalism provided for Black sailors in 1816.[51]

Adams became famous because of Cock's writing and his own relentless self-promotion. An employee of the Royal Africa Company, Cock saw a compelling political and financial opportunity in Adams's claim to having traveled to Timbuktu. Cock's company was none other than the royally chartered African slave-trading company that had for more than a century monopolized the trafficking of African bodies to slave ports in the Americas. A decade after the abolition of the slave trade, the company was struggling to reinvent itself as a mercantile force that might help open the interior of the African continent to a traffic in goods rather than people. Cock had formerly opposed the abolition of the slave trade, but he now eagerly sought the help of abolitionists like Thomas Clarkson, who had argued for an imperial project in Africa committed to a free trade in goods rather than people. An eyewitness account of Timbuktu, one that made the so-called dark continent legible to English investors, stood to benefit Cock's struggling company. Adams's storytelling capacities were evidently powerful and compelling, or so Cock

---

51. Robert Adams, "Interiour of Africa," *North American Review* . . . (Boston), May 1817, 11–26; Robert Adams, *The Narrative of Robert Adams, a Sailor, Who Was Wrecked on the Western Coast of Africa, in the Year 1810, Was Detained Three Years in Slavery by the Arabs of the Great Desert, and Resided Several Months in the City of Tombuctoo*, ed. S. Cock (London, 1816). On the significance of Timbuktu to British planners and Robert Adams's role in that work, see Brian Gardner, *The Quest for Timbuctoo* (New York, 1968), 20–32. Adams's narratives have been the subject of considerable political controversy ever since their appearance in 1816. Ann Fabian argues Adams might not have even existed, nor the African Company that editor Cook worked for. Charles Hanford Adams has critiqued Fabian's claim by verifying the existence and significance of the African Company, though acknowledging that Adams did not likely travel to Timbuktu. See Fabian, *The Unvarnished Truth: Personal Narratives in Nineteenth-Century America* (Berkeley, Calif., 2000); and Adams, ed., *The Narrative of Robert Adams, a Barbary Captive* (Cambridge, Mass., 2005), xxix. For a discussion of the competing national agendas within the two versions of Adams's accounts, see Stephen F. Wolfe, "Robert Adams in Transatlantic Review: Archiving the Barbary Captive and Traveller," *European Journal of American Studies*, VII, no.1 (Spring 2012), 1–13.

insisted to his readers, persuading him that "there was not one who was not struck with the artlessness and good sense of Adams's replies."[52]

Because Cock sought to attract financial investments, he resorted to familiar literary fabrications to sell Adams's narrative. They included an unlikely romance between the enslaved Adams and the daughter of his master, a woman named Isha, who demanded that he serve her supper in her tent, where "he remained . . . all night." That interlude featured a woodcut with a partially clad Adams running from the scene after being caught with Isha. Cock also added patriotic elements to Adams's narrative, a challenge given that he was, according to his own accounting, born in New York state. Cock featured a testimonial by the British vice consul Joseph Dupuis in the preface, verifying the authenticity of Adams's storytelling as well as underscoring that he, and British authorities more generally, had been responsible for Adams's emancipation from slavery in Africa. A sense of English righteousness infused numerous details within the narrative, from a description of the incompetence of the American ship captain, John Horton, whose inability to navigate produced the shipwreck, to the insinuation that Horton had been off course because he wished to violate the slave trade ban and traffic Africans. When Adams was rescued by Dupuis, the British consul, editor Cock included the only first-person testimony by Adams in the text. "Never," he stated, "shall I forget the kindness of this good gentleman." He "seemed to study how to make me comfortable and happy." British humanitarian virtue was so persuasive that Adams transferred his loyalties from America to Great Britain, answering that he was now "an Englishman." Ironmonger wardens could not have been happier with Adams's redemption.[53]

Yet ironies suffused the Englishman's portrayal of Adams's adventures. The editor maintained that Adams was an authentic source of information about Timbuktu, even while admitting he had also paid him for his testimony. The negotiations for his story were both financial and diplomatic in form. First,

52. Adams, *Narrative of Robert Adams*, ed. Cock, xvi, also cited in Paul Baepler, ed., *White Slaves, African Masters: An Anthology of American Barbary Captivity Narratives* (Chicago, 1999), 210. On the history of the Royal Africa Company before the abolition of the slave trade, see William A. Pettigrew, *Freedom's Debt: The Royal African Company and the Politics of the Atlantic Slave Trade, 1672–1752* (Williamsburg, Va., and Chapel Hill, N.C., 2013); and K[enneth] G[ordon] Davies, *The Royal African Company* (London, 1957). The question of Adam's race has also generated commentary with some scholars, like Baepler, classifying him as a white slave on the basis of his lighter complexion. See Gillian Weiss, *Captives and Corsairs: France and Slavery in the Early Modern Mediterranean* (Stanford, Calif., 2011), 154–155.

53. Adams, *Narrative of Robert Adams*, ed. Cock, 59, 78, 80.

"the Editor took measures to render Adams's situation more comfortable, by equipping him with decent clothes, of which he stood peculiarly in need." Second, and more revealing, Adams feared being hurt by the military conflict between the United States and Great Britain in 1814, so he exacted a promise that if "he, by any accident, be impressed" by the British Royal Navy, "his discharge, either by purchase or substitute, should be immediately effected." Adams's insistence on transactional freedom if impressed, a request that Ironmonger wardens would have understood even if they also would have refused to pay it, was indeed double-edged, as resisting British impressment had been the primary American justification for war in its recent conflict with Great Britain. It is impossible to know Cock's motives in broadcasting an antiimpressment argument, except perhaps that it helped him sell more stories. It is certain, however, that Cock and his fellow Royal African Company employees believed their future depended on finding a nationalist vehicle for rescuing the humanity and freedom of an African American sailor enslaved in Africa. That unlikely charge meant having to join with abolitionists in creating an enlightened capitalism in Africa, the company's best hope for remaining relevant to Great Britain's humanitarian empire in 1816.[54]

Although the Royal African Company would largely fail in its endeavor to secure a place for itself in the new humanitarian empire and would soon be formally disbanded by Parliament, the commercial success of Cock's narrative would spark a political debate about the authenticity of Adams's story, one that ironically brought to light a far more accurate portrait of Adams's experience as an enslaved Black sailor in Africa. At the heart of the dispute lay, not the improbable details of Adams's narrative, nor his romance with Isha, but, as the American editor Jared Sparks explained in a review of Adams's narrative, whether Adams had even been to Timbuktu, not to mention the true nature of his relationships with "negroes" en route. As the editor of a new national daily with the aspiration of challenging British cultural and political authority, Sparks sought to upend Adams's published account by attacking Adams's credibility. He published the older narrative that had come into his possession with little editorial comment, believing it provided self-evident proof that Adams had manufactured his celebrated account, the same story that Cock and his fellow British gentlemen were applauding in 1817.[55]

54. Ibid., xiv–xv, 209–210.
55. Adams, "Interiour of Africa," *North American Review*, 11–26. On Adams's second narrative, see Hester Blum, "Pirated Tars, Piratical Texts: Barbary Captivity and American Sea Narratives," *Early American Studies: An Interdisciplinary Journal*, I (2003), 133–158.

Gone in Sparks's account were any narrative details ratifying Britain's humanitarian authority. The American ship captain, John Norton instead of Horton, was an excellent officer according to Adams, and only struck ground because he had not been adequately warned of the impending danger by his crew. No mention was made of being on a secret slaving voyage, voyages that a great many American ships were engaged in at the time, nor was the first mate, a man named Dalby, deemed incompetent. Instead, he was portrayed as a fellow survivor, enslaved alongside Adams after they had been divided into lots by their captors. At no point did Adams claim to be an Englishman, nor was he ransomed solely by the British vice consul, Dupuis. Instead, Adams recounted being ransomed "by the consuls of the United States and of Great Britain at Mogadore," who were charged with redeeming "such Christian slaves as might be found in this district." In Sparks's version, Adams's ransom is secured in American currency: "To my unspeakable joy I found myself ransomed for one hundred and five dollars." A Black American sailor born in New York, Adams benefited from the same transactional freedom that he allegedly experienced in the better-known version of his life story published in London. Adams's emancipation as portrayed in the *North American Review*, however, represented a rare moment when a nation still dedicated to the legal practice of trafficking and enslaving African men and women funded one Black man's emancipation.[56]

The two narratives of Adams's journey, then, differed most significantly, not in their national claims, but in their portrayals of race, slavery, and trafficking within Africa. In the English version, Cock portrayed Adams in racially ambiguous terms, having a "Mulatto" mother but also being perceived as "a white man" while *"in the interior of Africa."* In the American version, by contrast, Adams is resolutely Black throughout. Speaking in the first person, the American Adams consistently notes his connections to local "negroes" wherever he travels across portions of the interior of North Africa. When he arrives in Timbuktu, he is freed, in sharp contrast to his Muslim masters, who are imprisoned. "Our whole party was ordered to Tombuctoo, under a guard of forty negroes, armed with bows and arrows," Adams observes. "During the whole of this journey," Adams explained, "my former masters were pinioned and closely guarded. I was left at liberty and walked with the negroes, or occasionally rested myself by riding on the camels." These carefully delineated contrasts between Adams and his former Muslim captors

---

56. Adams, "Interiour of Africa," *North American Review*, 12, 26.

remain when they leave Timbuktu. "They paid sixteen pounds of tobacco for each man," Adams remarks of a party of "Moorish traders," continuing, "the Moors, their countrymen, were bought to be restored to liberty, and I to my former condition as a slave." In the English version, by contrast, the transaction in Timbuktu is described as a humane and emancipatory one: "There arrived a company of trading Moors with tobacco, who after some weeks ransomed the whole party."[57]

The geographies of race, freedom, and enslavement within Africa are almost entirely reversed in the two accounts, a remarkable difference made visible at precisely the moment when Adams's body is trafficked for sale. In the American telling, Adams's suffering as an enslaved Black sailor leads him to express empathy for the numerous enslaved Africans that traveled with him in his arduous journey across the Saharan sand. "At the end of the fourth day" of their journey north after leaving Timbuktu, "a negro child died of hunger, thirst, and fatigue, and the body was thrown carelessly upon the sand. Two days afterwards the mother of the child died, being overcome with fatigue and grief for the loss of her child. Her body was left in the same manner as that of the child, exposed on the sand." Like William Nelson and Equiano, Adams expresses revulsion and horror at the ways deceased slaves were discarded, unburied, and unsung along his journey. The targets for his moral outrage were his Muslim captors, prompting Adams to make sweeping condemnations of them. The Moors, Adams concludes, "are much more wretched and uncivilized than the negroes." At the heart of Adams's critique was not only the suffering that Moorish masters caused but their devotion to trafficking people. Adams's journey north was punctuated by frequent sales to new Moorish masters, all of whom sought advantage through additional slave trafficking. On reaching southern Morocco, Adams describes the "inhabitants" as being "a few shades lighter in their complexion" but also "being an abandoned set of thieves and robbers. Their whole employment consists in plundering travellers and strangers." For the Adams who appeared in the *North American Review*, moral virtue existed in opposition to slavery,

---

57. Adams, *Narrative of Robert Adams*, ed. Cock, xi, xxviii, 24, 57; Adams, "Interiour of Africa," *North American Review*, 14, 22, 24. Robert Murray has historicized a similar racial ambiguity among African Americans who traveled to Liberia and were designated white by Africans. Such complexities were not generated by skin color but by the particular geographic contexts that shaped both trafficking and race. See Murray, "Bodies in Motion: Liberian Settlers, Medicine, and Mobility in the Atlantic World," *Journal of the Early Republic*, XXXIX (2019), 615–646.

trafficking, and white skin color. Adams exposed white racial privileges as a threat to a genuine American nationalism, one that was antislavery in word and in deed.[58]

Although it is tempting to valorize the first-person American version of Adams's story as the more truthful and certainly more just account, it would be better to view the striking disparities between the two texts as evidence of the powerful work that race and trafficking exacted on sailors and writers alike in both Great Britain and the young United States in 1816. Rather than conclude Adams did not exist or dismiss the accounts as fiction, the competing versions instead underscore the historical contingencies that shaped how an illiterate Black sailor might traffic his life story to two white editors keen on knowing what the heart of a Black continent looked like. Such aspirations would in time transform the African continent. In the short term, they contributed to a hardening of the category of race itself by which imperialists and European actors discerned the essential value of Black people. In the wake of the abolition of the Atlantic slave trade and the elimination of slave trafficking in the Mediterranean, questions about the relationship between trafficking and race remained more important than ever. As the sites of trafficking moved from oceans to continental and national interiors, so did race become imagined as an immutable and national identity, as objective and fixed as the boundaries that nations defended. If Adams's trip to the interior of Africa was a hoax, it was no more or less fraudulent than the increasingly pervasive notion that races were themselves immutable essences that could be divined by a single glance at someone's skin color. In that regard, both of Adams's stories were true, Cock's version especially so, as it became the dominant fiction shaping how imperial actors, whether sailors, slaves, or statesman, would see race and use it to redefine nations, slavery, and freedom over the ensuing century.

## Conclusion

Selling people on the basis of the color of their skin did not end with the abolition of the African slave trade, even if that campaign dramatically reduced the trafficking of newly enslaved African peoples to the Americas. To the

---

58. Adams, "Interiour of Africa," *North American Review*, 23–25. Adams's hostility to trafficking was more pronounced in the American version, a vantage that led the author to equate British impressment with enslavement. See Blum, "Pirated Tars, Piratical Texts," *Early American Studies*, I (2003), 154.

contrary, trafficking by race remained central to global economic work after 1807, as the interior of North America was further opened to conquest and plantation slavery. The ending of a legal transatlantic traffic in enslaved Africans had important consequences for how nations saw and understood freedom, traffic, and race. The focus of antitrafficking discourse shifted decisively from oceanic geographies to national interiors, from disputes over sovereignty and maritime solidarities to territorial anxieties about internalized national and imperial frontiers. Understanding the changing geography of human trafficking helps explain why racial and national discourses grew stronger with the abolition of the slave trade and how and why working classes in Great Britain and America began to engage in antislavery movements and nation-bound political formations simultaneously. Resistance to trafficking mattered more than ever, but efforts to do so increasingly occurred within national boundaries, tethering the meaning of rights to national and racial imaginaries.

Racism among the trafficked was not inevitable, even if racist thought and habits of mind among them were expanding after 1807. Black and white sailors continued to labor next to one another in the national navies of both Great Britain and the United States, and coercion among allegedly free workers remained conspicuous in both countries, with pecuniary coercions especially powerful in the United States and corporal punishment ubiquitous for servants and wage earners across Great Britain during the first half of the nineteenth century. As whiteness became more tightly linked to national policies such as the U.S. Naturalization Act of 1790, race became more territorial and impermeable in form, an ideology better able to delineate hierarchies among trafficked victims within nations. With the remarkable expansion of slavery across the American continent, white racial ideology also became more conspicuous, fusing the rhetoric of Native American conquest with anti-Black racism. In Great Britain, meanwhile, discussions of white slavery likewise became more prominent after 1807, a vehicle for separating trafficked classes at home from those on the margins of its empire. Critiques of economic injustice on both sides of the Atlantic increasingly foregrounded white racial categories at odds with older articulations of sailor and servant antislavery. Indeed, in the hands of Richard Alsop, the story of a white slave named John Jewitt transformed a lonely captive's survival chronicle into a defense of both slavery and capitalism.

The Black and white American sailors in Naples who successfully defended the freedom of their Black compatriot won a strategic victory in the fall of

1816. They proved ready and able to uphold hard-won rights and to fight for a nation that they hoped would, in turn, champion their rights. Yet their improbable victory, and the larger stakes that animated it, were only dimly visible to the British and American consular officials who recorded the documents that recounted these dramatic confrontations. Their struggle was invisible to would-be allies in the abolitionist movement on both sides of the Atlantic in 1816 as well as to subsequent historians. The successful abolition of the African slave trade in 1807 not only transformed the geography of race trafficking but deemphasized the importance of maritime workers. Sailors would continue to struggle against trafficking and, if Black, against reenslavement and life-threatening racism. At the very moment that Black and white American sailors were disarming a racist British ship's captain, sailors taken captive across the Mediterranean were becoming known as white slaves, regardless of their national origin or skin color. The resolution of the War of 1812, which had briefly elevated the importance of impressment to both American and British fleets, eliminated the leverage that sailors, Black and white, had briefly wielded. History, in turn, would be even less kind to these sailors, trapped as they were outside the geographic and conceptual borders of the Atlantic historiographies that valorized abolitionists on the one hand and industrial wage workers on the other. Yet their struggles were central to a key political question of the early nineteenth century: Could trafficked workers fight for one another across lines of color?[59]

Rather than being peripheral, the Mediterranean was central to the political and economic conflicts shaping global antislavery during the first two decades of the nineteenth century. Prize taking was vital to the implementation of the 1807 Abolition Act and to Great Britain's long-standing ambition to control trafficking in the region and to rescue national slaves there. Britain's enduring commitment to both prize taking and to antislavery suggests how and why the Mediterranean became so instrumental to the expansion of global antislavery campaigns after 1807. Prize taking and antislavery were indeed a combustible mixture, one that helped spark the fight between American and British sailors in Naples, Italy, in 1816. The flogging of a free Black sailor represented a fuse waiting to be lit. The only thing more remarkable than white and Black Americans successively disarming British ship's officers

---

59. On the broader significance of maritime solidarities to antebellum U.S. history, see Hester Blum, *The View from the Masthead: Maritime Imagination and Antebellum American Sea Narratives* (Chapel Hill, N.C., 2008), 58–63.

was that they did so without triggering a larger military or diplomatic war in 1816. The political stakes of mariner solidarities remained crucial to both nations' ambitions and aspirations, even if they also upended the very meaning and purpose of each nation's trafficking policies. National struggles over human trafficking and slavery were only beginning to intensify in 1816. And in those conflicts, white slavery and white victimhood had become unavoidable ideological artifacts, starting points for the formation of the English and American working classes.

CONCLUSION

# The Radical Challenge to Race Traffic

As great Britain strengthened its capacity to enforce the abolition of the African slave trade in the aftermath of Napoleon's final defeat, a formerly enslaved Jamaican named Robert Wedderburn launched one of the most ferocious critiques of human trafficking ever uttered by a British subject (Figure 17). "This Wedderburn, doth charge all potentates, governors, and governments of every description with felony," began a published letter entitled *The Axe Laid to the Root; or, A Fatal Blow to Oppressors*. Addressed to his half-sister, a slaveowner in Jamaica, Wedderburn's letter condemned the trafficking crimes that racial slavery sanctioned. He directed particular animus toward his father, a slaveowner born in Scotland, who had raped numerous enslaved women, including Robert's mother, to profit from the sale of the children, Robert's siblings. The most affecting moment in Wedderburn's letter came when he directly summoned the ghost of his deceased father. "You set a pattern to your slaves to treat your wife with contempt, by taking your negro wenches to your adulterous bed.... How can I forgive you? Oh! My father, what do you deserve at my hands?" Violence was portrayed intimately in Wedderburn's letter and in his weekly speeches to supporters in a barn in London's East End. His words stirred rumors of war that held the potential to incite resistance to British rule in both London and Jamaica. Wedderburn's conversations with his deceased father were so vivid and lifelike that when he was arrested in 1819, it was not for treason but for the charge of blasphemy. A radical and unruly Methodist, he was, to followers and enemies alike, one of the most dangerous men in Great Britain.[1]

---

1. Robert Wedderburn, *The Axe Laid to the Root; or, A Fatal Blow to Oppressors, Being an Address to the Planter and Negroes of the Island of Jamaica; No!* [1817], reprinted in Iain McCalman, ed., *The Horrors of Slavery and Other Writings by Robert Wedderburn* (New York, 1991), 81, 82 86. For abolitionist interest in the reproductive capacities of enslaved Jamaican women as well as abolitionist anxieties about sexual violence toward them, see

FIGURE 17. *Robert Wedderburn.* Frontispiece from Robert Wedderburn, *The Horrors of Slavery; Exemplified in the Life and History of the Rev. Robert Wedderburn* . . . (London, 1824). British Library, London

Wedderburn's rage against human trafficking led him to condemn trafficking absolutely and without conditions in all its forms. Trafficking, he believed, made visible the foundational thefts within slavery, ongoing violence that required immediate action. His hostility to human trafficking also fostered solidarities with dispossessed British commoners, whom he believed were being bought and sold as textile operatives without the power to vote or the benefit of common lands that had nurtured them for generations. Wedderburn used antitrafficking to challenge core tenets of British political economy: that commerce in people could ever be moral, that land could or should be sold, and that private property could ever be a source of independence and virtue. For Wedderburn, traffic in land, like commerce in people, was a form of theft. Both practices had to be abolished. Although Wedderburn never saw the ledger books for the Ironmongers' Slave Fund, he would not have been surprised by the revelation that enclosure at home and enslavement through the African trade had been linked financially. For Wedderburn, as for Ironmonger wardens, there was a single global economic system based on human trafficking. The core tenet of Ironmonger antislavery in the Mediterranean—that emancipations should be transactional—however, was, to Wedderburn, a sinful notion, a failure to see the crimes that made all British "potentates" guilty of felony. Here indeed was a dramatic adaptation of antislavery ideology beyond the African slave trade, an argument that cut to the very root of Anglo-American political economy and culture.

---

Sasha Turner, *Contested Bodies: Pregnancy, Childrearing, and Slavery in Jamaica* (Philadelphia, 2017), 18–43, 215–218. Until recently, Wedderburn's powerful political challenge was largely overlooked by leading historians of abolition and of labor. Edward P. Thompson dismissed Wedderburn, whom he described as an unknown tailor who "promoted a little ill-printed journal." See Thompson, *The Making of the English Working Class* (London, 1963), 886. David Brion Davis, meanwhile, made no mention of Wedderburn at all in Davis, *The Problem of Slavery in the Age of Revolution, 1770–1823* (Ithaca, N.Y., 1999). For a fuller explication of Wedderburn's neglected contributions to both labor and abolition, see Iain McCalman, "Anti-Slavery and Ultra-Radicalism in Early Nineteenth-Century England: The Case of Robert Wedderburn," *Slavery and Abolition*, VII (1986), 99–117. For a rich portrait of Wedderburn as an Atlantic religious radical, see Peter Linebaugh and Marcus Rediker, *The Many-Headed Hydra: Sailors, Slaves, Commoners, and the Hidden History of the Revolutionary Atlantic* (Boston, 2000), 287–326. For brief portraits of Wedderburn's contributions to Black abolitionism, see Manisha Sinha, *The Slave's Cause: A History of Abolition* (New Haven, Conn., 2016), 198–199; and Paul Gilroy, *The Black Atlantic: Modernity and Double Consciousness* (Cambridge, Mass., 1993), 12.

Like Thomas Lurting, Wedderburn's opposition to human trafficking led him to challenge British imperial power wherever it profited from commerce in people. Along the way, Wedderburn not only questioned how British subjects thought about markets but also whether markets were or ever could be natural, humane, or fair. Like the African-born servant John Punch who ran away with indentured servants in 1640; or the enslaved African, Ceasar, and his Irish wife, Peggy, in New York City in 1741, who refused to validate Daniel Horsmanden's racial conspiracies; or the writers Robert Barker, Olaudah Equiano, and Phillis Wheatley, each of whom turned personal suffering into potent weapons against imperial power, Wedderburn was effective because he attracted a diverse cohort of trafficked peoples. In his sermons, he confronted and exposed the self-serving bromides that defenders of Britain's blue water empire had long proffered in response to critics. He confronted strongly held beliefs that all markets were expressions of freedom, that antislavery was a uniquely British tradition, and that religious authorities know what's best for people. Wedderburn understood that emancipation could only be achieved through constant struggle with political authorities who were unwilling to give up power voluntarily.[2]

If Wedderburn's polemic drew on generations of antitrafficking insight, it was nonetheless specific to his moment. He grasped a fact of profound importance about the political economy of Great Britain and its current and former colonies in the decades after the abolition of the African slave trade in 1807: that in 1819, two centuries after the first Africans had been sold in Virginia and twelve years after the abolition of the slave trade, human trafficking remained vital to the growth and future of British power. Steadfastly committed to transactional freedom as well as transactional emancipation, a hallmark of centuries of trafficking policy in the Mediterranean, British officials addressed the ongoing labor demands of growing their empire after the abolition of the slave trade in 1807 by expanding their use of transported indentured labor. In 1819, penal transportation was also growing, while trafficked labor was proving vital to the building of Britain's Asian and African

---

2. Historians have not typically located Wedderburn's writings within a tradition of slave narratives because of uncertainty about whether he was literate as well as his focus on British workers. On efforts to locate Wedderburn's contributions within an African and Atlantic diaspora, see Nadine Hunt, "Remembering Africans in Diaspora: Robert Wedderburn's 'Freedom Narrative,'" in Olatunji Ojo and Hunt, eds., *Slavery in Africa and the Caribbean: A History of Enslavement and Identity since the 18th Century* (London, 2012), 175–198; and Edlie L. Wong, *Neither Fugitive nor Free: Atlantic Slavery, Freedom Suits, and the Legal Culture of Travel* (New York, 2009), 63–67.

imperial projects. The shift from enslaved to indentured labor would be most dramatic after the abolition of slavery across all of Britain's colonies in 1834. Antitrafficking might have fueled the growth of abolitionist sentiment in Great Britain, but it had not yet produced a commensurate movement against human trafficking more broadly. Here was another reason Wedderburn's message was so threatening.[3]

In the United States, the geography of human trafficking was also shifting and expanding, though in ways that would make it harder to sustain a broader coalition of trafficked peoples against slavery. With the end of convict transportation from Great Britain, a by-product of the American victory in the American Revolution, there were far fewer trafficked whites in the new nation. Moreover, in 1819, indentured servitude had all but ceased to exist in North America, surviving primarily within particular emigration streams or among Native American children in missionary schools. The trafficking of enslaved people within the United States meanwhile had become better organized, more visible to Americans of all statuses and backgrounds, and even more violent in the wake of the transatlantic slave trade's abolition. The internal slave trade between 1808 and 1860 trafficked twice as many enslaved

---

3. James J. Willis, "Transportation versus Imprisonment in Eighteenth- and Nineteenth-Century Britain: Penal Power, Liberty, and the State," *Law and Society Review*, XXXIX (2005), 171–210. On the importance of Indian convict labor to Britain's imperial work in the Indian subcontinent during the early nineteenth century, see Clare Anderson, "Convicts and Coolies: Rethinking Indentured Labor in the Nineteenth Century," *Slavery and Abolition*, XXX, no. 1 (2009), 93–109. On the role of Indian sailors, many of them trafficked and unfree, in building British imperial projects before, during, and after the abolition of the slave trade, see Michael H. Fisher, "Working across the Seas: Indian Maritime Labourers in India, Britain, and in Between, 1600–1857," *International Review of Social History*, LI, supplement 14 (2006), 21–45; Fisher, *Counterflows to Colonialism: Indian Travellers, and Settlers in Britain, 1600–1857* (Delhi, India, 2004), 137–179; and Aaron Jaffer, *Lascars and Indian Ocean Seafaring, 1780–1860: Shipboard Life, Unrest, and Mutiny* (Woodbridge, Suffolk, U.K., 2015). For an overview of Britain's transition to indentured labor from slavery, see David Northrup, *Indentured Labor in the Age of Imperialism, 1834–1922* (Cambridge, 1995). On the global origins of an indentured labor market that grew during the late eighteenth century across Asia, even as abolitionist projects gained prominence in the Americas and Africa, see Richard B. Allen, "Slaves, Convicts, Abolitionism, and the Global Origins of the Post-Emancipation Indentured Labor System," *Slavery and Abolition*, XXXV (2014), 328–348. On the continuity of indentured labor within nineteenth- and early twentieth-century global migration, see Cindy Hahamovitch, "Creating Perfect Immigrants: Guestworkers of the World in Historical Perspective," *Labor History*, XLIV (2003), 69–94.

people across North American interiors than had arrived from Africa in the previous century and a half, as trafficking became essential to the expansion of Southern slavery, the North's economy, and British industrialization.[4]

The abolition of the slave trade transformed how and where U.S. authorities commodified and policed the mobility of enslaved peoples. Replacing the slave ship as the factory were thousands of geographically dispersed commercial sites across the nation, where local militia, auctioneers, justices of the peace, and overseers commodified and transported the bodies of enslaved men, women, and children from slave plantations in the Upper South to booming projects across the Deep South. In the absence of newly arrived enslaved people from Africa on American soil, slave fungibility necessitated family separations to supply labor needs and build new plantations. The work of slavecatchers also became more extensive, invasive, and well financed, even if their work made some white Southerners uncomfortable. Trafficking the enslaved became the most powerful disciplinary tool for slaveholders as well as the best way for them to finance the expansion of the economy. As internal policing of Black bodies through trafficking expanded after 1808, the distinction between trafficking and enslavement also effectively shrank for African Americans. Rather than expanding freedom, the abolition of the

---

4. The decisive court case that ended the enforcement of contracts of indenture in North America was still in motion in 1817. Mary Clark, an African American servant in Indiana, ran from her master but was imprisoned in 1816. She sued for her freedom arguing that contracts of indenture could not be enforced because they created "a state of servitude as degrading and demoralizing in its consequences, as a state of absolute slavery." She won her freedom suit in 1821, a result of an abolitionist movement that helped indentured servants in states that had abolished slavery. The Clark case, David Montgomery writes, "produced the decisive final round of struggle against specific enforcement of labor contracts." See Montgomery, *Citizen Worker: The Experience of Workers in the United States with Democracy and the Free Market during the Nineteenth Century* (Cambridge, 1993), 36–37. On contracts of indenture among Native American children, see Vivien Rendleman, "Unfree Labor: Empire, Labor, and Coercion in the Upper Mississippi River Valley, 1812–1861" (Ph.D. diss., Duke University, 2024), Chapter Three. "Arguing that the history of (racial) capitalism began with the slave trade rather than the factory system," writes historian Walter Johnson, "does not necessarily pose any greater threat to historical and analytical precision than arguing that Harriet Tubman and John C. Calhoun were human beings." "There was no such thing as capitalism without slavery," he continues, for "the history of Manchester never happened without the history of Mississippi." See Johnson, "To Remake the World: Slavery, Racial Capitalism, and Justice," in Johnson with Robin D. G. Kelley, eds., *Race Capitalism Justice*, Forum 1, *Boston Review* (2017), 25.

African slave trade sparked escalating battles over the mobility of both free and enslaved African Americans across the United States.[5]

From Wedderburn's vantage, these changing political geographies created opportunities for resisting capitalism and slavery simultaneously. Widening disparities in the legal status of enslaved Blacks and trafficked whites necessitated collaborations among them. Rather than crafting separate narratives and prescriptions for factory workers and for the enslaved, Wedderburn embraced the harder challenge, articulating a critique of capitalism and slavery that posited common freedoms and independence in land. The fight for land would also be a fight for the nation and what it might do on behalf of its subjects, whether they were recognized as citizens by political authorities. That redemptive vision of the nation and of land could not be confined to colonial outposts but had to be taken into the very heart of the empire, into London's East End, where the people who had been turned into things in global marketplaces could become agents in their emancipation. Here is where the fight had to be fought and won, Wedderburn believed, a conviction both empowering and emboldening, even as he was charged with blasphemy.[6]

Although few architects of the labor movement in Great Britain or the United States had heard of Wedderburn by 1840, Wedderburn's antitrafficking

---

5. On the expansion of the domestic slave trade in the United States, see Ira Berlin, *Many Thousands Gone: The First Two Centuries of Slavery in North America* (Cambridge, Mass., 1998), 47–48, 264–266; Joshua D. Rothman, *The Ledger and the Chain: How Domestic Slave Traders Shaped America* (New York, 2021), 9–52; Edward E. Baptist, *The Half Has Never Been Told: Slavery and the Making of American Capitalism* (New York, 2014); Steven Deyle, *Carry Me Back: The Domestic Slave Trade in American Life* (New York, 2005); and W. E. B. Du Bois, *The Suppression of the African Slave-Trade to the United States of America, 1638–1870* (New York, 2007). Joshua Rothman writes that "between 1800 and 1860, American slaveholders sent roughly one million Black people from the upper South to the lower South, moving in the span of sixty years over twice as many people as were transported in two centuries to mainland North America via the transatlantic slave trade from Africa." See Rothman, *Ledger and the Chain*, 3. On the centrality of mobility to the meaning and practice of citizenship for African American freemen during the antebellum era, see R. J. M. Blackett, *The Captive's Quest for Freedom: Fugitive Slaves, the 1850 Fugitive Slave Law, and the Politics of Slavery* (New York, 2018); Stephen Kantrowitz, *More Than Freedom: Fighting for Black Citizenship in a White Republic, 1829–1889* (New York, 2012); Thomas D. Morris, *Free Men All: The Personal Liberty Laws of the North, 1780–1861* (Union, N.J., 1999); and Leon F. Litwack, *North of Slavery: The Negro in the Free States, 1790–1860* (Chicago, 1961).

6. Wedderburn has been characterized as an "ultra radical," a reflection of his political commitments to abolition and land reform as well his millenarian views and willingness to fight his political battles with firearms. See Eric Pencek, "Intolerable Anonymity: Robert

message anticipated key issues that would shape the emergence of working classes on both sides of the Atlantic. Land reform was central to Chartist messaging and organizing in Great Britain throughout the 1830s and 1840s, while antirent activists in the United States made land reform an important element within the young nation's first working-men's political parties. Antislavery and abolition likewise became essential components of working-class organizing and rhetoric on both sides of the Atlantic during the 1820s. Tory radical Richard Oastler, for instance, was motivated by both antislavery and "hatred of oppression" to fight for the immediate abolition of chattel slavery throughout Britain's empire, a ten-hour day for all factory workers in Great Britain, the elimination of child labor in all factories, universal manhood suffrage for British working people, and repeal of the Corn Laws that were accelerating land dispossession across Ireland. Oastler's radical vision, which made him a household name among working-class families during the 1830s, linked many of the same actors that Wedderburn had summoned into his East End barn. Known derisively as the "King of the Factory Children" to his detractors, Oastler was, like Wedderburn, enamored of melodrama and committed to justice through direct action and abolition, and he employed many of the same melodramatic rhetorical flourishes as Wedderburn.[7]

---

Wedderburn and the Discourse of Ultra-Radicalism," *Nineteenth-Century Contexts: An Interdisciplinary Journal*, XXXVII (2015), 61–77; and David Worrall, *Radical Culture: Discourse, Resistance, and Surveillance, 1790–1880* (Detroit, Mich., 1992).

7. The definitive biography of Richard Oastler remains Cecil Driver, *Tory Radical: The Life of Richard Oastler* (New York, 1946), 323, 443. On land reform's importance to the Chartists, see Jamie L. Bronstein, *Land Reform and Working-Class Experience in Britain and the United States, 1800–1862* (Stanford, Calif., 1999). On the connections between antislavery and efforts to repeal the corn law, see Simon Morgan, "The Anti-Corn Law League and British Anti-Slavery in Transatlantic Perspective, 1838–1846," *Historical Journal*, LII (2009), 87–107; and Paul A. Pickering and Alex Tyrrell, *The People's Bread: A History of the Anti-Corn Law League* (London, 2000). On Oastler's career in the context of working-class formation, see Thompson, *Making of the English Working Class*, 289–298, 342–348. On Oastler's radicalism, see Matthew Roberts, "Richard Oastler, Toryism, Radicalism, and the Limitations of Party, c.1807–46," *Parliamentary History*, XXXVII (2018), 250–273. For an analysis of family, gender, and class in the writings of Oastler, see Colin Creighton, "Richard Oastler, Factory Legislation, and the Working-Class Family," *Journal of Historical Sociology*, V (1992), 292–321. On Oastler and the passage of factory legislation more generally, see J. T. Ward, "Richard Oastler on Politics and Factory Reform, 1832–1833," *Northern History*, XXIV (1988), 124–145; and John A. Hargreaves and E. A. Hilary Haigh, eds., *Slavery in Yorkshire: Richard Oastler and the Campaign against Child Labour in the Industrial Revolution* (Queensgate, Huddersfield, U.K., 2012).

In the United States, opposition to trafficking similarly incubated political and moral insights that were foundational to critiques and protests against the emerging industrial order, one that stretched from the new textile mills of the Boston Manufacturing Company to booming cotton plantations in Alabama in 1819. For newspaper polemicist and labor instigator George Henry Evans, trafficking people and selling public lands to expand enslavement were related crimes, issues that he believed, with prescience, could be woven together to nurture militant opposition to both slavery and land monopolies across the United States. As the editor of the largest working-class publication in the nation by 1830, the *Workingman's Advocate,* Evans adopted a political platform that was strikingly similar to Wedderburn's arguments in *Axe Laid to the Root*. He called for the immediate abolition of slavery, radical land reform, the cessation of all trafficking of people or land, support for the ten-hour day for factory workers, the unionization of female factory operatives, and praise for Nat Turner in 1831, whose violence in defense of his personal liberty Evans deemed justified. In both the United States and in Great Britain, the working class came into being explicitly as an antislavery formation, a fact only partially appreciated by historians of either labor or abolition. Central to that political accomplishment was the tradition of antitrafficking, a deeply expansive critique of political economy that linked opposition to debt and land monopolies to the abolition of slavery and human trafficking.[8]

Yet to view Wedderburn's radicalism as the logical or inevitable culmination of plebeian resistance to racial capitalism obscures conflicts and complexities within that same tradition. Antitrafficking emerged slowly and

---

8. George Henry Evans has long been controversial to labor historians, though less so to historians of abolition. Much of the focus has been on his very public debate with abolitionist Gerrit Smith in 1844 over the comparative importance of abolition and labor reform, with both men debating the merits of the issues known as "white slavery." See Evans, "To Gerrit Smith," *Working Man's Advocate* (New York), July 6, 1844, [3]. For the significance of Evans and Smith's debate to abolitionist histories, see Jonathan H. Earle, *Jacksonian Antislavery and the Politics of Free Soil, 1824–1854* (Chapel Hill, N.C., 2004), 60–61; and John Stauffer, *The Black Hearts of Men: Radical Abolitionists and the Transformation of Race* (Cambridge, Mass., 2001), 136–137. For labor-based analyses of Evans's racism, see David R. Roediger, *Wages of Whiteness: Race and the Making of the American Working Class* (London, 1991), 71; and W[illiam] E[dward] Burghardt Du Bois, *Black Reconstruction: An Essay toward a History of the Part Which Black Folk Played in the Attempt to Reconstruct Democracy in America, 1860–1880* (New York, 1935), 17. For an exploration of what Evans learned from his debate with Smith, see Gunther Peck, "Labor Abolition and the Politics of White Victimhood: Rethinking the History of Working-Class Racism," *Journal of the Early Republic*, XXXIX (2019), 89–98.

in episodic fashion over the seventeenth and eighteenth centuries, even as it became a resource for challenging the British state's capacity to regulate markets in people. The political character of antitrafficking, like antislavery ideology, was inconsistent and geographically fragmented across most of the seventeenth and eighteenth centuries. In the Mediterranean, being sold represented the primary path to freedom for many captive sailors, hindering the articulation of systemic critiques of human trafficking. Although Thomas Lurting refused to sell any of his captors, risking his life and freedom for his principles, his example collided with the pragmatic reality that most captive sailors depended on human trafficking to survive as sailors or be redeemed if captured. Being trafficked across the Atlantic, by contrast, intensified the power of masters to control the lives, livelihoods, and bodies of unfree laborers, whether indentured, transported, or enslaved. More important, conflict among the trafficked—between sailors on slave ships and the enslaved as well as between servants and enslaved laborers on plantations—hampered collaboration among the trafficked against common ship captains or shared masters.

Alliances between transported servants, impressed sailors, and enslaved peoples occurred, but they were more often temporary and pragmatic rather than sustained and principled, adaptations to common cruelties at the hands of shared masters or particularly abusive ship captains, as in the case of Robert Barker. Nor were human trafficking and enslavement equivalent historical phenomena. Not every human bought and sold in the Americas became enslaved, even if every African who endured the Middle Passage across the Atlantic was offered for sale on arrival in the Americas. Across the Mediterranean, not all captives became slaves or thought of themselves as such, even if the booming traffic in captive sailors provided large numbers of enslaved peoples for both Muslim and Christian polities. Recognizing the historical differences between commerce in people and enslavement sharpens how we see key complexities among the trafficked and why there emerged no singular form of resistance to human trafficking.

At the same time, the history of antitrafficking clarifies how and why antislavery became so politically contested across the seventeenth and eighteenth centuries. Antislavery was not an incipient form of abolitionist thought and practice; rather, it was a language deployed by sovereigns when exercising power, a key vehicle for expanding control over newly conquered and trafficked subjects and goods. As such, antislavery was deployed by sovereign authorities to protect royal prerogatives and their protrafficking policies. Across much of the seventeenth century, antislavery functioned as a tool for sovereigns to assert power. Antitrafficking, by contrast, was a more protean political energy, one that critiqued political authority and exposed its ideological limits. Although antitrafficking would, in time, help to transform antislavery into a vehicle for articulating systemic economic critiques as well as proposals for creating emancipatory power in both the Mediterranean and the Atlantic, abolitionism was not the logical culmination of antislavery thought and practice. Rather, abolition was an unlikely consequence of the historical contingencies that trafficked and enslaved people themselves brought about by resisting human commerce.

When captive sailors in the Mediterranean and indentured servants across the Atlantic described themselves as slaves during the 1670s, they were rallying family members, religious societies, and political authorities to secure their freedom and to change the policies that had led to them being trafficked in the first place. Although the resulting Servant Registry of 1671 and the Royal Slave Fund of 1680 did not end the policies that enabled the trafficking of English subjects at home and abroad, the servants, captive sailors, and transported convicts who protested being sold as so-called slaves nonetheless transformed the possibilities of antislavery discourse in the late seventeenth century, exposing the mischief done in the name of fighting slavery along the way. That mischief included efforts by the English crown to mollify the antislavery demands of trafficked Atlantic servants and captive Mediterranean sailors by expanding participation in the African slave trade. Sequestering the trafficked from the enslaved and the Mediterranean from the Atlantic were imperial maneuvers meant to contain the challenges produced by antitrafficking across disparate parts of England's growing empire. The displaced Virginia-bound indentures who ended up trafficked into slavery in North Africa in 1679 created the perfect storm of unruly subjects for the architects of England's empire of trafficking.

Outlets for trafficked Atlantic servants and captive Mediterranean sailors to air their grievances at the beginning of the eighteenth century were rare and sporadic. With the exception of Aphra Behn's novel, *Oroonoko*, and Thomas Southerne's subsequent theatrical adaptation of Behn's work, which framed so-called white slaves as existential threats to British nobility and their allegedly superior antislavery sensibilities, English literary culture before 1750 provided few opportunities for them to be seen or heard. Over the first half of the eighteenth century, British print culture slowly became more accessible to trafficked individuals, especially those held captive and sold in the Mediterranean. Narratives about human trafficking yielded mixed results for the intrepid authors who published their stories. In the case of Robert Drury, collaboration with Daniel Defoe was a necessity, but it also saddled his story with a host of dubious literary forms and exotic romances as well as antislavery rhetoric and white racial tropes that complicated the question of the text's authorship for centuries thereafter. Commercial writer Richard Goadby similarly transformed the plebeian narrative of Bampfylde-Moore Carew, heightening both antislavery rhetoric and race talk while minimizing Carew's powerful critiques of human trafficking.

Expanding access to printing presses around mid-century, however, began to offer new platforms for authors who had been trafficked, even as trafficking one's story about trafficking generated both dilemmas and opportunities for authors. Carew and William Moraley each sought justice by advancing powerful critiques of British transportation and impressment, while Thomas Troughton zeroed in on a more personal target, calling out the calumny of his former ship captain in sanctioning sailor enslavements in North Africa. Robert Barker similarly sought a measure of justice against his former ship captain. Other plebeian writers published their narratives for material gain, such as Henry Grace and Peter Williamson, who both sought military pensions. Although Grace and Williamson failed in their attempt to obtain pensions and Grace's volume was never reprinted, Williamson nevertheless discovered the power of condemning an entire class of shipping merchants while dressed in the imagined head gear of a Delaware Indian. Commercial and political success could move in tandem for authors of such narratives, even if such results complicated what was historically true and knowable in their stories, a case in point illustrated by John Jewitt's eventual publishing success as the white slave of Maquinna. For commercial and untrained writers alike, print culture was associated with a complex mixture of political artifacts, including a greater likelihood to describe trafficking as slavery and an expanded facility after 1760 with tropes of racial suffering and white victimhood. Those who deployed both stood to obtain increased commercial success.

Even as print culture created a vital means for some writers to be heard, it also resulted in an uneven playing field for others that increased writers' dependence on supportive patrons. Phillis Wheatley's remarkable poetry challenged the emerging American nation to become the antislavery polity it claimed to be but was not in practice. Yet her second volume of poems, which contained her anticipated response to the racism and hypocrisy of the nation's founders, never found a publisher because of the scarcity of patrons in the nation she had so powerfully imagined. Olaudah Equiano, on the other hand, was more successful in harnessing commercial success and English patrons to abolitionist ends, a remarkable accomplishment in the history of antitrafficking and antislavery storytelling. His appreciation of an alternative political economy in the Mediterranean, one not organized as yet by racism in the 1770s, also spoke to the radical potential of the geographic imagination long displayed by trafficked and enslaved authors. Equiano's success, however, was the exception that proved a larger rule, that print culture could simultaneously serve to expand both antislavery and racist tropes in narratives of the trafficked.[9]

When Peter Williamson and later John Jewitt experimented with linking notions of white suffering to radical critiques of human trafficking, they furthered but did not complete a transformation that would make white victimhood a naturalized political fact. Yet Williamson and Jewitt were hardly the first to have conjured white suffering as their foundation for critiquing human trafficking. The efforts to divert, ignore, or transform the antitrafficking sentiments of plebeian actors into support for elite rule were almost as old as the imperial grammars of skin color manifest in the Servant Registry of 1671 and the literary efforts of Behn and later Defoe that vindicated aristocratic rule at the expense of trafficked peoples at home and abroad. It was among elites seeking to justify the policing of both enslaved and trafficked peoples that a notion of whiteness centered on racial suffering initially took hold. From its earliest articulations, whiteness was a mercantilist discourse, one used by its practitioners to mark, count, and commodify trafficked servants. The first stories about whiteness were revisionist in nature, novel narratives that effaced their origins in human trafficking by appropriating the powerful arguments against human trafficking that plebeian actors themselves articulated. Over time, white racial ideology became persuasive as a narrative of white suffering, one that stood in direct opposition to alliances between whites and Blacks, the men and women whose united actions against common masters terrified colonial, metropolitan, and later national authorities.

The success of white racial revisionism resided in the political necessities of imperial rule and governance: namely, the need to conjure a politics that could divide Blacks and whites from each other while simultaneously disciplining trafficked whites whose labor also remained vital to building empires and nations. Revisionism became an essential part of white racial ideology, not because white people were more prone to evasion than other groups of humans in history, but because imperial rule and the class-based ideologies that supported it required artifacts that could sunder ties between trafficked peoples while still policing trafficked whites. Stories and images of white

---

9. David Waldstreicher, *The Odyssey of Phillis Wheatley: A Poet's Journeys through American Slavery and Independence* (New York, 2023), 324–342.

victimhood along with conspiracies to kill white people like those conjured by Daniel Horsmanden grew powerful and persuasive, not through public executions, but when trafficked whites themselves began to embrace a politics of racial suffering during the late eighteenth and early nineteenth centuries. The belief that whites experienced suffering *because* of their skin color became an enduring and characteristic feature of white racial ideology through literary dramatization and repetition. White suffering became a habit of thought in both fiction and in policies, a social fact as natural as skin color itself with no apparent history.

Wars and their aftermath in North America, the Seven Years' War, the American Revolution, and the War of 1812, each elevated racialized suffering and antislavery ideology on both sides of the Atlantic. The prominence of antislavery sentiment in waging and making war did not alter the deep ambivalence North American elites possessed toward trafficked whites and enslaved peoples. The U.S. Naturalization Act adopted in 1790 during the early days of the new Republic codified two classes of whites, one worthy and the other trafficked, unfree, and therefore excludable. The imperative of keeping some whites out while letting others in, of creating a selective filter at odds with the fiction of a singular white race, was not new and certainly not original or unique to the American nation. The 1790 Naturalization Act nevertheless helped foster an enduring tradition of mutable whiteness and revision among immigrant groups inhabiting the United States that echoed the deep class ambivalence of mercantilist planners toward whites. Some whites remained worthy of emulation; others were threats to the very fabric of the nation. Whiteness within U.S. immigration law was revisable from its inception. An imperial instrument, white racial ideology was built to travel, to discriminate, and to traverse mercantile and later national boundaries. Yet it became hegemonic outside the confines of a single polity or the interests of a particular class or an exceptional nation, no matter how corrupted by the original sin of racial slavery. To see white racial ideology as the product of American exceptionalism is to reverse the historical sequence and to evade harder questions about the global origins of racism as well as the resistance to it enacted by trafficked peoples across the planet.

The global origins of the 1790 U.S. Naturalization Act might have been lost on its authors in the first U.S. Congress, but the idea of alien whiteness persisted in discourse about white races and would continue to provide opportunities for American jurists to revise and restrict the criteria for U.S. citizenship and naturalization over the next century and a half. When Takao Ozawa, an immigrant who had been born in Japan, insisted he was an American citizen in his pleading to the U.S. Supreme Court in 1922, he claimed he was white and American by virtue of his skin color and his culture, having raised children who were Christian and who spoke no Japanese. In so doing, Ozawa animated a centuries-old discourse about white skin color that used it to signify political virtues among peoples living outside the boundaries of a Christian nation. Supreme Court Justice George Sutherland dismissed Ozawa's case using racialized science, insisting Ozawa could not be Caucasian since he was born in Japan to Japanese parents. The same justices would reverse course a few months later when denying the citizenship claim of Bhagat Singh Thind, an Indian immigrant born in the Caucasus who argued that racial science and nativity proved he was white as a "Caucasian." Writing for the majority, Justice Marshall Harlan insisted only everyday perceptions of the "common man" should be used to define the boundaries of whiteness moving forward. The revisability of whiteness had rarely been so vivid in law, but this legal spectacle exemplified that political fact about the mercurial meaning of white skin color. Whiteness gained power not only by separating so-called whites from peoples of color but by ratifying hierarchies among whites, whether citizens or aliens. To the jurists shaping the imperial boundaries of the American nation in the early twentieth century, white racial revision was vital to defining the rights of citizens and noncitizens alike, whether excluded immigrants or lesser whites with immigrant surnames.[10]

How much of this political mischief was visible or foreseeable to Robert Wedderburn in 1819 is hard to know. He might have read John Jewitt's or even Peter Williamson's stories or even seen the authors perform their racial masquerades. Like them, Wedderburn told a powerful and deeply personal testimony about human trafficking using his body to make his story vivid and compelling. Unlike Jewitt or Williamson, Wedderburn said nothing about whiteness or race in his speeches or his published sermons. He might have taken pride in the fact that his arguments about land, human trafficking, and slavery were supported by key leaders of the emerging working classes

---

10. On Takao Ozawa's effort to win citizenship before the U.S. Supreme Court, see Ian Haney López, *White by Law: The Legal Construction of Race* (New York, 2006), 56–61. On Justice Harlan's ruling that the "free white person" standard of the 1790 Naturalization Act is a matter of "common speech" to be defined by "the common man," see United States v. Thind, 261 U.S. at 204 (1923), 204, 209; and López, *White by Law*, 64. For additional discussions of the Ozawa and Thind cases, see Doug Coulson, *Race, Nation, and Refuge: The Rhetoric of Race in Asian American Citizenship Cases* (Albany, N.Y., 2017); and Jennifer C. Snow, *Protestant Missionaries, Asian Immigrants, and Ideologies of Race in America, 1850–1924* (New York, 2007).

on both sides of the Atlantic. Yet the ideas of Oastler and Evans in the late 1820s, like Jewitt and Williamson, differed from Wedderburn's message in one very important respect. Oastler and Evans condemned the crimes of human trafficking in Britain and America as examples of white slavery, an injustice they claimed was as bad if not worse than the violence enacted on enslaved peoples of African descent across the Americas. Although Evans and Oastler insisted opposition to white slavery was compatible with immediate Black abolition, they animated a narrative that in time displaced Wedderburn's radical message. If antislavery could become a handmaiden for expanding imperial prerogatives over marketplaces for goods and people, so, too, could hostility to trafficking be remade into a vehicle ratifying elite power. This was, in fact, an old lesson, as the story of the Servant Registry in 1671 suggests. By the 1840s, the combustible mixture of radical economic critique and white victimhood was gaining collective strength, not only among working-class actors but among abolitionists on both sides of the Atlantic. By the 1850s, even a defender of slavery, George Fitzhugh, could champion a critique of white slavery in the North to defend the South's allegedly peculiar institution. Gender and melodrama were central to these transformations in antitrafficking and antislavery, as polemicists in both the U.S. South and the U.S. North weaponized images of white womanhood to defend arguments on behalf of trafficking and slavery.[11]

The differences between Wedderburn and the likes of Oastler and Evans, then, were profound, with consequential and enduring outcomes. Wedderburn exposed unavoidable facts about human trafficking within Great Brit-

---

11. Richard Oastler, "A Letter on the Horrors of White Slavery," *Leeds Mercury*, Oct. 16, 1830, original in Goldsmith Kress Collection, University of London Senate House Library. For George Henry Evans's first use of the term *white slavery*, see his debate with abolitionist Gerrit Smith in 1844 in Evans, "To Gerrit Smith," *Workingman's Advocate*, July 6, 1844, [3]. For a fuller explication of the relationship between American and British class formations and whiteness, see Gunther Peck, "White Slavery and Whiteness: A Transnational View of the Sources of Working-Class Radicalism and Racism," *Labor*, I, no. 2 (Summer 2004), 41–63. For a more damning portrait of Evans and his role in the creation of working-class racism, see Roediger, *Wages of Whiteness*, 77–80. The question of whether the abolitionists furthered white supremacy or effectively challenged it is a matter of vigorous debate. On abolitionists as pioneering antiracists, see Paul Goodman, *Of One Blood: Abolitionism and the Origins of Racial Equality* (Berkeley, Calif., 1998); and Henry Mayer, *All on Fire: William Lloyd Garrison and the Abolition of Slavery* (New York, 1998). For more sober assessments of the racism of white abolitionists, see David W. Blight, *Frederick Douglass: Prophet of Freedom* (New York, 2018); Martha S. Jones, *Birthright Citizens:*

ain's inhumane empire and economy, the animating thefts that immiserated the men, women, and children who were trafficked across the empire. Oastler and Evans, by contrast, built their critiques of slavery, trafficking, and nation around a revisionist narrative of white suffering, condemning child labor in factories as an expansive form of white slavery. Although Oastler and Evans supported abolition, their narrative innovations instead made white victimhood the starting point for political critique and for emancipation in both nations at the dawn of the industrial era. In both Great Britain and the United States, the working classes were raced from their inception. Whiteness did not so much co-opt or destroy working-class consciousness as constitute the political fabric from which it sprang across the Atlantic world.

The linking of racialism to radicalism was not new or unique to British and American working-class actors during the 1820s. That comingling had a long history among British elites, whether inventors of the antislavery novel or architects of transportation as an allegedly humane, antislavery policy. As in the late seventeenth century, elite actors continued to be far more likely to deploy grammars of skin color and race. Yet as Jewitt, and Williamson before him, demonstrated, plebeian images of white suffering changed what antislavery and class relations looked like. The eventual embrace of white slavery abolitionism by workers on both sides of the Atlantic by the 1840s would make racism and white supremacy far more dynamic, resilient, and enduring than at any point between 1619 and 1819. From then on, whiteness would become an emancipatory rhetoric for an already racialized working class as well as for powerful and privileged actors, an ideology disguised as an identity that was

---

*A History of Race and Rights in Antebellum America* (New York, 2018); and Kantrowitz, *More Than Freedom*. When southern proslavery polemicist George Fitzhugh embraced the cause of white slavery abolitionism to defend chattel slavery in the U.S. South in 1857, he appropriated the words and logic of both Evans and labor radical Sarah Bagley in 1846. Fitzhugh's theft of Bagley's words to valorize white patriarchal power exemplifies the challenges that white wage-earning women encountered in trying to turn antislavery and antitrafficking to their ends as a class. See Bagley and Evans, "The Factory Girls—White Slavery at Lowell," *Young America! Organ of the National Reform Association* (New York), Jan. 3, 1846, [2]; and [Fitzhugh], "The Conservative Principle; or, Social Evils and Their Remedies; Part II; Slave Trade," *DeBow's Review* (Columbia, S.C.), May 1857, 449–462. On the role of working-class women in the antebellum antislavery movement, see Julie Roy Jeffrey, *The Great Silent Army of Abolitionism: Ordinary Women in the Antislavery Movement* (Chapel Hill, N.C., 1998); Susan Zaeske, *Signatures of Citizenship: Petitioning, Antislavery, and Women's Political Identity* (Chapel Hill, N.C., 2003); and Bruce Laurie, *Beyond Garrison: Antislavery and Social Reform* (New York, 2005).

now capable of transcending the diverse forms of human trafficking that had birthed it. In the 1820s, these developments, however, were still in motion, narrative questions rather than conclusions about the political content of both antitrafficking and race.

Although there were several political causes at home and abroad in the early 1820s that the radical Wedderburn might have celebrated, one event in particular, the outbreak of the Greek Revolution of 1821, would link abolition, antitrafficking, and Christianity into a single compelling battle. The most dramatic moment in the Greek Revolution—the Siege of Missolonghi, which ended with the capture, enslavement, trafficking, and dispersal of thousands of Greeks in 1826—would lead European powers to intervene on behalf of the struggling Greek rebellion in the name of abolition and race, building on the rhetoric and sentiments established by European powers at the Congress of Vienna. The fight for Greek independence, one that had only recently pitted a diverse multitude of Muslims and Christians against one another, with Albanian fighters playing key roles for both sides, had now become a fight for Christianity and civilization against a newly racialized Ottoman enemy.[12]

French painter Victor Delacroix vividly brought the revisionist story of race and traffic in the Greek Revolution to life in his 1826 canvas *Greece on the Ruins of Missolonghi*. The work featured the nation of Greece as a bare-breasted white woman being captured by a dark-skinned African wearing a turban (Figure 18). Christianity, white womanhood, and the European nation had been enslaved by Africa and Islam. Previously, skin color had played little role in shaping conflicts between Turkish and Greek peoples. Now their religious and political conflicts were replaced by a timeless image of white suffering, with trafficking a one-sided predation by Africa and Islam against Europe and Christianity. The British architect of white slavery abolitionism in the Mediterranean, Sir Sydney Smith, was no doubt proud of that revision, though also likely anxious to prove his abolitionist credentials through war on Muslim people.[13]

Images of female Greek slaves would grow in importance in the United

---

12. Mark Mazower, *The Greek Revolution: 1821 and the Making of Modern Europe* (New York, 2021), xxxv.

13. On Delacroix's painting and the racism behind support for Greek independence, see ibid., 337–338. No definitive biography of Sir Sidney Smith exists. He lived until 1840. At the time of the Greek Revolution during the 1820s, he was living in Paris. There are no records of what he thought about that military campaign.

FIGURE 18. Eugène Delacroix. *La Grèce sur les ruines de Missolonghi (Greece on the Ruins of Missolonghi)*. 1826. Oil on canvas. Musée des Beaux-Arts de Bordeaux. Bx E 439. Courtesy of Wikimedia, https://commons.wikimedia.org/wiki/File:Eugène_Ferdinand_Victor_Delacroix_017.jpg

States over the ensuing decades. In 1843, the American sculptor Hiram Powers successfully crafted and then exhibited a white marble statue of a naked woman in chains entitled the *Greek Slave*. Embraced by abolitionists in cities across the U.S. North as a way of advancing a larger antislavery project that linked the Greek revolutionary struggle to feminist struggles on behalf of women and African American slaves, the statue was conversely received in the U.S. South as an image of white female purity, a figure whose innocence needed to be defended by all chaste and moral observers. Just so did the *Greek*

*Slave* enable abolitionism to be linked to white racism, a concession to race trafficking that paralleled the growing engagement by both abolitionists and working-class leaders with white slavery abolitionism. Indeed, despite the simmering regional tensions between the North and South in the United States, both sides collaborated in the 1840s in amplifying a vernacular of white suffering in the cause of region, a revision that rejected the broader antislavery project of working-class women and enslaved African Americans then concurrently lobbying for women's rights and abolition. Mediterranean whiteness had become central to the power and meaning of white victimhood and white racism the world over.[14]

In retrospect, the outlines of defeat for Wedderburn and his motley crew seem clear, even as he sharpened his metaphorical axe in 1817. Many of the leaders of the emerging labor and abolitionist movements did not seek to fashion a broader movement of labor abolition but talked past one another. The outlines of a transoceanic project of white supremacy built on narratives of white victimhood, in turn, were clearly visible in both the Atlantic and the Mediterranean in the wake of Napoleon's defeat. Imperial innovations in the name of antislavery and whiteness were unleashing reactionary responses to trafficked and enslaved actors across the expanding reaches of Anglo-American power. Conflicts among trafficked people remained profound and enduring, providing few examples for how a child laborer in York, an impressed sailor in the Mediterranean, or an enslaved artisan from Africa toiling in South Carolina might forge common cause against the same wealthy classes who benefited from their labors. Nor were Britain and America's factory workers, however impoverished and unfree, enslaved, even if many were trafficked. Factory workers who claimed to be enslaved could just as easily express resentment toward the enslaved as solidarity with them. There were good reasons to believe collaboration between the labor and abolitionist movements around an expansive antislavery vision would falter.[15]

---

14. On the significance of the *Greek Slave* to the histories of women's rights, race, and abolition, see Jean Fagan Yellin, *Women and Sisters: The Antislavery Feminists in American Culture* (New Haven, Conn., 1989), 99–124; Joy S. Kasson, *Marble Queens and Captives: Women in Nineteenth-Century American Sculpture* (New Haven, Conn., 1990), 46–72; and Mazower, *Greek Revolution*, 452.

15. For a fuller analysis of labor abolition, see Peck, "Labor Abolition and the Politics of White Victimhood," *Journal of the Early Republic*, XXXIX (2019), 89–98; Sinha, *Slave's Cause*, 339–380; and Roediger, *Wages of Whiteness*, 80–87.

In his final years, Wedderburn himself struggled to stay true to the arguments he proffered in *The Axe Laid to the Root*. The last thing Wedderburn published in 1831, an address to Britain's new lord chancellor Henry Brougham, first baron Brougham and Vaux, recanted his earlier radicalism, calling for compensation to all slaveholders for the loss of their human property should the government emancipate enslaved Jamaicans. That "disturbing change of heart," as one historian recently put it, was as unexpected and remarkable as the radical vision Wedderburn had articulated in his hayloft fifteen years earlier. Why would Wedderburn, so fearless and determined to stop human trafficking, turn aside from the justice project he had so powerfully championed? Few immediate answers emerge from the documentary record, but the longer history of plebeian antitrafficking provides some clues. Like Henry Grace, Robert Barker, and other penniless authors before him who had struggled to traffic their narratives of human suffering, Wedderburn sought security in his final published missive, a kind of pension that might protect him from absolute destitution. He was seventy when he wrote his appeal to Lord Brougham and had just been "sentenced to twelve months imprisonment, and hard labour" at sea. Wedderburn clarified the purpose of his address to Lord Brougham in the very next sentence of his appeal. "I then would be most happy to be forwarded in the same ship . . . to gain much more information for the government" about slavery and emancipation in Jamaica. Spied on by government detectives during his prime, Wedderburn now proposed becoming a spy on behalf of a government he hoped would ship him back to his place of birth. To bolster his case, Wedderburn again recounted the horrific trauma of watching his mother being beaten as a young man: "My mother was . . . stretched on the ground, and actually flogged before me, while she was in a state of pregnancy." For Wedderburn, a lifetime of recounting this tale of outrage had left him penniless but also with a deep sense of longing to return to his community of origin as it experienced emancipation. Why not have the British government pay his way to Jamaica?[16]

That strategic sensibility linked Wedderburn to generations of trafficked sailors, servants, and enslaved peoples every bit as much as his radical rhetoric

---

16. [Robert Wedderburn], *An Address to the Right Honourable Lord Brougham and Vaux* . . . (London, 1831), [3], [16], as reprinted in Ryan Hanley, "A Radical Change of Heart: Robert Wedderburn's Last Word on Slavery," *Slavery and Abolition*, XXXVII (2016), 423–445, esp. 433, 441. On Brougham's conservative approach to abolition, see Robin Blackburn, *The Overthrow of Colonial Slavery, 1776–1848* (London, 1988), 436–459.

on behalf of the trafficked and the landless in 1817. Like them, Wedderburn was no stranger to the contradictions inherent in trafficking. As a storyteller, he had to persuade his readers and listeners of his sincerity, whatever their views and outlook. Like a sailor redeemed from Barbary, the only thing Wedderburn still possessed was his story. Recounting it had become a necessity for his survival. That the British state should be the object of Wedderburn's desire in his final missive should come as no surprise, for he had long enlisted the loyalties of the powerful with the force of his suffering. When in prison for blasphemy, Wedderburn had met none other than William Wilberforce, who with him had planned the publication of *The Horrors of Slavery* on his return to London's East End in 1824. Seven years later, an ailing Wedderburn told Lord Brougham what he thought Brougham wanted to hear, that emancipation should be transactional and gradual in form and that slaves should pay the costs of their individual freedom. Wedderburn likely never met any wardens of the Ironmongers' Company, but he certainly understood their ethic, that only transactional emancipations could be truly humanitarian.

What Wedderburn did not tell Lord Brougham in his appeal was also significant, that he had been convicted of running a brothel in London's East End earlier that year. On that charge, Wedderburn offered no contrary evidence or explanation. Trafficking the sexual labor of women had apparently become his only reliable livelihood, despite his origin story as a product of rape and sexual theft. If Wedderburn perceived any inconsistencies between the charge against him and his narrative, he did not reveal them. Nor is it likely Lord Brougham perceived any hypocrisy, for Brougham was an expedient abolitionist, a powerful man who cared little about the rights of enslaved people, the status of sex workers, whether free or enslaved, or the needs of a radical Black preacher. Indeed, he ignored Wedderburn's appeal entirely, refusing even to recognize his political standing as a British subject with a reply. So, Wedderburn did not return to his Jamaican homeland as a government spy or as a celebrant in the coming jubilee. Instead, he performed another year of hard labor at sea and slipped into obscurity on his return, dying just months after the emancipation of his Jamaican patriots from slavery on January 5, 1835. He was buried in London in a pauper's grave.

Remembering Robert Wedderburn and the radical antitrafficking and antislavery narrative he and others crafted represents an ongoing political challenge. A victim himself of racial revisionism, Wedderburn's legacy matters because he so sharply confronted the harms of human trafficking to British experience and identity, to the enslaved African and the British commoner alike, to the church and its believers, to the nation and its advocates, and to the land and its occupants. Between 1815 and 1820, on the eve of working-class formation, Wedderburn brilliantly exposed the state authorities who were making enormous profits from selling people and dispossessing their lands. Because of the power of his words and the humanity he embodied, he provided a road map to a redeemed political economy without racism or Faustian bargains with white suffering at its core. He did not pit Black against white in his speeches, even if he underscored just how exceptionally violent human trafficking within chattel slavery was for enslaved Black women, men, and their children. If abolition and labor were to enhance one another in a broader emancipatory project, racial identities of necessity mattered, but they could not serve as the end point for political organizing and action. For those listening to Wedderburn in his seedy hayloft, a genuinely transformed world still seemed imminent, a jubilee borne of unshakable religious aspiration and unflinching critique of the hypocrisies of antislavery nations. National and spiritual redemption could not be abandoned in that pressing struggle any more than antislavery could be left to the imperial planners who had labored so long to control and suppress it. Nation and faith constituted foundational tools for ending human trafficking, Wedderburn believed. On that point, he agreed with trafficked sailors, many enslaved people, and political elites like William Wilberforce, Lord Brougham, and the romantic defenders of the Greek Revolution.

Wedderburn's vision of a just nation and a religious tradition that could liberate the trafficked and the enslaved did not die in 1835. On the contrary, it continued to move men and women of every hue, creed, and faith to action. We live with the consequences of these unfinished battles over race traffic and the fate of our own humanity into the present.

## APPENDIX A

# The Colonial State Papers

The Colonial State Papers (CSP) is an online database pairing more than forty thousand bibliographic entries compiled and published by British civil servants in the 1870s as *The Calendar of State Papers, Colonial: America and the West Indies, 1574–1739* with full-page scans of the original documents housed at the British National Archives in the Colonial Office record series CO 1, "Privy Council and Related Bodies: America and West Indies, Colonial Papers," one of several records series on which the *Calendar* is based. The papers contained therein include largely correspondence between colonial entities and metropolitan administrators presented to the Board of Trade and the Privy Council in London between 1574 and 1739. The efforts of the *Calendar*'s early cataloguers to systematize Britain's imperial history made imperial records legible to British political leaders and researchers at the peak of British power. Now, researchers can link *Calendar* summaries to page scans of the original documents.

Keyword searches of the CSP constitute an invaluable tool for researchers studying British colonial expansion, but they can also be challenging to use for at least two reasons. First, the *Calendar* entries, a mixture of summaries and partial transcriptions, constitute the entirety of the database's searchable text. Although researchers can access page scans of the original documents on which the *Calendar* entries are based, the text of those documents is not searchable, which limits the archival range and representativeness of keyword searching. The second factor is that British civil servants, while conscientious and faithful bibliographers of British imperial correspondence, introduced occasional errors into the *Calendar*, changing language in the handwritten originals and even omitting passages or including phrases that were not in the original documents. These errors were often associated with white grammar, the adjectives assigned to varied human actors over the course of the late seventeenth and early eighteenth centuries (see Table 7). All of these revisionist keywords have been excluded from my tabulations of white grammar and my comparison of white servants and Christian servants, with only keywords in the original sources tabulated and analyzed. Rather than viewing keyword searches in the *Calendar* as the actual words of British imperial actors in the seventeenth and eighteenth centuries, then, I have used keyword searches to establish which original primary documents to read in the British National Archives. I have created separate databases for the following keywords: *Christian servant(s)*, *white servant(s)*, *whites*, *white people*, *white m(e)n*, *white wom(e)n*, and *white slave(s)*. I have recorded each utterance in the original documents as a separate entry within the respective keyword databases.

To discern the political work associated with white grammar, I have kept careful track of the timing and context for the appearance of each keyword, asking a series of "yes" or "no" questions of each reference. "Numbered" indicates whether a particular keyword was accompanied by a numeric integer. "Militia" denotes whether the designated keyword was described in association with the militia. "With Black" tracks whether the particular keyword was accompanied by any mention of Black or "Negro" subjects. "Rights" measures whether specific benefits or political privileges, however minimal, were mentioned in connection to the designated subject. When Christian servants were owed land on completing their indentures or when white men were described as being able to protest abusive treatment or violence by a colonial master in a legal proceeding, for example, I have coded these subjects as possessing rights. "Humanity" assesses whether the specific language of humanity or inhumanity, that is, humane or inhumane treatment, was mentioned in connection to a particular subject. The most common example of language associated with "Humanity" involved the efforts of metropolitan officials to restrain "inhumane severity" by masters toward their servants. "Unruly," in turn, denotes whether colonial or metropolitan authorities noted any rebellious behavior associated with a particular subject. Such behavior included running away from a master, abusive speech toward political or religious authorities, violating local ordinances policing the mobility of colonial subjects, becoming a pirate, or, in rarer instances, joining with enslaved actors in rebellion against shared masters.

I have chosen to adopt these thematic categories owing to their preponderance in the original sources as well as their historical significance for trafficked actors. For certain keywords like *whites* and *Blacks*, I have also kept track of whether they were paired with one another or appeared on their own. The tables are descriptive tabulations of both the frequency of particular terms as well as their changing meanings and context. The absence of a given theme such as "Rights" does not indicate a particular subject did not possess them, only that a discussion of rights did not appear in that specific textual reference. The databases do not reveal why meanings waxed or waned over time, moreover, only that such semantic patterns and trends existed. The relatively infrequent articulation of imperial anxieties about the unruly behavior of Christian servants after 1690, for example, does not mean individual Christian servants had become happier with their masters, only that colonial leaders articulated their anxieties about servants using white grammar instead. These tables highlight the specific kinds of political work that colonial and metropolitan elites associated with white grammar regarding trafficked whites and white subjecthood.

TABLE 1. Mentions of White Grammar by Keyword in the Colonial State Papers, 1661–1720

| | KEYWORD | | | | | | | | | | |
|---|---|---|---|---|---|---|---|---|---|---|---|
| | White servants | | Whites | | White men | | White women | | White people | | Total | |
| Decades | N | % | N | % | N | % | N | % | N | % | N | % |
| 1661–1670 | 0 | 0 | 12 | 75 | 3 | 19 | 0 | 0 | 1 | 6 | 16 | 100 |
| 1671–1680 | 89 | 59 | 36 | 24 | 19 | 13 | 1 | 1 | 7 | 5 | 152 | 102 |
| 1681–1690 | 28 | 50 | 13 | 23 | 14 | 25 | 1 | 2 | 0 | 0 | 56 | 100 |
| 1691–1700 | 92 | 61 | 11 | 7 | 42 | 28 | 3 | 2 | 4 | 3 | 152 | 101 |
| 1701–1710 | 59 | 44 | 12 | 9 | 48 | 36 | 5 | 4 | 9 | 7 | 133 | 100 |
| 1711–1720 | 24 | 13 | 16 | 9 | 76 | 42 | 14 | 8 | 50 | 28 | 180 | 100 |
| Total | 292 | — | 100 | — | 202 | — | 24 | — | 71 | — | 689 | — |
| % of total | — | 42 | — | 15 | — | 29 | — | 3 | — | 10 | — | 99 |

*Note:* Some total percentages do not equal 100 owing to rounding.

TABLE 2. Mentions of White Servants by Category in the Colonial State Papers, 1661–1720

| Decades | INDIVIDUAL SERVANTS | | CATEGORY | | | | | | | | | | |
|---|---|---|---|---|---|---|---|---|---|---|---|---|---|
| | Total no. | Numbered | % of total no. | Militia | % of total no. | With Black | % of total no. | Rights | % of total no. | Humanity | % of total no. | Unruly | % of total no. |
| 1661–1670 | 0 | 0 | 0 | 0 | 0 | 0 | 0 | 0 | 0 | 0 | 0 | 0 | 0 |
| 1671–1680 | 89 | 80 | 90 | 8 | 9 | 83 | 93 | 0 | 0 | 0 | 0 | 4 | 4 |
| 1681–1690 | 28 | 9 | 32 | 19 | 68 | 9 | 32 | 0 | 0 | 3 | 11 | 7 | 25 |
| 1691–1700 | 92 | 17 | 18 | 38 | 41 | 17 | 18 | 9 | 10 | 4 | 4 | 23 | 25 |
| 1701–1710 | 59 | 16 | 27 | 23 | 39 | 20 | 34 | 18 | 31 | 1 | 2 | 3 | 5 |
| 1711–1720 | 24 | 7 | 29 | 9 | 38 | 9 | 38 | 6 | 25 | 0 | 0 | 3 | 13 |
| Total | 292 | 129 | — | 97 | — | 138 | — | 33 | — | 8 | — | 40 | — |
| % of total no. | — | — | 44 | — | 33 | — | 47 | — | 11 | — | 3 | — | 14 |

*Note:* Depending on the context in which the keyword appeared, it might be counted under several categories. The phrase "fifty white servants and 100 negroes," for example, yielded thematic hits for "Numbered" and "With Black."

TABLE 3. Mentions of Christian Servants by Category in the Colonial State Papers, 1661–1720

| Decades | INDIVIDUAL SERVANTS | | | CATEGORY | | | | | | | | | |
|---|---|---|---|---|---|---|---|---|---|---|---|---|---|
| | Total no. | Numbered | % of total no. | Militia | % of total no. | With Black | % of total no. | Rights | % of total no. | Humanity | % of total no. | Unruly | % of total no. |
| 1661–1670 | 11 | 4 | 36 | 6 | 55 | 5 | 45 | 5 | 45 | 0 | 0 | 2 | 18 |
| 1671–1680 | 22 | 1 | 5 | 7 | 32 | 12 | 55 | 8 | 36 | 3 | 14 | 6 | 27 |
| 1681–1690 | 29 | 3 | 10 | 10 | 34 | 17 | 59 | 7 | 24 | 8 | 28 | 1 | 3 |
| 1691–1700 | 44 | 2 | 5 | 19 | 43 | 19 | 43 | 22 | 50 | 22 | 50 | 4 | 9 |
| 1701–1710 | 16 | 1 | 6 | 2 | 13 | 5 | 31 | 11 | 69 | 9 | 56 | 0 | 0 |
| 1711–1720 | 0 | 0 | 0 | 0 | 0 | 0 | 0 | 0 | 0 | 0 | 0 | 0 | 0 |
| Total | 122 | 11 | — | 44 | — | 58 | — | 53 | — | 42 | — | 13 | — |
| % of total no. | — | — | 9 | — | 36 | — | 48 | — | 43 | — | 34 | — | 11 |

*Note:* Depending on the context in which the keyword appeared, it might be counted under several categories.

TABLE 4. Mentions of Blacks by Category in the Colonial State Papers, 1661–1720

| Decades | INDIVIDUAL BLACKS | | | CATEGORY | | | | | | | | |
|---|---|---|---|---|---|---|---|---|---|---|---|---|
| | Total no. | Numbered | % of total no. | Militia | % of total no. | With whites | % of total no. | Rights | % of total no. | Humanity | % of total no. | Unruly | % of total no. |
| 1661–1670 | 34 | 17 | 50 | 2 | 6 | 8 | 24 | 1 | 3 | 0 | 0 | 11 | 32 |
| 1671–1680 | 49 | 35 | 71 | 8 | 16 | 23 | 47 | 2 | 4 | 0 | 0 | 9 | 18 |
| 1681–1690 | 14 | 7 | 50 | 1 | 7 | 8 | 57 | 0 | 0 | 0 | 0 | 4 | 29 |
| 1691–1700 | 23 | 17 | 74 | 14 | 61 | 12 | 52 | 0 | 0 | 0 | 0 | 14 | 61 |
| 1701–1710 | 17 | 9 | 53 | 6 | 35 | 11 | 65 | 1 | 6 | 0 | 0 | 5 | 29 |
| 1711–1720 | 10 | 9 | 90 | 4 | 40 | 8 | 80 | 0 | 0 | 0 | 0 | 2 | 20 |
| Total | 147 | 94 | — | 35 | — | 70 | — | 4 | — | 0 | — | 45 | — |
| % of total no. | — | — | 64 | — | 24 | — | 48 | — | 3 | — | 0 | — | 31 |

*Note:* Depending on the context in which the keyword appeared, it might be counted under several categories.

TABLE 5. Mentions of Whites by Category in the Colonial State Papers, 1661–1720

| Decades | INDIVIDUAL WHITES | | | | | | CATEGORY | | | | | | |
|---|---|---|---|---|---|---|---|---|---|---|---|---|---|
| | Total no. | Numbered | % of total no. | Militia | % of total no. | With Black | % of total no. | Rights | % of total no. | Humanity | % of total no. | Unruly | % of total no. |
| 1661–1670 | 12 | 8 | 67 | 1 | 8 | 9 | 75 | 1 | 8 | 0 | 0 | 2 | 17 |
| 1671–1680 | 36 | 35 | 97 | 20 | 56 | 27 | 75 | 1 | 3 | 0 | 0 | 0 | 0 |
| 1681–1690 | 13 | 10 | 77 | 5 | 38 | 10 | 77 | 0 | 0 | 0 | 0 | 2 | 15 |
| 1691–1700 | 11 | 10 | 91 | 9 | 82 | 7 | 64 | 0 | 0 | 0 | 0 | 1 | 9 |
| 1701–1710 | 12 | 10 | 83 | 10 | 83 | 5 | 42 | 0 | 0 | 0 | 0 | 0 | 0 |
| 1711–1720 | 16 | 14 | 88 | 14 | 88 | 4 | 25 | 0 | 0 | 0 | 0 | 3 | 19 |
| Total | 100 | 87 | — | 59 | — | 62 | — | 2 | — | 0 | — | 8 | — |
| % of total no. | — | — | 87 | — | 59 | — | 62 | — | 2 | — | 0 | — | 8 |

*Note:* Depending on the context in which the keyword appeared, it might be counted under several categories.

TABLE 6. Mentions of Unruly Christian Servants versus White Servants in the Colonial State Papers, 1661–1720

|  | TYPE | | | | | |
|---|---|---|---|---|---|---|
|  | Christian | | White | | Total | |
| Decades | N | % | N | % | N | % |
| 1661–1680 | 8 | 67 | 4 | 33 | 12 | 100 |
| 1681–1700 | 5 | 14 | 30 | 86 | 35 | 100 |
| 1701–1720 | 0 | 0 | 6 | 100 | 6 | 100 |
| Total | 13 | — | 40 | — | 53 | — |
| % of total | — | 25 | — | 75 | — | 100 |

TABLE 7. Revisions to White Grammar in the *Calendar of State Papers* by Keyword, 1870s

|  | KEYWORDS | | | | | | | | | | |
|---|---|---|---|---|---|---|---|---|---|---|---|
|  | White servants | | Whites | | White men | | White immigrants | | White women | | Total | |
| Types of revision | N | % | N | % | N | % | N | % | N | % | N | % |
| Revisions to original sources | 67 | 80 | 12 | 14 | 2 | 2 | 1 | 1 | 2 | 2 | 84 | 99 |
| Revisions adding whiteness | 52 | 93 | 1 | 2 | 1 | 2 | 1 | 2 | 1 | 2 | 56 | 101 |

*Note:* Total percentages do not equal 100 owing to rounding.

TABLE 8. Mentions of White People by Category in the Colonial State Papers, 1661–1720

| Decades | INDIVIDUALS | | | CATEGORY | | | | | | | | | |
|---|---|---|---|---|---|---|---|---|---|---|---|---|---|
| | Total no. | Numbered | % of total no. | Militia | % of total no. | With Black | % of total no. | Rights | % of total no. | Humanity | % of total no. | Unruly | % of total no. |
| 1661–1680 | 8 | 1 | 13 | 2 | 25 | 8 | 100 | 0 | 0 | 0 | 0 | 4 | 50 |
| 1681–1700 | 4 | 1 | 25 | 3 | 75 | 1 | 25 | 0 | 0 | 0 | 0 | 2 | 50 |
| 1701–1720 | 59 | 23 | 39 | 25 | 42 | 19 | 32 | 25 | 42 | 0 | 0 | 3 | 5 |
| Total | 71 | 25 | — | 30 | — | 28 | — | 25 | — | 0 | — | 9 | — |
| % of total no. | — | — | 35 | — | 42 | — | 39 | — | 35 | — | 0 | — | 13 |

*Note:* Depending on the context in which the keyword appeared, it might be counted under several categories.

APPENDIX B

# Early English Books Online

The database known as Early English Books Online (EEBO) constitutes more than sixty thousand books printed in the English language, beginning with the first book printed in the English language in 1475 and running through 1700. EEBO has taken more than two decades to complete, with phase one encompassing 25,368 English language texts digitized by 2009 and an additional 34,963 texts digitized and added to the database by 2020. The project is largely complete, although EEBO will continue to expand by a few thousand volumes as the participating libraries in the text-creation partnership work to finish digitizing their remaining holdings not already in the collection. The keyword searches that form the basis of the following tables were initially run in 2014 and repeated in the summer of 2023 to capture the many new entries that have been added to the database since 2014. Fortunately, the semantic patterns have remained consistent. For the tables below, all keyword searches were completed by September 15, 2023.

Each printed utterance of a particular keyword has been recorded as a separate entry, while words that were not connected to people have been excluded from the results. Instances of the word *white* and *whites* when referring to particular kinds of commodities such as white sugar or egg whites, for example, have been omitted from the tables. For each appearance of a keyword referring to people, I have recorded the date of publication as well as information focused on two criteria: where the subject originated and whether that subject was Christian based on the context of the passage. Geographic origin designates the continent from which the subject's ancestors originated, not the nativity of the given subject, a fact much harder to discern from the texts. When determining the geographic origin of keyword subjects, I have used contemporary boundaries, with Africa comprising the entire African continent up to the western shores of the Red Sea and Asia comprising the European continent east of the Ural Mountains running to the Pacific Ocean, south to the Indian Sea, and west, including the land mass known as Asia Minor and the Arabian Peninsula. I have designated Europe to be the territories north of the Mediterranean Ocean, east of Iceland and the Atlantic Ocean, and west of the Ural Mountains and the Bosporus Strait. By mapping the geographic origins of keyword subjects as well as their location within each text, I track where and when white grammar became closely associated with Christianity and the European continent.

If the text was fictional, I have recorded the geographic origin and religious affiliation of the white character(s) as if he, she, or they were real historical actors. If the geographic origin and religious affiliation of the keyword subject is not known or knowable from the passage, I have recorded it as unknown. Some texts were reprinted repeatedly over the course of the seventeenth century. I have recorded the keyword for each reprinting as a new entry to capture the frequency as well as the evolving meaning(s) of white grammar over time. The category *non-Christian* includes peoples of many religious affiliations, some of them well-known to English writers but others unknown to them as well. The numbers of Christian and non-Christian actors should be understood as English perceptions of the varied people linked by white grammar in the seventeenth century, not as objective criteria or as the actual identities that the historical actors in question themselves adopted.

TABLE 9. Changing Religious Affiliations and Geographic Origins of Whites Mentioned in Early English Books Online, 1651–1700

| Decades | Total no. | RELIGIOUS AFFILIATION | | | | ORIGIN | | | | | | | |
| --- | --- | --- | --- | --- | --- | --- | --- | --- | --- | --- | --- | --- | --- |
| | | Christian | | Non-Christian | | Europe | | Africa | | Asia | | Unknown | |
| | | N | % | N | % | N | % | N | % | N | % | N | % |
| 1651–1660 | 6 | 1 | 17 | 5 | 83 | 2 | 33 | 3 | 50 | 1 | 17 | 0 | 0 |
| 1661–1670 | 88 | 60 | 68 | 28 | 32 | 60 | 68 | 28 | 32 | 0 | 0 | 0 | 0 |
| 1671–1680 | 17 | 11 | 65 | 6 | 35 | 11 | 65 | 4 | 24 | 2 | 12 | 0 | 0 |
| 1681–1690 | 47 | 24 | 51 | 23 | 49 | 29 | 62 | 6 | 13 | 11 | 23 | 1 | 2 |
| 1691–1700 | 69 | 48 | 70 | 21 | 30 | 51 | 74 | 16 | 23 | 2 | 3 | 0 | 0 |
| Total | 227 | 144 | — | 83 | — | 153 | — | 57 | — | 16 | — | 1 | — |
| % of total no. | — | — | 63 | — | 37 | — | 67 | — | 25 | — | 7 | — | .4 |

*Note*: Although several hundred mentions of the keyword *whites* appear before 1650, they refer to egg whites, the whites of eyes, and the like. None are to people as whites. The first half century has been excluded from the table, since there are no keyword references to whites as people from 1600 to 1650.

TABLE 10. Religious Affiliations and Geographic Origins of White People Mentioned in Early English Books Online, 1601–1700

| Decades | Total no. | RELIGIOUS AFFILIATION | | | | ORIGIN | | | | | | | |
| --- | --- | --- | --- | --- | --- | --- | --- | --- | --- | --- | --- | --- | --- |
| | | Christian | | Non-Christian | | Europe | | Africa | | Asia | | Unknown | |
| | | N | % | N | % | N | % | N | % | N | % | N | % |
| 1601–1620 | 9 | 2 | 22 | 7 | 78 | 2 | 22 | 3 | 33 | 4 | 44 | 0 | 0 |
| 1621–1640 | 21 | 10 | 48 | 11 | 52 | 10 | 48 | 5 | 24 | 5 | 24 | 1 | 5 |
| 1641–1660 | 3 | 1 | 33 | 2 | 67 | 1 | 33 | 1 | 33 | 1 | 33 | 0 | 0 |
| 1661–1680 | 25 | 9 | 36 | 16 | 64 | 9 | 36 | 9 | 36 | 7 | 28 | 0 | 0 |
| 1681–1700 | 33 | 24 | 73 | 9 | 27 | 24 | 73 | 4 | 12 | 4 | 12 | 1 | 3 |
| Total | 91 | 46 | — | 45 | — | 46 | — | 22 | — | 21 | — | 2 | — |
| % of total no. | — | — | 51 | — | 49 | — | 51 | — | 24 | — | 23 | — | 2 |

TABLE 11. Religious Affiliations and Geographic Origins of White Men Mentioned in Early English Books Online, 1601–1700

| Years | Total no. | RELIGIOUS AFFILIATION | | | | ORIGIN | | | | | | | |
|---|---|---|---|---|---|---|---|---|---|---|---|---|---|
| | | Christian | | Non-Christian | | Europe | | Africa | | Asia | | Unknown | |
| | | N | % | N | % | N | % | N | % | N | % | N | % |
| 1601–1625 | 85 | 64 | 75 | 21 | 25 | 58 | 68 | 13 | 15 | 12 | 14 | 2 | 2 |
| 1626–1650 | 36 | 16 | 44 | 20 | 56 | 14 | 39 | 8 | 22 | 11 | 31 | 3 | 8 |
| 1651–1675 | 46 | 32 | 70 | 14 | 30 | 39 | 85 | 2 | 4 | 3 | 7 | 2 | 4 |
| 1676–1700 | 160 | 138 | 86 | 22 | 14 | 141 | 88 | 8 | 5 | 6 | 4 | 5 | 3 |
| Total | 327 | 250 | — | 77 | — | 252 | — | 31 | — | 32 | — | 12 | — |
| % of total no. | — | — | 76 | — | 24 | — | 77 | — | 9 | — | 10 | — | 4 |

TABLE 12. Aggregate Religious and Geographic Identities of White Subjects by Keyword Mentioned in Early English Books Online, 1601–1700

| Keyword | Total no. | RELIGIOUS AFFILIATION | | | | ORIGIN | | | | | | | |
| --- | --- | --- | --- | --- | --- | --- | --- | --- | --- | --- | --- | --- | --- |
| | | Christian | | Non-Christian | | Europe | | Africa | | Asia | | Unknown | |
| | | N | % | N | % | N | % | N | % | N | % | N | % |
| White slaves | 7 | 0 | 0 | 7 | 100 | 0 | 0 | 7 | 100 | 0 | 0 | 0 | 0 |
| White women | 79 | 34 | 43 | 45 | 57 | 44 | 56 | 17 | 22 | 16 | 20 | 2 | 3 |
| White people | 91 | 46 | 51 | 45 | 49 | 46 | 51 | 22 | 24 | 21 | 23 | 2 | 2 |
| Whites | 227 | 144 | 63 | 83 | 37 | 153 | 67 | 57 | 25 | 16 | 7 | 1 | .4 |
| White men | 327 | 250 | 76 | 77 | 24 | 252 | 77 | 31 | 9 | 32 | 10 | 12 | 4 |
| White servants | 28 | 28 | 100 | 0 | 0 | 28 | 100 | 0 | 0 | 0 | 0 | 0 | 0 |
| Total | 759 | 502 | — | 257 | — | 523 | — | 134 | — | 85 | — | 17 | — |
| % of total | — | — | 66 | — | 34 | — | 69 | — | 18 | — | 11 | — | 2 |

438

APPENDIX C

# Eighteenth Century Collections Online

Eighteenth Century Collections Online (ECCO) is the largest and most complete digitized database of English-language texts published between 1701 and 1800 in existence. Comprising more than 180,000 books, pamphlets, and broadsides, the collection began as the English Short Title Catalogue in 1976, an effort by librarians, scholars, and bibliographers to create a comprehensive catalog of all English-language publications produced during the eighteenth century. I have searched ECCO not only for older forms of white grammar, including keywords such as *Christian slaves, white servants, whites, white m(e)n, white wom(e)n, white people,* and *white slaves,* but also for newer terms that emerged after 1700, such as *white race* and *English slave(s).* Because new titles have been added to ECCO throughout the writing of the book, all the tables in Appendix C were updated during the summer of 2023 and completed by September 15, 2023.

I have recorded the appearance of each keyword in ECCO as a separate entry for my respective keyword databases. Non-human references to whites as well as typographical anomalies such as "white staves," ceremonial statecraft objects which appear as *white slaves* in keyword searches, have been excluded from my findings. I have recorded the date of publication and the author and place of the larger publication in which each keyword appeared. I have also tracked four criteria for each keyword: where the particular keyword subject originated, whether the subject was Christian, whether the text and the keyword subjects were fictional, and whether the language of blackness accompanied the reference. I have recorded new editions of texts in ECCO that formerly appeared in Early English Books Online as new entries to capture the frequency as well as the evolving meaning(s) of white grammar moving into the eighteenth century.

As in Appendix B, I have used contemporary boundaries when determining the geographic origin of keyword subjects: Africa comprises the entire African continent up to the western shores of the Red Sea; Asia comprises the European continent east of the Ural Mountains running to the Pacific Ocean, south to the Indian Sea, and west, including the land mass known as Asia Minor and the Arabian Peninsula. I have designated Europe to be the territories north of the Mediterranean Ocean, east of Iceland and the Atlantic Ocean, and west of the Ural Mountains and the Bosporus Strait. By mapping the geographic origins of keyword subjects as well as their location within each text, I track where and when white grammar became closely associated with Christianity and the European continent.

In Tables 5, 6, 7, and 8, I have tracked whether keywords appeared in fictional or nonfictional texts. For the keywords *white women* and *white slaves,* I have also asked whether these white subjects were objects of policing, designated in Tables 5 and 6 by the category "Policed." Additionally, I examine whether white women and white slaves were discussed in connection to sexual acts across lines of skin color, described by the category "Interracial sex." Last, I examine whether skin color grammar appears adjacent to the numerous references to Christian slaves. By skin color grammar, I include any mentions of white, Moor, "negro," or Black that appear in the same sentence with references to Christian slaves. As it turns out, there are no mentions of white grammar in any of the 1,058 references to Christian slaves during the eighteenth century.

TABLE 13. Religious Affiliations and Geographic Origins of Whites Mentioned in Eighteenth Century Collections Online, 1701–1800

| Decades | Total no. | RELIGIOUS AFFILIATION | | | | ORIGIN | | | | | | | |
|---|---|---|---|---|---|---|---|---|---|---|---|---|---|
| | | Christian | | Non–Christian | | Europe | | Africa | | Asia | | Unknown | |
| | | N | % | N | % | N | % | N | % | N | % | N | % |
| 1701–1720 | 77 | 59 | 77 | 18 | 23 | 64 | 83 | 8 | 10 | 5 | 6 | 0 | 0 |
| 1721–1740 | 118 | 100 | 85 | 18 | 15 | 104 | 88 | 11 | 9 | 3 | 3 | 0 | 0 |
| 1741–1760 | 545 | 482 | 88 | 63 | 12 | 490 | 90 | 43 | 8 | 12 | 2 | 0 | 0 |
| 1761–1780 | 1415 | 1323 | 93 | 92 | 7 | 1328 | 94 | 69 | 5 | 18 | 1 | 0 | 0 |
| 1781–1800 | 2551 | 2494 | 98 | 57 | 2 | 2512 | 98 | 21 | 1 | 18 | 1 | 0 | 0 |
| Total | 4706 | 4458 | — | 248 | — | 4498 | — | 152 | — | 56 | — | 0 | — |
| % of Total no. | — | — | 95 | — | 5 | — | 96 | — | 3 | — | 1 | — | 0 |

TABLE 14. Religious Affiliations and Geographic Origins of White Women Mentioned in Eighteenth Century Collections Online, 1701–1800

| Decades | Total No. | RELIGIOUS AFFILIATION ||||| ORIGIN ||||||||
| | | Christian || Non–Christian || Europe || Africa || Asia || Unknown ||
| | | N | % | N | % | N | % | N | % | N | % | N | % |
| 1701–1720 | 34 | 15 | 44 | 19 | 56 | 28 | 82 | 1 | 3 | 0 | 0 | 5 | 15 |
| 1721–1740 | 67 | 45 | 67 | 22 | 33 | 57 | 85 | 5 | 7 | 1 | 1 | 4 | 6 |
| 1741–1760 | 54 | 49 | 91 | 5 | 9 | 52 | 96 | 0 | 0 | 0 | 0 | 2 | 4 |
| 1761–1780 | 129 | 122 | 95 | 7 | 5 | 128 | 99 | 0 | 0 | 1 | 1 | 0 | 0 |
| 1781–1800 | 355 | 324 | 91 | 31 | 9 | 332 | 94 | 7 | 2 | 14 | 4 | 2 | 1 |
| Total | 639 | 555 | — | 84 | — | 597 | — | 13 | — | 16 | — | 13 | — |
| % of Total no. | — | — | 87 | — | 13 | — | 93 | — | 2 | — | 3 | — | 2 |

TABLE 15. Religious Affiliations and Geographic Origins of White Slaves Mentioned in Eighteenth Century Collections Online, 1701–1800

| Decades | Total No. | RELIGIOUS AFFILIATION | | | | ORIGIN | | | | | | | |
| --- | --- | --- | --- | --- | --- | --- | --- | --- | --- | --- | --- | --- | --- |
| | | Christian | | Non–Christian | | Europe | | Africa | | Asia | | Unknown | |
| | | N | % | N | % | N | % | N | % | N | % | N | % |
| 1701–1720 | 5 | 3 | 60 | 2 | 40 | 3 | 60 | 0 | 0 | 2 | 40 | 0 | 0 |
| 1721–1740 | 37 | 14 | 38 | 23 | 62 | 23 | 62 | 2 | 5 | 12 | 32 | 0 | 0 |
| 1741–1760 | 23 | 11 | 48 | 12 | 52 | 17 | 74 | 0 | 0 | 6 | 26 | 0 | 0 |
| 1761–1780 | 48 | 10 | 21 | 38 | 79 | 10 | 21 | 0 | 0 | 38 | 79 | 0 | 0 |
| 1781–1800 | 81 | 34 | 42 | 47 | 58 | 36 | 44 | 2 | 2 | 43 | 53 | 0 | 0 |
| Total | 194 | 72 | — | 122 | — | 89 | — | 4 | — | 101 | — | 0 | — |
| % of Total no. | — | — | 37 | — | 63 | — | 46 | — | 2 | — | 52 | — | 0 |

TABLE 16. Geographic Origins of Individuals of White Race Mentioned in Eighteenth Century Collections Online, 1701–1800

|  |  | ORIGIN | | | | | | | |
|---|---|---|---|---|---|---|---|---|---|
|  |  | Europe | | Africa | | Asia | | Unknown | |
| Decades | Total no. | N | % | N | % | N | % | N | % |
| 1701–1720 | 1 | 0 | 0 | 1 | 100 | 0 | 0 | 0 | 0 |
| 1721–1740 | 3 | 2 | 67 | 0 | 0 | 1 | 33 | 0 | 0 |
| 1741–1760 | 1 | 1 | 100 | 0 | 0 | 0 | 0 | 0 | 0 |
| 1761–1780 | 13 | 2 | 15 | 1 | 8 | 4 | 31 | 6 | 46 |
| 1781–1800 | 35 | 24 | 69 | 2 | 6 | 0 | 0 | 9 | 26 |
| Total | 53 | 29 | — | 4 | — | 5 | — | 15 | — |
| % of Total no. | — | — | 55 | — | 8 | — | 9 | — | 28 |

TABLE 17. Nonfictional versus Fictional White Women Mentioned in Eighteenth Century Collections Online, 1701–1800

| | | NONFICTIONAL | | | | | | | | FICTIONAL | | | | | | | |
|---|---|---|---|---|---|---|---|---|---|---|---|---|---|---|---|---|---|
| | | Religious affiliation | | | | Sexuality | | | | | Religious affiliation | | | | Sexuality | | |
| | | Christian | | Non-Christian | | Policed | | Interracial sex | | | Christian | | Non-Christian | | Policed | | Interracial sex |
| Decades | Total no. | N | % | N | % | N | % | N | % | Total no. | N | % | N | % | N | % | N | % |
| 1701–1720 | 11 | 10 | 91 | 1 | 9 | 1 | 9 | 3 | 27 | 23 | 4 | 17 | 19 | 83 | 0 | 0 | 12 | 52 |
| 1721–1740 | 48 | 43 | 90 | 5 | 10 | 29 | 60 | 27 | 56 | 19 | 2 | 11 | 17 | 89 | 0 | 0 | 16 | 84 |
| 1741–1760 | 47 | 45 | 96 | 2 | 4 | 12 | 26 | 29 | 62 | 7 | 4 | 57 | 3 | 43 | 0 | 0 | 5 | 71 |
| 1761–1780 | 124 | 119 | 96 | 5 | 4 | 42 | 34 | 79 | 64 | 5 | 3 | 60 | 2 | 40 | 0 | 0 | 0 | 0 |
| 1781–1800 | 314 | 288 | 92 | 26 | 8 | 26 | 8 | 136 | 43 | 43 | 38 | 88 | 5 | 12 | 0 | 0 | 18 | 42 |
| Total | 544 | 505 | 93 | 39 | 7 | 110 | 20 | 274 | 50 | 97 | 51 | 53 | 46 | 47 | 0 | 0 | 51 | 53 |

TABLE 18. Nonfictional versus Fictional White Slaves Mentioned in Eighteenth Century Collections Online, 1701–1800

| Decades | Total no. | NONFICTIONAL | | | | | | | | | Total no. | FICTIONAL | | | | | | | |
|---|---|---|---|---|---|---|---|---|---|---|---|---|---|---|---|---|---|---|---|
| | | Religious affiliation | | | | Sexuality | | | | | | Religious affiliation | | | | Sexuality | | | |
| | | Christian | | Non-Christian | | Policed | | Interracial sex | | | | Christian | | Non-Christian | | Policed | | Interracial sex | |
| | | N | % | N | % | N | % | N | % | | | N | % | N | % | N | % | N | % |
| 1701–1720 | 2 | 0 | 0 | 2 | 100 | 0 | 0 | 0 | 0 | | 3 | 3 | 100 | 0 | 0 | 0 | 0 | 0 | 0 |
| 1721–1740 | 14 | 1 | 7 | 13 | 93 | 0 | 0 | 1 | 7 | | 23 | 13 | 57 | 10 | 43 | 0 | 0 | 1 | 4 |
| 1741–1760 | 15 | 3 | 20 | 12 | 80 | 0 | 0 | 2 | 13 | | 8 | 5 | 63 | 3 | 38 | 0 | 0 | 0 | 0 |
| 1761–1780 | 30 | 3 | 10 | 27 | 90 | 0 | 0 | 0 | 0 | | 18 | 7 | 39 | 11 | 61 | 1 | 6 | 0 | 0 |
| 1781–1800 | 52 | 23 | 44 | 29 | 56 | 13 | 25 | 1 | 2 | | 29 | 11 | 38 | 18 | 62 | 3 | 10 | 0 | 0 |
| Total | 113 | 30 | 27 | 83 | 73 | 13 | 12 | 4 | 4 | | 81 | 39 | 48 | 42 | 52 | 4 | 5 | 1 | 1 |

TABLE 19. Nonfictional versus Fictional Christian Slaves Mentioned in Eighteenth Century Collections Online, 1701–1800

| Decades | Total no. | No. nonfictional | % nonfictional of total no. | No. nonfictional with racial descriptors | % nonfictional with racial descriptors of no. nonfictional | No. fictional | % fictional of total no. | No. fictional with racial descriptors | % fictional with racial descriptors of no. fictional |
|---|---|---|---|---|---|---|---|---|---|
| 1701–1720 | 99 | 73 | 74 | 3 | 4 | 26 | 26 | 4 | 15 |
| 1721–1740 | 138 | 79 | 57 | 3 | 4 | 59 | 43 | 3 | 5 |
| 1741–1760 | 197 | 143 | 73 | 6 | 4 | 54 | 27 | 12 | 22 |
| 1761–1780 | 269 | 146 | 54 | 11 | 8 | 123 | 46 | 7 | 6 |
| 1781–1800 | 350 | 270 | 77 | 7 | 3 | 80 | 23 | 10 | 13 |
| Total | 1053 | 711 | | 30 | | 342 | | 36 | |
| % of total no. | | | 68 | | 4 | | 32 | | 11 |

TABLE 20. Grammars of Bondage in the Mediterranean by Keyword in Eighteenth Century Collections Online, 1701–1800

| Decades | CHRISTIAN SLAVES (C.S.) | | WHITE SLAVES (W.S.) | | ENGLISH SLAVES (E.S.) | | Ratio of C.S. to W.S. + E.S. |
|---|---|---|---|---|---|---|---|
| | Total no. | No. fictional | Total no. | No. fictional | Total no. | No. fictional | |
| 1701–1720 | 99 | 26 | 2 | 0 | 2 | 0 | 24.8/1 |
| 1721–1740 | 138 | 59 | 24 | 11 | 2 | 0 | 5.3/1 |
| 1741–1760 | 197 | 54 | 13 | 0 | 7 | 1 | 9.4/1 |
| 1761–1780 | 269 | 123 | 39 | 12 | 7 | 0 | 5.8/1 |
| 1781–1800 | 350 | 80 | 60 | 22 | 38 | 11 | 3.6/1 |
| Total | 1053 | 342 | 138 | 45 | 56 | 12 | 5.4/1 |

APPENDIX D

# Daniel Horsmanden's *Journal of the Proceedings in the Detection of the Conspiracy* (1744)

In 1744, Daniel Horsmanden, the chief justice for New York's Supreme Court, published the proceedings of the New York Conspiracy of 1741. During the trial, Horsmanden served as both the principal public prosecutor and its main documentarian. Thirty-four conspirators were executed, eighty-four enslaved people were transported to the Caribbean, and seven white conspirators were permanently exiled from New York. Not all of those who were executed or transported produced confessions that were recorded in the Horsmanden's *A Journal of the Proceedings in the Detection of the Conspiracy Formed by Some White People, in Conjunction with Negro and Other Slaves, for Burning the City of New-York in America, and Murdering the Inhabitants . . .* (New York, 1744), however, though many did, and some confessed more than once as part of the prosecution's effort to convict more people. I have identified a total of 111 confessions or final statements in the *Proceedings* given by eighty-four individuals. Some of the final statements were not confessions but final words attributed to conspirators just before being executed. Peggy, Ceasar, and John Hughson, for example, each refused to confess to a conspiracy even as they awaited the gallows. Their words matter, however, and I have included their final statements in my analysis of confession discourse in New York City in 1741.

I have counted each of the confessions or final statements as a separate entry and kept track of who conducted the interrogation, when the testimony was recorded and by whom, and what happened to the conspirator or the accused after making their statement. In analyzing the language of these testimonies, I have asked a series of "yes" or "no" questions that identify the presence or absence of particular thematic material in the testimonies. Some confessions possessed none of these themes while others contained several, enabling me to track ideological differences among the conspirators as well as to observe how court interrogators might have encouraged revisions to confessions. "Killing white people" denotes whether that language or violence against white actors was explicitly articulated as a motive in the confession or final statement. "Killing masters" indicates an explicit motive to kill masters, either their own or others, as part of the conspiracy, whether racial language was apparent. "Antislavery aspirations" signals that the confessor included language about desiring freedom or resisting slavery and servitude as a motive for their participation in the conspiracy. "Foreign alliances" means that the accused conspirator mentioned the possibility of Spanish or French intervention in their confession. Of the eighty-four individuals whose testimonies survived, twenty-three provided multiple confessions over the course of the trial, creating the opportunity to examine changing thematic emphases in conspirator testimonies. Table 1 makes such progressions visible by listing all the confessions for a given individual by date.

TABLE 21. Confessions and Final Statements of New York's Conspirators, 1741, in Horsmanden's *Proceedings*

| | Conspirator (owner if enslaved) | Status | Date | Justice | Killing white people | Killing masters | Antislavery aspirations | Foreign alliances | Sentence | Page no. in *Proceedings* |
|---|---|---|---|---|---|---|---|---|---|---|
| 1. | Adam (Murray's) | Enslaved | 6/27 | Horsmanden | Y | Y | N | Y | Transported | 102 |
| b. | Adam (Murray's) | Enslaved | 7/7 | Horsmanden | Y | N | N | N | Transported | 129 |
| 2. | Bastian | Free Black | 6/11 | Before the grand jury | N | Y | Y | Y | Death by burning | 69 |
| b. | Bastian | Free Black | 6/15 | Horsmanden | Y | Y | N | Y | Transported | 80 |
| c. | Bastian | Free Black | 7/15 | Horsmanden | Y | Y | N | N | Transported | 141 |
| 3. | Brash (Peter Jay's) | Enslaved | 6/25 | Horsmanden | N | Y | N | N | Transported | 97 |
| b. | Brash (Peter Jay's) | Enslaved | 7/15 | Horsmanden | Y | N | N | N | Transported | 141 |
| 4. | Braveboy (Kierstede's) | Enslaved | 6/30 | 2d Justice | N | Y | N | N | Transported | 114 |

450

TABLE 21. (continued)

| | Conspirator (owner if enslaved) | Status | Date | Justice | Killing white people | Killing masters | Antislavery aspirations | Foreign alliances | Sentence | Page no. in *Proceedings* |
|---|---|---|---|---|---|---|---|---|---|---|
| 5. | Bridgewater (Van Horn's) | Enslaved | 6/27 | George Moore | Y | N | N | Y | Transported | 110 |
| 6. | Cajoe (Gomez's) | Enslaved | 6/28 | "By a Private Hand" | Y | Y | N | N | Transported | 111 |
| 7. | Cambridge (Codweis's) | Enslaved | 6/30 | Nichols and Lodge | N | N | N | N | Transported | 115 |
| b. | Cambridge (Codweiss's) | Enslaved | 7/10 | John Schutz | N | N | N | N | Transported | 133 |
| 8. | Cato (Moore's) | Enslaved | 6/22 | Horsmanden | Y | Y | Y | N | Transported | 90 |
| b. | Cato (Moore's) | Enslaved | 6/26 | Horsmanden | N | Y | N | N | Transported | 98 |
| 9. | Cato (Shurmur's) | Enslaved | 6/27 | Horsmanden | N | Y | N | N | Death by hanging | 106 |
| 10. | Ceasar | Free Black | 5/11 | Horsmanden | N | N | N | N | Death by hanging | 25 |
| 11. | Ceasar (Horsfield's) | Enslaved | 6/27 | George Moore | N | N | N | N | Transported | 110 |

TABLE 21. (continued)

| | Conspirator (owner if enslaved) | Status | Date | Justice | Killing white people | Killing masters | Antislavery aspirations | Foreign alliances | Sentence | Page no. in *Proceedings* |
|---|---|---|---|---|---|---|---|---|---|---|
| 12. | Ceasar (Kortrecht's) | Enslaved | 7/2 | Nichols and Lodge | Y | N | N | Y | Transported | 121 |
| 13. | Ceasar (Pintard's) | Enslaved | 6/22 | Horsmanden | Y | N | N | N | Transported | 89 |
| 14. | Cuffee | Free Black | 5/30 | At the stake | N | Y | N | N | Death by burning | 47 |
| 15. | David Johnson | Free White | 7/14 | Before the grand jury | Y | N | N | N | Transported | 139 |
| 16. | Deptford (Cruger's) | Enslaved | 6/27 | Nichols and Lodge | N | N | N | N | Transported | 109 |
| 17. | Dick (Van Eyck's) | Enslaved | 6/30 | Nichols and Lodge | N | N | N | N | Transported | 116 |
| 18. | Dundee (Todd's) | Enslaved | 6/24 | "By a Private Hand" | N | Y | N | Y | Transported | 93 |
| b. | Dundee (Todd's) | Enslaved | 7/6 | 2d justice | N | Y | N | N | Transported | 122 |
| 19. | Emmanuel (Wendover's) | Enslaved | 6/27 | "By a Private Hand" | Y | N | N | Y | Transported | 111 |

452

TABLE 21. (continued)

| | Conspirator (owner if enslaved) | Status | Date | Justice | Killing white people | Killing masters | Antislavery aspirations | Foreign alliances | Sentence | Page no. in *Proceedings* |
|---|---|---|---|---|---|---|---|---|---|---|
| 20. | Fortune (Clarkson's) | Enslaved | 7/2 | Nichols and Lodge | N | Y | N | N | Transported | 121 |
| 21. | Guy (Horsfield's) | Enslaved | 6/27 | Nichols and Lodge | N | N | N | N | Transported | 108 |
| 22. | Harry | Free White | 7/18 | At the stake | N | N | N | N | Death by burning | 148 |
| 23. | Harry (Farman's) | Enslaved | 6/22 | Horsmanden | N | Y | N | N | Transported | 91 |
| 24. | Harry (Kip's) | Enslaved | 6/27 | Horsmanden | N | Y | N | N | Death by hanging | 106 |
| 25. | Jack (Abrahamse's) | Enslaved | 7/2 | Nichols and Lodge | Y | Y | N | N | Transported | 121 |
| 26. | Jack (Breaston's) | Enslaved | 6/27 | Nichols and Lodge | N | Y | N | N | Transported | 108 |
| 27. | Jack (Comfort's) | Enslaved | 6/6 | Horsmanden | N | Y | N | Y | Transported | 64 |
| b. | Jack (Comfort's) | Enslaved | 6/15 | Horsmanden | N | Y | N | Y | Transported | 80 |

TABLE 21. (*continued*)

| | Conspirator (owner if enslaved) | Status | Date | Justice | Killing white people | Killing masters | Antislavery aspirations | Foreign alliances | Sentence | Page no. in *Proceedings* |
|---|---|---|---|---|---|---|---|---|---|---|
| 28. | Jack (Murray's) | Enslaved | 6/26 | Horsmanden | Y | Y | Y | Y | Transported | 100 |
| 29. | Jack (Sleydall's) | Enslaved | 6/12 | Before his master | Y | N | N | N | Transported | 72 |
| b. | Jack (Sleydall's) | Enslaved | 6/26 | Horsmanden | Y | N | N | N | Transported | 98 |
| 30. | Jack (Tiebout's) | Enslaved | 6/24 | Alderman Bancker | N | N | Y | Y | Pardoned | 94 |
| 31. | Jacob (Rutger's) | Enslaved | 6/24 | Horsmanden | Y | N | N | N | Transported | 93 |
| 32. | Jeffrey (Cap. Brown's) | Enslaved | 6/27 | Nichols and Lodge | N | N | N | N | Transported | 108 |
| b. | Jeffrey (Cap. Brown's) | Enslaved | 6/29 | Before the grand jury | N | Y | N | N | Transported | 113 |
| 33. | John Hughson | Free White | 6/6 | Horsmanden | N | N | Y | N | Death by hanging | 72 |
| 34. | John Ury | Free White | 8/29 | Horsmanden | N | N | Y | N | Death by Hanging | 174 |

454

TABLE 21. (continued)

| | Conspirator (owner if enslaved) | Status | Date | Justice | Killing white people | Killing masters | Antislavery aspirations | Foreign alliances | Sentence | Page no. in *Proceedings* |
|---|---|---|---|---|---|---|---|---|---|---|
| 35. | Jonneau | Free Black | 7/2 | Nichols and Lodge | N | N | N | N | Transported | 121 |
| 36. | Lewis (Schuyler's) | Enslaved | 7/1 | Nichols and Lodge | N | Y | N | N | Transported | 118 |
| 37. | London (French's) | Enslaved | 6/24 | Before his master | N | Y | N | N | Transported | 94 |
| 38. | London (Kelly's) | Enslaved | 7/2 | Nichols and Lodge | Y | N | N | Y | Transported | 120 |
| 39. | London (Marschalk's) | Enslaved | 6/20 | Horsmanden | Y | Y | N | Y | Transported | 88 |
| 40. | London (Wynkoop's) | Enslaved | 6/25 | Horsmanden | N | Y | N | Y | Transported | 96 |
| 41. | Low (Provost's) | Enslaved | 6/27 | Nichols and Lodge | N | N | N | N | Transported | 108 |
| 42. | Mars | Free Black | 6/29 | Before the grand jury | N | Y | N | N | Transported | 113 |
| b. | Mars | Free Black | 7/6 | Nichols and Lodge | Y | N | N | N | Transported | 122 |

TABLE 21. (continued)

| | Conspirator (owner if enslaved) | Status | Date | Justice | Killing white people | Killing masters | Antislavery aspirations | Foreign alliances | Sentence | Page no. in Proceedings |
|---|---|---|---|---|---|---|---|---|---|---|
| 43. | Mink (Groesbeck's) | Enslaved | 6/18 | Before the grand jury | N | N | N | N | Transported | 83 |
| b. | Mink (Groesbeck's) | Enslaved | 6/27 | Nichols and Lodge | N | N | N | N | Transported | 108 |
| 44. | Othello | Free Black | 6/29 | Horsmanden | N | N | N | N | Death by hanging | 116 |
| b. | Othello | Free Black | 7/12 | Horsmanden | N | N | Y | N | Death by hanging | 136 |
| c. | Othello | Free Black | 7/18 | John Schultz | N | Y | Y | Y | Death by hanging | 145 |
| 45. | Patrick (English's) | Enslaved | 6/27 | Nichols and Lodge | N | N | Y | N | Transported | 108 |
| 46. | Pedro (De Peyster's) | Enslaved | 6/29 | John Schultz | Y | Y | N | N | Pardoned | 113 |
| 47. | Peggy | Indentured | 5/9 | Horsmanden | N | N | Y | N | Death by Hanging | 22 |
| b. | Peggy | Indentured | 5/20 | Horsmanden | N | N | Y | N | Death by hanging | 72 |

456

TABLE 21. (continued)

| | Conspirator (owner if enslaved) | Status | Date | Justice | Killing white people | Killing masters | Antislavery aspirations | Foreign alliances | Sentence | Page no. in *Proceedings* |
|---|---|---|---|---|---|---|---|---|---|---|
| 48. | Pompey | Free Black | 6/22 | Horsmanden | Y | N | N | Y | Transported | 88 |
| 49. | Pompey (Bayard's) | Enslaved | 6/30 | Nichols and Lodge | N | N | N | Y | Transported | 115 |
| 50. | Pompey (Gilbert's) | Enslaved | 6/27 | Nichols and Lodge | Y | N | N | N | Transported | 109 |
| 51. | Pompey (Leffert's) | Enslaved | 6/9 | Before the grand jury | N | N | Y | N | Transported | 66 |
| 52. | Primus (Debrosse's) | Enslaved | 6/19 | Before the grand jury | Y | Y | N | N | Transported | 87 |
| b. | Primus (Debrosse's) | Enslaved | 7/6 | Nichols and Lodge | Y | Y | N | Y | Transported | 122 |
| 53. | Prince | Free Black | 5/11 | Horsmanden | N | N | Y | N | Death by hanging | 25 |
| 54. | Prince (Crooke's) | Enslaved | 6/27 | Nichols and Lodge | Y | N | N | N | Pardoned | 109 |
| 55. | Quack | Free Black | 5/30 | At the stake | N | Y | N | N | Death by burning | 45 |

TABLE 21. *(continued)*

| | Conspirator (owner if enslaved) | Status | Date | Justice | Killing white people | Killing masters | Antislavery aspirations | Foreign alliances | Sentence | Page no. in *Proceedings* |
|---|---|---|---|---|---|---|---|---|---|---|
| 56. | Quack (Walter's) | Enslaved | 6/23 | By a private hand | N | N | Y | N | Death by burning | 109 |
| b. | Quack (Walter's) | Enslaved | 6/27 | George Moore | N | N | Y | N | Death by burning | 136 |
| c. | Quack (Walter's) | Enslaved | 7/12 | Horsmanden | N | N | Y | N | Death by burning | 92 |
| 57. | Sam (Cortlandt's) | Enslaved | 7/1 | Horsmanden | Y | N | N | N | Transported | 118 |
| 58. | Sam (Lowe's) | Enslaved | 7/6 | Nichols and Lodge | N | N | N | N | Transported | 122 |
| b. | Sam (Lowe's) | Enslaved | 7/7 | Horsmanden | N | N | N | N | Transported | 123 |
| 59. | Sarah (Mrs. Burk's) | Enslaved | 6/1 | Horsmanden | Y | Y | N | Y | Transported | 50 |
| 60. | Sarah Hughson | Free White | 7/8 | Horsmanden | Y | Y | N | Y | Pardoned | 130 |
| 61. | Sawney (Niblett's) | Enslaved | 6/6 | Horsmanden | Y | Y | N | Y | Transported | 62 |
| 62. | Scipio (Bound's) | Enslaved | 7/2 | Nichols and Lodge | Y | Y | Y | Y | Transported | 120 |

TABLE 21. (*continued*)

| | Conspirator (owner if enslaved) | Status | Date | Justice | Killing white people | Killing masters | Antislavery aspirations | Foreign alliances | Sentence | Page no. in *Proceedings* |
|---|---|---|---|---|---|---|---|---|---|---|
| 63. | Scipio (Abrahamse's) | Enslaved | 6/27 | Nichols and Lodge | N | Y | N | N | Transported | 109 |
| 64. | Scotland (Marston's) | Enslaved | 6/29 | Horsmanden | Y | N | N | N | Transported | 113 |
| 65. | Starling (St. Lawrence's) | Enslaved | 6/23 | Horsmanden | Y | Y | N | N | Transported | 92 |
| 66. | Titus (Phoenix's) | Enslaved | 6/27 | Nichols and Lodge | Y | N | N | N | Transported | 116 |
| b. | Titus (Phoenix's) | Enslaved | 6/30 | Nichols and Lodge | N | Y | N | N | Transported | 109 |
| 67. | Tom (Ben Moore's) | Enslaved | 6/18 | Before the grand jury | N | N | N | Y | Transported | 84 |
| 68. | Tom (Livingstone's) | Enslaved | 6/27 | Nichols and Lodge | N | Y | N | N | Transported | 112 |
| b. | Tom (Livingstone's) | Enslaved | 6/28 | Horsmanden | Y | Y | N | N | Transported | 109 |
| 69. | Tom (Rowe's) | Enslaved | 7/2 | Nichols and Lodge | Y | N | N | N | Transported | 120 |

459

TABLE 21. (continued)

| | Conspirator (owner if enslaved) | Status | Date | Justice | Killing white people | Killing masters | Antislavery aspirations | Foreign alliances | Sentence | Page no. in Proceedings |
|---|---|---|---|---|---|---|---|---|---|---|
| 70. | Tom (Soumain's) | Enslaved | 6/26 | By a private hand | N | Y | Y | N | Transported | 99 |
| b. | Tom (Soumain's) | Enslaved | 6/27 | Nichols and Lodge | N | Y | N | N | Transported | 109 |
| 71. | Tony Brazier | Free Black | 6/30 | Nichols and Lodge | Y | N | N | N | Transported | 115 |
| b. | Tony Brazier | Free Black | 7/2 | Nichols and Lodge | N | Y | N | N | Transported | 120 |
| 72. | Wan (Mr. Love's) | Enslaved | 6/19 | Before the grand jury | Y | Y | N | N | Transported | 86 |
| 73. | Warwick (Hunt's) | Enslaved | 7/1 | Nichols and Lodge | N | Y | N | N | Transported | 118 |
| 74. | Will (Lush's) | Enslaved | 6/27 | Nichols and Lodge | N | N | N | N | Transported | 108 |
| 75. | Will (Ten Eyck's) | Enslaved | 6/30 | Nichols and Lodge | N | Y | N | Y | Transported | 116 |
| 76. | Will Ticklepitcher | Free Black | 6/12 | Horsmanden | Y | Y | N | N | Transported | 71 |
| b. | Will Ticklepitcher | Free Black | 6/15 | Horsmanden | Y | N | N | N | Transported | 80 |
| c. | Will Ticklepitcher | Free Black | 6/26 | Horsmanden | N | Y | N | N | Transported | 98 |

TABLE 21. *(continued)*

| | Conspirator (owner if enslaved) | Status | Date | Justice | Killing white people | Killing masters | Antislavery aspirations | Foreign alliances | Sentence | Page no. in *Proceedings* |
|---|---|---|---|---|---|---|---|---|---|---|
| 77. | Will (Ward's) | Enslaved | 7/4 | At the stake | N | N | Y | Y | Death by burning | 125 |
| 78. | William Kane | Free White | 7/5 | Before the grand jury | N | Y | N | Y | Death by hanging | 127 |
| b. | William Kane | Free White | 7/29 | Horsmanden | N | N | N | Y | Death by hanging | 158 |
| 79. | Windsor (Cohen's) | Enslaved | 6/30 | John Schultz | Y | Y | N | N | Transported | 115 |
| 80. | Worcester (Varian's) | Enslaved | 6/22 | Horsmanden | Y | N | N | N | Transported | 91 |
| b. | Worcester (Varian's) | Enslaved | 6/30 | Nichols and Lodge | N | N | N | N | Transported | 115 |
| 81. | York (Crooke's) | Enslaved | 6/27 | George Moore | N | N | Y | N | Transported | 110 |
| 82. | York (Marschalk's) | Enslaved | 6/20 | At the stake | Y | Y | N | Y | Death by burning | 87 |
| 83. | York (Peck's) | Enslaved | 6/27 | Nichols and Lodge | N | N | N | N | Transported | 108 |
| 84. | York (Thompson's) | Enslaved | 6/27 | Nichols and Lodge | N | N | N | N | Transported | 109 |

TABLE 22. Thematic References within Confessions and Final Statements by Sentencing, 1741, in Horsmanden's *Proceedings*

| | | THEMES | | | | | | | |
|---|---|---|---|---|---|---|---|---|---|
| | | Killing white people | | Killing masters | | Antislavery aspirations | | Foreign alliances | |
| Sentence | Total no. confessions | N | % | N | % | N | % | N | % |
| Execution | 22 | 1 | 5 | 9 | 41 | 12 | 55 | 6 | 27 |
| Transportation | 85 | 39 | 46 | 41 | 48 | 7 | 8 | 20 | 24 |
| Pardon | 4 | 3 | 75 | 2 | 50 | 1 | 25 | 2 | 50 |
| Total | 111 | 43 | — | 52 | — | 20 | — | 28 | — |
| % of total | — | — | 39 | — | 47 | — | 18 | — | 25 |

TABLE 23. Thematic Differences within Confessions and Final Statements by Court Interrogators, 1741, in Horsmanden's *Proceedings*

| Court interrogators | Sentence | Number | THEMES | | | | | | | |
| --- | --- | --- | --- | --- | --- | --- | --- | --- | --- | --- |
| | | | Killing white people | | Killing masters | | Antislavery aspirations | | Foreign alliances | |
| | | | N | % | N | % | N | % | N | % |
| Horsmanden | Execution | 12 | 1 | 8 | 3 | 25 | 7 | 58 | 2 | 17 |
| Horsmanden | Transportation | 30 | 20 | 67 | 19 | 63 | 2 | 7 | 10 | 33 |
| Nichols and Lodge | Execution | 0 | 0 | 0 | 0 | 0 | 0 | 0 | 0 | 0 |
| Nichols and Lodge | Transportation | 36 | 10 | 28 | 13 | 36 | 2 | 6 | 6 | 17 |
| Grand jury and others | Execution | 10 | 0 | 0 | 6 | 60 | 5 | 50 | 4 | 40 |
| Grand jury and others | Transportation | 23 | 12 | 52 | 11 | 48 | 4 | 17 | 6 | 26 |

TABLE 24. Thematic Differences in Confessions and Final Statements Recorded by Nichols and Lodge by Date, 1741, in Horsmanden's *Proceedings*

| | | THEMES | | | | | | | |
|---|---|---|---|---|---|---|---|---|---|
| | | Killing white people | | Killing masters | | Antislavery aspirations | | Foreign alliances | |
| Dates | No. of confessions | N | % | N | % | N | % | N | % |
| 6/27 | 16 | 2 | 13 | 4 | 25 | 1 | 6 | 0 | 0 |
| 6/30–7/1 | 9 | 1 | 11 | 4 | 44 | 0 | 0 | 2 | 22 |
| 7/2–7/6 | 11 | 7 | 64 | 5 | 45 | 1 | 9 | 4 | 36 |
| Total | 36 | 10 | — | 13 | — | 2 | — | 6 | — |
| % of total | — | — | 28 | — | 36 | — | 6 | — | 17 |

TABLE 25. Correlations between Themes in Confessions and Final Statements, 1741, in Horsmanden's *Proceedings*

| Primary theme | Total no. of 111 | % (of 111) | OVERLAPPING THEMES ||||||||
| | | | Killing white people || Killing masters || Antislavery aspirations || Foreign alliances ||
| | | | N | % | N | % | N | % | N | % |
|---|---|---|---|---|---|---|---|---|---|---|
| Killing white people | 43 | 39 | 43 | 100 | 20 | 47 | 3 | 7 | 14 | 33 |
| Killing masters | 52 | 47 | 20 | 38 | 52 | 100 | 6 | 12 | 18 | 35 |
| Antislavery aspirations | 20 | 18 | 3 | 15 | 6 | 30 | 20 | 100 | 6 | 30 |
| Foreign alliances | 28 | 25 | 14 | 50 | 18 | 64 | 6 | 21 | 28 | 100 |

465

TABLE 26. Sentencing Differences between Free and Enslaved Conspirators, 1741, in Horsmanden's *Proceedings*

|  | SENTENCE | | | | | | Total | |
|---|---|---|---|---|---|---|---|---|
|  | Transported | | Executed | | Pardoned | | | |
| Status | N | % | N | % | N | % | N | % |
| Free | 7 | 39 | 10 | 56 | 1 | 6 | 18 | 101 |
| Enslaved | 58 | 88 | 5 | 8 | 3 | 5 | 66 | 101 |
| Total | 65 | 77 | 15 | 18 | 4 | 5 | 84 | 100 |

*Note:* Some total percentages do not equal 100 owing to rounding.

# INDEX

Abdallah, Mulay, 214, 234, 242, 244–245
Aberdeen, Scotland, 251, 253, 278, 280, 284, 286–289, 291
Abolitionism: British, 1, 2, 5, 18, 20–22, 78, 80, 314, 316, 323–329, 332, 352, 355, 368, 397, 406; contemporary, 2, 3, 5; connections of, to white suffering and white slavery, 4, 5, 22, 146, 314–315, 365–373, 417–418; and Black abolitionists, 20, 146, 295–297, 300–305, 325, 329–335, 382–383, 397, 399–403, 414–421; and white abolitionists, 85–90, 95, 107, 115, 119, 126–129, 287, 324–329, 332, 355, 368, 397, 406, 414–415; and national relations of rescue, 223–229; transatlantic scope of, 292–295, 297, 348, 352, 397; American, 323–324, 329, 397, 406, 414–415, 417; and gospel of free labor, 328–329; and Christian slavery, 363–365, 384–385; and class biases within, 368–369; radical, 406; and antitrafficking, 408–410
Abolition of the African Slave Trade, 295–297, 323–329, 351–359, 366–368, 373–374, 385–386, 389, 393, 402–403
*Act concerning Servants and Slaves, An* (Virginia, 1705), 75–76
*Act for Encouraging the Importation of White Servants, An* (Leeward Islands, 1693), 36
*Act for the Abolition of the Slave Trade, An* (London, 1807), 352, 354–355, 397
*Act for the Better Encouragement of Seamen in His Majesty's Service, An* (London, 1744), 216–217
*Act for the Better Settlement and Relief of the Poor, An* (New York, 1788), 296–297
*Act for the Encouragement of Seamen to Enter into His Majesty's Service, An* (London, 1740), 248
*Act to Prevent Stealing and Transporting Other Children, An* (London, 1670), 62–65
Adams, Robert, 389–395
*Address to the Inhabitants of the British Settlements in America, upon Slave-Keeping, An* (Rush), 301–302
Adis, Henry, 126
*Adventures of Robinson Crusoe, The* (Defoe), 151, 154, 157, 161
Africa, 12, 13, 22, 25, 30, 65, 80, 92, 149, 153, 179, 195, 213, 270, 300, 311, 316, 326, 352, 358, 391, 393, 416; North, 2, 13, 16, 18, 21, 85, 86n, 89n, 90n, 96, 100, 103, 108–110, 115–117, 125, 128, 130, 132, 155–156, 162, 196, 220, 223, 230, 233, 235, 240, 248, 250, 260–261, 329, 340–341, 345, 347, 365, 372, 377, 380, 384, 386–387, 393; sub-Saharan, 182–183, 221; French West, 221; South, 309; interior of, 389–395. *See also* Barbary Coast
African Americans, 3, 71, 76, 171, 184, 186, 299, 322, 362, 366–367, 392, 404–405, 417–418
Africans, 6, 7, 8, 12, 14, 20–21, 29, 34, 49, 53–55, 59, 72, 78–79, 87, 139, 171–172, 178, 184, 258, 299, 322, 388, 393, 402; collaborations of, with white servants, 49, 68–73, 171–173, 183–199; as sailors, 216, 241, 280, 317, 325
Alabama, 407
Aladdin, 149

Alexandria, Egypt, 386
Algiers, 16, 85–86, 97, 99, 104–110, 113–116, 121–122, 124, 131, 223, 231, 343, 349, 363, 366, 386–389; sailors of, 96, 101, 336; slave market in, 96; merchants of, 118; ships from, 223; subjects of, 223; treaties of, with England, 223, 340; pirates from, 325, 389; British–Dutch bombardment of, 363, 386. *See also* Barbary Coast
Algonquin people, 279, 281
Alien whiteness. *See* Whiteness: alien
Almenara, Alonso Tellez de, 260–261
Almeria, Don Roderigo de, 261
Alsop, Richard, 374, 379–381, 384, 388, 396. See also Jewitt, John; *Narrative of the Adventures and Sufferings of John R. Jewitt*
*American Citizen* (New York), 360
American Revolution, 295–298, 340, 347, 362, 403, 412
Annesley, James, 173–174, 199–211, 256, 265, 268–269
Annesley, Richard, 199–200, 203, 205–207, 210
Annesley, Sir Arthur, first earl of Anglesey, 59
Annesley trial, 174, 200–209
Annis, John, 332
Antigua, 31, 67
Antirent movement, 406
Antisemitism, 2
Antislavery: historical uses of, 3, 16, 20, 117; elite actors and, 5, 16, 20–21, 59–60, 68, 201–209, 271, 293, 414; enslaved and trafficked persons and, 8, 15, 16–17, 20–23, 39, 46, 56–58, 68, 141, 190–191, 253, 320, 399–403; markets and, 17–18, 110, 233, 239, 270; as language of national sovereignty, 18, 21–22, 47, 336–340, 347, 358, 360, 408; as English birthright, 46–47, 49, 117, 124, 128–129, 133, 137, 153, 182, 207, 226–227, 344–345, 362; political traditions of, 49n, 56–59, 298; elite, 60–72, 87–88, 117, 124, 140, 146, 209, 240; and race traffic, 79–80, 261; and whiteness, 80, 135, 142–145, 271, 370, 412; conversion to Islam as, 118; as transactional, 238–239, 363–364; and nationalism, 247, 295–299, 300, 302, 304, 320, 324, 346–348, 350–351, 358–364, 390, 420–421; radical, 280, 296, 320, 399–403, 420–421; geography of, 298–305; and racism, 299, 382; American, 360–361; working-class formation and, 401. *See also* Antitrafficking; Sailor antislavery; Servant antislavery
Antitrafficking, 7–8, 20, 22, 62–65, 81, 85–90, 133, 247, 264–267, 295, 297, 322, 329, 331, 348, 380, 399–403, 406–408, 416; in Thomas Lurting's *Fighting Sailor*, 85–90; and resistance to impressment, 266–267, 293, 362–363, 367, 385; in Olaudah Equiano's *Narrative*, 334; in John Jewitt's *Journal*, 378, 380; in Robert Wedderburn's *Axe*, 399–403; and working-class formation, 404–405. *See also* Antislavery
*Apology for the Life of Mr. Bampfylde-Moore Carew, Commonly Called the King of the Beggars, An* [Goadby], 268–270. *See also* Carew, Bampfylde-Moore; Goadby, Robert; *Life and Adventures of Bampfylde-Moore Carew* (Carew)
Apprenticeships, 40, 356
*Arabian Nights Entertainments, Consisting of One Thousand and One Stories*, 148–150, 218, 275, 382
Armatage, John, 241
*Armourer's Escape; or, Three Years at Nootka Sound, The* (Jewitt), 381–382
Arne, Thomas, 211–212
Arrais, Amet, 106
*Arrival and Intertainements of the Embassador, The* (Blake), 111–113

Arson, 171, 178–179, 183–184, 186, 190
Articles of Confederation, 296
Articles of War, 281–282
Atkins, Sir Jonathan (governor of Barbados), 41
Atkinson, Anthony, 321
Atlantic, the, 2, 6, 11, 18, 21–22, 25, 40, 80–81, 89–90, 125, 129, 131, 139, 183, 222, 248, 250, 272, 294, 336, 348, 406, 408; political economy of, 5–6, 9–10, 25, 54–55, 65, 240, 291, 385; and racial slavery, 6, 23, 25, 54–55, 59, 68–73, 81, 89, 93, 147, 149, 155, 203, 222, 259, 311, 346; and enslaved Africans, 30–31, 34–36, 76, 88–89, 141, 150, 183, 307, 408; and trafficking servants, 39, 40, 125, 183, 408
*Atlas Geographus*, 147
Attucks, Crispus, 299
*Axe Laid to the Root; or, A Fatal Blow to Oppressors, The* (Wedderburn), 399, 407, 419

Bacon, Nathaniel, 69–70
Bacon's Rebellion, 9n, 40n, 68–73, 75n, 76, 82, 85, 114–116, 143
Bales, Kevin, 1–2
Bannister, the Irishman (in Behn's *Oroonoko*), 140
Baptists, 126–127
Barbados, 6, 7, 26, 27n, 32–34, 36, 40–42, 46–47, 49–50, 54, 56–59, 61, 63, 71, 74–75, 78–79, 136, 146, 155, 167, 175, 222, 328
Barbados Slave and Servant Code of 1661, 27n
*Barbarian Cruelty . . .* (Troughton), 213–214, 241–242
Barbary Coast, 13n, 98, 109, 119, 156, 220, 230, 246, 250, 260, 327, 343–344, 372, 420
Bargrave, John (Captain), 44
Barker, Robert, 316–320, 402, 408, 410, 419
Barnard, Richard, 109

Bastinado, 101, 388. *See also* Corporal punishment
Batstone, David, 1
Battle of Acre (1799), 370
Battle of Trafalgar (1805), 385–386
Battle of Waterloo (1815), 363
Bayley, Robert, 63
Beake, Robert (Major), 58
Beauty: in interracial romances, 71, 141, 163–165, 210, 312; as revealed by trafficking, 163–164; and blackness, 171; and alien whiteness, 270–271, 276, 379–380; and white slavery, 278; and *The Greek Slave*, 417–418
Behn, Aphra, 133–142, 146–147, 151, 157–158, 162–164, 169, 203, 268, 380, 382, 409, 411
Bell, John (ship's master), 349–350
Bentham, Jeremy, 315
Berkeley, Sir William, 69–70
Bermuda, 61, 276
Best, Thomas, 43–44, 46
Betton, Thomas, 18, 230; will of, 230, 235, 237–239. *See also* Worshipful Company of Ironmongers
Bight of Benin, 65
Bill of Rights (English), 78
*Bill to Prevent the Importation of Slaves, by Any of His Majesty's Subjects, A* (1805), 353n
Black, David, 176
Black Guard, 196, 221, 260. *See also* Africa: North; Soldiers: Black
Black Kate, 206, 211
Blackness: as commodity, 29–30; prominence of, before whiteness, 30–31, 134; policing of, and interracial sex, 71, 75–76, 81, 202, 276–278; and nobility, 133–140, 163–164; theft of, through trafficking, 163–164; as distinct from skin color, 172, 299; and Irish commoners, 206–207; and national honor, 299, 350–351

Blacks: enslaved, 1, 6–8, 12, 14, 20–21, 26, 34, 37, 49–51, 53, 55, 65, 70–71, 79, 82, 89, 133, 138–139, 155, 158–160, 171, 184, 188–193, 198, 212, 222, 232, 258, 260, 276, 290, 294, 295, 300, 315–316, 322–324, 328, 355, 382; trafficked, 2, 6, 7, 30–31, 34–36, 76, 141, 307; as militia, 35, 260, 297; as fathers, 75; women, 75–76, 142, 146, 163, 277, 421; men, 164, 276–277, 421; as prison laborers, 176; as pirates, 179; free, 189, 332, 347, 382–383; Spanish, 196–197; as sailors, 216, 240–241, 280, 317, 326, 332, 339–340, 361; as overseers, 260; as soldiers in the Continental army, 297, 303; as soldiers for Britain, 303; as artisans, 347; in the Colonial State Papers, 428
Blake, Robert, 111
Blue Water Empire, 132, 154, 159, 180, 231–232, 252, 402. *See also* British Empire
Bonaparte, Napoleon, 370, 372, 385, 387, 418
Bon Sàam, Moses, 382–383
Boranguet, Sam, 345
Boscawen, Edward, 59
Boston, Massachusetts, 131, 217, 299–302, 346, 389
*Boston Evening Post*, 299
Boston Manufacturing Company, 407
Boston Massacre, 299, 303. *See also* Attucks, Crispus
Braithwaite, John, 181
Braudel, Ferdinand, 22n
Brazil, 153–154
Bridewell. *See* Prisons
British Admiralty Office, 234
British Army, 251, 281, 283, 298, 303
British Empire, 17, 20, 37–38, 83, 95, 129, 135, 151, 153, 155, 158, 167, 169, 216, 250, 252, 279; racism within, 2, 293; subjects of, 82–83, 212, 230, 238; trafficking and enslavement within, 136, 145, 153–154, 169, 293, 327, 409; treaty of, with Algiers, 223, 336; treaty of, with Morocco, 226–227, 336; diplomatic efforts of, to emancipate Christian slaves, 242–247; as humanitarian, 332, 362, 392
*British Evening Post* (London), 383
British Impress Service, 249, 265–266, 271, 281, 337, 359. *See also* Impressment
British National Party, 2, 3
Brougham, Henry, first baron Brougham and Vaux, 419–421
Brown, Christopher, 205
Brown, William, 237
Browne, Joseph, 219
Browne, Richard (Major General), 58
Buffon, George-Louis Leclerc, comte de, 309
Burnett, John, 289
Burt, N., 311
Burton, Mary, 183, 190–196, 198, 211

Cadiz, Spain, 389
Caer, Richard, 47
Cairo, Egypt, 147
*Calendar of State Papers*, 7n, 32n, 37–38, 423, 430
Callao, Chile, 179
Calvert, Frederick, 147–148
Canada, 251, 281
Cape Fear River, 191
Cape Verde Islands, 53
Captives: sailors as, 9, 10, 13, 14, 15, 102, 138–139, 341, 348, 377, 409; English, 18, 87–88, 110–111, 117, 119, 131, 158, 214–215; Christian, 90n, 103, 376; religious, 109, 147, 260; British, 228, 230–231, 234, 373–385; Spanish, 228; Irish, 240
Carew, Bampfylde-Moore, 262–271, 293, 310, 320, 410
"Caribbee," 31
Carnegie, Alexander, 291
Carter, George, 238

Casi, Juan (John Casey), 48–49
Cason, Master (agent for Parliament), 110
Catholicism, 50, 66, 77, 136, 228
Catholics, 47–48, 50, 76, 81, 113, 121; Irish, in New York, 126, 186n, 190, 191, 192; Irish, in Northern Ireland, 126, 200, 204, 206, 208–209; English, 136, 138
Caucasian, 413
Caucasus region, 147, 413
Ceasar, 171–173, 189–192, 198, 209, 211, 328, 402
Ceuta, Morocco, 107
Chardin, Jean-Baptiste, 94
Charles I, 111, 113, 139
Charles II, 62, 81, 85–88, 113, 115–117, 123–124, 129–130, 132, 136, 235
Charleston, South Carolina, 302
Chartist Party, 406
Chesapeake Affair, 359–621
Child labor reform, 406. *See also* Oastler, Richard
Chile, 179
Christendom, 92, 133
Christianity, 50, 71, 78, 81, 92, 115, 118, 120, 156, 162, 295, 324; and antislavery, 50–51, 295, 304, 313–314, 322, 324, 328, 332; and English political identity, 80–83, 324, 332; gospel of, 80, 87–88, 304; and free labor, 328–329; transcendence of, across lines of color or nation, 388. *See also* Methodism, radical
Christians, 50, 71, 93–94, 102, 125, 162, 176, 181, 245, 283; enslaved, 6, 88, 104, 106–107, 110–111, 115, 118–119, 122, 129–130, 132, 148, 218, 220, 341, 343–445, 349, 363; and political authorities, 267; radical, 303–304, 312, 322, 324, 328–329. *See also* Baptists; Christianity; Christian slavery; Protestants; Quakers
Christian slavery, 6, 16, 89, 101, 104, 107, 111, 129, 217–218, 220, 223, 367; in North Africa, 130, 155; abolition of, 365; replacement of, by white slavery in Mediterranean, 365–373; changing contours of, 366–367
Clarkson, Thomas, 287, 324–329, 348, 355, 390
Clement, Stephen, 249–250, 261
Cobbett, William, 368–369
Cock, Samuel, 389–392
Cockayne, Francis (lord mayor of London), 242
Cockrell, Dan (merchant), 231
Colley, Linda, 239–240
Collins, Mary, 63
Colonial State Papers, 6n, 30–38, 72–75, 91, 158, 199, 423–431
Committee of Council for Foreign Plantations, 34
Commoners, 232, 255, 264, 267–268, 291–292, 401; Irish, 206–207; British, 238, 420–421; policing of, 255, 258; mobility of, 264–267, 286
Commons, enclosure of, 238, 270
Company of Royal Adventurers, 65
Congo River, 92
Congress of Vienna, 16, 363, 365, 370, 372, 383, 416
Connecticut, 381, 383
Conspiracy, servant-slave (1741). *See* New York Servant-Slave Conspiracy of 1741
Constantinople, 147
Consular officials: English, 108, 122, 242; British, 215, 223–224, 227, 245, 340–341, 343–344, 349, 358, 364, 391, 420; French, 365; American, 393, 397
Continental Army, 303
Convicts: English, 6–7, 139, 157, 159, 169, 189–190, 270; transported, 7, 11, 13, 14, 23, 26, 34, 59, 64, 72, 74, 159, 178–179, 222, 315, 320–323, 388, 403; sale of, 27, 32n, 321, 323–324; enslavement of, 43, 57–59; Irish, 157. *See also* Felons

Coole, Richard, 109
Corn Laws, 406
Cornwallis, Thomas (Captain), 60, 63
Coromantee people, 279–281
Corporal punishment, 40–42, 70–71, 74–77, 97, 114, 160, 171–172, 179, 183, 185–187, 191, 245, 267, 276; of Black men, 71, 75–76, 81, 202, 276–278, 349; dismemberment as, 74–75, 114, 150, 179, 284–285, 325, 326–327, 334, 361, 387–388; torture as, 75, 97, 101, 114–116, 245, 271, 284, 317, 352, 387–388; branding as, 77–78, 271; executions as, 171–172, 183, 185–187, 191, 198, 210; and whipping post, 179, 273, 276, 349; flogging as, 276–277, 349–350, 362, 388, 397–398; of white women, 276–277; of kidnapped children, 286, 290; of sailors, 316–320, 349–351, 362. *See also* Bastinado; Galleys
Corsairs. *See* Pirates
Council of the Lords of Trade and Plantation, 67–68, 178
Crasset, Jean, 180
Creole, 272
Cromwell, Oliver, 47–48, 56, 58, 60, 111, 126
Cromwell, Richard, 56
Crusoe, Robinson, 151, 153–157
Cushnie, Alexander, 284, 286

D'Aranda, Emanuel, 99–107, 118–121
Dartmouth, William, earl of, 295, 302
Deaan Meverrow, 161, 164–165, 168
De Bruyn, Cornelius, 147
Defoe, Daniel, 66–67, 151–164, 169, 272, 380, 409–411. *See also* individual novels
Delacroix, Eugène: *Greece on the Ruins of Missolonghi*, 416–417
Delano, Henry, 344
Delaware, 276
Delaware people, 251, 253, 274, 284, 293, 410

Delaware River, 208
*Delineation of Curious Foreign Beasts and Birds, in Their Natural Colours* (Burt), 311–313
Dellon, Charles Gabriel, 176
Deportation: Irish, 65–66, 126; of Monmouth rebels, 76–77
Devon, England, 262
Dickinson, Jane, 45–46
Dorset, England, 282
Dorsey, Nicholas, 249
Douglass, William, 181
Downs, Michael, 206
Downward, John, 343
Doyle, Mary, 207
Drury, Robert, 160–170, 378, 382, 409–410
Dublin, 199, 203, 207, 265
Duke of York, 128
Dunbar, Scotland, 58
Duncan, George (ship captain), 344
Duncombe, Daniel, 41
Dunkirk, France, 105–106, 119
Dupuis, Joseph, 391, 393
Durham, England, 58
Dutch: and African slave trade, 26; and Mediterranean slave trafficking, 267

Early English Books Online, 6n, 30, 90–95, 433–438
*Ebenezer; or, A Small Monument of Great Mercy* (Okeley), 15–16, 97
Eckstein, John: *Sir Sidney Smith* (1801), 371
Edinburgh, Scotland, 290
Egypt, 270, 306
Eighteenth Century Collections Online, 6n, 147, 174–175, 218, 275, 439–448
Eldridge, John (mayor of London), 250
Emancipation: of Christian slaves, 100, 108, 112, 120, 154, 216, 363–364, 391; and racial hierarchies, 173–174; of Black sailors, 216, 241, 386, 391; national, 223–229, 281, 336–345; Black,

240–241, 281, 391; of white servants, 273; and the gospel, 295; in the Mediterranean, 336–345; of British felons, 342; as transactional in form, 343, 364; of Africans on slaving vessels, 354–355, 358; self-, 402; geographies of, 405

Enclosure, 264, 266

England, 5, 14, 15, 25–28, 30–31, 35, 40–42, 44–45, 48, 57, 64, 67, 74, 81, 85, 100, 110, 113, 116–117, 120, 122, 124, 129, 157, 162, 169, 251, 257, 264, 383, 409; political authorities of, 22, 46, 83, 95, 121, 264–266; Crown of, 65, 111, 117, 130, 217

English Army, 35, 47, 56–59, 112

English Empire, 21, 136

Englishness, 47, 49, 65, 117, 128, 155, 228, 324–327, 344

Enlightenment, 295, 307–308, 311, 314; critiques of, 314

Enslaved: Africans, 1, 6–8, 12, 14, 20–21, 26, 34, 37, 49–51, 53, 55, 65, 70–71, 79, 82, 89, 133, 138–139, 155, 158–160, 171, 184, 188–193, 198, 212, 222, 232, 258, 260, 276, 290, 294, 295, 300, 315–316, 322–324, 328, 355, 382, 402; Blacks, 6, 7, 30–31, 34–36, 76, 141, 143, 145, 260, 276–278, 338, 353; Christians, 6, 88, 104, 106–107, 110–111, 115, 118–119, 122, 129–130, 132, 148, 218, 220, 341, 343–345, 349, 364, 387, 447–448; Muslims, 6, 16, 103–104, 107, 132, 148, 153, 218; English, 18, 108, 112–113, 122, 124, 131, 132, 155, 162, 212, 216–217, 220–221, 228–229, 231–233, 239, 364, 387; comparison of, to beasts, when sold, 56–57, 96, 139, 147, 228, 321–322; whites, 74–75, 89, 93–95, 143, 145, 147–150, 162, 167, 197, 201, 210, 218, 368–370; French, 103, 364; Flemings, 105; Turks, 106–107, 119; Dutch, 113, 364; Irish, 113; Scots, 113; Spaniards, 113, 188, 195–197, 227–228; as Royal slaves, 136; Spanish, 188, 195–197, 227–228; nobility of, 202; British, 227, 230–233, 235, 238–239, 250, 340–341, 347; Protestants, 228; Jamaicans, 292; American sailors, 338–340, 363; Germans, 364; Greeks, 364; Swedes, 388

Equiano, Olaudah, 329–335, 345–346, 348, 388, 394, 402, 410–411

Evans, George Henry, 407, 414–415

Ewan, Charles, 290–291

Exeter, England, 57, 312

Exodus (book of), 78

Faria e Sousa, Manuel de, 92

Farril, Gerrat, 239

Fazakerley, Nicholas, 236–237, 240

Felons: transported, 26, 32, 64, 72, 76–78, 95, 139, 158–159, 177–178, 200, 212, 265, 272, 320, 323, 327, 337, 344, 382–383; enslavement of, 43; petitions of, to Parliament, 56–59; antislavery demands of, 320–324; as slave ship sailors, 323–327; Spanish, 344–345. *See also* Convicts; Putney Debates

Fez, Morocco, 181, 242

Fielding, Henry, 270–271

*Fighting Sailor Turn'd Peaceable Christian* (Lurting), 87

Finch, Sir Heneage, 61

Fitzhugh, George, 414

Five Nations, 282–283

Flanders, 104–105, 107, 289

Florida, 191

Florus, Julius, 182–183

Ford, Mary, 60–61

*Fortunate Transport* (Anon.), 271–274

*Fortunes and Misfortunes of the Famous Moll Flanders* (Defoe), 158–159

Fox, George, 86, 88n, 115, 126

Foyle, Oxenbridge, 56–59, 77

France, 191, 217, 251, 279, 304, 359, 362, 372; and African slave trade, 168, 372; soldiers of, 171, 280–282; colonies of, 186; race theorists in, 304, 309

Franklin, Benjamin, 307–308, 367–368; as Ibrahim, Sidi Mohamet, 367–368
Fraser, Francis, 289
Free labor, 348
Freeland, Peter, 179
"Free white persons," 337–338. *See also* Naturalization Law: in United States (1790)
*French and Indian Cruelty* (Williamson), 251, 253, 274, 278, 280, 284, 291
French Navy, 370, 385–386
French Revolution, 324, 337
Frethorne, Richard, 45
Frezier, Amedee, 175–176
Friday (Defoe's character), 154–157
Furlong, Bartholomew, 205–206

Galland, Antoine, 148–150, 275. *See also Arabian Nights Entertainments*
Galleys, 176, 322, 373. *See also* Galley slavery
Galley slavery, 101–105, 119, 123, 132, 175–176, 322, 335, 342, 373. *See also* Galleys
Gee, Joshua, 131
*Generall Historie of Virginia, New England, and the Summer Isles* (Smith), 39
George I, 152
George II, 216–217, 231, 233, 235, 241–242
Georgia, region of, 93, 147–148, 332
Germany, 47
Gibraltar, Straights of, 107, 213, 231, 244–246, 342–344, 347
Glasgow, Scotland, 364
Goadby, Robert, 268–271, 293, 310, 410
Godshall, Robert, 231
Gomberville, Marin Le Roy Sieur de, 94, 149–150
Gooch, William, 178
Gordon, William, second earl of Aberdeen, 289
Gouge, William, 120
Grace, Henry, 282–283, 293, 316, 410, 419
Great Britain, 2, 22, 108, 160, 163, 173–174, 232, 247, 255, 264, 283, 323, 350, 352, 399, 405; and nationalism, 2–3, 368; sovereignty of, 47, 49, 81–83, 110–111, 115, 136, 145, 159, 227, 282, 307, 348, 358; and antitrafficking, 85–90, 262–271, 293, 362–363, 367, 385, 399–408; and antislavery, 108, 123, 238, 240, 272, 320, 347, 397; trafficking policies of, 252, 282, 420; expansion of sovereignty of, through abolition, 280–282, 356–358
Greece, 149, 335, 346, 416
*Greece on the Ruins of Missolonghi. See* Delacroix, Eugène
Greek Revolution, 416–417, 421
*Greek Slave, The. See* Powers, Hiram
Green, James, 358–359
Green, William, 320–322, 324
Greenland, 120
Grey, Alexander, 287
Grimlin, Charles, 41
Gullett, Daniel, 213
Gypsies, 64, 267–270

Habeas corpus, 57–58, 332
Haiti, 281
Hakluyt, Richard, the Elder, 67
Hamet, Bashaw, 245–246
Hants, England, 262
Harlan, Marshall, 413
Haselrig, Sir Arthur, 57
Hatsell, Henry (Captain), 56–57
Haverland, William, 63
Haycock, Polly (heroine of *The Fortunate Transport*), 271–274
Hegemony, of race, 3, 30, 280, 412; of nations, 385, 412
Hilton, Edward, 326–327
*History and Remarkable Life of the Truly Honourable Col. Jacque* (Defoe), 157, 159
*History of Algiers* (d'Aranda), 99–107, 119
*History of Polexander, The* [Gomberville], 149–150

*History of the Revolution in the Empire of Morocco* (Braithwaite), 181
*History of Tom Jones, a Foundling* (Fielding), 270–271
Hodgers, Margaret, 205
Holland, 47, 54
Hopkins, Stephen, 298
*Horrors of Slavery, The* (Wedderburn), 400, 420
Horsmanden, Daniel, 171–173, 183–199, 209–210, 256, 260, 277, 401–402, 449–466
Horton, John, 391. *See also* Norton, John
Hottentots, 309
House of Commons, 60
Hughson, John, 171–173, 189, 192, 196, 209; as race traitor, 189–190, 198
Humanitarianism: and Christian servants, 33–34, 37, 73–75; origins of, 54, 59n, 100, 153, 165–166, 168, 229, 231–232, 234, 246, 335, 420; and transportation policy, 66–67, 159–160; and trafficking, 133, 139, 159, 163–164, 328, 332, 335; and corporal punishment, 160, 273; and white servants, 177; and Britishness, 272–273, 362, 391; and empire and race, 292–293, 320; of Black Africans, 317–320, 335, 399–403
Human rights, 173–174, 311, 335, 339–403. *See also* Humanitarianism; Rights
Human trafficking, 1, 3, 4, 8, 20–23, 43, 51, 59, 64–65, 86, 98, 157, 168, 210–211, 292, 310–311, 314, 316, 355; political economy of, 5–6, 9–10, 25–28, 54–55, 65, 86–90, 98, 107, 132, 146, 215, 217, 224, 240, 258, 291, 385; critiques of, 7–8, 20, 22, 77–78, 133, 135, 247, 264–267, 295, 297, 322, 329, 331, 348, 380, 399–403; defined, 11; and British sovereignty, 47, 49, 81–83, 108–110, 117, 136, 145, 159, 197, 225, 282, 316, 355; emancipatory promise of, 88, 107; and race formation, 210–211, 292, 310–311, 314–315; and British policy, 252, 267, 282, 316; and U.S. sovereignty, 316, 385; within national interiors, 404–405. *See also* Kidnapping; Man stealing; Ransom traffic; Spiriting; Transportation

Imoinda, 137–138, 142–144, 163, 275, 278; as a Black woman, 137–138; as a white woman, 142–144
Impressment, 87–88, 118, 122–123, 126–127, 129, 211–212, 216–217, 241, 249, 255, 271, 281, 333, 341, 345, 347, 360–361, 369, 397, 408, 418; critiques of, 266–267, 293, 367, 385, 392; expansion of, 337, 359. *See also* British Impress Service
Indentured servitude, 11–13, 31, 38–41, 49, 56–59, 158, 173, 177, 258, 261, 356, 402; and sexual subjugation of female servants, 41–42, 276–277; changes to, in North America, 42–43, 46; comparisons of, to slavery, 56–59, 64, 67; expansion of, in British colonies after slave trade abolition, 356–357, 402
India, 306
Indian Ocean, 179
Indians. *See* Native Americans
Indian-Settler Violence, 251–253, 270, 281–282, 284–285
Industrial Revolution, 254
*Infortunate: The Voyage and Adventures of William Moraley, The* (Moraley), 256
Inhumanity, 159, 215, 246, 323, 325. *See also* Humanitarianism
*Inquiry into the Nature and Causes of the Wealth of Nations* (Smith), 341
Insurrection. *See* Bacon's Rebellion; New York Servant-Slave Conspiracy of 1741; Rebellion; Stono Rebellion
*Interesting Narrative of the Life of Olaudah Equiano, The*, 329–335

Ireland, 7, 34, 48, 66, 101, 121–122, 126, 157, 200, 211, 269, 368–369, 383, 406; Northern, 199, 209, 269

Irish: as transported servants, 6–7, 29–30, 43, 173, 342; as soldiers, 47, 190, 192, 194; as white slaves, 74–75, 368–369, 383; as sailors, 101, 121, 239, 267, 325, 344; as renegades, 121; as indentured servants, 171, 173, 177, 188; collaboration of, with enslaved Africans, 177–178, 183–199, 402; as witnesses in court, 190–194, 196, 198, 205–209, 211; as priests, 192; women, 200, 203, 206, 208, 211, 402; nobility of, as race, 201; as laundry maids, 206–207; as peasantry, 240; as gentry, 269

Irish colonization, 65, 126

Ironmongers Company. *See* Worshipful Company of Ironmongers

Ironmongers Slave Fund. *See* Worshipful Company of Ironmongers: and Slave Fund

Iroquois Nation, 201

Islam, conversion to, 118, 220, 224, 245, 365, 416; as "turning Turk," 122, 224

Islamophobia, 3n, 16, 21, 365, 394

Isle of Wight, 96

Israel, 2, 91, 92n

Italy, 101, 104, 109, 267, 349, 351

*Jack the Giant-Killer*, 264

Jamaica, 33–36, 47, 59, 63, 67, 146, 177, 179, 241, 279–281, 292, 312, 317, 332, 399, 419–420

James II, 76–77, 136

Jamestown, Virginia, 39, 44, 70

Jamison, William, 289

Japan, 412

Jefferson, Thomas, 304–305, 315

Jemma. *See* Annesley, James

Jerusalem Garters, 131

Jesus Christ, 106, 126, 312

Jewish people, 2, 87, 100–101, 106, 109, 181, 240, 247; as merchants, 100, 106, 109; as prison keepers in Italy, 101, 109; as a race, 181; as naturalized in England, 240

Jewitt, John, 373–384, 386, 388, 410. *See also* Alsop, Richard

Johnson, David, 190

Johnson, Samuel, 298

Johnston, George, 290

Jones, Thomas, 216, 240, 248, 281

Jope, John Colyn (Captain), 25–27

Jorey, Joseph, 75

*Journal Kept at Nootka Sound, A* (Jewitt), 376–378

*Journal of the Proceedings in the Detection of the Conspiracy* (Horsmanden), 183, 185–187, 197–199, 209–210, 449–466

Juggy Landy, 200, 206–207, 211

Jukes, Vincent, 119–120

Kane, William, 190, 192–193

Kelsey, Thomas (Major General), 58–59

Kent, England, 262

Kidnapping, 12, 18, 29, 36, 48–49, 61, 63, 66, 78, 80, 121, 139, 158–159, 163, 203, 207–208, 253, 279, 293, 331–333; role of British state in, 65–66, 203, 207–208, 331, 333–334; as form of slavery, 67–68, 253, 331; of children, 203, 208, 253, 334; archive of, 286–292, 318. *See also* Human trafficking; Man stealing; Trafficking

King Philip's War, 143

Kneefe, Martin, 206

Knight, Major (New Model Army), 58

Knowles Riot, 217

Koran, The, 118

Lady Altham, 205–207

La Galera, 176

Land reform, 406

Langhorne, John, 300

Latton, William (ambassador), 244–245
Laud, William, 120
Lawrence, Richard, 71
Lee, Thomas, 178
Leeward Islands, 36, 67, 179
Leghorn, Italy, 101, 104, 109, 335
Lepore, Jill, 27n, 186n, 194–195
*Les mille et une nuit* (Galland), 148. See also *Arabian Nights Entertainments*; Galland, Antoine
Levelers, 50–51, 58n
Ley, Peter, 288
Libya, 306
*Life and Adventures of Bampfylde-Moore Carew* (Carew), 262–267
Ligon, Richard, 50–54
Linnaeus, Carl, 314
Liverpool, England, 326, 343
Locke, John, 165
Lodge, Mr., 187, 190
Logic, Charles (British consul), 341, 343–344
London, 15, 35–36, 42, 47, 61, 86, 109, 111, 131, 147, 159, 161, 182, 199, 213, 230, 235, 238, 240, 242, 257, 272, 279, 298–299, 302, 309, 312, 332, 339, 346, 383, 386, 389; East End, 63, 399, 405–406, 420; Saint Giles parish, 63; Saint Katherine's parish, 63, 67
*London Magazine: and Monthly Chronologer*, 182–183
Lord Altham, 204
Lord Exmouth, 386. See also Pellew, Sir Edward
Loughton, William, 176–177
Love: and colonization, 25; in interracial unions, 71, 141, 163–165, 191–192, 201–202, 210–211, 312; as political resistance, 191–192, 211, 402; between master and servant, 273–274, 321
Lurting, Thomas, 85–90, 95, 107, 115, 119, 126–129, 132, 168, 225, 228, 247, 325, 402, 408
Lyttelton, Sir Charles, 34

Mackett, William (Captain), 166–167
Madagascar, 161–163, 165
*Madagascar; or, Robert Drury's Journal during Fifteen Years Captivity on That Island* (Drury), 161–162
Magna Carta, 59
Malefactors: English, 31–32, 36, 38–39, 64, 158, 181–182, 189–190, 315, 342; as white servants, 36, 38; as white sufferers, 314–315; Spanish, 342–345. See also Convicts; Transportation; White servants
Mallorca, 85
Manhood: English, 115–117, 128–129, 155; American, 361
Mann Act, 3
Man stealing, 78, 283, 286, 292. See also Spiriting; Trafficking
Manucci, Niccolao, 180
Manumission, 128
Maquinna, Chief, 374, 376–381, 410. See also Nootkan people
Markets: and violence, 55; connection of, to humanitarian sensibility, 59n–60n; values of, 153; universal prices set by, 165, 261; morality of, 334, 399–403
Maroon War, 177
Marriage: and slave trafficking, 46, 163–165; interracial, 71, 163–165, 210, 312, 402; in North Africa, 246; in London's marketplace, 312; within Indian captivity, 378, 380; within North African captivity, 387. See also Beauty; Love; Sex trafficking
Martyrdom (Christian), 120–121
Maryland, 31, 54–55, 60, 159, 249, 270, 276–277, 289, 320, 322, 360
Massachusetts, 80, 298, 360

Mauritania, 306
McGuire, John, 239
Mediterranean, the, 6, 11, 16, 18, 21–22, 27, 85, 88–90, 105, 107, 121, 125, 129–130, 139, 212, 247, 306, 335–336, 345, 402, 409; English slaves in, 18, 108, 112–113, 122, 124, 132, 155, 162, 212, 220–221, 228–229, 231–233, 239, 364; slavery in, 89, 196, 322, 367–368; prize taking in, 167, 213, 217, 224–225, 227, 354–358, 397; and antislavery, 336, 349–351; as proving ground for slave trade abolition, 357–359; and racial revisionism, 370–372, 418
*Memoirs of an Unfortunate Nobleman* (Annesley), 201
Mendoza, Juan González de, 93
Mercantilism, 8, 11, 13, 18, 20, 60, 64, 71, 80, 150–151, 153, 169, 224, 231, 282, 293, 309, 390, 412
Methodism, radical, 399
Middle Passage, 141, 167, 322, 346, 408; in *Oroonoko*, 141; from Madagascar to Virginia, 167; in Equiano's *Interesting Narrative*, 332
Militia: with indentured labor, 31; Christian servants as, 32; white servants as, 33–34, 36, 178; Blacks as, 35
Minstrelsy, 254, 291, 293
Mittelberger, Gottlieb, 283–284, 293
Mohammed esh-Sheikh es Seghir, 111
Mohawk people, 191
*Moll Flanders* (Defoe), 157–159, 272
Monmouth rebels, 76–78, 136
Montreal, 251, 283
Montserrat, 67
Moore, George, 187
Moors, 94
Moraley, William, 256–261, 293, 410
Morgan, Edmund, 27n, 69n, 258–259
Moroccan ships, 336
Morocco, 99, 106, 111–112, 132, 181–182, 214, 221–222, 226–227, 231, 233–234, 240, 242, 245–246, 260, 267, 281, 336, 340, 343–344, 358, 366, 394
Moscow, 267
Mumping, 264–267, 268–271
Murphy, Elinor, 207
Murray, John, fourth earl of Dunmore, 303
Muslims: as white, 2; as racialized, 12; and Mediterranean slave trade, 87, 92, 102, 220; as masters, 89, 95, 366, 393–394; as ship captains, 102; as merchants, 107, 244; as enslaved, 118; as pirates, 121, 267; as white slaves, 147–148, 150, 384; women, 205, 384; as trafficked prisoners of war, 267; as political authorities, 267
Mutiny, 213, 316

Nakedness: and trafficking, 51–53, 167; and racial essence, 204–205, 210, 274; and whiteness, 273–274, 284; and Christian purity, 387–388
Naples, Italy, 349, 351, 396–397
*Narrative of the Adventures and Sufferings of John R. Jewitt; Only Survivor of the Crew of the Ship Boston, A* (Jewitt), 374–375, 379–382. *See also* Alsop, Richard
*Narrative of the Shipwreck of the British Brig "Surprise," of Glasgow, A*, 364
Native Americans: wars against, 44–45, 68–73, 143; enslavement of, 70–72; collaboration of, with enslaved, 191; appropriations of, 253–256, 283–284, 293–294, 372, 381–382; "friendly," 270; trafficking of, 403. *See also* individual peoples
Naturalization law: in United States (1790), 336–339, 412; in England (1674), 337–339
"Negroes," 5, 25–26, 30–31, 36, 39, 53, 55, 71, 160, 163, 184, 222, 258–259, 355, 392–393; prominence of, in the seventeenth century, 30–31; collaboration of, with white servants, 36–37, 68–73,

184; Spanish, 186; treatment of, 259, 272, 394; white, 309–315
Nelson, Horatio, 385–386, 389
Nelson, William, 385–389, 394; and race, in narrative of, 387
Ness, Christopher, 126
Newcastle, England, 256, 265
Newfoundland, 262
Newgate prison. *See* Prisons
New Jersey, 276, 281
New Model Army, 58–60
New Salley. *See* Sale, Republic of
Newsham, Amelia, 312–315
New World, plantations, 147
New York City, 8n, 14, 180, 188, 190, 195, 296, 302, 391, 393
*New York Packet*, 383
New York Servant-Slave Conspiracy of 1741, 8n, 14, 171–174, 178, 183–199, 296, 328, 449–466. *See also* Arson
Niagara Falls, 282–283
Nice, France, 335
Nichols, Mr., 187–188, 190
Nobility: as race, 135–137, 139, 140–142, 145, 204–205; of white womanhood, 141, 149–151; English, 145
Noble, Ozborn, 242
Noell, Martin, 56–57
Nonviolence, as strategy, 87, 127–228
Nootkan people, 374–383
Norfolk, Virginia, 360
*North American Review*, 389–390, 392, 394–395
North Carolina, 36, 191, 211
Northey, Edward 74–75, 77, 79–80
Norton, John, 393. *See also* Horton, John
*Notes on the State of Virginia* (Jefferson), 304–305
Novel, the English, 132, 138, 170; origins of, 138; adaptations of, by plebeian authors, 162; relationship of, to white grammar and antislavery, 170. *See also* Print culture; Racial revisionism
Numidia, Africa, 306

Oastler, Richard, 406, 414–415
*Observations concerning the Increase in Mankind* (Franklin), 307–308
Ogilby, John, 92
Okeley, William, 15–16, 21, 95–97, 124–125, 129
Omdurman, 3n. *See also* White nationalism
*One Thousand and One Arabian Nights.* See *Arabian Nights Entertainments*
Oran, Africa, 342, 344
Order of Malta, 365
Orientalism, 51, 151, 203, 380
*Oroonoko* (Behn), 133–142, 150, 155, 203, 211, 380, 409
*Oroonoko: A Tragedy* (Southerne), 142–147, 201, 209, 275, 278, 409
Ottoman Empire, 147, 180, 230, 365, 380; connection of, to skin color and race, 169–170
Overton, Richard, 122–123, 126
Ozawa, Takao, 412–413

Painter, Nell Irvin, 30n, 93–94
Palatine immigrants, 308
Palermo Protocol (2000), 1, 11, 12n
Palestine, 306
Pamunkey people, 45
Parliament, British, 1, 15, 18, 42–43, 56–66, 78, 81, 109–110, 114, 122–123, 126, 152, 182, 236, 240, 290, 320, 339, 352, 389, 392
*Particulars of the Hardships and Sufferings of William Nelson* (Nelson), 386–388
Pass system: between England and Algiers, 1698, 224–226; for policing commoners' mobility in Great Britain, 264–266
Pegelin, Alli ("General of the Gallies"), 101, 103, 106
Peggy, 189–192, 194–195, 198, 209, 328, 402; as race traitor, 190–191
Pellew, Sir Edward, 363, 386

Pennsylvania, 199, 208, 276–277, 279–280, 283, 287, 308
Penny press, 293
Penon de Velez, 118
People's Party, 254
Pepys, Samuel, 339
Persians, 180
Peters, John, 347
Peters, Thomas, 178
Pettigrew, William (British consul), 242–246
Peunio, Anthony, 345–346
Phelps, Thomas, 98–99, 124, 128
Philadelphia, 260–261, 284, 381
Phipeny, Israel, 179
Piracy, 25–26, 31, 44, 85, 90n, 102, 106, 110, 119, 121, 179, 221, 260, 354, 369, 386, 389. *See also* Privateers; Prize taking; Renegades
Pirates: English, 119, 121, 145, 224, 226, 282; French, 121; Irish, 121, 224, 226; Muslim, 121, 148, 225; Turkish, 121–122; in Madagascar, 165; in Indian Ocean, 179; in Jamaica, 179; white and Black, 179; in Mediterranean, 221; as enemies of British sovereignty, 225; Algerine, 226, 386, 389; North African, 226, 260
Pitman, Henry, 76–82, 136
Pitts, Joseph, 98–99
Plebeian authors, 251–256, 260–271, 273–275, 278–280, 282–294, 293, 310, 316, 318, 320, 373–395. *See also* Adams, Robert; Barker, Robert; Carew, Bampfylde-Moore; Grace, Henry; Green, William; Jewitt, John; Mittelberger, Gottlieb; Nelson, William; Revel, James; Williamson, Peter
Plymouth, England, 56–57, 251
Pocahontas, 25
Pocock, Thomas, 228
Political economy, 5, 10, 20, 28, 38, 60, 67, 69, 72, 151, 153, 169, 216, 231, 262, 278, 297, 336, 346, 356, 401–402, 407, 410–411, 421
*Poor Unhappy Transported Felon's Sorrowful Account, The*, 322–324
Pornography, 273–275
Portuguese, as leaders in the slave trade, 26, 154, 244
Potts, Dr. John, 45–46
Powers, Hiram: *Greek Slave, The*, 417–418
Powhatan people, 25, 44–45, 70
Powhatan uprising, 44–45
Pownall, Thomas, 307
*Practical Grammar of the English Tongue, A* (Loughton), 176
*Present State of the Republick of Letters*, 306
Press gang, 202, 221. *See also* British Impress Service; Impressment
Print culture, 255, 293, 316, 380, 409, 411. *See also* Penny press; Plebeian authors
Prisoner exchanges, 107–108
Prison labor, 176. *See also* Convicts; Felons; Galleys; Galley slavery
Prisons: Bridewell (London), 56, 145; in Leghorn, Italy, 101–102, 104, 109; Penon de Veles (in Spain), 118–119; British, 157; Newgate (London), 158, 243; Valdivia, Chile, 175–176; in London, 180, 273–274; in New York, 1741, 196–197; in Montreal, 251
Privateers, 86, 354. *See also* Piracy; Pirates
Prize taking, 167, 213, 217, 224–225, 227, 354–358, 397; changes to, 282; and slave trade abolition, 354–356, 397
Prophet Muhammad, 106
Protestants, 47, 50, 77, 81, 240
Providence, island of, 95–96, 102
Prynne, William, 126
Puerto Rico, 48
Punch, John, 54–55, 81, 402
Puritan, Republic, 56

Puritans, 56–59, 113, 126
Putney Debates, 9n, 56–60, 219

Quakers, 86, 127, 132, 168, 225, 228, 251, 368

Race: white, emergence of, 6, 175, 304, 306–315; as skin color, 9, 28, 172; as inheritance, 10; and slavery, 17, 28–30, 90, 147; conceptions of, 134, 141, 302–304, 306–315; and phenotype, 134; narrative dimensions of, 135, 143, 273; as nobility, 141, 201–209, 273; and human trafficking, 210–211, 292, 310–311, 314; nations as, 222, 302; plebeian adaptations of, 252; as a tool, 279–280; Black, emergence of, 279–281, 307, 309, 314; during Seven Years' War, 281–282, 284; emergence of red, 307–308; essence of, as deeper than skin color, 309–310; in U.S. Naturalization law, 336–337; geographies of, 393–394; hardening of, as category, 395–398
Race traffic: and political economy, 1, 16, 20–21, 79, 155, 216, 218, 222, 252, 310, 351, 353, 390, 421; defined, 28; and the Mediterranean, 216, 218, 222, 252, 363, 365, 370, 372–373, 384, 417–418; in political culture, 253–256, 283–284, 293–294, 372, 381–382, 417–418; expansion of, after slave trade abolition, 395–396; and Hiram Powers's *The Greek Slave*, 417–418
Racial capitalism, 10, 17–18, 18n, 20, 22–23, 407
Racial revisionism, 5, 10, 12, 16, 19, 21, 38n, 137–138, 142–144, 198, 206, 271, 308, 332, 364, 366, 369, 380–383, 411–413, 415, 420–421; in the Mediterranean, 151, 364, 369; in English print culture, 268, 270–271, 380–383; and discourse about white race, 308; and working class, 414–415. *See also* Racism; Whiteness
Racism: contemporary formations of, in white victimhood, 2–5; links of, to antislavery, 5, 80, 146, 253; and Atlantic slavery, 6, 23, 25, 54–55, 59, 68–73, 81, 89, 93, 155, 203, 259, 311, 336; origins of, 6–7, 25, 27n, 74, 307–308; as a geographic angle of vision, 19, 20n, 21–23; as antiblackness, 90, 155, 290, 299–300; and humanitarianism, 160, 173, 273; in pornography, 273, 417–418; and radicalism, 278–279, 415; resistance of, by Blacks, 300–305, 333; as scientific, 308–310; resistance of, by abolitionists, 327–328; imperial context of, 365–373; and white womanhood, 416–418
Rainsborough, William (Captain), 112
Ransom traffic, 12n, 13, 86–87, 89–90, 95–108, 110, 114–117, 134, 166, 223, 228, 231, 234, 243, 245, 247, 336, 341, 343, 391, 393–394. *See also* Human trafficking; Trafficking
Rappahannock River, 167
Ravel, Italy, 267
Ravenna, Italy, 267
Rebellion: slave, 7, 22, 68–73, 407; servant-slave, 7–8, 22, 33–34, 36–37, 49–50, 54–55, 68–73, 75, 146, 296; servant, 22, 37, 68–73, 76–78; of white servants, 37, 75–78; servant-slave, in fiction, 137–138; and white women, 276–279. *See also* Bacon's Rebellion; New York Servant-Slave Conspiracy of 1741; Stono Rebellion
Refuse sailors, 317, 327, 389. *See also* Barker, Robert
Refuse slaves, 331, 334, 346
Reid, Robert, 288
Renegades, 11n, 103, 106, 109–110, 118–122, 145, 148, 163, 228; French, 109, 121; English, 119, 121, 145, 224, 226, 282;

Renegades (*continued*)
  Irish, 121, 224; Turkish, 121–122; Imoinda as female, 142–144; as diplomatic, 372. *See also* Piracy
Reparations, 2, 5n
Rer Moume, 166
Rer Vove, 166
Rescue, aristocratic, 145–146; as expression of whiteness, 141, 146; female, 145, 274–275; British relations of, 231–236, 336–337, 343, 345, 397
Revel, chevalier de (governor of Genoa), 372
Revel, James, 322–324, 327
Rhode Island, 298
Riffardeau, Charles Francois de, Marquis de Riviere, 365
Rights: and human trafficking, 29, 37, 173; of white subjects, 29, 37, 73–74, 173, 178–179, 193–194, 277, 338, 351, 361, 373, 413, 418, 424, 429; of Christian servants, 34, 53–54, 73, 177, 427; English context of, 40–41, 60, 68, 78, 113, 255, 339; of servants, 40–41, 53–54, 60, 68, 177, 255; to traffic goods, 65; origins of, 73–74, 182; sailors', 113, 117, 347, 351, 359–364, 369, 373, 382, 385, 389, 396–397; to national rescue, 113; and sovereign authority, 128; human, 173–174, 311, 314, 335, 399–403; transactional origins of, 173, 348, 369; as rooted in skin color, 182, 193, 277; Spanish, 186, 345, 347; of sovereign subjects, 196; of noble birth, 202, 207, 209; to land, 266; for the enslaved and the trafficked, 296, 302, 335, 348, 351, 382, 420; of American citizenship, 338, 359, 361, 369, 373, 413; Black, 347, 351, 361, 373, 396–397, 424, 428; British, 351, 359, 361, 369, 373, 382, 389, 396–397; of women, 418; of white servants, 424, 426; of white people, 431. *See also* Bill of Rights (English)
Rinuccini, Monsignor, Archbishop of Fermo, Italy, 66–67
Rivers, Marcellus, 56–59, 77
Robe, Thomas, 67
Robin John, Amboe, 325
Robin John, Ancona, 325
Robin John, Ephraim, 325
Rolfe, John, 25–27, 39
Romance, interracial, 202, 391, 410
Rome, Italy, 47
Romme, John, 191
Ross, James, 287
Ross, Margaret, 287–289
Royal African Company, 65, 81, 389–390
Royal ancestry, 146, 150
Royal Exchange, London, 257
Royalists, 53, 115, 139
Royal Navy, 127, 216–217, 227, 241, 265, 320, 337, 340, 349, 351, 355, 361, 370, 385–386, 392, 396; deserters from, 359, 362
Royal Slave Fund, 116–117, 124, 130–131, 409
Royal Society, London, 310
"Rule Britannia" (Arne), 211–212, 373
Run aways: as servants, 37, 40–42, 54–55, 77–78, 270, 290; as Irish servants, 48; as enslaved, 51, 54–55; as Dutch servants, 54–55; as Scottish servants, 54–55; policing of, 54–55, 77, 81, 270, 290; as English servants, 55
Rush, Benjamin, 301–302
Russia, 267

Sahara Desert, 394
Said, Edward, 151n
Sailor antislavery, 86, 117, 123, 128, 130, 147, 215–223, 320, 348, 396. *See also* Abolitionism; Antislavery; Servant antislavery
Sailors: trafficked, 5, 13, 15, 21, 82, 103, 130, 161–169; captive, 9, 10, 13, 14,

15, 102, 138–139, 341, 348, 377, 409; English, 85, 88, 96, 116, 147–148, 159, 161, 197, 213, 223, 226, 228, 240, 267, 318, 326, 344, 387; Muslim, 85–86, 103, 148, 365; Turkish, 86, 128; Algerine, 96; Irish, 101, 239, 326; Christian, 103, 365–366; French, 186, 188; Spanish, 211, 261, 346, 364; Black, 216, 240–241, 280, 317, 326, 339, 347, 349–351, 353, 366, 373, 385, 387–398; British (white and Black), 226–227, 230, 241, 248, 252, 281–282, 316, 320, 329, 337, 339, 341, 347, 349–351, 356, 361–362, 373, 385, 387–396; African, 241, 316–318, 325, 335; Native American, 241; enslaved, 316, 326, 364, 387–395; American (white and Black), 336–337, 339, 347, 349–351, 359–364, 373–374, 385, 389–398; rights of, 359–364, 385, 389; Dutch, 364, 388; French, 364, 387; German, 364; Greek, 364; Neapolitan (Italian), 364; Swedish, 387–388; African-American, 392–395  
Saint Helena, 167  
Saint Johns (Leeward Islands), 179  
Saint Kitts, 48, 332  
Saint Patrick's Day, 190  
Saint Martin, Caribbean, 48  
Sale, Republic of, 111–113, 153  
Salem Witch Trials, 79  
Sallee Rover, 153  
Sampson, George, 213  
San Domingo, 47  
Sardinia, 370, 372  
Savannah, Georgia, 177–178  
Scetti, Aurelio, 102  
Schultz, John, 187  
Scotland, 7, 34, 47, 54, 159, 253, 342, 399  
*Second Part of the Unfortunate Shipwright; or, The Blind Man's Travels* (Barker), 320  
*Selling of Joseph: A Memorial, The* (Sewall), 78  

Seraglio, 94, 148n  
Servant antislavery, 46–49, 56–60, 64, 68, 72, 80–82, 147, 157, 159, 258–259, 268, 272, 396. *See also* Abolitionism; Antislavery; Sailor antislavery  
Servant registry, 64–65, 72, 116, 139, 224, 258, 409, 411, 414  
Servants: indentured 2–3, 6, 7, 12–15, 18, 31, 33, 39, 41–43, 45, 49, 51, 54, 64, 71, 74, 76, 82, 89, 95, 114–115, 125, 130, 139, 177, 182–183, 199–200, 243, 252, 255–256, 276–277, 282–284, 290, 320, 337, 356, 380, 409; transportation of, to North America, 5, 8, 12–13, 29, 34, 103, 140, 200, 207, 252, 272, 320, 323, 408; Christian, 6, 15, 32–34, 36–38, 51, 53–54, 72–75, 177, 218, 273, 427; from England, 6–7, 36, 39, 45, 55, 60, 68, 81, 114, 143, 145, 197–298, 224, 243, 272, 297; from Ireland, 6–7, 29–30, 41, 48–49, 60, 143, 183, 189, 195, 209; from Scotland, 6–7, 54, 286–291, 342; white 7, 29, 31–38, 73–74, 77, 79, 140, 147, 158–159, 177, 180, 193, 218, 273–274, 276–278, 328; hired, 7; Christian vs. white, 36–38, 73–74, 177, 273; resistance of, to masters, 37, 40–42, 189–195, 272, 323; from Holland, 54; female, 159, 272–274, 276–277; Black, 277; from Germany, 283–284  
Servant-slave collaboration, 13n, 50, 54–55, 68–73, 81–82, 140, 146–147, 171, 189, 198, 296–297, 323–324, 405. *See also* New York Slave-Servant Conspiracy of 1741n  
Seven Years' War, 251, 274, 279, 281–282, 307, 320, 412  
Sewall, Samuel, 78–80, 131  
Sex: as labor, 42n; between servants and slaves, 54, 71, 81; interracial, 71, 75–76, 81, 202, 276–278; policing of, 71, 75–76, 81, 158, 202, 276–278;

Sex (*continued*)
  in the seraglio, 94, 148; as violence in the slave trade, 150, 168–169, 399; and colonial encounters, 163–164, 202; between servants and masters, 272–274, 277–278, 391; and scientific racism, 311–312
Sex trafficking, 3, 41–42, 53, 64, 148–149, 207, 378
Sharp, Granville, 332
Sherwood Forest, England, 270
Ships: *White Lion* (English), 25; *Mary of London* (English), 95–96; *Ogden, Tristram of Liverpool* (English), 179; *La bella morea* (French), 213; *Inspector Privateer* (English), 213–214, 247; HMS *Phoenix*, 243; HMS *Sea Horse*, 246; *Thetis Snow* (British), 316–317; *Indian Queen* (British), 325; *Lark* (British), 343; *Sally* (British) 344; *Alexander* (British) 345; *Hydra* (British) 345; *Speculator* (British) 345; *Ann* (British) 349; HMS *Leopard*, 359–360; USS *Chesapeake*, 360; USS *Essex*, 361; *Surprise* (British), 364; *Boston* (American), 374–375, 381; HMS *Belona*, 386
Siege of Missolonghi, 416–417
Siege of Oswego, 280–281
Skin color: history of, 10n, 17; as distinct from race, 28–29, 90, 92–93, 143, 181, 309; Black, 30–31, 34–36, 155, 162, 296, 305, 307; white, 30–31, 34–36, 134, 140, 143, 145, 149, 156, 162–165, 169, 193, 253, 278, 308, 333, 412; historical association of, with numeracy, 35; and branding, 77–78; as linked to antislavery, 80, 142; and alien whiteness, 92–93, 143–144, 181; disconnection of, from race in the Mediterranean, 129–130, 181, 221–222; and transactional values, 129, 149–150, 181–182, 205–206; changing taxonomies of, 133–142, 169–170, 172–173, 179, 181, 261; as sign of nobility, 140–141, 145, 205; and racial suffering, 255, 278; absence of, in plebeian narratives, 292–293; in U.S. Constitution, 296
Slave markets, Muslim, 148, 205, 384
Slavery: modern, 1, 6, 12n; racial, 6, 23, 25, 54–55, 59, 68–73, 81, 89, 93, 155, 203, 259, 311, 346; definitions of, 11–12, 43, 55–59, 82, 345–346; English, 18, 154–155, 217–219; domestic, 43, 55, 66–67, 157–158, 217; New World, 54–55, 81, 93, 346; African, 65, 89, 155, 261; kidnapping as, 67–68; Mediterranean, 89, 100, 203, 261; galley, 101–105, 119, 123, 126, 132, 175–176, 322, 335, 342, 373; Danish, 219; French, 219, 387–388; Italian, 219; British, 248; as *"Barbarian,"* 260. *See also* Christian slavery; Turkish slavery; White slavery
Slave ship captains, English, 137–138, 316–320, 324–327, 331–332, 355
Slave ships: English, 65, 324–325, 327, 343; Portuguese, 154, 241
Slave trade: Atlantic, 1, 2, 4n, 8, 11, 15, 18, 21, 25–26, 30, 60, 65, 79, 81, 93, 129, 131, 138–139, 141, 152, 154, 159, 162, 165, 168, 198, 232, 247, 280, 295, 307, 324, 347, 357, 388; Mediterranean, 6, 95, 205; expansion of, in 1680s, 71–72, 93; Algerine, 96, 99; violence of, 138–139; in Cairo, 147; in Constantinople, 147; in Madagascar, 162, 168; and humanity, 234; North African, 366. *See also* Middle Passage
Smith, Adam, 131, 341
Smith, John, 39, 43
Smith, Sir William Sidney, 16, 365–374, 383–384, 416; at the Congress of Vienna, 363, 365, 370, 372; as diplomatic renegade, 372; as race trafficker, 372–373; and Islamophobia, 373; and white slavery abolitionism, 416
Smithie, Lawrence, 326

Sodomy, 114–115
Soldiers: English, 27, 47, 51, 57, 66, 70, 112, 126; trafficked, 27, 35, 47, 147, 150; Black, 35, 69–70, 297, 355–356; enslaved, 35, 69–70, 76, 103–104, 118, 297, 382; white, 35, 69–70, 150, 382; British, 47, 216–217, 252, 274, 280–282, 355–356; Irish, 47, 190, 192–194; American, 69–70, 72, 76, 297, 303; in Bacon's Army, 69–70, 76; Georgia (Russian), 147; across the Mediterranean, 103–104; as symbols of sovereignty, 112; Spanish, 118; forced labor of, 252, 382; and traffic in goods, 280–282; Albanian, 416
Solidarity: among trafficked and enslaved, 12–13, 398, 418; among sailors across racial lines, 350–351, 385
Sollicoffre, John Leonard, 231, 245
Somerset, England, 262
South America, 233
South Carolina, 36, 177–178, 191, 418
Southerne, Thomas, 142–147, 163, 201, 209, 275, 278, 382; and antislavery, 144–145
South Sea Bubble, 152
South Sea Trading Company, 152, 232–233, 240
Sovereignty, 18, 21, 47, 49, 81–83, 110–111, 115, 136, 139, 145, 159, 196–197, 307, 348, 369, 387; expansion of, through abolition, 227, 354, 359; changes in geography of, 282, 307, 364; and slave trade abolition, 359–387. *See also* Antislavery
Spain, 47–48, 101, 175–176, 191, 216–217, 232; and Florida, 177; colonies of, 186; subjects of, Muslim and Christian, 227–228
Spaniards, 156, 244
Spanish Army, 47, 171
Spanish Navy, 385
Sparks, Jared, 389–390, 392–394

Spiriting, 15, 18, 36, 61–64, 67–68, 100, 145, 147, 202, 208, 223, 257–258, 288, 290, 293–294, 328
Spiriting Act, 62–65, 81, 223, 249. See also *Act to Prevent Stealing and Transporting Other Children, An* (London, 1670); Servant antislavery
Stamp Act, 198–199
*State of the Process* [Williamson and Cushnie], 286–291
Stede, Edwyn, 7
Steward, John, 63
Stono Rebellion, 177–178, 191
Stuart Monarchy, 65
Stuart Restoration, 123, 140
*Substance of the Evidence, The* (Clarkson), 324–328
Sugar, 26, 31, 40, 49, 154, 198, 278
Sultan, 149, 151
Surinam, 133, 137
Sutherland, George (U.S. Supreme Court justice), 413
Sweden, 265, 370, 373; national navy of, 373
Sweet, Thomas, 108–110, 121–122, 130
Symonds, John, 41

Tackey's Revolt, 279–281
*Taken* (2008), 4n
Tangier, colony of, 85, 132, 213–214, 243–244, 343, 354
Tavernier, Jean-Baptiste, 92
*Taxation No Tyranny* (Johnson), 298
Tellez, Balthazar, 306
Terence (poet), 295
Tetuan, Morocco, 105–106, 234
Thames River, 112
Thevenot, Jean de, 94–95
Thiene, William, 63
Thind, Bhagat Singh, 413
Thompson, James, 211–212
Thompson, John, 377–383
Thomson, Robert, 291

Thornton, Robert John, 314
"Ticklepitcher," 186
Timbuktu, 389–390, 392–394
Tiverton, Ireland, 269
Tobacco, 26, 39, 154, 159, 167, 278, 300, 323, 394
Toms, Nathaniel, 349–350
*Tom Thumb*, 264
*Topographicall Description and Admeasurement of the Ysland of Barbados in the West Indyaes with the M[aste]rs of the Severall Plantacons, A* (Ligon), 51–52
*To the Great Turk, and His King at Argiers* (Fox), 115
*Tour to the East, A* (Calvert), 147
Trafficking: of Black people, 2, 6, 7, 30–31, 34–36, 76, 141, 307; and white victimhood, 4, 5, 22, 146, 365–373, 414–416; of servants, 20, 22, 29, 38–39, 42, 46, 61–62, 64, 74, 83, 125, 139, 211, 258–259, 296; of enslaved peoples, 29, 56–59, 112, 133, 137, 152, 164–166, 197, 259, 282, 353, 393; and soldiers, 35; and white people, 37, 74–75, 89, 93–95, 143, 145, 147–150, 162, 167, 197, 201, 210, 218, 278, 364–365, 368–370, 379–380, 382–384, 396; of children, 63–64, 66–68, 147–148, 251, 253, 287–291, 403, 418; of goods, 70–71, 282, 331; and sailors, 85, 207, 224; and national and religious identities, 86–87, 89–90, 95–108, 110, 114–117, 222; and royal slaves, 136; humanity of, 163–164; and captives, 196; and debt, 258, 288; and white womanhood, 273–275, 416–418; and prizes in war, 282, 378
Trafficking Violence Protection Act (2000), 1, 11
Transportation: to North America, 11, 13, 23, 31–32, 34, 57–59, 64, 74, 76–78, 95, 126, 148, 159, 175, 177, 186, 200, 207–208, 255, 258, 266, 270–271, 322–324, 337, 347, 383, 388, 402–403; as kidnapping, 65–66, 287–291; as humanitarian policy, 66–67, 157–158, 207, 209, 260, 272; Italian, 102; from America to Caribbean, 187, 197–198, 209; condemnation of, as policy, 264–267, 323–324; as admonition to youth, 322; Spanish, across the Mediterranean, 336, 342; to Australia, 341–342
Transportation Act of 1718, 157–159
Travel writing, English, 162, 261, 306
Treaty of 1602, 113
Treaty of Utrecht, 232
Trefry, Mr. (Oroonoko's master), 141
Trelawney, Edward, 241
Trent, Henry, 231. *See also* Worshipful Company of Ironmongers: trustees and wardens of
Troughton, Thomas, 213–216, 219–222, 240–248, 281, 283, 341, 343–344, 410
Turkey, 230, 335
Turkey Company, 345
Turkish slavery, 66, 102, 104, 106, 119–120, 123, 125–126, 129, 203, 248, 260, 267–268, 271
Turks, 105, 120, 126, 128, 267, 271, 380; as captains, 121; as renegades, 122; as masters, 125; as enslaved by Europeans, 267; as slaveholders, 271; as prisoners, 373; fleet manned by, 373
Turner, John, 205
Turner, Nat, 407
*Two Dialogues on the Man-Trade* (Philmore), 292–293

*Unfortunate Shipwright: or, Cruel Captain* [Barker], 319
Union Jack (British flag), 227, 241, 280, 343, 358. *See also* Royal Navy
United States, 254, 337, 350, 362, 396, 405; diplomatic conflicts of, with Algiers, 336–337; and nationalism, 367; and antitrafficking, 407–412. *See*

*also* Naturalization law: in United States (1790)
United States Congress, 412
United States Constitution, 296; and Three-Fifths Compromise, 296, 338; and slavery, 296, 338
United States Department of State, 3
United States Navy, 350, 359, 361–363, 386, 396; ships, 359–361; and nationalism, 367; and antitrafficking, 407. *See also* American Revolution
Ury, John, 189, 192–194

Vagrancy Statute, 1547, 43, 55
Vagrants, 64; as defined by transportation policy, 66–67; as footloose commoners, 263–265, 270; in Articles of Confederation, 296
Valdivia, Chile, 175–176
Vancouver, Canada, 374
Vane, Sir Henry, 57
Vatican, the, 66
Veale, Captain Richard, 113–115, 142, 243, 246, 248
Venice, Italy, 102
Virgil, 295
Virginia, 8n, 25, 26, 36, 42, 44, 46, 54, 61, 63, 68, 71–72, 75–76, 113, 116, 130, 143, 146, 158, 167, 249, 276, 290, 300, 303, 323, 331, 360, 402
Virginia Company, 25–27, 44
Virginia General Assembly, 71–72, 75–76
Virginia Statute of 1661, 55
Voltaire, M. de, 304, 309–311

Wager, Charles, Sir, 233–239, 248
Waldstreicher, David, 299
War for American Independence. *See* American Revolution
War of 1812, 350–351, 359–361, 363, 369, 397, 412
War of Jenkin's Ear, 216, 241, 281
Washbutt, Captain, 316–318, 320
Washington, George, 297, 338

Wedderburn, Robert, 399–403, 405–407, 413–416, 418–421. See also *Axe Laid to the Root; or, A Fatal Blow to Oppressors, The* (Wedderburn)
Wesley, Samuel, 91
Western Design, 47, 59
West Indies, 208
Wharfingers, 327, 389
Wheatley, John, 301
Wheatley, Phillis, 295–297, 300–305, 325, 345–348, 402, 410; and critique of white racism, 302, 304–305; patriotism of, 302–303; letter from, to George Washington, 303; "On Being Brought from Africa to America," 304; response of, to Thomas Jefferson, 304–305
Wheatley, Susannah, 304
White grammar: origins of, 6–8, 10, 16; as discourse, 71–80, 83, 91–95, 129–130, 147–151, 156, 158, 162, 174–175, 177–181, 193, 210, 275, 277–278, 318, 372; in the Colonial State Papers, 425
White men, 31, 73, 95, 156, 173, 181, 197, 333–334; in the Colonial State Papers, 431; in Early English Books Online, 435–438
White nationalism, 2, 3, 5, 8, 19, 140; American 2; British 2
White negroes, 309–315
Whiteness, 5, 6, 19, 22–23, 27, 82, 133–134, 141–144, 146, 155, 273, 279; and antislavery, 4, 5, 22, 142–146, 188, 365–373, 418; as racial revisionism, 5, 10, 12, 16, 19, 21, 38n, 143, 198, 206, 271, 308, 332, 364, 366, 369, 380–383, 411–413; as heritable privilege, 7–8, 189; as ideology, 8, 10, 189, 198, 273, 279, 380, 411–412; historiography of, 29n; alien, 90–95, 162, 169, 180–182, 306, 308–309, 379–380, 412; imperial, 38, 92–93, 273; and human trafficking, 160–170, 309; as a colonial virus, 273–274; as pornography of racial suffering, 273–274, 284;

Whiteness (*continued*)
　scientific conceptions of, 309–310; as political currency in the United States, 338, 367; as response to radical antislavery, 380–381, 396

White people, 6, 14, 16, 31, 73, 91–92, 94–95, 140, 142, 162–163, 169, 171–172, 181, 187–188, 190, 193, 197, 253, 283, 290, 307, 411; in the Colonial State Papers, 425–431; in Early English Books Online, 435–438

White race, 6, 175, 304, 306–315, 412; geographies of, 315; in Eighteenth Century Collections Online, 444

Whites, 10, 30–31, 71–80, 279, 290; as trafficked people, 6, 7, 22, 31, 34–37, 73, 129, 159, 169, 176–177, 179, 278, 403, 411–412; as convicts, 7, 11, 13, 14, 23, 26, 34, 64, 72, 74, 159, 178–179, 222, 315, 327; as militia, 36, 278; in the Colonial State Papers, 429–430; in Early English Books Online, 435–438; in Eighteenth Century Collections Online, 441

White servants, 30–34, 36, 73, 148, 177, 181, 276, 278; in the Colonial State Papers, 426; in Early English Books Online, 438

White slavery: as discourse about white victimhood, 2, 3, 5, 8, 10, 351, 364–373, 384; as moral panic during the Progressive Era, 3; as shorthand for indentured servitude, 3n, 8n, 15, 74–75, 93–95, 143; and European bombardment of Tripoli in 1815, 10, 18, 364; as Muslim slavery in the Mediterranean, 94–95, 139, 142–146, 150–151, 182, 364; as imperial romance of the African slave trade, 160–169; and critique of radical abolitionists, 368–369. *See also* White slavery abolitionism; White victimhood

White slavery abolitionism, 4, 5, 22, 146, 365–373, 414–416

White slaves, 2, 4, 5, 8, 10, 16, 18, 20, 22, 74–75, 89, 93–95, 143, 145, 147–150, 162, 167, 197, 201, 210, 218, 278, 364–365, 368–370, 379–380, 382–384, 396; in Early English Books Online, 438; in Eighteenth Century Collections Online, 443, 446

White supremacy: followers of, 2–3, 6, 19, 21–23, 155, 182n, 277, 418; defined, 5; hegemony of, 8; origins of, 10, 22, 254; as narrative of white suffering, 253–254, 279, 290, 411–412; as female in form, 274–275, 278; absence of, in plebeian narratives, 318; and military aggression, 373; and formation of British and American working classes, 398, 405–406; as global narrative of white victimhood, 412–418

White victimhood, 2–4, 6–8, 10, 12–14, 16, 18–19, 22, 155, 159, 253, 274, 279, 374, 388, 410, 414; and white slavery, 2, 4, 5, 8, 10, 16, 18, 20, 22, 74–75, 89, 93–95, 143, 145, 147–150, 162, 167, 197, 201, 210, 218, 278, 364–365, 368–370, 379–380, 382–384, 396; globalization of, 18, 21, 365–385

White womanhood: as sexual purity, 143; and masculine rescue, 274–275, 284; and war, 274–275, 416–418; and unruly behavior, 277–279; as metonym, 279; and white racism, 418

White women, 31, 71, 73, 93–94, 145, 158–159, 173, 175, 178, 181, 253, 273, 275–278, 379; unruly, 158, 178–179; in the Colonial State Papers, 425–431; in Early English Books Online, 438; in Eighteenth Century Collections Online, 442, 445

Wilberforce, William, 368, 420

Williams, John, 374–376

Williamson, James, 289

Williamson, Peter, 251–256, 260–261, 264, 273–275, 278–280, 282–294, 315,

318, 320, 372–373, 381–382, 388–389, 410–411, 413–415
William Wilberforce Act, 1. *See also* Trafficking Violence Protection Act (2000)
Wills, James, 259
Wilson, Isobel, 288
Wood, Abraham, 73
Wooldridge, Thomas, 302
Worcester, England, 58
Working class: British, 396, 405–406; American, 396, 405–406; origin of, as antislavery formation, 396–398, 407; and race, 415
*Workingman's Advocate* (New York), 407
Worshipful Company of Ironmongers, 232, 235–238, 240–241, 248–249, 261, 332, 340, 343–345, 347, 358, 420; and Slave Fund, 18, 215, 230–231, 235–236, 238, 250, 340, 343–345, 401; trustees and wardens of, 232–237, 239–241, 261, 341, 344, 347, 358, 363–364, 385, 391, 401; humanitarian transactions on behalf of, 232; Hall of, in London, 235; and British courts, 236–237; and charity schools, 238; investments of, 238, 401; antislavery ideology of, 239; refusal of, to emancipate Irish sailors, 239

Xury, 153–154

Yarborough, Lady, 61–62, 64
York, England, 418

Zabaim, 150
Zelopa, 150